The Disney Afternoon

ADVENTURES

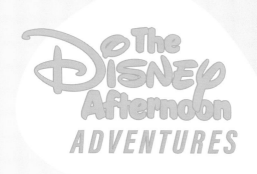

FANTAGRAPHICS BOOKS, INC.
7563 Lake City Way NE
Seattle WA 98115
(800) 657-1100

Visit us at fantagraphics.com.
Follow us on Twitter at @fantagraphics and
on Facebook at facebook.com/fantagraphics.

Publisher: GARY GROTH
Editor: DAVID GERSTEIN
Design: CHELSEA WIRTZ
Production: PAUL BARESH
and CHRISTINA HWANG
Associate Publisher: ERIC REYNOLDS

The Disney Afternoon Adventures showcases classic comics based on TV cartoons from *The Disney Afternoon* programming block, first published in *Disney Adventures* magazine or around the world. This is *The Disney Afternoon Adventures* Volume 2. Permission to quote or reproduce material for reviews must be obtained from the publisher.

Thanks to Jonathan H. Gray, Thomas Jensen, Iliana Lopez, Erik Rosengarten, and Ken Shue.

First printing: March 2023 • ISBN 978-168396-570-1
Printed in China • Library of Congress Control Number: 2021951602

The stories in this volume were originally created in English in the United States, except where noted, and were first published in the following magazines: "Flight of the Sky-Raker" in American *TaleSpin* #1 and 2, June and July 1991 (KV 0990 and KJB 001-1), "Your Bridges Are Hangin' Down" in Brazilian *Almanaque Disney* #228, May 1990 (S 87022), "Dime After Dime" in American *Disney Adventures* Vol. 1, No. 6, April 8, 1991 (KZ 3590), "Good Dog Card" in American *Disney Adventures* Vol. 6, No. 9, July 1996 (Kus/DG 6-09B), "For the Love of Cheese" in American *Chip 'n' Dale Rescue Rangers* [series I] #17, October 1991 (Kus/CDR 17B), "Isle of Kablooey!" in American *Disney Adventures* Vol. 7, No. 11, July 1997 (KJZ 291), "Shake!" (created in English in Denmark) in Swedish *Kalle Anka & C:o* 1993-34, August 23, 1993; first American publication in *Uncle Scrooge* #352, April 2006 (D 92373), "It's a Plunderful Life!" in American Disney Adventures Vol. 1, No. 11, September 1991 (KZ 4990), "Salad Daze!" in American *Disney Adventures* Vol. 2, No. 6, April 1992 (KJZ 047b), "Duke Igthorn's Bridge" in Brazilian *Disneylândia* #2, February 1990 (S 88174), "The Long Flight Home" in American *TaleSpin* #7, December 1991 (KJB 011), "Vogue's Gallery" in American *Disney Adventures* Vol. 3, No. 10, August 1993 (KJZ 125), "Catch of the Day" in American *TaleSpin* #7, December 1991 (KZ 7390)

Cover art by Rick Hoover, color by Gail Bailey. Title page art by Rick Hoover, color by Gail Bailey, restoration by David Gerstein and Henrieke Goorhuis

TITLES IN THIS SERIES

Darkwing Duck: Just Us Justice Ducks (*The Disney Afternoon Adventures* Vol. 1)
TaleSpin: Flight of the Sky-Raker (*The Disney Afternoon Adventures* Vol. 2)

COMING SOON

Chip 'n Dale Rescue Rangers: The Count Roquefort Case (*The Disney Afternoon Adventures* Vol. 3)

ALSO AVAILABLE

Walt Disney's Donald Duck: Duck Luck (Carl Barks)
Donald Duck: 20,000 Leaks Under the Sea (Dick Kinney and Al Hubbard) (*Disney Masters* Vol. 20)
Mickey Mouse: The Monster of Sawtooth Mountain (Paul Murry) *(Disney Masters Vol. 21)*
Donald Duck: Donald's Happiest Adventures (Lewis Trondheim and Nicolas Keramidas)
Walt Disney Uncle Scrooge and Donald Duck: Bear Mountain Tales (20 American and international artists, including Carl Barks, Don Rosa, Daniel Branca, and Giorgio Cavazzano)
Walt Disney's Uncle Scrooge: The Diamond Jubilee Collection (Carl Barks with William Van Horn and Daan Jippes)
The Complete Life and Times of Scrooge McDuck Deluxe Edition (Don Rosa)

FROM OUR NON-DISNEY CATALOG

Nuft and the Last Dragons: By Balloon to the North Pole (Freddy Milton)

Disney

TaleSpin

FLIGHT OF THE SKY-RAKER

AND OTHER STORIES

The Disney Afternoon ADVENTURES

CONTENTS

This content was first created in 1990-1997.

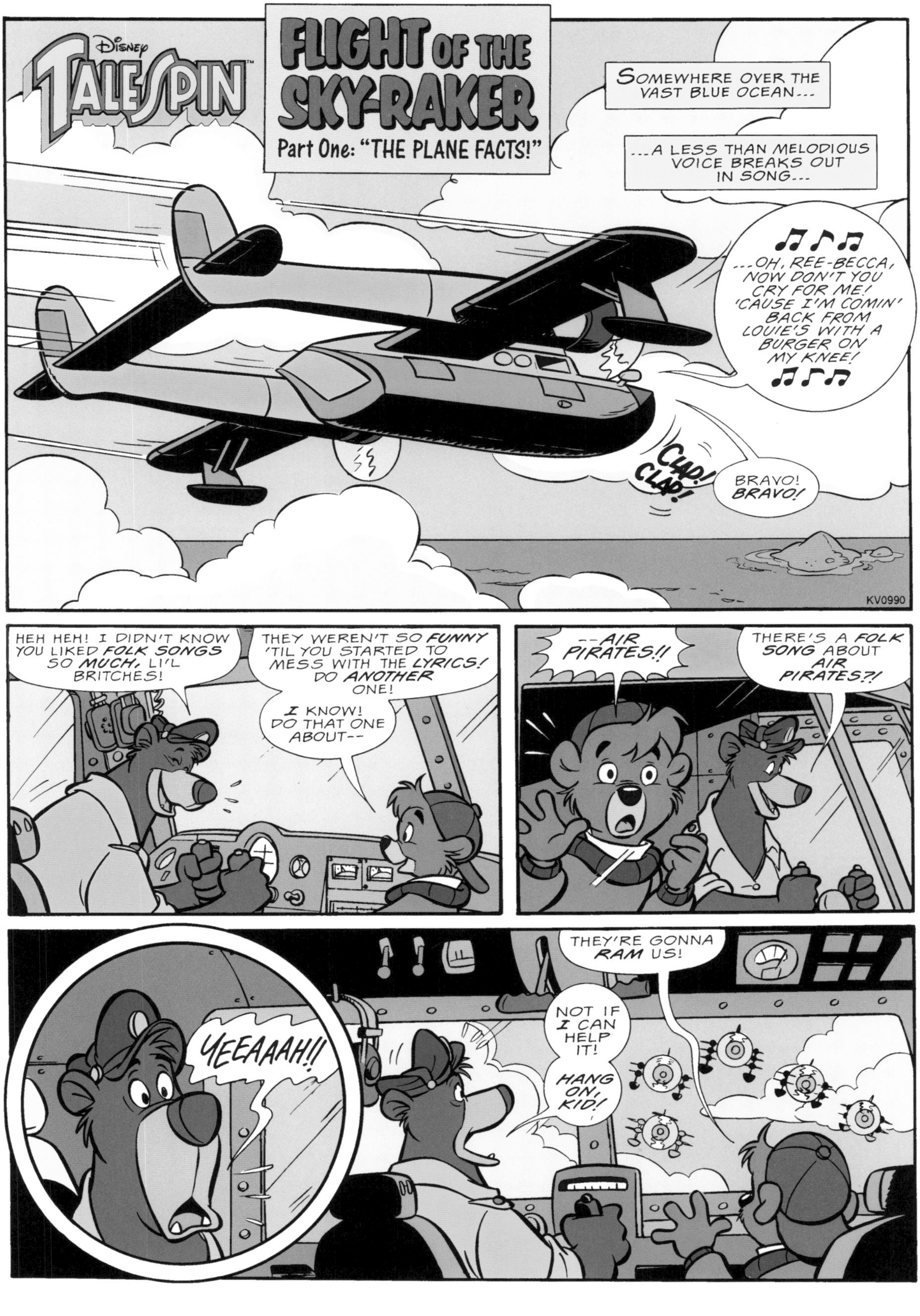
DISNEY TALESPIN
FLIGHT OF THE SKY-RAKER
Part One: "THE PLANE FACTS!"
SOMEWHERE OVER THE VAST BLUE OCEAN...
...A LESS THAN MELODIOUS VOICE BREAKS OUT IN SONG...
...OH, REE-BECCA, NOW DON'T YOU CRY FOR ME! 'CAUSE I'M COMIN' BACK FROM LOUIE'S WITH A BURGER ON MY KNEE!
CLAP! CLAP!
BRAVO! BRAVO!
KV0990
HEH HEH! I DIDN'T KNOW YOU LIKED FOLK SONGS SO MUCH, LI'L BRITCHES!
THEY WEREN'T SO FUNNY 'TIL YOU STARTED TO MESS WITH THE LYRICS! DO ANOTHER ONE!
I KNOW! DO THAT ONE ABOUT--
--AIR PIRATES!!
THERE'S A FOLK SONG ABOUT AIR PIRATES?!
YEEAAAH!!
THEY'RE GONNA RAM US!
NOT IF I CAN HELP IT!
HANG ON, KID!

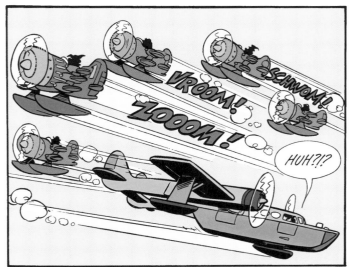

VROOM!

SCHWOM!

ZOOOM!

HUH?!?

DID I JUST *MISS* SOMETHIN'?

NO, I'D SAY *SOMETHING* JUST MISSED *US!*

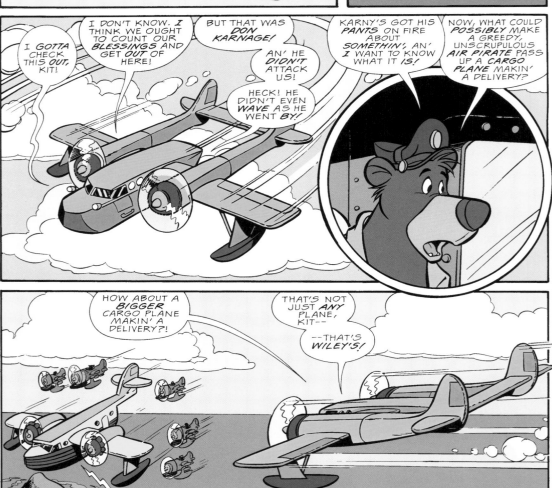

I GOTTA CHECK THIS *OUT*, KIT!

I DON'T KNOW. *I* THINK WE OUGHT TO COUNT OUR *BLESSINGS* AND GET *OUT* OF HERE!

BUT THAT WAS *DON KARNAGE!*

AN' HE *DIDN'T* ATTACK US!

HECK! HE DIDN'T EVEN *WAVE* AS HE WENT *BY!!*

KARNY'S GOT HIS *PANTS* ON FIRE ABOUT *SOMETHIN'*, AN' *I* WANT TO KNOW WHAT IT *IS!*

NOW, WHAT COULD *POSSIBLY* MAKE A GREEDY, UNSCRUPULOUS *AIR PIRATE* PASS UP A *CARGO PLANE* MAKIN' A DELIVERY?

HOW ABOUT A *BIGGER* CARGO PLANE MAKIN' A DELIVERY?!

THAT'S NOT JUST *ANY* PLANE, KIT—

—THAT'S *WILEY'S!*

MAYDAY! MAYDAY! THIS IS *WILEY POLE!* I'M UNDER ATTACK! MAYDAY! *MAYDAY!!*

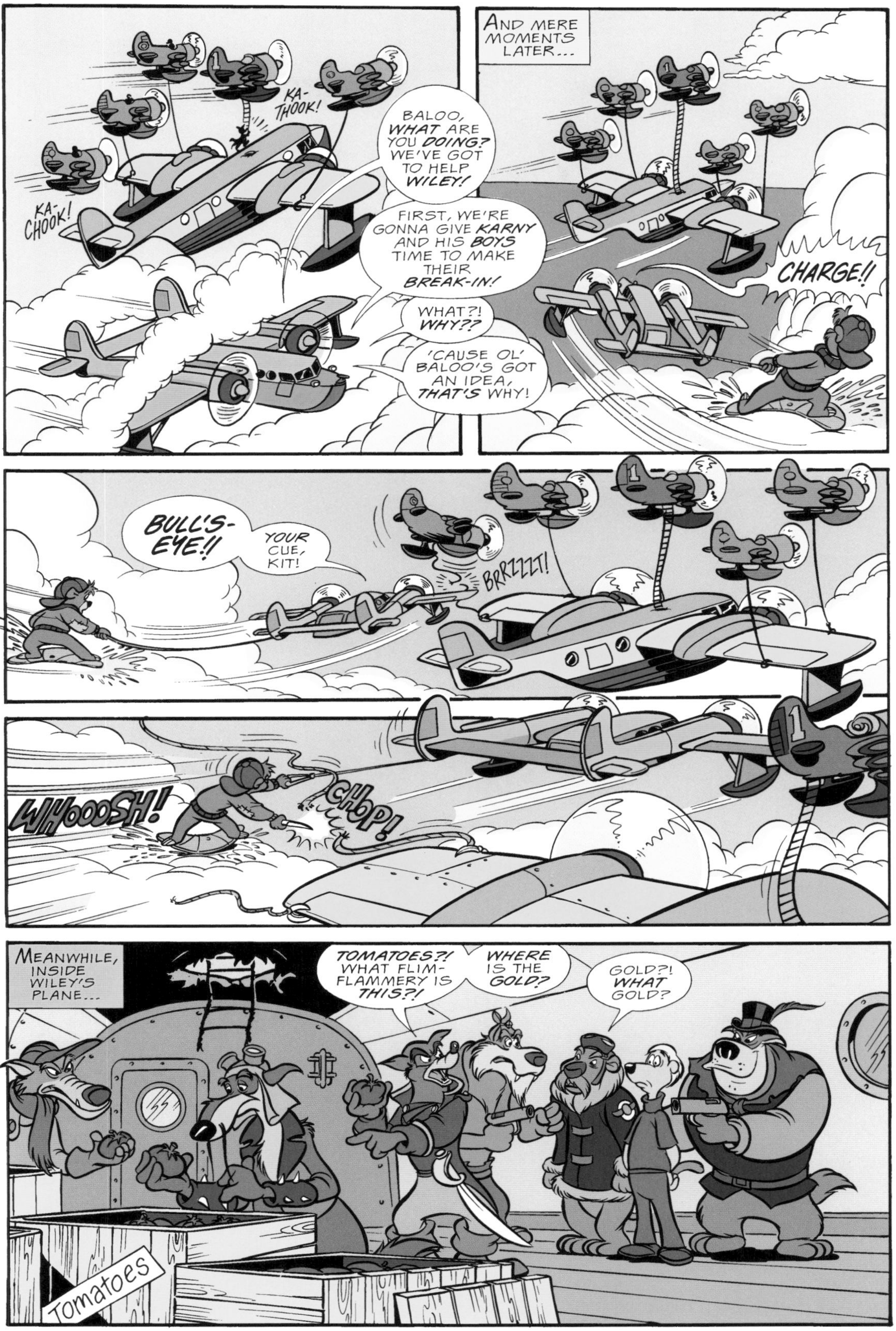
KA-THOOK!
KA-CHOOK!
BALOO, WHAT ARE YOU DOING? WE'VE GOT TO HELP WILEY!
FIRST, WE'RE GONNA GIVE KARNY AND HIS BOYS TIME TO MAKE THEIR BREAK-IN!
WHAT?! WHY??
'CAUSE OL' BALOO'S GOT AN IDEA, THAT'S WHY!
AND MERE MOMENTS LATER...
CHARGE!!
BULL'S-EYE!!
YOUR CUE, KIT!
BRRZZZT!
WHOOOSH!
CHOP!
MEANWHILE, INSIDE WILEY'S PLANE...
TOMATOES?! WHAT FLIM-FLAMMERY IS THIS?!
WHERE IS THE GOLD?
GOLD?! WHAT GOLD?
Tomatoes

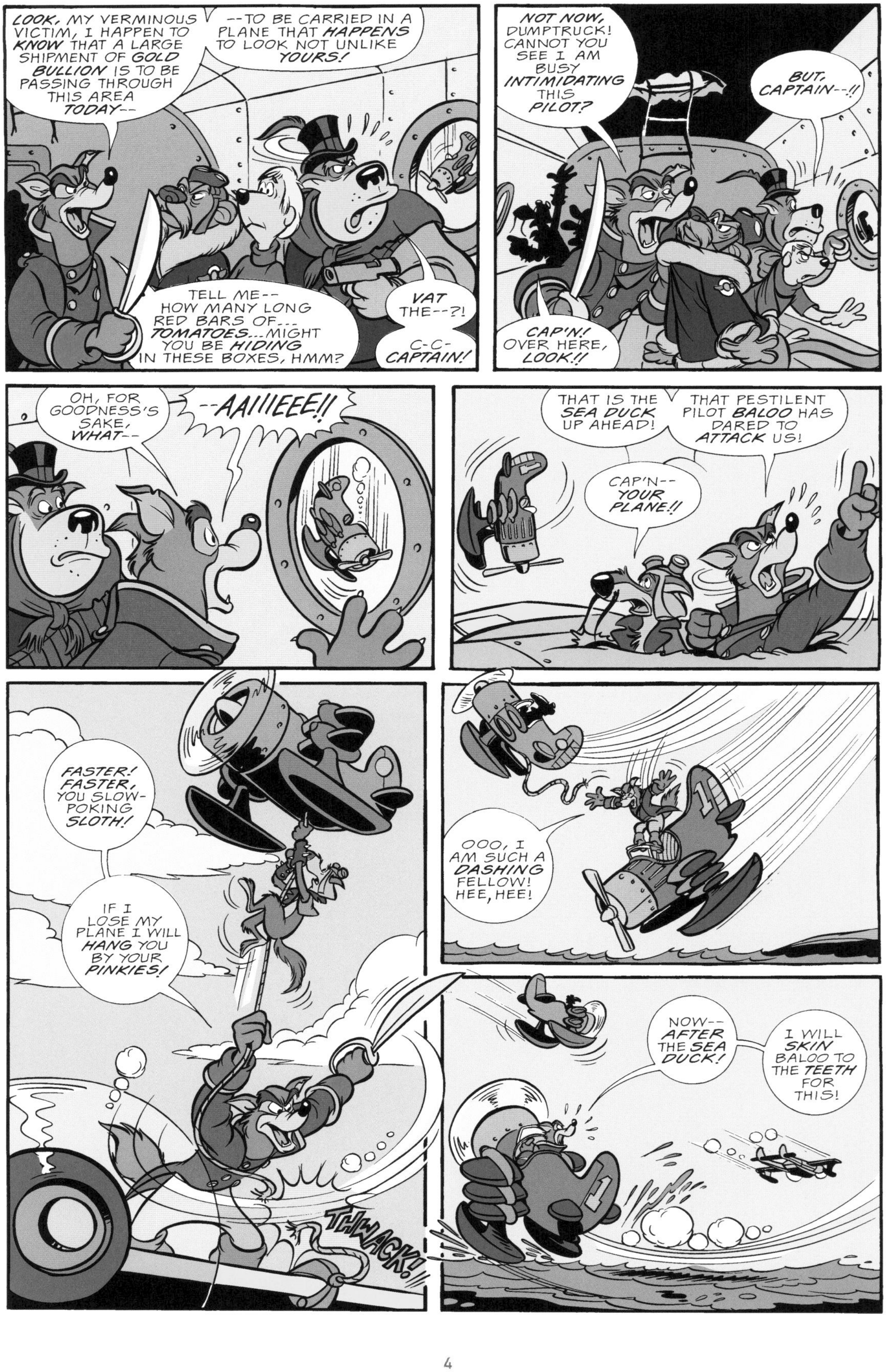
LOOK, MY VERMINOUS VICTIM, I HAPPEN TO KNOW THAT A LARGE SHIPMENT OF GOLD BULLION IS TO BE PASSING THROUGH THIS AREA TODAY--
--TO BE CARRIED IN A PLANE THAT HAPPENS TO LOOK NOT UNLIKE YOURS!
TELL ME-- HOW MANY LONG RED BARS OF--- TOMATOES... MIGHT YOU BE HIDING IN THESE BOXES, HMM?
VAT THE--?!
C-C-CAPTAIN!
NOT NOW, DUMPTRUCK! CANNOT YOU SEE I AM BUSY INTIMIDATING THIS PILOT?
BUT, CAPTAIN--!!
CAP'N! OVER HERE, LOOK!!
OH, FOR GOODNESS'S SAKE, WHAT--
--AAIIIEEE!!
THAT IS THE SEA DUCK UP AHEAD!
THAT PESTILENT PILOT BALOO HAS DARED TO ATTACK US!
CAP'N-- YOUR PLANE!!
FASTER! FASTER, YOU SLOW-POKING SLOTH!
IF I LOSE MY PLANE I WILL HANG YOU BY YOUR PINKIES!
THWACK!
OOO, I AM SUCH A DASHING FELLOW! HEE, HEE!
NOW-- AFTER THE SEA DUCK!
I WILL SKIN BALOO TO THE TEETH FOR THIS!

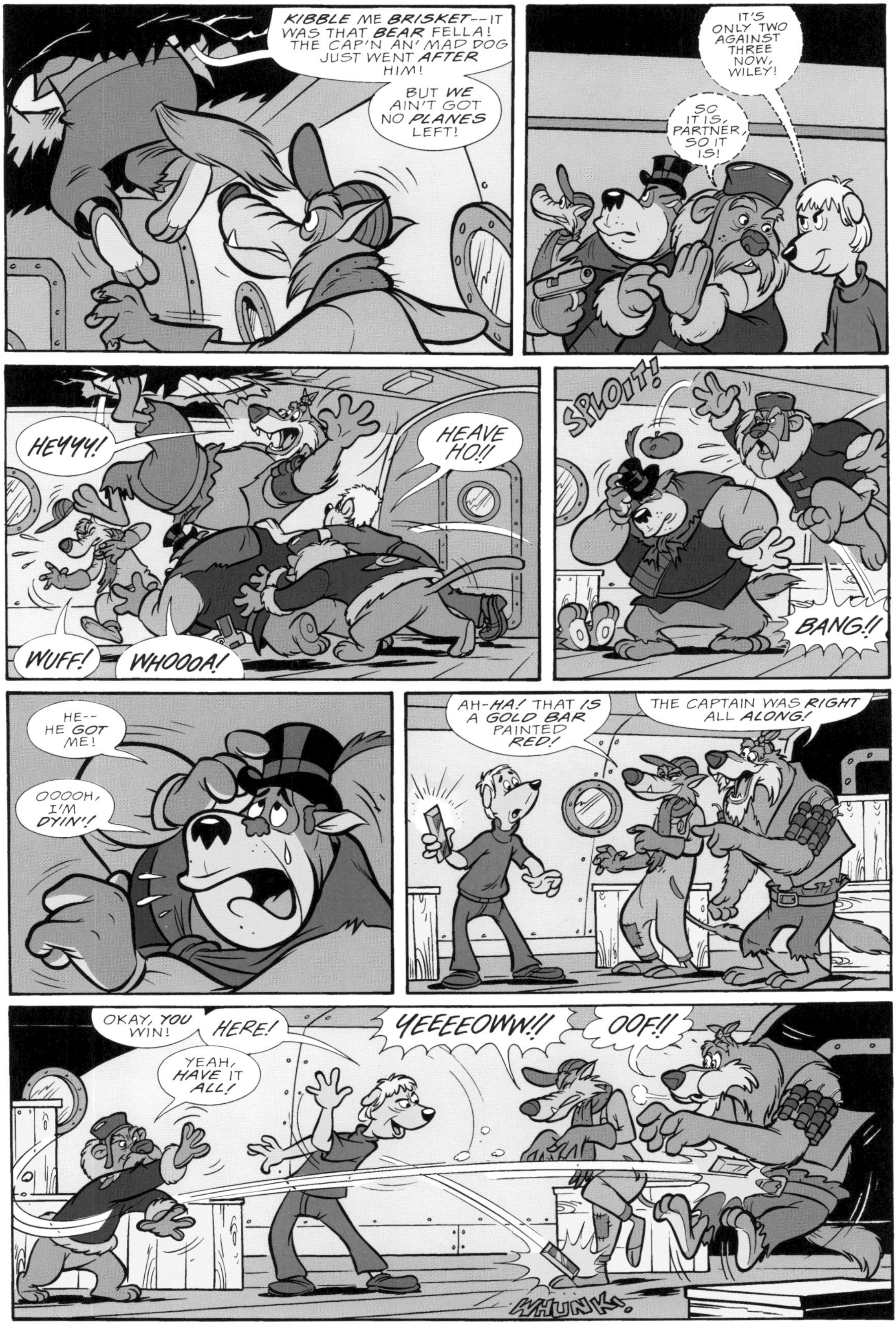

KIBBLE ME BRISKET--IT WAS THAT BEAR FELLA! THE CAP'N AN' MAD DOG JUST WENT AFTER HIM!
BUT WE AIN'T GOT NO PLANES LEFT!
IT'S ONLY TWO AGAINST THREE NOW, WILEY!
SO IT IS, PARTNER, SO IT IS!
HEYYY!
HEAVE HO!!
WUFF!
WHOOOA!
SPLOIT!
BANG!!
HE-- HE GOT ME!
OOOOH, I'M DYIN'!
AH-HA! THAT IS A GOLD BAR PAINTED RED!
THE CAPTAIN WAS RIGHT ALL ALONG!
OKAY, YOU WIN!
HERE!
YEAH, HAVE IT ALL!
YEEEEOWW!!
OOF!!
WHUNK!

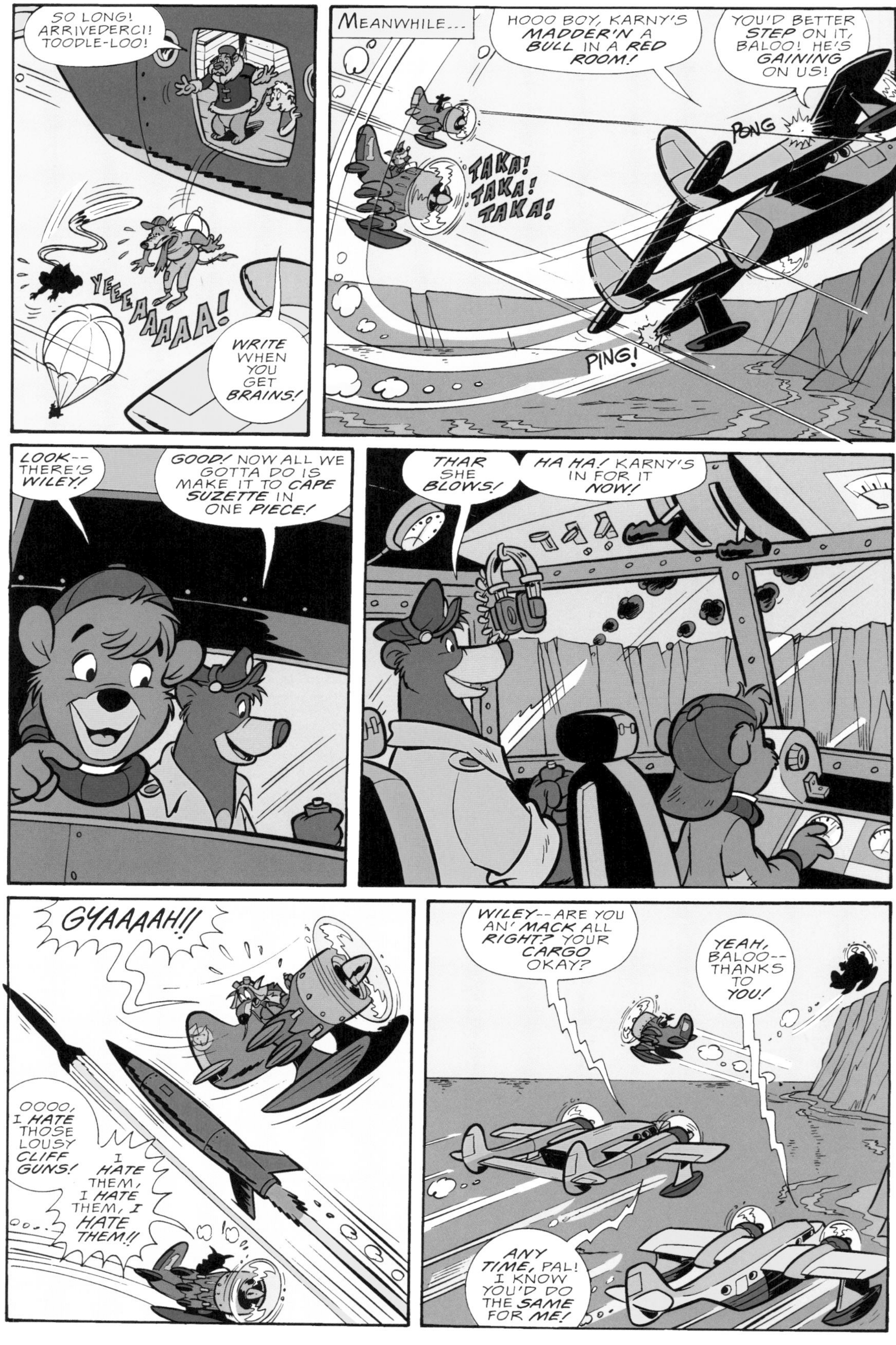
SO LONG! ARRIVEDERCI! TOODLE-LOO!
YEEEAAAAAA!
WRITE WHEN YOU GET BRAINS!
MEANWHILE...
HOOO BOY, KARNY'S MADDER'N A BULL IN A RED ROOM!
YOU'D BETTER STEP ON IT, BALOO! HE'S GAINING ON US!
PONG
TAKA! TAKA! TAKA!
PING!
LOOK-- THERE'S WILEY!
GOOD! NOW ALL WE GOTTA DO IS MAKE IT TO CAPE SUZETTE IN ONE PIECE!
THAR SHE BLOWS!
HA HA! KARNY'S IN FOR IT NOW!
GYAAAAH!!
OOOO, I HATE THOSE LOUSY CLIFF GUNS!
I HATE THEM, I HATE THEM, I HATE THEM!!
WILEY-- ARE YOU AN' MACK ALL RIGHT? YOUR CARGO OKAY?
YEAH, BALOO-- THANKS TO YOU!
ANY TIME, PAL! I KNOW YOU'D DO THE SAME FOR ME!

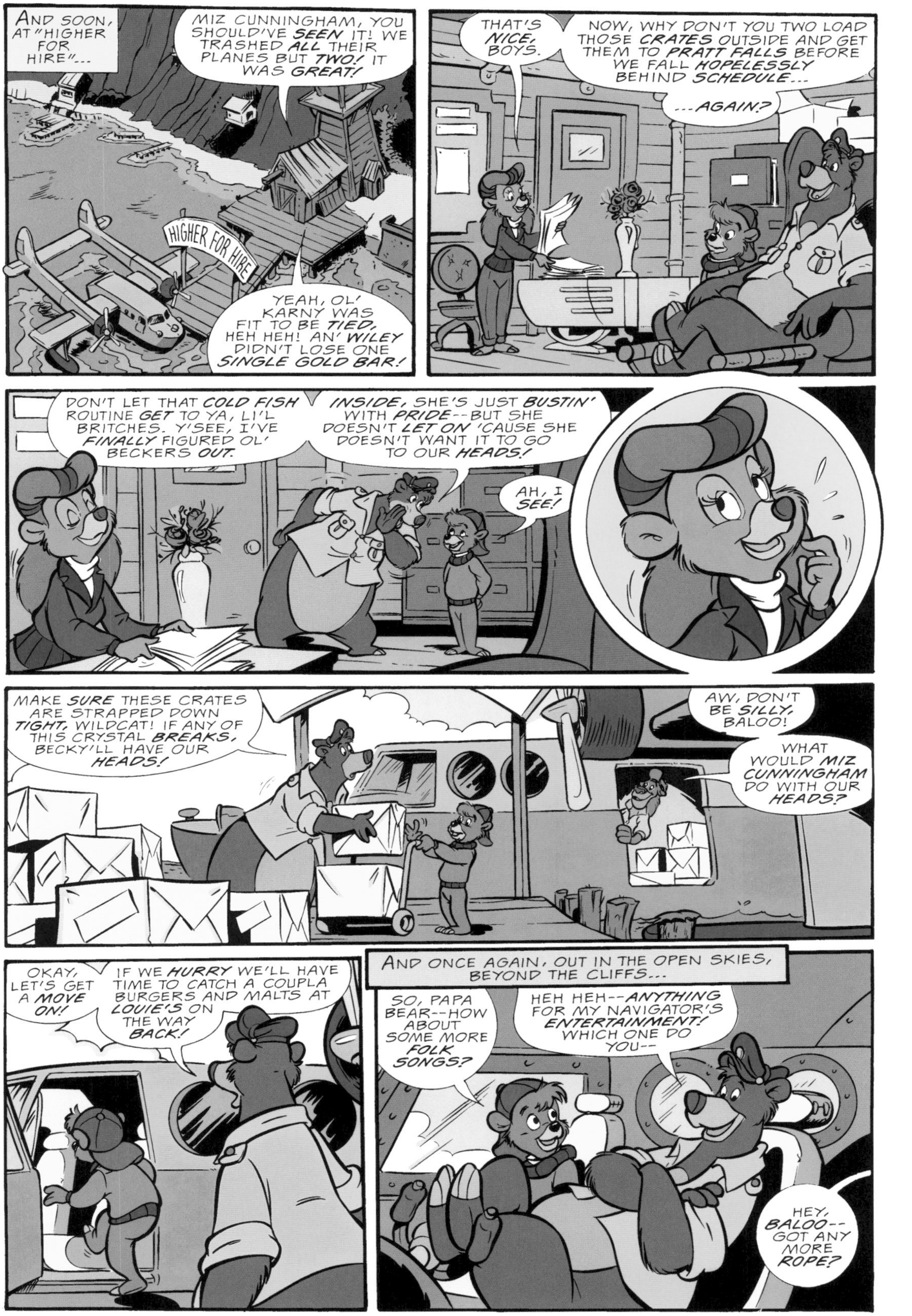
AND SOON, AT "HIGHER FOR HIRE"...
MIZ CUNNINGHAM, YOU SHOULD'VE SEEN IT! WE TRASHED ALL THEIR PLANES BUT TWO! IT WAS GREAT!
HIGHER FOR HIRE
YEAH, OL' KARNY WAS FIT TO BE TIED, HEH HEH! AN' WILEY DIDN'T LOSE ONE SINGLE GOLD BAR!
THAT'S NICE, BOYS.
NOW, WHY DON'T YOU TWO LOAD THOSE CRATES OUTSIDE AND GET THEM TO PRATT FALLS BEFORE WE FALL HOPELESSLY BEHIND SCHEDULE...
...AGAIN?
DON'T LET THAT COLD FISH ROUTINE GET TO YA, LI'L BRITCHES. Y'SEE, I'VE FINALLY FIGURED OL' BECKERS OUT.
INSIDE, SHE'S JUST BUSTIN' WITH PRIDE--BUT SHE DOESN'T LET ON 'CAUSE SHE DOESN'T WANT IT TO GO TO OUR HEADS!
AH, I SEE!
MAKE SURE THESE CRATES ARE STRAPPED DOWN TIGHT, WILDCAT! IF ANY OF THIS CRYSTAL BREAKS, BECKY'LL HAVE OUR HEADS!
AW, DON'T BE SILLY, BALOO!
WHAT WOULD MIZ CUNNINGHAM DO WITH OUR HEADS?
OKAY, LET'S GET A MOVE ON!
IF WE HURRY WE'LL HAVE TIME TO CATCH A COUPLA BURGERS AND MALTS AT LOUIE'S ON THE WAY BACK!
AND ONCE AGAIN, OUT IN THE OPEN SKIES, BEYOND THE CLIFFS...
SO, PAPA BEAR--HOW ABOUT SOME MORE FOLK SONGS?
HEH HEH--ANYTHING FOR MY NAVIGATOR'S ENTERTAINMENT! WHICH ONE DO YOU--
HEY, BALOO--GOT ANY MORE ROPE?

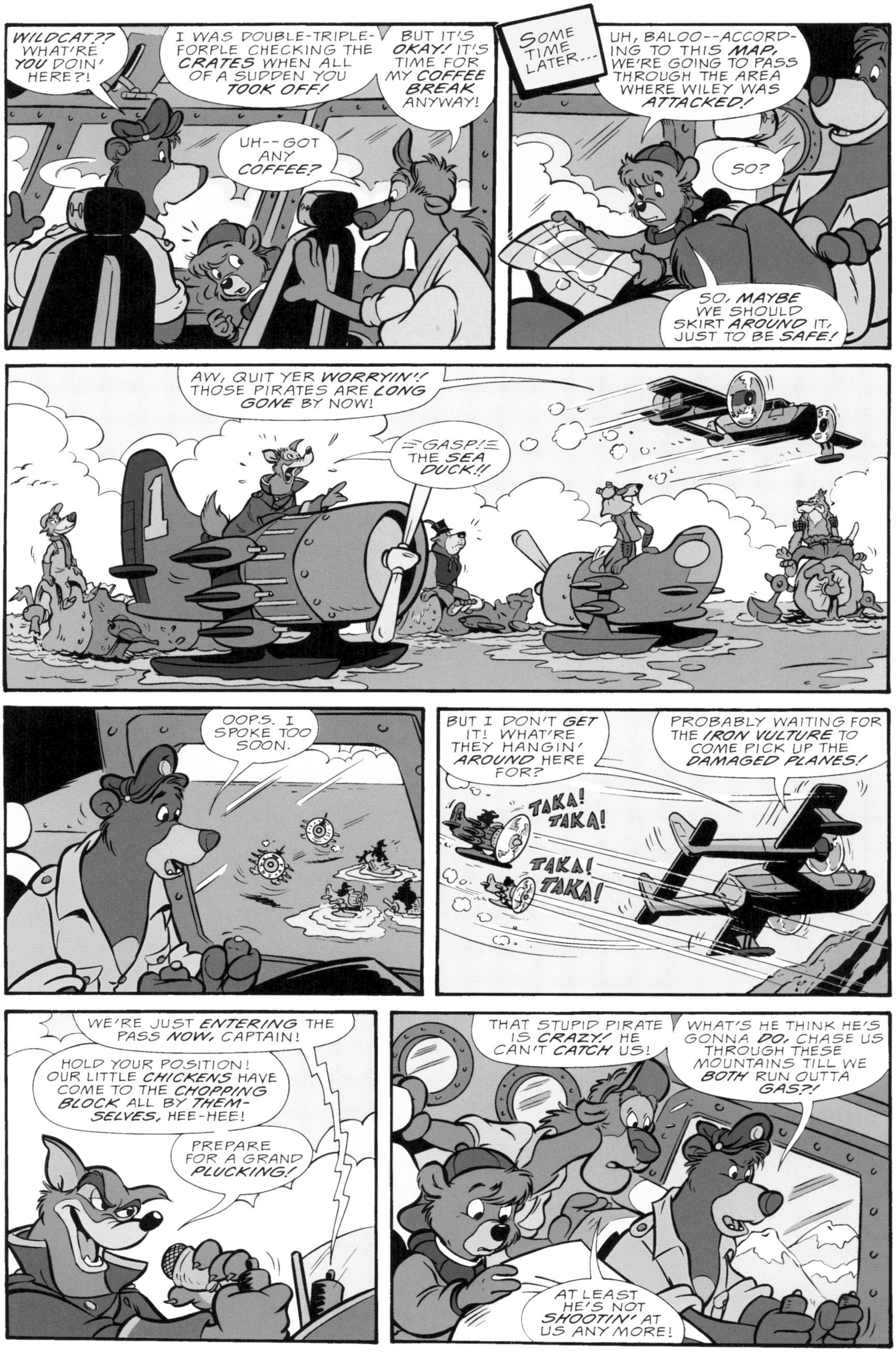
WILDCAT?? WHAT'RE YOU DOIN' HERE?!
I WAS DOUBLE-TRIPLE-FORPLE CHECKING THE CRATES WHEN ALL OF A SUDDEN YOU TOOK OFF!
BUT IT'S OKAY! IT'S TIME FOR MY COFFEE BREAK ANYWAY!
UH-- GOT ANY COFFEE?
SOME TIME LATER...
UH, BALOO--ACCORDING TO THIS MAP, WE'RE GOING TO PASS THROUGH THE AREA WHERE WILEY WAS ATTACKED!
SO?
SO, MAYBE WE SHOULD SKIRT AROUND IT, JUST TO BE SAFE!
AW, QUIT YER WORRYIN'! THOSE PIRATES ARE LONG GONE BY NOW!
GASP! THE SEA DUCK!!
OOPS. I SPOKE TOO SOON.
BUT I DON'T GET IT! WHAT'RE THEY HANGIN' AROUND HERE FOR?
PROBABLY WAITING FOR THE IRON VULTURE TO COME PICK UP THE DAMAGED PLANES!
TAKA! TAKA!
TAKA! TAKA!
WE'RE JUST ENTERING THE PASS NOW, CAPTAIN!
HOLD YOUR POSITION! OUR LITTLE CHICKENS HAVE COME TO THE CHOPPING BLOCK ALL BY THEMSELVES, HEE-HEE!
PREPARE FOR A GRAND PLUCKING!
THAT STUPID PIRATE IS CRAZY! HE CAN'T CATCH US!
WHAT'S HE THINK HE'S GONNA DO, CHASE US THROUGH THESE MOUNTAINS TILL WE BOTH RUN OUTTA GAS?!
AT LEAST HE'S NOT SHOOTIN' AT US ANY MORE!

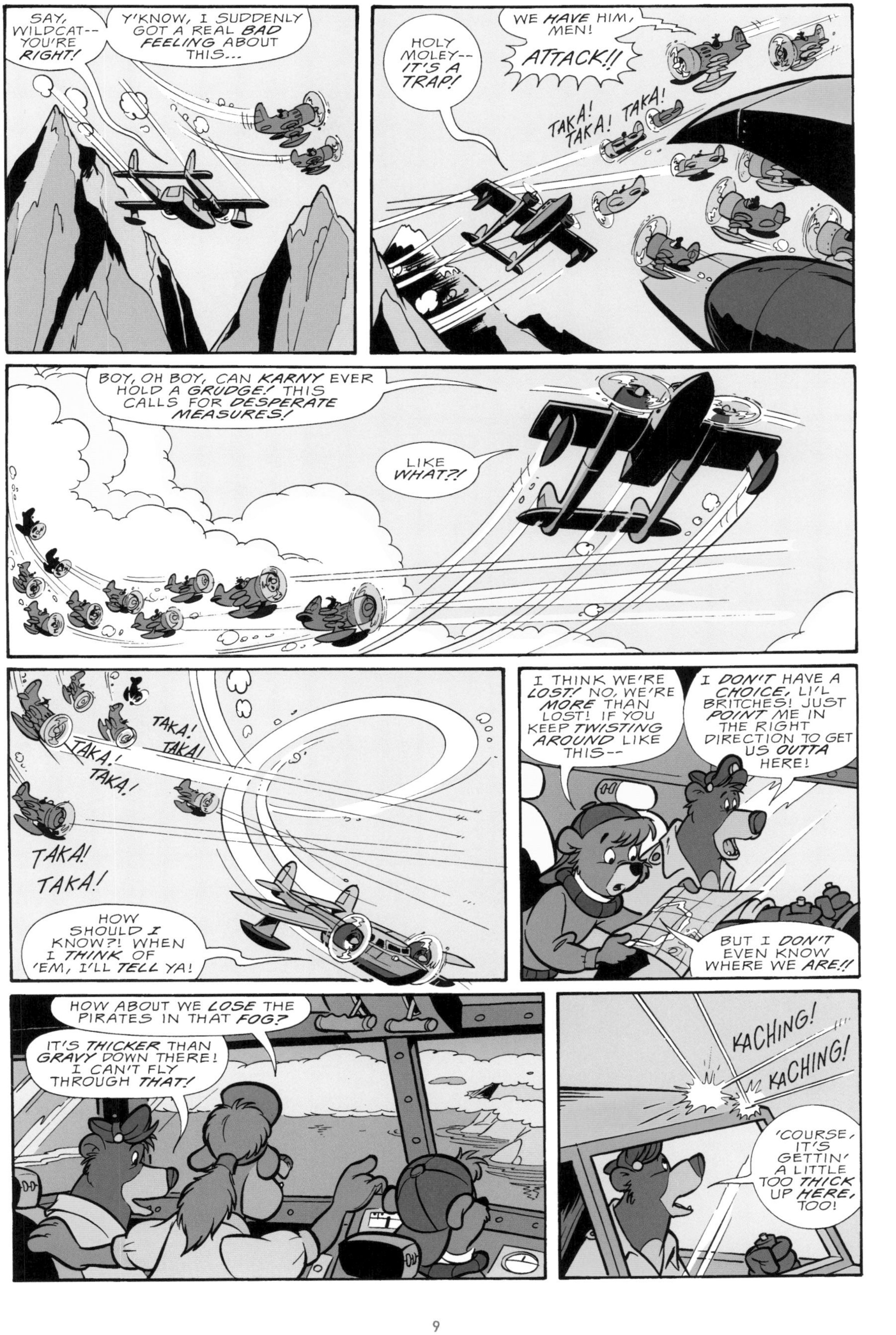

SAY, WILDCAT-- YOU'RE RIGHT!
Y'KNOW, I SUDDENLY GOT A REAL BAD FEELING ABOUT THIS...
HOLY MOLEY-- IT'S A TRAP!
WE HAVE HIM, MEN!
ATTACK!!
TAKA! TAKA! TAKA!
BOY, OH BOY, CAN KARNY EVER HOLD A GRUDGE! THIS CALLS FOR DESPERATE MEASURES!
LIKE WHAT?!
TAKA! TAKA! TAKA! TAKA!
TAKA! TAKA!
HOW SHOULD I KNOW?! WHEN I THINK OF 'EM, I'LL TELL YA!
I THINK WE'RE LOST! NO, WE'RE MORE THAN LOST! IF YOU KEEP TWISTING AROUND LIKE THIS--
I DON'T HAVE A CHOICE, LI'L BRITCHES! JUST POINT ME IN THE RIGHT DIRECTION TO GET US OUTTA HERE!
BUT I DON'T EVEN KNOW WHERE WE ARE!!
HOW ABOUT WE LOSE THE PIRATES IN THAT FOG?
IT'S THICKER THAN GRAVY DOWN THERE! I CAN'T FLY THROUGH THAT!
KACHING!
KACHING!
'COURSE, IT'S GETTIN' A LITTLE TOO THICK UP HERE, TOO!

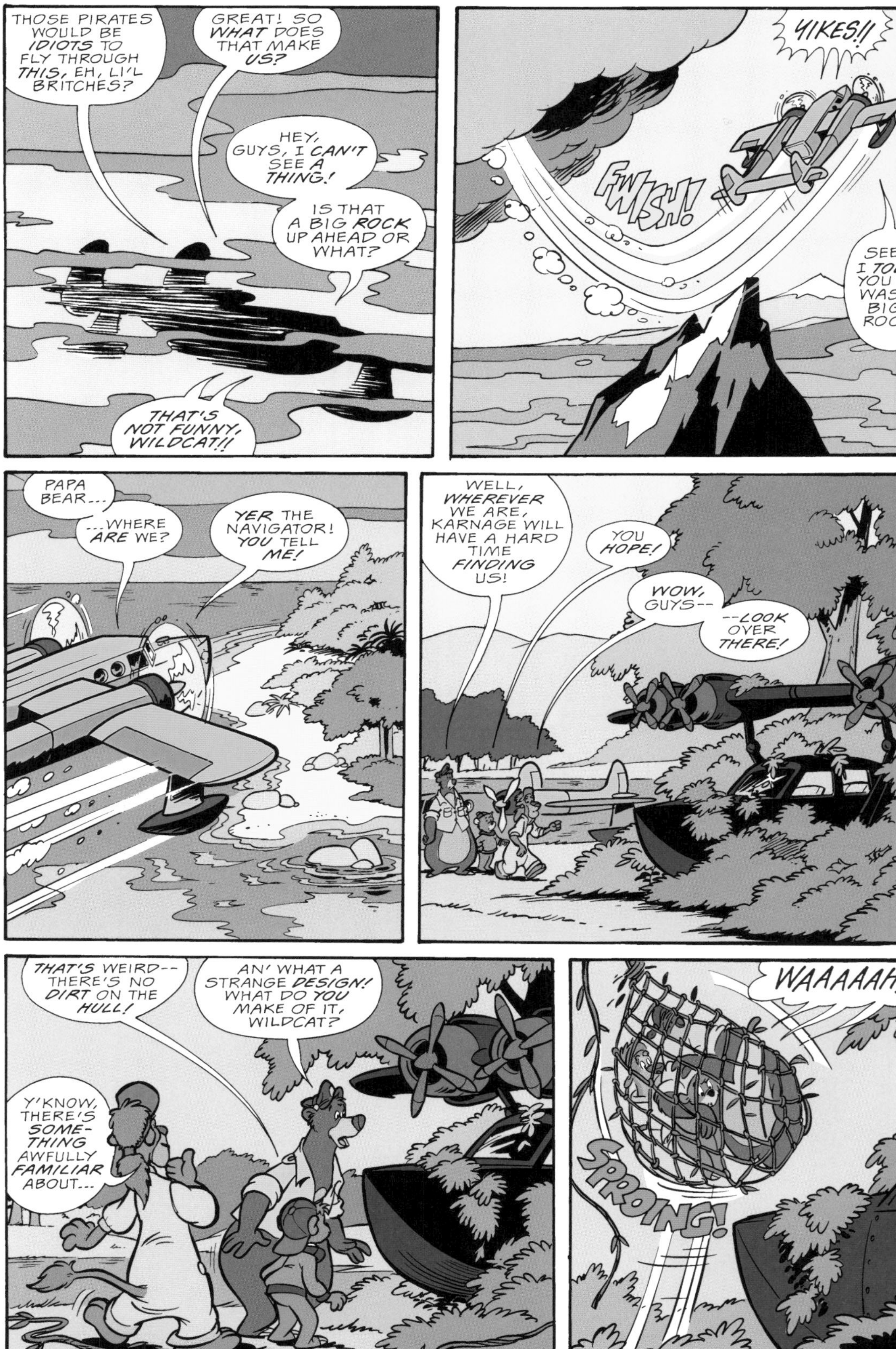
THOSE PIRATES WOULD BE IDIOTS TO FLY THROUGH THIS, EH, LI'L BRITCHES?
GREAT! SO WHAT DOES THAT MAKE US?
HEY, GUYS, I CAN'T SEE A THING!
IS THAT A BIG ROCK UP AHEAD OR WHAT?
THAT'S NOT FUNNY, WILDCAT!!
YIKES!!
FWISH!
SEE? I TOLD YOU IT WAS A BIG ROCK!
PAPA BEAR...
...WHERE ARE WE?
YER THE NAVIGATOR! YOU TELL ME!
WELL, WHEREVER WE ARE, KARNAGE WILL HAVE A HARD TIME FINDING US!
YOU HOPE!
WOW, GUYS--
--LOOK OVER THERE!
THAT'S WEIRD-- THERE'S NO DIRT ON THE HULL!
AN' WHAT A STRANGE DESIGN! WHAT DO YOU MAKE OF IT, WILDCAT?
Y'KNOW, THERE'S SOME-THING AWFULLY FAMILIAR ABOUT...
WAAAAAH!!
SPROING!

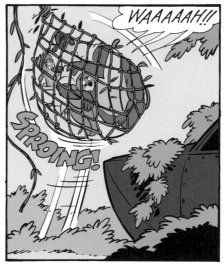

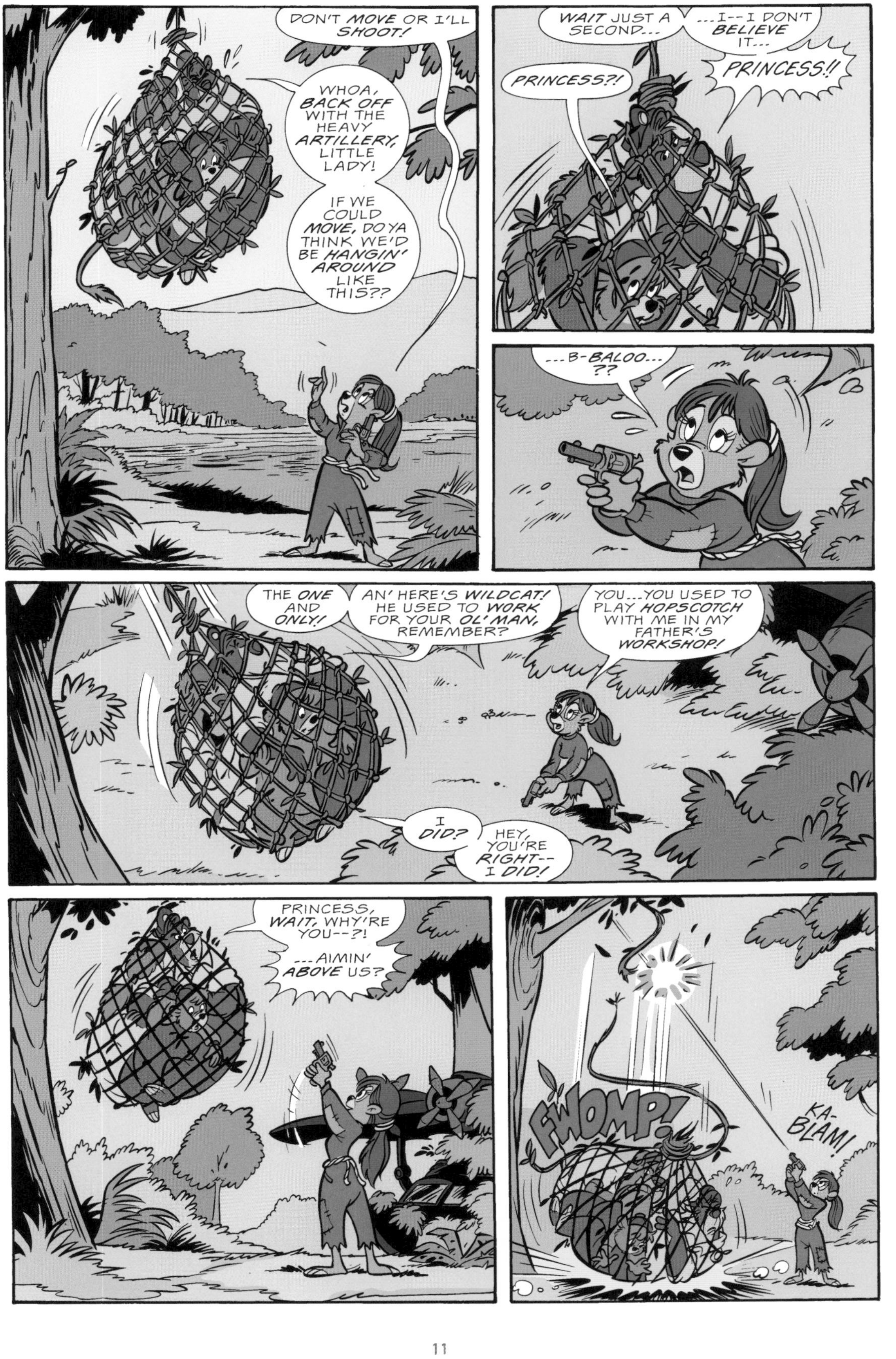
DON'T MOVE OR I'LL SHOOT!
WHOA, BACK OFF WITH THE HEAVY ARTILLERY, LITTLE LADY!
IF WE COULD MOVE, DO YA THINK WE'D BE HANGIN' AROUND LIKE THIS??
WAIT JUST A SECOND...
...I--I DON'T BELIEVE IT...
PRINCESS?!
PRINCESS!!
...B-BALOO...??
THE ONE AND ONLY!
AN' HERE'S WILDCAT! HE USED TO WORK FOR YOUR OL' MAN, REMEMBER?
YOU...YOU USED TO PLAY HOPSCOTCH WITH ME IN MY FATHER'S WORKSHOP!
I DID?
HEY, YOU'RE RIGHT-- I DID!
PRINCESS, WAIT, WHY'RE YOU--?!
...AIMIN' ABOVE US?
FWOMP!
KA-BLAM!

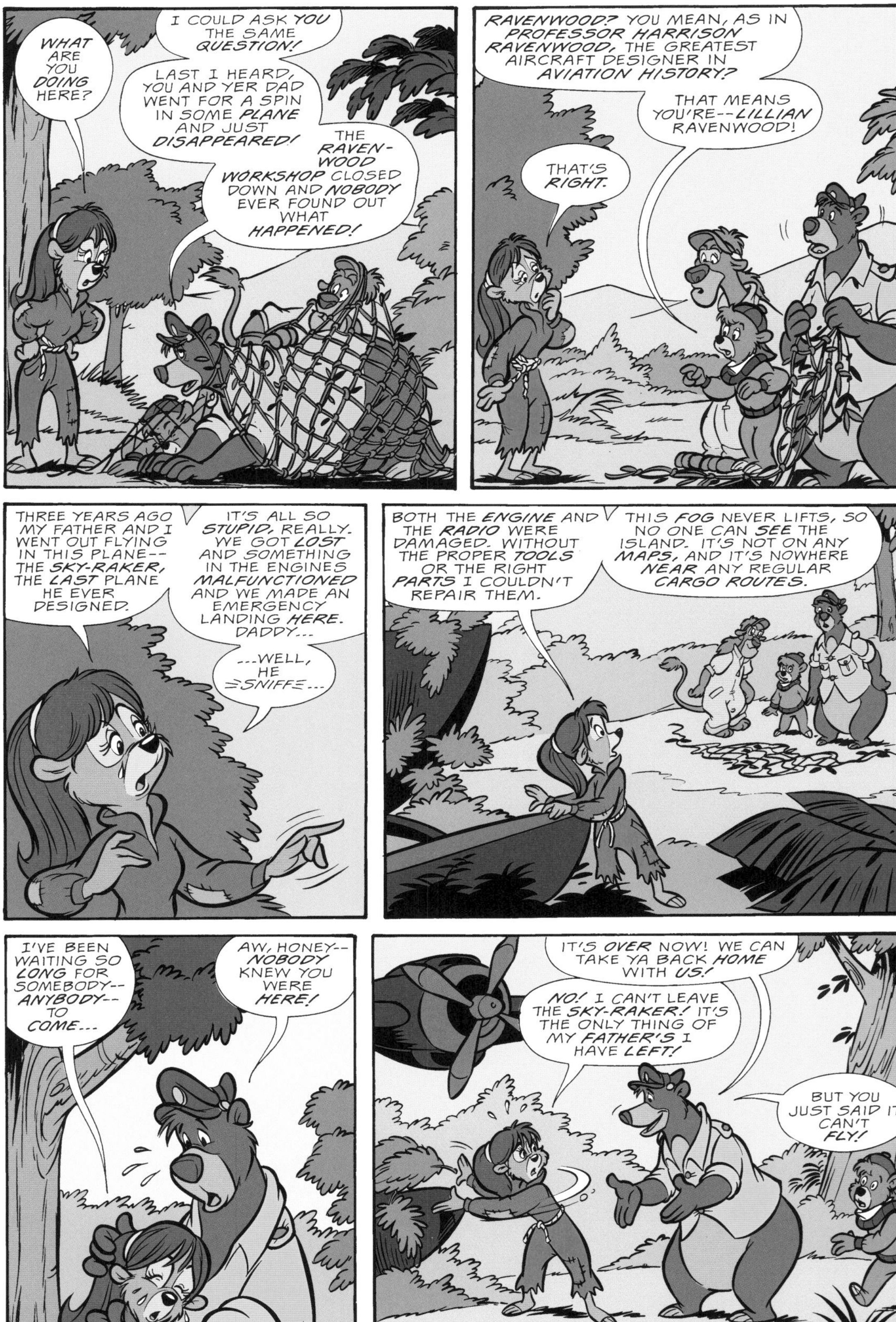
WHAT ARE YOU DOING HERE?
I COULD ASK YOU THE SAME QUESTION!
LAST I HEARD, YOU AND YER DAD WENT FOR A SPIN IN SOME PLANE AND JUST DISAPPEARED!
THE RAVEN-WOOD WORKSHOP CLOSED DOWN AND NOBODY EVER FOUND OUT WHAT HAPPENED!
RAVENWOOD? YOU MEAN, AS IN PROFESSOR HARRISON RAVENWOOD, THE GREATEST AIRCRAFT DESIGNER IN AVIATION HISTORY?
THAT MEANS YOU'RE--LILLIAN RAVENWOOD!
THAT'S RIGHT.
THREE YEARS AGO MY FATHER AND I WENT OUT FLYING IN THIS PLANE-- THE SKY-RAKER, THE LAST PLANE HE EVER DESIGNED.
IT'S ALL SO STUPID, REALLY. WE GOT LOST AND SOMETHING IN THE ENGINES MALFUNCTIONED AND WE MADE AN EMERGENCY LANDING HERE. DADDY...
--WELL, HE =SNIFF=--
BOTH THE ENGINE AND THE RADIO WERE DAMAGED. WITHOUT THE PROPER TOOLS OR THE RIGHT PARTS I COULDN'T REPAIR THEM.
THIS FOG NEVER LIFTS, SO NO ONE CAN SEE THE ISLAND. IT'S NOT ON ANY MAPS, AND IT'S NOWHERE NEAR ANY REGULAR CARGO ROUTES.
I'VE BEEN WAITING SO LONG FOR SOMEBODY-- ANYBODY-- TO COME...
AW, HONEY-- NOBODY KNEW YOU WERE HERE!
IT'S OVER NOW! WE CAN TAKE YA BACK HOME WITH US!
NO! I CAN'T LEAVE THE SKY-RAKER! IT'S THE ONLY THING OF MY FATHER'S I HAVE LEFT!
BUT YOU JUST SAID IT CAN'T FLY!

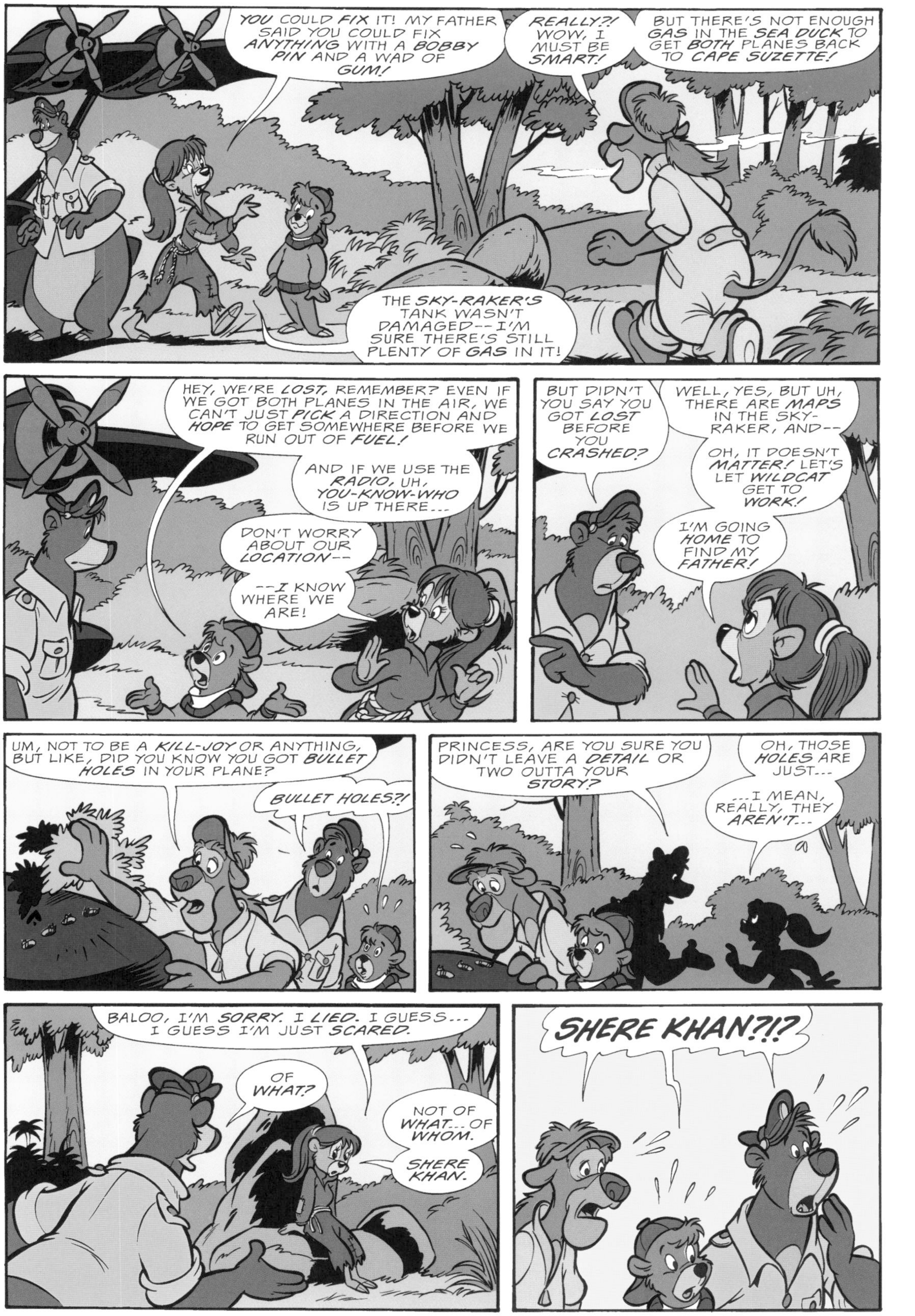
YOU COULD FIX IT! MY FATHER SAID YOU COULD FIX ANYTHING WITH A BOBBY PIN AND A WAD OF GUM!
REALLY?! WOW, I MUST BE SMART!
BUT THERE'S NOT ENOUGH GAS IN THE SEA DUCK TO GET BOTH PLANES BACK TO CAPE SUZETTE!
THE SKY-RAKER'S TANK WASN'T DAMAGED-- I'M SURE THERE'S STILL PLENTY OF GAS IN IT!
HEY, WE'RE LOST, REMEMBER? EVEN IF WE GOT BOTH PLANES IN THE AIR, WE CAN'T JUST PICK A DIRECTION AND HOPE TO GET SOMEWHERE BEFORE WE RUN OUT OF FUEL!
AND IF WE USE THE RADIO, UH, YOU-KNOW-WHO IS UP THERE...
DON'T WORRY ABOUT OUR LOCATION--
--I KNOW WHERE WE ARE!
BUT DIDN'T YOU SAY YOU GOT LOST BEFORE YOU CRASHED?
WELL, YES, BUT UH, THERE ARE MAPS IN THE SKY-RAKER, AND--
OH, IT DOESN'T MATTER! LET'S LET WILDCAT GET TO WORK!
I'M GOING HOME TO FIND MY FATHER!
UM, NOT TO BE A KILL-JOY OR ANYTHING, BUT LIKE, DID YOU KNOW YOU GOT BULLET HOLES IN YOUR PLANE?
BULLET HOLES?!
PRINCESS, ARE YOU SURE YOU DIDN'T LEAVE A DETAIL OR TWO OUTTA YOUR STORY?
OH, THOSE HOLES ARE JUST...
...I MEAN, REALLY, THEY AREN'T...
BALOO, I'M SORRY. I LIED. I GUESS... I GUESS I'M JUST SCARED.
OF WHAT?
NOT OF WHAT... OF WHOM.
SHERE KHAN.
SHERE KHAN?!?

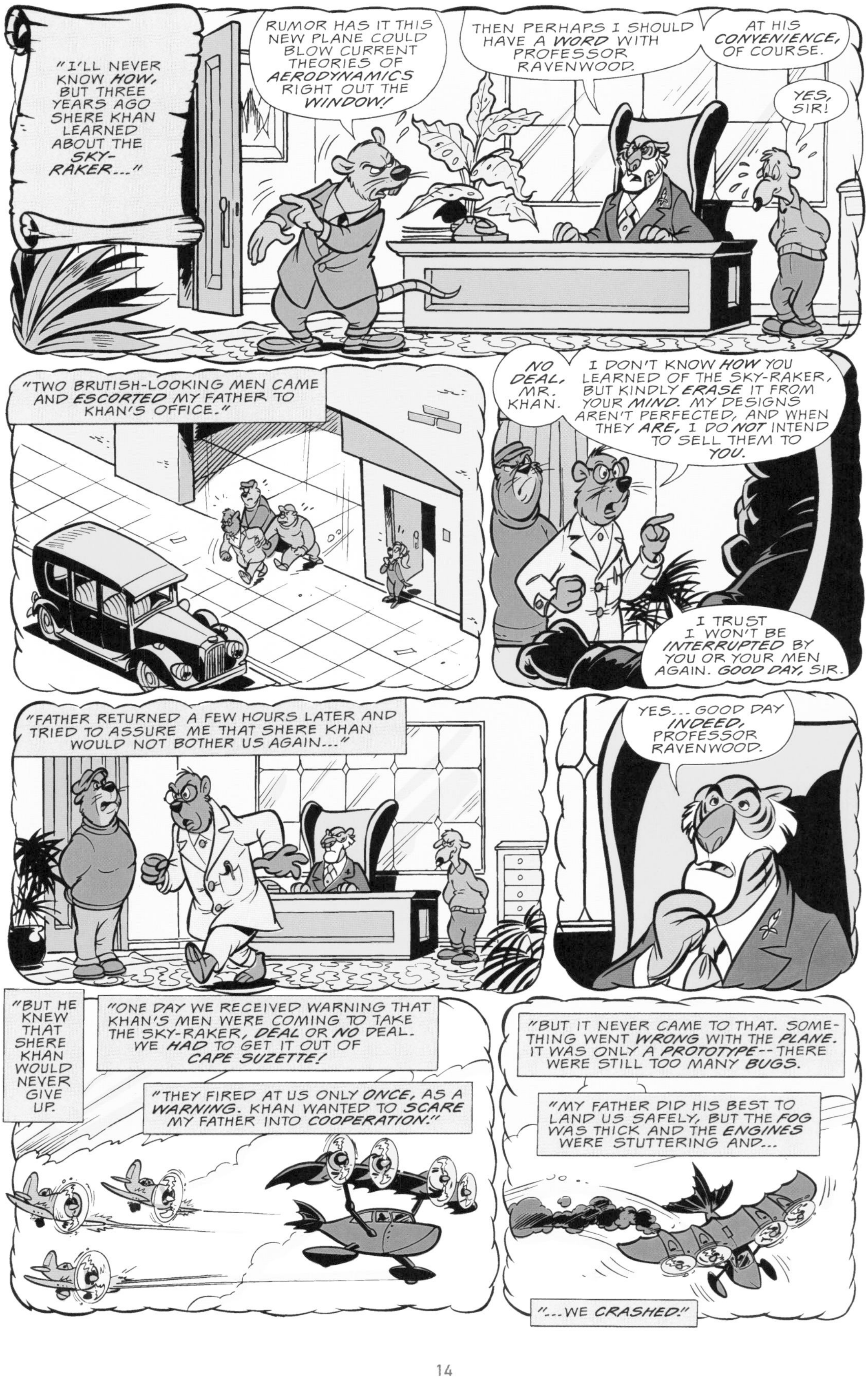
"I'LL NEVER KNOW HOW, BUT THREE YEARS AGO SHERE KHAN LEARNED ABOUT THE SKY-RAKER..."
RUMOR HAS IT THIS NEW PLANE COULD BLOW CURRENT THEORIES OF AERODYNAMICS RIGHT OUT THE WINDOW!
THEN PERHAPS I SHOULD HAVE A WORD WITH PROFESSOR RAVENWOOD.
AT HIS CONVENIENCE, OF COURSE.
YES, SIR!
"TWO BRUTISH-LOOKING MEN CAME AND ESCORTED MY FATHER TO KHAN'S OFFICE."
NO DEAL, MR. KHAN.
I DON'T KNOW HOW YOU LEARNED OF THE SKY-RAKER, BUT KINDLY ERASE IT FROM YOUR MIND. MY DESIGNS AREN'T PERFECTED, AND WHEN THEY ARE, I DO NOT INTEND TO SELL THEM TO YOU.
I TRUST I WON'T BE INTERRUPTED BY YOU OR YOUR MEN AGAIN. GOOD DAY, SIR.
"FATHER RETURNED A FEW HOURS LATER AND TRIED TO ASSURE ME THAT SHERE KHAN WOULD NOT BOTHER US AGAIN..."
YES... GOOD DAY INDEED, PROFESSOR RAVENWOOD.
"BUT HE KNEW THAT SHERE KHAN WOULD NEVER GIVE UP.
"ONE DAY WE RECEIVED WARNING THAT KHAN'S MEN WERE COMING TO TAKE THE SKY-RAKER, DEAL OR NO DEAL. WE HAD TO GET IT OUT OF CAPE SUZETTE!
"THEY FIRED AT US ONLY ONCE, AS A WARNING. KHAN WANTED TO SCARE MY FATHER INTO COOPERATION."
"BUT IT NEVER CAME TO THAT. SOMETHING WENT WRONG WITH THE PLANE. IT WAS ONLY A PROTOTYPE--THERE WERE STILL TOO MANY BUGS.
"MY FATHER DID HIS BEST TO LAND US SAFELY, BUT THE FOG WAS THICK AND THE ENGINES WERE STUTTERING AND...
"...WE CRASHED!"

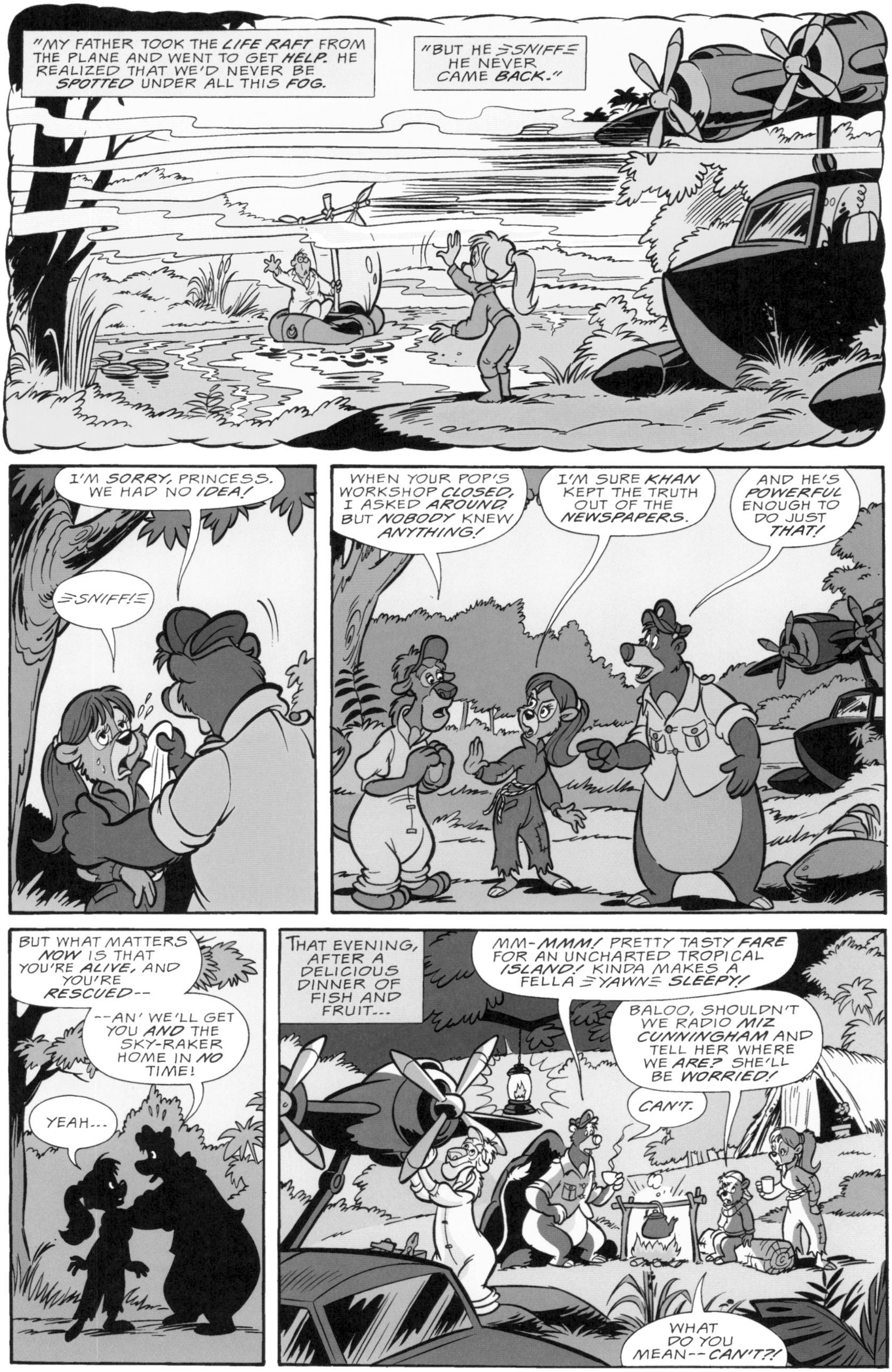
"MY FATHER TOOK THE LIFE RAFT FROM THE PLANE AND WENT TO GET HELP. HE REALIZED THAT WE'D NEVER BE SPOTTED UNDER ALL THIS FOG.
"BUT HE =SNIFF= HE NEVER CAME BACK."
I'M SORRY, PRINCESS. WE HAD NO IDEA!
=SNIFF!=
WHEN YOUR POP'S WORKSHOP CLOSED, I ASKED AROUND, BUT NOBODY KNEW ANYTHING!
I'M SURE KHAN KEPT THE TRUTH OUT OF THE NEWSPAPERS.
AND HE'S POWERFUL ENOUGH TO DO JUST THAT!
BUT WHAT MATTERS NOW IS THAT YOU'RE ALIVE, AND YOU'RE RESCUED--
--AN' WE'LL GET YOU AND THE SKY-RAKER HOME IN NO TIME!
YEAH...
THAT EVENING, AFTER A DELICIOUS DINNER OF FISH AND FRUIT...
MM-MMM! PRETTY TASTY FARE FOR AN UNCHARTED TROPICAL ISLAND! KINDA MAKES A FELLA =YAWN= SLEEPY!
BALOO, SHOULDN'T WE RADIO MIZ CUNNINGHAM AND TELL HER WHERE WE ARE? SHE'LL BE WORRIED!
CAN'T.
WHAT DO YOU MEAN--CAN'T?!

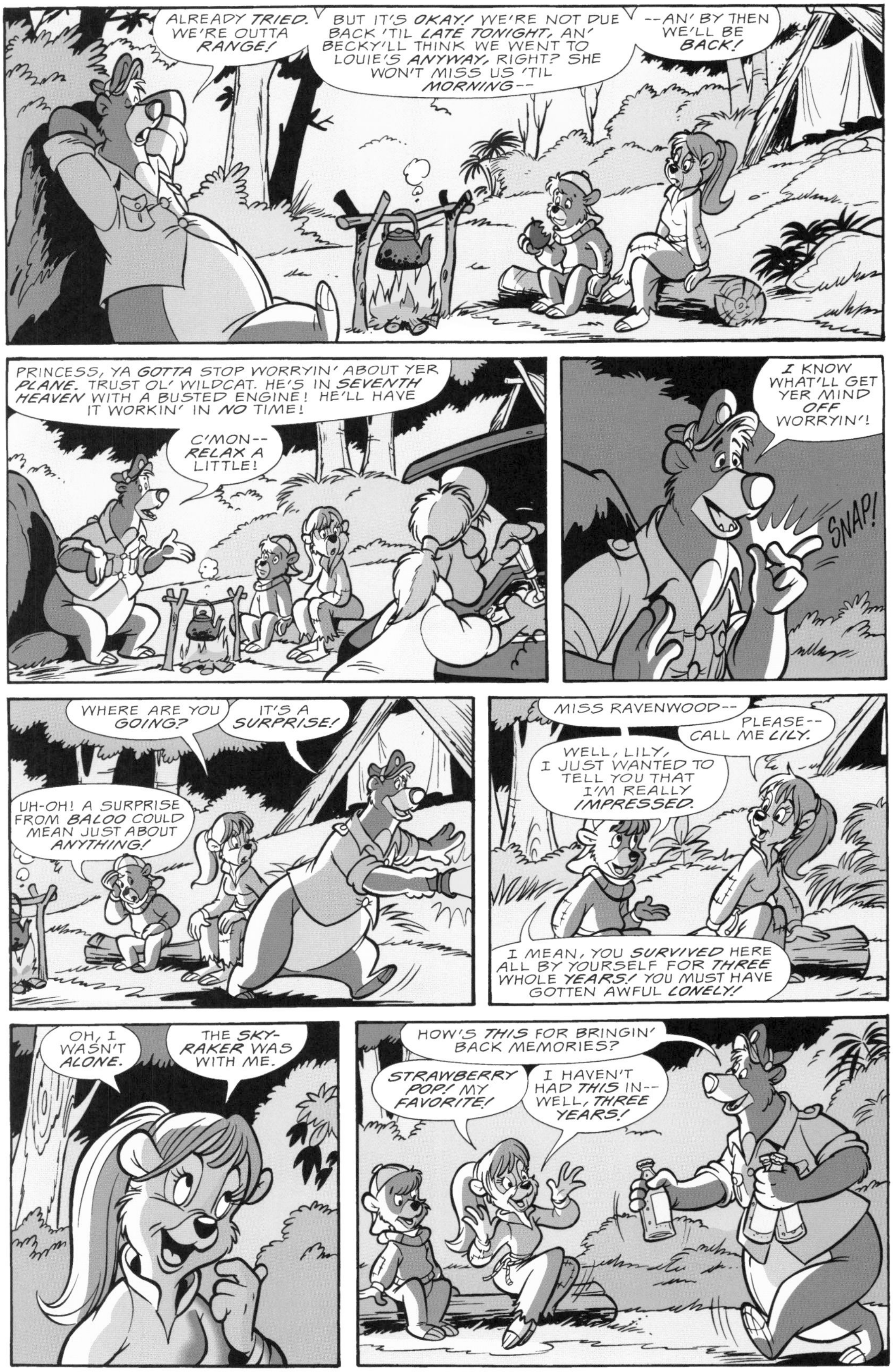

ALREADY TRIED. WE'RE OUTTA RANGE!
BUT IT'S OKAY! WE'RE NOT DUE BACK 'TIL LATE TONIGHT, AN' BECKY'LL THINK WE WENT TO LOUIE'S ANYWAY, RIGHT? SHE WON'T MISS US 'TIL MORNING--
--AN' BY THEN WE'LL BE BACK!
PRINCESS, YA GOTTA STOP WORRYIN' ABOUT YER PLANE. TRUST OL' WILDCAT. HE'S IN SEVENTH HEAVEN WITH A BUSTED ENGINE! HE'LL HAVE IT WORKIN' IN NO TIME!
C'MON-- RELAX A LITTLE!
I KNOW WHAT'LL GET YER MIND OFF WORRYIN'!
SNAP!
WHERE ARE YOU GOING?
IT'S A SURPRISE!
UH-OH! A SURPRISE FROM BALOO COULD MEAN JUST ABOUT ANYTHING!
MISS RAVENWOOD--
PLEASE-- CALL ME LILY.
WELL, LILY, I JUST WANTED TO TELL YOU THAT I'M REALLY IMPRESSED.
I MEAN, YOU SURVIVED HERE ALL BY YOURSELF FOR THREE WHOLE YEARS! YOU MUST HAVE GOTTEN AWFUL LONELY!
OH, I WASN'T ALONE.
THE SKY-RAKER WAS WITH ME.
HOW'S THIS FOR BRINGIN' BACK MEMORIES?
STRAWBERRY POP! MY FAVORITE!
I HAVEN'T HAD THIS IN-- WELL, THREE YEARS!

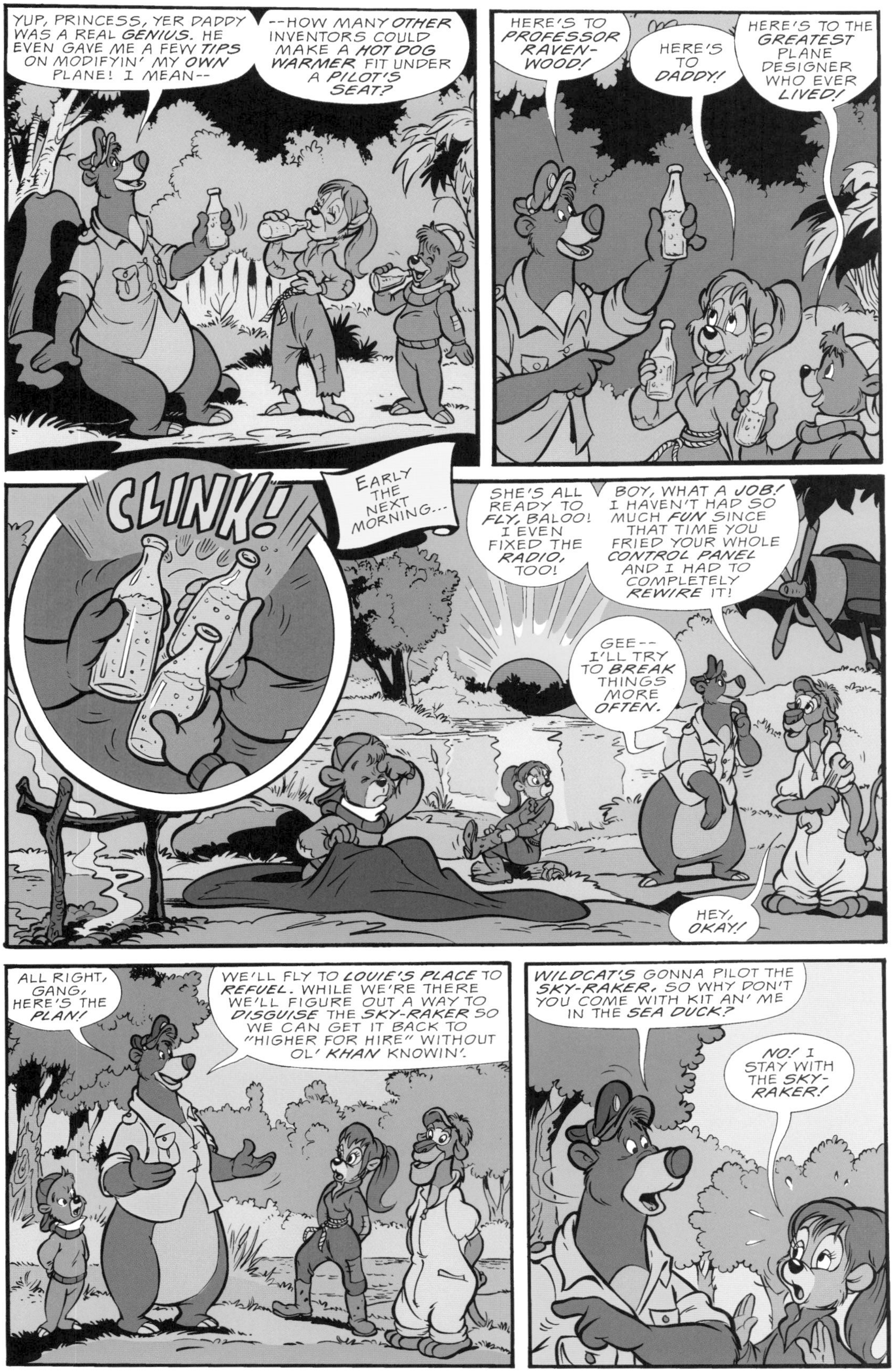

YUP, PRINCESS, YER DADDY WAS A REAL GENIUS. HE EVEN GAVE ME A FEW TIPS ON MODIFYIN' MY OWN PLANE! I MEAN--
--HOW MANY OTHER INVENTORS COULD MAKE A HOT DOG WARMER FIT UNDER A PILOT'S SEAT?
HERE'S TO PROFESSOR RAVEN-WOOD!
HERE'S TO DADDY!
HERE'S TO THE GREATEST PLANE DESIGNER WHO EVER LIVED!
CLINK!
EARLY THE NEXT MORNING...
SHE'S ALL READY TO FLY, BALOO! I EVEN FIXED THE RADIO, TOO!
BOY, WHAT A JOB! I HAVEN'T HAD SO MUCH FUN SINCE THAT TIME YOU FRIED YOUR WHOLE CONTROL PANEL AND I HAD TO COMPLETELY REWIRE IT!
GEE-- I'LL TRY TO BREAK THINGS MORE OFTEN.
HEY, OKAY!
ALL RIGHT, GANG, HERE'S THE PLAN!
WE'LL FLY TO LOUIE'S PLACE TO REFUEL. WHILE WE'RE THERE WE'LL FIGURE OUT A WAY TO DISGUISE THE SKY-RAKER SO WE CAN GET IT BACK TO "HIGHER FOR HIRE" WITHOUT OL' KHAN KNOWIN'.
WILDCAT'S GONNA PILOT THE SKY-RAKER, SO WHY DON'T YOU COME WITH KIT AN' ME IN THE SEA DUCK?
NO! I STAY WITH THE SKY-RAKER!

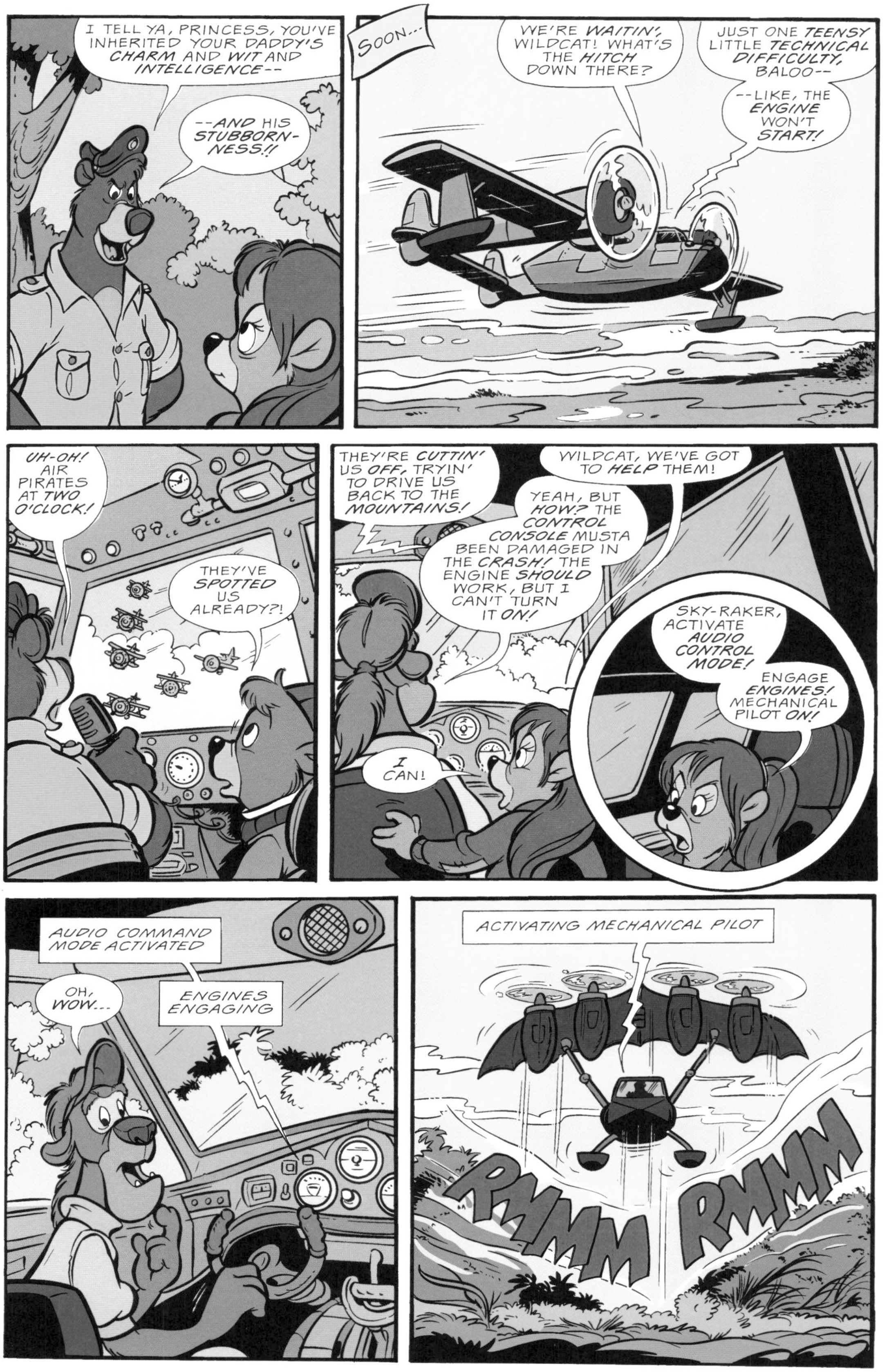

I TELL YA, PRINCESS, YOU'VE INHERITED YOUR DADDY'S CHARM AND WIT AND INTELLIGENCE--
--AND HIS STUBBORN-NESS!!
SOON...
WE'RE WAITIN', WILDCAT! WHAT'S THE HITCH DOWN THERE?
JUST ONE TEENSY LITTLE TECHNICAL DIFFICULTY, BALOO--
--LIKE, THE ENGINE WON'T START!
UH-OH! AIR PIRATES AT TWO O'CLOCK!
THEY'VE SPOTTED US ALREADY?!
THEY'RE CUTTIN' US OFF, TRYIN' TO DRIVE US BACK TO THE MOUNTAINS!
WILDCAT, WE'VE GOT TO HELP THEM!
YEAH, BUT HOW? THE CONTROL CONSOLE MUSTA BEEN DAMAGED IN THE CRASH! THE ENGINE SHOULD WORK, BUT I CAN'T TURN IT ON!
I CAN!
SKY-RAKER, ACTIVATE AUDIO CONTROL MODE!
ENGAGE ENGINES! MECHANICAL PILOT ON!
AUDIO COMMAND MODE ACTIVATED
OH, WOW...
ENGINES ENGAGING
ACTIVATING MECHANICAL PILOT
RMMM RMMM

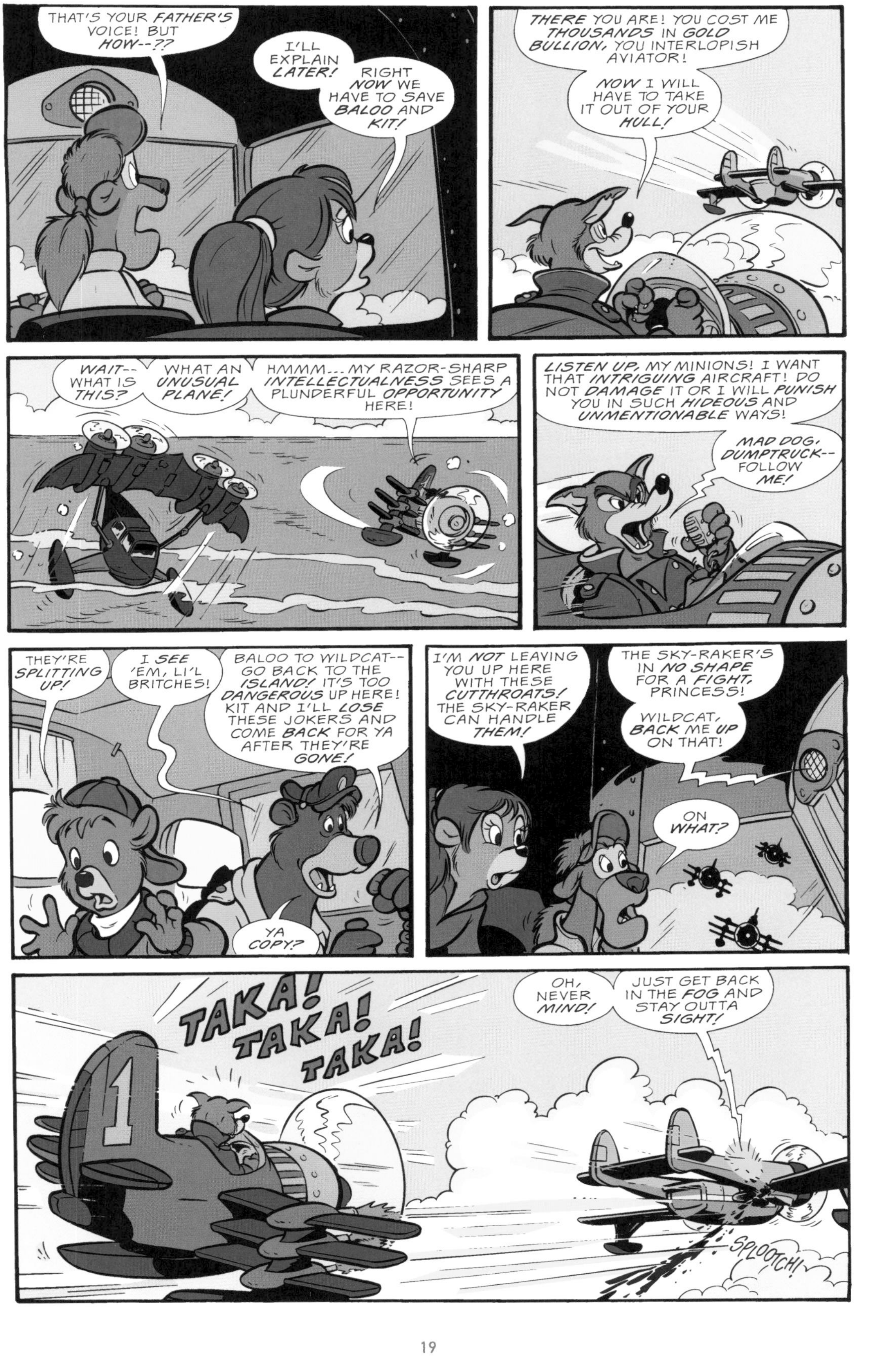
THAT'S YOUR FATHER'S VOICE! BUT HOW--??
I'LL EXPLAIN LATER!
RIGHT NOW WE HAVE TO SAVE BALOO AND KIT!
THERE YOU ARE! YOU COST ME THOUSANDS IN GOLD BULLION, YOU INTERLOPISH AVIATOR!
NOW I WILL HAVE TO TAKE IT OUT OF YOUR HULL!
WAIT-- WHAT IS THIS?
WHAT AN UNUSUAL PLANE!
HMMM... MY RAZOR-SHARP INTELLECTUALNESS SEES A PLUNDERFUL OPPORTUNITY HERE!
LISTEN UP, MY MINIONS! I WANT THAT INTRIGUING AIRCRAFT! DO NOT DAMAGE IT OR I WILL PUNISH YOU IN SUCH HIDEOUS AND UNMENTIONABLE WAYS!
MAD DOG, DUMPTRUCK-- FOLLOW ME!
THEY'RE SPLITTING UP!
I SEE 'EM, LI'L BRITCHES!
BALOO TO WILDCAT-- GO BACK TO THE ISLAND! IT'S TOO DANGEROUS UP HERE! KIT AND I'LL LOSE THESE JOKERS AND COME BACK FOR YA AFTER THEY'RE GONE!
YA COPY?
I'M NOT LEAVING YOU UP HERE WITH THESE CUTTHROATS! THE SKY-RAKER CAN HANDLE THEM!
THE SKY-RAKER'S IN NO SHAPE FOR A FIGHT, PRINCESS!
WILDCAT, BACK ME UP ON THAT!
ON WHAT?
TAKA! TAKA! TAKA!
OH, NEVER MIND!
JUST GET BACK IN THE FOG AND STAY OUTTA SIGHT!
SPLOOTCH!

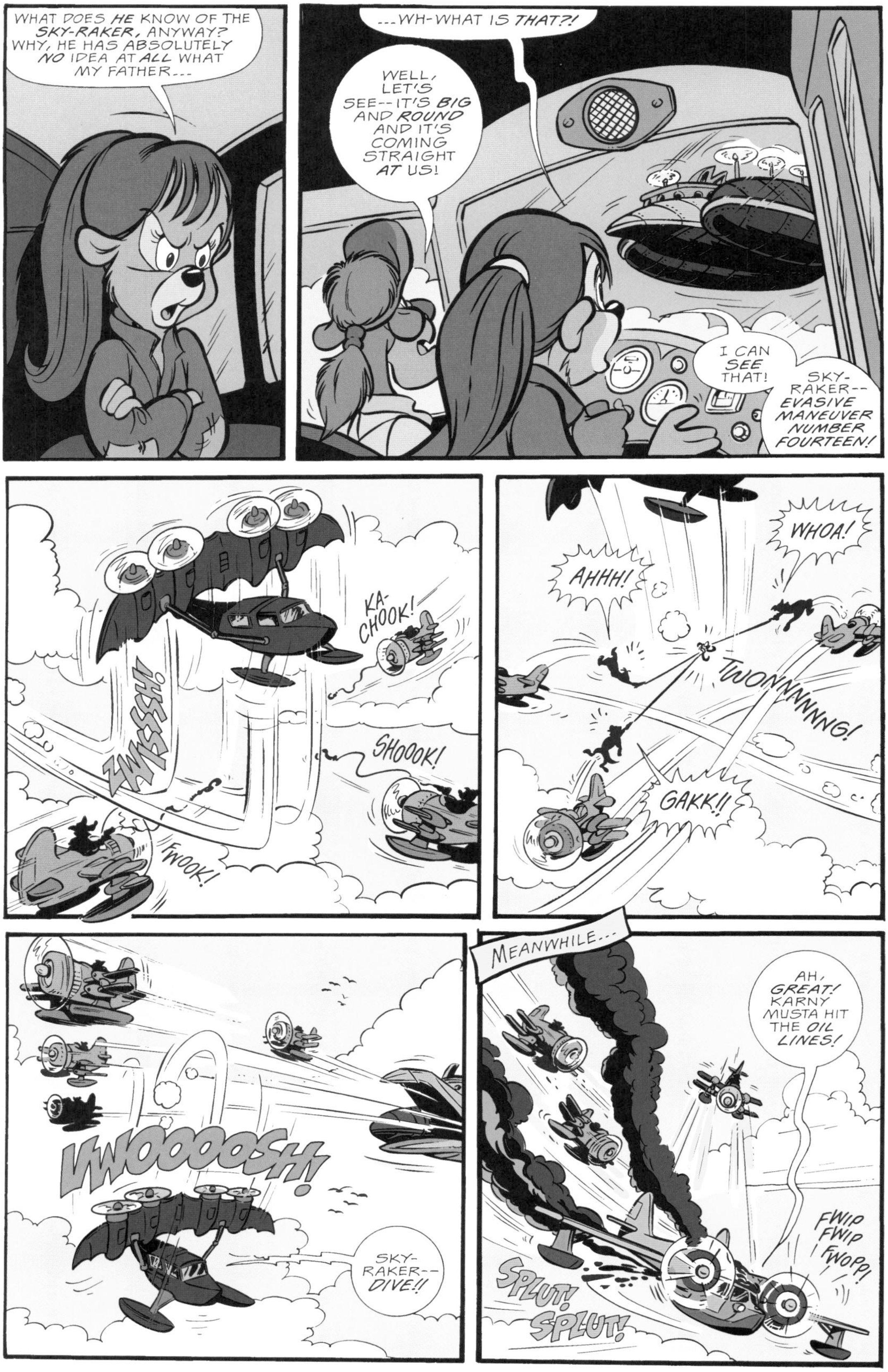

WHAT DOES HE KNOW OF THE SKY-RAKER, ANYWAY? WHY, HE HAS ABSOLUTELY NO IDEA AT ALL WHAT MY FATHER---
---WH-WHAT IS THAT?!
WELL, LET'S SEE--IT'S BIG AND ROUND AND IT'S COMING STRAIGHT AT US!
I CAN SEE THAT!
SKY-RAKER--EVASIVE MANEUVER NUMBER FOURTEEN!
KA-CHOOK!
ZWISSH!
SHOOOK!
FWOOK!
WHOA!
AHHH!
TWONNNNNNG!
GAKK!!
VWOOOOSH!
SKY-RAKER--DIVE!!
MEANWHILE...
AH, GREAT! KARNY MUSTA HIT THE OIL LINES!
FWIP FWIP FWOPP!
SPLUT! SPLUT!

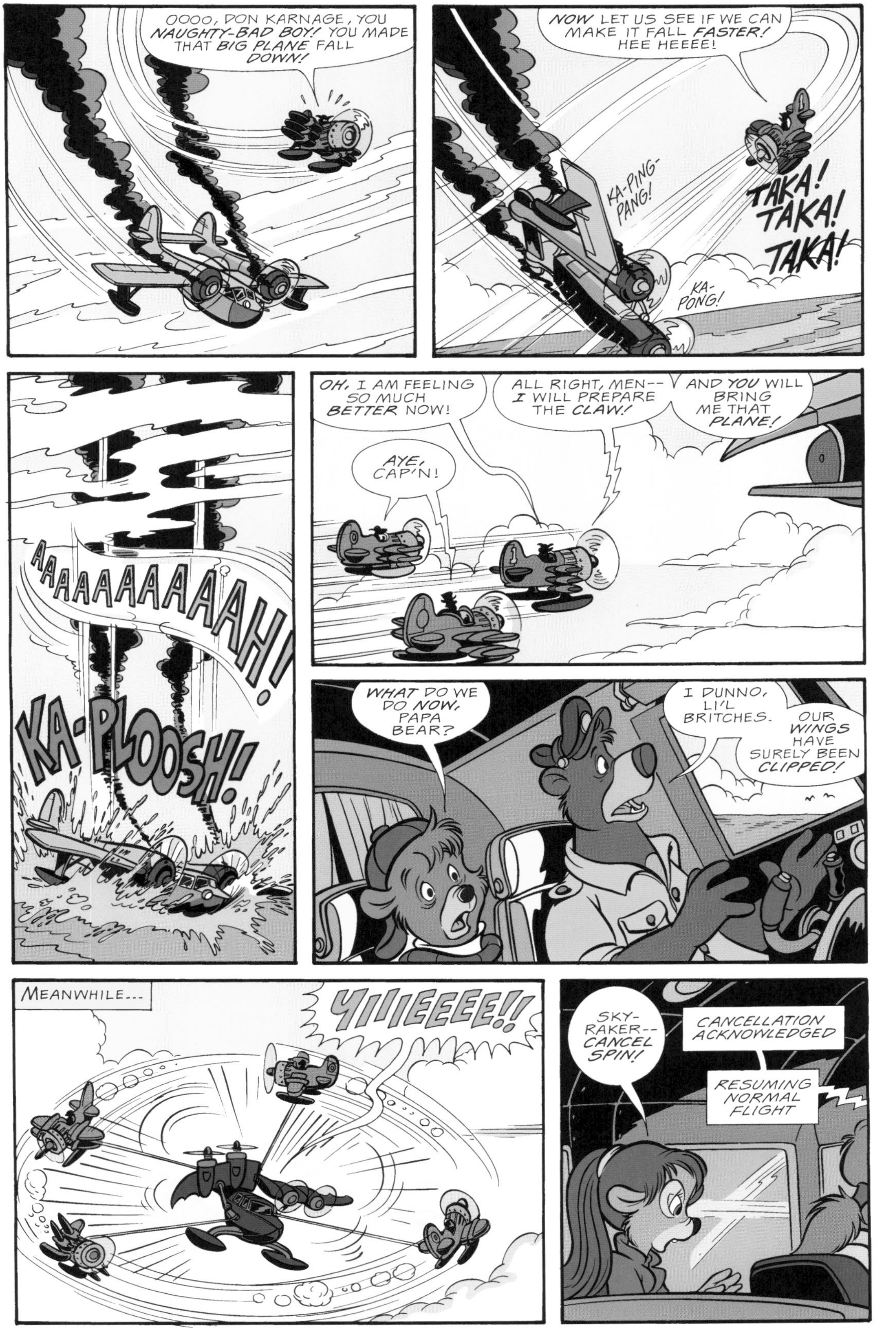

OOOO, DON KARNAGE, YOU NAUGHTY-BAD BOY! YOU MADE THAT BIG PLANE FALL DOWN!
NOW LET US SEE IF WE CAN MAKE IT FALL FASTER! HEE HEEEE!
KA-PING-PANG!
TAKA! TAKA! TAKA!
KA-PONG!
AAAAAAAAAAAH!
KA-PLOOSH!
OH, I AM FEELING SO MUCH BETTER NOW!
ALL RIGHT, MEN-- I WILL PREPARE THE CLAW!
AND YOU WILL BRING ME THAT PLANE!
AYE, CAP'N!
WHAT DO WE DO NOW, PAPA BEAR?
I DUNNO, LI'L BRITCHES.
OUR WINGS HAVE SURELY BEEN CLIPPED!
MEANWHILE...
YIIIEEEE!!
SKY-RAKER-- CANCEL SPIN!
CANCELLATION ACKNOWLEDGED
RESUMING NORMAL FLIGHT

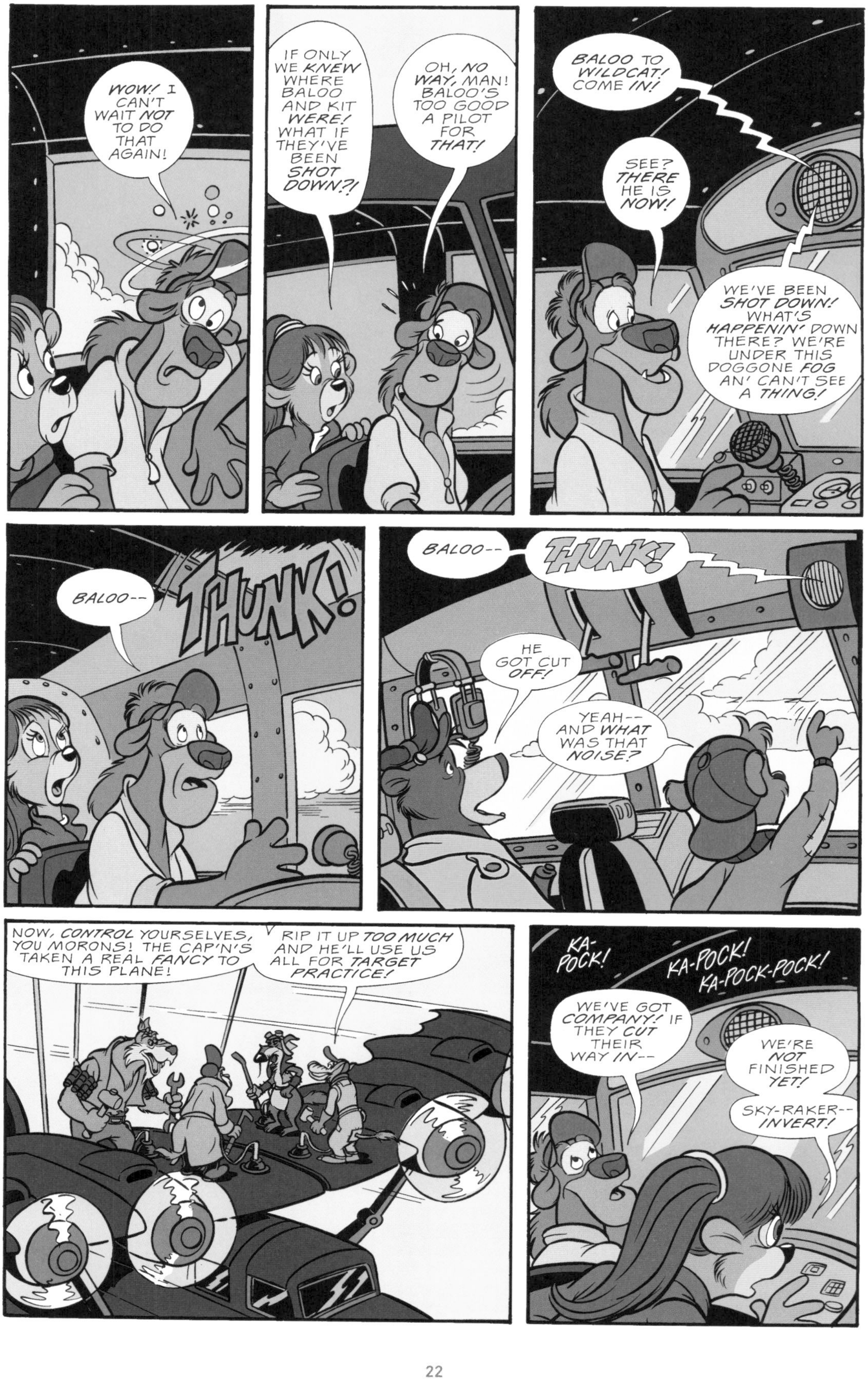
WOW! I CAN'T WAIT NOT TO DO THAT AGAIN!
IF ONLY WE KNEW WHERE BALOO AND KIT WERE! WHAT IF THEY'VE BEEN SHOT DOWN?!
OH, NO WAY, MAN! BALOO'S TOO GOOD A PILOT FOR THAT!
BALOO TO WILDCAT! COME IN!
SEE? THERE HE IS NOW!
WE'VE BEEN SHOT DOWN! WHAT'S HAPPENIN' DOWN THERE? WE'RE UNDER THIS DOGGONE FOG AN' CAN'T SEE A THING!
BALOO--
THUNK!
BALOO--
THUNK!
HE GOT CUT OFF!
YEAH-- AND WHAT WAS THAT NOISE?
NOW, CONTROL YOURSELVES, YOU MORONS! THE CAP'N'S TAKEN A REAL FANCY TO THIS PLANE!
RIP IT UP TOO MUCH AND HE'LL USE US ALL FOR TARGET PRACTICE!
KA-POCK!
KA-POCK!
KA-POCK-POCK!
WE'VE GOT COMPANY! IF THEY CUT THEIR WAY IN--
WE'RE NOT FINISHED YET!
SKY-RAKER-- INVERT!

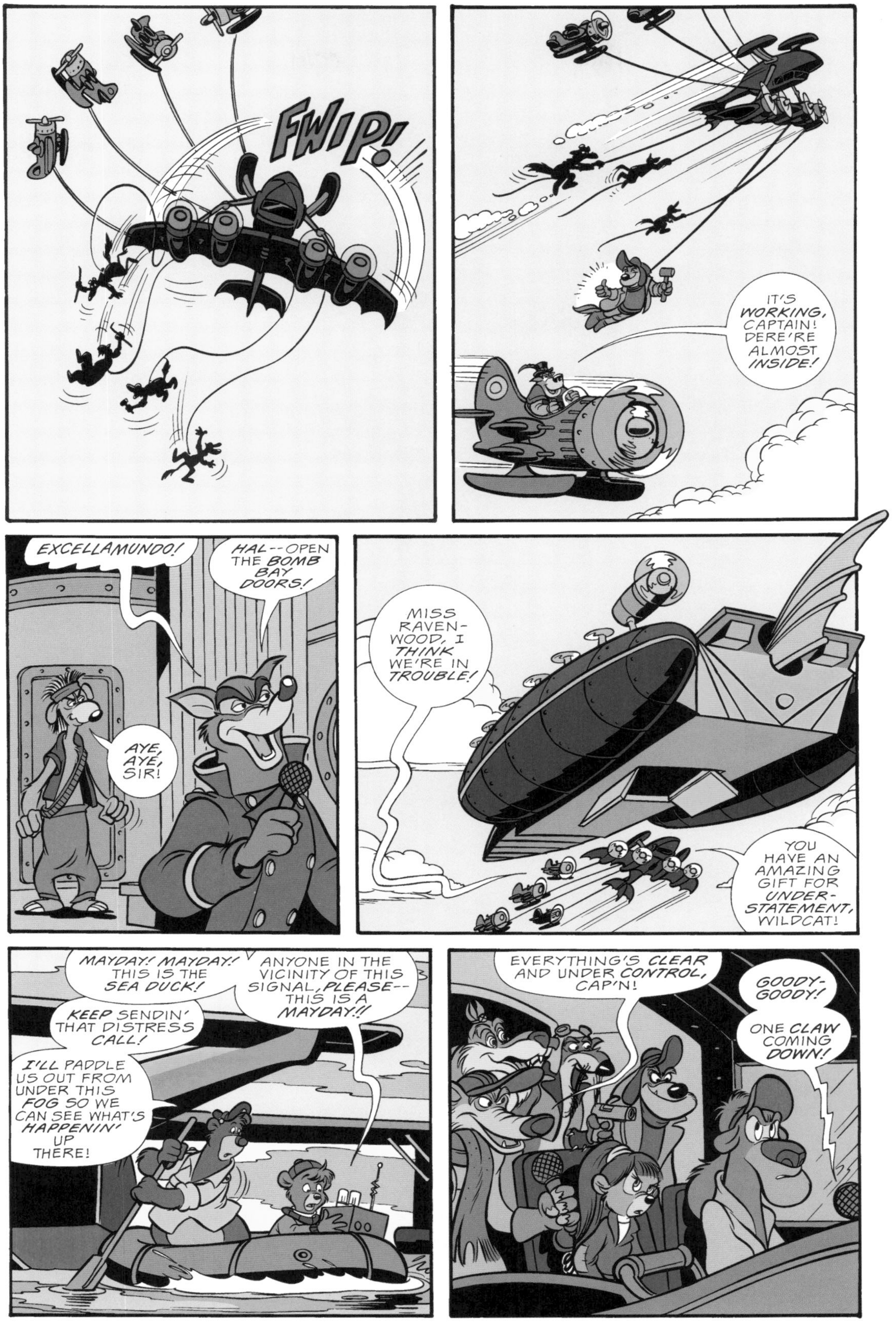
FWIP!
IT'S WORKING, CAPTAIN! DERE'RE ALMOST INSIDE!
EXCELLAMUNDO!
HAL--OPEN THE BOMB BAY DOORS!
AYE, AYE, SIR!
MISS RAVEN-WOOD, I THINK WE'RE IN TROUBLE!
YOU HAVE AN AMAZING GIFT FOR UNDER-STATEMENT, WILDCAT!
MAYDAY! MAYDAY! THIS IS THE SEA DUCK!
ANYONE IN THE VICINITY OF THIS SIGNAL, PLEASE-- THIS IS A MAYDAY!!
KEEP SENDIN' THAT DISTRESS CALL!
I'LL PADDLE US OUT FROM UNDER THIS FOG SO WE CAN SEE WHAT'S HAPPENIN' UP THERE!
EVERYTHING'S CLEAR AND UNDER CONTROL, CAP'N!
GOODY-GOODY!
ONE CLAW COMING DOWN!

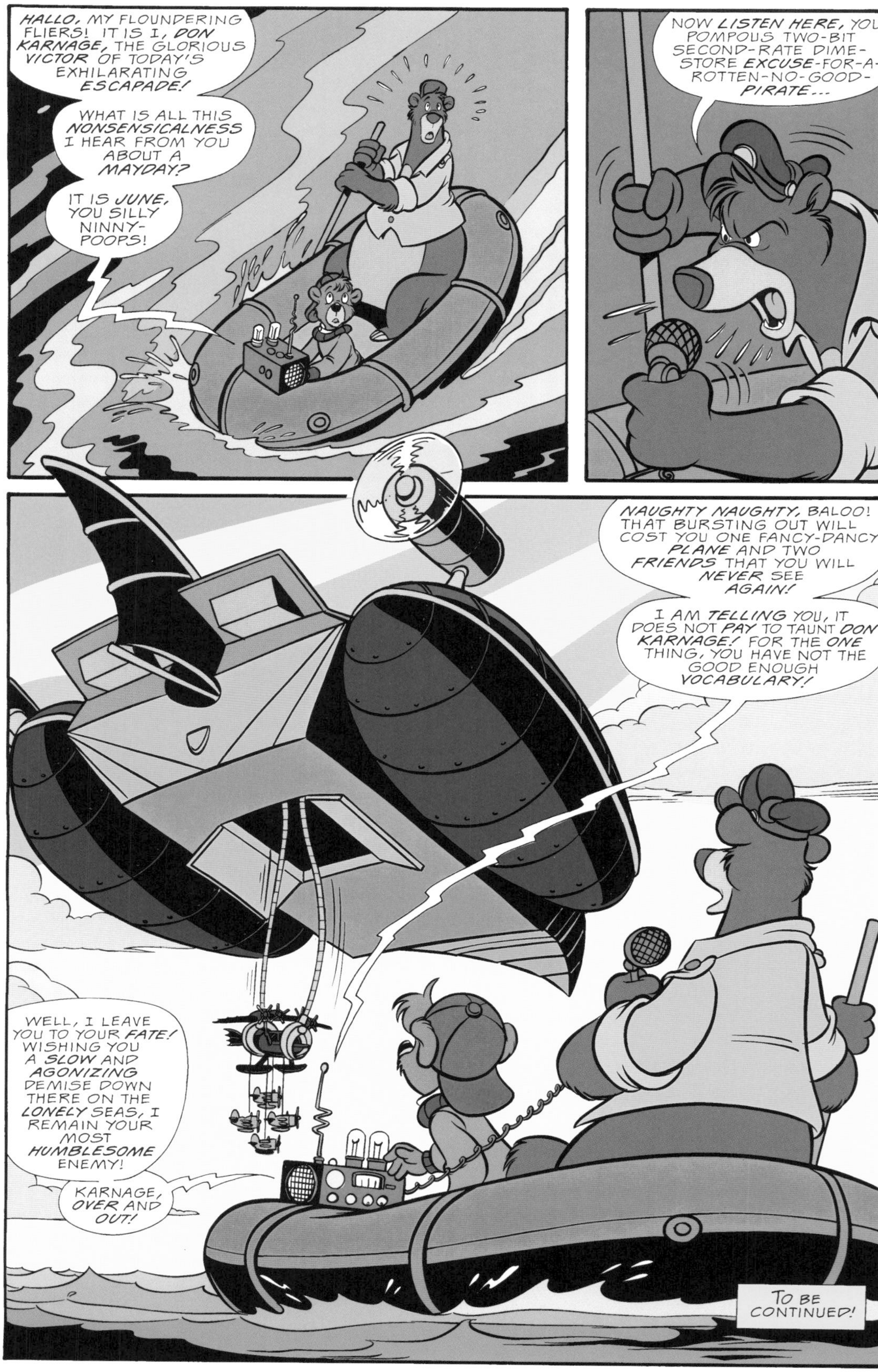
HALLO, MY FLOUNDERING FLIERS! IT IS I, DON KARNAGE, THE GLORIOUS VICTOR OF TODAY'S EXHILARATING ESCAPADE!
WHAT IS ALL THIS NONSENSICALNESS I HEAR FROM YOU ABOUT A MAYDAY?
IT IS JUNE, YOU SILLY NINNY-POOPS!
NOW LISTEN HERE, YOU POMPOUS TWO-BIT SECOND-RATE DIME-STORE EXCUSE-FOR-A-ROTTEN-NO-GOOD-PIRATE...
NAUGHTY NAUGHTY, BALOO! THAT BURSTING OUT WILL COST YOU ONE FANCY-DANCY PLANE AND TWO FRIENDS THAT YOU WILL NEVER SEE AGAIN!
I AM TELLING YOU, IT DOES NOT PAY TO TAUNT DON KARNAGE! FOR THE ONE THING, YOU HAVE NOT THE GOOD ENOUGH VOCABULARY!
WELL, I LEAVE YOU TO YOUR FATE! WISHING YOU A SLOW AND AGONIZING DEMISE DOWN THERE ON THE LONELY SEAS, I REMAIN YOUR MOST HUMBLESOME ENEMY!
KARNAGE, OVER AND OUT!
TO BE CONTINUED!

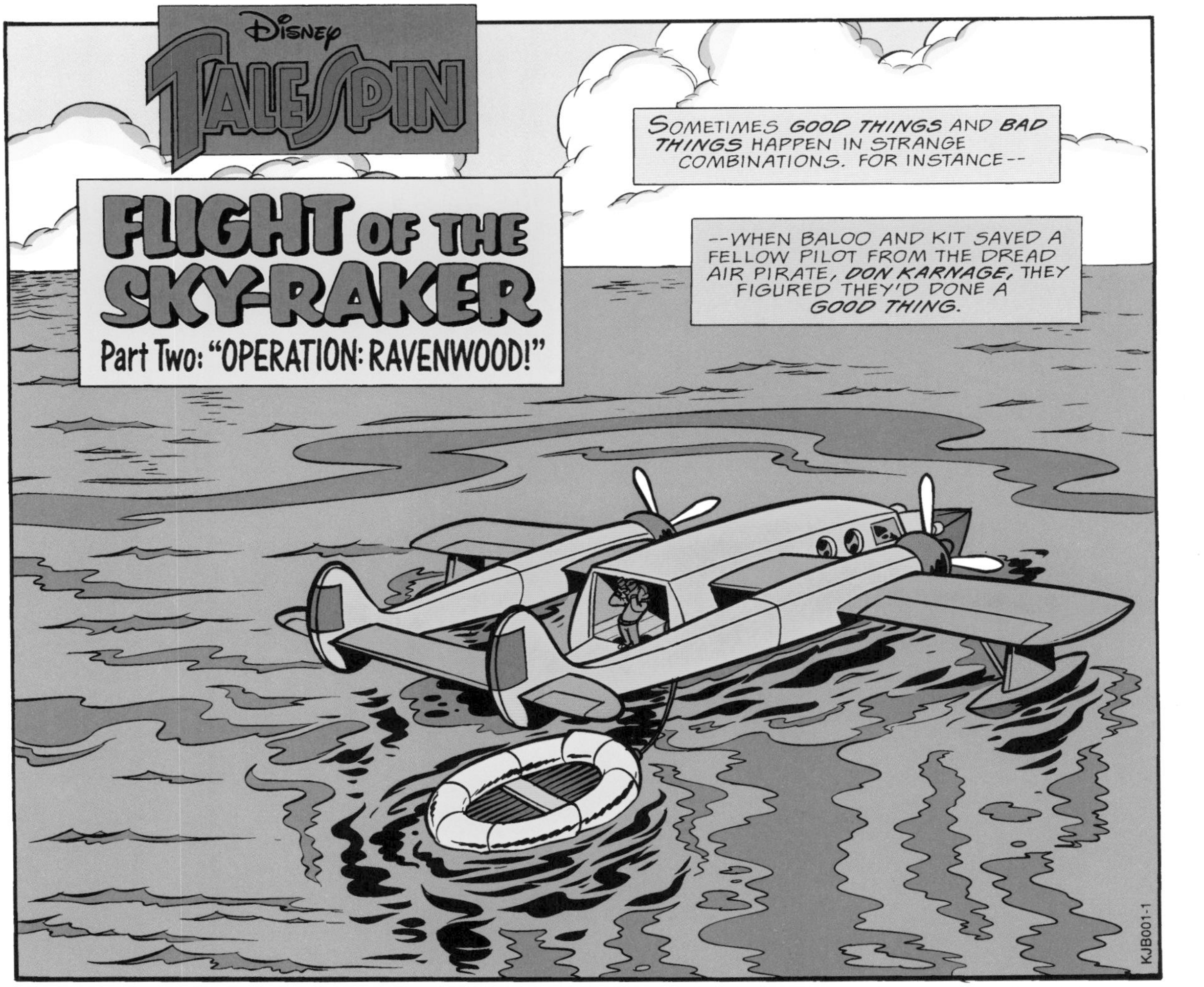
Disney
TaleSpin
FLIGHT OF THE SKY-RAKER
Part Two: "OPERATION: RAVENWOOD!"
SOMETIMES GOOD THINGS AND BAD THINGS HAPPEN IN STRANGE COMBINATIONS. FOR INSTANCE--
--WHEN BALOO AND KIT SAVED A FELLOW PILOT FROM THE DREAD AIR PIRATE, DON KARNAGE, THEY FIGURED THEY'D DONE A GOOD THING.
KJB001-1

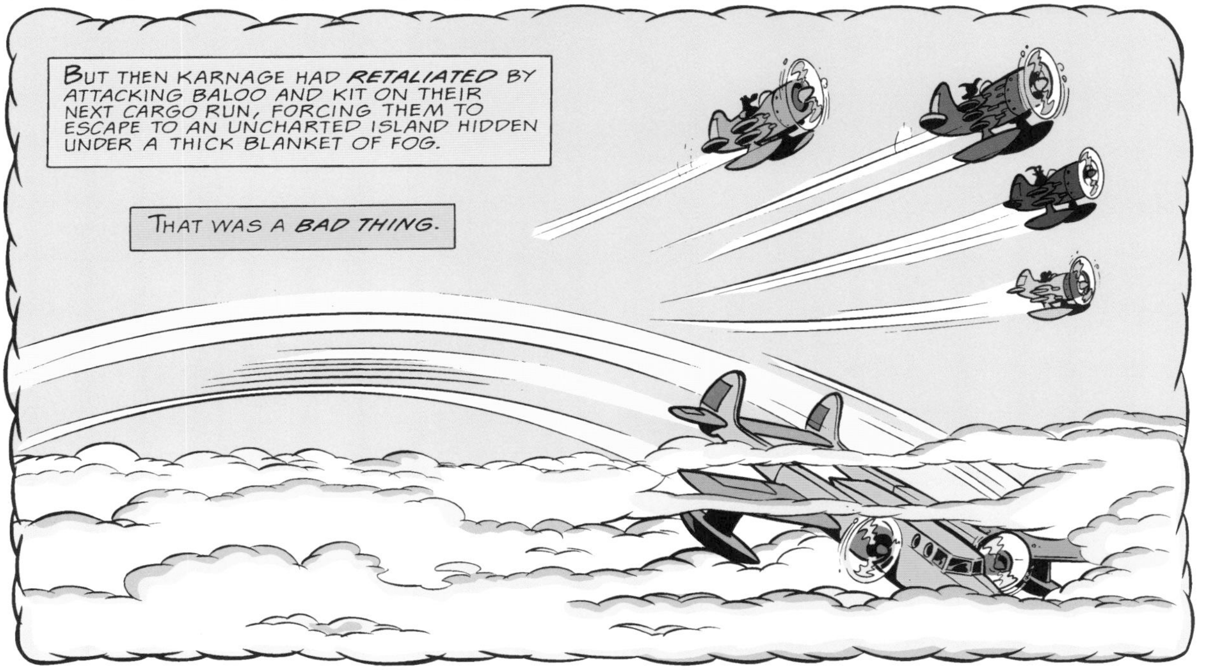
BUT THEN KARNAGE HAD RETALIATED BY ATTACKING BALOO AND KIT ON THEIR NEXT CARGO RUN, FORCING THEM TO ESCAPE TO AN UNCHARTED ISLAND HIDDEN UNDER A THICK BLANKET OF FOG.
THAT WAS A BAD THING.

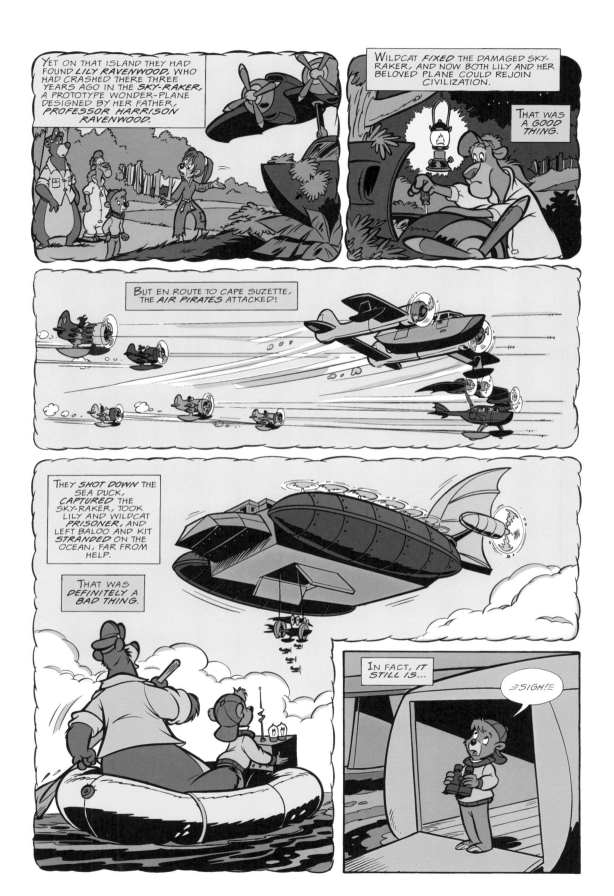

YET ON THAT ISLAND THEY HAD FOUND *LILY RAVENWOOD*, WHO HAD CRASHED THERE THREE YEARS AGO IN THE *SKY-RAKER*, A PROTOTYPE WONDER-PLANE DESIGNED BY HER FATHER, *PROFESSOR HARRISON RAVENWOOD*.

WILDCAT *FIXED* THE DAMAGED SKY-RAKER, AND NOW BOTH LILY AND HER BELOVED PLANE COULD REJOIN CIVILIZATION.

THAT WAS A GOOD THING.

BUT EN ROUTE TO CAPE SUZETTE, THE *AIR PIRATES* ATTACKED!

THEY *SHOT DOWN* THE SEA DUCK, *CAPTURED* THE SKY-RAKER, TOOK LILY AND WILDCAT *PRISONER*, AND LEFT BALOO AND KIT *STRANDED* ON THE OCEAN, FAR FROM HELP.

THAT WAS DEFINITELY A BAD THING.

IN FACT, IT STILL IS...

≡SIGH!≡

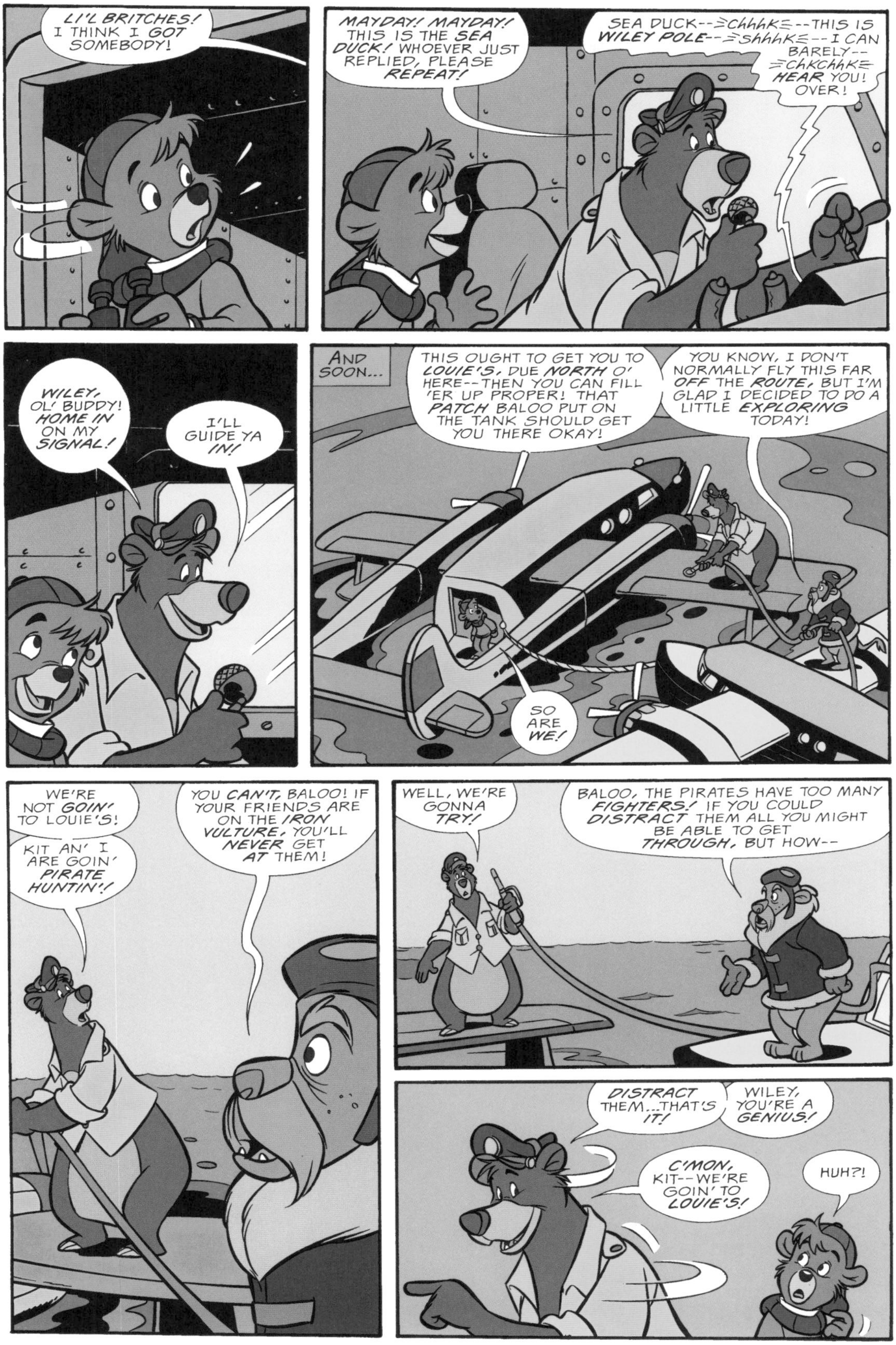
LI'L BRITCHES! I THINK I GOT SOMEBODY!
MAYDAY! MAYDAY! THIS IS THE SEA DUCK! WHOEVER JUST REPLIED, PLEASE REPEAT!
SEA DUCK-- CHHHK --THIS IS WILEY POLE-- SHHHK --I CAN BARELY-- CHKCHHK HEAR YOU! OVER!
WILEY, OL' BUDDY! HOME IN ON MY SIGNAL!
I'LL GUIDE YA IN!
AND SOON...
THIS OUGHT TO GET YOU TO LOUIE'S, DUE NORTH O' HERE--THEN YOU CAN FILL 'ER UP PROPER! THAT PATCH BALOO PUT ON THE TANK SHOULD GET YOU THERE OKAY!
YOU KNOW, I DON'T NORMALLY FLY THIS FAR OFF THE ROUTE, BUT I'M GLAD I DECIDED TO DO A LITTLE EXPLORING TODAY!
SO ARE WE!
WE'RE NOT GOIN' TO LOUIE'S!
KIT AN' I ARE GOIN' PIRATE HUNTIN'!
YOU CAN'T, BALOO! IF YOUR FRIENDS ARE ON THE IRON VULTURE, YOU'LL NEVER GET AT THEM!
WELL, WE'RE GONNA TRY!
BALOO, THE PIRATES HAVE TOO MANY FIGHTERS! IF YOU COULD DISTRACT THEM ALL YOU MIGHT BE ABLE TO GET THROUGH, BUT HOW--
DISTRACT THEM...THAT'S IT!
WILEY, YOU'RE A GENIUS!
C'MON, KIT--WE'RE GOIN' TO LOUIE'S!
HUH?!

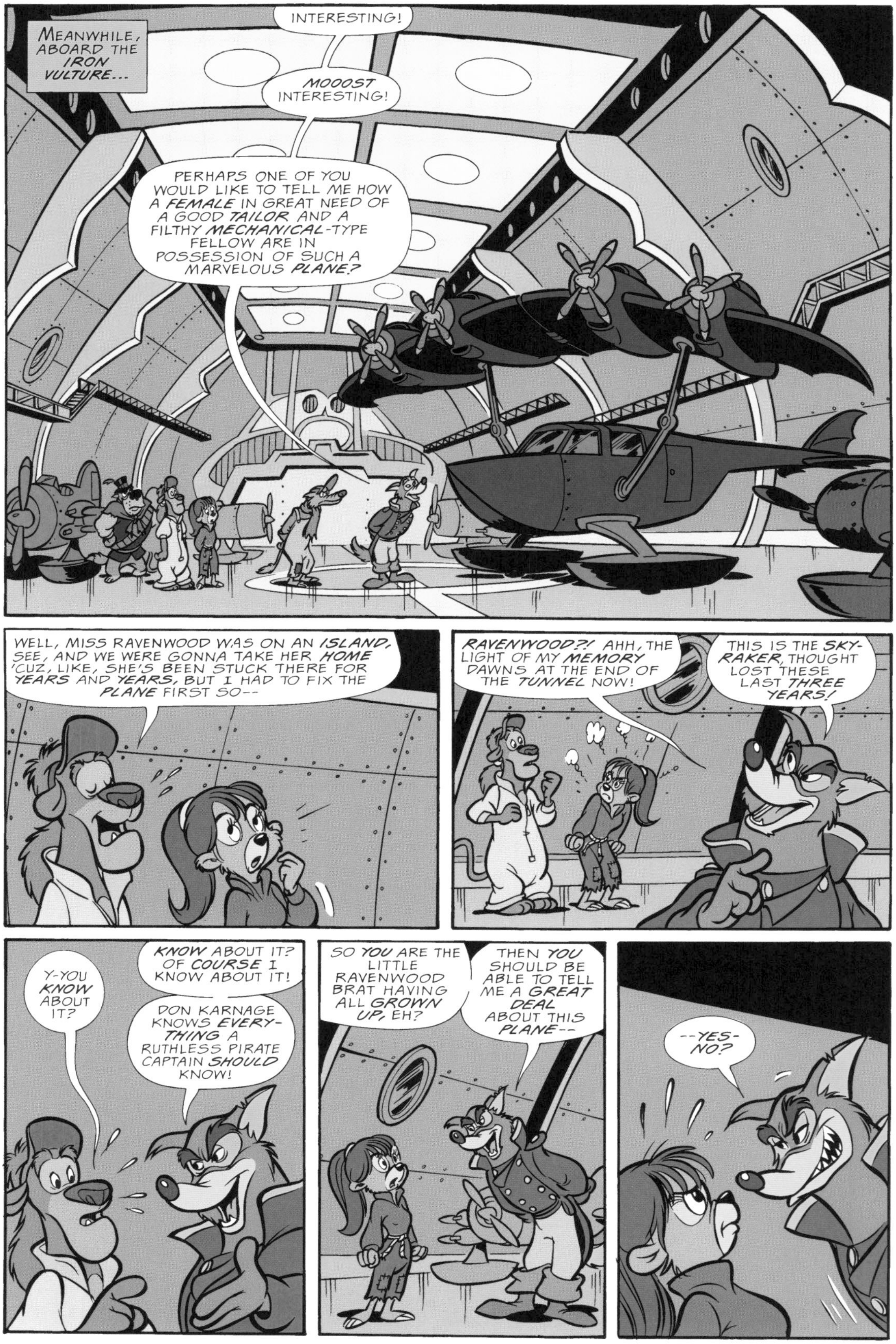
MEANWHILE, ABOARD THE IRON VULTURE...
INTERESTING!
MOOOST INTERESTING!
PERHAPS ONE OF YOU WOULD LIKE TO TELL ME HOW A FEMALE IN GREAT NEED OF A GOOD TAILOR AND A FILTHY MECHANICAL-TYPE FELLOW ARE IN POSSESSION OF SUCH A MARVELOUS PLANE?
WELL, MISS RAVENWOOD WAS ON AN ISLAND, SEE, AND WE WERE GONNA TAKE HER HOME 'CUZ, LIKE, SHE'S BEEN STUCK THERE FOR YEARS AND YEARS, BUT I HAD TO FIX THE PLANE FIRST SO--
RAVENWOOD?! AHH, THE LIGHT OF MY MEMORY DAWNS AT THE END OF THE TUNNEL NOW!
THIS IS THE SKY-RAKER, THOUGHT LOST THESE LAST THREE YEARS!
Y-YOU KNOW ABOUT IT?
KNOW ABOUT IT? OF COURSE I KNOW ABOUT IT!
DON KARNAGE KNOWS EVERY-THING A RUTHLESS PIRATE CAPTAIN SHOULD KNOW!
SO YOU ARE THE LITTLE RAVENWOOD BRAT HAVING ALL GROWN UP, EH?
THEN YOU SHOULD BE ABLE TO TELL ME A GREAT DEAL ABOUT THIS PLANE--
--YES-NO?

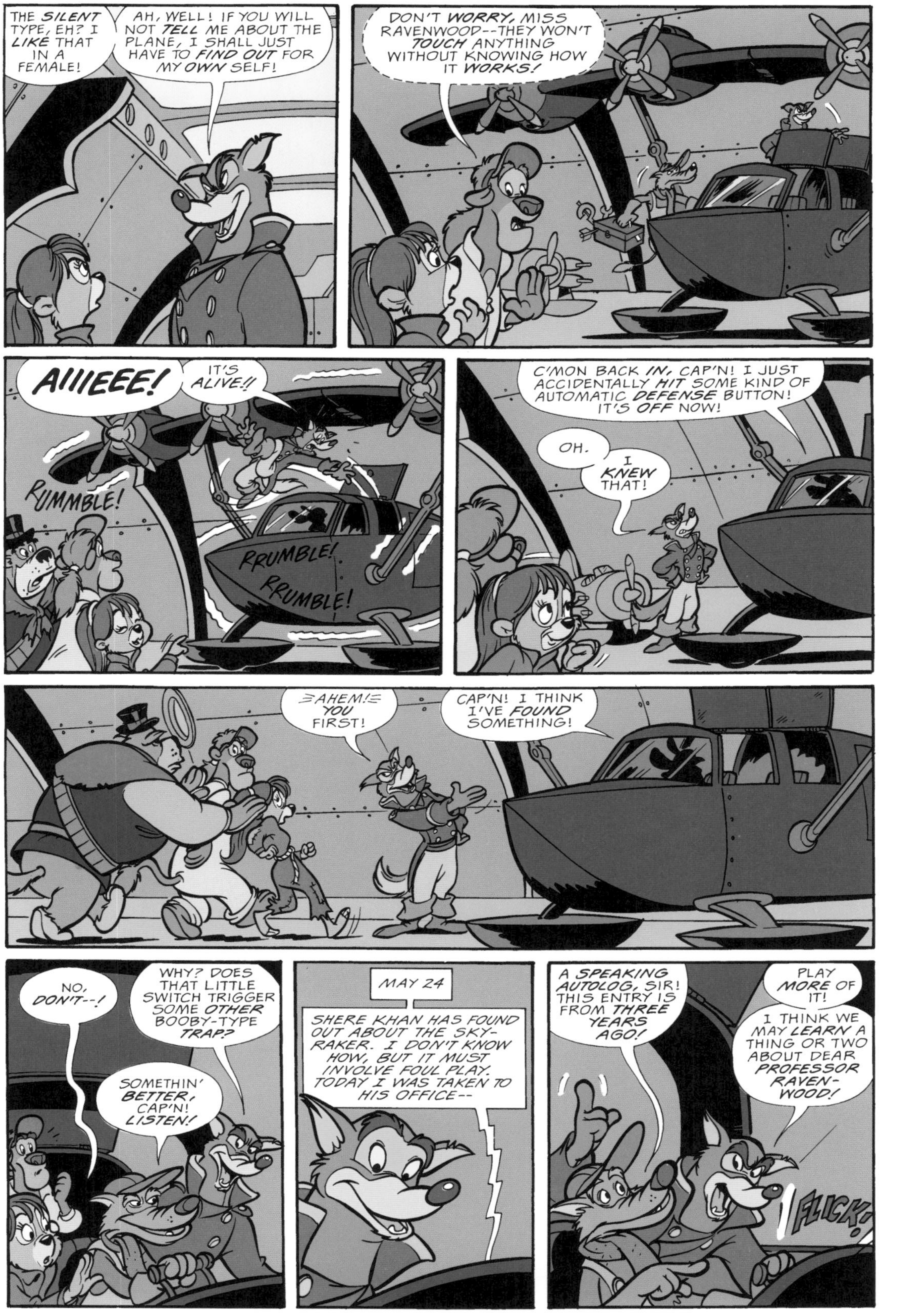
THE SILENT TYPE, EH? I LIKE THAT IN A FEMALE!
AH, WELL! IF YOU WILL NOT TELL ME ABOUT THE PLANE, I SHALL JUST HAVE TO FIND OUT FOR MY OWN SELF!
DON'T WORRY, MISS RAVENWOOD--THEY WON'T TOUCH ANYTHING WITHOUT KNOWING HOW IT WORKS!
AIIIEEE!
IT'S ALIVE!!
RUMMBLE!
RRUMBLE!
RRUMBLE!
C'MON BACK IN, CAP'N! I JUST ACCIDENTALLY HIT SOME KIND OF AUTOMATIC DEFENSE BUTTON! IT'S OFF NOW!
OH.
I KNEW THAT!
AHEM! YOU FIRST!
CAP'N! I THINK I'VE FOUND SOMETHING!
NO, DON'T--!
WHY? DOES THAT LITTLE SWITCH TRIGGER SOME OTHER BOOBY-TYPE TRAP?
SOMETHIN' BETTER, CAP'N! LISTEN!
MAY 24
SHERE KHAN HAS FOUND OUT ABOUT THE SKY-RAKER. I DON'T KNOW HOW, BUT IT MUST INVOLVE FOUL PLAY. TODAY I WAS TAKEN TO HIS OFFICE--
A SPEAKING AUTOLOG, SIR! THIS ENTRY IS FROM THREE YEARS AGO!
PLAY MORE OF IT!
I THINK WE MAY LEARN A THING OR TWO ABOUT DEAR PROFESSOR RAVENWOOD!
FLICK!

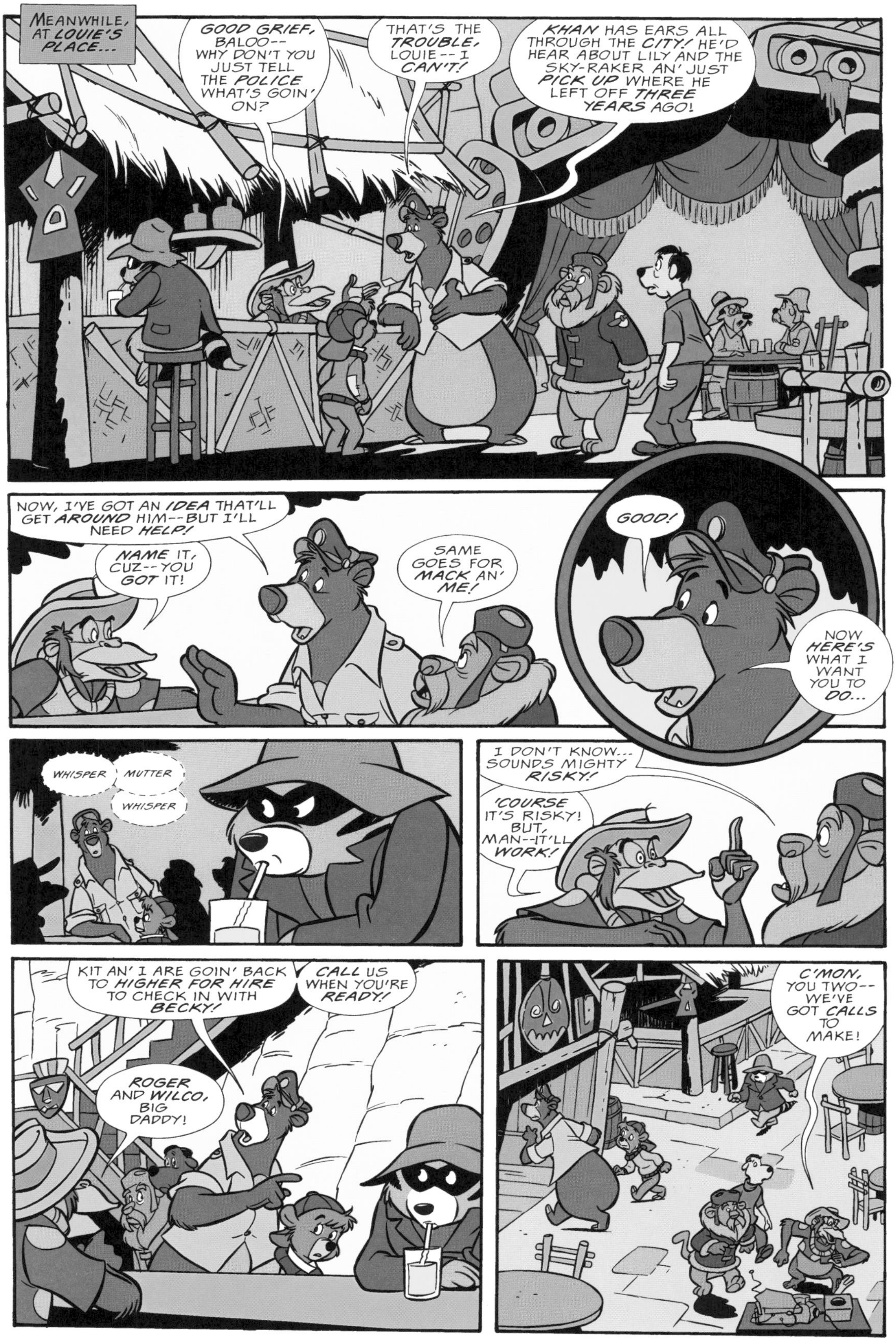
MEANWHILE, AT LOUIE'S PLACE...
GOOD GRIEF, BALOO-- WHY DON'T YOU JUST TELL THE POLICE WHAT'S GOIN' ON?
THAT'S THE TROUBLE, LOUIE-- I CAN'T!
KHAN HAS EARS ALL THROUGH THE CITY! HE'D HEAR ABOUT LILY AND THE SKY-RAKER AN' JUST PICK UP WHERE HE LEFT OFF THREE YEARS AGO!
NOW, I'VE GOT AN IDEA THAT'LL GET AROUND HIM--BUT I'LL NEED HELP!
NAME IT, CUZ--YOU GOT IT!
SAME GOES FOR MACK AN' ME!
GOOD!
NOW HERE'S WHAT I WANT YOU TO DO...
WHISPER
MUTTER
WHISPER
I DON'T KNOW... SOUNDS MIGHTY RISKY!
'COURSE IT'S RISKY! BUT, MAN--IT'LL WORK!
KIT AN' I ARE GOIN' BACK TO HIGHER FOR HIRE TO CHECK IN WITH BECKY!
CALL US WHEN YOU'RE READY!
ROGER AND WILCO, BIG DADDY!
C'MON, YOU TWO-- WE'VE GOT CALLS TO MAKE!

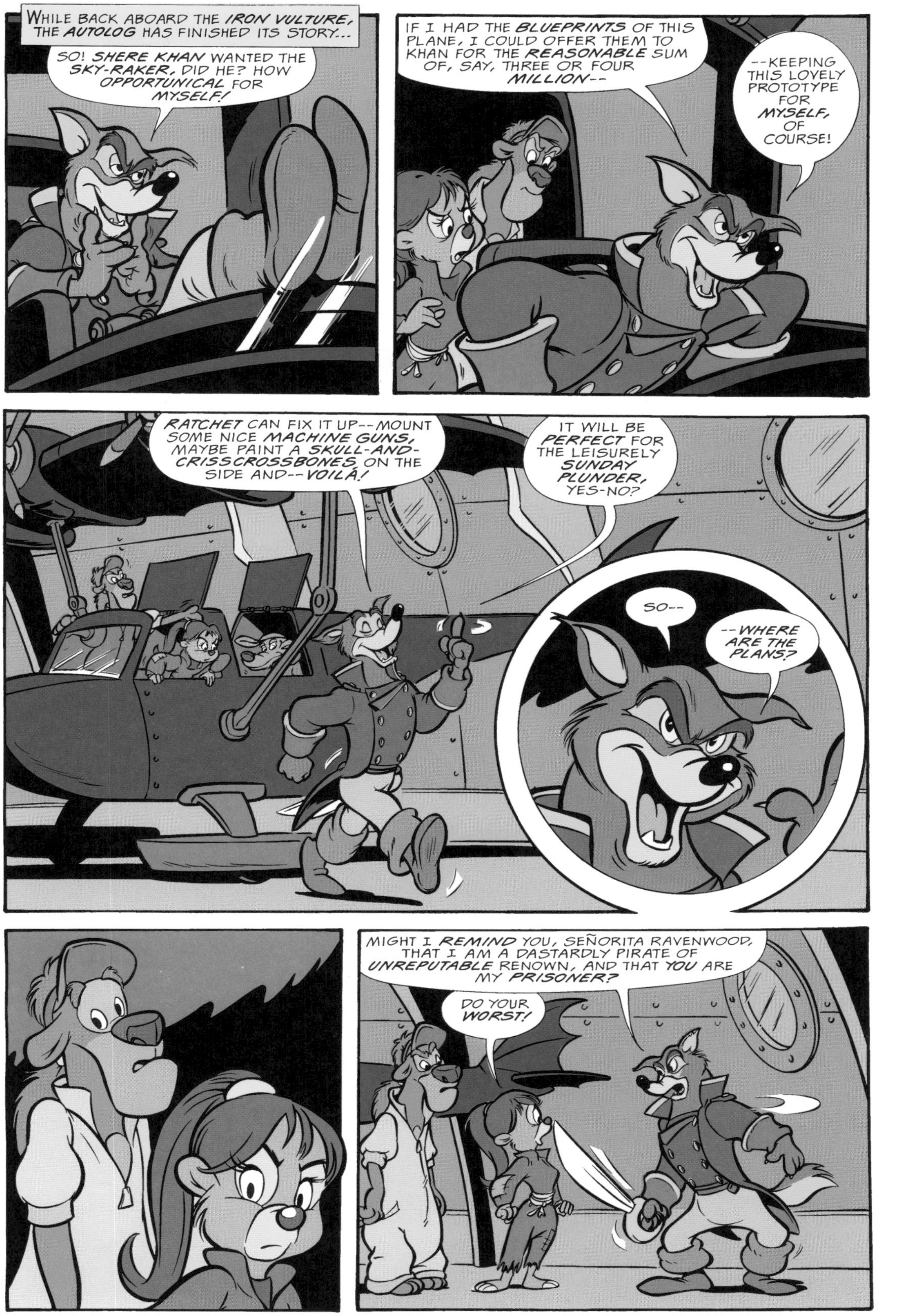
WHILE BACK ABOARD THE IRON VULTURE, THE AUTOLOG HAS FINISHED ITS STORY...
SO! SHERE KHAN WANTED THE SKY-RAKER, DID HE? HOW OPPORTUNICAL FOR MYSELF!
IF I HAD THE BLUEPRINTS OF THIS PLANE, I COULD OFFER THEM TO KHAN FOR THE REASONABLE SUM OF, SAY, THREE OR FOUR MILLION--
--KEEPING THIS LOVELY PROTOTYPE FOR MYSELF, OF COURSE!
RATCHET CAN FIX IT UP--MOUNT SOME NICE MACHINE GUNS, MAYBE PAINT A SKULL-AND-CRISSCROSSBONES ON THE SIDE AND--VOILÁ!
IT WILL BE PERFECT FOR THE LEISURELY SUNDAY PLUNDER, YES-NO?
SO--
--WHERE ARE THE PLANS?
MIGHT I REMIND YOU, SEÑORITA RAVENWOOD, THAT I AM A DASTARDLY PIRATE OF UNREPUTABLE RENOWN, AND THAT YOU ARE MY PRISONER?
DO YOUR WORST!

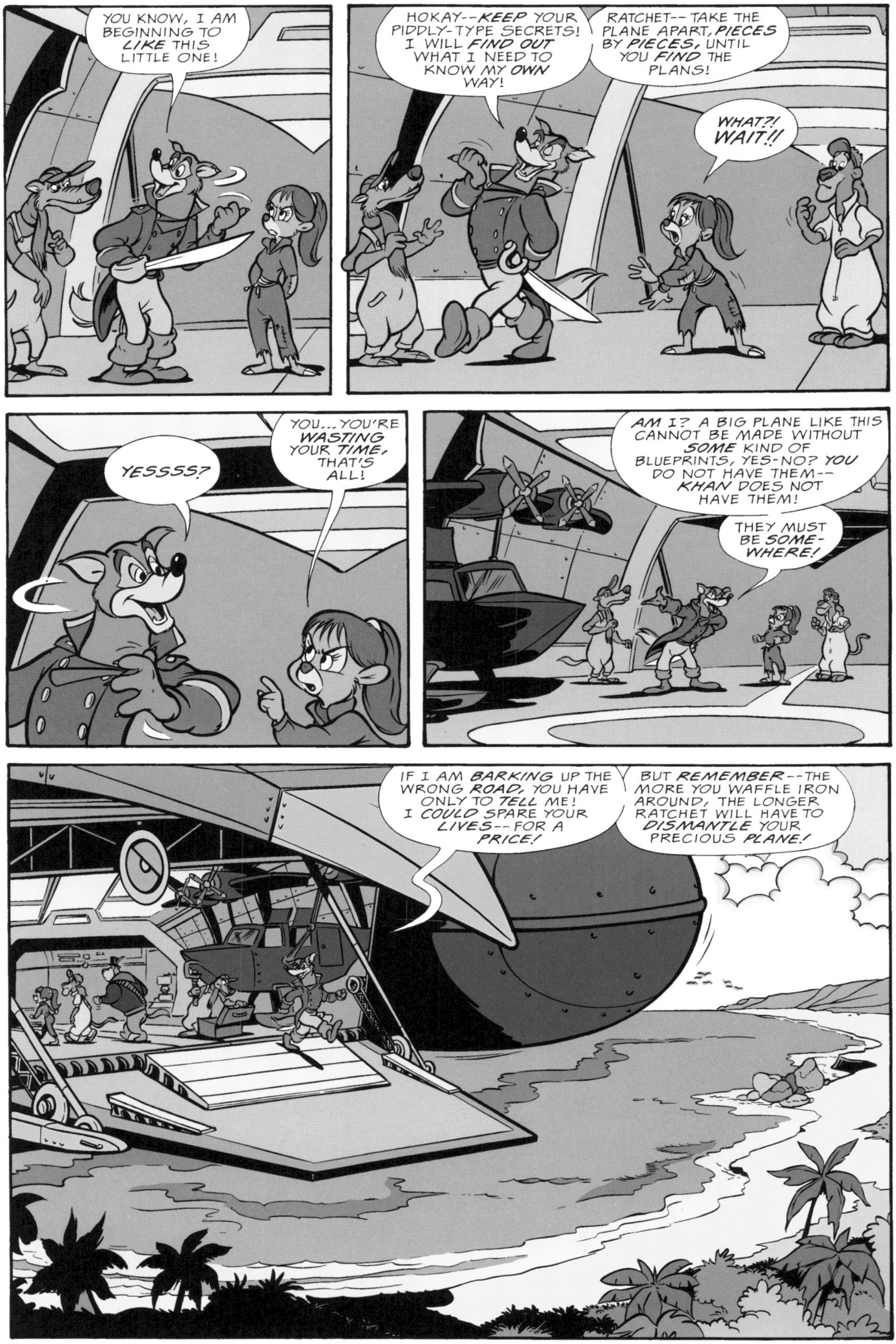
YOU KNOW, I AM BEGINNING TO LIKE THIS LITTLE ONE!
HOKAY--KEEP YOUR PIDDLY-TYPE SECRETS! I WILL FIND OUT WHAT I NEED TO KNOW MY OWN WAY!
RATCHET--TAKE THE PLANE APART, PIECES BY PIECES, UNTIL YOU FIND THE PLANS!
WHAT?! WAIT!!
YESSSS?
YOU...YOU'RE WASTING YOUR TIME, THAT'S ALL!
AM I? A BIG PLANE LIKE THIS CANNOT BE MADE WITHOUT SOME KIND OF BLUEPRINTS, YES-NO? YOU DO NOT HAVE THEM--KHAN DOES NOT HAVE THEM!
THEY MUST BE SOME-WHERE!
IF I AM BARKING UP THE WRONG ROAD, YOU HAVE ONLY TO TELL ME! I COULD SPARE YOUR LIVES--FOR A PRICE!
BUT REMEMBER--THE MORE YOU WAFFLE IRON AROUND, THE LONGER RATCHET WILL HAVE TO DISMANTLE YOUR PRECIOUS PLANE!

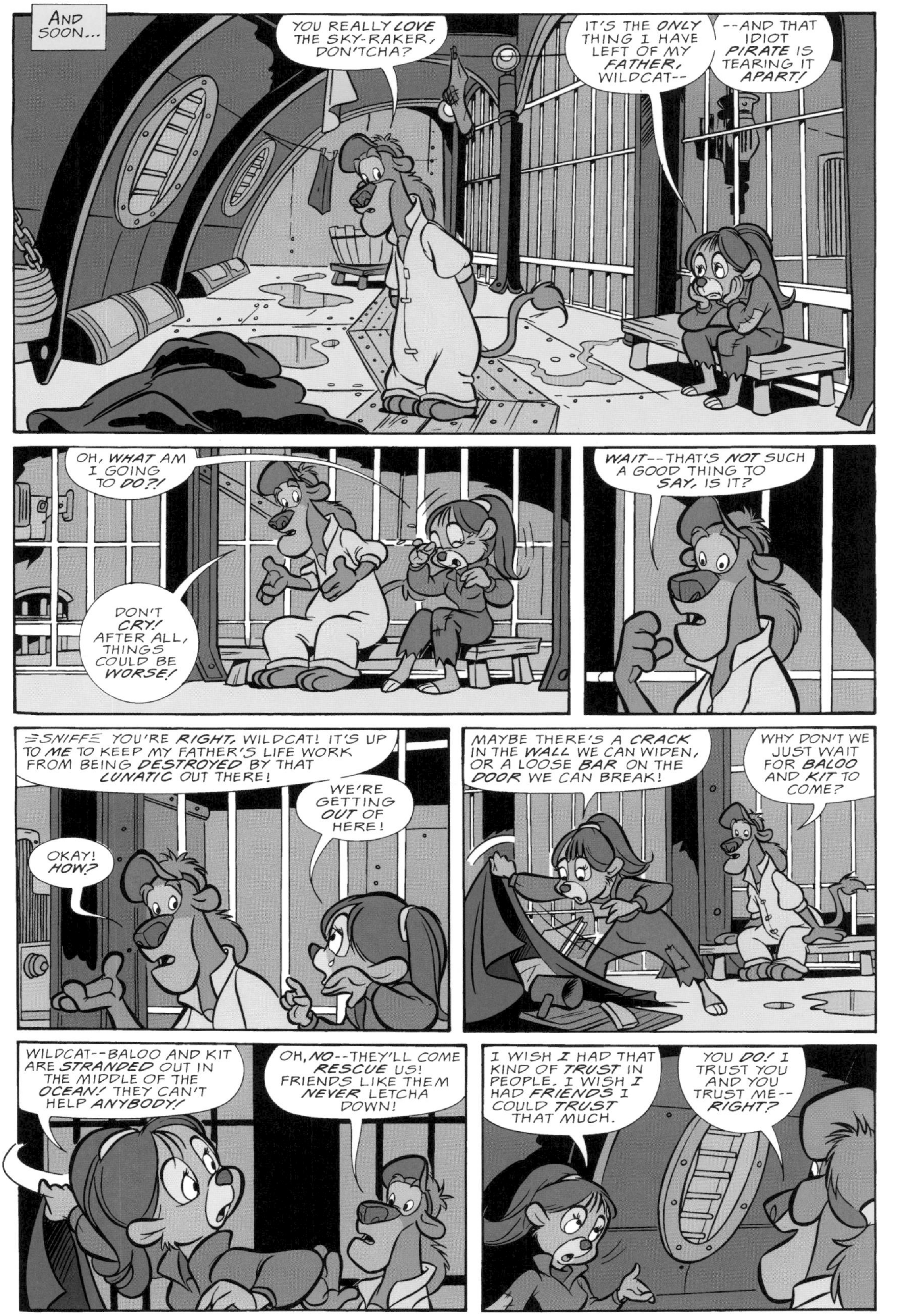
AND SOON...
YOU REALLY LOVE THE SKY-RAKER, DON'TCHA?
IT'S THE ONLY THING I HAVE LEFT OF MY FATHER, WILDCAT--
--AND THAT IDIOT PIRATE IS TEARING IT APART!
OH, WHAT AM I GOING TO DO?!
DON'T CRY! AFTER ALL, THINGS COULD BE WORSE!
WAIT--THAT'S NOT SUCH A GOOD THING TO SAY, IS IT?
SNIFF YOU'RE RIGHT, WILDCAT! IT'S UP TO ME TO KEEP MY FATHER'S LIFE WORK FROM BEING DESTROYED BY THAT LUNATIC OUT THERE!
WE'RE GETTING OUT OF HERE!
OKAY! HOW?
MAYBE THERE'S A CRACK IN THE WALL WE CAN WIDEN, OR A LOOSE BAR ON THE DOOR WE CAN BREAK!
WHY DON'T WE JUST WAIT FOR BALOO AND KIT TO COME?
WILDCAT--BALOO AND KIT ARE STRANDED OUT IN THE MIDDLE OF THE OCEAN! THEY CAN'T HELP ANYBODY!
OH, NO--THEY'LL COME RESCUE US! FRIENDS LIKE THEM NEVER LETCHA DOWN!
I WISH I HAD THAT KIND OF TRUST IN PEOPLE. I WISH I HAD FRIENDS I COULD TRUST THAT MUCH.
YOU DO! I TRUST YOU AND YOU TRUST ME-- RIGHT?

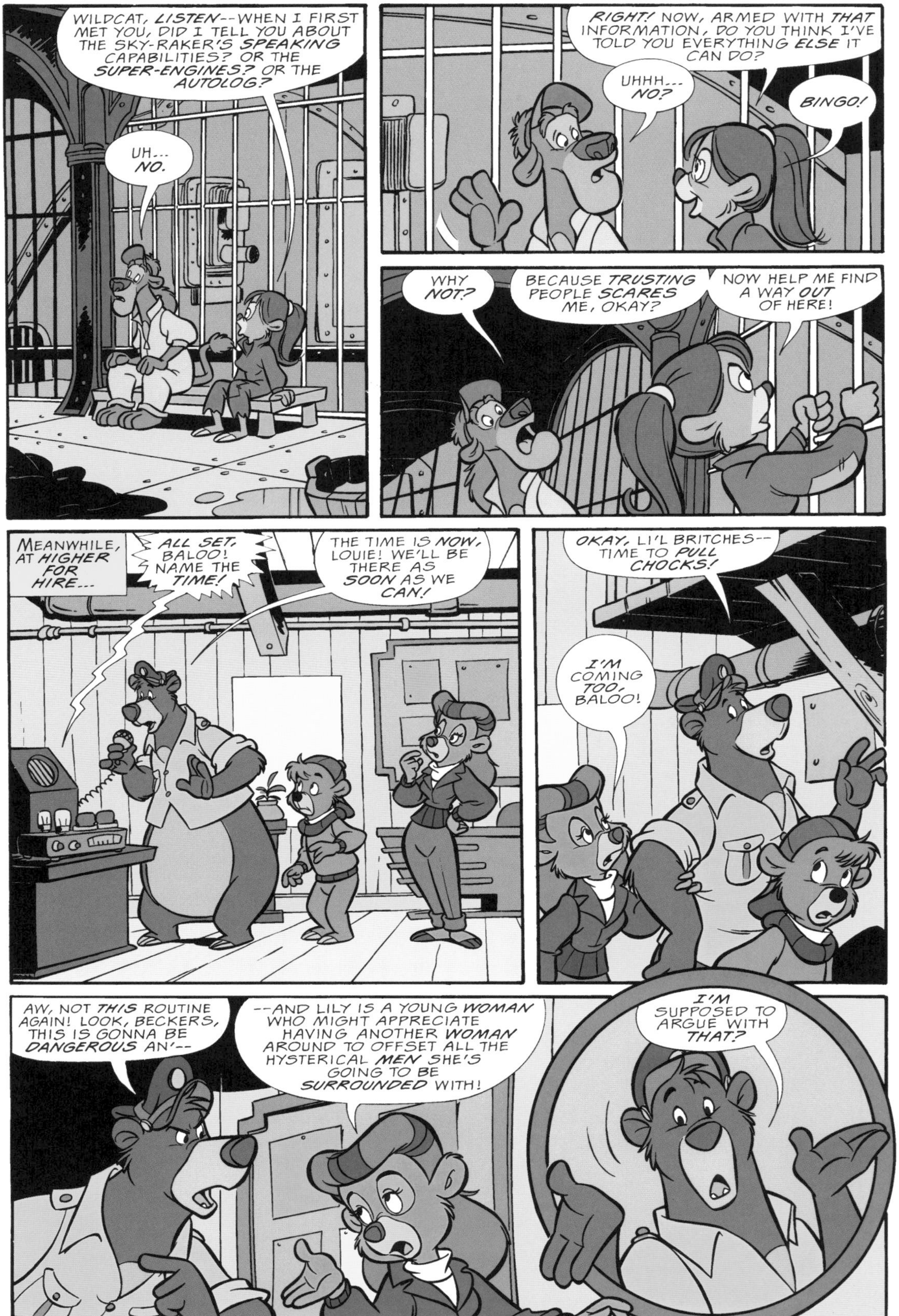

WILDCAT, LISTEN--WHEN I FIRST MET YOU, DID I TELL YOU ABOUT THE SKY-RAKER'S SPEAKING CAPABILITIES? OR THE SUPER-ENGINES? OR THE AUTOLOG?
UH... NO.
RIGHT! NOW, ARMED WITH THAT INFORMATION, DO YOU THINK I'VE TOLD YOU EVERYTHING ELSE IT CAN DO?
UHHH... NO?
BINGO!
WHY NOT?
BECAUSE TRUSTING PEOPLE SCARES ME, OKAY?
NOW HELP ME FIND A WAY OUT OF HERE!
MEANWHILE, AT HIGHER FOR HIRE...
ALL SET, BALOO! NAME THE TIME!
THE TIME IS NOW, LOUIE! WE'LL BE THERE AS SOON AS WE CAN!
OKAY, LI'L BRITCHES--TIME TO PULL CHOCKS!
I'M COMING TOO, BALOO!
AW, NOT THIS ROUTINE AGAIN! LOOK, BECKERS, THIS IS GONNA BE DANGEROUS AN'--
--AND LILY IS A YOUNG WOMAN WHO MIGHT APPRECIATE HAVING ANOTHER WOMAN AROUND TO OFFSET ALL THE HYSTERICAL MEN SHE'S GOING TO BE SURROUNDED WITH!
I'M SUPPOSED TO ARGUE WITH THAT?

IN THE PENTHOUSE SUITE HIGH ATOP THE *KHAN INDUSTRIES BUILDING...*

SO THE *SKY-RAKER* HAS BEEN *FOUND*-- AND BY NONE OTHER THAN *MISTER BALOO.*

YOU HAVE DONE *WELL.*

I BELIEVE *THIS* SHOULD PROVE *ADEQUATE* COMPENSATION FOR YOUR EFFORTS.

OH, I DO BELIEVE IT *WILL, MISTER KHAN!*

ONE MORE THING.

NO ONE IS TO HEAR OF THE *SKY-RAKER. IS* THAT *CLEAR?*

CLEAR AS *GLASS, MISTER KHAN!* NOBODY'LL HEAR A PEEP OUTTA *ME,* NO SIREE! WHY, I'LL--

GOOD.

GET ME *CAPTAIN QUARRY.*

QUARRY, SIR? =ULP!=

Y-YES, SIR!

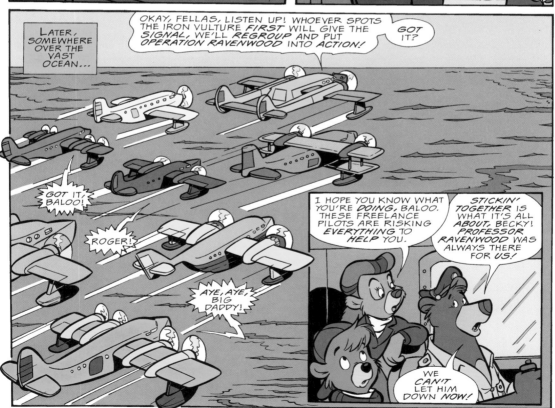

LATER, SOMEWHERE OVER THE VAST OCEAN...

OKAY, FELLAS, LISTEN UP! WHOEVER SPOTS THE IRON VULTURE *FIRST* WILL GIVE THE SIGNAL, WE'LL REGROUP AND PUT *OPERATION RAVENWOOD* INTO *ACTION!*

GOT IT?

GOT IT, BALOO!

ROGER!

AYE, AYE, BIG DADDY!

I HOPE YOU KNOW WHAT YOU'RE *DOING,* BALOO. THESE FREELANCE PILOTS ARE RISKING *EVERYTHING* TO HELP YOU.

STICKIN' TOGETHER IS WHAT IT'S ALL *ABOUT, BECKY! PROFESSOR RAVENWOOD* WAS ALWAYS THERE FOR *US!*

WE *CAN'T* LET HIM DOWN *NOW!*

35

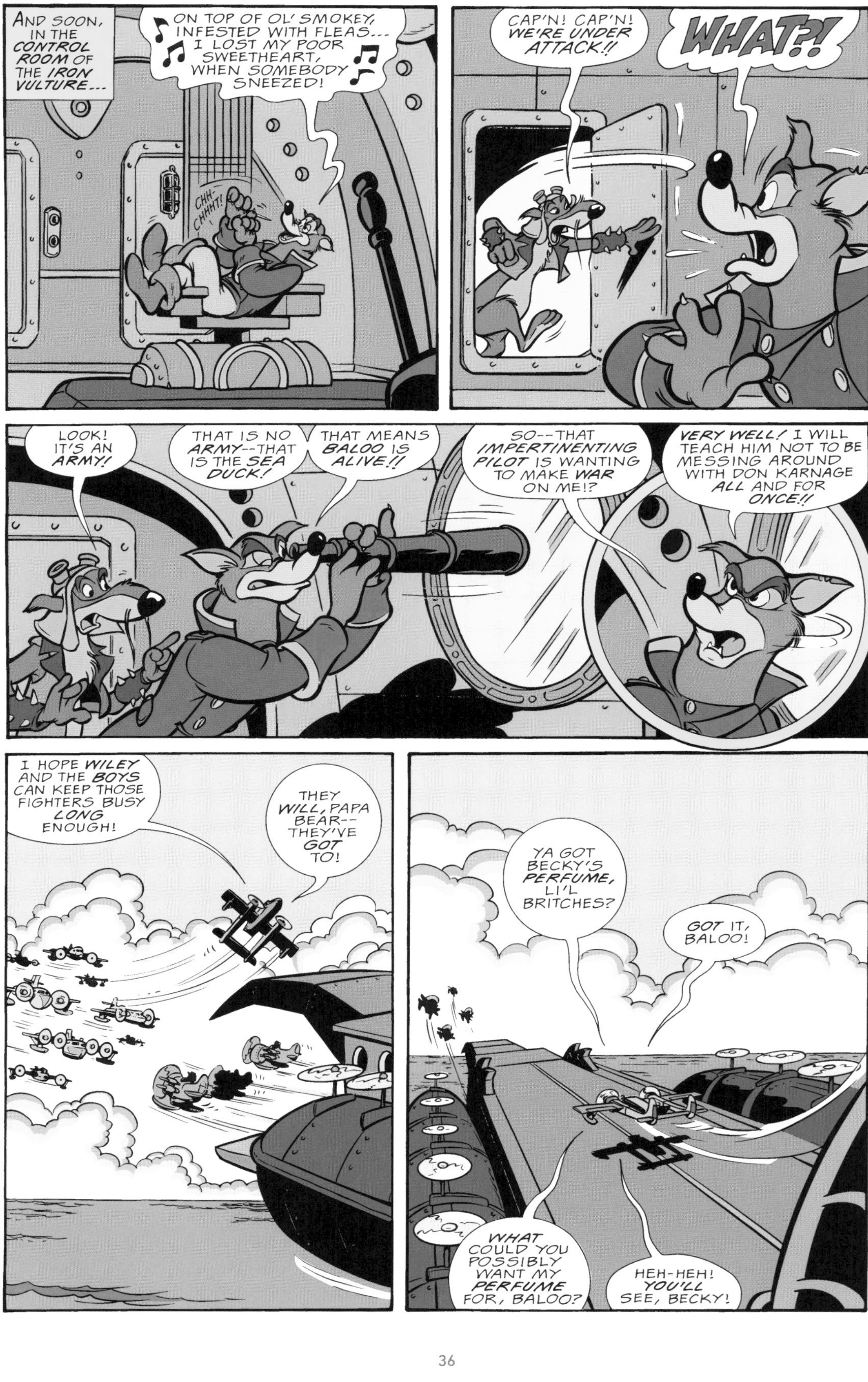
AND SOON, IN THE CONTROL ROOM OF THE IRON VULTURE...
ON TOP OF OL' SMOKEY, INFESTED WITH FLEAS... I LOST MY POOR SWEETHEART, WHEN SOMEBODY SNEEZED!
CHH-CHHHT!
CAP'N! CAP'N! WE'RE UNDER ATTACK!!
WHAT?!
LOOK! IT'S AN ARMY!
THAT IS NO ARMY--THAT IS THE SEA DUCK!
THAT MEANS BALOO IS ALIVE!!
SO--THAT IMPERTINENTING PILOT IS WANTING TO MAKE WAR ON ME!?
VERY WELL! I WILL TEACH HIM NOT TO BE MESSING AROUND WITH DON KARNAGE ALL AND FOR ONCE!!
I HOPE WILEY AND THE BOYS CAN KEEP THOSE FIGHTERS BUSY LONG ENOUGH!
THEY WILL, PAPA BEAR--THEY'VE GOT TO!
YA GOT BECKY'S PERFUME, LI'L BRITCHES?
GOT IT, BALOO!
WHAT COULD YOU POSSIBLY WANT MY PERFUME FOR, BALOO?
HEH-HEH! YOU'LL SEE, BECKY!

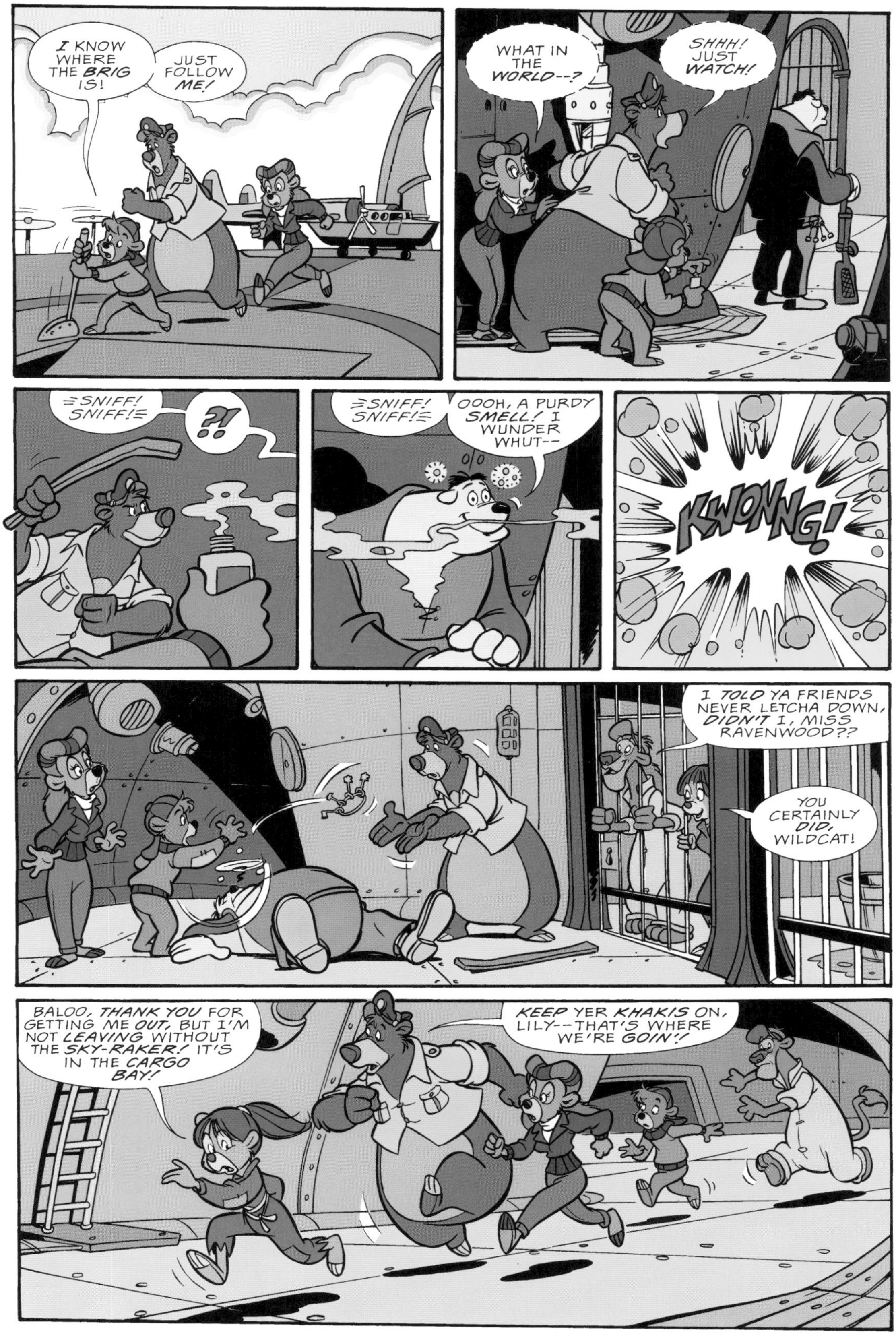
I KNOW WHERE THE BRIG IS!
JUST FOLLOW ME!
WHAT IN THE WORLD--?
SHHH! JUST WATCH!
≡SNIFF! SNIFF!≡
?!
≡SNIFF! SNIFF!≡
OOOH, A PURDY SMELL! I WUNDER WHUT--
KWONNG!
I TOLD YA FRIENDS NEVER LETCHA DOWN, DIDN'T I, MISS RAVENWOOD??
YOU CERTAINLY DID, WILDCAT!
BALOO, THANK YOU FOR GETTING ME OUT, BUT I'M NOT LEAVING WITHOUT THE SKY-RAKER! IT'S IN THE CARGO BAY!
KEEP YER KHAKIS ON, LILY--THAT'S WHERE WE'RE GOIN'!

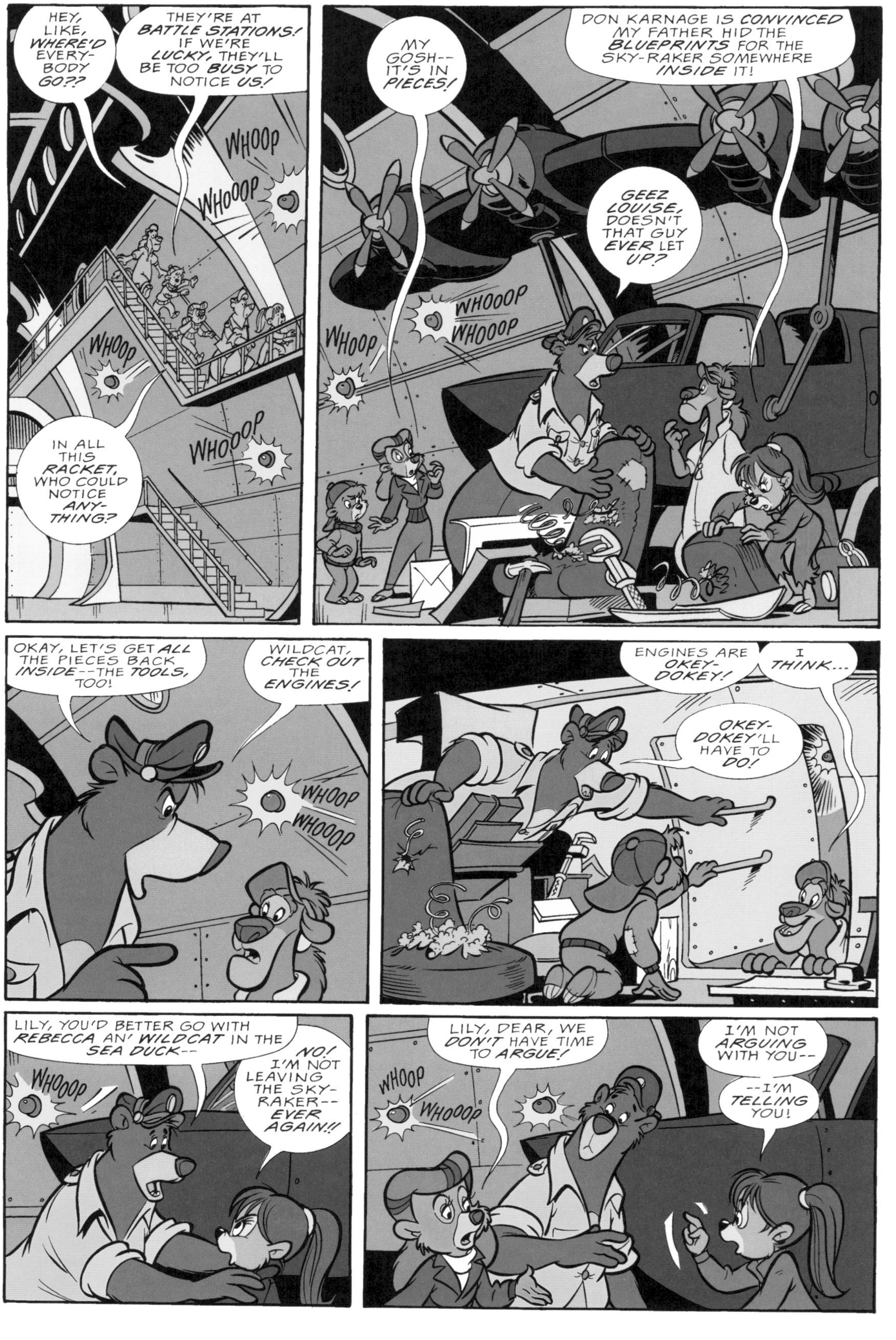
HEY, LIKE, WHERE'D EVERY-BODY GO??
THEY'RE AT BATTLE STATIONS! IF WE'RE LUCKY, THEY'LL BE TOO BUSY TO NOTICE US!
WHOOP
WHOOOP
WHOOP
IN ALL THIS RACKET, WHO COULD NOTICE ANY-THING?
WHOOOP
MY GOSH-- IT'S IN PIECES!
DON KARNAGE IS CONVINCED MY FATHER HID THE BLUEPRINTS FOR THE SKY-RAKER SOMEWHERE INSIDE IT!
GEEZ LOUISE, DOESN'T THAT GUY EVER LET UP?
WHOOOP
WHOOOP
WHOOP
OKAY, LET'S GET ALL THE PIECES BACK INSIDE--THE TOOLS, TOO!
WILDCAT, CHECK OUT THE ENGINES!
WHOOP
WHOOOP
ENGINES ARE OKEY-DOKEY!
I THINK...
OKEY-DOKEY'LL HAVE TO DO!
LILY, YOU'D BETTER GO WITH REBECCA AN' WILDCAT IN THE SEA DUCK--
WHOOOP
NO! I'M NOT LEAVING THE SKY-RAKER-- EVER AGAIN!!
WHOOP
WHOOOP
LILY, DEAR, WE DON'T HAVE TIME TO ARGUE!
I'M NOT ARGUING WITH YOU--
--I'M TELLING YOU!

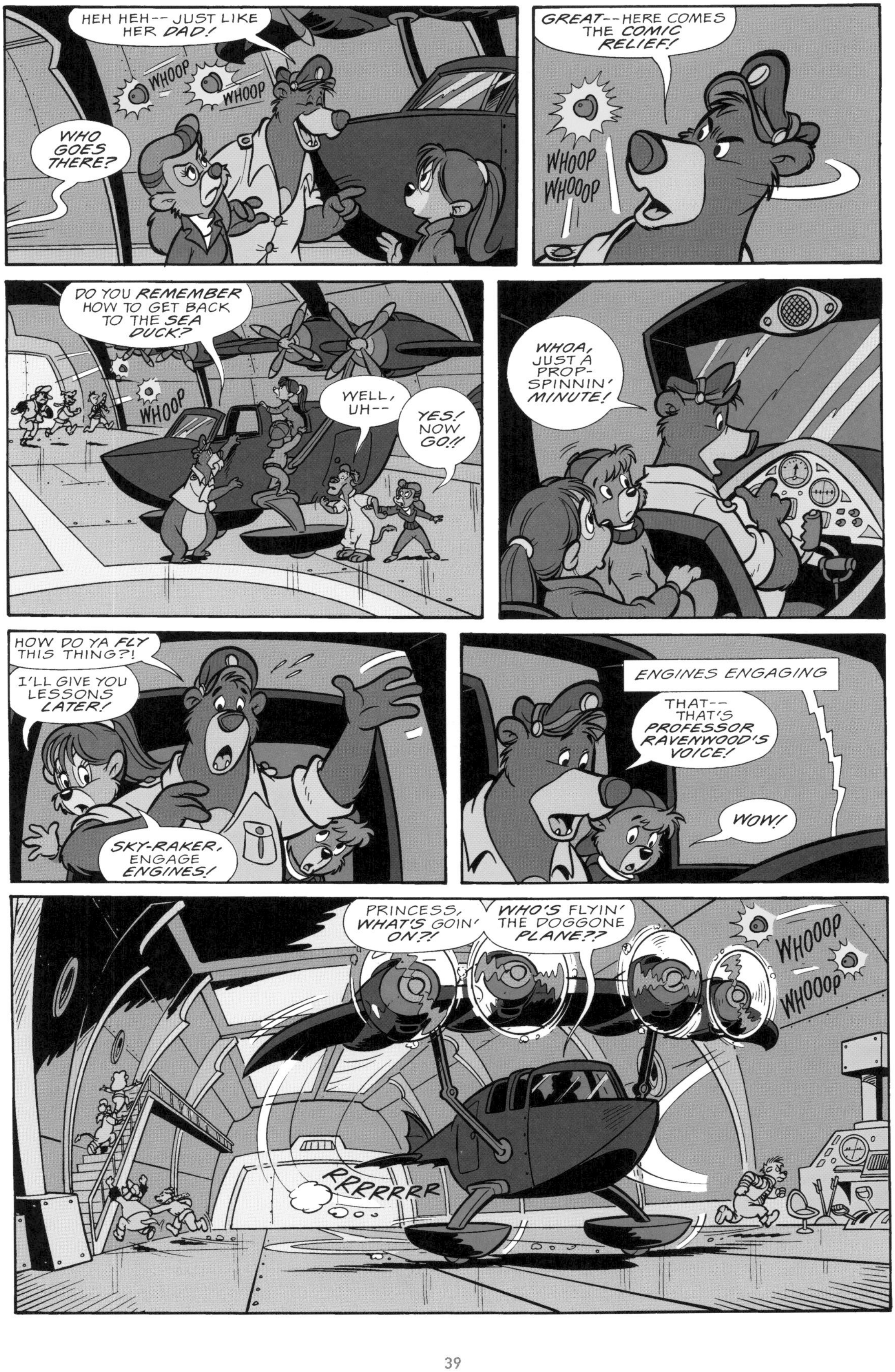
HEH HEH-- JUST LIKE HER DAD!
WHOOP
WHOOP
WHO GOES THERE?
GREAT--HERE COMES THE COMIC RELIEF!
WHOOP
WHOOOP
DO YOU REMEMBER HOW TO GET BACK TO THE SEA DUCK?
WHOOP
WELL, UH--
YES! NOW GO!!
WHOA, JUST A PROP-SPINNIN' MINUTE!
HOW DO YA FLY THIS THING?!
I'LL GIVE YOU LESSONS LATER!
SKY-RAKER, ENGAGE ENGINES!
ENGINES ENGAGING
THAT-- THAT'S PROFESSOR RAVENWOOD'S VOICE!
WOW!
PRINCESS, WHAT'S GOIN' ON?!
WHO'S FLYIN' THE DOGGONE PLANE??
WHOOOP
WHOOOP
RRRRRRR

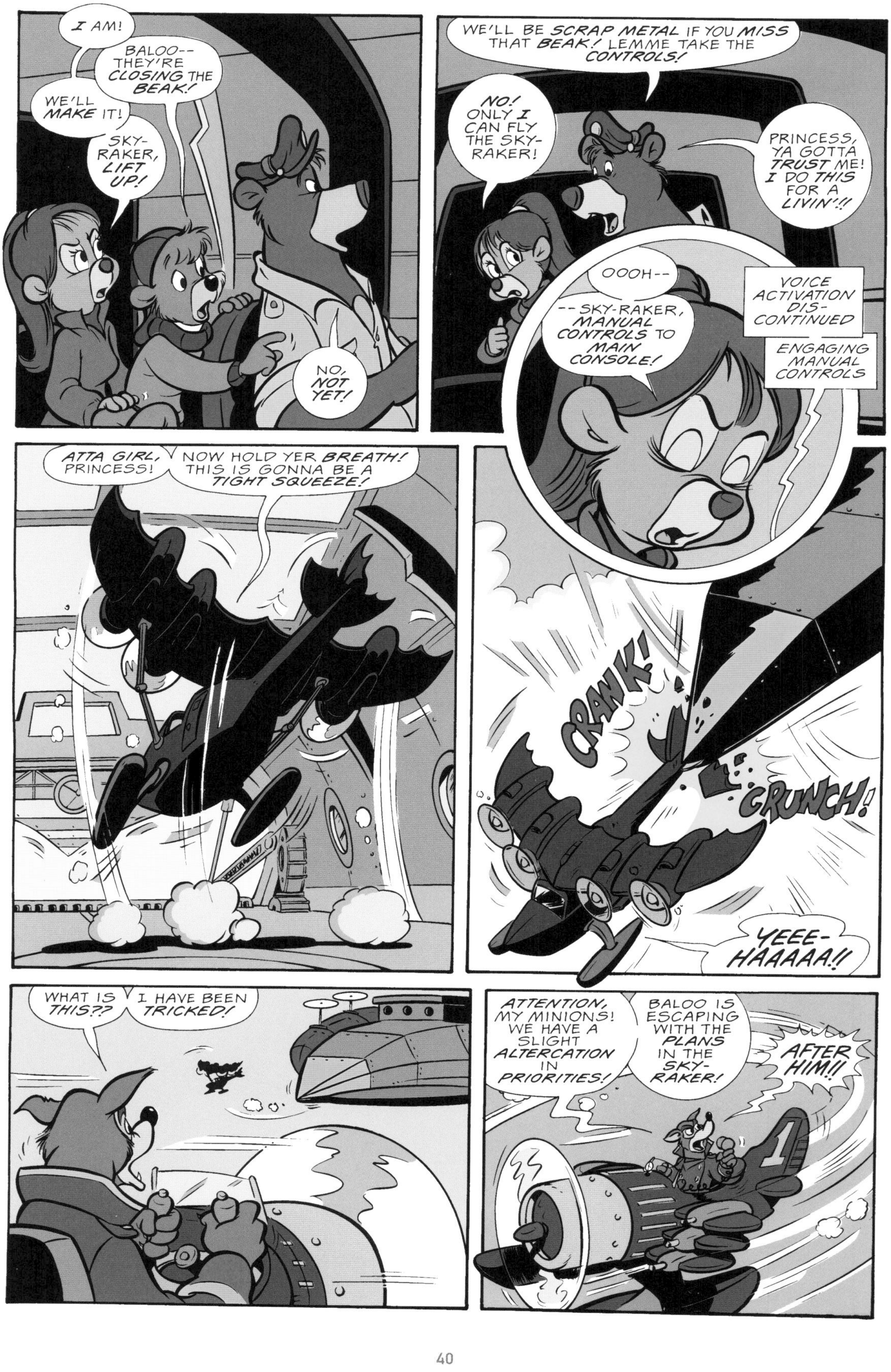

I AM!
BALOO-- THEY'RE CLOSING THE BEAK!
WE'LL MAKE IT!
SKY-RAKER, LIFT UP!
NO, NOT YET!
WE'LL BE SCRAP METAL IF YOU MISS THAT BEAK! LEMME TAKE THE CONTROLS!
NO! ONLY I CAN FLY THE SKY-RAKER!
PRINCESS, YA GOTTA TRUST ME! I DO THIS FOR A LIVIN'!!
OOOH--
--SKY-RAKER, MANUAL CONTROLS TO MAIN CONSOLE!
VOICE ACTIVATION DIS-CONTINUED
ENGAGING MANUAL CONTROLS
ATTA GIRL, PRINCESS!
NOW HOLD YER BREATH! THIS IS GONNA BE A TIGHT SQUEEZE!
CRANK!
CRUNCH!
YEEE-HAAAAA!!
WHAT IS THIS??
I HAVE BEEN TRICKED!
ATTENTION, MY MINIONS! WE HAVE A SLIGHT ALTERCATION IN PRIORITIES!
BALOO IS ESCAPING WITH THE PLANS IN THE SKY-RAKER!
AFTER HIM!!

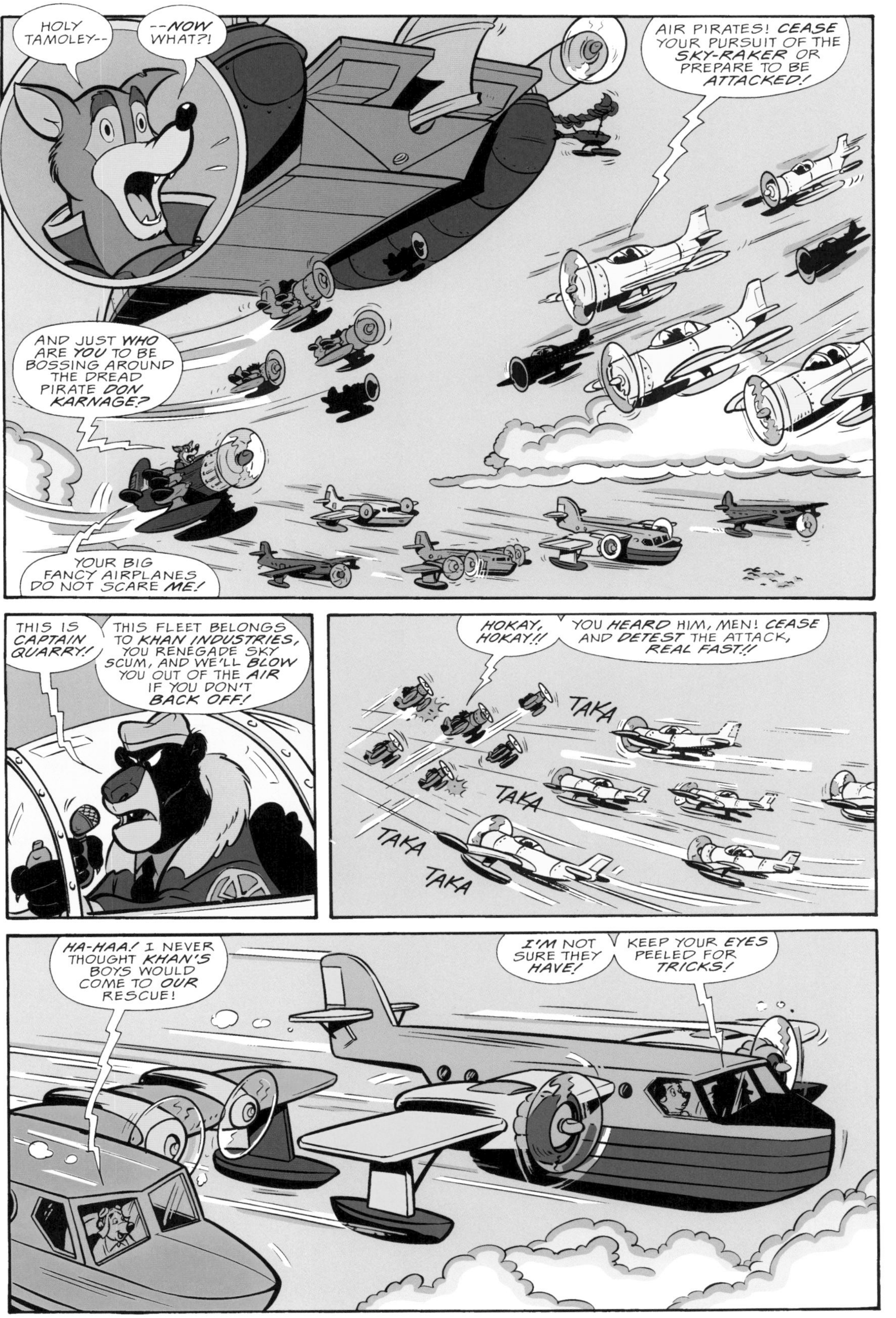

HOLY TAMOLEY--
--NOW WHAT?!
AIR PIRATES! CEASE YOUR PURSUIT OF THE SKY-RAKER OR PREPARE TO BE ATTACKED!
AND JUST WHO ARE YOU TO BE BOSSING AROUND THE DREAD PIRATE DON KARNAGE?
YOUR BIG FANCY AIRPLANES DO NOT SCARE ME!
THIS IS CAPTAIN QUARRY!
THIS FLEET BELONGS TO KHAN INDUSTRIES, YOU RENEGADE SKY SCUM, AND WE'LL BLOW YOU OUT OF THE AIR IF YOU DON'T BACK OFF!
HOKAY, HOKAY!!
YOU HEARD HIM, MEN! CEASE AND DETEST THE ATTACK, REAL FAST!!
TAKA
TAKA
TAKA
TAKA
HA-HAA! I NEVER THOUGHT KHAN'S BOYS WOULD COME TO OUR RESCUE!
I'M NOT SURE THEY HAVE!
KEEP YOUR EYES PEELED FOR TRICKS!

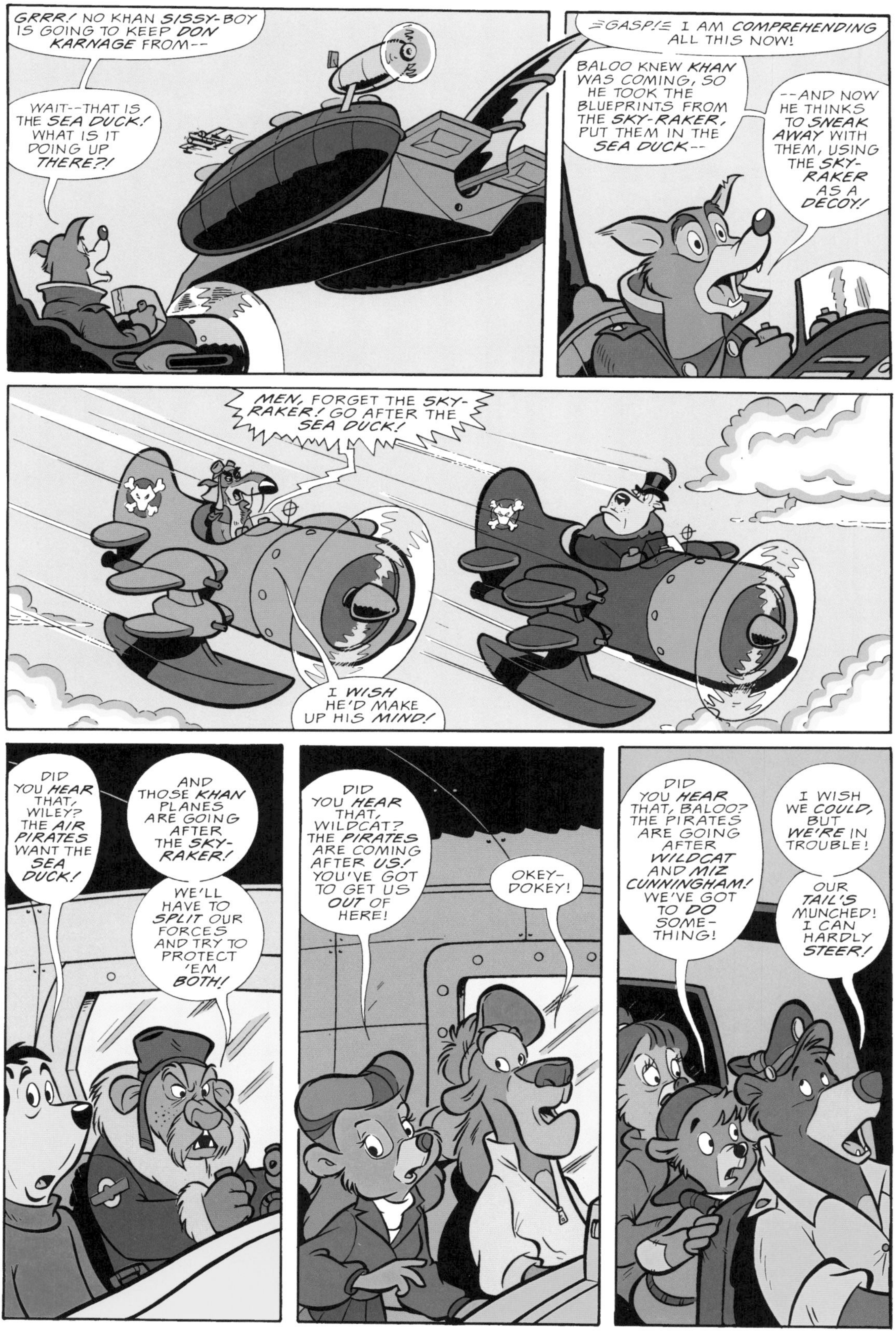
GRRR! NO KHAN SISSY-BOY IS GOING TO KEEP DON KARNAGE FROM--
WAIT--THAT IS THE SEA DUCK! WHAT IS IT DOING UP THERE?!
GASP! I AM COMPREHENDING ALL THIS NOW!
BALOO KNEW KHAN WAS COMING, SO HE TOOK THE BLUEPRINTS FROM THE SKY-RAKER, PUT THEM IN THE SEA DUCK--
--AND NOW HE THINKS TO SNEAK AWAY WITH THEM, USING THE SKY-RAKER AS A DECOY!
MEN, FORGET THE SKY-RAKER! GO AFTER THE SEA DUCK!
I WISH HE'D MAKE UP HIS MIND!
DID YOU HEAR THAT, WILEY? THE AIR PIRATES WANT THE SEA DUCK!
AND THOSE KHAN PLANES ARE GOING AFTER THE SKY-RAKER!
WE'LL HAVE TO SPLIT OUR FORCES AND TRY TO PROTECT 'EM BOTH!
DID YOU HEAR THAT, WILDCAT? THE PIRATES ARE COMING AFTER US! YOU'VE GOT TO GET US OUT OF HERE!
OKEY-DOKEY!
DID YOU HEAR THAT, BALOO? THE PIRATES ARE GOING AFTER WILDCAT AND MIZ CUNNINGHAM! WE'VE GOT TO DO SOME-THING!
I WISH WE COULD, BUT WE'RE IN TROUBLE!
OUR TAIL'S MUNCHED! I CAN HARDLY STEER!

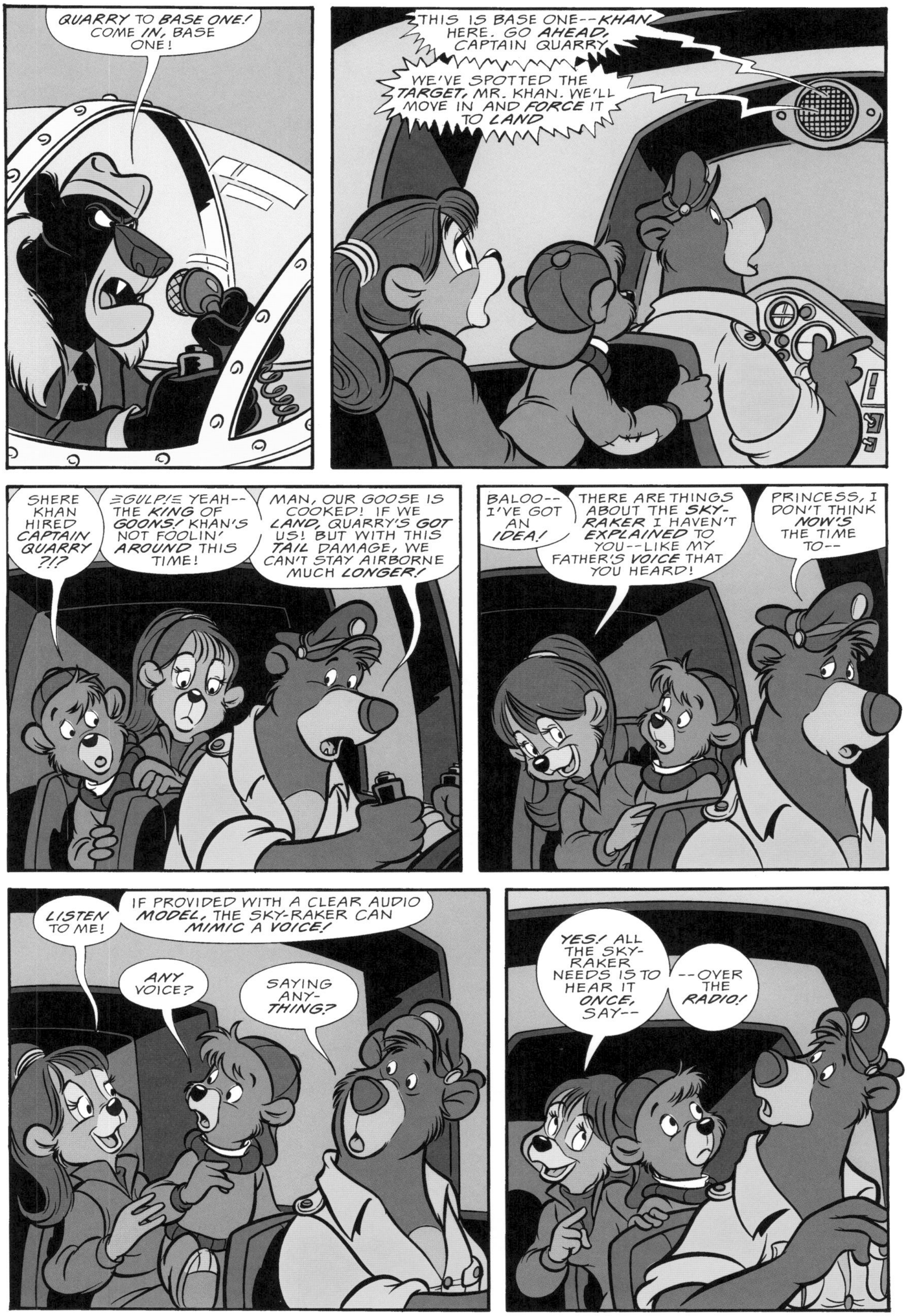
QUARRY TO BASE ONE! COME IN, BASE ONE!
THIS IS BASE ONE--KHAN HERE. GO AHEAD, CAPTAIN QUARRY.
WE'VE SPOTTED THE TARGET, MR. KHAN. WE'LL MOVE IN AND FORCE IT TO LAND.
SHERE KHAN HIRED CAPTAIN QUARRY ?!?
=GULP!= YEAH-- THE KING OF GOONS! KHAN'S NOT FOOLIN' AROUND THIS TIME!
MAN, OUR GOOSE IS COOKED! IF WE LAND, QUARRY'S GOT US! BUT WITH THIS TAIL DAMAGE, WE CAN'T STAY AIRBORNE MUCH LONGER!
BALOO-- I'VE GOT AN IDEA!
THERE ARE THINGS ABOUT THE SKY-RAKER I HAVEN'T EXPLAINED TO YOU--LIKE MY FATHER'S VOICE THAT YOU HEARD!
PRINCESS, I DON'T THINK NOW'S THE TIME TO--
LISTEN TO ME!
IF PROVIDED WITH A CLEAR AUDIO MODEL, THE SKY-RAKER CAN MIMIC A VOICE!
ANY VOICE?
SAYING ANY-THING?
YES! ALL THE SKY-RAKER NEEDS IS TO HEAR IT ONCE, SAY--
--OVER THE RADIO!

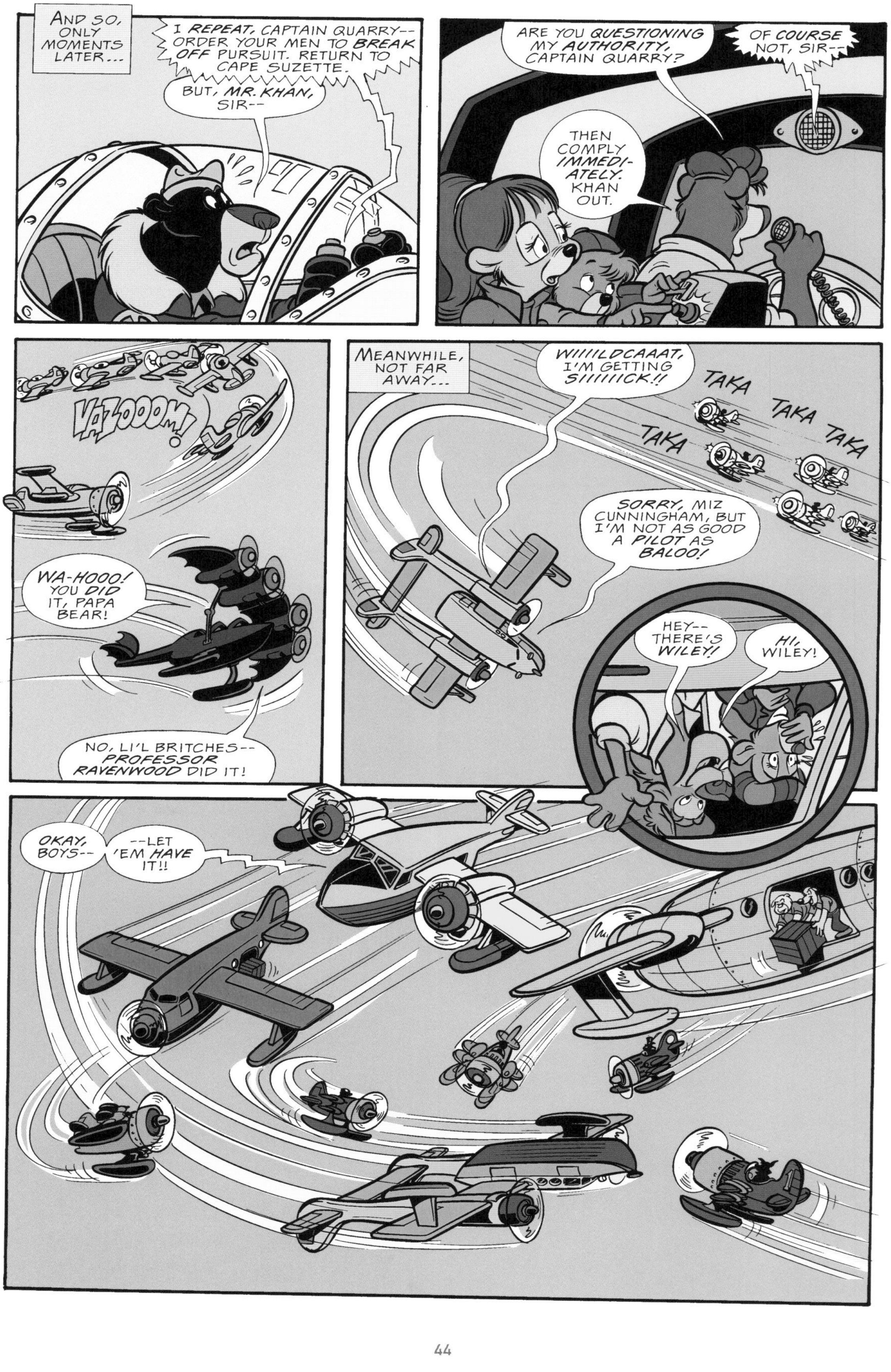

AND SO, ONLY MOMENTS LATER...
I REPEAT, CAPTAIN QUARRY-- ORDER YOUR MEN TO BREAK OFF PURSUIT. RETURN TO CAPE SUZETTE.
BUT, MR. KHAN, SIR--
ARE YOU QUESTIONING MY AUTHORITY, CAPTAIN QUARRY?
OF COURSE NOT, SIR--
THEN COMPLY IMMEDI-ATELY. KHAN OUT.
VAZOOOM!
WA-HOOO! YOU DID IT, PAPA BEAR!
NO, LI'L BRITCHES-- PROFESSOR RAVENWOOD DID IT!
MEANWHILE, NOT FAR AWAY...
WIIIILDCAAAT, I'M GETTING SIIIIIICK!!
TAKA TAKA TAKA TAKA
SORRY, MIZ CUNNINGHAM, BUT I'M NOT AS GOOD A PILOT AS BALOO!
HEY-- THERE'S WILEY!!
HI, WILEY!
OKAY, BOYS--
--LET 'EM HAVE IT!!

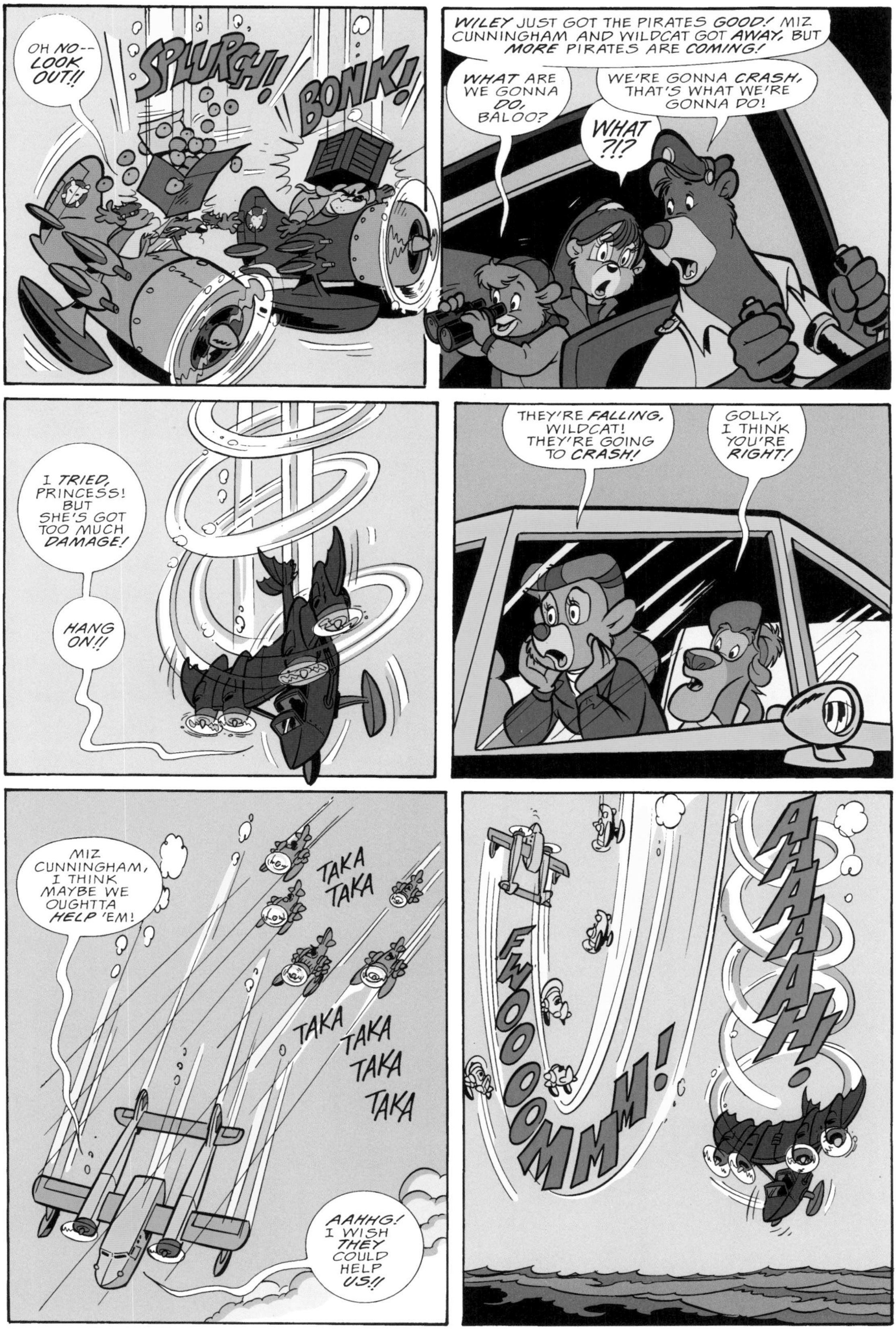

OH NO-- LOOK OUT!!
SPLURGH!
BONK!
WILEY JUST GOT THE PIRATES GOOD! MIZ CUNNINGHAM AND WILDCAT GOT AWAY, BUT MORE PIRATES ARE COMING!
WHAT ARE WE GONNA DO, BALOO?
WE'RE GONNA CRASH, THAT'S WHAT WE'RE GONNA DO!
WHAT ?!?
I TRIED, PRINCESS! BUT SHE'S GOT TOO MUCH DAMAGE!
HANG ON!!
THEY'RE FALLING, WILDCAT! THEY'RE GOING TO CRASH!
GOLLY, I THINK YOU'RE RIGHT!
MIZ CUNNINGHAM, I THINK MAYBE WE OUGHTTA HELP 'EM!
TAKA TAKA
TAKA TAKA TAKA TAKA
AAHHG! I WISH THEY COULD HELP US!!
FWOOOOMMM!
AAAAAAH!

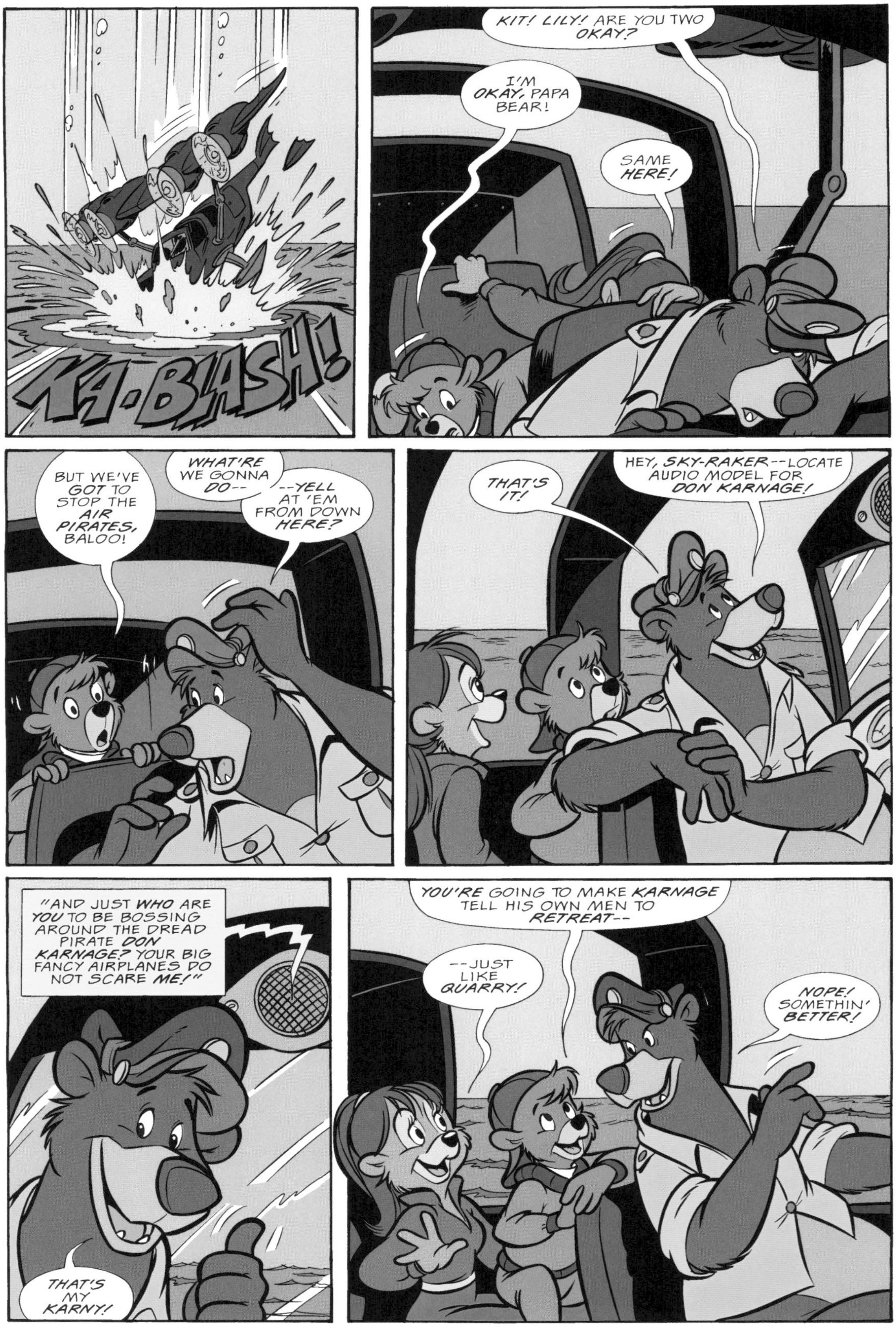
KA-BLASH!
KIT! LILY! ARE YOU TWO OKAY?
I'M OKAY, PAPA BEAR!
SAME HERE!
BUT WE'VE GOT TO STOP THE AIR PIRATES, BALOO!
WHAT'RE WE GONNA DO--
--YELL AT 'EM FROM DOWN HERE?
THAT'S IT!
HEY, SKY-RAKER--LOCATE AUDIO MODEL FOR DON KARNAGE!
"AND JUST WHO ARE YOU TO BE BOSSING AROUND THE DREAD PIRATE DON KARNAGE? YOUR BIG FANCY AIRPLANES DO NOT SCARE ME!"
THAT'S MY KARNY!
YOU'RE GOING TO MAKE KARNAGE TELL HIS OWN MEN TO RETREAT--
--JUST LIKE QUARRY!
NOPE! SOMETHIN' BETTER!

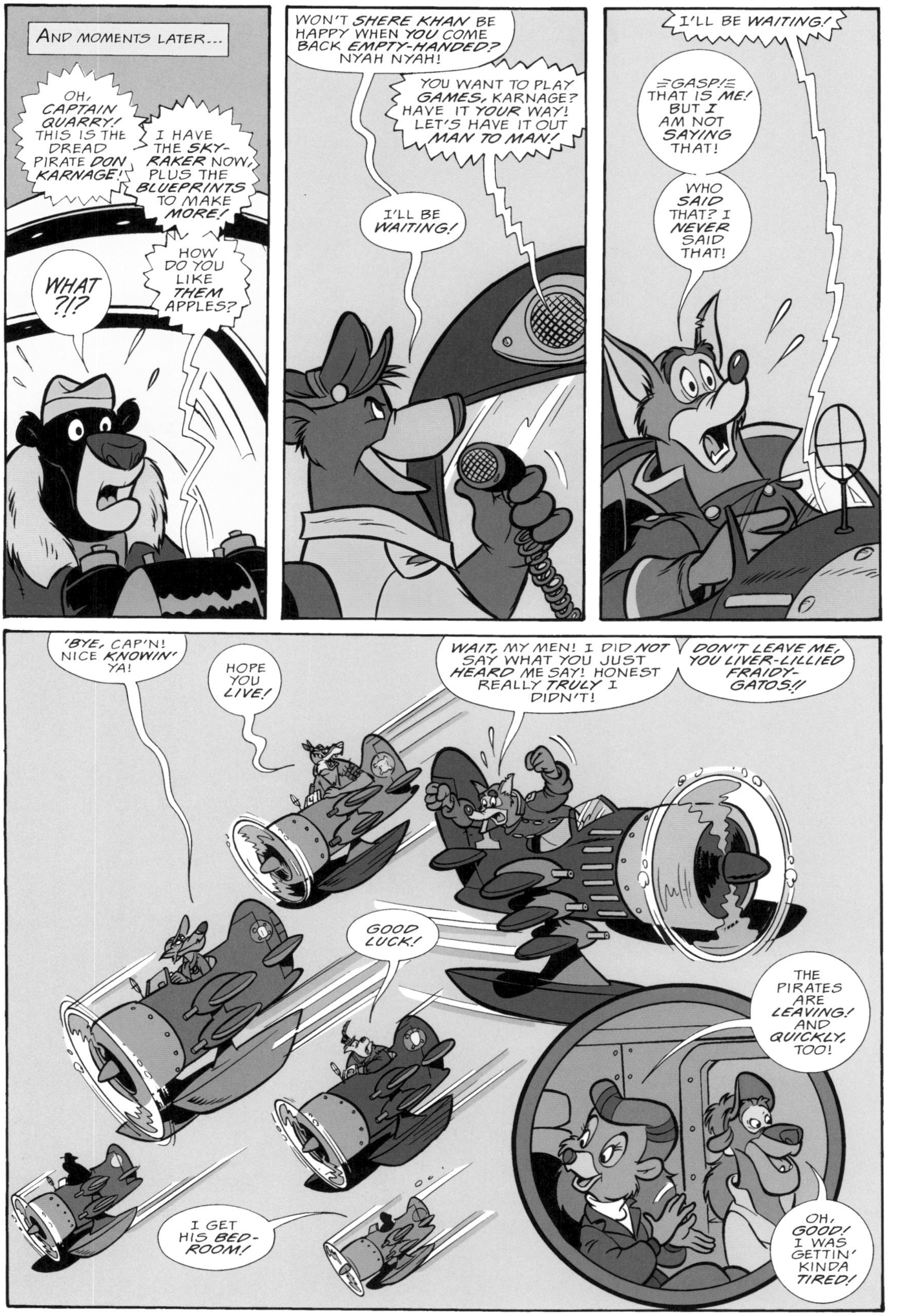
AND MOMENTS LATER...
OH, CAPTAIN QUARRY! THIS IS THE DREAD PIRATE DON KARNAGE!
I HAVE THE SKY-RAKER NOW, PLUS THE BLUEPRINTS TO MAKE MORE!
HOW DO YOU LIKE THEM APPLES?
WHAT ?!?
WON'T SHERE KHAN BE HAPPY WHEN YOU COME BACK EMPTY-HANDED? NYAH NYAH!
YOU WANT TO PLAY GAMES, KARNAGE? HAVE IT YOUR WAY! LET'S HAVE IT OUT MAN TO MAN!
I'LL BE WAITING!
I'LL BE WAITING!
≡GASP!≡ THAT IS ME! BUT I AM NOT SAYING THAT!
WHO SAID THAT? I NEVER SAID THAT!
'BYE, CAP'N! NICE KNOWIN' YA!
HOPE YOU LIVE!
WAIT, MY MEN! I DID NOT SAY WHAT YOU JUST HEARD ME SAY! HONEST REALLY TRULY I DIDN'T!
DON'T LEAVE ME, YOU LIVER-LILLIED FRAIDY-GATOS!!
GOOD LUCK!
THE PIRATES ARE LEAVING! AND QUICKLY, TOO!
I GET HIS BED-ROOM!
OH, GOOD! I WAS GETTIN' KINDA TIRED!

AND SOON...

WELL, PRINCESS—I THINK *WE* OUGHTTA GET YOU *HOME!*

OH, *BALOO!*

SSSPK! FZZZK! CRKRL!

OH *NO*—THE *CONSOLE!*

SKY-RAKER! SKY-RAKER, ARE YOU *OKAY?*

DADDY?! ANSWER *ME!!*

¡SSSPK! FZZZK!

H-HE'S *GONE...*

PRINCESS—THE *CONSOLE* JUST SHORTED *OUT.*

WE'LL *TOW* THE SKY-RAKER BACK TO HIGHER FOR HIRE AND *WILDCAT* WILL FIX IT UP IN A *JIFFY.*

THAT STUPID *PIRATE!* IF HE HADN'T BEEN SO DEAD SET ABOUT FINDING *BLUE-PRINTS* THAT DON'T *EXIST,* NONE OF THIS WOULD'VE *HAPPENED!*

BUT HE WAS *RIGHT,* BALOO.

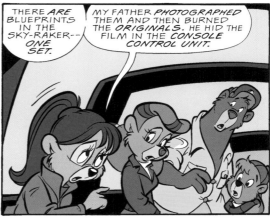

THERE *ARE* BLUEPRINTS IN THE SKY-RAKER— *ONE* SET.

MY FATHER *PHOTOGRAPHED* THEM AND THEN BURNED THE *ORIGINALS.* HE HID THE FILM IN THE *CONSOLE CONTROL UNIT.*

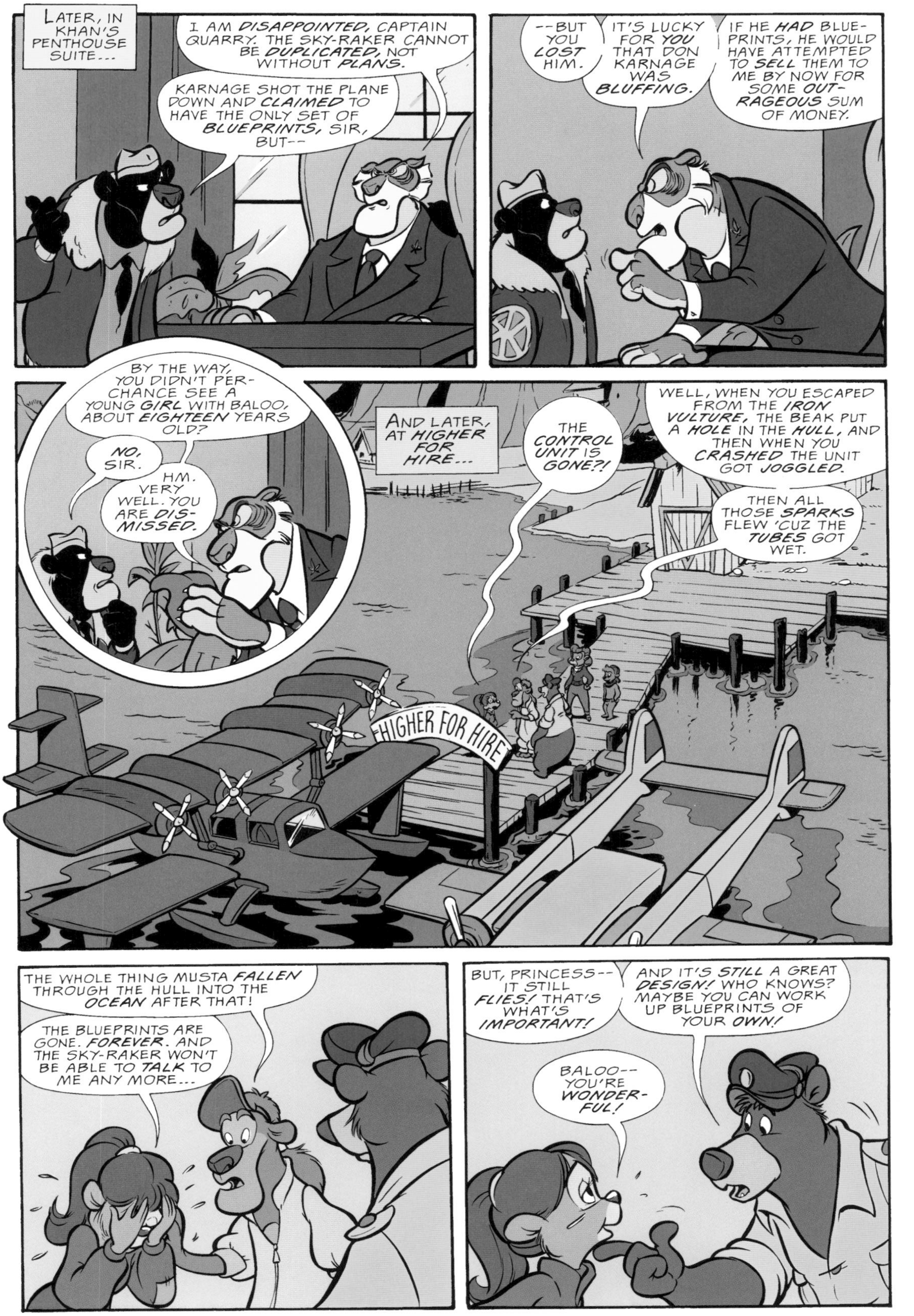
LATER, IN KHAN'S PENTHOUSE SUITE...
I AM *DISAPPOINTED*, CAPTAIN QUARRY. THE SKY-RAKER CANNOT BE *DUPLICATED*, NOT WITHOUT *PLANS*.
KARNAGE SHOT THE PLANE DOWN AND *CLAIMED* TO HAVE THE ONLY SET OF *BLUEPRINTS*, SIR, BUT--
--BUT YOU *LOST* HIM.
IT'S LUCKY FOR *YOU* THAT DON KARNAGE WAS *BLUFFING*.
IF HE *HAD* BLUEPRINTS, HE WOULD HAVE ATTEMPTED TO *SELL* THEM TO ME BY NOW FOR SOME *OUTRAGEOUS* SUM OF MONEY.
BY THE WAY, YOU DIDN'T PERCHANCE SEE A YOUNG *GIRL* WITH BALOO, ABOUT *EIGHTEEN* YEARS OLD?
NO, SIR.
HM. VERY WELL. YOU ARE *DISMISSED*.
AND LATER, AT *HIGHER FOR HIRE*...
THE *CONTROL UNIT* IS *GONE?!*
WELL, WHEN YOU ESCAPED FROM THE *IRON VULTURE*, THE BEAK PUT A *HOLE* IN THE *HULL*, AND THEN WHEN YOU *CRASHED* THE UNIT GOT *JOGGLED*.
THEN ALL THOSE *SPARKS* FLEW 'CUZ THE *TUBES* GOT WET.
HIGHER FOR HIRE
THE WHOLE THING MUSTA *FALLEN* THROUGH THE HULL INTO THE *OCEAN* AFTER THAT!
THE BLUEPRINTS ARE GONE. *FOREVER*. AND THE SKY-RAKER WON'T BE ABLE TO *TALK* TO ME ANY MORE...
BUT, PRINCESS-- IT STILL *FLIES!* THAT'S WHAT'S *IMPORTANT!*
AND IT'S *STILL* A GREAT *DESIGN!* WHO KNOWS? MAYBE YOU CAN WORK UP BLUEPRINTS OF YOUR *OWN!*
BALOO-- YOU'RE *WONDERFUL!*

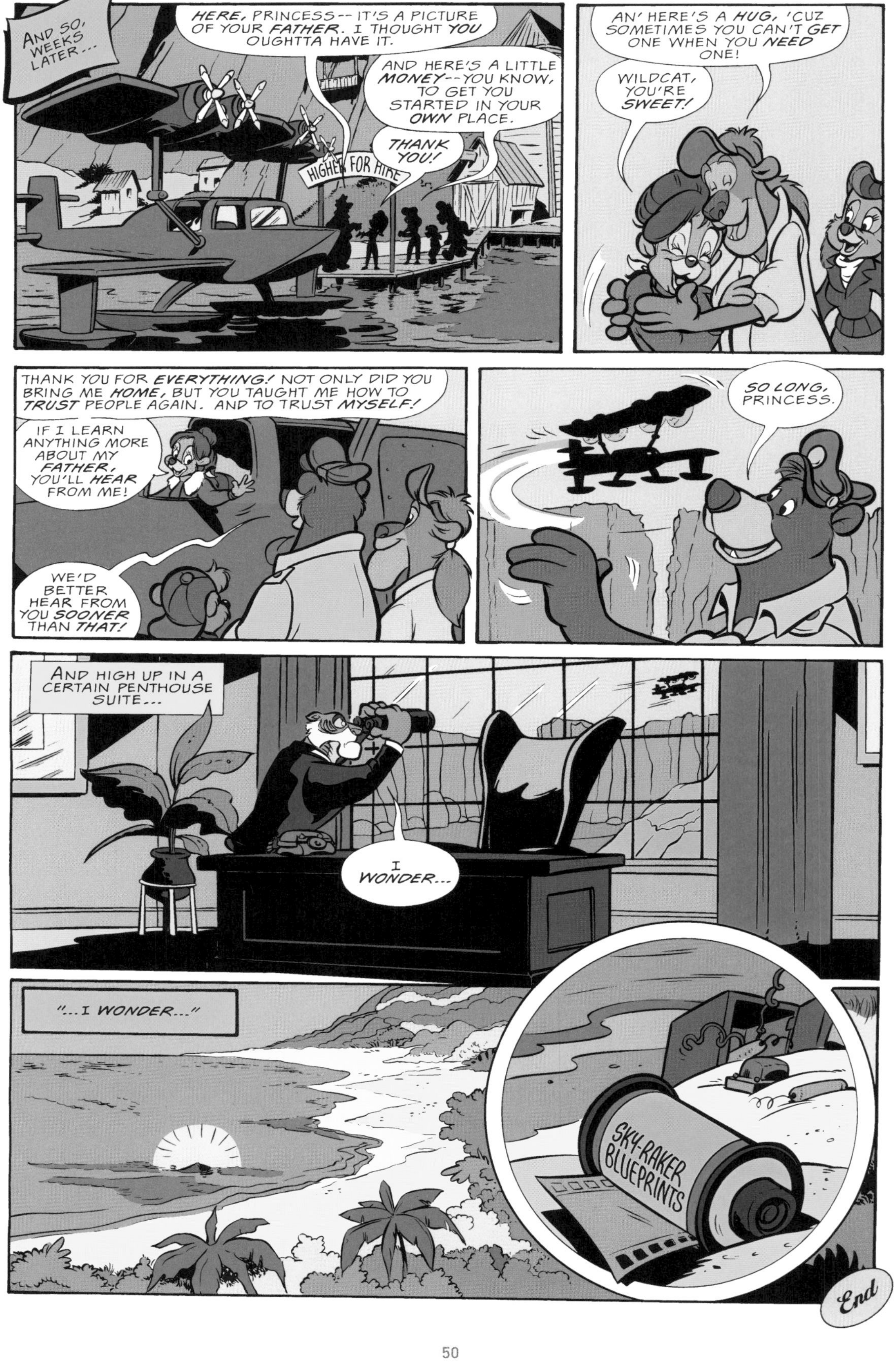

AND SO, WEEKS LATER...
HERE, PRINCESS-- IT'S A PICTURE OF YOUR FATHER. I THOUGHT YOU OUGHTTA HAVE IT.
AND HERE'S A LITTLE MONEY--YOU KNOW, TO GET YOU STARTED IN YOUR OWN PLACE.
THANK YOU!
HIGHER FOR HIRE
AN' HERE'S A HUG, 'CUZ SOMETIMES YOU CAN'T GET ONE WHEN YOU NEED ONE!
WILDCAT, YOU'RE SWEET!
THANK YOU FOR EVERYTHING! NOT ONLY DID YOU BRING ME HOME, BUT YOU TAUGHT ME HOW TO TRUST PEOPLE AGAIN. AND TO TRUST MYSELF!
IF I LEARN ANYTHING MORE ABOUT MY FATHER, YOU'LL HEAR FROM ME!
WE'D BETTER HEAR FROM YOU SOONER THAN THAT!
SO LONG, PRINCESS.
AND HIGH UP IN A CERTAIN PENTHOUSE SUITE...
I WONDER...
"...I WONDER..."
SKY-RAKER BLUEPRINTS
End

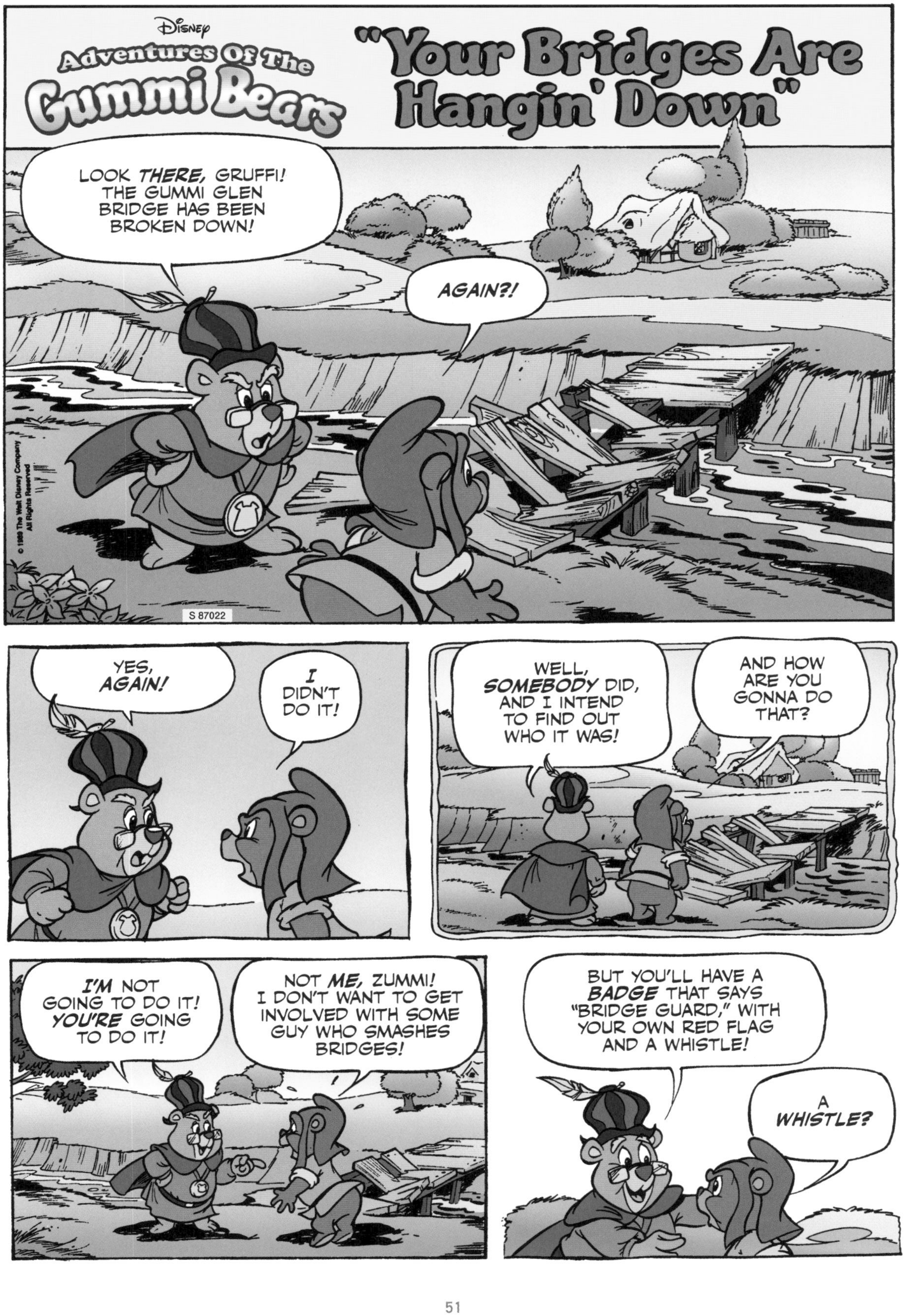
DISNEY
Adventures Of The Gummi Bears
"Your Bridges Are Hangin' Down"
LOOK THERE, GRUFFI! THE GUMMI GLEN BRIDGE HAS BEEN BROKEN DOWN!
AGAIN?!
© 1989 The Walt Disney Company All Rights Reserved
S 87022
YES, AGAIN!
I DIDN'T DO IT!
WELL, SOMEBODY DID, AND I INTEND TO FIND OUT WHO IT WAS!
AND HOW ARE YOU GONNA DO THAT?
I'M NOT GOING TO DO IT! YOU'RE GOING TO DO IT!
NOT ME, ZUMMI! I DON'T WANT TO GET INVOLVED WITH SOME GUY WHO SMASHES BRIDGES!
BUT YOU'LL HAVE A BADGE THAT SAYS "BRIDGE GUARD," WITH YOUR OWN RED FLAG AND A WHISTLE!
A WHISTLE?

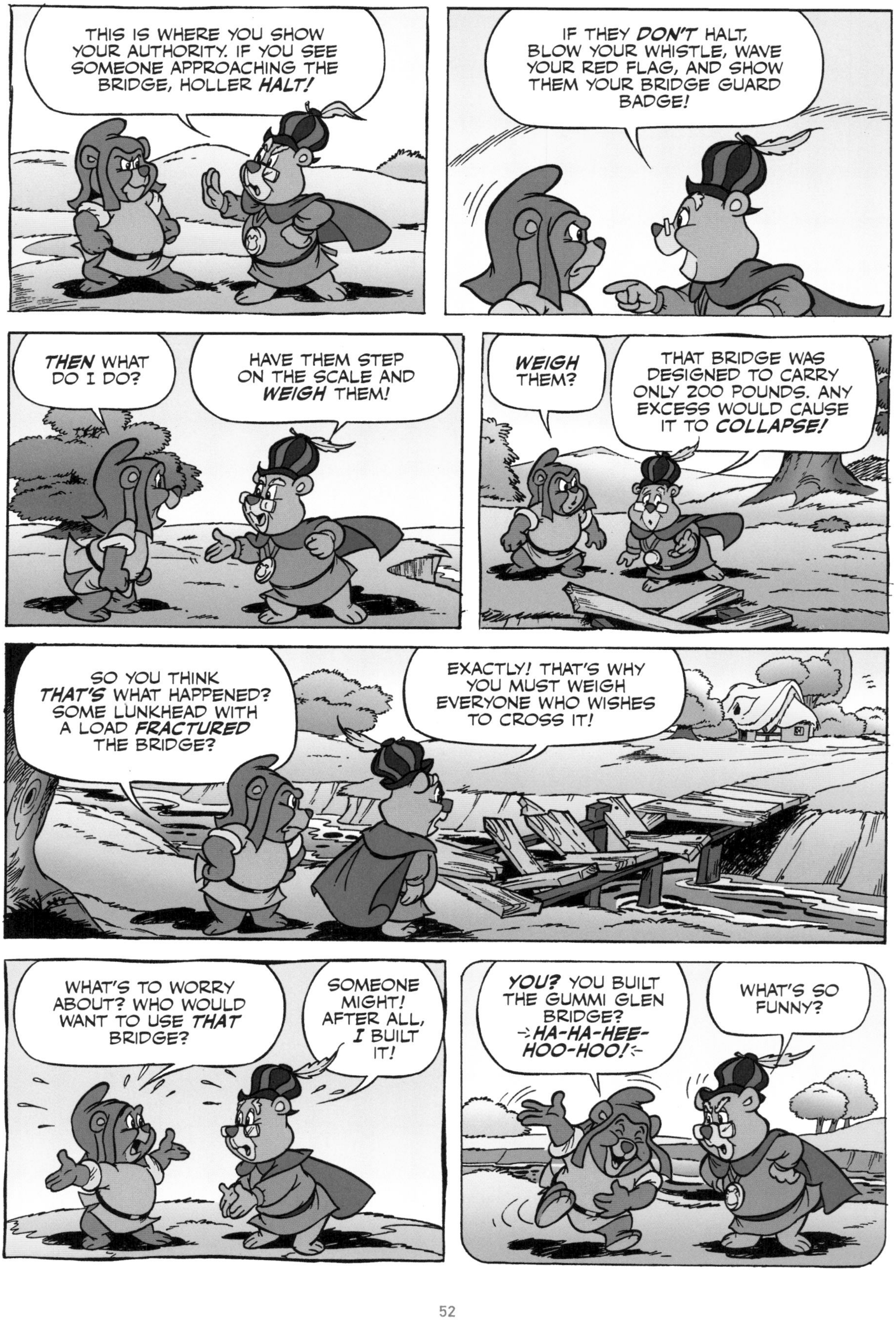
THIS IS WHERE YOU SHOW YOUR AUTHORITY. IF YOU SEE SOMEONE APPROACHING THE BRIDGE, HOLLER *HALT!*
IF THEY *DON'T* HALT, BLOW YOUR WHISTLE, WAVE YOUR RED FLAG, AND SHOW THEM YOUR BRIDGE GUARD BADGE!
THEN WHAT DO I DO?
HAVE THEM STEP ON THE SCALE AND *WEIGH* THEM!
WEIGH THEM?
THAT BRIDGE WAS DESIGNED TO CARRY ONLY 200 POUNDS. ANY EXCESS WOULD CAUSE IT TO *COLLAPSE!*
SO YOU THINK *THAT'S* WHAT HAPPENED? SOME LUNKHEAD WITH A LOAD *FRACTURED* THE BRIDGE?
EXACTLY! THAT'S WHY YOU MUST WEIGH EVERYONE WHO WISHES TO CROSS IT!
WHAT'S TO WORRY ABOUT? WHO WOULD WANT TO USE *THAT* BRIDGE?
SOMEONE MIGHT! AFTER ALL, *I* BUILT IT!
YOU? YOU BUILT THE GUMMI GLEN BRIDGE? *HA-HA-HEE-HOO-HOO!*
WHAT'S SO FUNNY?

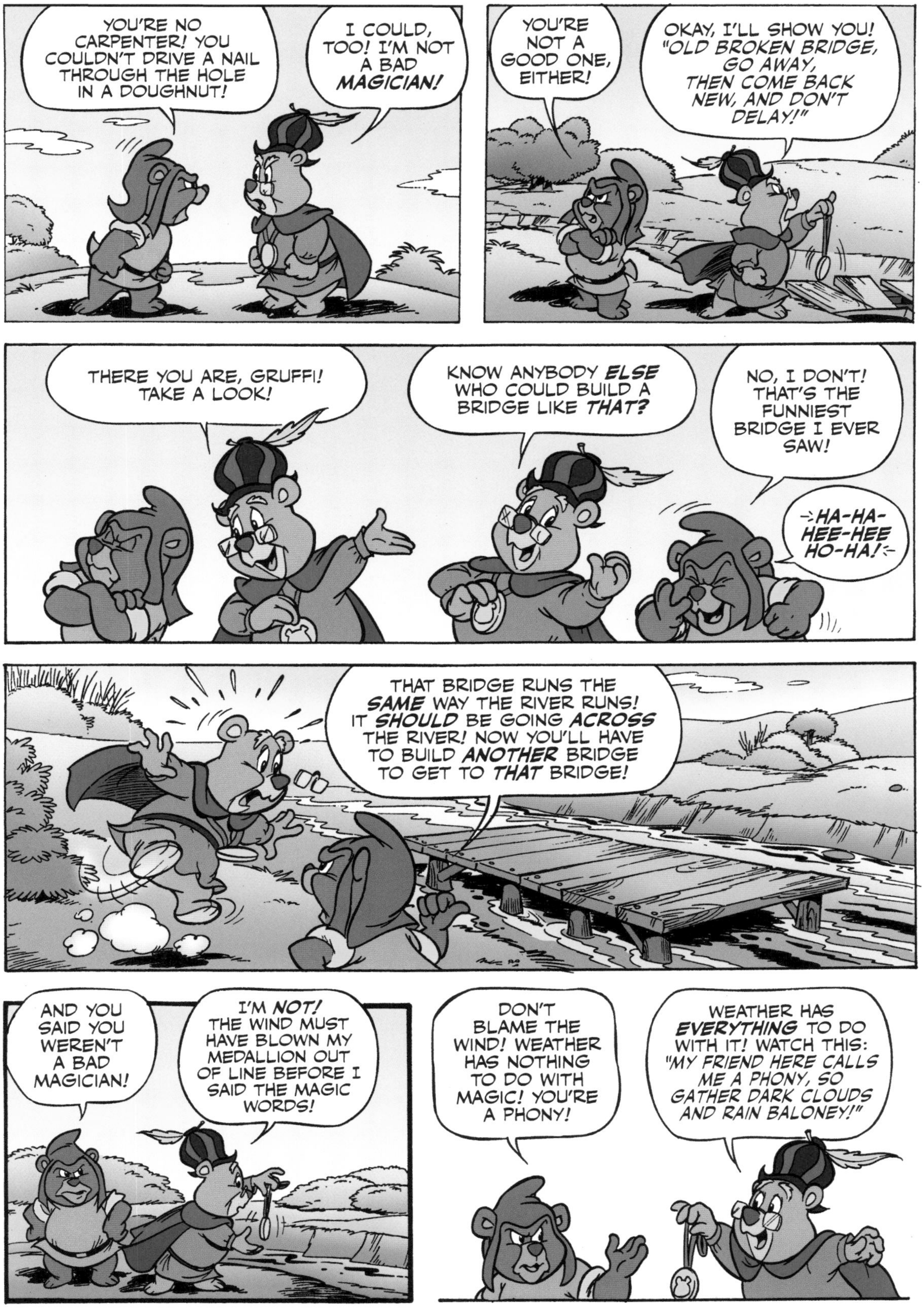
YOU'RE NO CARPENTER! YOU COULDN'T DRIVE A NAIL THROUGH THE HOLE IN A DOUGHNUT!
I COULD, TOO! I'M NOT A BAD MAGICIAN!
YOU'RE NOT A GOOD ONE, EITHER!
OKAY, I'LL SHOW YOU! "OLD BROKEN BRIDGE, GO AWAY, THEN COME BACK NEW, AND DON'T DELAY!"
THERE YOU ARE, GRUFFI! TAKE A LOOK!
KNOW ANYBODY ELSE WHO COULD BUILD A BRIDGE LIKE THAT?
NO, I DON'T! THAT'S THE FUNNIEST BRIDGE I EVER SAW!
HA-HA-HEE-HEE HO-HA!
THAT BRIDGE RUNS THE SAME WAY THE RIVER RUNS! IT SHOULD BE GOING ACROSS THE RIVER! NOW YOU'LL HAVE TO BUILD ANOTHER BRIDGE TO GET TO THAT BRIDGE!
AND YOU SAID YOU WEREN'T A BAD MAGICIAN!
I'M NOT! THE WIND MUST HAVE BLOWN MY MEDALLION OUT OF LINE BEFORE I SAID THE MAGIC WORDS!
DON'T BLAME THE WIND! WEATHER HAS NOTHING TO DO WITH MAGIC! YOU'RE A PHONY!
WEATHER HAS EVERYTHING TO DO WITH IT! WATCH THIS: "MY FRIEND HERE CALLS ME A PHONY, SO GATHER DARK CLOUDS AND RAIN BALONEY!"

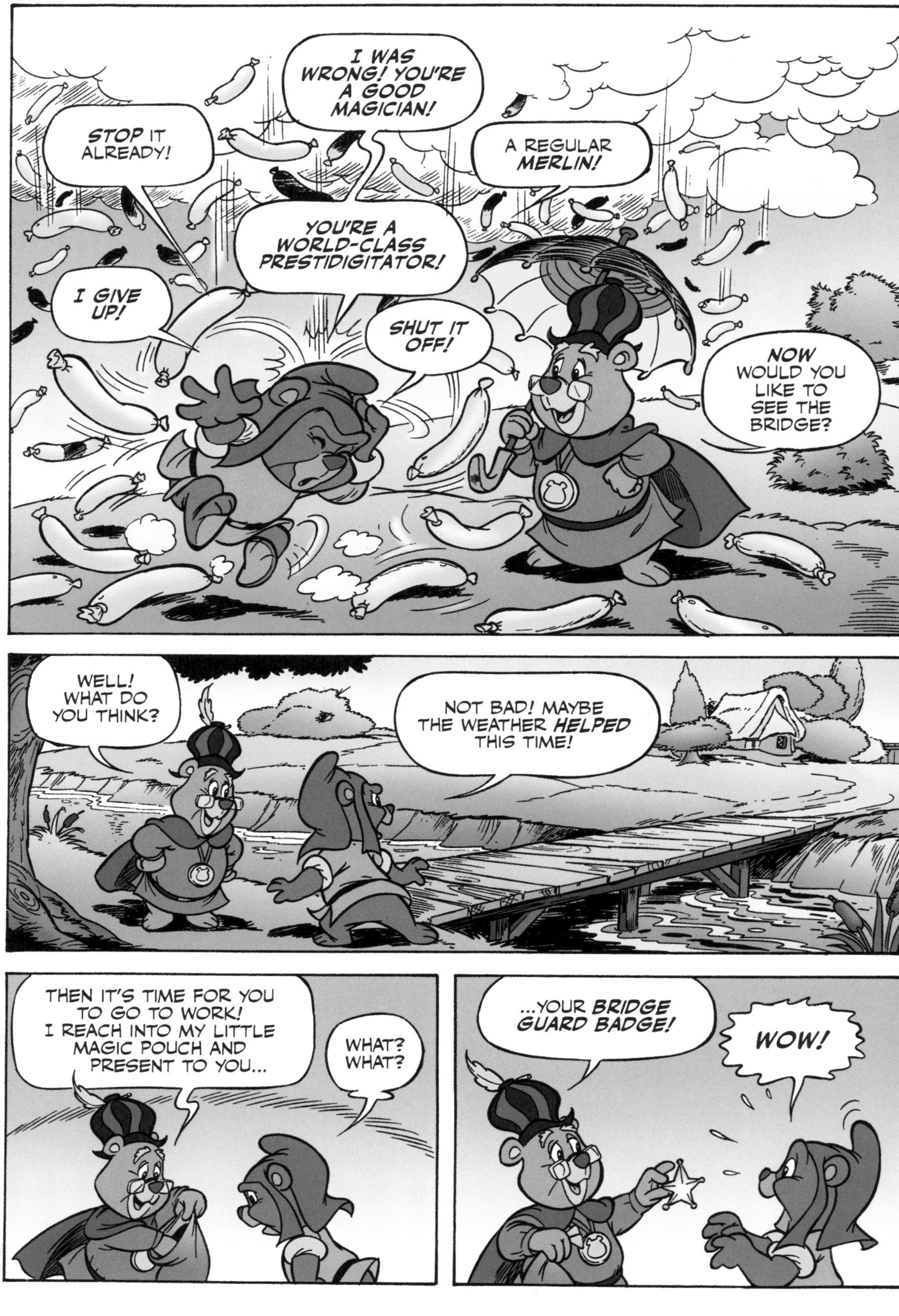
I WAS WRONG! YOU'RE A GOOD MAGICIAN!
STOP IT ALREADY!
A REGULAR MERLIN!
YOU'RE A WORLD-CLASS PRESTIDIGITATOR!
I GIVE UP!
SHUT IT OFF!
NOW WOULD YOU LIKE TO SEE THE BRIDGE?
WELL! WHAT DO YOU THINK?
NOT BAD! MAYBE THE WEATHER HELPED THIS TIME!
THEN IT'S TIME FOR YOU TO GO TO WORK! I REACH INTO MY LITTLE MAGIC POUCH AND PRESENT TO YOU...
WHAT? WHAT?
...YOUR BRIDGE GUARD BADGE!
WOW!

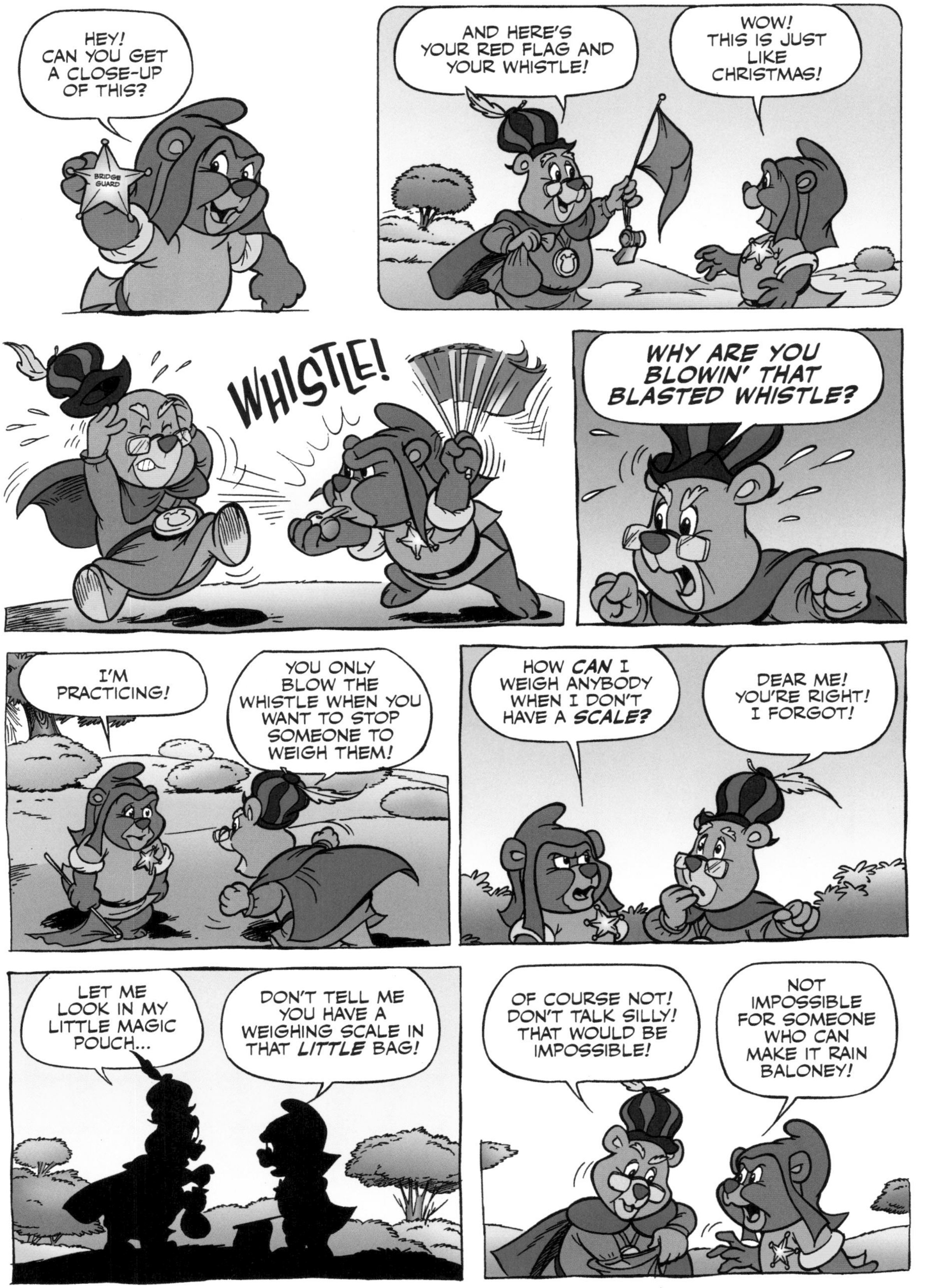
HEY! CAN YOU GET A CLOSE-UP OF THIS?
BRIDGE GUARD
AND HERE'S YOUR RED FLAG AND YOUR WHISTLE!
WOW! THIS IS JUST LIKE CHRISTMAS!
WHISTLE!
WHY ARE YOU BLOWIN' THAT BLASTED WHISTLE?
I'M PRACTICING!
YOU ONLY BLOW THE WHISTLE WHEN YOU WANT TO STOP SOMEONE TO WEIGH THEM!
HOW CAN I WEIGH ANYBODY WHEN I DON'T HAVE A SCALE?
DEAR ME! YOU'RE RIGHT! I FORGOT!
LET ME LOOK IN MY LITTLE MAGIC POUCH...
DON'T TELL ME YOU HAVE A WEIGHING SCALE IN THAT LITTLE BAG!
OF COURSE NOT! DON'T TALK SILLY! THAT WOULD BE IMPOSSIBLE!
NOT IMPOSSIBLE FOR SOMEONE WHO CAN MAKE IT RAIN BALONEY!

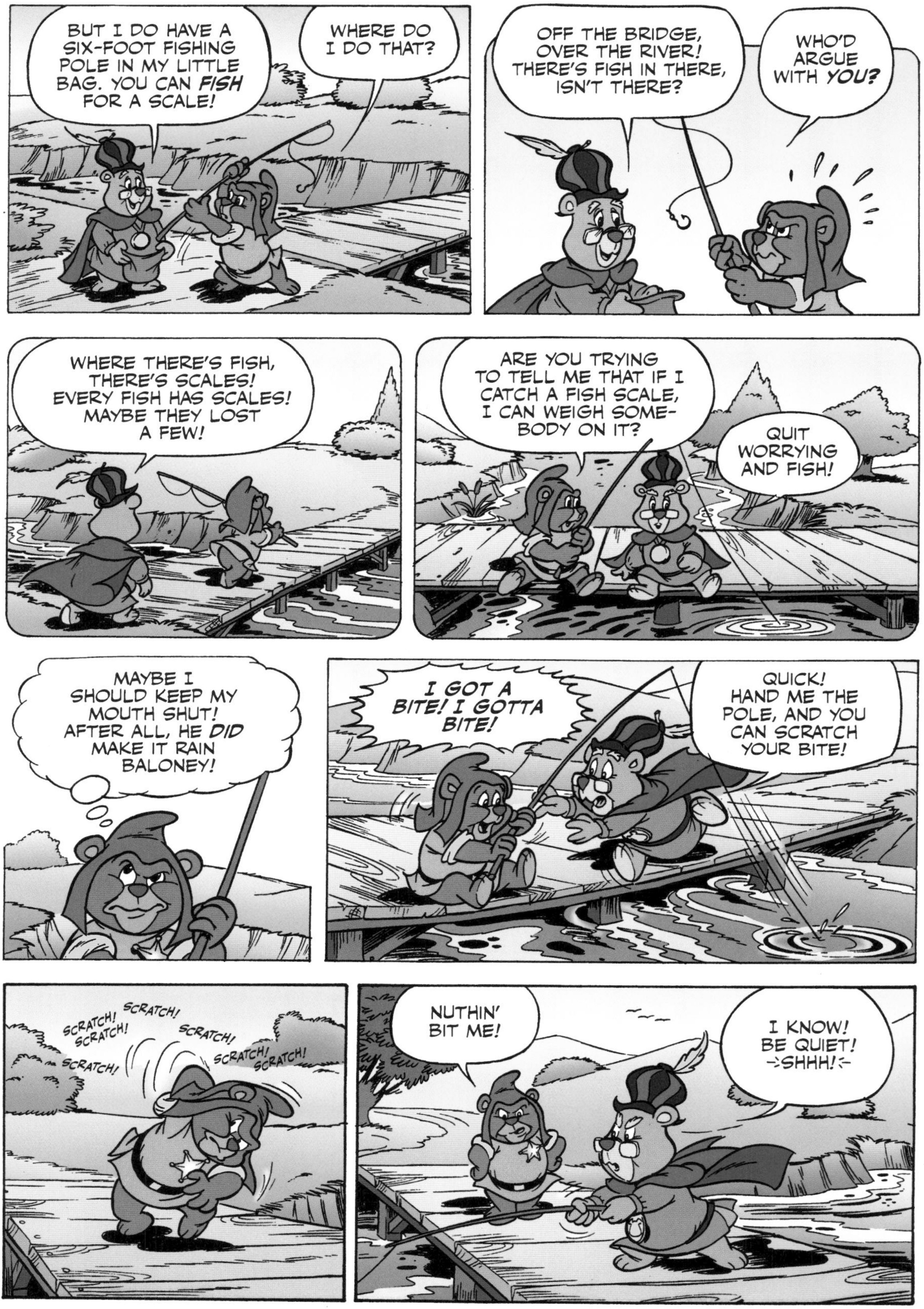
BUT I DO HAVE A SIX-FOOT FISHING POLE IN MY LITTLE BAG. YOU CAN *FISH* FOR A SCALE!
WHERE DO I DO THAT?
OFF THE BRIDGE, OVER THE RIVER! THERE'S FISH IN THERE, ISN'T THERE?
WHO'D ARGUE WITH *YOU?*
WHERE THERE'S FISH, THERE'S SCALES! EVERY FISH HAS SCALES! MAYBE THEY LOST A FEW!
ARE YOU TRYING TO TELL ME THAT IF I CATCH A FISH SCALE, I CAN WEIGH SOME-BODY ON IT?
QUIT WORRYING AND FISH!
MAYBE I SHOULD KEEP MY MOUTH SHUT! AFTER ALL, HE *DID* MAKE IT RAIN BALONEY!
I GOT A BITE! I GOTTA BITE!
QUICK! HAND ME THE POLE, AND YOU CAN SCRATCH YOUR BITE!
SCRATCH! SCRATCH! SCRATCH! SCRATCH! SCRATCH! SCRATCH! SCRATCH!
NUTHIN' BIT ME!
I KNOW! BE QUIET! SHHH!

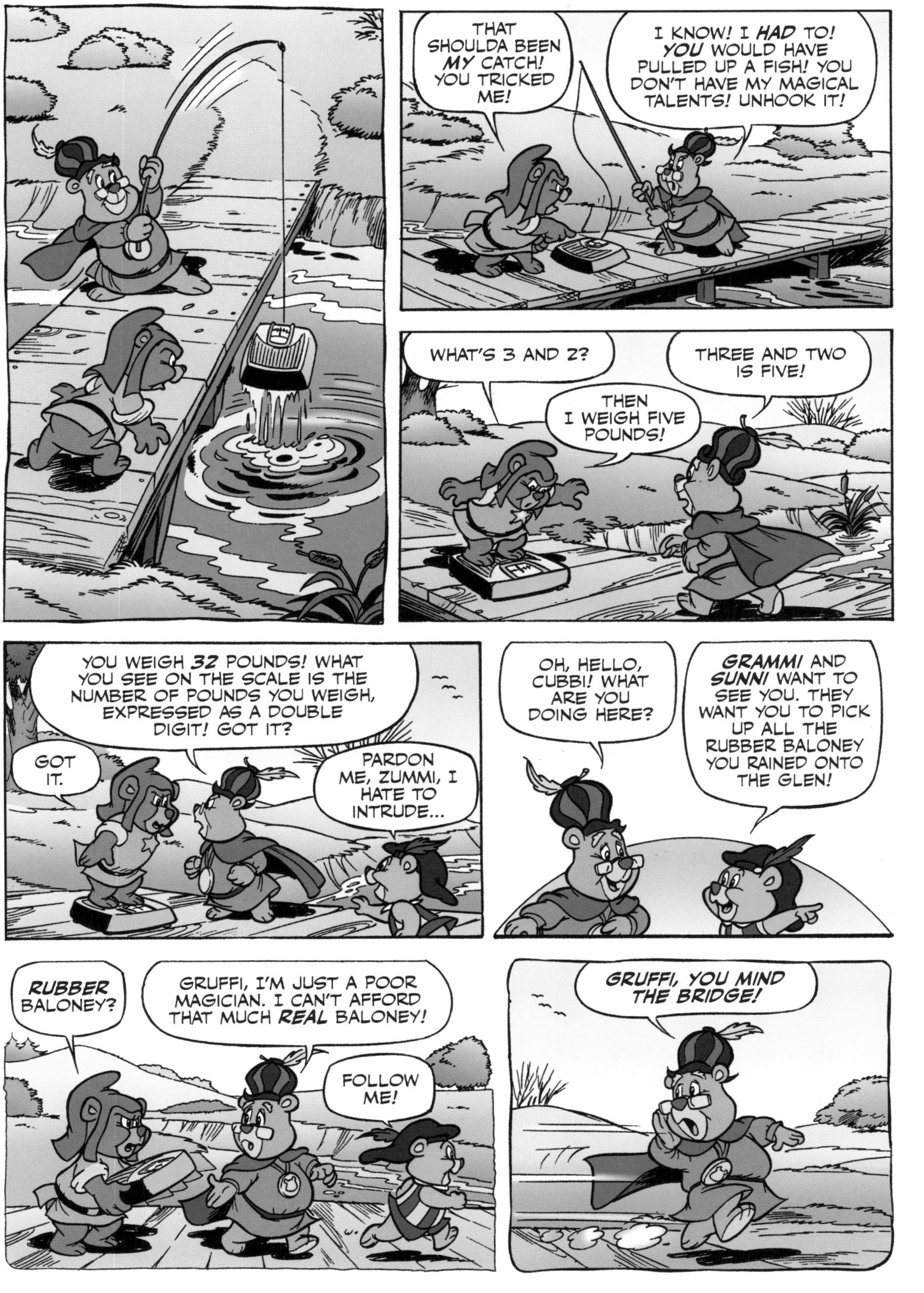
THAT SHOULDA BEEN MY CATCH! YOU TRICKED ME!
I KNOW! I HAD TO! YOU WOULD HAVE PULLED UP A FISH! YOU DON'T HAVE MY MAGICAL TALENTS! UNHOOK IT!
WHAT'S 3 AND 2?
THREE AND TWO IS FIVE!
THEN I WEIGH FIVE POUNDS!
YOU WEIGH 32 POUNDS! WHAT YOU SEE ON THE SCALE IS THE NUMBER OF POUNDS YOU WEIGH, EXPRESSED AS A DOUBLE DIGIT! GOT IT?
GOT IT.
PARDON ME, ZUMMI, I HATE TO INTRUDE...
OH, HELLO, CUBBI! WHAT ARE YOU DOING HERE?
GRAMMI AND SUNNI WANT TO SEE YOU. THEY WANT YOU TO PICK UP ALL THE RUBBER BALONEY YOU RAINED ONTO THE GLEN!
RUBBER BALONEY?
GRUFFI, I'M JUST A POOR MAGICIAN. I CAN'T AFFORD THAT MUCH REAL BALONEY!
FOLLOW ME!
GRUFFI, YOU MIND THE BRIDGE!

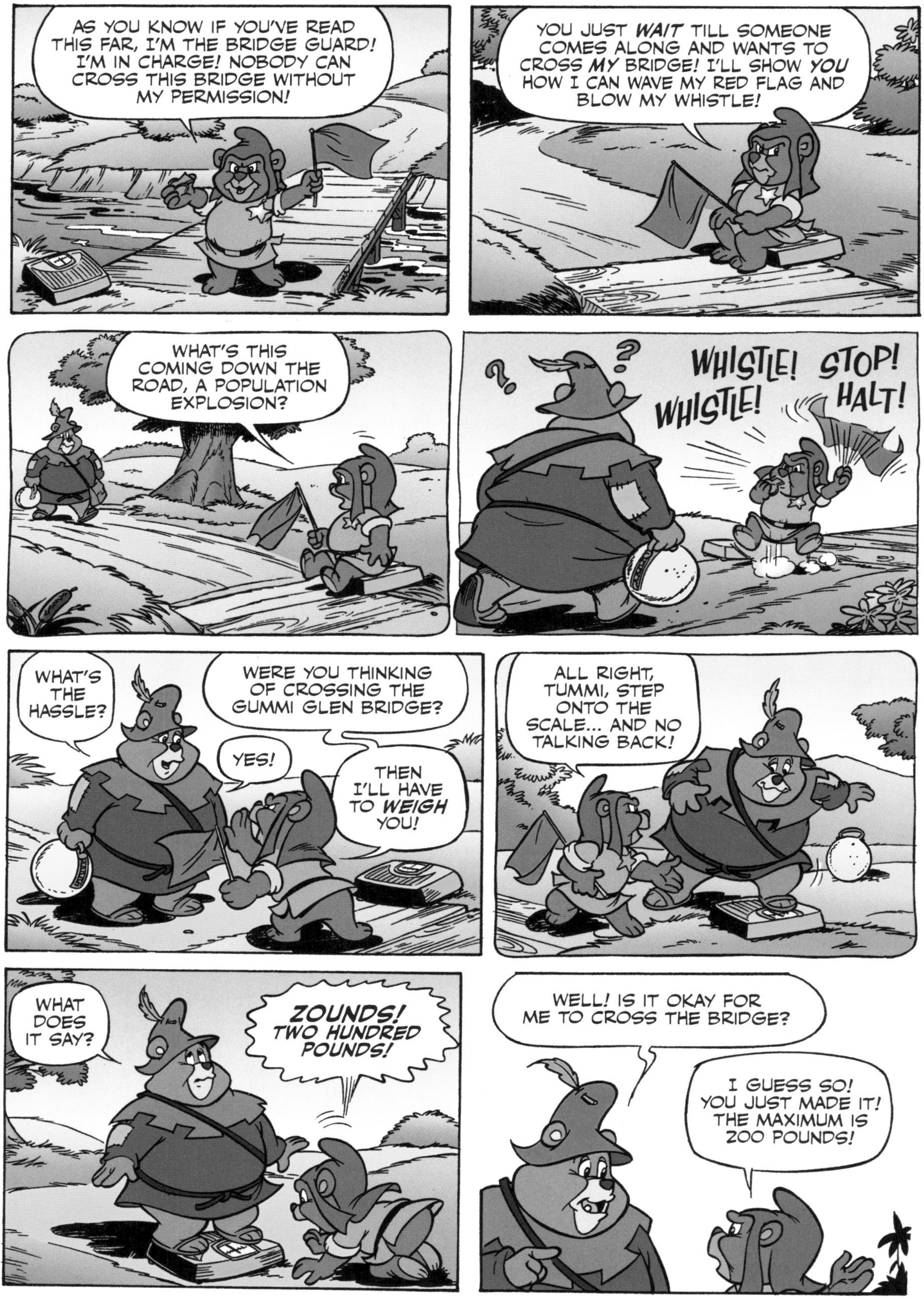
AS YOU KNOW IF YOU'VE READ THIS FAR, I'M THE BRIDGE GUARD! I'M IN CHARGE! NOBODY CAN CROSS THIS BRIDGE WITHOUT MY PERMISSION!
YOU JUST WAIT TILL SOMEONE COMES ALONG AND WANTS TO CROSS MY BRIDGE! I'LL SHOW YOU HOW I CAN WAVE MY RED FLAG AND BLOW MY WHISTLE!
WHAT'S THIS COMING DOWN THE ROAD, A POPULATION EXPLOSION?
?
?
WHISTLE!
WHISTLE!
STOP!
HALT!
WHAT'S THE HASSLE?
WERE YOU THINKING OF CROSSING THE GUMMI GLEN BRIDGE?
YES!
THEN I'LL HAVE TO WEIGH YOU!
ALL RIGHT, TUMMI, STEP ONTO THE SCALE... AND NO TALKING BACK!
WHAT DOES IT SAY?
ZOUNDS! TWO HUNDRED POUNDS!
WELL! IS IT OKAY FOR ME TO CROSS THE BRIDGE?
I GUESS SO! YOU JUST MADE IT! THE MAXIMUM IS 200 POUNDS!

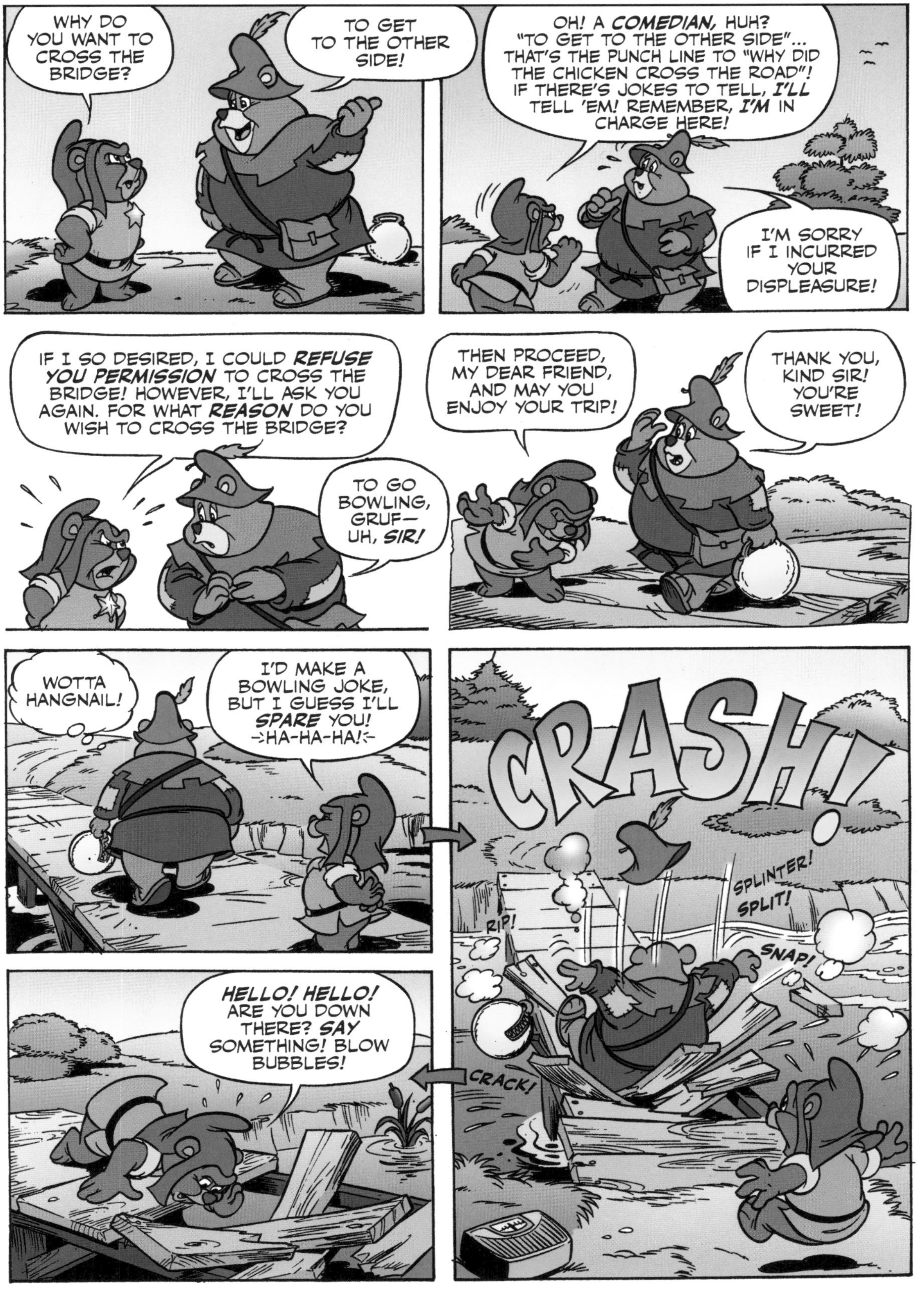
WHY DO YOU WANT TO CROSS THE BRIDGE?
TO GET TO THE OTHER SIDE!
OH! A COMEDIAN, HUH? "TO GET TO THE OTHER SIDE"... THAT'S THE PUNCH LINE TO "WHY DID THE CHICKEN CROSS THE ROAD"! IF THERE'S JOKES TO TELL, I'LL TELL 'EM! REMEMBER, I'M IN CHARGE HERE!
I'M SORRY IF I INCURRED YOUR DISPLEASURE!
IF I SO DESIRED, I COULD REFUSE YOU PERMISSION TO CROSS THE BRIDGE! HOWEVER, I'LL ASK YOU AGAIN. FOR WHAT REASON DO YOU WISH TO CROSS THE BRIDGE?
TO GO BOWLING, GRUF— UH, SIR!
THEN PROCEED, MY DEAR FRIEND, AND MAY YOU ENJOY YOUR TRIP!
THANK YOU, KIND SIR! YOU'RE SWEET!
WOTTA HANGNAIL!
I'D MAKE A BOWLING JOKE, BUT I GUESS I'LL SPARE YOU! HA-HA-HA!
CRASH!
SPLINTER!
SPLIT!
RIP!
SNAP!
CRACK!
HELLO! HELLO! ARE YOU DOWN THERE? SAY SOMETHING! BLOW BUBBLES!

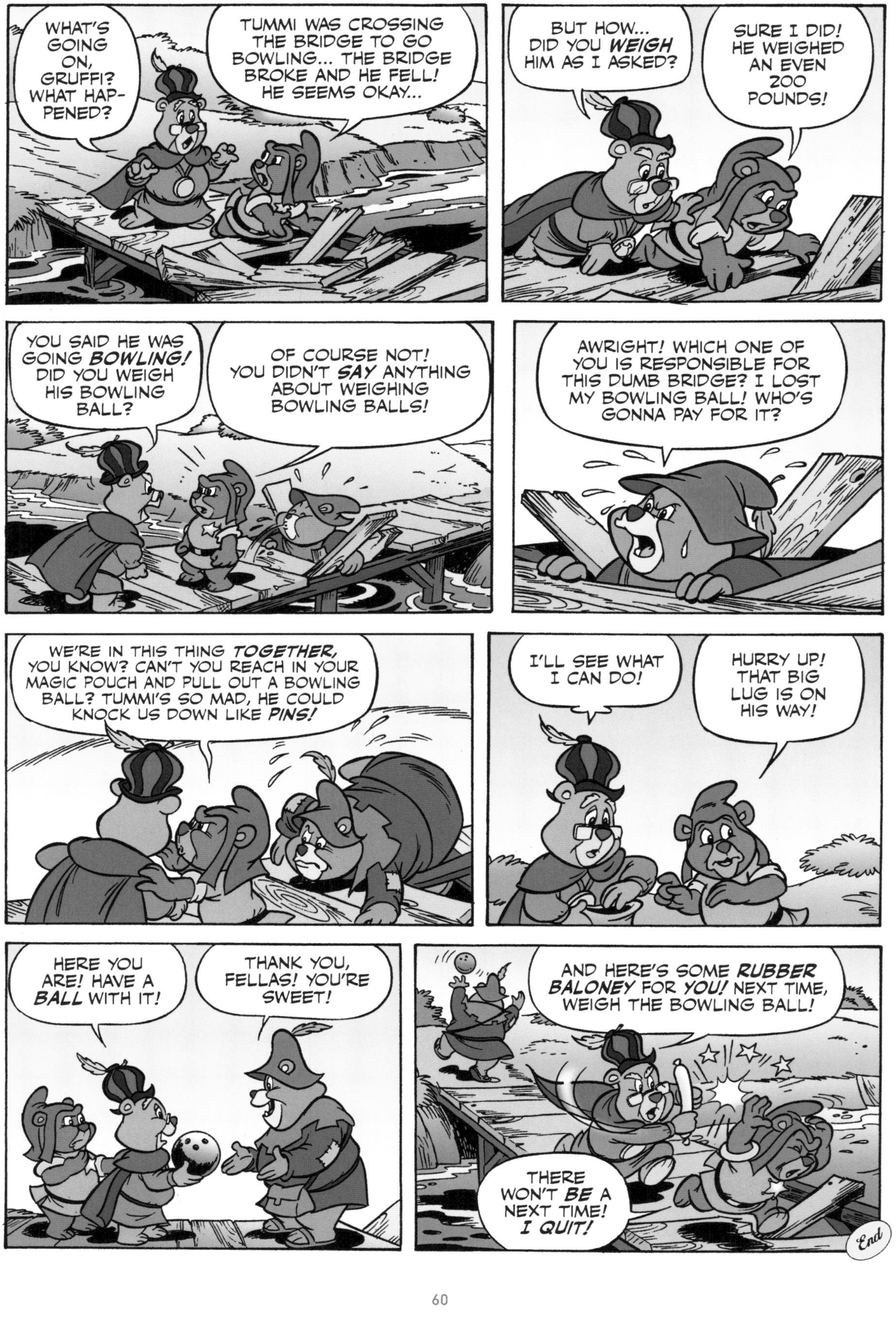
WHAT'S GOING ON, GRUFFI? WHAT HAP-PENED?
TUMMI WAS CROSSING THE BRIDGE TO GO BOWLING... THE BRIDGE BROKE AND HE FELL! HE SEEMS OKAY...
BUT HOW... DID YOU WEIGH HIM AS I ASKED?
SURE I DID! HE WEIGHED AN EVEN 200 POUNDS!
YOU SAID HE WAS GOING BOWLING! DID YOU WEIGH HIS BOWLING BALL?
OF COURSE NOT! YOU DIDN'T SAY ANYTHING ABOUT WEIGHING BOWLING BALLS!
AWRIGHT! WHICH ONE OF YOU IS RESPONSIBLE FOR THIS DUMB BRIDGE? I LOST MY BOWLING BALL! WHO'S GONNA PAY FOR IT?
WE'RE IN THIS THING TOGETHER, YOU KNOW? CAN'T YOU REACH IN YOUR MAGIC POUCH AND PULL OUT A BOWLING BALL? TUMMI'S SO MAD, HE COULD KNOCK US DOWN LIKE PINS!
I'LL SEE WHAT I CAN DO!
HURRY UP! THAT BIG LUG IS ON HIS WAY!
HERE YOU ARE! HAVE A BALL WITH IT!
THANK YOU, FELLAS! YOU'RE SWEET!
AND HERE'S SOME RUBBER BALONEY FOR YOU! NEXT TIME, WEIGH THE BOWLING BALL!
THERE WON'T BE A NEXT TIME! I QUIT!
End

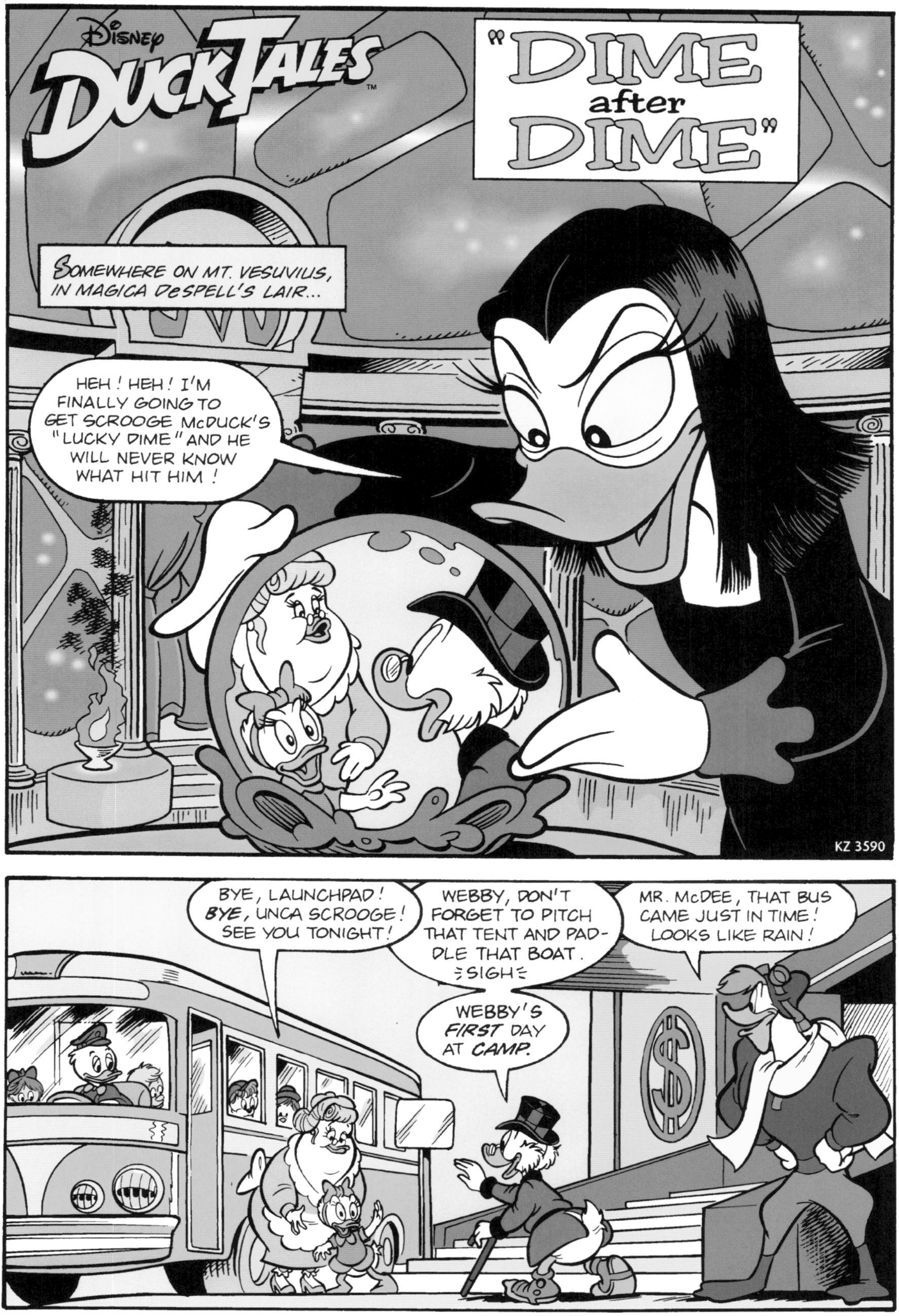
Disney
DuckTales™
"DIME after DIME"
SOMEWHERE ON MT. VESUVIUS, IN MAGICA DeSPELL'S LAIR...
HEH! HEH! I'M FINALLY GOING TO GET SCROOGE McDUCK'S "LUCKY DIME" AND HE WILL NEVER KNOW WHAT HIT HIM!
KZ 3590
BYE, LAUNCHPAD! BYE, UNCA SCROOGE! SEE YOU TONIGHT!
WEBBY, DON'T FORGET TO PITCH THAT TENT AND PADDLE THAT BOAT. SIGH
WEBBY'S FIRST DAY AT CAMP.
MR. McDEE, THAT BUS CAME JUST IN TIME! LOOKS LIKE RAIN!

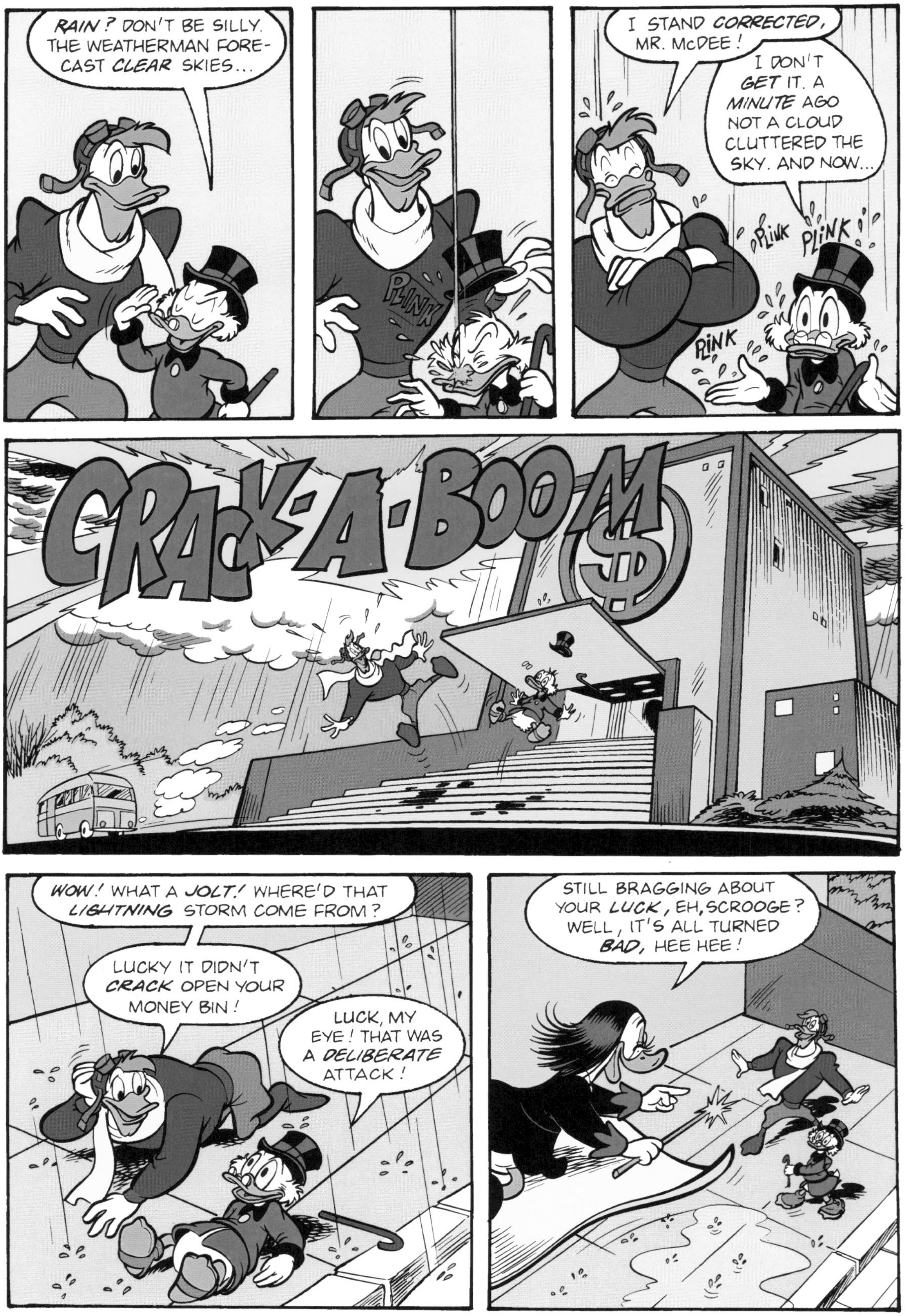

RAIN? DON'T BE SILLY. THE WEATHERMAN FORECAST CLEAR SKIES...
PLINK
I STAND CORRECTED, MR. McDEE!
I DON'T GET IT. A MINUTE AGO NOT A CLOUD CLUTTERED THE SKY. AND NOW...
PLINK
PLINK
PLINK
CRACK-A-BOOM
WOW! WHAT A JOLT! WHERE'D THAT LIGHTNING STORM COME FROM?
LUCKY IT DIDN'T CRACK OPEN YOUR MONEY BIN!
LUCK, MY EYE! THAT WAS A DELIBERATE ATTACK!
STILL BRAGGING ABOUT YOUR LUCK, EH, SCROOGE? WELL, IT'S ALL TURNED BAD, HEE HEE!

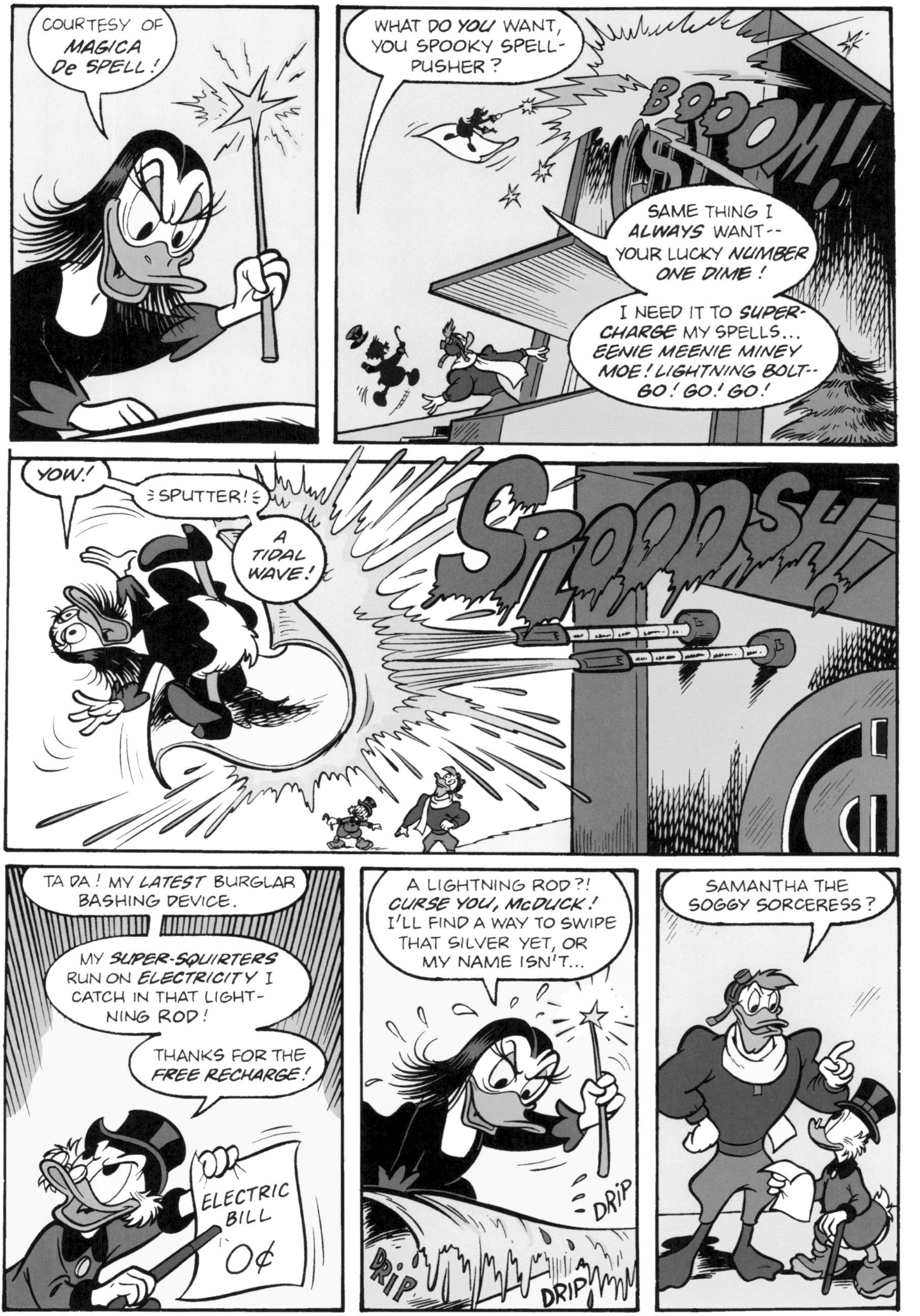
COURTESY OF MAGICA De SPELL!
WHAT DO YOU WANT, YOU SPOOKY SPELL-PUSHER?
BOOOM!
SAME THING I ALWAYS WANT-- YOUR LUCKY NUMBER ONE DIME!
I NEED IT TO SUPER-CHARGE MY SPELLS... EENIE MEENIE MINEY MOE! LIGHTNING BOLT-- GO! GO! GO!
YOW!
SPUTTER!
A TIDAL WAVE!
SPLOOOSH!
TA DA! MY LATEST BURGLAR BASHING DEVICE.
MY SUPER-SQUIRTERS RUN ON ELECTRICITY I CATCH IN THAT LIGHT-NING ROD!
THANKS FOR THE FREE RECHARGE!
ELECTRIC BILL 0¢
A LIGHTNING ROD?! CURSE YOU, McDUCK! I'LL FIND A WAY TO SWIPE THAT SILVER YET, OR MY NAME ISN'T...
DRIP
DRIP
DRIP
SAMANTHA THE SOGGY SORCERESS?

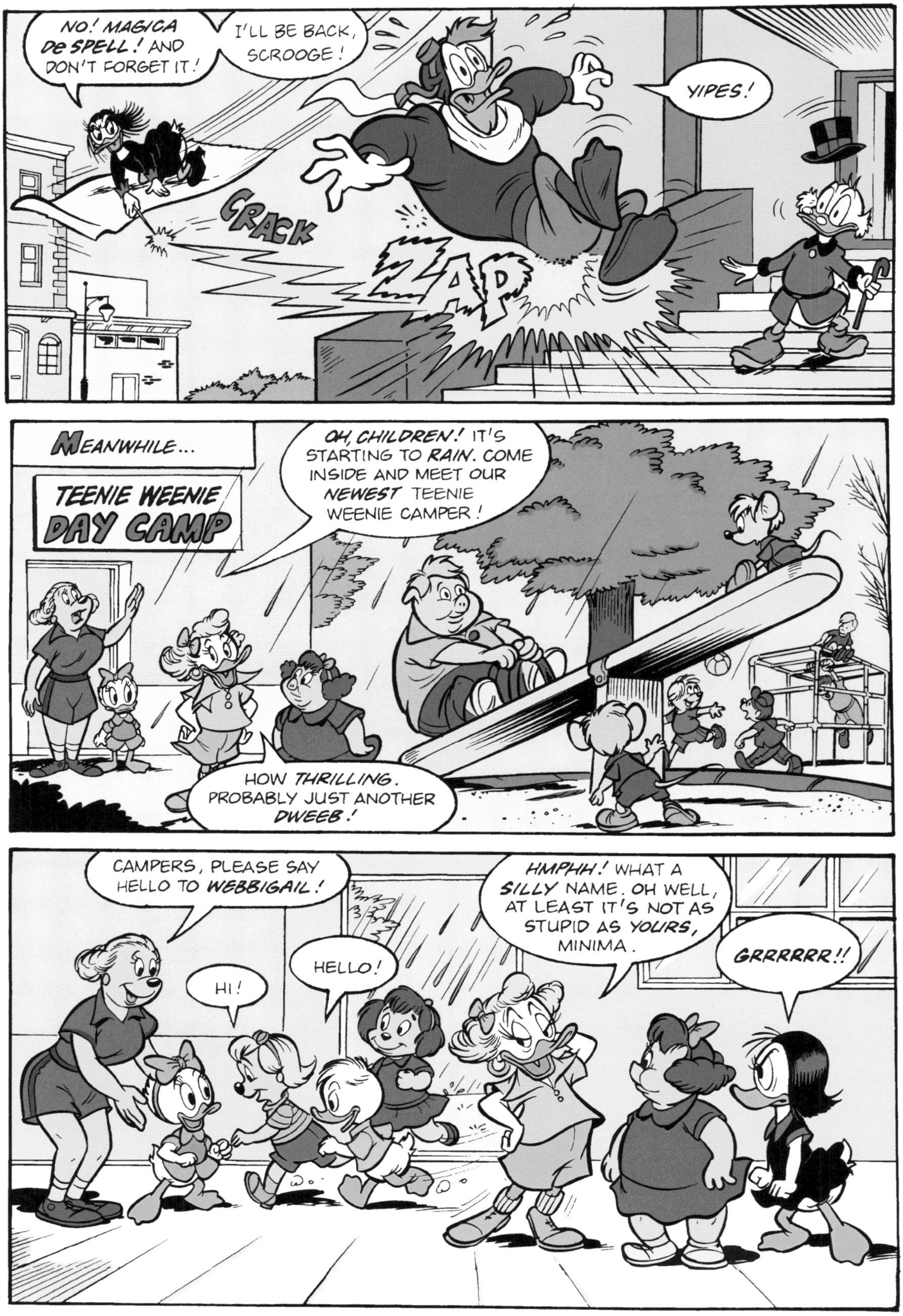
NO! MAGICA De SPELL! AND DON'T FORGET IT!
I'LL BE BACK, SCROOGE!
YIPES!
CRACK
ZAP
MEANWHILE...
TEENIE WEENIE DAY CAMP
OH, CHILDREN! IT'S STARTING TO RAIN. COME INSIDE AND MEET OUR NEWEST TEENIE WEENIE CAMPER!
HOW THRILLING. PROBABLY JUST ANOTHER DWEEB!
CAMPERS, PLEASE SAY HELLO TO WEBBIGAIL!
HI!
HELLO!
HMPHH! WHAT A SILLY NAME. OH WELL, AT LEAST IT'S NOT AS STUPID AS YOURS, MINIMA.
GRRRRRR!!

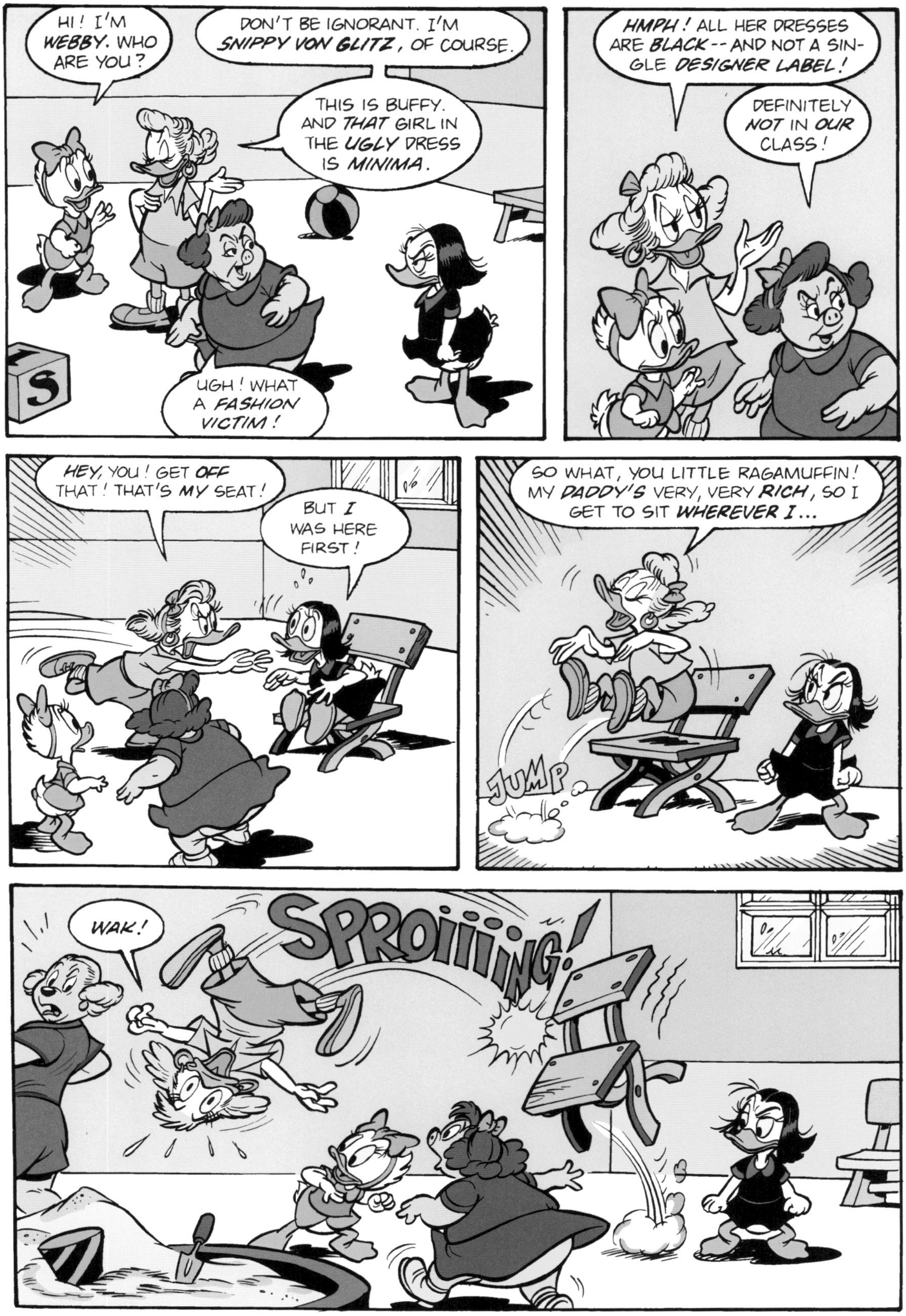
HI! I'M WEBBY. WHO ARE YOU?
DON'T BE IGNORANT. I'M SNIPPY VON GLITZ, OF COURSE.
THIS IS BUFFY. AND THAT GIRL IN THE UGLY DRESS IS MINIMA.
UGH! WHAT A FASHION VICTIM!
S
HMPH! ALL HER DRESSES ARE BLACK-- AND NOT A SINGLE DESIGNER LABEL!
DEFINITELY NOT IN OUR CLASS!
HEY, YOU! GET OFF THAT! THAT'S MY SEAT!
BUT I WAS HERE FIRST!
SO WHAT, YOU LITTLE RAGAMUFFIN! MY DADDY'S VERY, VERY RICH, SO I GET TO SIT WHEREVER I...
JUMP
WAK!
SPROiiiiiNG!

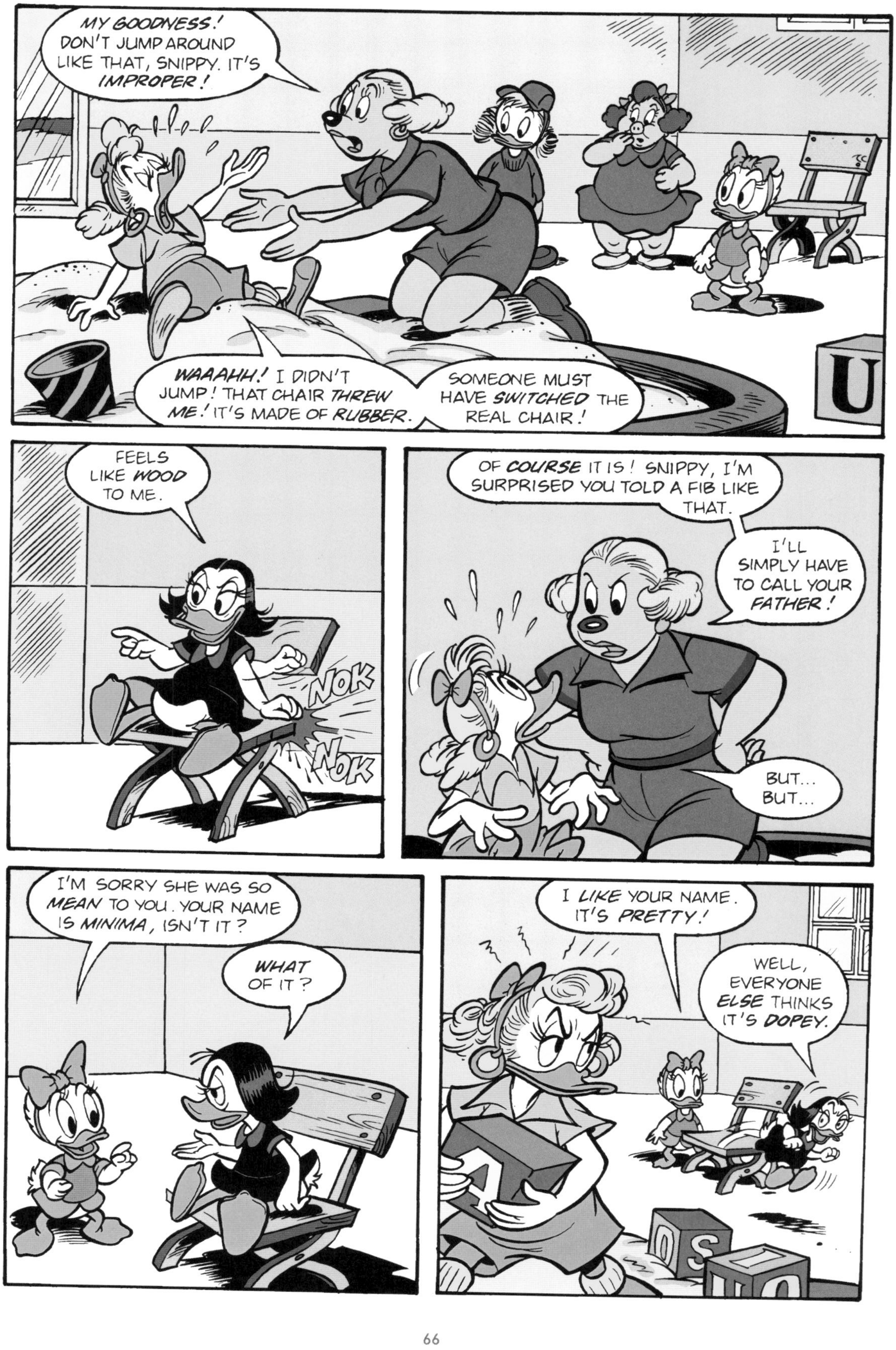
MY GOODNESS! DON'T JUMP AROUND LIKE THAT, SNIPPY. IT'S IMPROPER!
WAAAHH! I DIDN'T JUMP! THAT CHAIR THREW ME! IT'S MADE OF RUBBER.
SOMEONE MUST HAVE SWITCHED THE REAL CHAIR!
U
FEELS LIKE WOOD TO ME.
NOK
NOK
OF COURSE IT IS! SNIPPY, I'M SURPRISED YOU TOLD A FIB LIKE THAT.
I'LL SIMPLY HAVE TO CALL YOUR FATHER!
BUT... BUT...
I'M SORRY SHE WAS SO MEAN TO YOU. YOUR NAME IS MINIMA, ISN'T IT?
WHAT OF IT?
I LIKE YOUR NAME. IT'S PRETTY!
WELL, EVERYONE ELSE THINKS IT'S DOPEY.

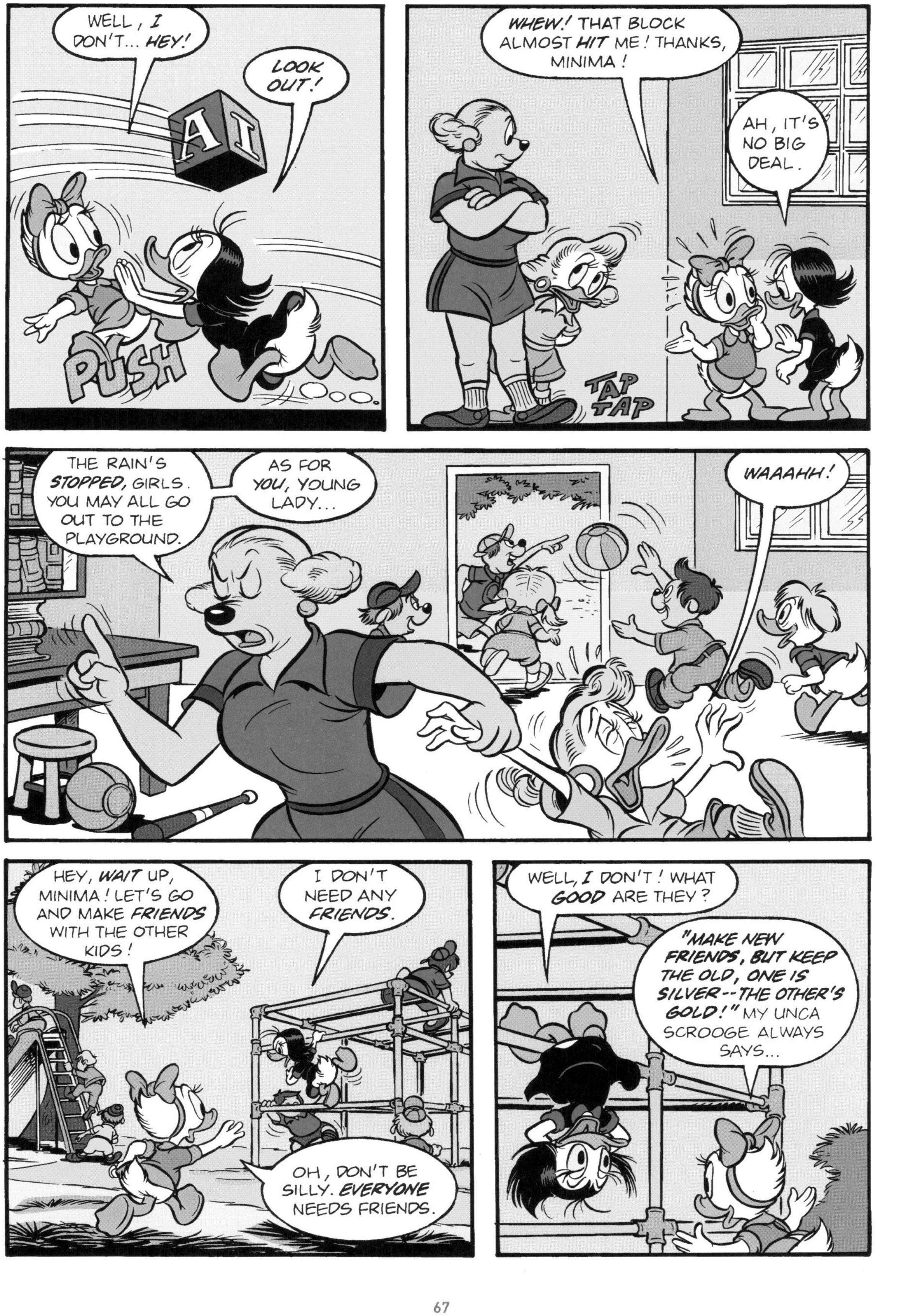
WELL, I DON'T... HEY!
LOOK OUT!
PUSH
WHEW! THAT BLOCK ALMOST HIT ME! THANKS, MINIMA!
AH, IT'S NO BIG DEAL.
TAP TAP
THE RAIN'S STOPPED, GIRLS. YOU MAY ALL GO OUT TO THE PLAYGROUND.
AS FOR YOU, YOUNG LADY...
WAAAHH!
HEY, WAIT UP, MINIMA! LET'S GO AND MAKE FRIENDS WITH THE OTHER KIDS!
I DON'T NEED ANY FRIENDS.
OH, DON'T BE SILLY. EVERYONE NEEDS FRIENDS.
WELL, I DON'T! WHAT GOOD ARE THEY?
"MAKE NEW FRIENDS, BUT KEEP THE OLD, ONE IS SILVER--THE OTHER'S GOLD!" MY UNCA SCROOGE ALWAYS SAYS...

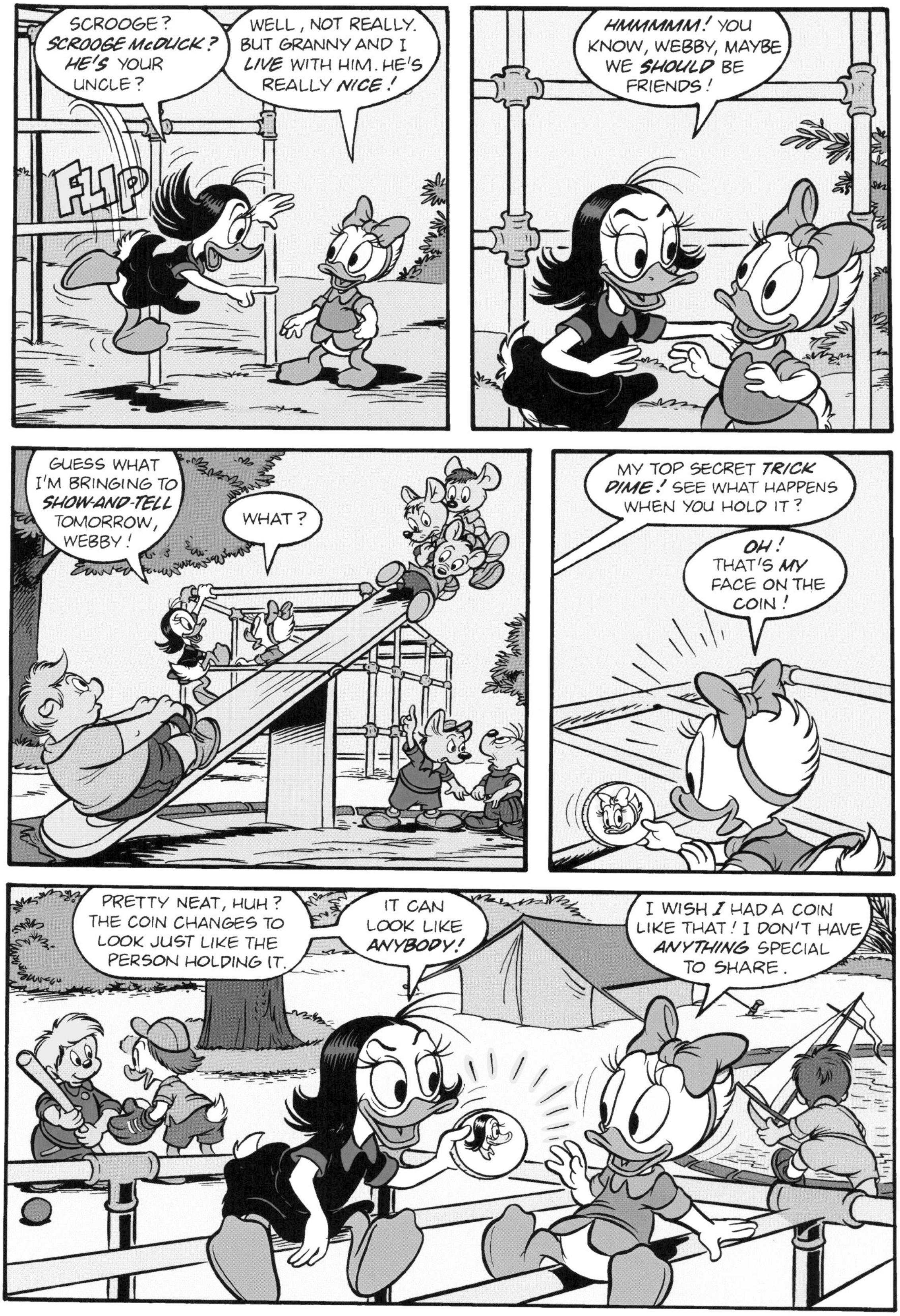

SCROOGE? SCROOGE McDUCK? HE'S YOUR UNCLE?
WELL, NOT REALLY. BUT GRANNY AND I LIVE WITH HIM. HE'S REALLY NICE!
FLIP
HMMMMM! YOU KNOW, WEBBY, MAYBE WE SHOULD BE FRIENDS!
GUESS WHAT I'M BRINGING TO SHOW-AND-TELL TOMORROW, WEBBY!
WHAT?
MY TOP SECRET TRICK DIME! SEE WHAT HAPPENS WHEN YOU HOLD IT?
OH! THAT'S MY FACE ON THE COIN!
PRETTY NEAT, HUH? THE COIN CHANGES TO LOOK JUST LIKE THE PERSON HOLDING IT.
IT CAN LOOK LIKE ANYBODY!
I WISH I HAD A COIN LIKE THAT! I DON'T HAVE ANYTHING SPECIAL TO SHARE.

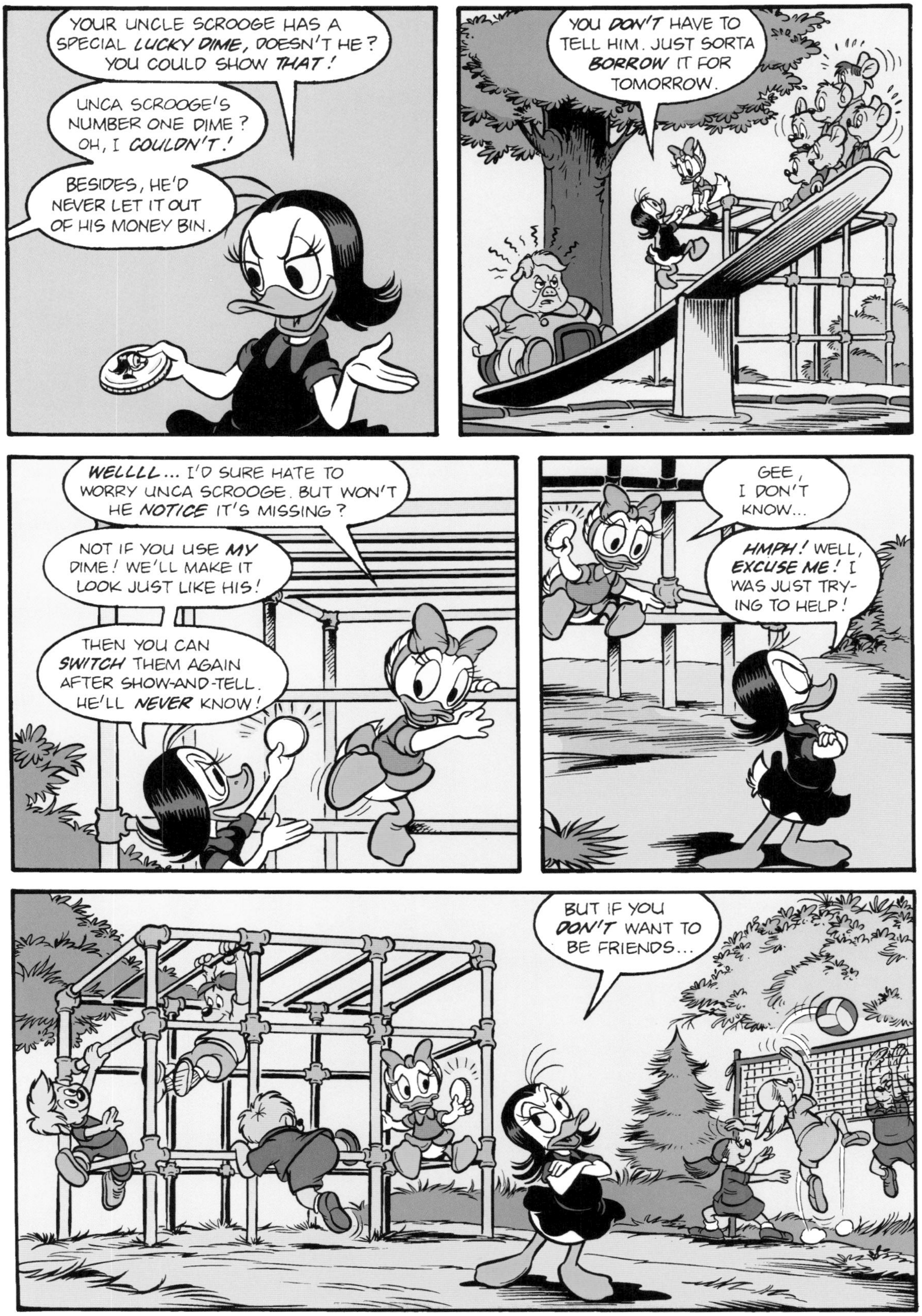
YOUR UNCLE SCROOGE HAS A SPECIAL LUCKY DIME, DOESN'T HE? YOU COULD SHOW THAT!
UNCA SCROOGE'S NUMBER ONE DIME? OH, I COULDN'T!
BESIDES, HE'D NEVER LET IT OUT OF HIS MONEY BIN.
YOU DON'T HAVE TO TELL HIM. JUST SORTA BORROW IT FOR TOMORROW.
WELLLL... I'D SURE HATE TO WORRY UNCA SCROOGE. BUT WON'T HE NOTICE IT'S MISSING?
NOT IF YOU USE MY DIME! WE'LL MAKE IT LOOK JUST LIKE HIS!
THEN YOU CAN SWITCH THEM AGAIN AFTER SHOW-AND-TELL. HE'LL NEVER KNOW!
GEE, I DON'T KNOW...
HMPH! WELL, EXCUSE ME! I WAS JUST TRYING TO HELP!
BUT IF YOU DON'T WANT TO BE FRIENDS...

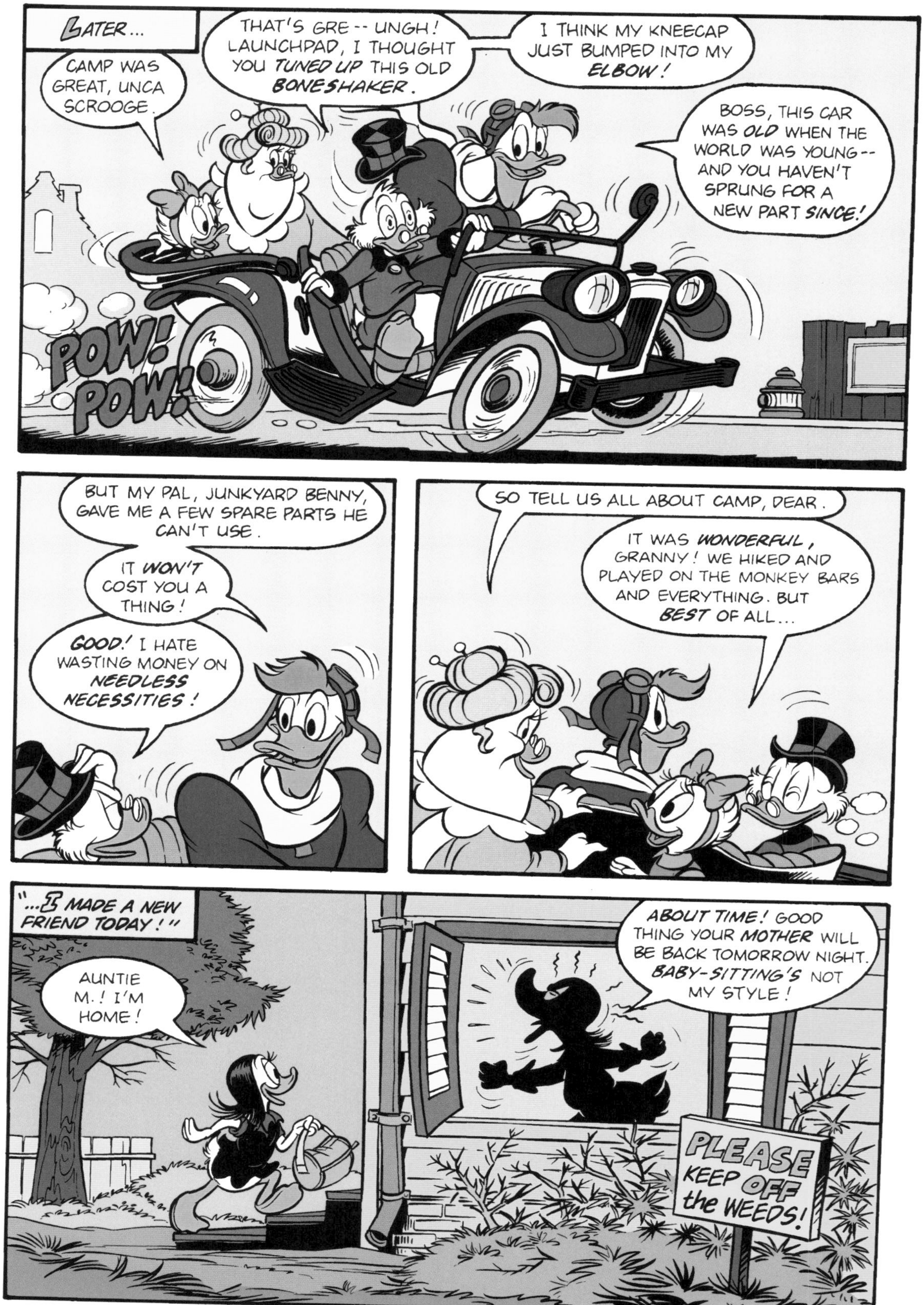
LATER...
CAMP WAS GREAT, UNCA SCROOGE.
THAT'S GRE -- UNGH! LAUNCHPAD, I THOUGHT YOU TUNED UP THIS OLD BONESHAKER.
I THINK MY KNEECAP JUST BUMPED INTO MY ELBOW!
BOSS, THIS CAR WAS OLD WHEN THE WORLD WAS YOUNG -- AND YOU HAVEN'T SPRUNG FOR A NEW PART SINCE!
POW! POW!
BUT MY PAL, JUNKYARD BENNY, GAVE ME A FEW SPARE PARTS HE CAN'T USE.
IT WON'T COST YOU A THING!
GOOD! I HATE WASTING MONEY ON NEEDLESS NECESSITIES!
SO TELL US ALL ABOUT CAMP, DEAR.
IT WAS WONDERFUL, GRANNY! WE HIKED AND PLAYED ON THE MONKEY BARS AND EVERYTHING. BUT BEST OF ALL...
"...I MADE A NEW FRIEND TODAY!"
AUNTIE M.! I'M HOME!
ABOUT TIME! GOOD THING YOUR MOTHER WILL BE BACK TOMORROW NIGHT. BABY-SITTING'S NOT MY STYLE!
PLEASE KEEP OFF the WEEDS!

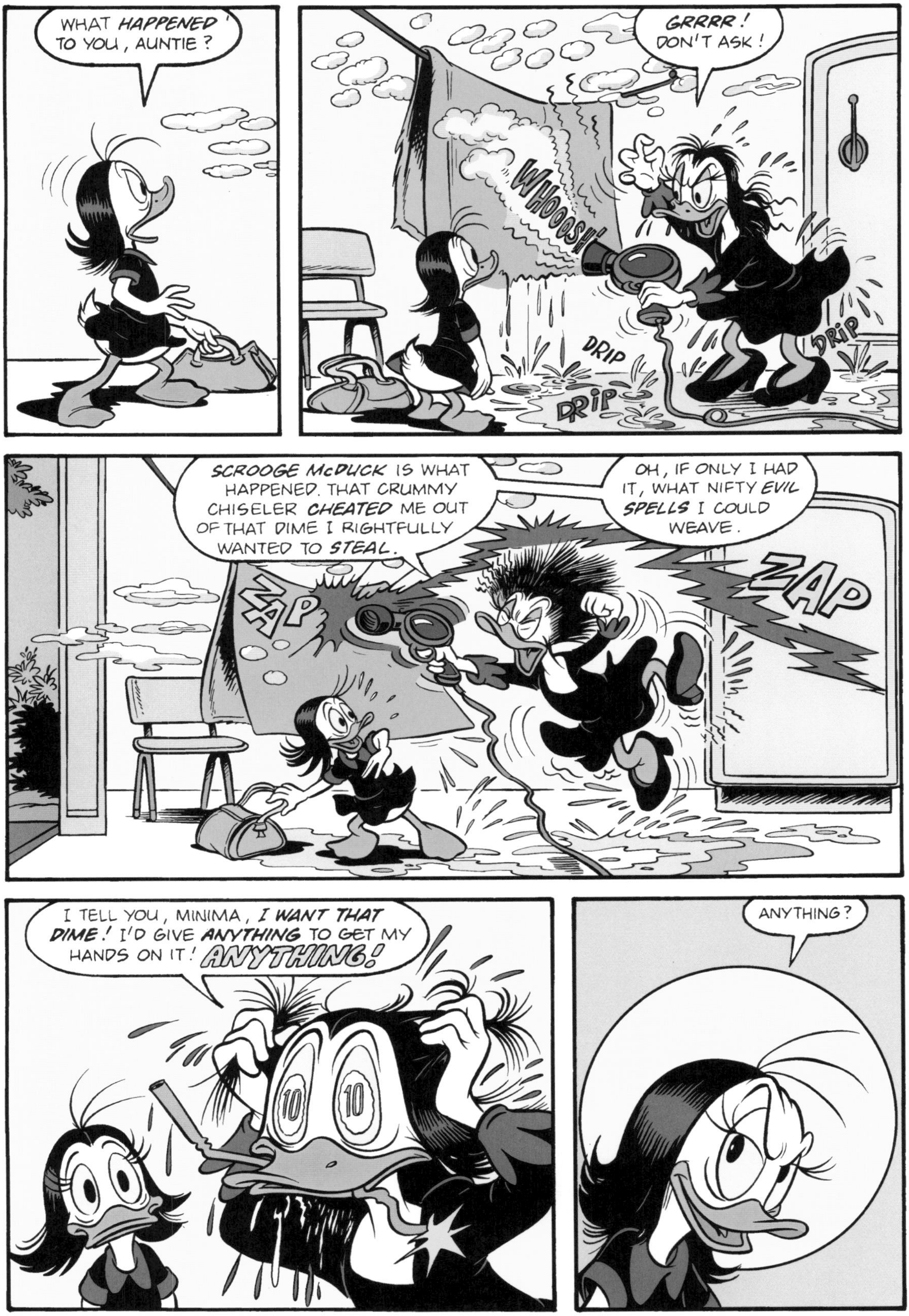
WHAT HAPPENED TO YOU, AUNTIE?
GRRRR! DON'T ASK!
WHOOOSH!
DRIP
DRIP
DRIP
SCROOGE McDUCK IS WHAT HAPPENED. THAT CRUMMY CHISELER CHEATED ME OUT OF THAT DIME I RIGHTFULLY WANTED TO STEAL.
OH, IF ONLY I HAD IT, WHAT NIFTY EVIL SPELLS I COULD WEAVE.
ZAP
ZAP
I TELL YOU, MINIMA, I WANT THAT DIME! I'D GIVE ANYTHING TO GET MY HANDS ON IT! ANYTHING!
10
10
ANYTHING?

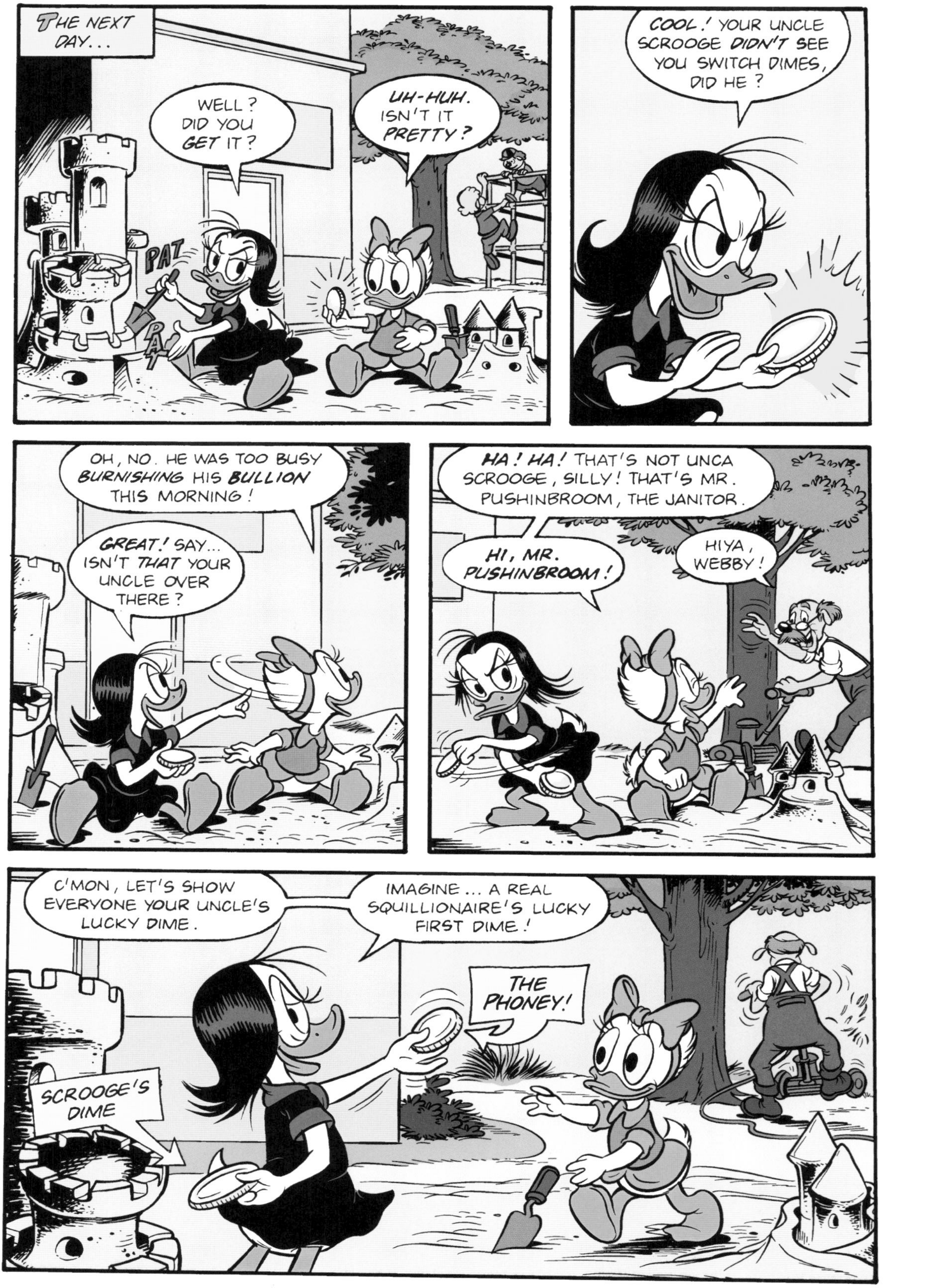
THE NEXT DAY...
WELL? DID YOU GET IT?
UH-HUH. ISN'T IT PRETTY?
PAT
PAT
COOL! YOUR UNCLE SCROOGE DIDN'T SEE YOU SWITCH DIMES, DID HE?
OH, NO. HE WAS TOO BUSY BURNISHING HIS BULLION THIS MORNING!
GREAT! SAY... ISN'T THAT YOUR UNCLE OVER THERE?
HA! HA! THAT'S NOT UNCA SCROOGE, SILLY! THAT'S MR. PUSHINBROOM, THE JANITOR.
HI, MR. PUSHINBROOM!
HIYA, WEBBY!
C'MON, LET'S SHOW EVERYONE YOUR UNCLE'S LUCKY DIME.
IMAGINE... A REAL SQUILLIONAIRE'S LUCKY FIRST DIME!
THE PHONEY!
SCROOGE'S DIME

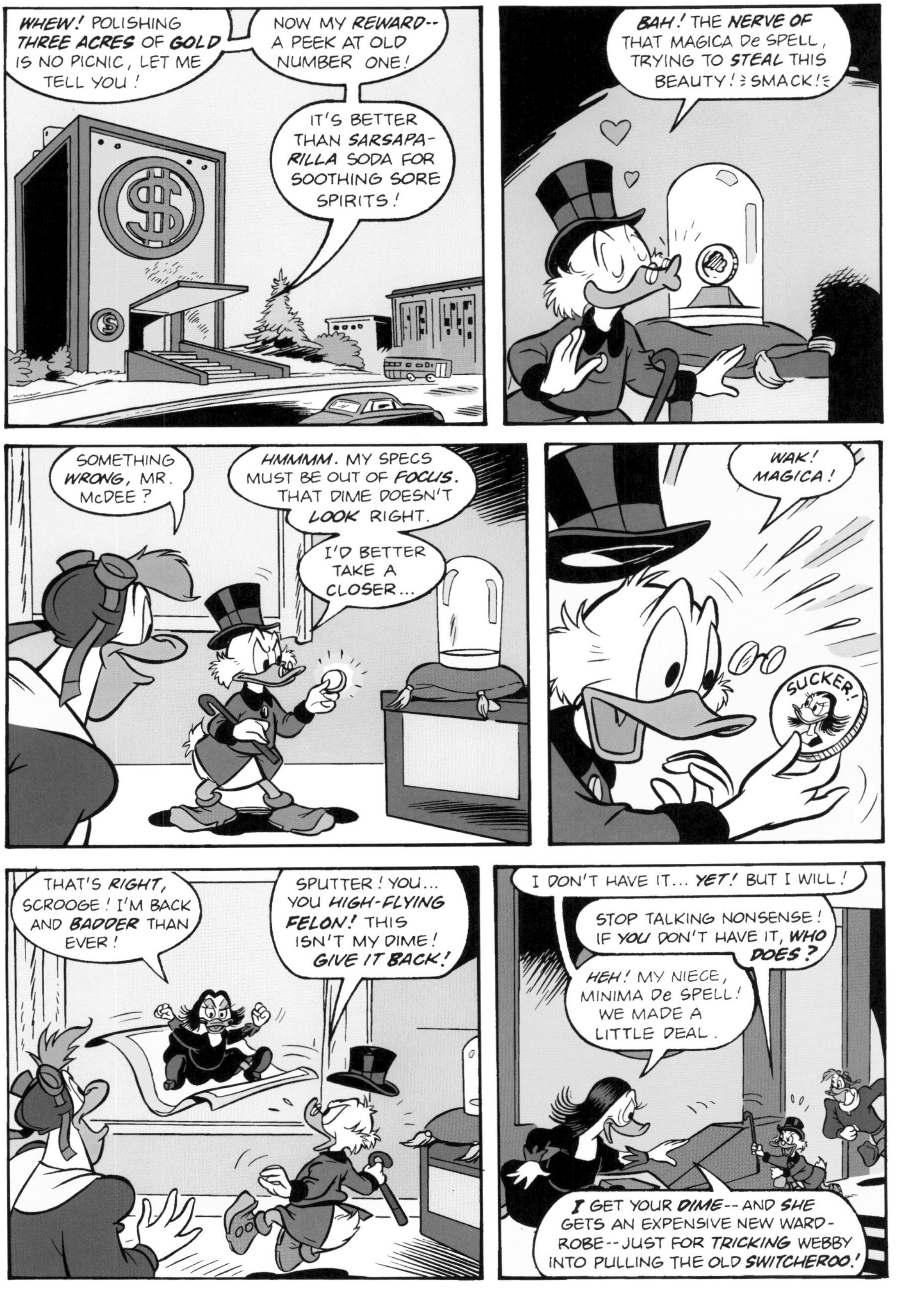
WHEW! POLISHING THREE ACRES OF GOLD IS NO PICNIC, LET ME TELL YOU!
NOW MY REWARD-- A PEEK AT OLD NUMBER ONE!
IT'S BETTER THAN SARSAPARILLA SODA FOR SOOTHING SORE SPIRITS!
BAH! THE NERVE OF THAT MAGICA De SPELL, TRYING TO STEAL THIS BEAUTY! SMACK!
SOMETHING WRONG, MR. McDEE?
HMMMM. MY SPECS MUST BE OUT OF FOCUS. THAT DIME DOESN'T LOOK RIGHT.
I'D BETTER TAKE A CLOSER...
WAK! MAGICA!
SUCKER!
THAT'S RIGHT, SCROOGE! I'M BACK AND BADDER THAN EVER!
SPUTTER! YOU... YOU HIGH-FLYING FELON! THIS ISN'T MY DIME! GIVE IT BACK!
I DON'T HAVE IT... YET! BUT I WILL!
STOP TALKING NONSENSE! IF YOU DON'T HAVE IT, WHO DOES?
HEH! MY NIECE, MINIMA De SPELL! WE MADE A LITTLE DEAL.
I GET YOUR DIME-- AND SHE GETS AN EXPENSIVE NEW WARDROBE-- JUST FOR TRICKING WEBBY INTO PULLING THE OLD SWITCHEROO!

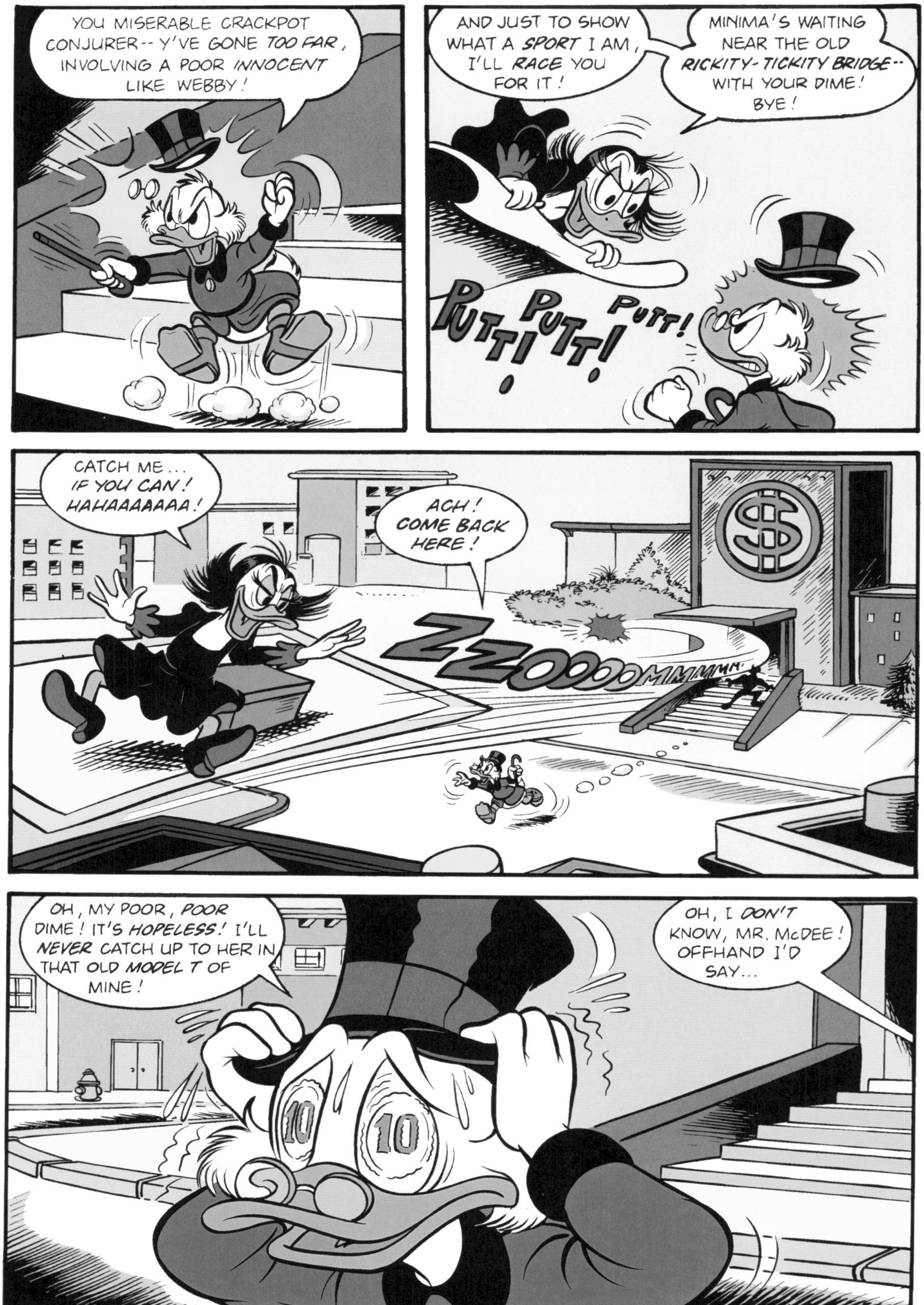
YOU MISERABLE CRACKPOT CONJURER -- Y'VE GONE TOO FAR, INVOLVING A POOR INNOCENT LIKE WEBBY!
AND JUST TO SHOW WHAT A SPORT I AM, I'LL RACE YOU FOR IT!
MINIMA'S WAITING NEAR THE OLD RICKITY-TICKITY BRIDGE -- WITH YOUR DIME! BYE!
PUTT! PUTT! PUTT!
CATCH ME... IF YOU CAN! HAHAAAAAAA!
ACH! COME BACK HERE!
ZZOOOOOMMMMM
OH, MY POOR, POOR DIME! IT'S HOPELESS! I'LL NEVER CATCH UP TO HER IN THAT OLD MODEL T OF MINE!
OH, I DON'T KNOW, MR. McDEE! OFFHAND I'D SAY...
10
10

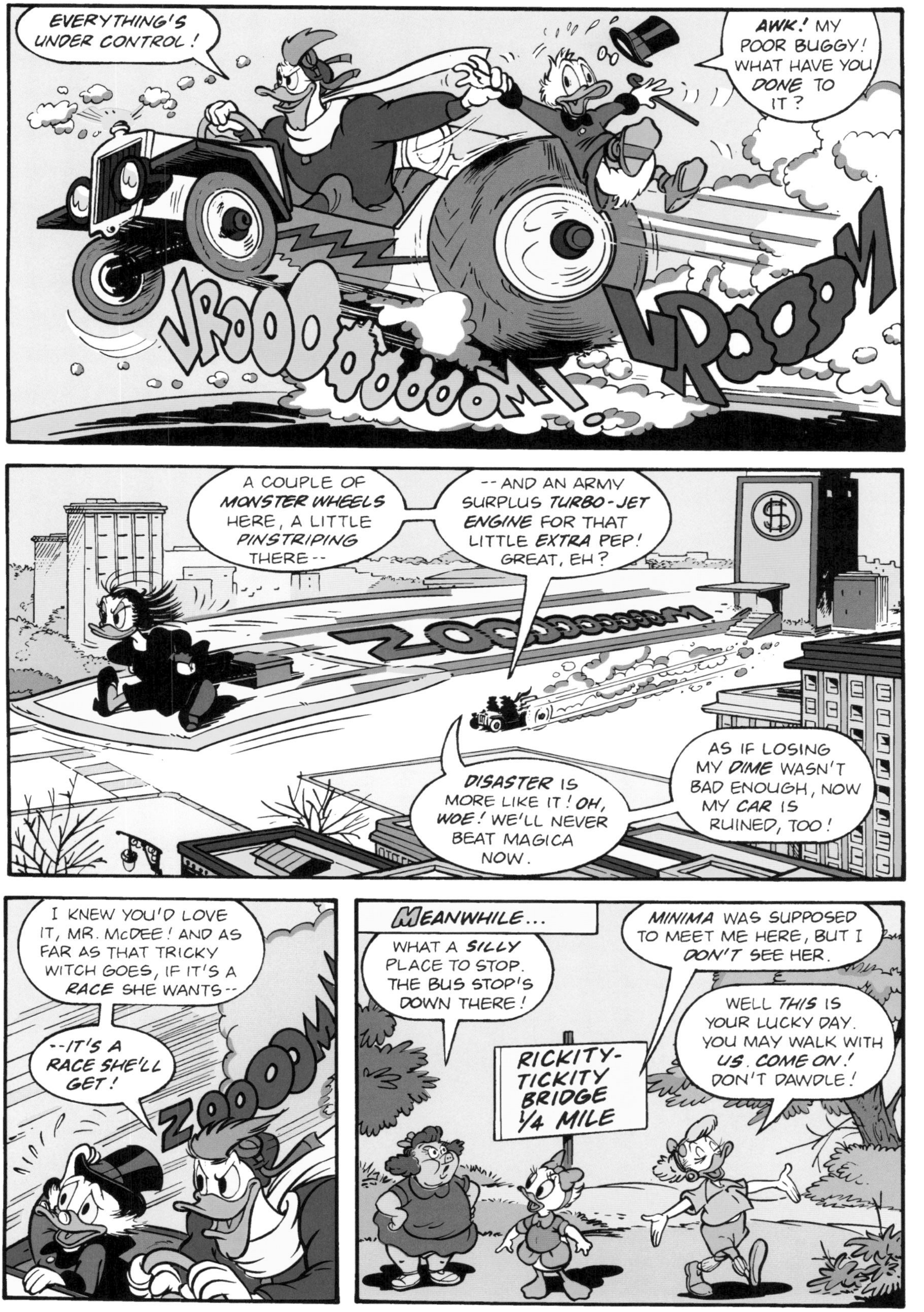
EVERYTHING'S UNDER CONTROL!
AWK! MY POOR BUGGY! WHAT HAVE YOU DONE TO IT?
A COUPLE OF MONSTER WHEELS HERE, A LITTLE PINSTRIPING THERE--
--AND AN ARMY SURPLUS TURBO-JET ENGINE FOR THAT LITTLE EXTRA PEP! GREAT, EH?
DISASTER IS MORE LIKE IT! OH, WOE! WE'LL NEVER BEAT MAGICA NOW.
AS IF LOSING MY DIME WASN'T BAD ENOUGH, NOW MY CAR IS RUINED, TOO!
I KNEW YOU'D LOVE IT, MR. McDEE! AND AS FAR AS THAT TRICKY WITCH GOES, IF IT'S A RACE SHE WANTS--
--IT'S A RACE SHE'LL GET!
MEANWHILE...
WHAT A SILLY PLACE TO STOP. THE BUS STOP'S DOWN THERE!
MINIMA WAS SUPPOSED TO MEET ME HERE, BUT I DON'T SEE HER.
RICKITY-TICKITY BRIDGE 1/4 MILE
WELL THIS IS YOUR LUCKY DAY. YOU MAY WALK WITH US. COME ON! DON'T DAWDLE!

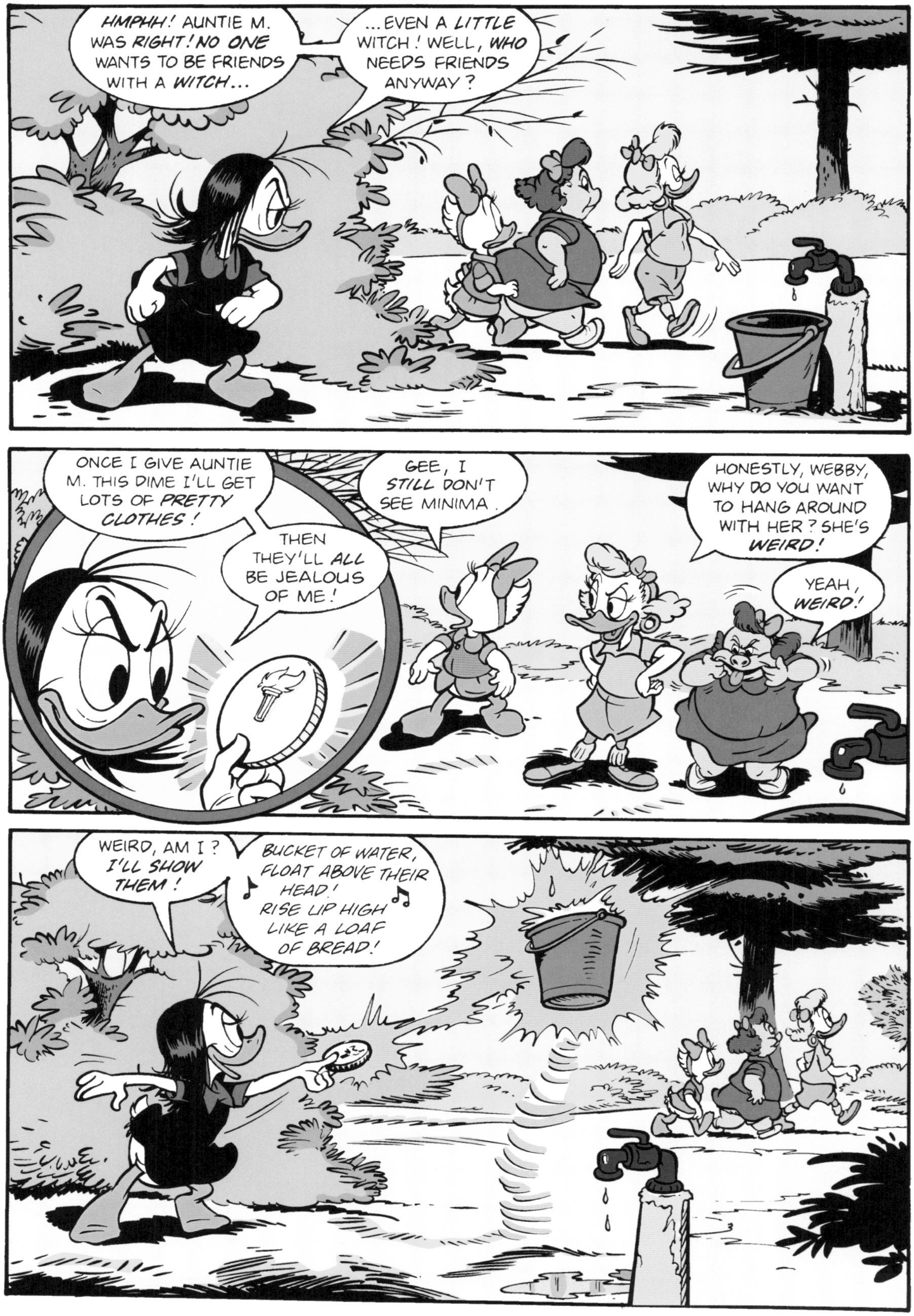
HMPHH! AUNTIE M. WAS RIGHT! NO ONE WANTS TO BE FRIENDS WITH A WITCH...
...EVEN A LITTLE WITCH! WELL, WHO NEEDS FRIENDS ANYWAY?
ONCE I GIVE AUNTIE M. THIS DIME I'LL GET LOTS OF PRETTY CLOTHES!
THEN THEY'LL ALL BE JEALOUS OF ME!
GEE, I STILL DON'T SEE MINIMA.
HONESTLY, WEBBY, WHY DO YOU WANT TO HANG AROUND WITH HER? SHE'S WEIRD!
YEAH, WEIRD!
WEIRD, AM I? I'LL SHOW THEM!
BUCKET OF WATER, FLOAT ABOVE THEIR HEAD! RISE UP HIGH LIKE A LOAF OF BREAD!

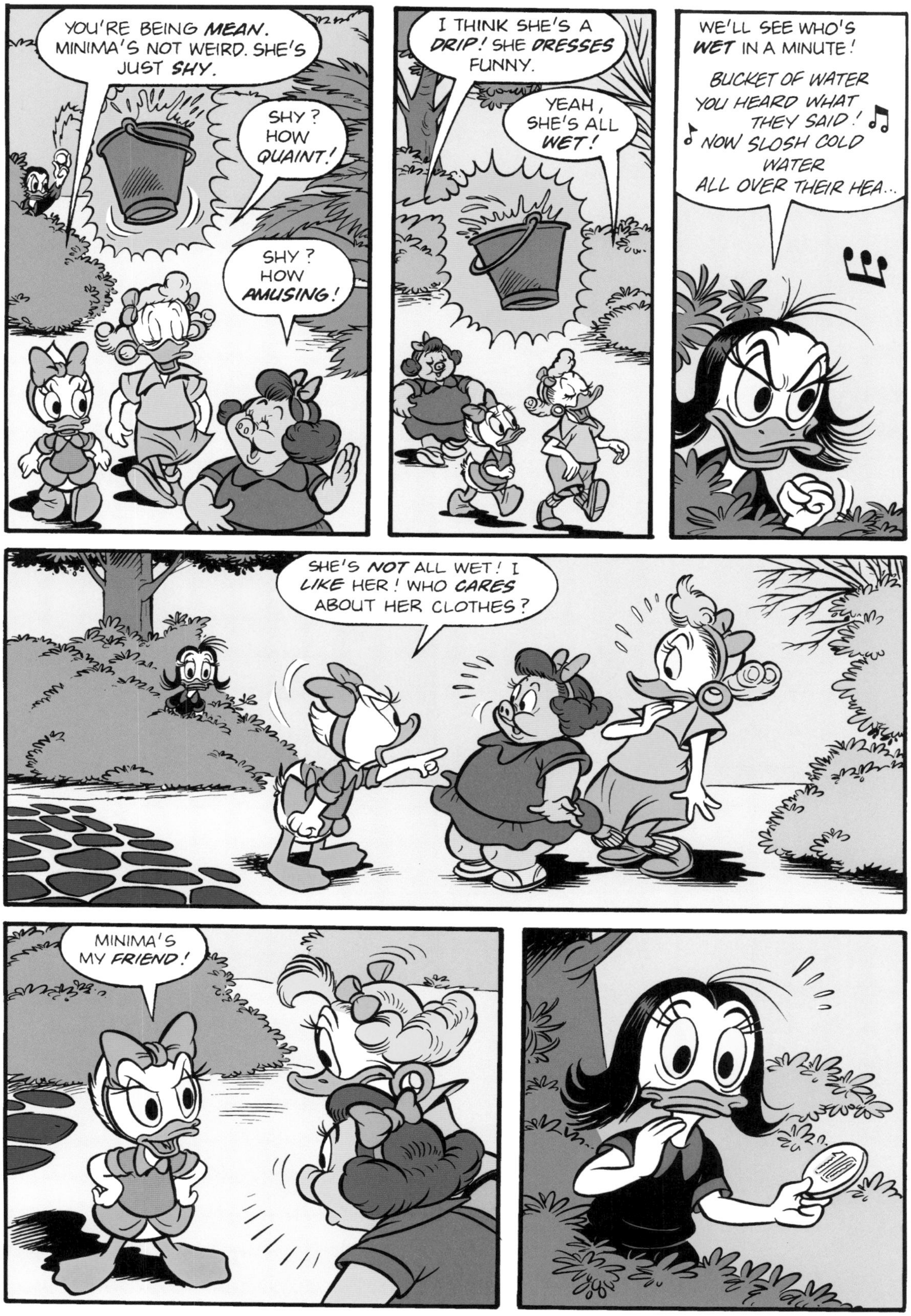

YOU'RE BEING MEAN. MINIMA'S NOT WEIRD. SHE'S JUST SHY.
SHY? HOW QUAINT!
SHY? HOW AMUSING!
I THINK SHE'S A DRIP! SHE DRESSES FUNNY.
YEAH, SHE'S ALL WET!
WE'LL SEE WHO'S WET IN A MINUTE!
BUCKET OF WATER YOU HEARD WHAT THEY SAID! NOW SLOSH COLD WATER ALL OVER THEIR HEA...
SHE'S NOT ALL WET! I LIKE HER! WHO CARES ABOUT HER CLOTHES?
MINIMA'S MY FRIEND!

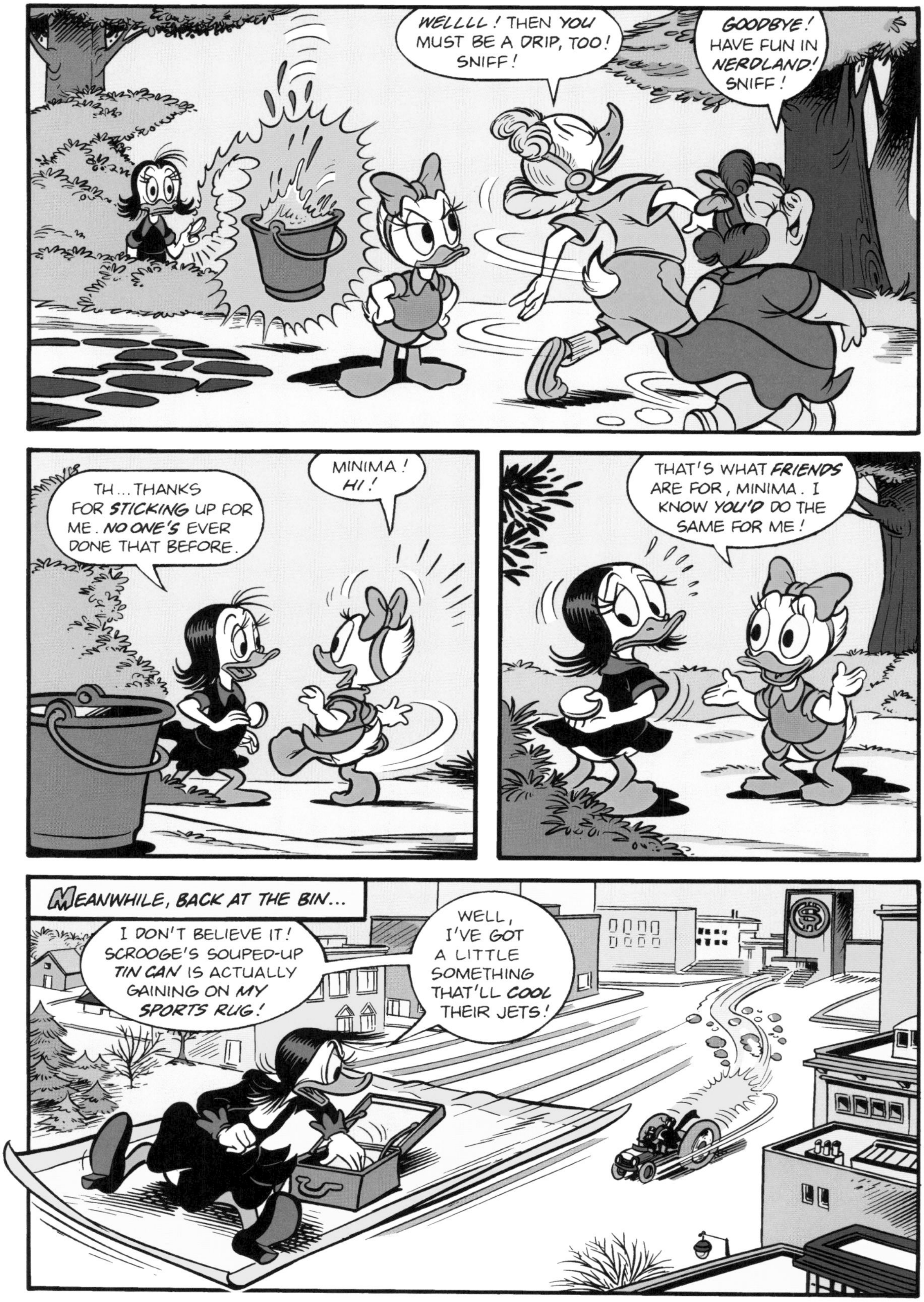
WELLLL! THEN YOU MUST BE A DRIP, TOO! SNIFF!
GOODBYE! HAVE FUN IN NERDLAND! SNIFF!
TH...THANKS FOR STICKING UP FOR ME. NO ONE'S EVER DONE THAT BEFORE.
MINIMA! HI!
THAT'S WHAT FRIENDS ARE FOR, MINIMA. I KNOW YOU'D DO THE SAME FOR ME!
MEANWHILE, BACK AT THE BIN...
I DON'T BELIEVE IT! SCROOGE'S SOUPED-UP TIN CAN IS ACTUALLY GAINING ON MY SPORTS RUG!
WELL, I'VE GOT A LITTLE SOMETHING THAT'LL COOL THEIR JETS!

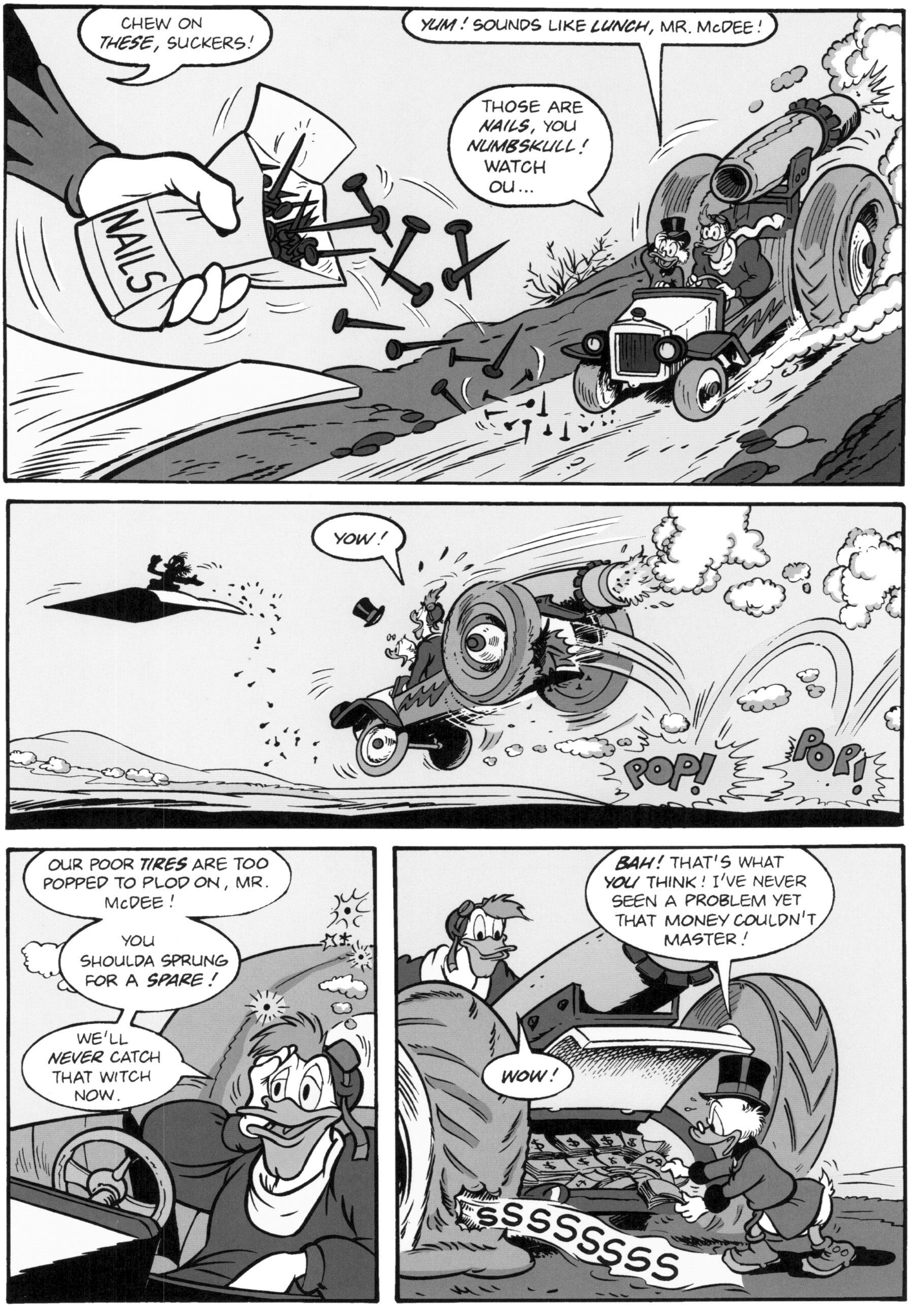
CHEW ON THESE, SUCKERS!
YUM! SOUNDS LIKE LUNCH, MR. McDEE!
THOSE ARE NAILS, YOU NUMBSKULL! WATCH OU...
NAILS
YOW!
POP!
POP!
OUR POOR TIRES ARE TOO POPPED TO PLOD ON, MR. McDEE!
YOU SHOULDA SPRUNG FOR A SPARE!
WE'LL NEVER CATCH THAT WITCH NOW.
BAH! THAT'S WHAT YOU THINK! I'VE NEVER SEEN A PROBLEM YET THAT MONEY COULDN'T MASTER!
WOW!
SSSSSSSSS

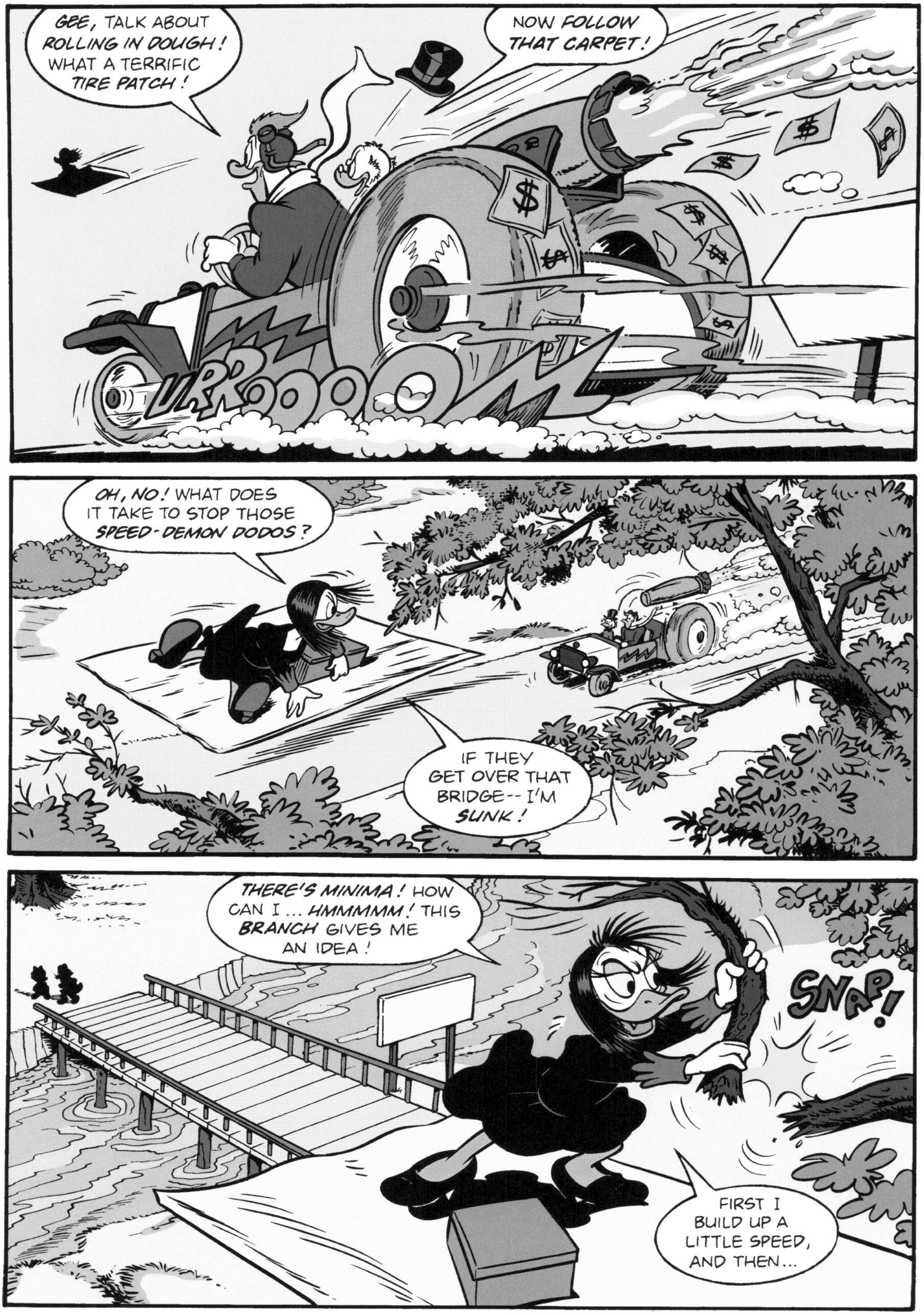
GEE, TALK ABOUT ROLLING IN DOUGH! WHAT A TERRIFIC TIRE PATCH!
NOW FOLLOW THAT CARPET!
VRROOOOOM
OH, NO! WHAT DOES IT TAKE TO STOP THOSE SPEED-DEMON DODOS?
IF THEY GET OVER THAT BRIDGE-- I'M SUNK!
THERE'S MINIMA! HOW CAN I ... HMMMMM! THIS BRANCH GIVES ME AN IDEA!
SNAP!
FIRST I BUILD UP A LITTLE SPEED, AND THEN...

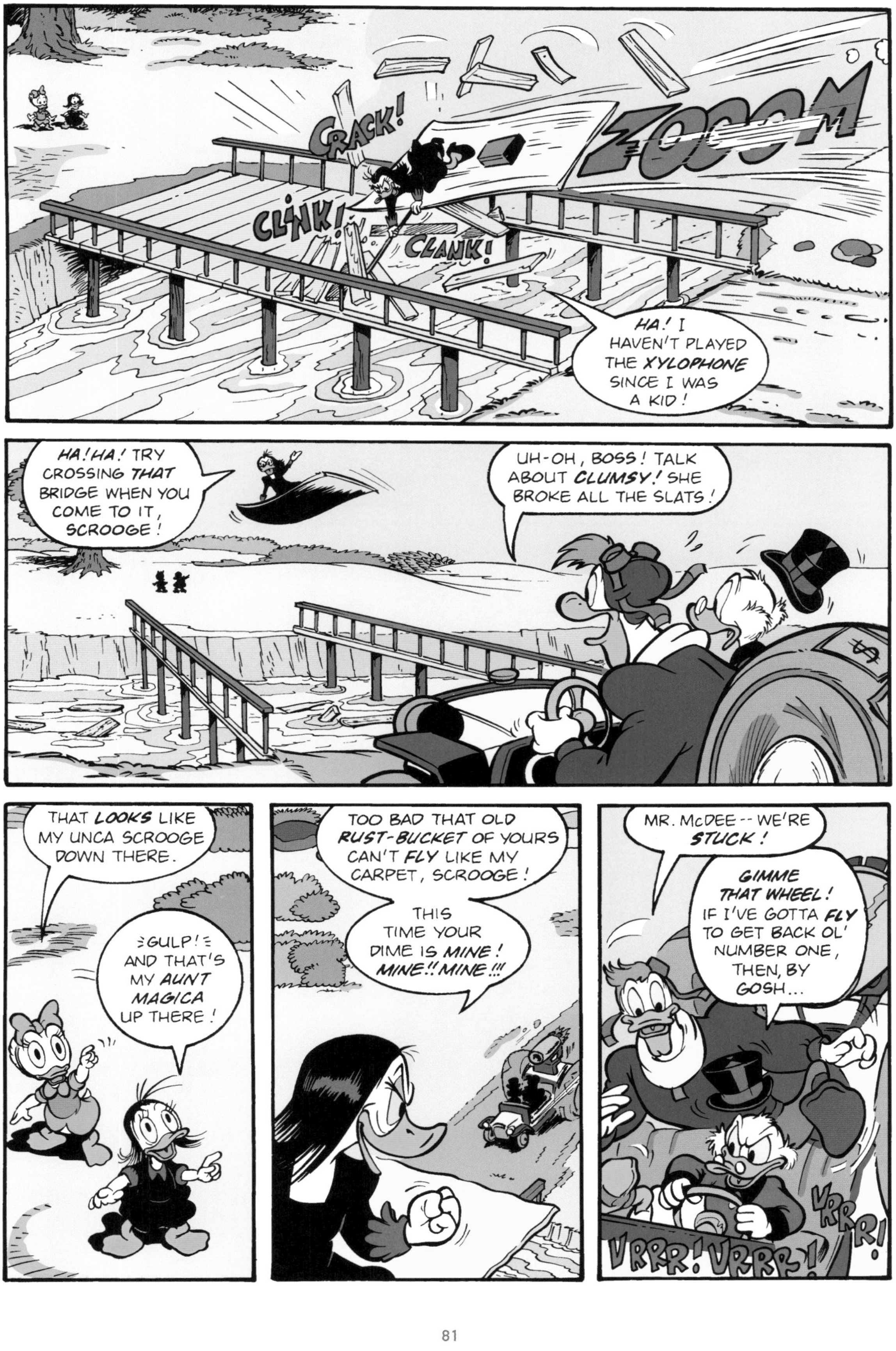
CRACK!
ZOOOOM
CLINK!
CLANK!
HA! I HAVEN'T PLAYED THE XYLOPHONE SINCE I WAS A KID!
HA! HA! TRY CROSSING THAT BRIDGE WHEN YOU COME TO IT, SCROOGE!
UH-OH, BOSS! TALK ABOUT CLUMSY! SHE BROKE ALL THE SLATS!
THAT LOOKS LIKE MY UNCA SCROOGE DOWN THERE.
GULP! AND THAT'S MY AUNT MAGICA UP THERE!
TOO BAD THAT OLD RUST-BUCKET OF YOURS CAN'T FLY LIKE MY CARPET, SCROOGE!
THIS TIME YOUR DIME IS MINE! MINE!! MINE!!!
MR. McDEE -- WE'RE STUCK!
GIMME THAT WHEEL! IF I'VE GOTTA FLY TO GET BACK OL' NUMBER ONE, THEN, BY GOSH...
VRRRR!
VRRR! VRRR!

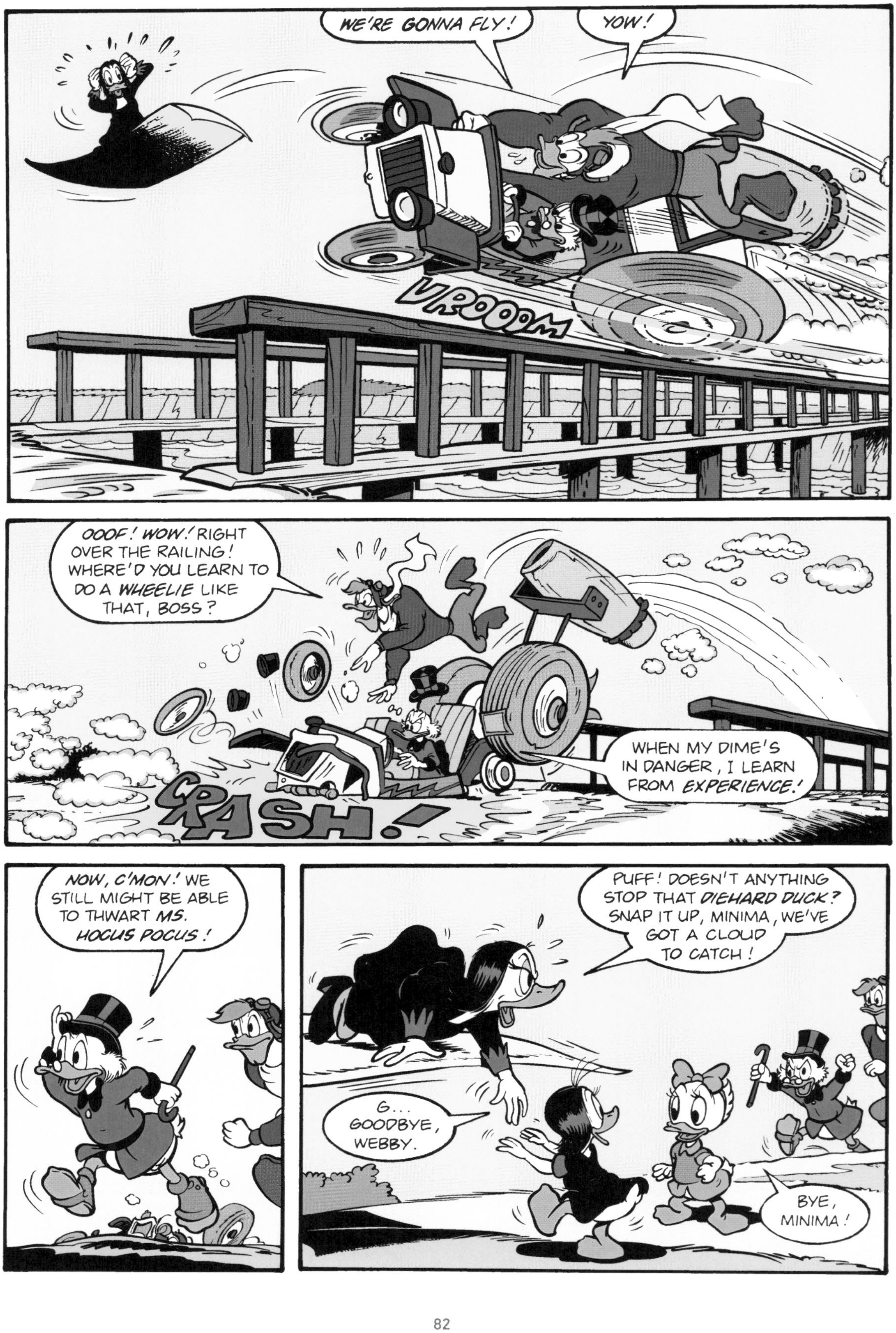
WE'RE GONNA FLY!
YOW!
VROOOM
OOOF! WOW! RIGHT OVER THE RAILING! WHERE'D YOU LEARN TO DO A WHEELIE LIKE THAT, BOSS?
WHEN MY DIME'S IN DANGER, I LEARN FROM EXPERIENCE!
CRASH!
NOW, C'MON! WE STILL MIGHT BE ABLE TO THWART MS. HOCUS POCUS!
PUFF! DOESN'T ANYTHING STOP THAT DIEHARD DUCK? SNAP IT UP, MINIMA, WE'VE GOT A CLOUD TO CATCH!
G... GOODBYE, WEBBY.
BYE, MINIMA!

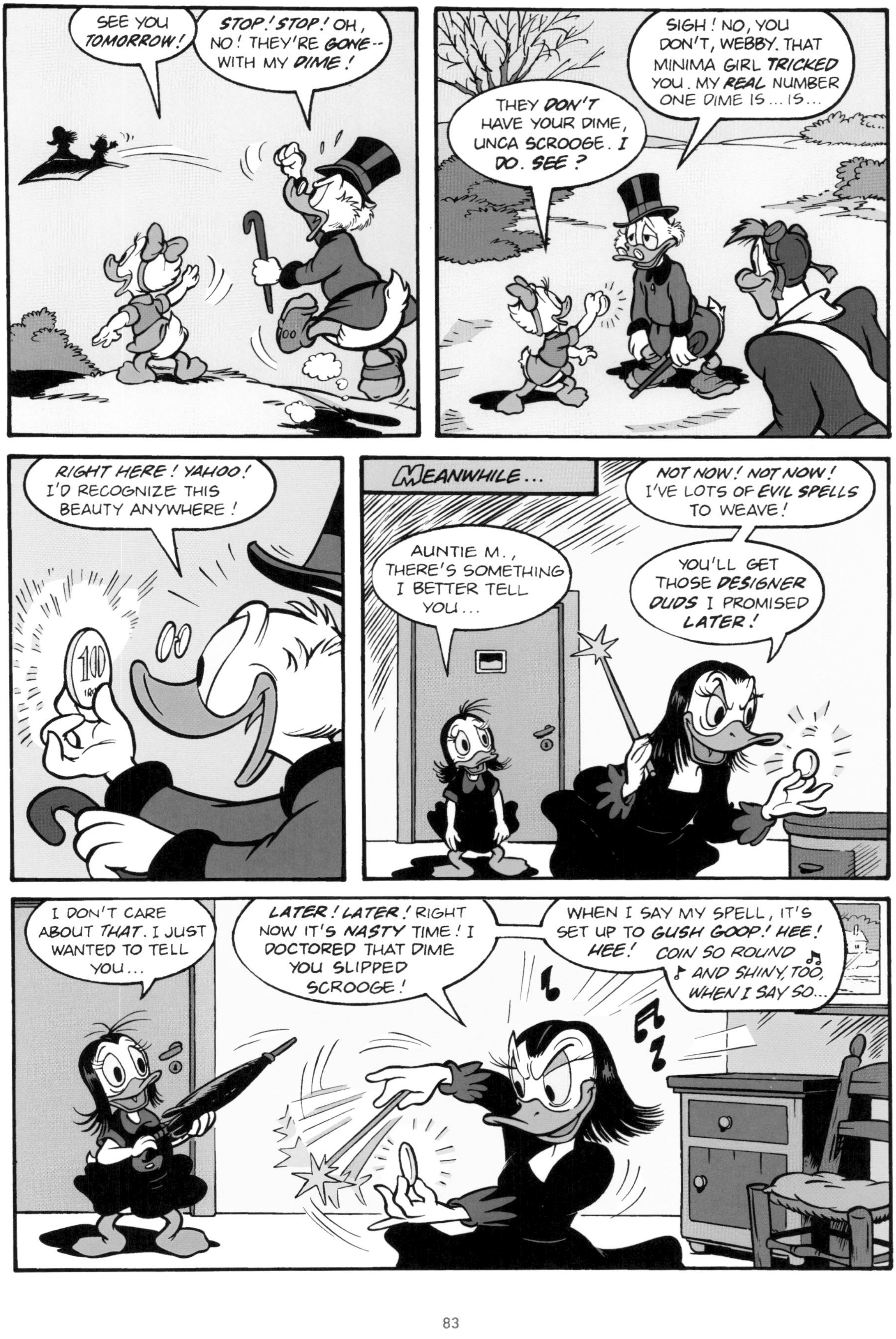

SEE YOU TOMORROW!
STOP! STOP! OH, NO! THEY'RE GONE-- WITH MY DIME!
THEY DON'T HAVE YOUR DIME, UNCA SCROOGE. I DO. SEE?
SIGH! NO, YOU DON'T, WEBBY. THAT MINIMA GIRL TRICKED YOU. MY REAL NUMBER ONE DIME IS... IS...
RIGHT HERE! YAHOO! I'D RECOGNIZE THIS BEAUTY ANYWHERE!
MEANWHILE...
NOT NOW! NOT NOW! I'VE LOTS OF EVIL SPELLS TO WEAVE!
AUNTIE M., THERE'S SOMETHING I BETTER TELL YOU...
YOU'LL GET THOSE DESIGNER DUDS I PROMISED LATER!
I DON'T CARE ABOUT THAT. I JUST WANTED TO TELL YOU...
LATER! LATER! RIGHT NOW IT'S NASTY TIME! I DOCTORED THAT DIME YOU SLIPPED SCROOGE!
WHEN I SAY MY SPELL, IT'S SET UP TO GUSH GOOP! HEE! HEE!
COIN SO ROUND AND SHINY, TOO, WHEN I SAY SO...

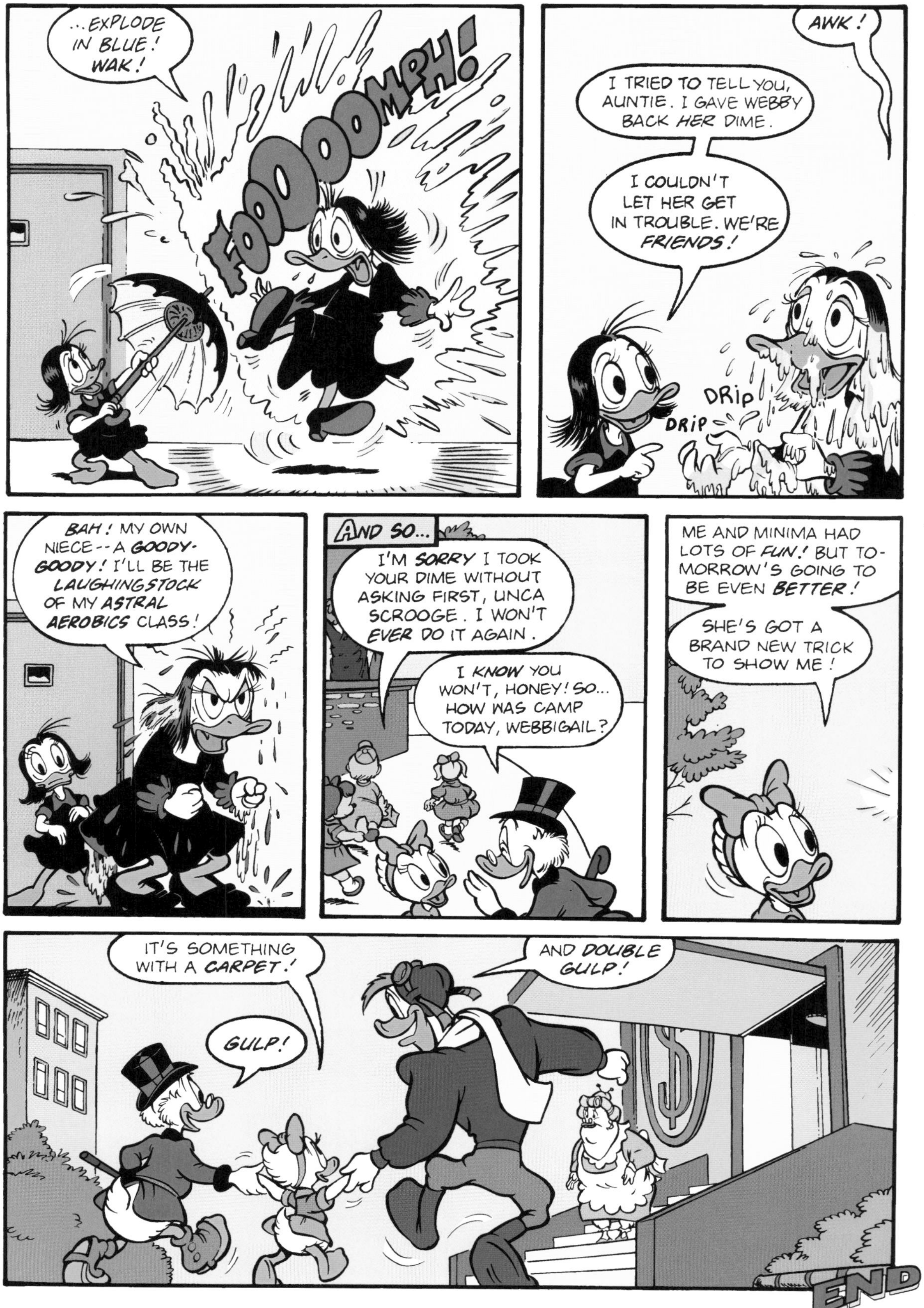
...EXPLODE IN BLUE! WAK!
FOOOOOOMPH!
AWK!
I TRIED TO TELL YOU, AUNTIE. I GAVE WEBBY BACK HER DIME.
I COULDN'T LET HER GET IN TROUBLE. WE'RE FRIENDS!
DRIP
DRIP
BAH! MY OWN NIECE--A GOODY-GOODY! I'LL BE THE LAUGHINGSTOCK OF MY ASTRAL AEROBICS CLASS!
AND SO...
I'M SORRY I TOOK YOUR DIME WITHOUT ASKING FIRST, UNCA SCROOGE. I WON'T EVER DO IT AGAIN.
I KNOW YOU WON'T, HONEY! SO... HOW WAS CAMP TODAY, WEBBIGAIL?
ME AND MINIMA HAD LOTS OF FUN! BUT TO-MORROW'S GOING TO BE EVEN BETTER!
SHE'S GOT A BRAND NEW TRICK TO SHOW ME!
IT'S SOMETHING WITH A CARPET!
GULP!
AND DOUBLE GULP!
END

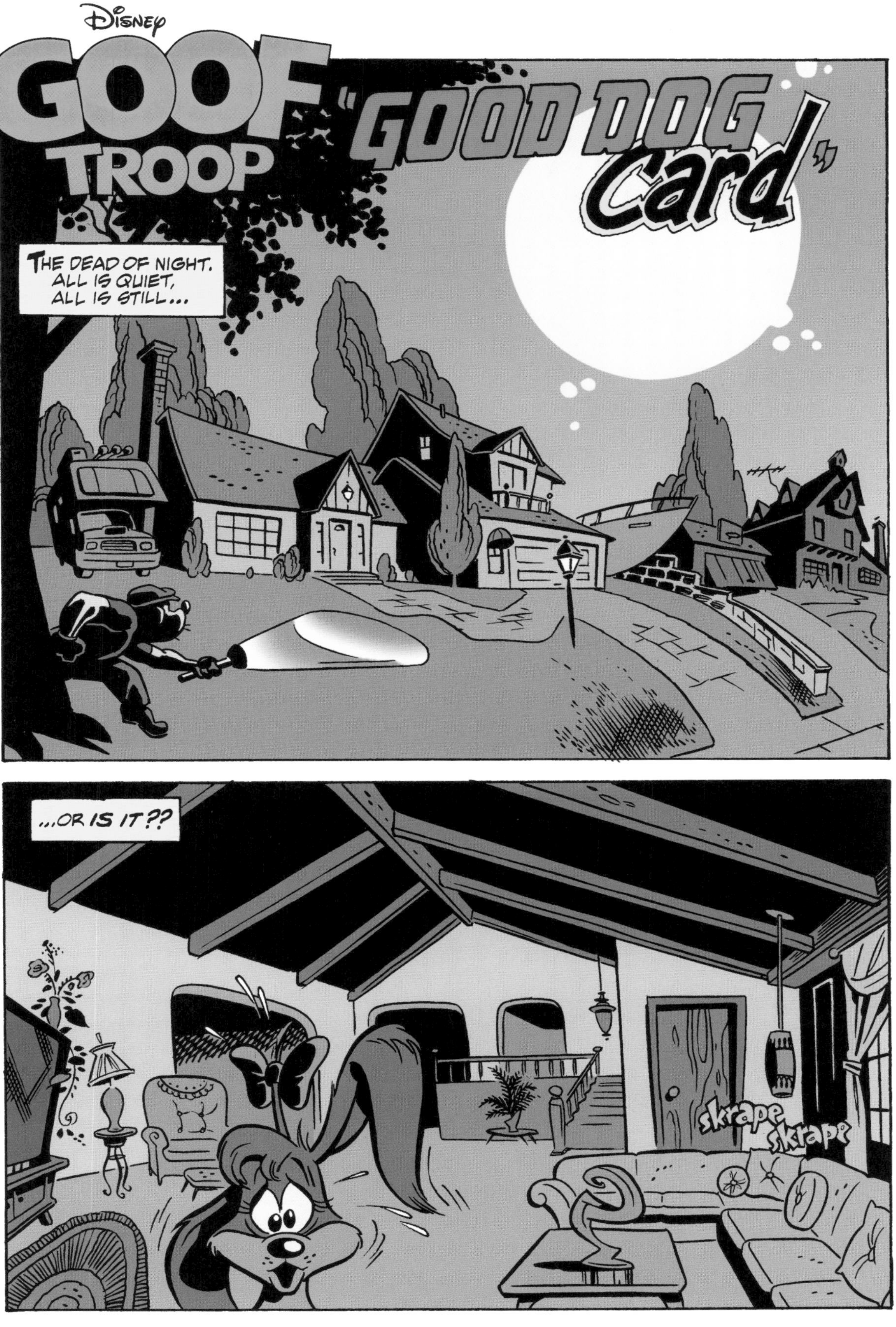
Disney
GOOF TROOP
"GOOD DOG Card"
THE DEAD OF NIGHT. ALL IS QUIET, ALL IS STILL...
...OR IS IT??
skrape skrape

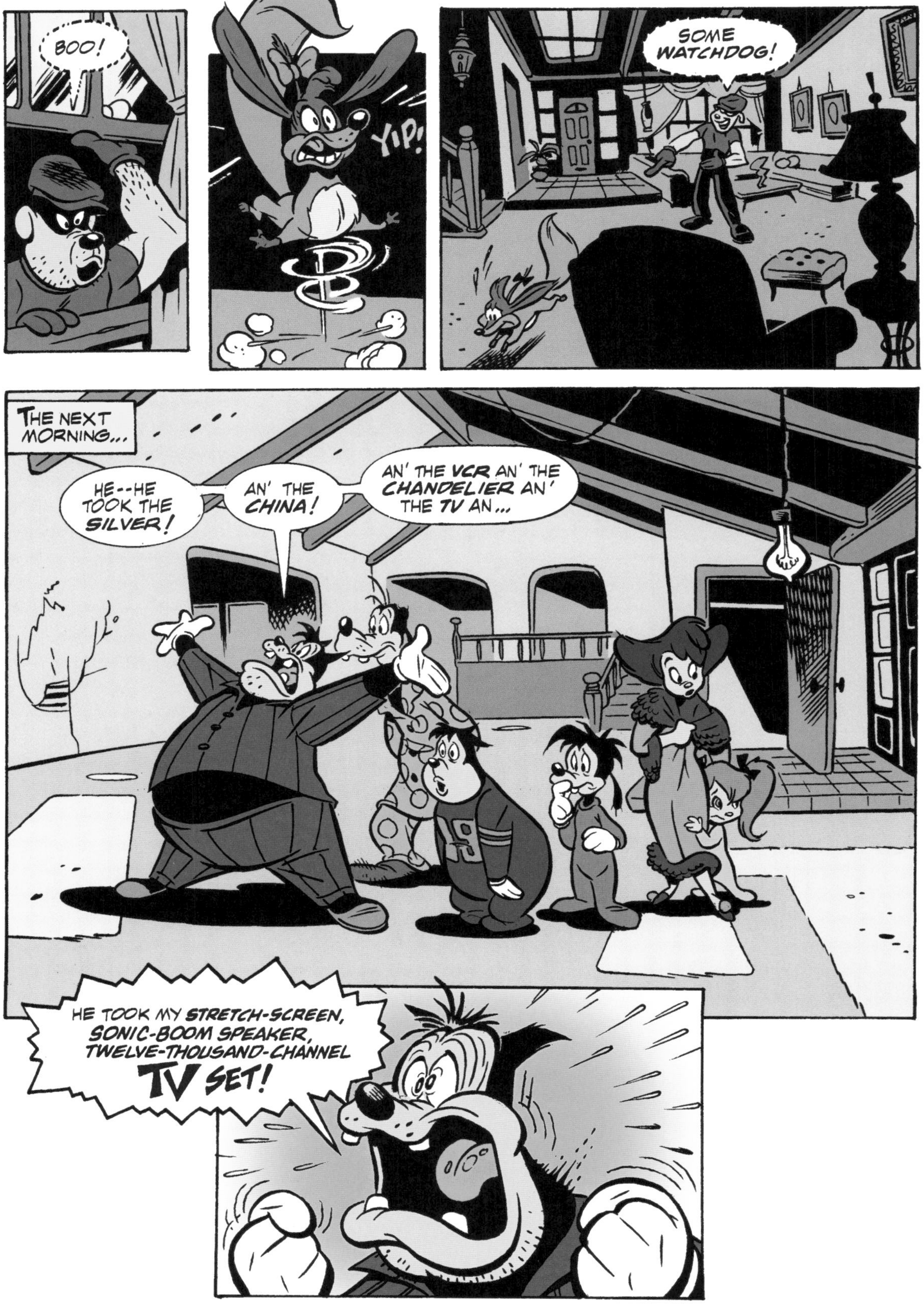
BOO!
YIP!
SOME WATCHDOG!
THE NEXT MORNING...
HE--HE TOOK THE SILVER!
AN' THE CHINA!
AN' THE VCR AN' THE CHANDELIER AN' THE TV AN...
HE TOOK MY STRETCH-SCREEN, SONIC-BOOM SPEAKER, TWELVE-THOUSAND-CHANNEL TV SET!

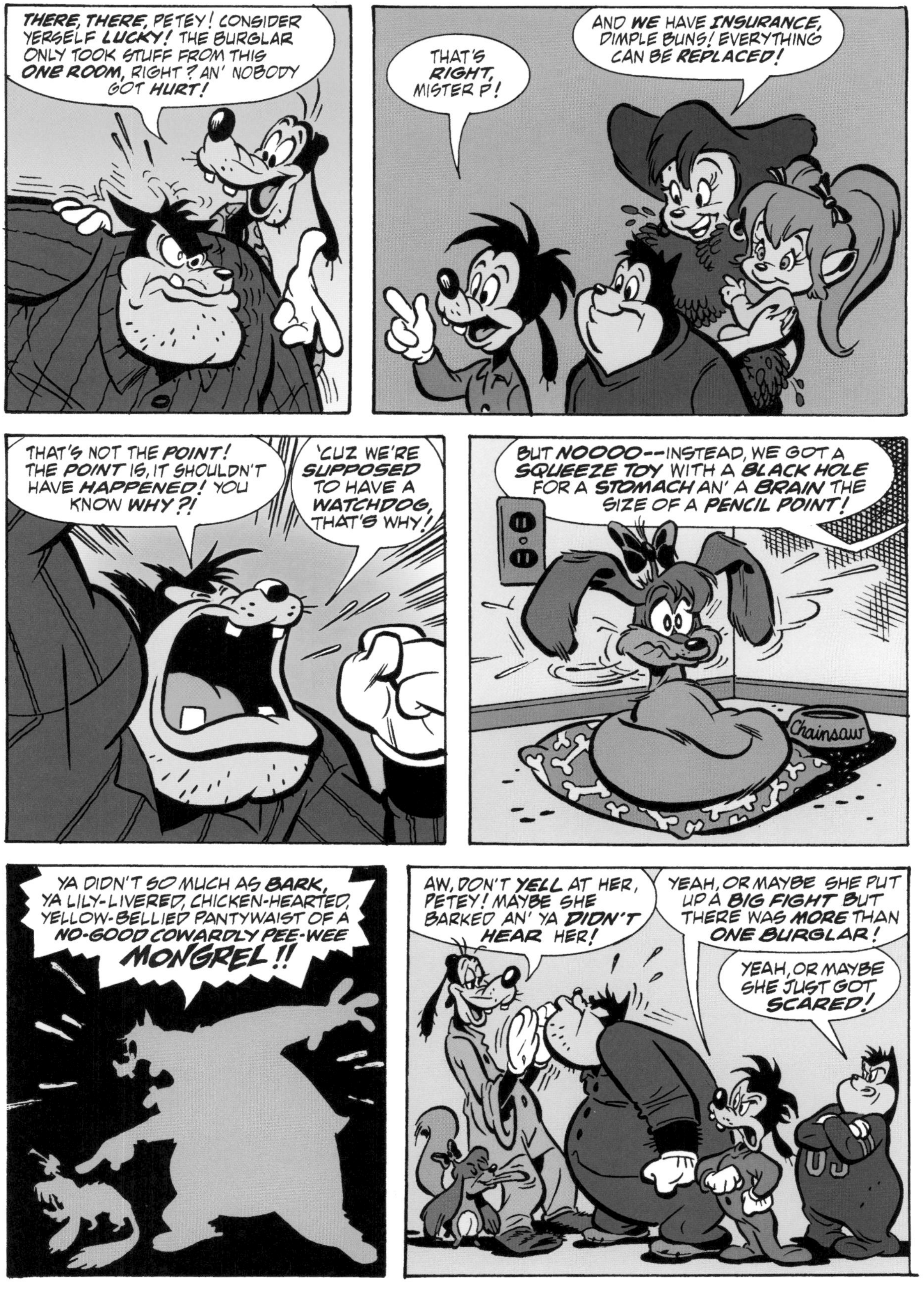
THERE, THERE, PETEY! CONSIDER YERSELF LUCKY! THE BURGLAR ONLY TOOK STUFF FROM THIS ONE ROOM, RIGHT? AN' NOBODY GOT HURT!
THAT'S RIGHT, MISTER P!
AND WE HAVE INSURANCE, DIMPLE BUNS! EVERYTHING CAN BE REPLACED!
THAT'S NOT THE POINT! THE POINT IS, IT SHOULDN'T HAVE HAPPENED! YOU KNOW WHY?!
'CUZ WE'RE SUPPOSED TO HAVE A WATCHDOG, THAT'S WHY!
BUT NOOOO--INSTEAD, WE GOT A SQUEEZE TOY WITH A BLACK HOLE FOR A STOMACH AN' A BRAIN THE SIZE OF A PENCIL POINT!
Chainsaw
YA DIDN'T SO MUCH AS BARK, YA LILY-LIVERED, CHICKEN-HEARTED, YELLOW-BELLIED PANTYWAIST OF A NO-GOOD COWARDLY PEE-WEE MONGREL!!
AW, DON'T YELL AT HER, PETEY! MAYBE SHE BARKED AN' YA DIDN'T HEAR HER!
YEAH, OR MAYBE SHE PUT UP A BIG FIGHT BUT THERE WAS MORE THAN ONE BURGLAR!
YEAH, OR MAYBE SHE JUST GOT SCARED!

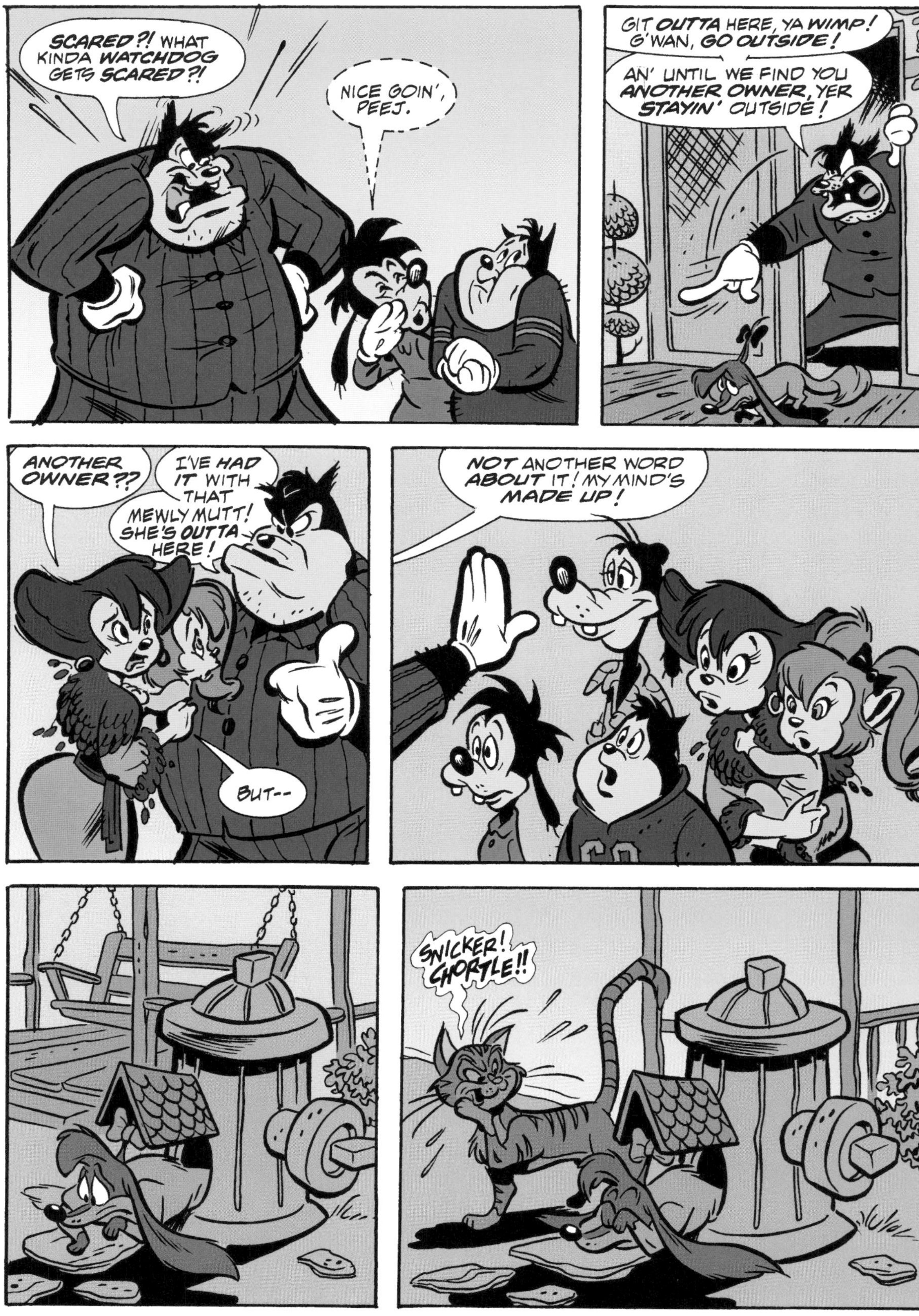
SCARED?! WHAT KINDA WATCHDOG GETS SCARED?!
NICE GOIN', PEEJ.
GIT OUTTA HERE, YA WIMP! G'WAN, GO OUTSIDE!
AN' UNTIL WE FIND YOU ANOTHER OWNER, YER STAYIN' OUTSIDE!
ANOTHER OWNER??
I'VE HAD IT WITH THAT MEWLY MUTT! SHE'S OUTTA HERE!
BUT--
NOT ANOTHER WORD ABOUT IT! MY MIND'S MADE UP!
SNICKER! CHORTLE!!

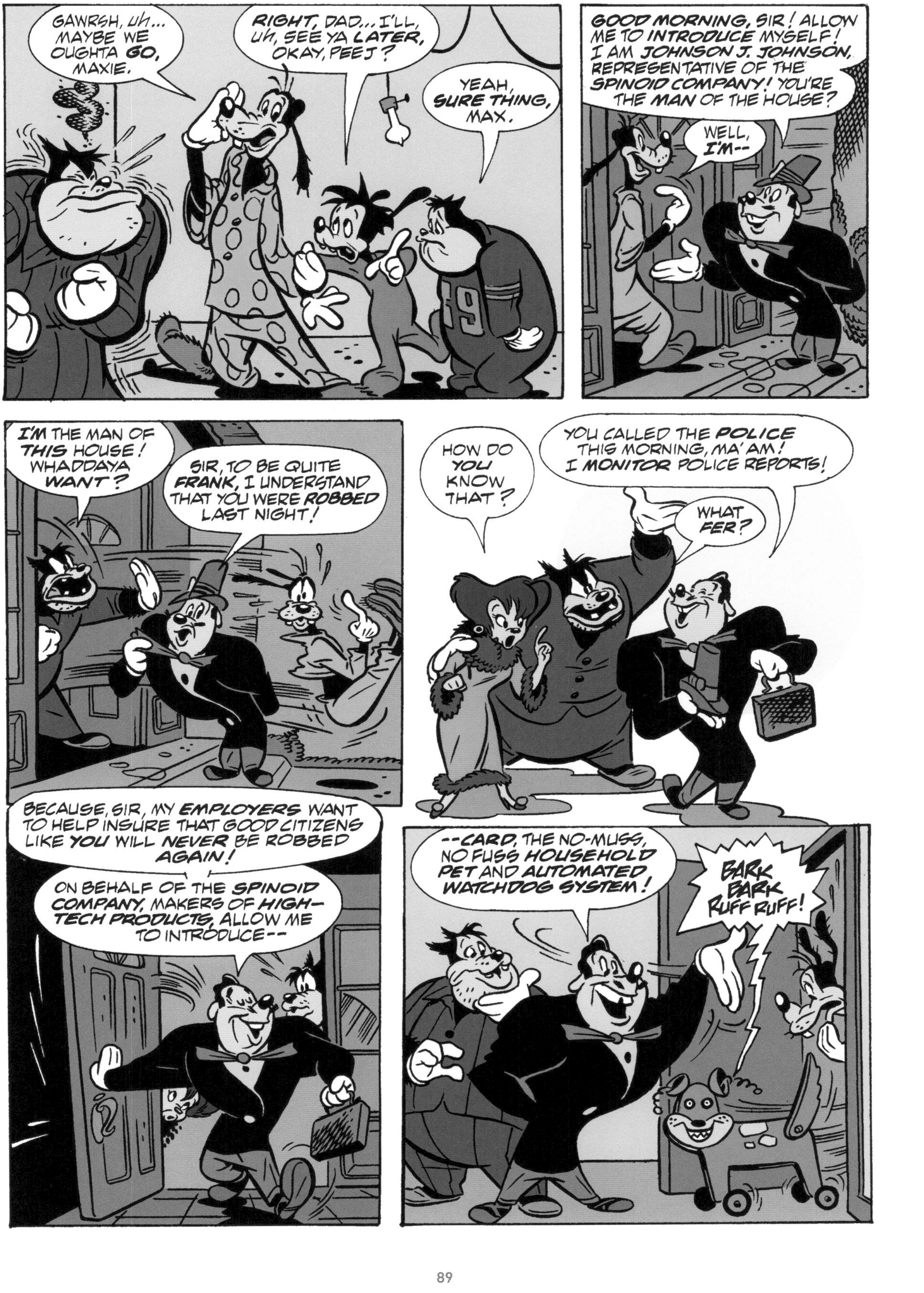
GAWRSH, UH... MAYBE WE OUGHTA GO, MAXIE.
RIGHT, DAD... I'LL, UH, SEE YA LATER, OKAY, PEEJ?
YEAH, SURE THING, MAX.
GOOD MORNING, SIR! ALLOW ME TO INTRODUCE MYSELF! I AM JOHNSON J. JOHNSON, REPRESENTATIVE OF THE SPINOID COMPANY! YOU'RE THE MAN OF THE HOUSE?
WELL, I'M--
I'M THE MAN OF THIS HOUSE! WHADDAYA WANT?
SIR, TO BE QUITE FRANK, I UNDERSTAND THAT YOU WERE ROBBED LAST NIGHT!
HOW DO YOU KNOW THAT?
YOU CALLED THE POLICE THIS MORNING, MA'AM! I MONITOR POLICE REPORTS!
WHAT FER?
BECAUSE, SIR, MY EMPLOYERS WANT TO HELP INSURE THAT GOOD CITIZENS LIKE YOU WILL NEVER BE ROBBED AGAIN!
ON BEHALF OF THE SPINOID COMPANY, MAKERS OF HIGH-TECH PRODUCTS, ALLOW ME TO INTRODUCE--
--CARD, THE NO-MUSS, NO FUSS HOUSEHOLD PET AND AUTOMATED WATCHDOG SYSTEM!
BARK BARK RUFF RUFF!

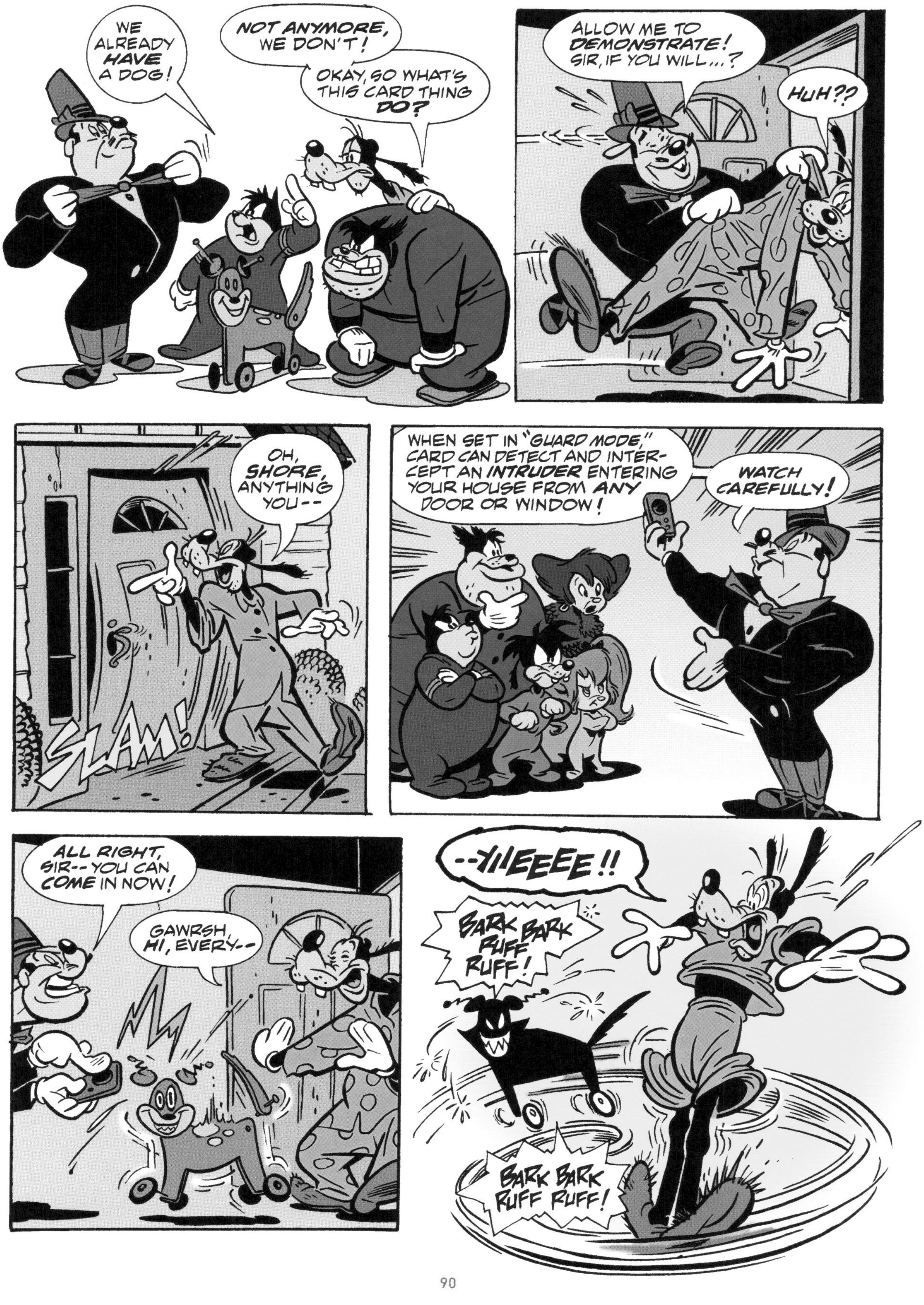
WE ALREADY HAVE A DOG!
NOT ANYMORE, WE DON'T!
OKAY, SO WHAT'S THIS CARD THING DO?
ALLOW ME TO DEMONSTRATE! SIR, IF YOU WILL...?
HUH??
OH, SHORE, ANYTHING YOU--
SLAM!
WHEN SET IN "GUARD MODE," CARD CAN DETECT AND INTERCEPT AN INTRUDER ENTERING YOUR HOUSE FROM ANY DOOR OR WINDOW!
WATCH CAREFULLY!
ALL RIGHT, SIR--YOU CAN COME IN NOW!
GAWRSH, HI, EVERY--
--YIIEEEEE!!
BARK BARK RUFF RUFF!
BARK BARK RUFF RUFF!

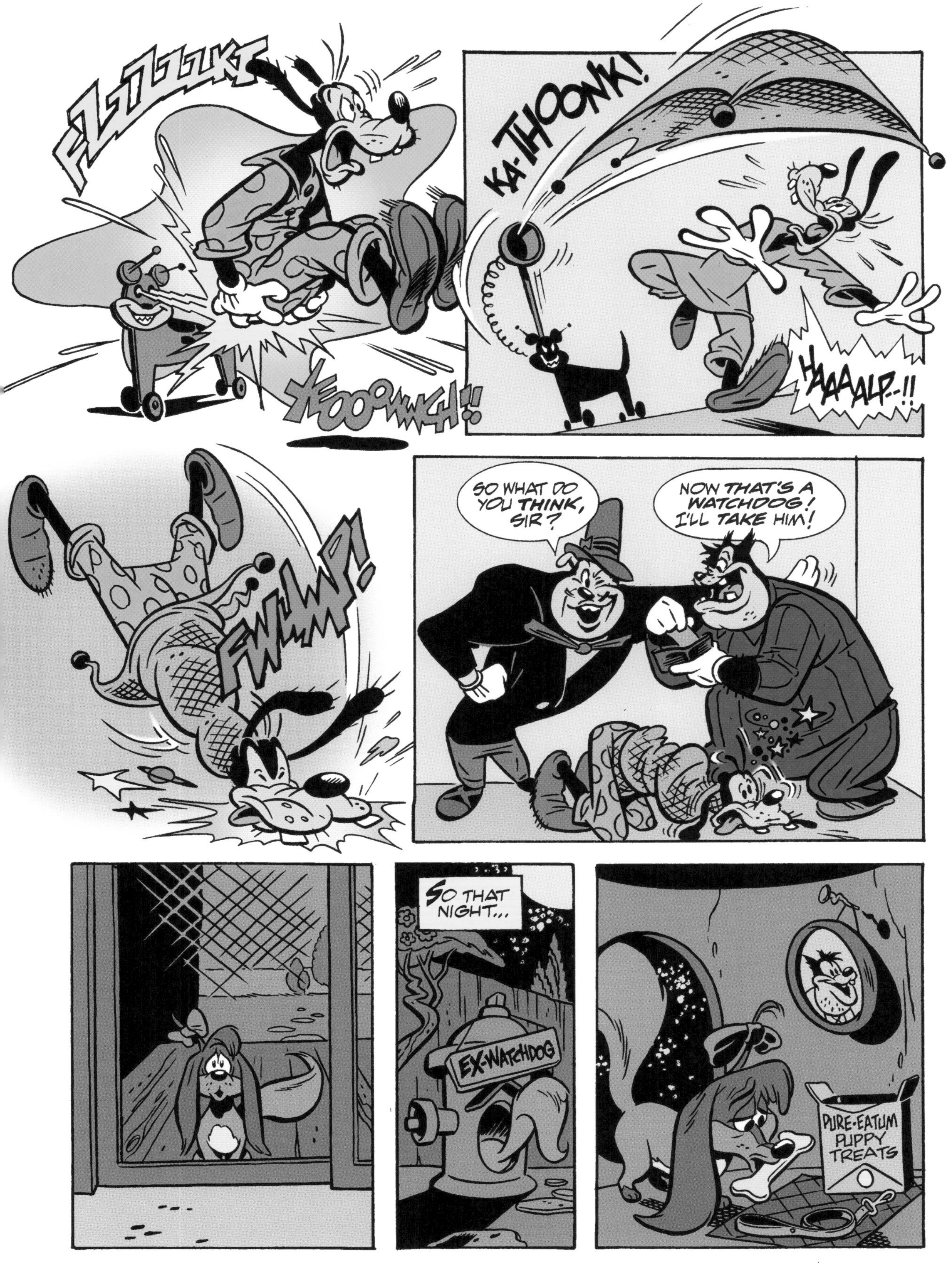
FZZZLLKT
YEOOOWWCH!!
KA-THOONK!
HAAAALP--!!
FWUMP!
SO WHAT DO YOU THINK, SIR?
NOW THAT'S A WATCHDOG! I'LL TAKE HIM!
SO THAT NIGHT...
EX-WATCHDOG
PURE-EATUM PUPPY TREATS

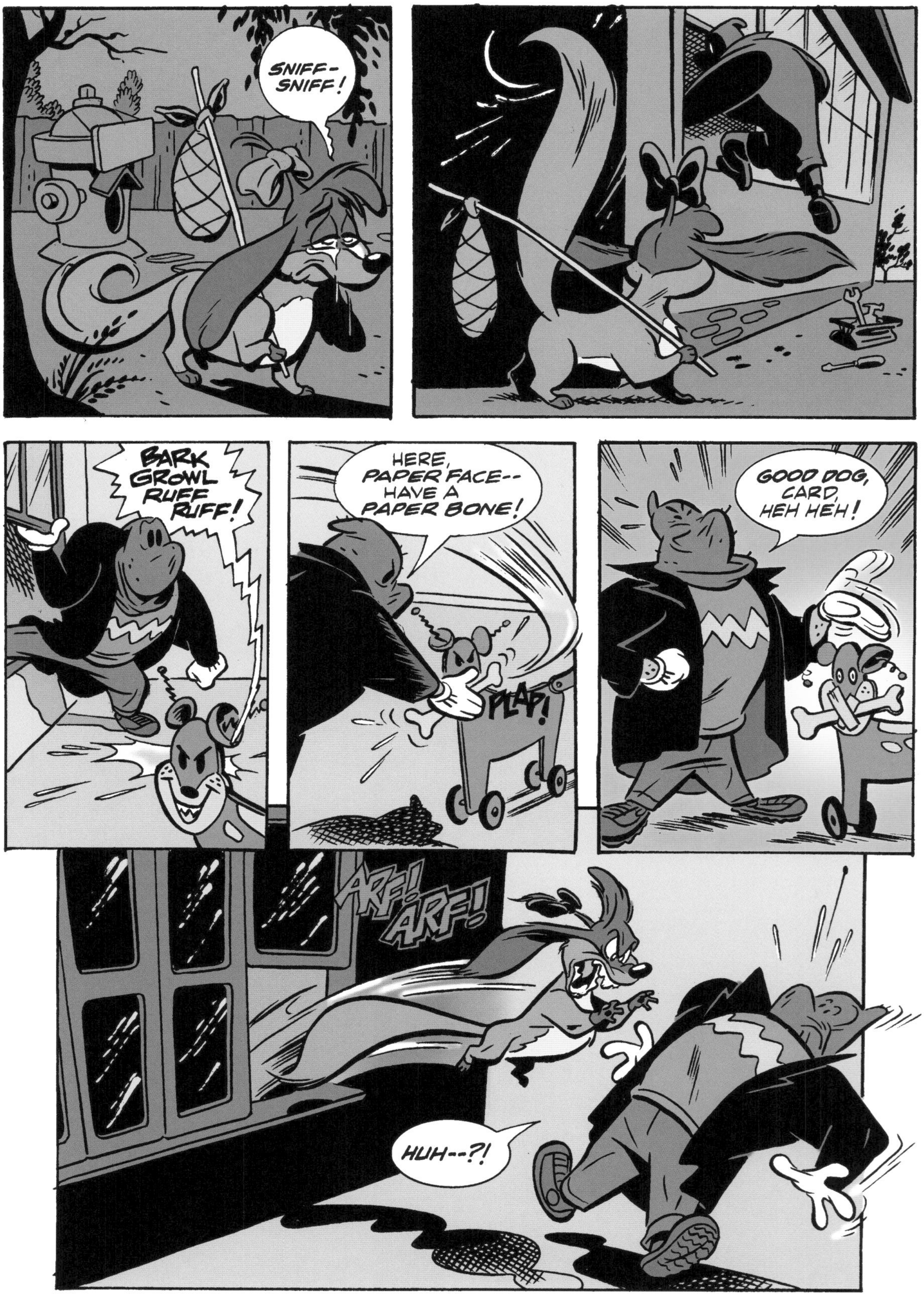
SNIFF-SNIFF!
BARK GROWL RUFF RUFF!
HERE, PAPER FACE-- HAVE A PAPER BONE!
PLAP!
GOOD DOG, CARD, HEH HEH!
ARF! ARF!
HUH--?!

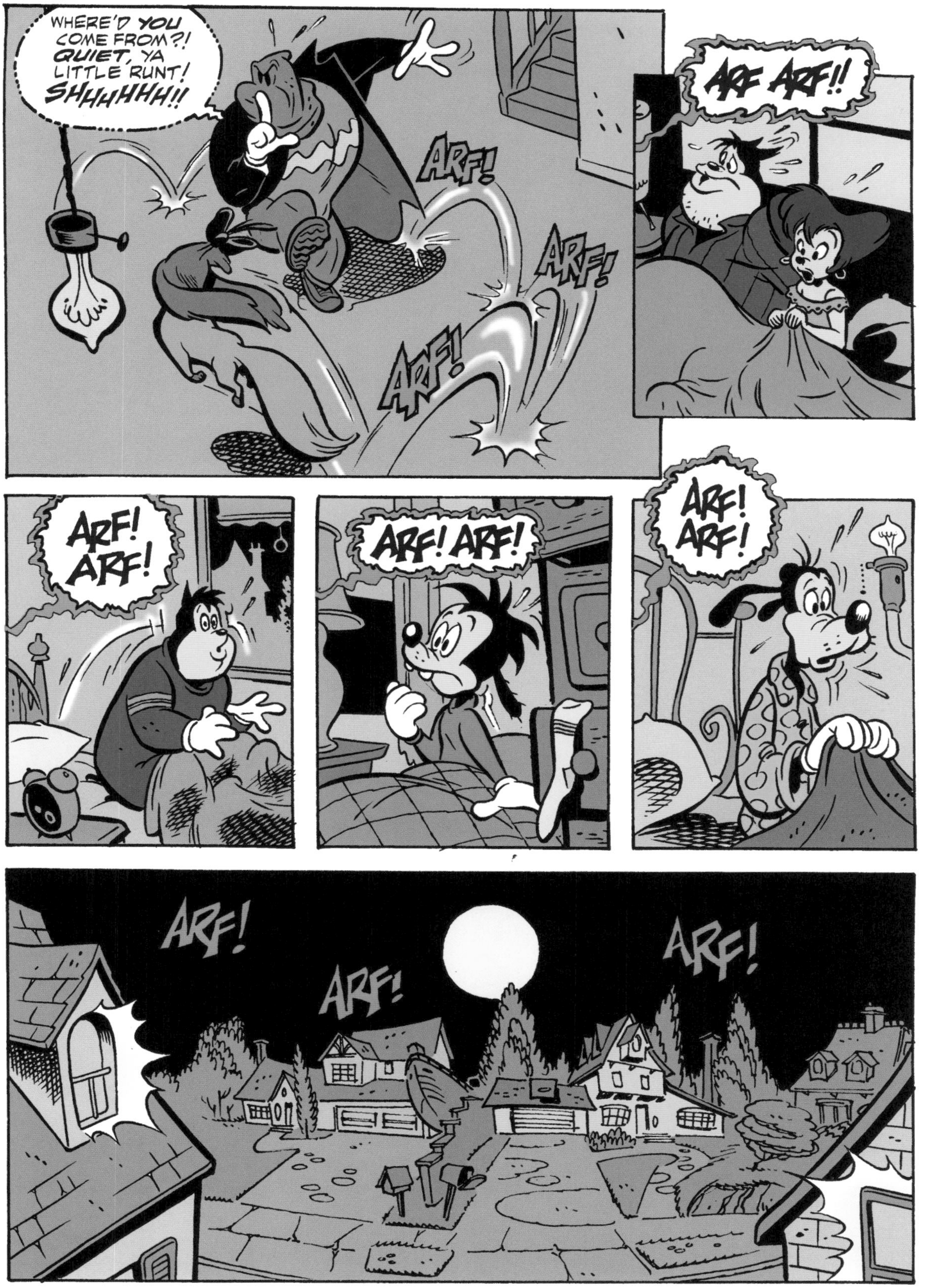
WHERE'D YOU COME FROM?! QUIET, YA LITTLE RUNT! SHHHHHH!!
ARF!
ARF!
ARF!
ARF ARF!!
ARF! ARF!
ARF! ARF!
ARF! ARF!
ARF!
ARF!
ARF!

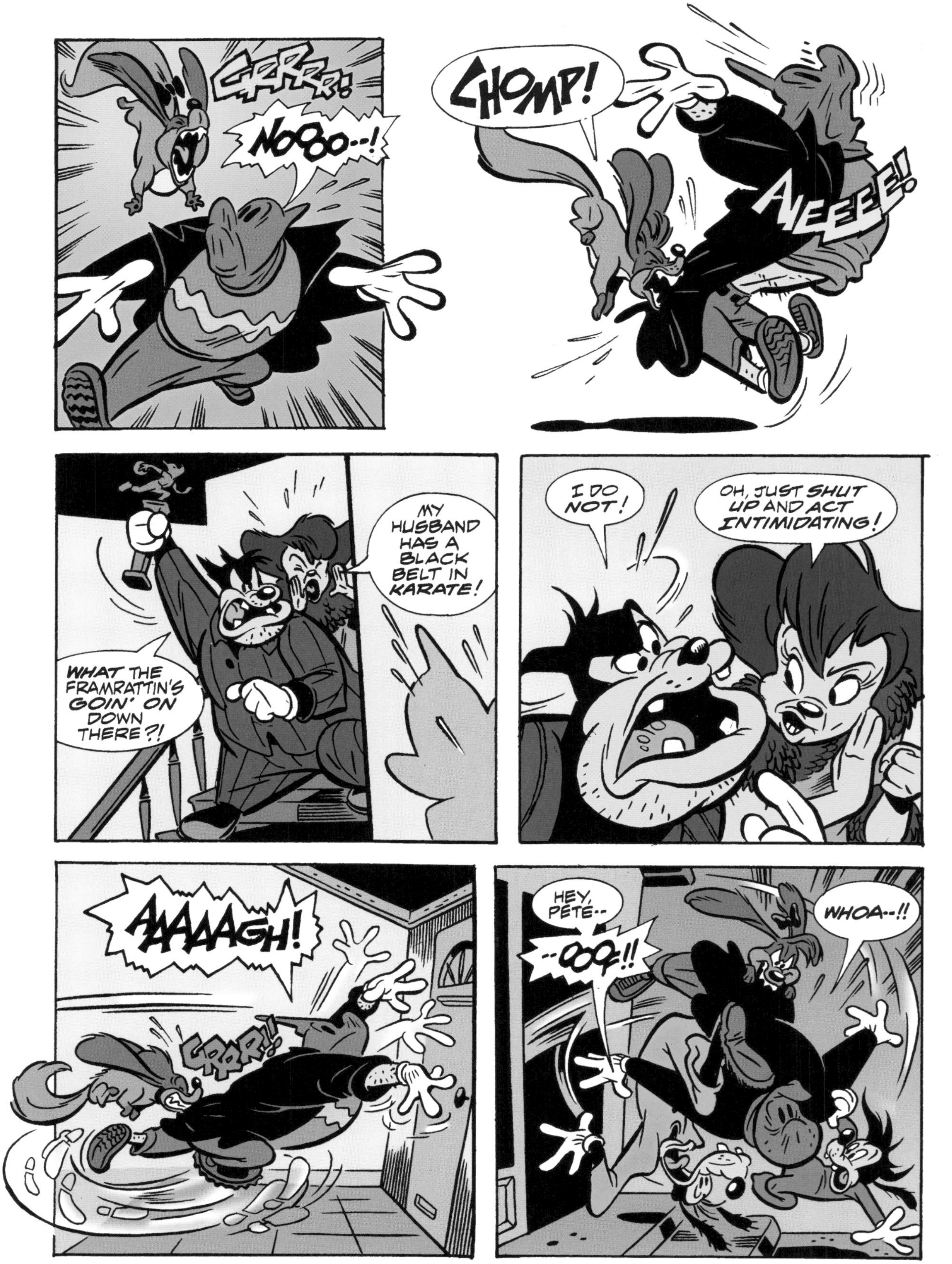
GRRRR!
NOOOOO--!
CHOMP!
AIEEEE!
MY HUSBAND HAS A BLACK BELT IN KARATE!
WHAT THE FRAMRATTIN'S GOIN' ON DOWN THERE?!
I DO NOT!
OH, JUST SHUT UP AND ACT INTIMIDATING!
AAAAAAGH!
GRRR!!
HEY, PETE--
--OOF!!
WHOA--!!

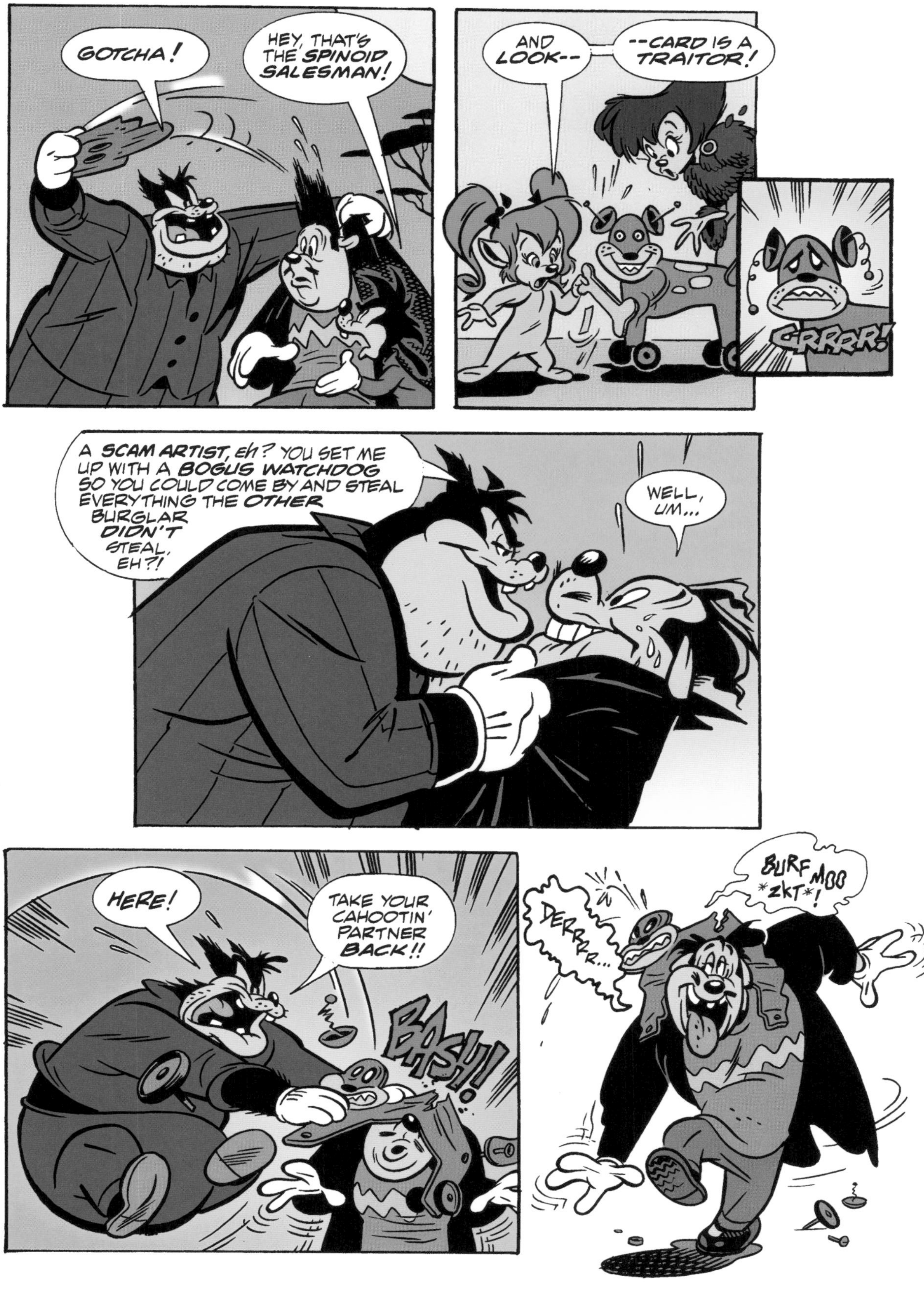
GOTCHA!
HEY, THAT'S THE SPINOID SALESMAN!
AND LOOK--
--CARD IS A TRAITOR!
GRRRR!
A SCAM ARTIST, eh? YOU SET ME UP WITH A BOGUS WATCHDOG SO YOU COULD COME BY AND STEAL EVERYTHING THE OTHER BURGLAR DIDN'T STEAL, EH?!
WELL, UM...
HERE!
TAKE YOUR CAHOOTIN' PARTNER BACK!!
BASH!!
DERRRR...
BURF MOO *ZKT*!

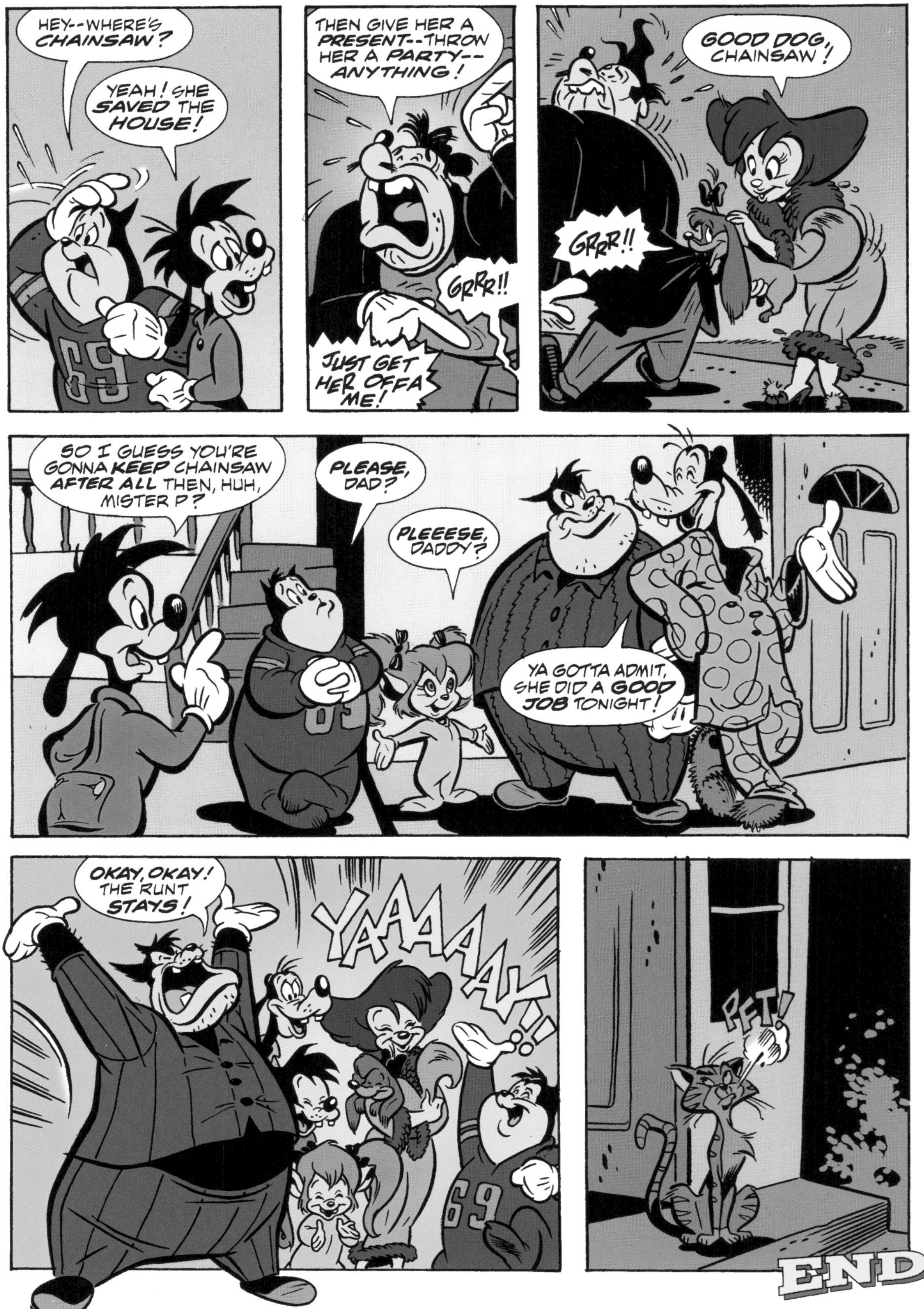
HEY--WHERE'S CHAINSAW?
YEAH! SHE SAVED THE HOUSE!
THEN GIVE HER A PRESENT--THROW HER A PARTY--ANYTHING!
GRRR!!
JUST GET HER OFFA ME!
GOOD DOG, CHAINSAW!
GRRR!!
SO I GUESS YOU'RE GONNA KEEP CHAINSAW AFTER ALL THEN, HUH, MISTER P?
PLEASE, DAD?
PLEEESE, DADDY?
YA GOTTA ADMIT, SHE DID A GOOD JOB TONIGHT!
OKAY, OKAY! THE RUNT STAYS!
YAAAAAY!!
PFT!
END

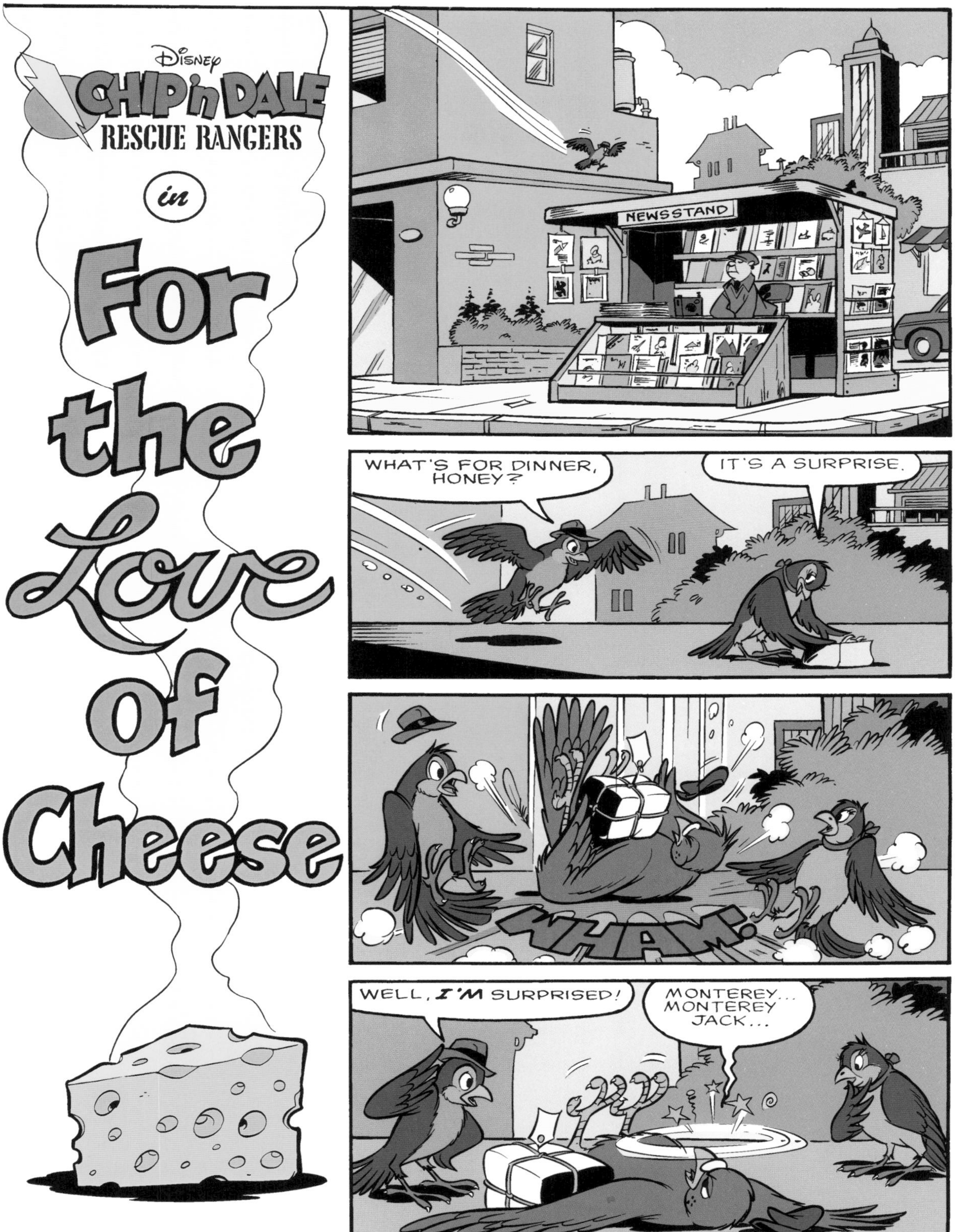
DISNEY
CHIP 'n DALE
RESCUE RANGERS
in
For the Love of Cheese
NEWSSTAND
WHAT'S FOR DINNER, HONEY?
IT'S A SURPRISE.
WHAM!
WELL, I'M SURPRISED!
MONTEREY... MONTEREY JACK...

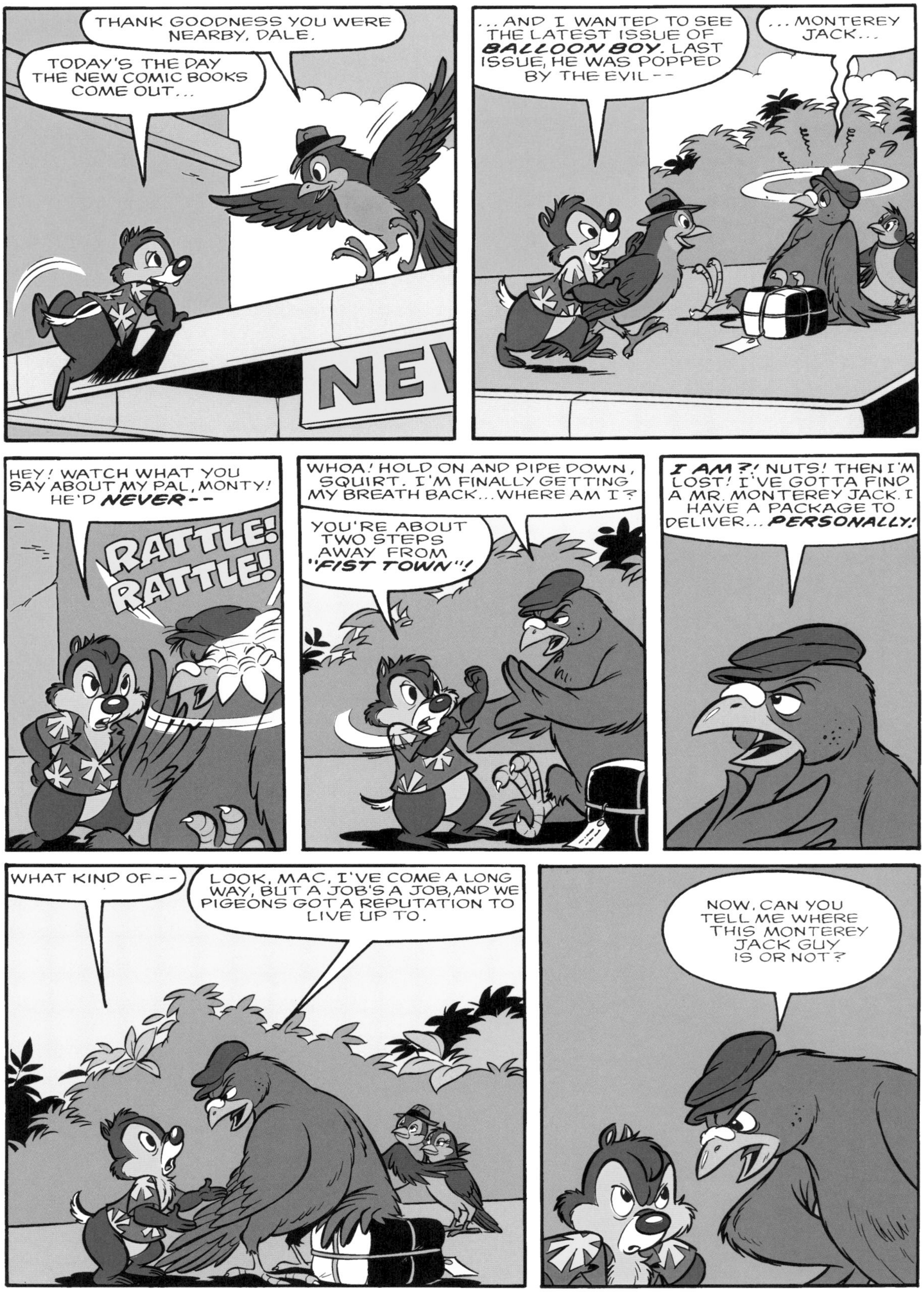
TODAY'S THE DAY THE NEW COMIC BOOKS COME OUT...
THANK GOODNESS YOU WERE NEARBY, DALE.
NEW
...AND I WANTED TO SEE THE LATEST ISSUE OF BALLOON BOY. LAST ISSUE, HE WAS POPPED BY THE EVIL--
...MONTEREY JACK...
HEY! WATCH WHAT YOU SAY ABOUT MY PAL, MONTY! HE'D NEVER--
RATTLE! RATTLE!
WHOA! HOLD ON AND PIPE DOWN, SQUIRT. I'M FINALLY GETTING MY BREATH BACK... WHERE AM I?
YOU'RE ABOUT TWO STEPS AWAY FROM "FIST TOWN"!
I AM?! NUTS! THEN I'M LOST! I'VE GOTTA FIND A MR. MONTEREY JACK. I HAVE A PACKAGE TO DELIVER... PERSONALLY!
WHAT KIND OF--
LOOK, MAC, I'VE COME A LONG WAY, BUT A JOB'S A JOB, AND WE PIGEONS GOT A REPUTATION TO LIVE UP TO.
NOW, CAN YOU TELL ME WHERE THIS MONTEREY JACK GUY IS OR NOT?

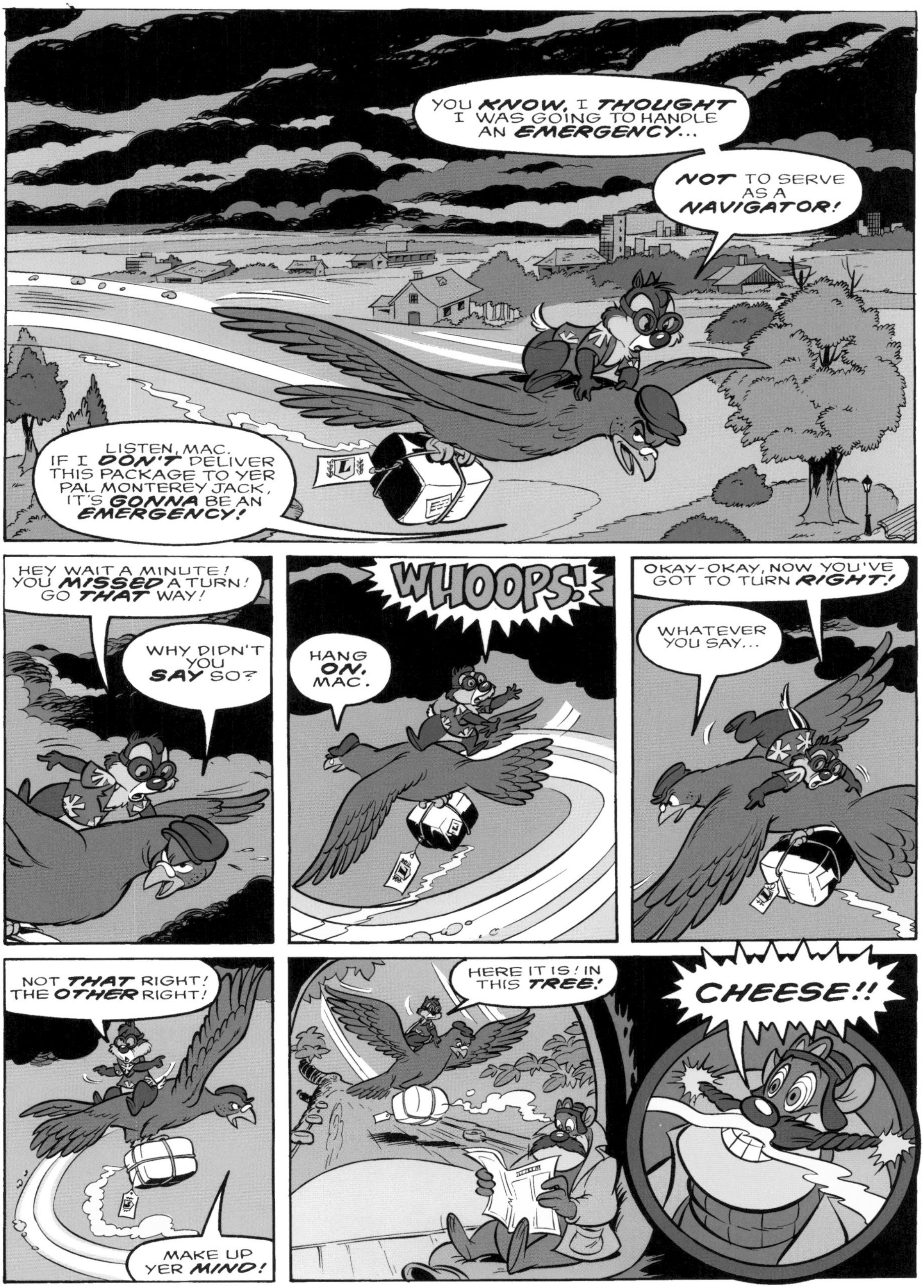

YOU KNOW, I THOUGHT I WAS GOING TO HANDLE AN EMERGENCY...
NOT TO SERVE AS A NAVIGATOR!
LISTEN, MAC. IF I DON'T DELIVER THIS PACKAGE TO YER PAL MONTEREY JACK, IT'S GONNA BE AN EMERGENCY!
HEY WAIT A MINUTE! YOU MISSED A TURN! GO THAT WAY!
WHY DIDN'T YOU SAY SO?
WHOOPS!
HANG ON, MAC.
OKAY-OKAY, NOW YOU'VE GOT TO TURN RIGHT!
WHATEVER YOU SAY...
NOT THAT RIGHT! THE OTHER RIGHT!
MAKE UP YER MIND!
HERE IT IS! IN THIS TREE!
CHEESE!!

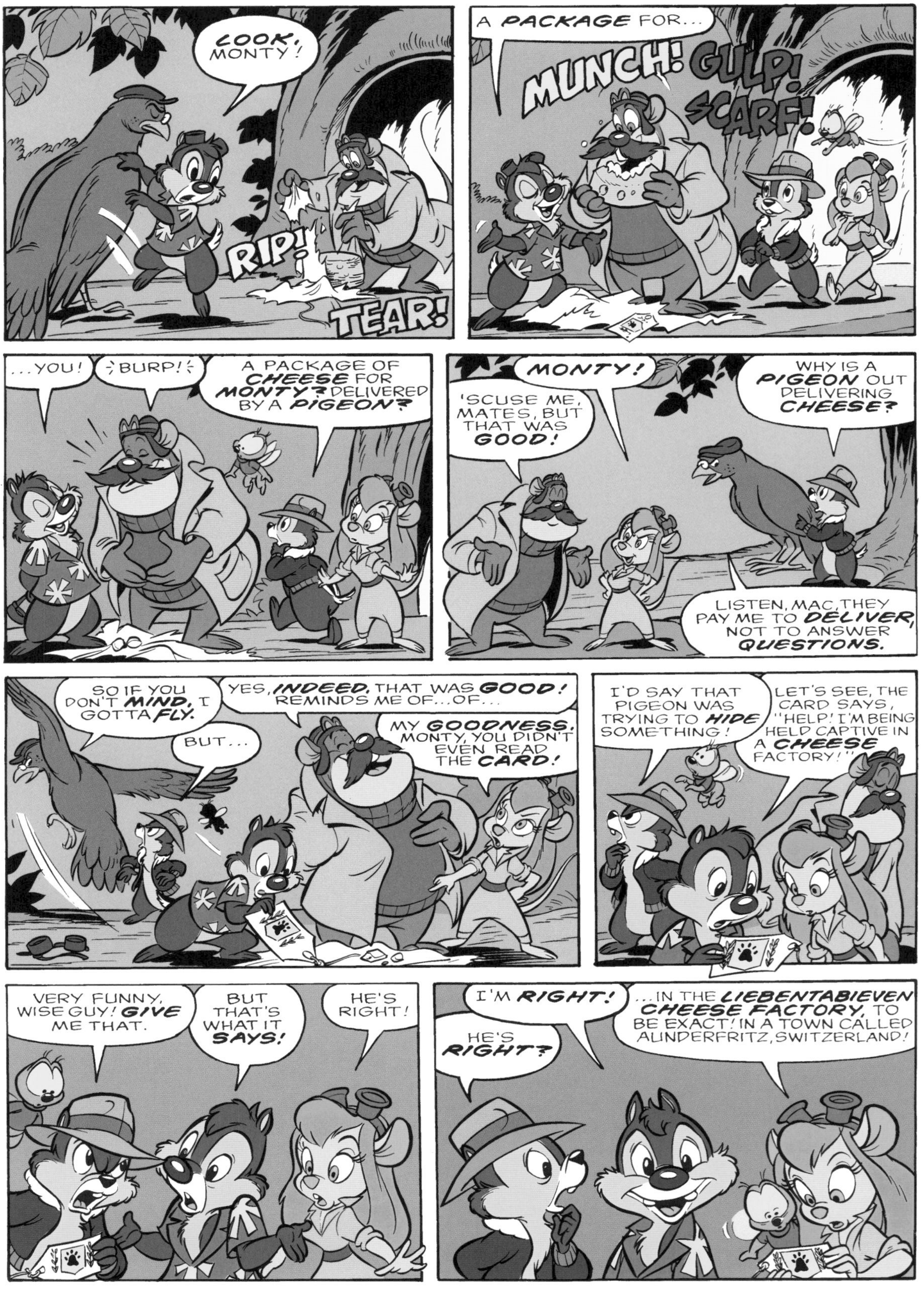
LOOK, MONTY!
RIP!
TEAR!
A PACKAGE FOR...
MUNCH! GULP! SCARF!
...YOU!
BURP!
A PACKAGE OF CHEESE FOR MONTY? DELIVERED BY A PIGEON?
MONTY!
'SCUSE ME, MATES, BUT THAT WAS GOOD!
WHY IS A PIGEON OUT DELIVERING CHEESE?
LISTEN, MAC, THEY PAY ME TO DELIVER, NOT TO ANSWER QUESTIONS.
SO IF YOU DON'T MIND, I GOTTA FLY.
BUT...
YES, INDEED. THAT WAS GOOD! REMINDS ME OF...OF...
MY GOODNESS. MONTY, YOU DIDN'T EVEN READ THE CARD!
I'D SAY THAT PIGEON WAS TRYING TO HIDE SOMETHING!
LET'S SEE, THE CARD SAYS, "HELP! I'M BEING HELD CAPTIVE IN A CHEESE FACTORY!"
VERY FUNNY, WISE GUY! GIVE ME THAT.
BUT THAT'S WHAT IT SAYS!
HE'S RIGHT!
HE'S RIGHT?
I'M RIGHT!
...IN THE LIEBENTABIEVEN CHEESE FACTORY, TO BE EXACT! IN A TOWN CALLED AUNDERFRITZ, SWITZERLAND!

I DON'T *BELIEVE* IT!

YOU'VE *HEARD* OF IT?

HEARD OF IT? LUV, THE *LIEBENTABIEVEN* CHEESE FACTORY *ONLY* PRODUCES THE BEST CHEESE ON *EARTH*!

BUT ITS LOCATION IS A *SECRET!* IT'S KIND OF A *LEGEND* AMONG US *CHEESE FANCIERS!*

A *CHEESE FACTORY* NOBODY CAN *FIND?*

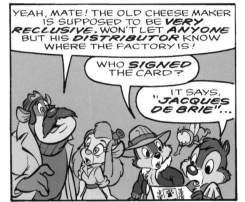

YEAH, MATE! THE OLD CHEESE MAKER IS SUPPOSED TO BE *VERY RECLUSIVE*. WON'T LET *ANYONE* BUT HIS *DISTRIBUTOR* KNOW WHERE THE FACTORY IS!

WHO *SIGNED* THE CARD?

IT SAYS, *"JACQUES DE BRIE"*...

JACQUES DE BRIE! BUT THAT'S *IMPOSSIBLE!*

IT *CAN'T* BE!

HUH?

WHAT'S THE BIG *MYSTERY* ABOUT A GUY CALLED JACQUES DE BRIE?

M-MONTY TOLD ME-- MONTY'S *CERTAIN*-- THAT JACQUES DE BRIE IS *DEAD!*

GASP!

IT'S *TRUE*, LADS. WITH ME OWN *EYES*, I SAW POOR JACQUES FALL TO HIS DEATH OVER REICHENROLL FALLS.

YOU WERE CROSSING *REICHENROLL FALLS?* WHY?

BECAUSE JACQUES AND I WERE ON A *SEARCH*...

...A *SEARCH* FOR THE LIEBENTABIEVEN *CHEESE* FACTORY!

RANGERS, I'D SAY WE HAVE A *MYSTERY* ON OUR HANDS!

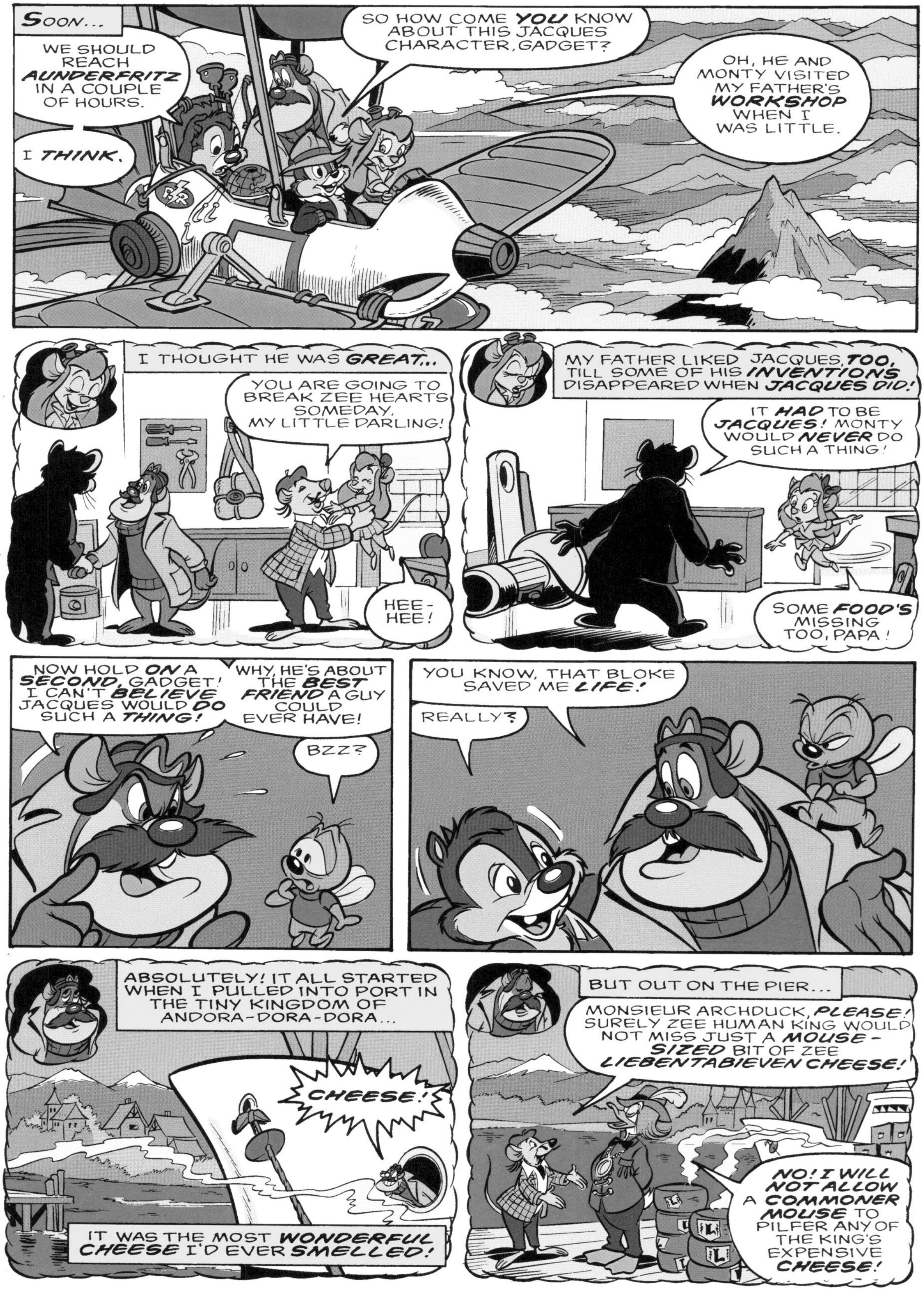
SOON...
WE SHOULD REACH AUNDERFRITZ IN A COUPLE OF HOURS.
I THINK.
SO HOW COME YOU KNOW ABOUT THIS JACQUES CHARACTER, GADGET?
OH, HE AND MONTY VISITED MY FATHER'S WORKSHOP WHEN I WAS LITTLE.
I THOUGHT HE WAS GREAT...
YOU ARE GOING TO BREAK ZEE HEARTS SOMEDAY, MY LITTLE DARLING!
HEE-HEE!
MY FATHER LIKED JACQUES, TOO, TILL SOME OF HIS INVENTIONS DISAPPEARED WHEN JACQUES DID!
IT HAD TO BE JACQUES! MONTY WOULD NEVER DO SUCH A THING!
SOME FOOD'S MISSING TOO, PAPA!
NOW HOLD ON A SECOND, GADGET! I CAN'T BELIEVE JACQUES WOULD DO SUCH A THING!
WHY, HE'S ABOUT THE BEST FRIEND A GUY COULD EVER HAVE!
BZZ?
YOU KNOW, THAT BLOKE SAVED ME LIFE!
REALLY?
ABSOLUTELY! IT ALL STARTED WHEN I PULLED INTO PORT IN THE TINY KINGDOM OF ANDORA-DORA-DORA...
CHEESE!
IT WAS THE MOST WONDERFUL CHEESE I'D EVER SMELLED!
BUT OUT ON THE PIER...
MONSIEUR ARCHDUCK, PLEASE! SURELY ZEE HUMAN KING WOULD NOT MISS JUST A MOUSE-SIZED BIT OF ZEE LIEBENTABIEVEN CHEESE!
NO! I WILL NOT ALLOW A COMMONER MOUSE TO PILFER ANY OF THE KING'S EXPENSIVE CHEESE!

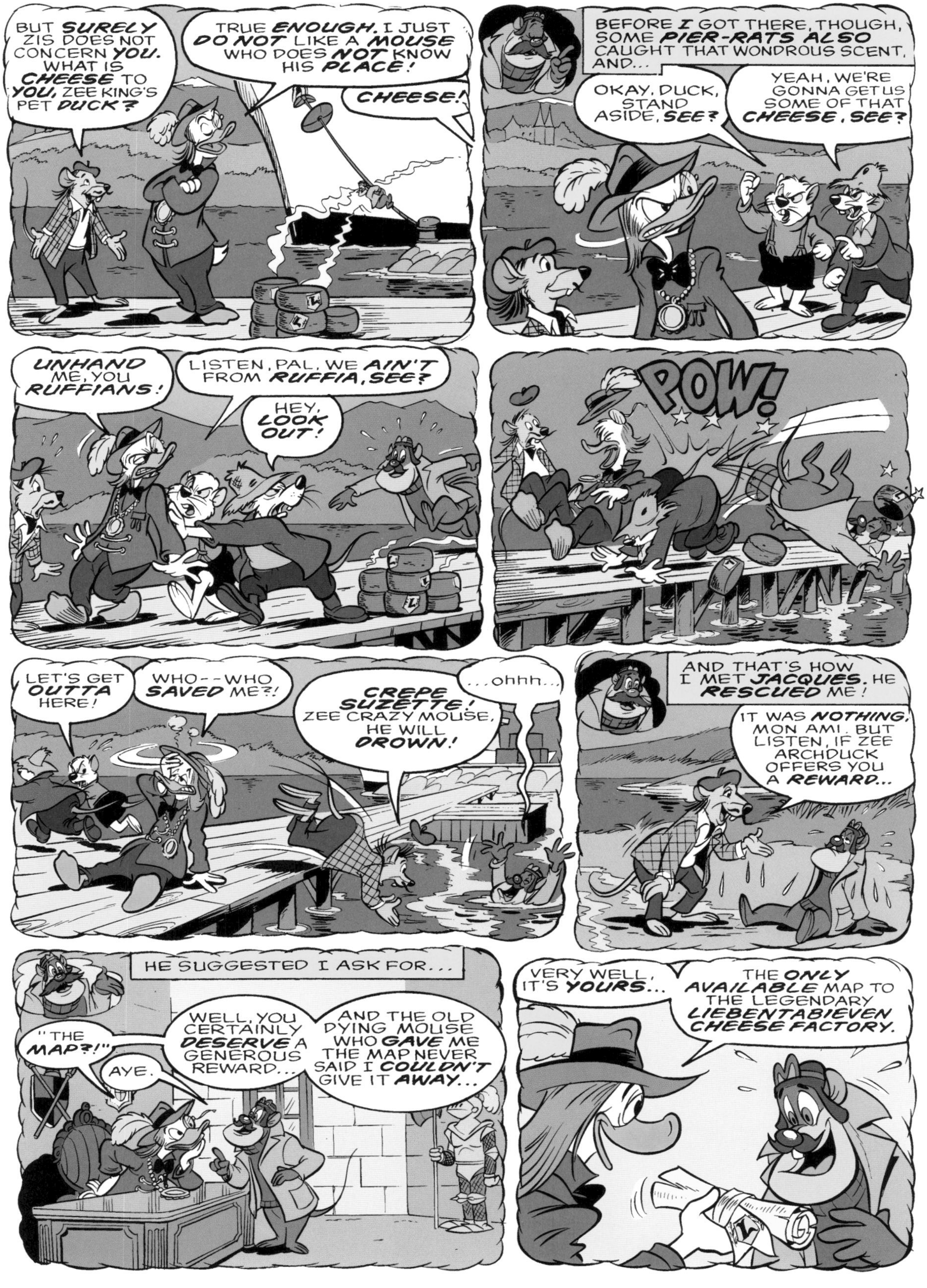

BUT SURELY ZIS DOES NOT CONCERN YOU. WHAT IS CHEESE TO YOU, ZEE KING'S PET DUCK?
TRUE ENOUGH. I JUST DO NOT LIKE A MOUSE WHO DOES NOT KNOW HIS PLACE!
CHEESE!
BEFORE I GOT THERE, THOUGH, SOME PIER-RATS ALSO CAUGHT THAT WONDROUS SCENT, AND...
OKAY, DUCK, STAND ASIDE, SEE?
YEAH, WE'RE GONNA GET US SOME OF THAT CHEESE, SEE?
UNHAND ME, YOU RUFFIANS!
LISTEN, PAL, WE AIN'T FROM RUFFIA, SEE?
HEY, LOOK OUT!
POW!
LET'S GET OUTTA HERE!
WHO--WHO SAVED ME?!
CREPE SUZETTE! ZEE CRAZY MOUSE, HE WILL DROWN!
...ohhh...
AND THAT'S HOW I MET JACQUES. HE RESCUED ME!
IT WAS NOTHING, MON AMI. BUT LISTEN, IF ZEE ARCHDUCK OFFERS YOU A REWARD...
HE SUGGESTED I ASK FOR...
"THE MAP?!"
AYE.
WELL, YOU CERTAINLY DESERVE A GENEROUS REWARD...
AND THE OLD DYING MOUSE WHO GAVE ME THE MAP NEVER SAID I COULDN'T GIVE IT AWAY...
VERY WELL, IT'S YOURS...
THE ONLY AVAILABLE MAP TO THE LEGENDARY LIEBENTABIEVEN CHEESE FACTORY.

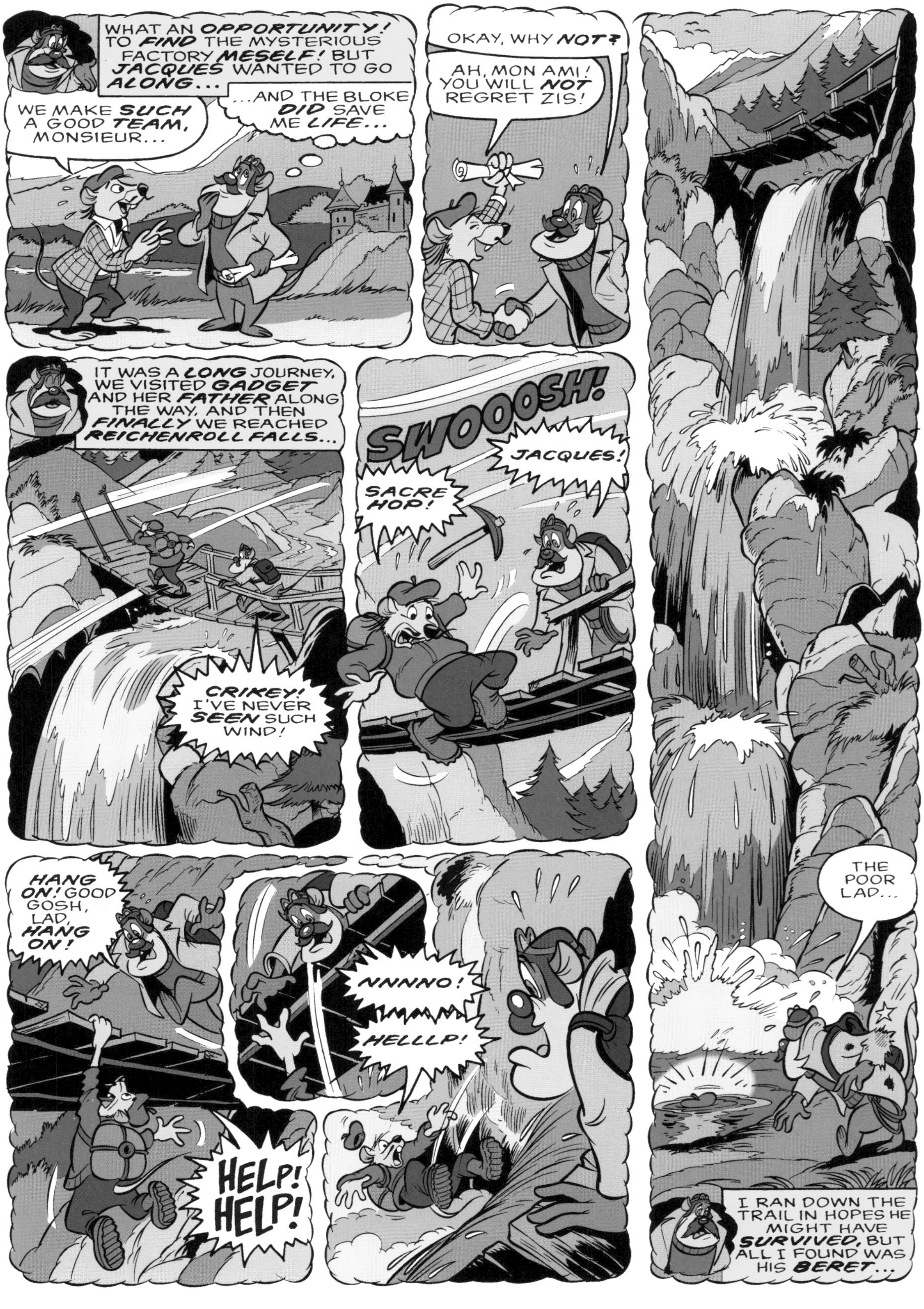

WHAT AN OPPORTUNITY! TO FIND THE MYSTERIOUS FACTORY MESELF! BUT JACQUES WANTED TO GO ALONG...
WE MAKE SUCH A GOOD TEAM, MONSIEUR...
...AND THE BLOKE DID SAVE ME LIFE...
OKAY, WHY NOT?
AH, MON AMI! YOU WILL NOT REGRET ZIS!
IT WAS A LONG JOURNEY, WE VISITED GADGET AND HER FATHER ALONG THE WAY, AND THEN FINALLY WE REACHED REICHENROLL FALLS...
CRIKEY! I'VE NEVER SEEN SUCH WIND!
SWOOOOSH!
JACQUES!
SACRE HOP!
HANG ON! GOOD GOSH, LAD, HANG ON!
HELP! HELP!
NNNNO!
HELLLP!
THE POOR LAD...
I RAN DOWN THE TRAIL IN HOPES HE MIGHT HAVE SURVIVED, BUT ALL I FOUND WAS HIS BERET...

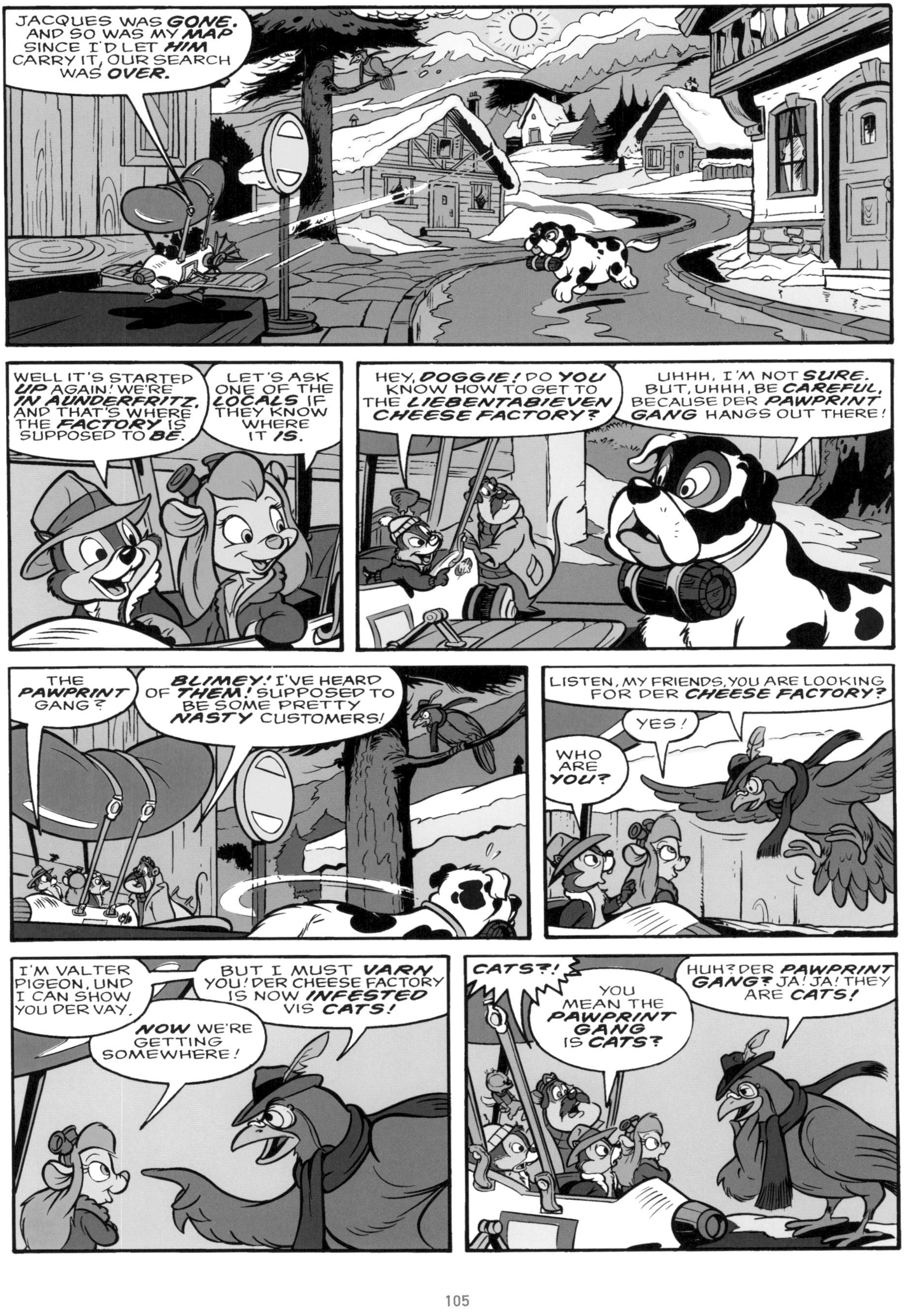
JACQUES WAS GONE. AND SO WAS MY MAP SINCE I'D LET HIM CARRY IT, OUR SEARCH WAS OVER.
WELL IT'S STARTED UP AGAIN! WE'RE IN AUNDERFRITZ, AND THAT'S WHERE THE FACTORY IS SUPPOSED TO BE.
LET'S ASK ONE OF THE LOCALS IF THEY KNOW WHERE IT IS.
HEY, DOGGIE! DO YOU KNOW HOW TO GET TO THE LIEBENTABIEVEN CHEESE FACTORY?
UHHH, I'M NOT SURE. BUT, UHHH, BE CAREFUL, BECAUSE DER PAWPRINT GANG HANGS OUT THERE!
THE PAWPRINT GANG?
BLIMEY! I'VE HEARD OF THEM! SUPPOSED TO BE SOME PRETTY NASTY CUSTOMERS!
LISTEN, MY FRIENDS, YOU ARE LOOKING FOR DER CHEESE FACTORY?
YES!
WHO ARE YOU?
I'M VALTER PIGEON, UND I CAN SHOW YOU DER VAY.
NOW WE'RE GETTING SOMEWHERE!
BUT I MUST VARN YOU! DER CHEESE FACTORY IS NOW INFESTED VIS CATS!
CATS?!
YOU MEAN THE PAWPRINT GANG IS CATS?
HUH? DER PAWPRINT GANG? JA! JA! THEY ARE CATS!

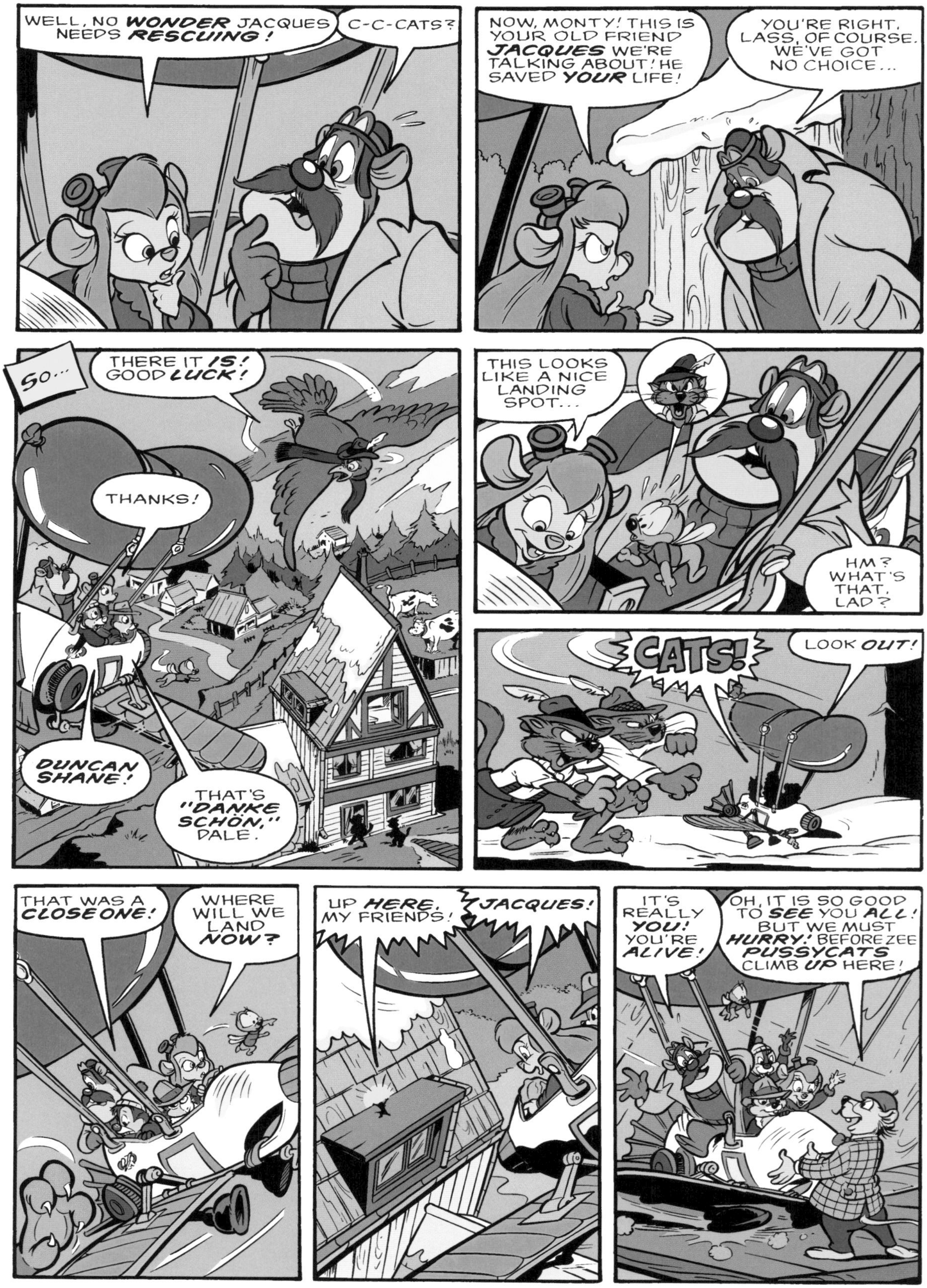
WELL, NO WONDER JACQUES NEEDS RESCUING!
C-C-CATS?
NOW, MONTY! THIS IS YOUR OLD FRIEND JACQUES WE'RE TALKING ABOUT! HE SAVED YOUR LIFE!
YOU'RE RIGHT, LASS, OF COURSE. WE'VE GOT NO CHOICE...
SO...
THERE IT IS! GOOD LUCK!
THANKS!
DUNCAN SHANE!
THAT'S "DANKE SCHÖN," DALE.
THIS LOOKS LIKE A NICE LANDING SPOT...
HM? WHAT'S THAT, LAD?
CATS!
LOOK OUT!
THAT WAS A CLOSE ONE!
WHERE WILL WE LAND NOW?
UP HERE, MY FRIENDS!
JACQUES!
IT'S REALLY YOU! YOU'RE ALIVE!
OH, IT IS SO GOOD TO SEE YOU ALL! BUT WE MUST HURRY! BEFORE ZEE PUSSYCATS CLIMB UP HERE!

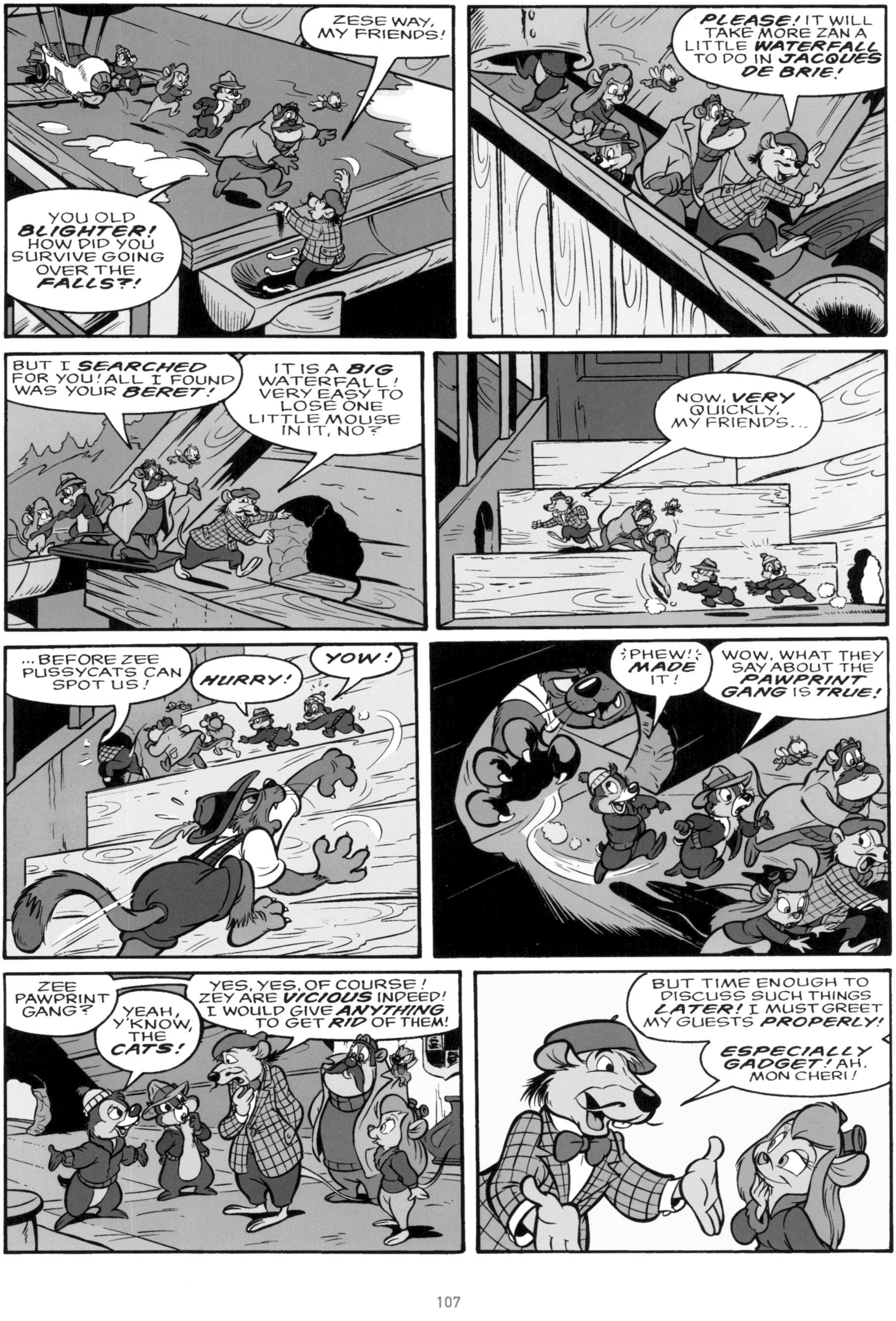
ZESE WAY, MY FRIENDS!
YOU OLD BLIGHTER! HOW DID YOU SURVIVE GOING OVER THE FALLS?!
PLEASE! IT WILL TAKE MORE ZAN A LITTLE WATERFALL TO DO IN JACQUES DE BRIE!
BUT I SEARCHED FOR YOU! ALL I FOUND WAS YOUR BERET!
IT IS A BIG WATERFALL! VERY EASY TO LOSE ONE LITTLE MOUSE IN IT, NO?
NOW, VERY QUICKLY, MY FRIENDS...
...BEFORE ZEE PUSSYCATS CAN SPOT US!
HURRY!
YOW!
PHEW! MADE IT!
WOW, WHAT THEY SAY ABOUT THE PAWPRINT GANG IS TRUE!
ZEE PAWPRINT GANG?
YEAH, Y'KNOW, THE CATS!
YES, YES, OF COURSE! ZEY ARE VICIOUS INDEED! I WOULD GIVE ANYTHING TO GET RID OF THEM!
BUT TIME ENOUGH TO DISCUSS SUCH THINGS LATER! I MUST GREET MY GUESTS PROPERLY!
ESPECIALLY GADGET! AH, MON CHERI!

OH, JACQUES, IT'S SO GOOD TO **SEE** YOU AGAIN!

ZEE PLEASURE IS **MINE**, TRULY! YOU HAVE **BLOSSOMED** INTO SUCH A **BEAUTIFUL FLOWER!**

OH, BROTHER!

AND SHE'S **FALLING** FOR IT!

BZZ!

BUT SUCH AN **HONOR** IT IS TO BE VISITED BY **CHIP** AND **DALE!**

HUH?

MY FRIENDS, I HAVE HEARD **SUCH** STORIES ABOUT YOUR **HEROIC EXPLOITS!**

REALLY?

BZZ?

I WILL **ALWAYS** BE IN YOUR **DEBT** FOR COMING TO MY **AID!** TRULY!

WELL, GEE, ALWAYS GLAD TO HELP!

YEAH! **ANY** TIME!

...BZZZ...

CRIKEY! THIS PLACE IS **FANTASTIC!**

I'VE NEVER **SEEN** SO MANY WONDERFUL **THINGS** UNDER ONE **ROOF!**

YOU CERTAINLY HAVE DONE **WELL** FOR YOURSELF, MATE!

ZESE TRIFLES? **PEH!** OLD MAN LIEBENTABIEVEN, HE IS **FOND** OF ME!

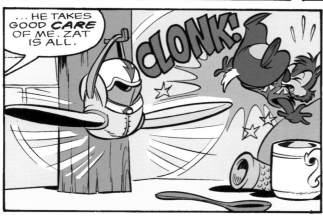

...HE TAKES GOOD **CARE** OF ME. ZAT IS ALL.

CLONK!

CRASH! SMASH! BAM! TINKLE!

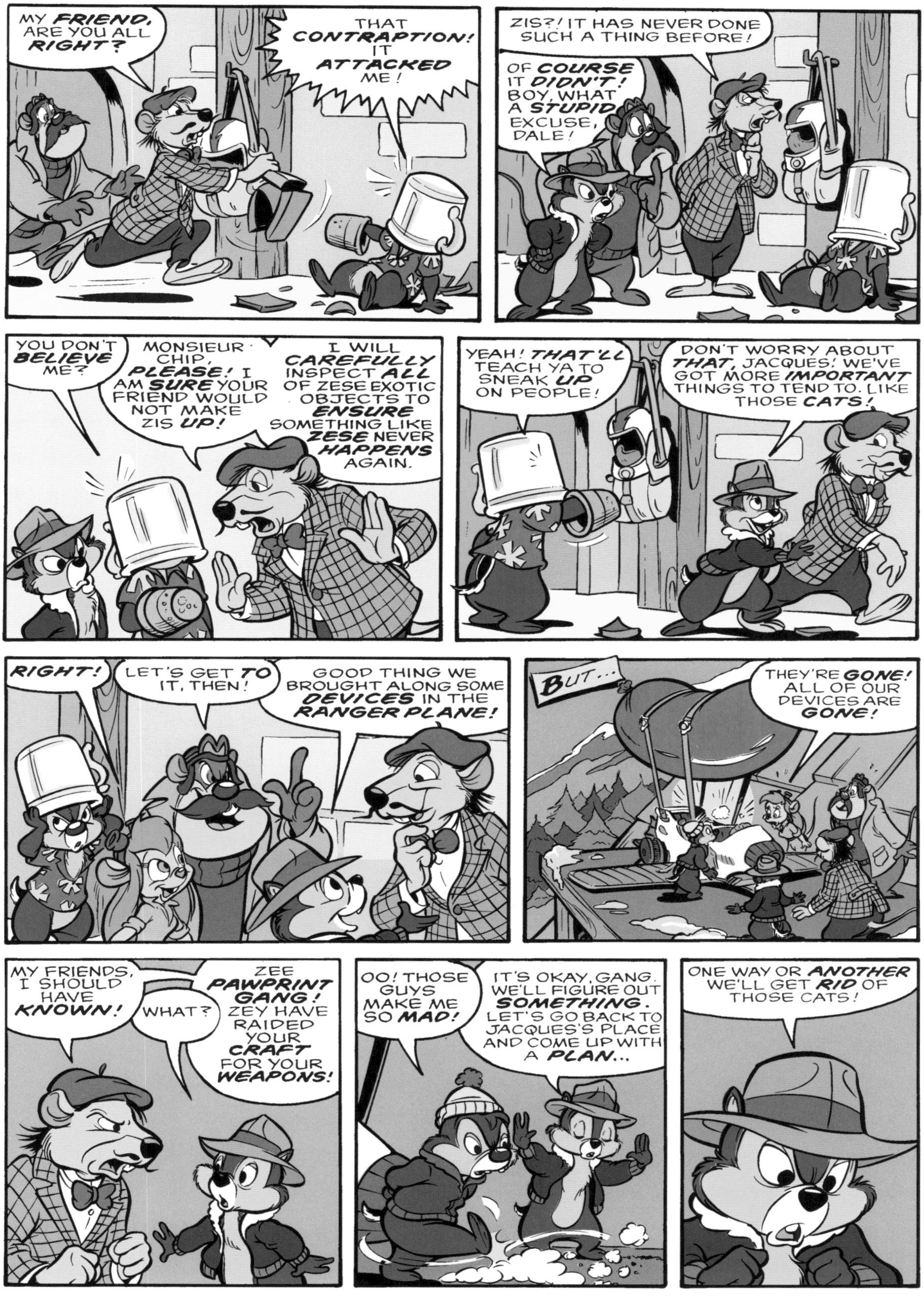

MY FRIEND, ARE YOU ALL RIGHT?
THAT CONTRAPTION! IT ATTACKED ME!
ZIS?! IT HAS NEVER DONE SUCH A THING BEFORE!
OF COURSE IT DIDN'T! BOY, WHAT A STUPID EXCUSE, DALE!
YOU DON'T BELIEVE ME?
MONSIEUR CHIP, PLEASE! I AM SURE YOUR FRIEND WOULD NOT MAKE ZIS UP!
I WILL CAREFULLY INSPECT ALL OF ZESE EXOTIC OBJECTS TO ENSURE SOMETHING LIKE ZESE NEVER HAPPENS AGAIN.
YEAH! THAT'LL TEACH YA TO SNEAK UP ON PEOPLE!
DON'T WORRY ABOUT THAT, JACQUES! WE'VE GOT MORE IMPORTANT THINGS TO TEND TO. LIKE THOSE CATS!
RIGHT!
LET'S GET TO IT, THEN!
GOOD THING WE BROUGHT ALONG SOME DEVICES IN THE RANGER PLANE!
BUT...
THEY'RE GONE! ALL OF OUR DEVICES ARE GONE!
MY FRIENDS, I SHOULD HAVE KNOWN!
WHAT?
ZEE PAWPRINT GANG! ZEY HAVE RAIDED YOUR CRAFT FOR YOUR WEAPONS!
OO! THOSE GUYS MAKE ME SO MAD!
IT'S OKAY, GANG. WE'LL FIGURE OUT SOMETHING. LET'S GO BACK TO JACQUES'S PLACE AND COME UP WITH A PLAN...
ONE WAY OR ANOTHER WE'LL GET RID OF THOSE CATS!

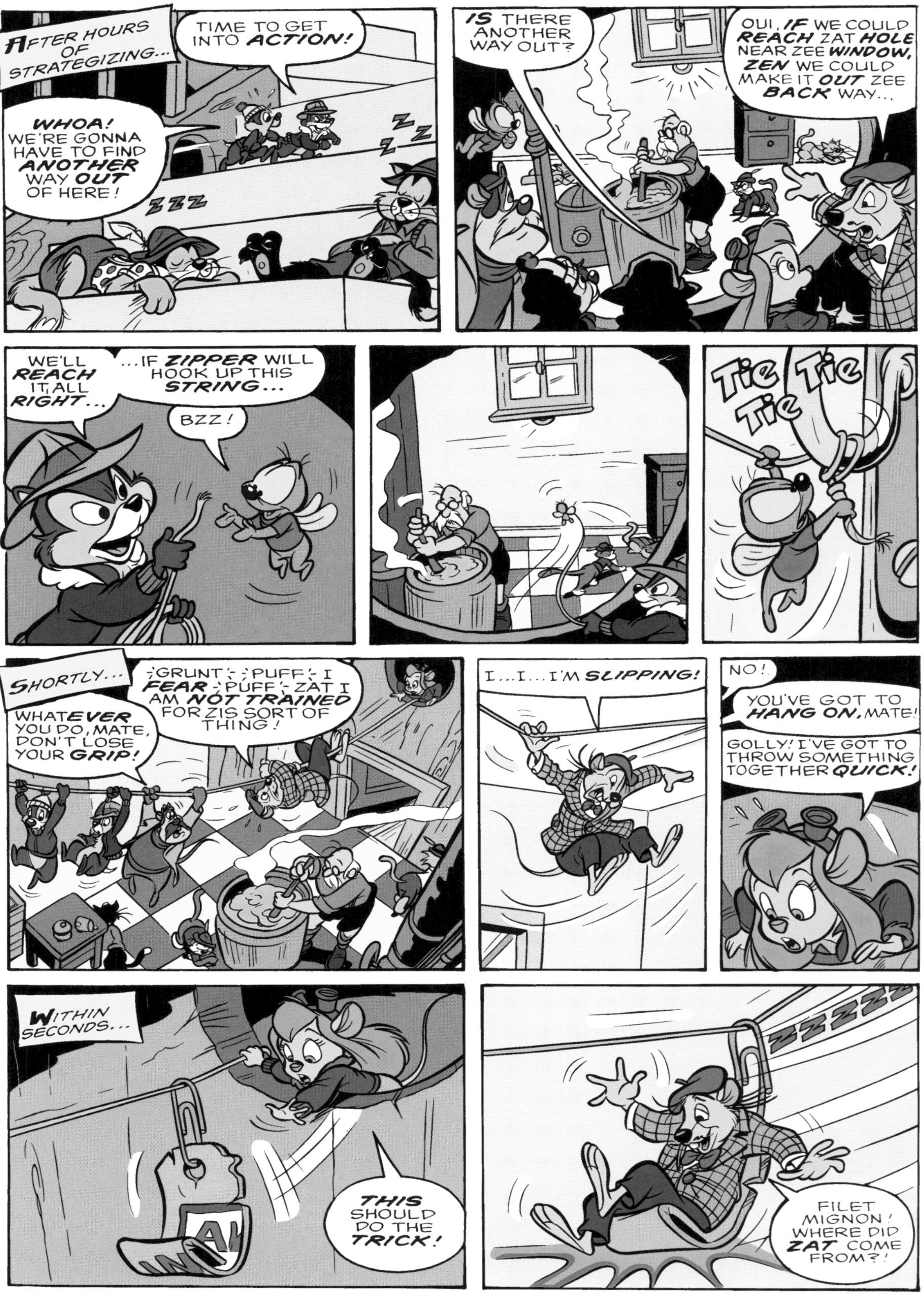

AFTER HOURS OF STRATEGIZING...
TIME TO GET INTO ACTION!
WHOA! WE'RE GONNA HAVE TO FIND ANOTHER WAY OUT OF HERE!
ZZZ
ZZZ
IS THERE ANOTHER WAY OUT?
OUI, IF WE COULD REACH ZAT HOLE NEAR ZEE WINDOW, ZEN WE COULD MAKE IT OUT ZEE BACK WAY...
WE'LL REACH IT, ALL RIGHT...
...IF ZIPPER WILL HOOK UP THIS STRING...
BZZ!
Tie Tie Tie
SHORTLY...
WHATEVER YOU DO, MATE, DON'T LOSE YOUR GRIP!
GRUNT PUFF I FEAR PUFF ZAT I AM NOT TRAINED FOR ZIS SORT OF THING!
I...I...I'M SLIPPING!
NO!
YOU'VE GOT TO HANG ON, MATE!
GOLLY! I'VE GOT TO THROW SOMETHING TOGETHER QUICK!
WITHIN SECONDS...
THIS SHOULD DO THE TRICK!
FILET MIGNON! WHERE DID ZAT COME FROM?!

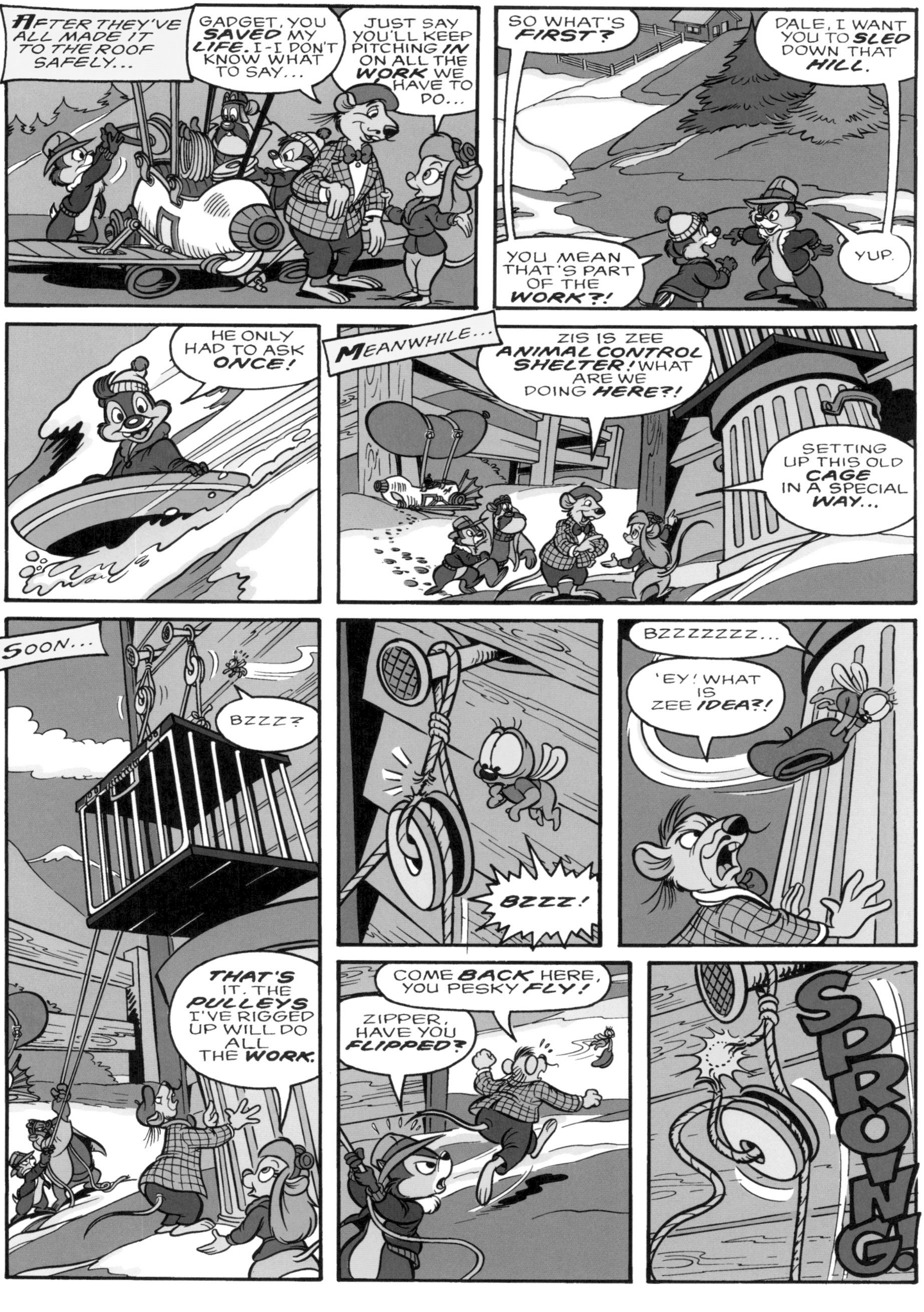
AFTER THEY'VE ALL MADE IT TO THE ROOF SAFELY...
GADGET, YOU SAVED MY LIFE. I-I DON'T KNOW WHAT TO SAY...
JUST SAY YOU'LL KEEP PITCHING IN ON ALL THE WORK WE HAVE TO DO...
SO WHAT'S FIRST?
DALE, I WANT YOU TO SLED DOWN THAT HILL.
YOU MEAN THAT'S PART OF THE WORK?!
YUP.
HE ONLY HAD TO ASK ONCE!
MEANWHILE...
ZIS IS ZEE ANIMAL CONTROL SHELTER! WHAT ARE WE DOING HERE?!
SETTING UP THIS OLD CAGE IN A SPECIAL WAY...
SOON...
BZZZ?
THAT'S IT. THE PULLEYS I'VE RIGGED UP WILL DO ALL THE WORK.
BZZZ!
BZZZZZZZ...
'EY! WHAT IS ZEE IDEA?!
COME BACK HERE, YOU PESKY FLY!
ZIPPER, HAVE YOU FLIPPED?
SPROING!

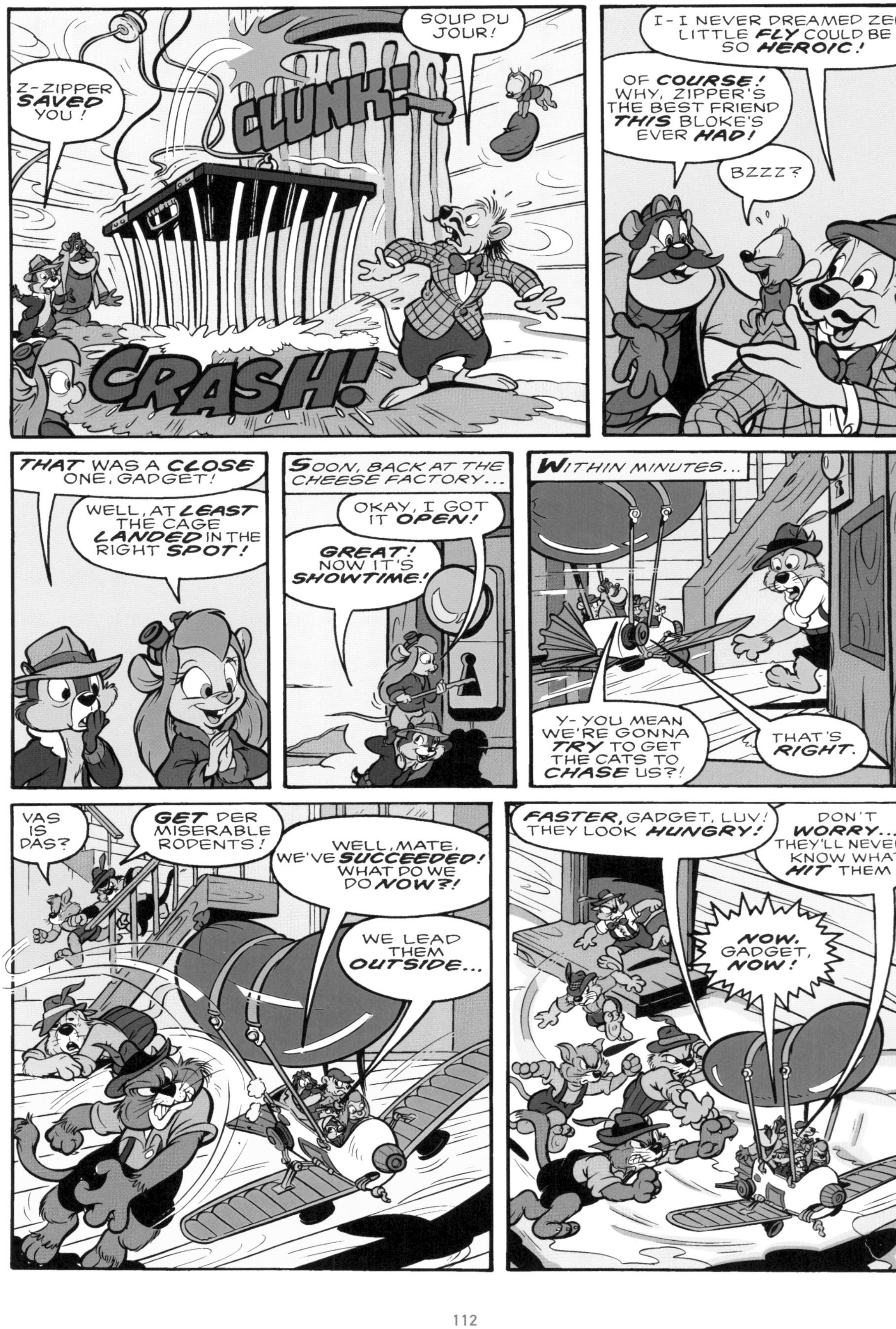
Z-ZIPPER SAVED YOU!
SOUP DU JOUR!
CLUNK!
CRASH!
I-I NEVER DREAMED ZEE LITTLE FLY COULD BE SO HEROIC!
OF COURSE! WHY, ZIPPER'S THE BEST FRIEND THIS BLOKE'S EVER HAD!
BZZZ?
THAT WAS A CLOSE ONE, GADGET!
WELL, AT LEAST THE CAGE LANDED IN THE RIGHT SPOT!
SOON, BACK AT THE CHEESE FACTORY...
OKAY, I GOT IT OPEN!
GREAT! NOW IT'S SHOWTIME!
WITHIN MINUTES...
Y-YOU MEAN WE'RE GONNA TRY TO GET THE CATS TO CHASE US?!
THAT'S RIGHT.
VAS IS DAS?
GET DER MISERABLE RODENTS!
WELL, MATE, WE'VE SUCCEEDED! WHAT DO WE DO NOW?!
WE LEAD THEM OUTSIDE...
FASTER, GADGET, LUV! THEY LOOK HUNGRY!
DON'T WORRY... THEY'LL NEVER KNOW WHAT HIT THEM!
NOW. GADGET, NOW!

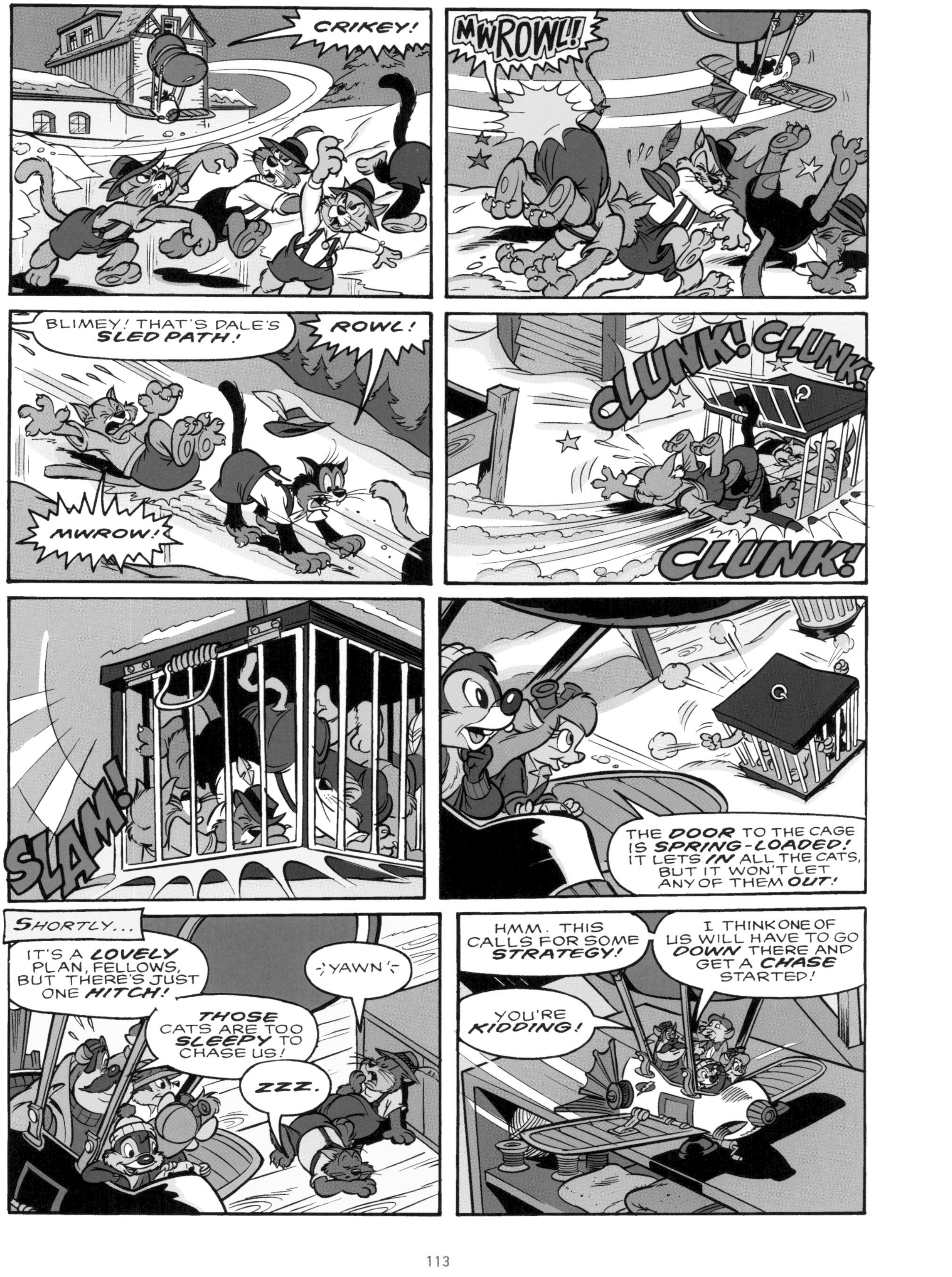

CRIKEY!
MWROWL!!
BLIMEY! THAT'S DALE'S SLED PATH!
ROWL!
MWROW!
CLUNK! CLUNK!
CLUNK!
SLAM!
THE DOOR TO THE CAGE IS SPRING-LOADED! IT LETS IN ALL THE CATS, BUT IT WON'T LET ANY OF THEM OUT!
SHORTLY...
IT'S A LOVELY PLAN, FELLOWS, BUT THERE'S JUST ONE HITCH!
YAWN
THOSE CATS ARE TOO SLEEPY TO CHASE US!
ZZZ.
HMM. THIS CALLS FOR SOME STRATEGY!
I THINK ONE OF US WILL HAVE TO GO DOWN THERE AND GET A CHASE STARTED!
YOU'RE KIDDING!

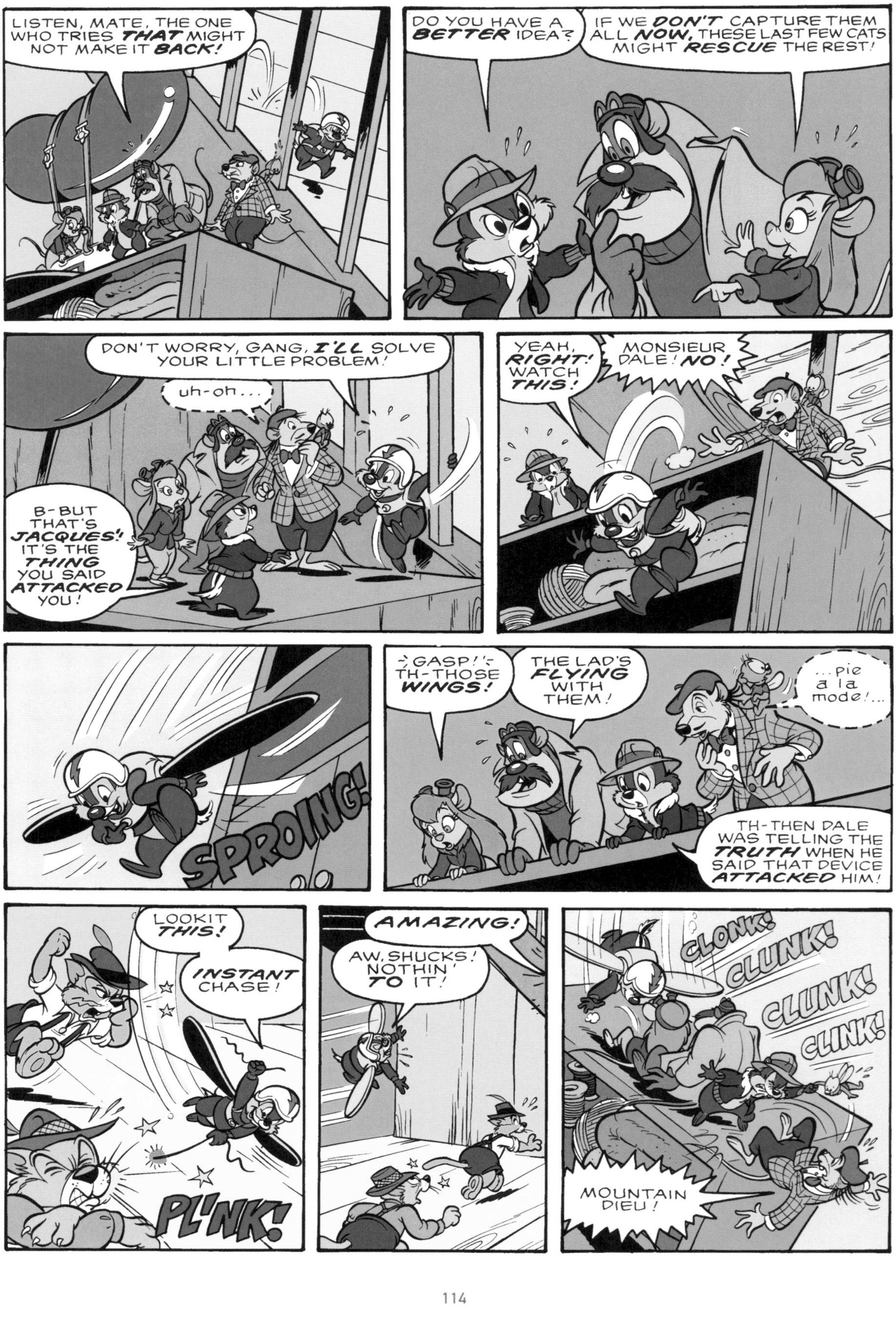
LISTEN, MATE, THE ONE WHO TRIES THAT MIGHT NOT MAKE IT BACK!
DO YOU HAVE A BETTER IDEA?
IF WE DON'T CAPTURE THEM ALL NOW, THESE LAST FEW CATS MIGHT RESCUE THE REST!
DON'T WORRY, GANG, I'LL SOLVE YOUR LITTLE PROBLEM!
uh-oh...
B-BUT THAT'S JACQUES! IT'S THE THING YOU SAID ATTACKED YOU!
YEAH, RIGHT! WATCH THIS!
MONSIEUR DALE! NO!
SPROING!
-GASP!- TH-THOSE WINGS!
THE LAD'S FLYING WITH THEM!
...pie a la mode!...
TH-THEN DALE WAS TELLING THE TRUTH WHEN HE SAID THAT DEVICE ATTACKED HIM!
LOOKIT THIS!
INSTANT CHASE!
PL'NK!
AMAZING!
AW, SHUCKS! NOTHIN' TO IT!
CLONK!
CLUNK!
CLUNK!
CLINK!
MOUNTAIN DIEU!

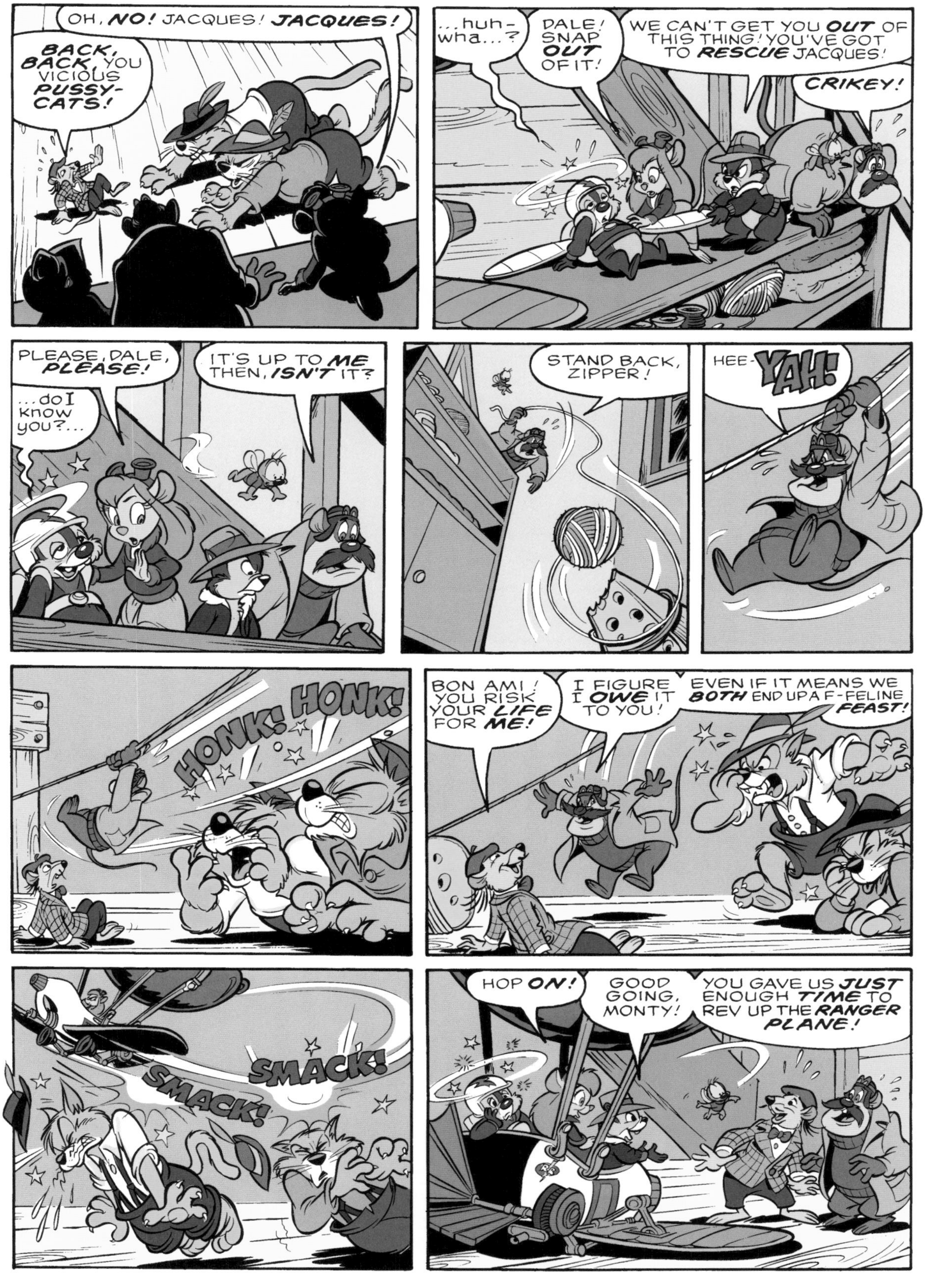
OH, NO! JACQUES! JACQUES!
BACK, BACK, YOU VICIOUS PUSSY-CATS!
...huh-wha...?
DALE! SNAP OUT OF IT!
WE CAN'T GET YOU OUT OF THIS THING! YOU'VE GOT TO RESCUE JACQUES!
CRIKEY!
PLEASE, DALE, PLEASE!
...do I know you?...
IT'S UP TO ME THEN, ISN'T IT?
STAND BACK, ZIPPER!
HEE-YAH!
HONK! HONK!
BON AMI! YOU RISK YOUR LIFE FOR ME!
I FIGURE I OWE IT TO YOU!
EVEN IF IT MEANS WE BOTH END UP A F-FELINE FEAST!
SMACK!
SMACK!
HOP ON!
GOOD GOING, MONTY!
YOU GAVE US JUST ENOUGH TIME TO REV UP THE RANGER PLANE!

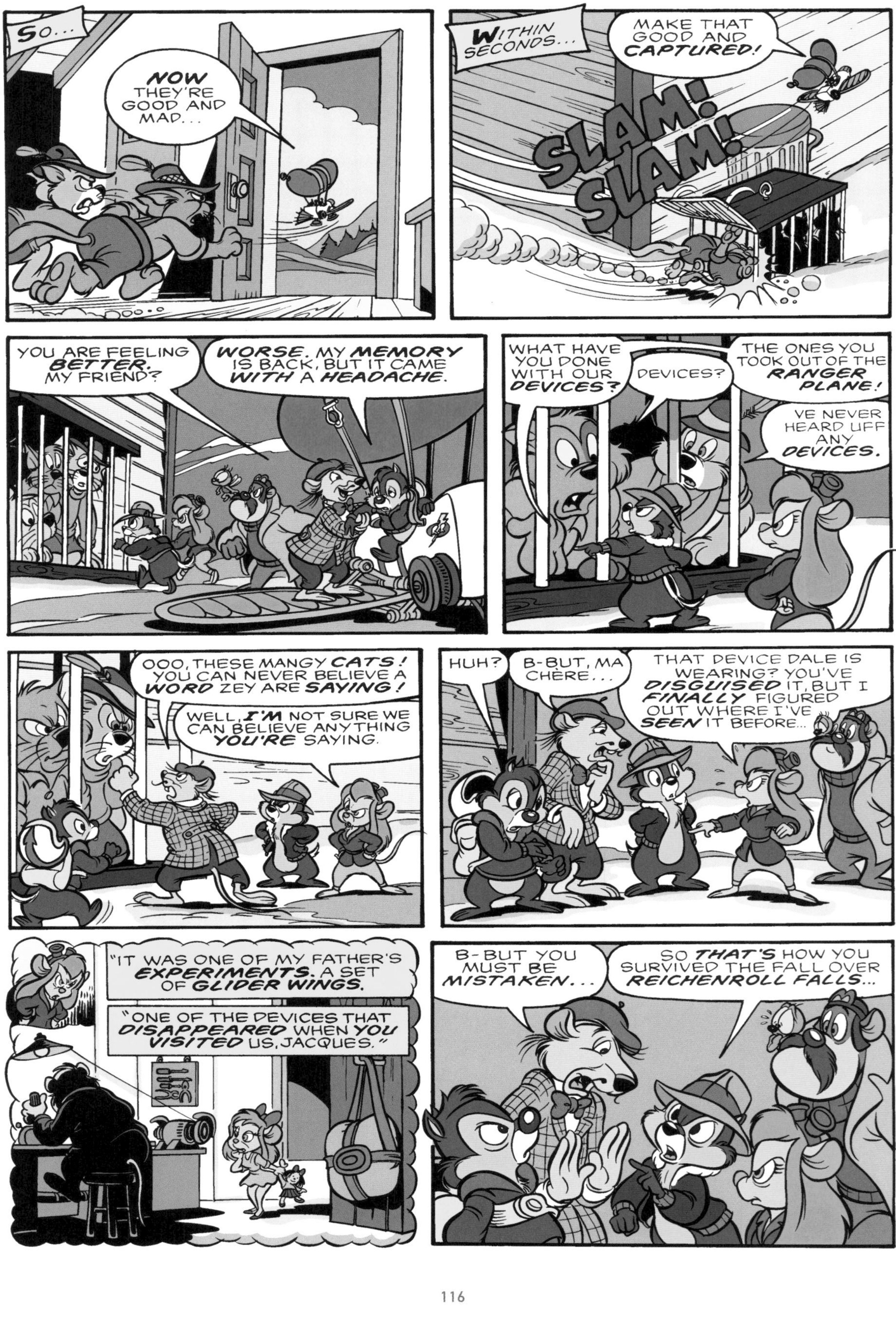

SO...
NOW THEY'RE GOOD AND MAD...
WITHIN SECONDS...
MAKE THAT GOOD AND CAPTURED!
SLAM! SLAM!
YOU ARE FEELING BETTER, MY FRIEND?
WORSE. MY MEMORY IS BACK, BUT IT CAME WITH A HEADACHE.
WHAT HAVE YOU DONE WITH OUR DEVICES?
DEVICES?
THE ONES YOU TOOK OUT OF THE RANGER PLANE!
VE NEVER HEARD UFF ANY DEVICES.
OOO, THESE MANGY CATS! YOU CAN NEVER BELIEVE A WORD ZEY ARE SAYING!
WELL, I'M NOT SURE WE CAN BELIEVE ANYTHING YOU'RE SAYING.
HUH?
B-BUT, MA CHÈRE...
THAT DEVICE DALE IS WEARING? YOU'VE DISGUISED IT, BUT I FINALLY FIGURED OUT WHERE I'VE SEEN IT BEFORE...
"IT WAS ONE OF MY FATHER'S EXPERIMENTS. A SET OF GLIDER WINGS.
"ONE OF THE DEVICES THAT DISAPPEARED WHEN YOU VISITED US, JACQUES."
B-BUT YOU MUST BE MISTAKEN...
SO THAT'S HOW YOU SURVIVED THE FALL OVER REICHENROLL FALLS...

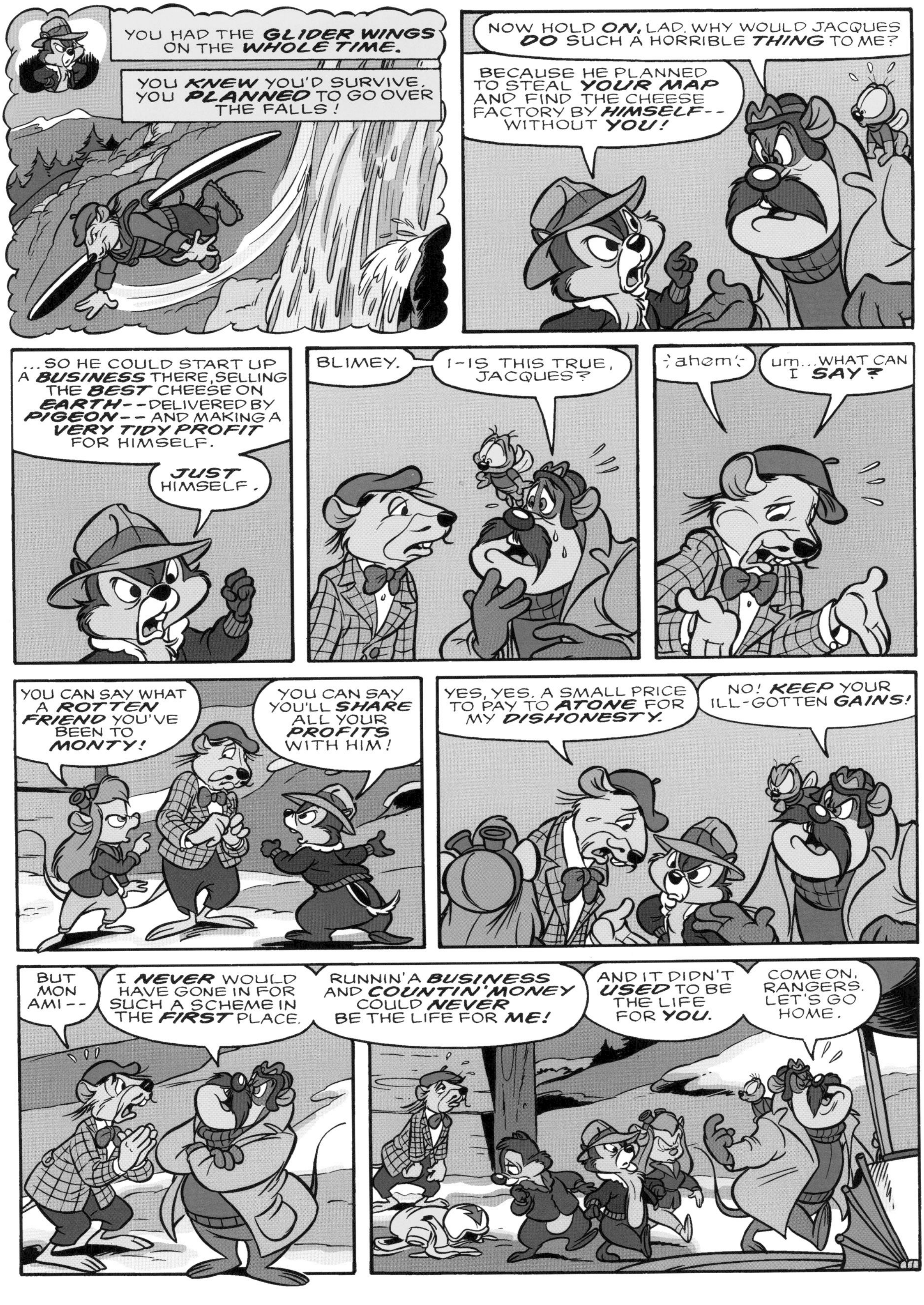

YOU HAD THE GLIDER WINGS ON THE WHOLE TIME.
YOU KNEW YOU'D SURVIVE. YOU PLANNED TO GO OVER THE FALLS!
NOW HOLD ON, LAD. WHY WOULD JACQUES DO SUCH A HORRIBLE THING TO ME?
BECAUSE HE PLANNED TO STEAL YOUR MAP AND FIND THE CHEESE FACTORY BY HIMSELF-- WITHOUT YOU!
...SO HE COULD START UP A BUSINESS THERE, SELLING THE BEST CHEESE ON EARTH--DELIVERED BY PIGEON-- AND MAKING A VERY TIDY PROFIT FOR HIMSELF.
JUST HIMSELF.
BLIMEY.
I-IS THIS TRUE, JACQUES?
ahem
um...WHAT CAN I SAY?
YOU CAN SAY WHAT A ROTTEN FRIEND YOU'VE BEEN TO MONTY!
YOU CAN SAY YOU'LL SHARE ALL YOUR PROFITS WITH HIM!
YES, YES. A SMALL PRICE TO PAY TO ATONE FOR MY DISHONESTY.
NO! KEEP YOUR ILL-GOTTEN GAINS!
BUT MON AMI--
I NEVER WOULD HAVE GONE IN FOR SUCH A SCHEME IN THE FIRST PLACE.
RUNNIN' A BUSINESS AND COUNTIN' MONEY COULD NEVER BE THE LIFE FOR ME!
AND IT DIDN'T USED TO BE THE LIFE FOR YOU.
COME ON, RANGERS. LET'S GO HOME.

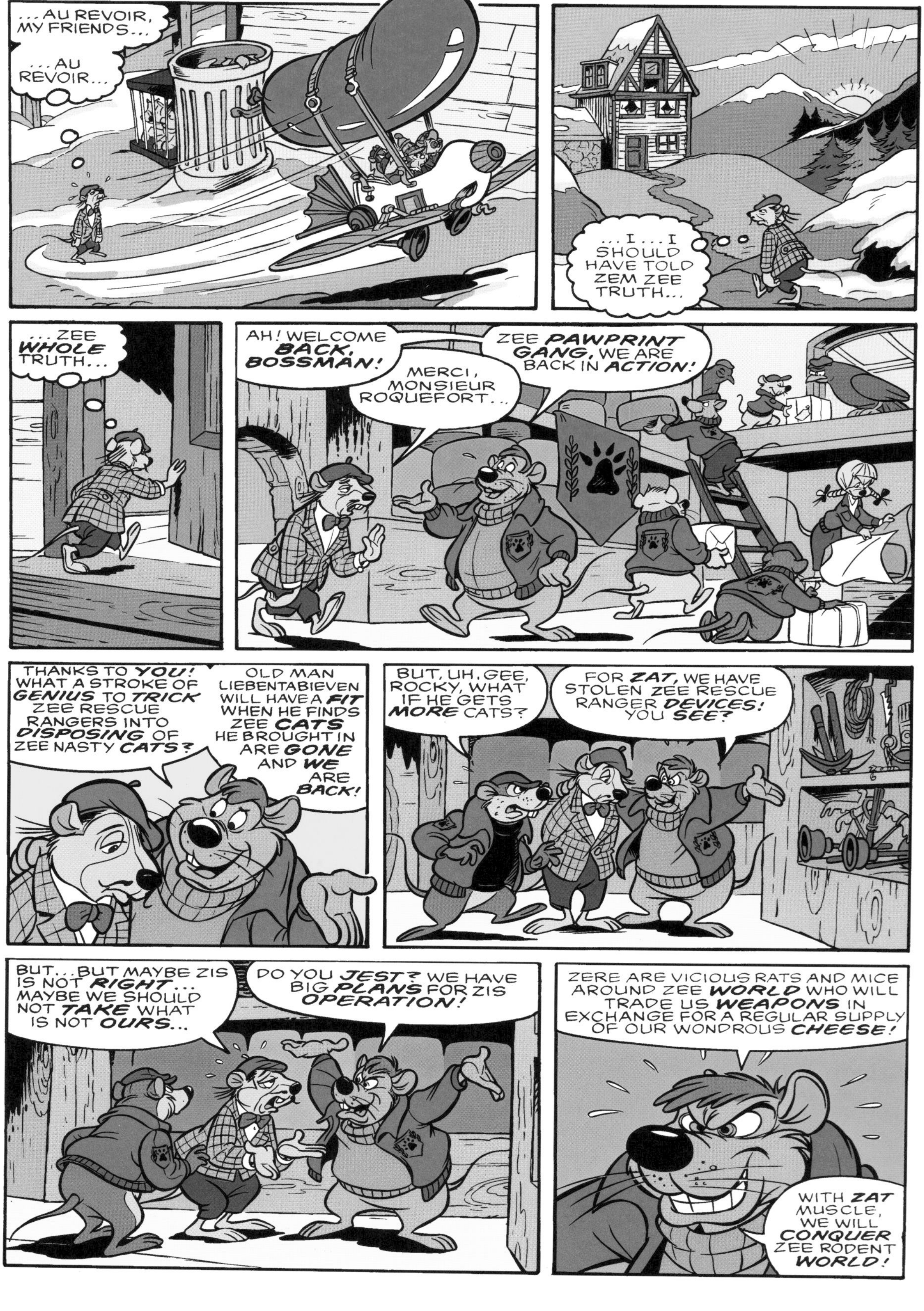
...AU REVOIR, MY FRIENDS...
...AU REVOIR...
...I...I SHOULD HAVE TOLD ZEM ZEE TRUTH...
...ZEE WHOLE TRUTH...
AH! WELCOME BACK, BOSSMAN!
MERCI, MONSIEUR ROQUEFORT...
ZEE PAWPRINT GANG, WE ARE BACK IN ACTION!
THANKS TO YOU! WHAT A STROKE OF GENIUS TO TRICK ZEE RESCUE RANGERS INTO DISPOSING OF ZEE NASTY CATS?
OLD MAN LIEBENTABIEVEN WILL HAVE A FIT WHEN HE FINDS ZEE CATS HE BROUGHT IN ARE GONE AND WE ARE BACK!
BUT, UH, GEE, ROCKY, WHAT IF HE GETS MORE CATS?
FOR ZAT, WE HAVE STOLEN ZEE RESCUE RANGER DEVICES! YOU SEE?
BUT...BUT MAYBE ZIS IS NOT RIGHT... MAYBE WE SHOULD NOT TAKE WHAT IS NOT OURS...
DO YOU JEST? WE HAVE BIG PLANS FOR ZIS OPERATION!
ZERE ARE VICIOUS RATS AND MICE AROUND ZEE WORLD WHO WILL TRADE US WEAPONS IN EXCHANGE FOR A REGULAR SUPPLY OF OUR WONDROUS CHEESE!
WITH ZAT MUSCLE, WE WILL CONQUER ZEE RODENT WORLD!

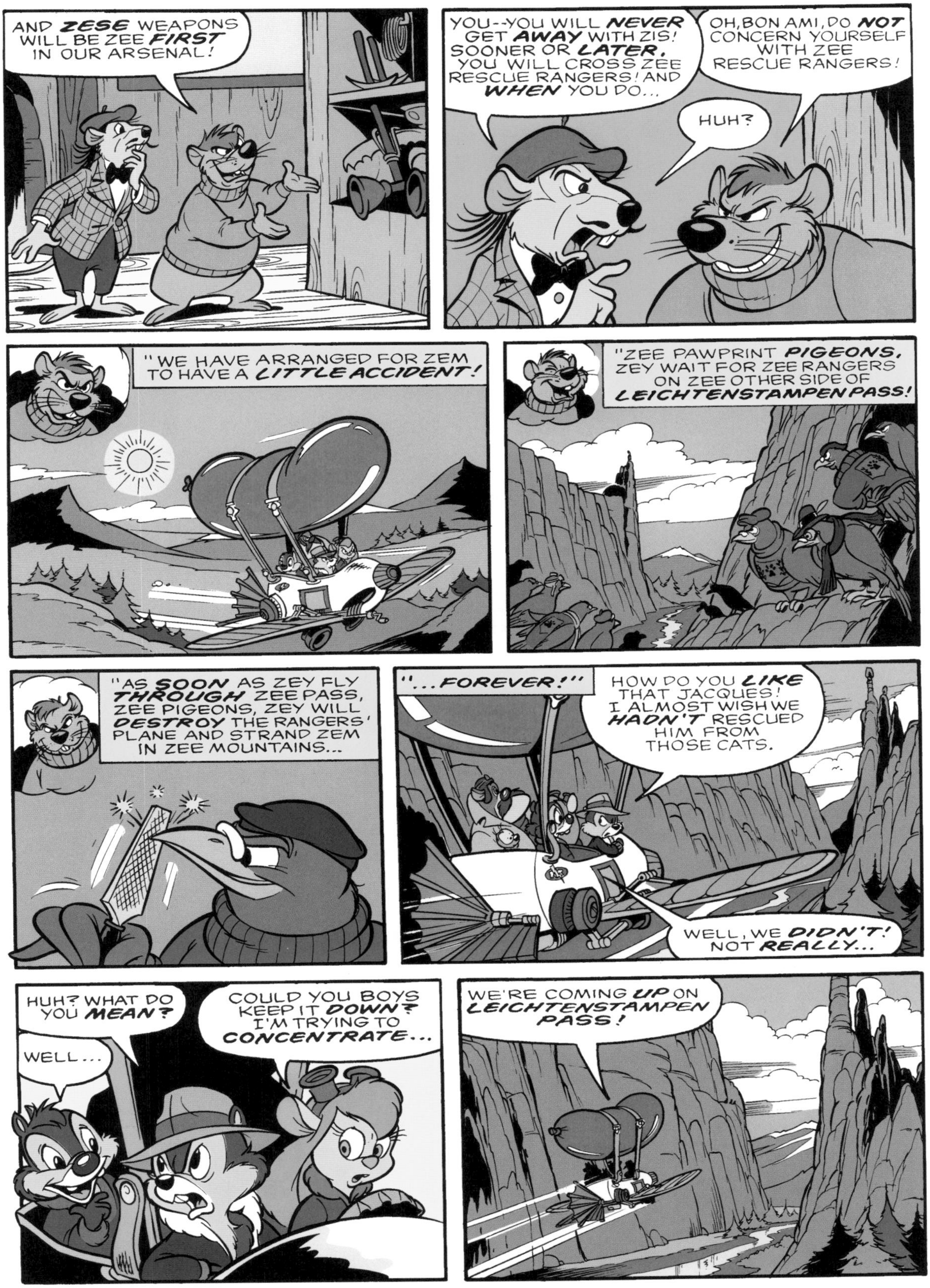

AND ZESE WEAPONS WILL BE ZEE FIRST IN OUR ARSENAL!
YOU--YOU WILL NEVER GET AWAY WITH ZIS! SOONER OR LATER, YOU WILL CROSS ZEE RESCUE RANGERS! AND WHEN YOU DO...
OH, BON AMI, DO NOT CONCERN YOURSELF WITH ZEE RESCUE RANGERS!
HUH?
"WE HAVE ARRANGED FOR ZEM TO HAVE A LITTLE ACCIDENT!
"ZEE PAWPRINT PIGEONS, ZEY WAIT FOR ZEE RANGERS ON ZEE OTHER SIDE OF LEICHTENSTAMPEN PASS!
"AS SOON AS ZEY FLY THROUGH ZEE PASS, ZEE PIGEONS, ZEY WILL DESTROY THE RANGERS' PLANE AND STRAND ZEM IN ZEE MOUNTAINS...
"...FOREVER!"
HOW DO YOU LIKE THAT JACQUES! I ALMOST WISH WE HADN'T RESCUED HIM FROM THOSE CATS.
WELL, WE DIDN'T! NOT REALLY...
HUH? WHAT DO YOU MEAN?
WELL...
COULD YOU BOYS KEEP IT DOWN? I'M TRYING TO CONCENTRATE...
WE'RE COMING UP ON LEICHTENSTAMPEN PASS!

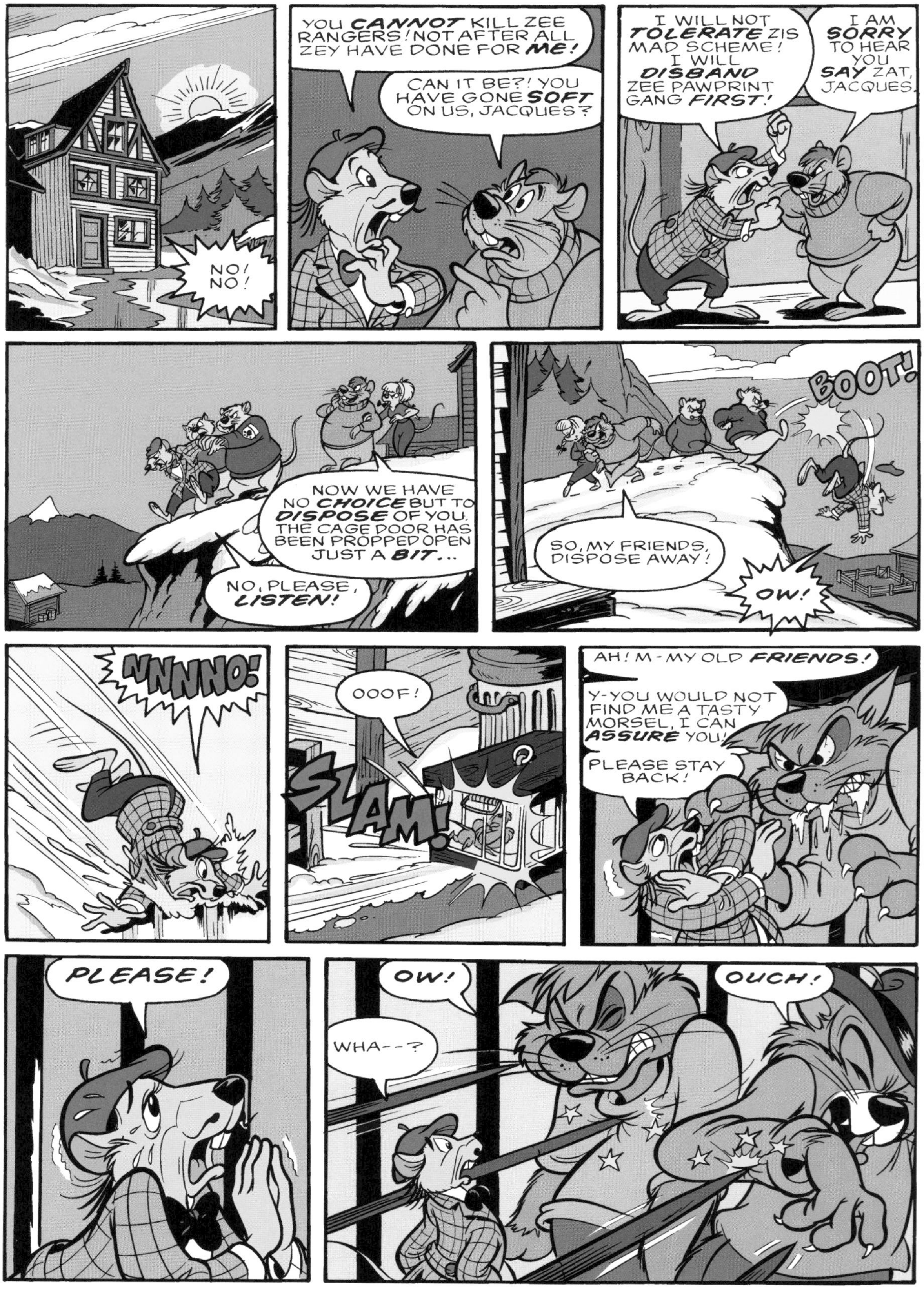
NO! NO!
YOU CANNOT KILL ZEE RANGERS! NOT AFTER ALL ZEY HAVE DONE FOR ME!
CAN IT BE?! YOU HAVE GONE SOFT ON US, JACQUES?
I WILL NOT TOLERATE ZIS MAD SCHEME! I WILL DISBAND ZEE PAWPRINT GANG FIRST!
I AM SORRY TO HEAR YOU SAY ZAT, JACQUES.
NOW WE HAVE NO CHOICE BUT TO DISPOSE OF YOU. THE CAGE DOOR HAS BEEN PROPPED OPEN JUST A BIT...
NO, PLEASE, LISTEN!
BOOT!
SO, MY FRIENDS, DISPOSE AWAY!
OW!
NNNNO!
OOOF!
SLAM!
AH! M-MY OLD FRIENDS!
Y-YOU WOULD NOT FIND ME A TASTY MORSEL, I CAN ASSURE YOU!
PLEASE STAY BACK!
PLEASE!
OW!
OUCH!
WHA--?

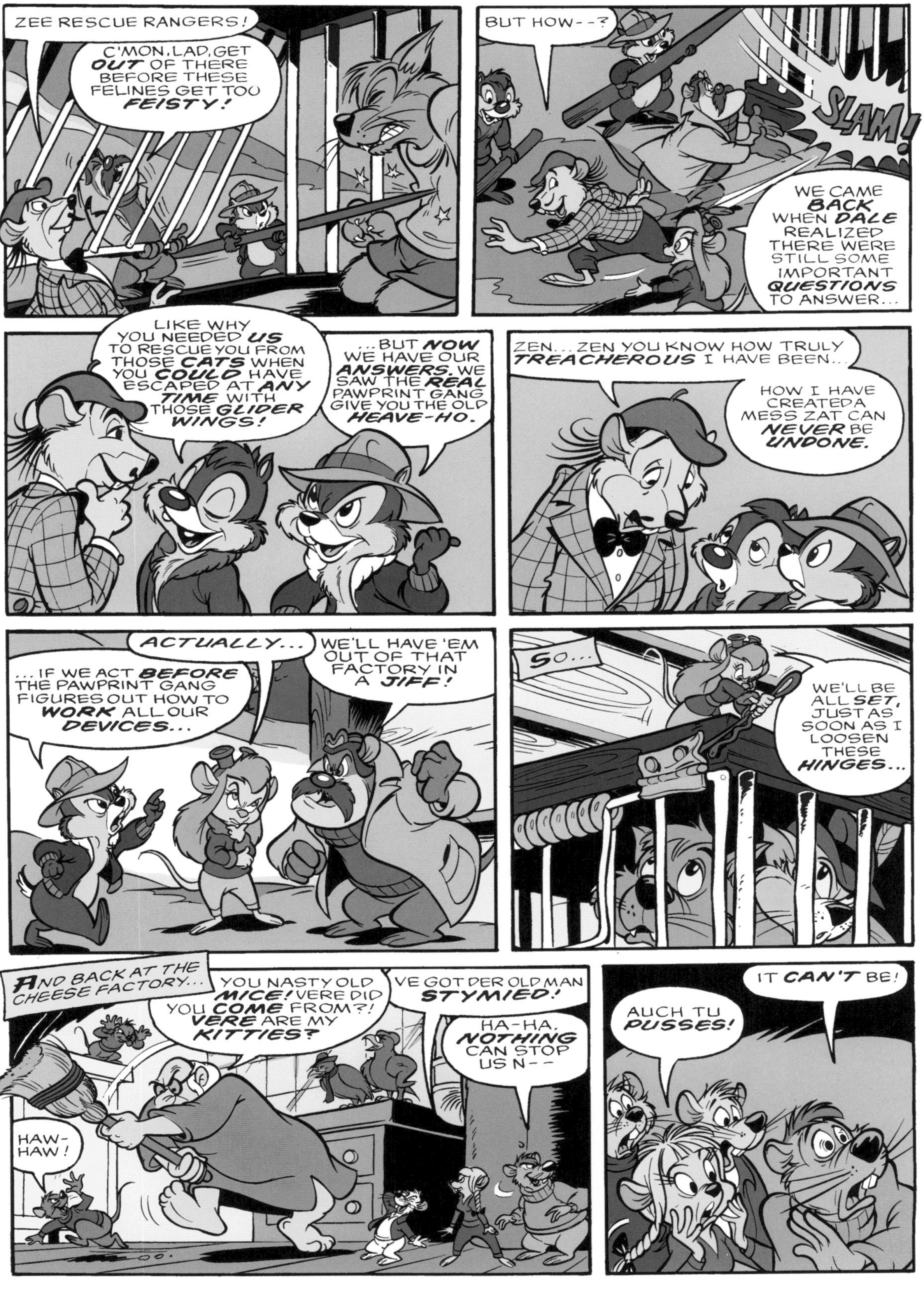
ZEE RESCUE RANGERS!
C'MON, LAD, GET OUT OF THERE BEFORE THESE FELINES GET TOO FEISTY!
BUT HOW--?
SLAM!
WE CAME BACK WHEN DALE REALIZED THERE WERE STILL SOME IMPORTANT QUESTIONS TO ANSWER...
LIKE WHY YOU NEEDED US TO RESCUE YOU FROM THOSE CATS WHEN YOU COULD HAVE ESCAPED AT ANY TIME WITH THOSE GLIDER WINGS!
...BUT NOW WE HAVE OUR ANSWERS. WE SAW THE REAL PAWPRINT GANG GIVE YOU THE OLD HEAVE-HO.
ZEN... ZEN YOU KNOW HOW TRULY TREACHEROUS I HAVE BEEN...
HOW I HAVE CREATED A MESS ZAT CAN NEVER BE UNDONE.
ACTUALLY...
...IF WE ACT BEFORE THE PAWPRINT GANG FIGURES OUT HOW TO WORK ALL OUR DEVICES...
WE'LL HAVE 'EM OUT OF THAT FACTORY IN A JIFF!
SO...
WE'LL BE ALL SET, JUST AS SOON AS I LOOSEN THESE HINGES...
AND BACK AT THE CHEESE FACTORY...
YOU NASTY OLD MICE! VERE DID YOU COME FROM?! VERE ARE MY KITTIES?
VE GOT DER OLD MAN STYMIED!
HA-HA. NOTHING CAN STOP US N--
HAW-HAW!
IT CAN'T BE!
AUCH TU PUSSES!

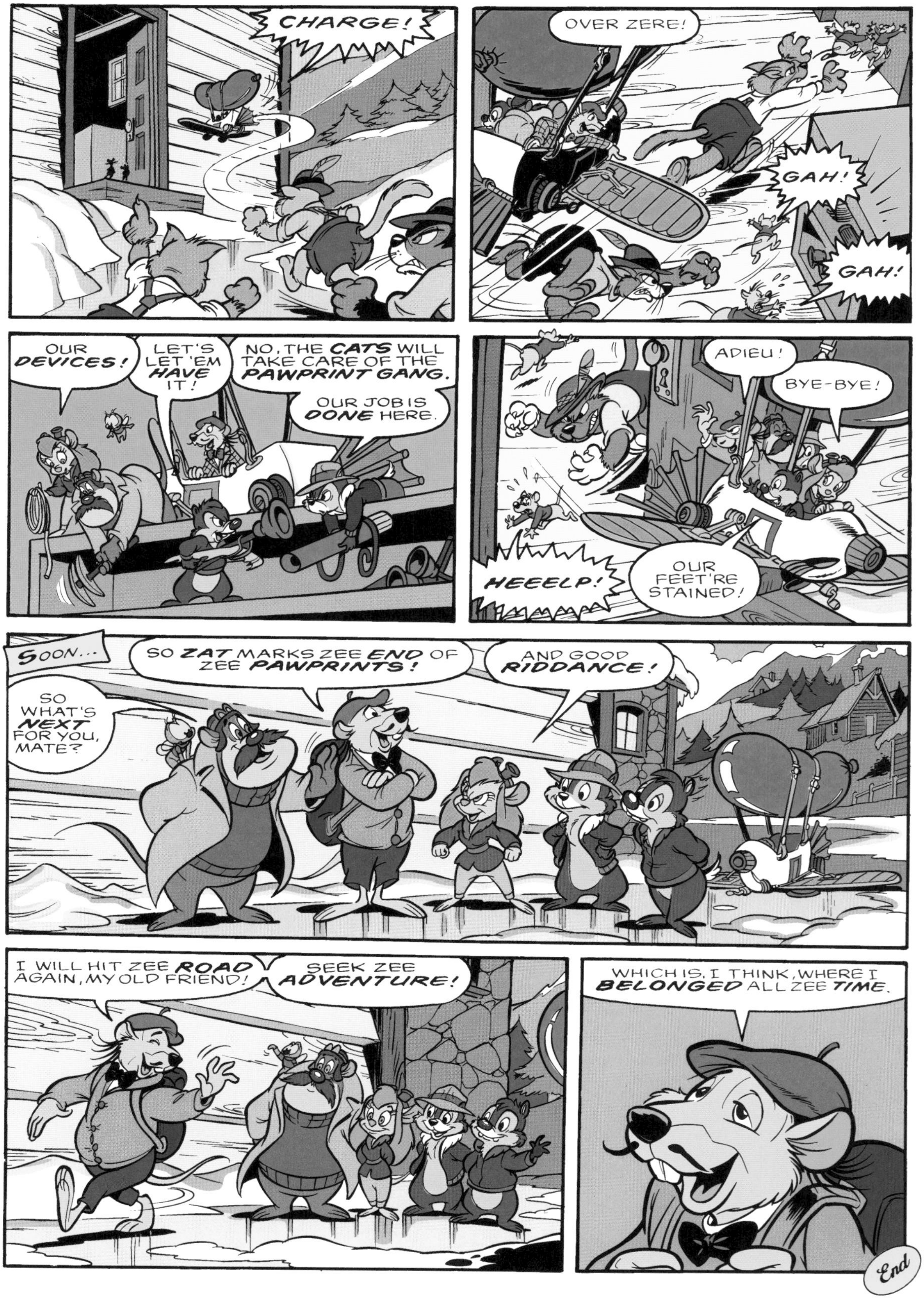
CHARGE!
OVER ZERE!
GAH!
GAH!
OUR DEVICES!
LET'S LET 'EM HAVE IT!
NO, THE CATS WILL TAKE CARE OF THE PAWPRINT GANG.
OUR JOB IS DONE HERE.
ADIEU!
BYE-BYE!
HEEEELP!
OUR FEET'RE STAINED!
SOON...
SO ZAT MARKS ZEE END OF ZEE PAWPRINTS!
AND GOOD RIDDANCE!
SO WHAT'S NEXT FOR YOU, MATE?
I WILL HIT ZEE ROAD AGAIN, MY OLD FRIEND!
SEEK ZEE ADVENTURE!
WHICH IS, I THINK, WHERE I BELONGED ALL ZEE TIME.
End

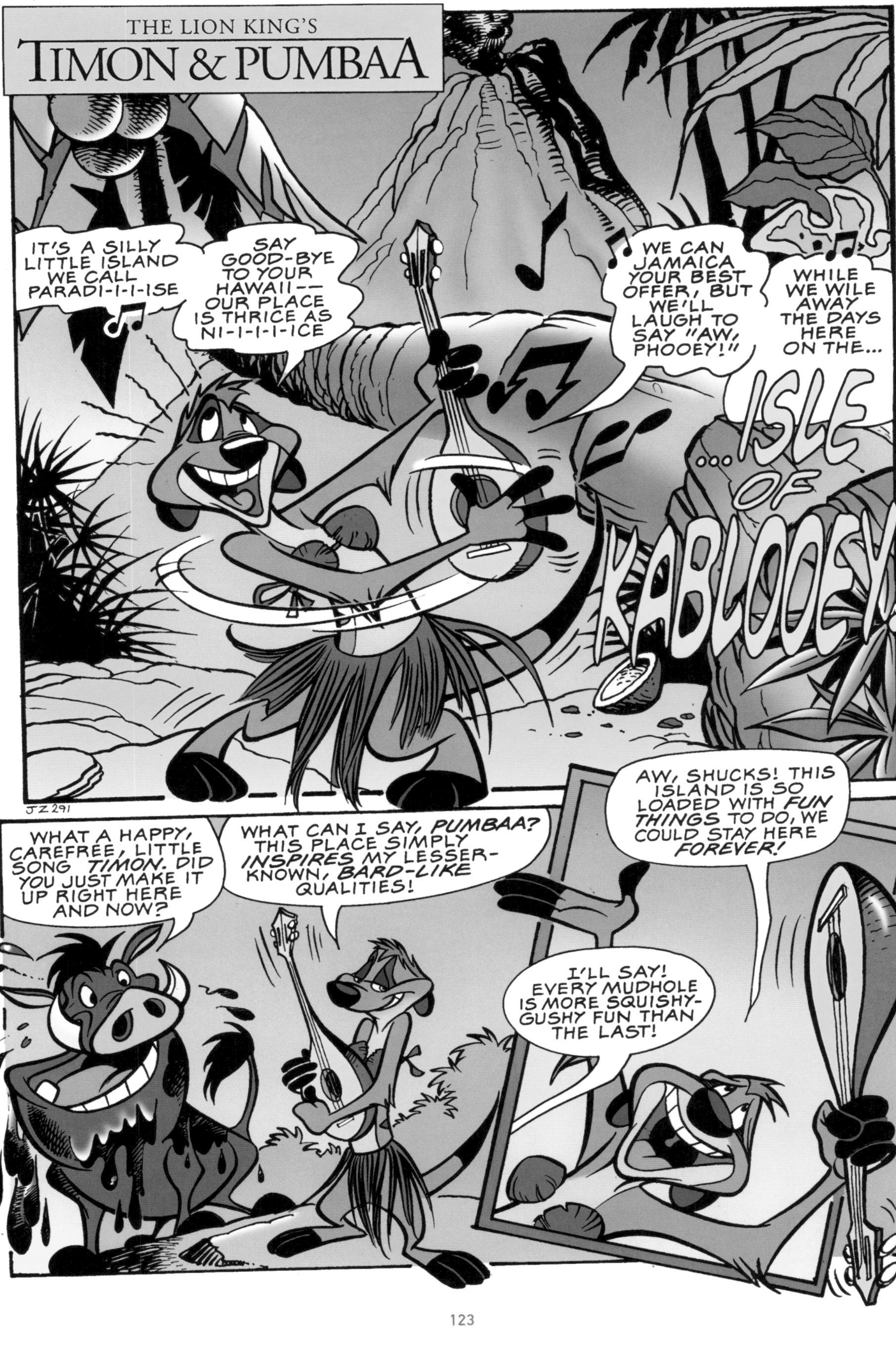

THE LION KING'S
TIMON & PUMBAA
IT'S A SILLY LITTLE ISLAND WE CALL PARADI-I-I-ISE
SAY GOOD-BYE TO YOUR HAWAII -- OUR PLACE IS THRICE AS NI-I-I-I-ICE
WE CAN JAMAICA YOUR BEST OFFER, BUT WE'LL LAUGH TO SAY "AW, PHOOEY!"
WHILE WE WILE AWAY THE DAYS HERE ON THE...
...ISLE OF KABLOOEY!!"
JZ 291
WHAT A HAPPY, CAREFREE, LITTLE SONG TIMON. DID YOU JUST MAKE IT UP RIGHT HERE AND NOW?
WHAT CAN I SAY, PUMBAA? THIS PLACE SIMPLY INSPIRES MY LESSER-KNOWN, BARD-LIKE QUALITIES!
AW, SHUCKS! THIS ISLAND IS SO LOADED WITH FUN THINGS TO DO, WE COULD STAY HERE FOREVER!
I'LL SAY! EVERY MUDHOLE IS MORE SQUISHY-GUSHY FUN THAN THE LAST!

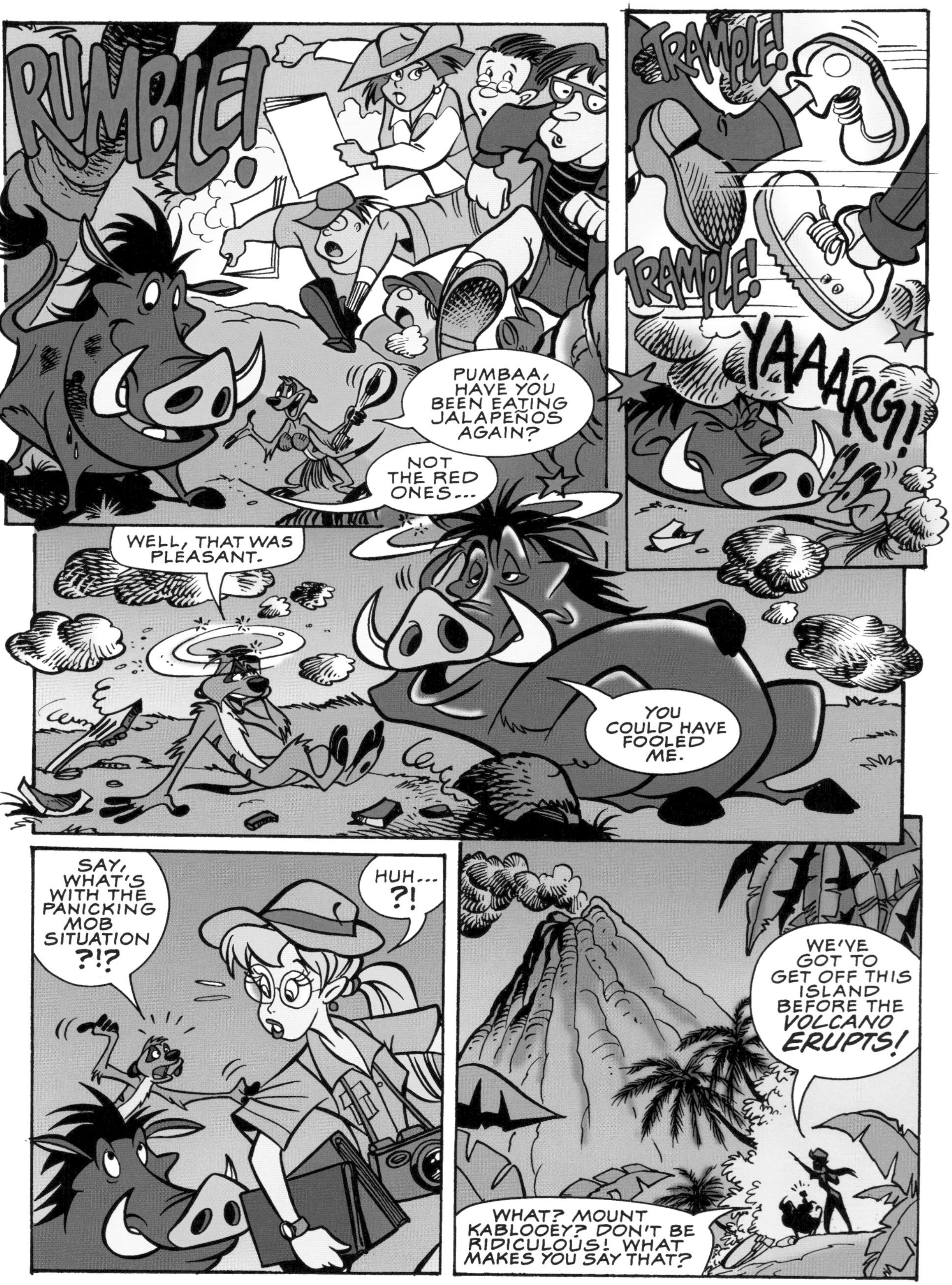

RUMBLE!
PUMBAA, HAVE YOU BEEN EATING JALAPEÑOS AGAIN?
NOT THE RED ONES...
TRAMPLE!
TRAMPLE!
YAAAARG!!
WELL, THAT WAS PLEASANT.
YOU COULD HAVE FOOLED ME.
SAY, WHAT'S WITH THE PANICKING MOB SITUATION ?!?
HUH... ?!
WE'VE GOT TO GET OFF THIS ISLAND BEFORE THE VOLCANO ERUPTS!
WHAT? MOUNT KABLOOEY? DON'T BE RIDICULOUS! WHAT MAKES YOU SAY THAT?

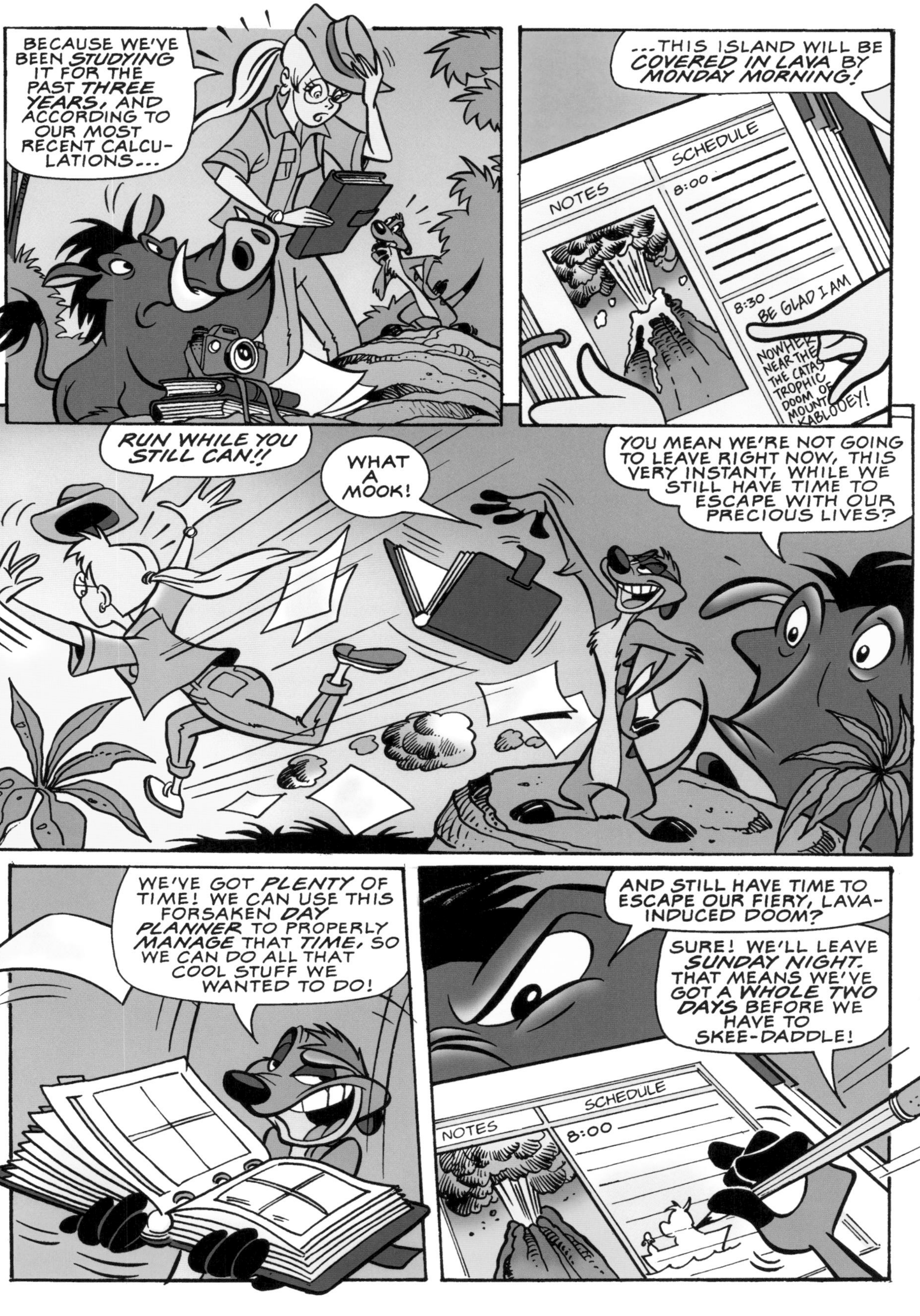
BECAUSE WE'VE BEEN STUDYING IT FOR THE PAST THREE YEARS, AND ACCORDING TO OUR MOST RECENT CALCU-LATIONS...
...THIS ISLAND WILL BE COVERED IN LAVA BY MONDAY MORNING!
SCHEDULE
NOTES
8:00
8:30
BE GLAD I AM
NOWHER NEAR THE CATAS TROPHIC DOOM OF MOUNT KABLOOEY!
RUN WHILE YOU STILL CAN!!
WHAT A MOOK!
YOU MEAN WE'RE NOT GOING TO LEAVE RIGHT NOW, THIS VERY INSTANT, WHILE WE STILL HAVE TIME TO ESCAPE WITH OUR PRECIOUS LIVES?
WE'VE GOT PLENTY OF TIME! WE CAN USE THIS FORSAKEN DAY PLANNER TO PROPERLY MANAGE THAT TIME, SO WE CAN DO ALL THAT COOL STUFF WE WANTED TO DO!
AND STILL HAVE TIME TO ESCAPE OUR FIERY, LAVA-INDUCED DOOM?
SURE! WE'LL LEAVE SUNDAY NIGHT. THAT MEANS WE'VE GOT A WHOLE TWO DAYS BEFORE WE HAVE TO SKEE-DADDLE!
SCHEDULE
NOTES
8:00

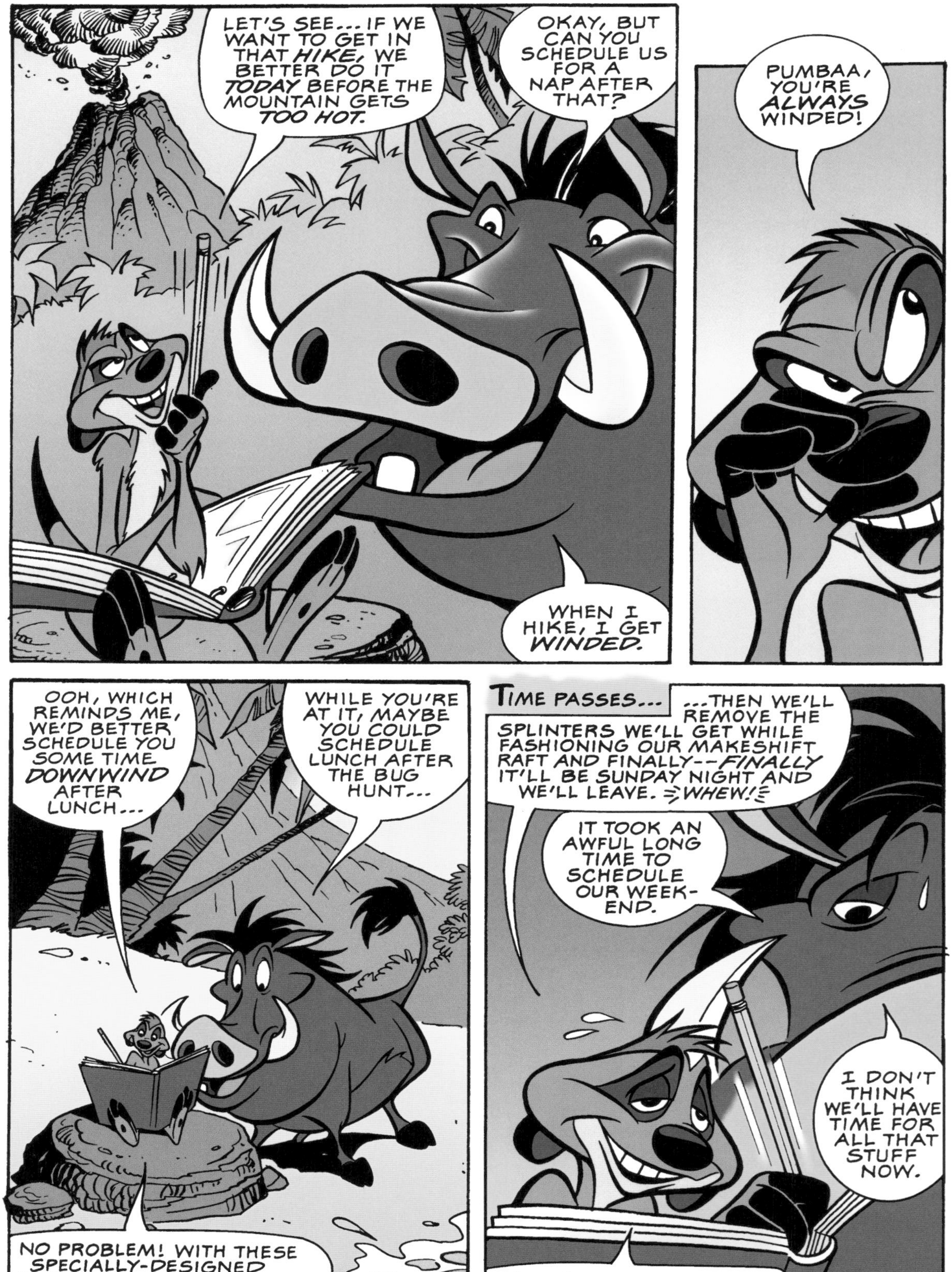
LET'S SEE... IF WE WANT TO GET IN THAT *HIKE,* WE BETTER DO IT *TODAY* BEFORE THE MOUNTAIN GETS *TOO HOT.*
OKAY, BUT CAN YOU SCHEDULE US FOR A NAP AFTER THAT?
WHEN I HIKE, I GET *WINDED.*
PUMBAA, YOU'RE *ALWAYS* WINDED!
OOH, WHICH REMINDS ME, WE'D BETTER SCHEDULE YOU SOME TIME *DOWNWIND* AFTER LUNCH...
WHILE YOU'RE AT IT, MAYBE YOU COULD SCHEDULE LUNCH AFTER THE BUG HUNT...
NO PROBLEM! WITH THESE SPECIALLY-DESIGNED PAGES, TIME MANAGEMENT IS A SNAP!
TIME PASSES...
...THEN WE'LL REMOVE THE SPLINTERS WE'LL GET WHILE FASHIONING OUR MAKESHIFT RAFT AND FINALLY--*FINALLY* IT'LL BE SUNDAY NIGHT AND WE'LL LEAVE. *WHEW!*
IT TOOK AN AWFUL LONG TIME TO SCHEDULE OUR WEEK-END.
I DON'T THINK WE'LL HAVE TIME FOR ALL THAT STUFF NOW.
YOU'RE PROBABLY RIGHT. WHAT TIME IS IT?

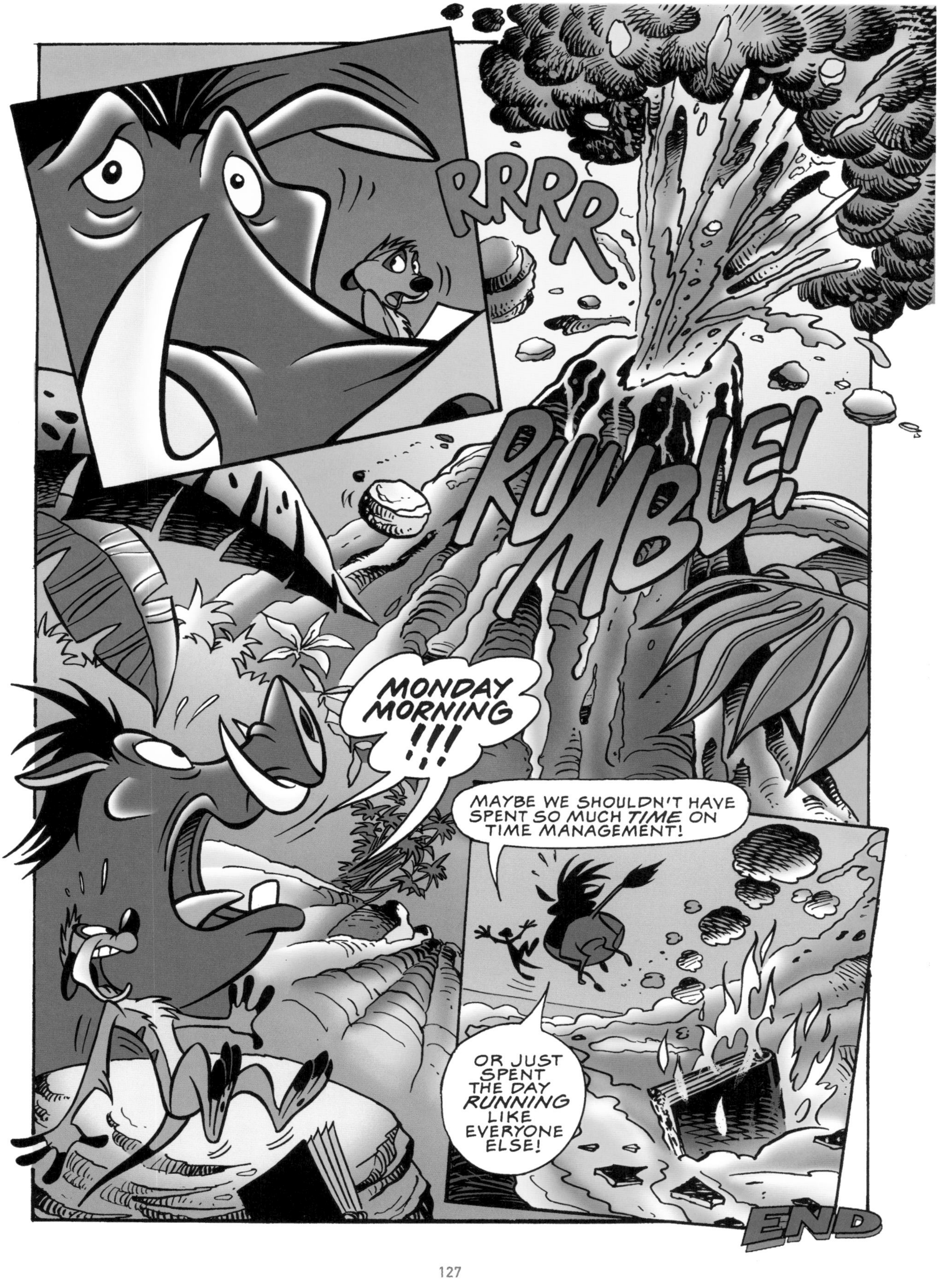
RRRR
RUMBLE!
MONDAY MORNING !!!
MAYBE WE SHOULDN'T HAVE SPENT SO MUCH *TIME* ON TIME MANAGEMENT!
OR JUST SPENT THE DAY *RUNNING* LIKE EVERYONE ELSE!
END

DISNEY
DUCKTALES
SHAKE
I'LL HAVE THE LAUNCHPAD SPECIAL, MR. DRAKE!
DRAKE'S SHAKES
LAUNCHPAD SPECIAL
$1.00
ONE LAUNCHPAD SPECIAL!
D92373
ONE LAUNCHPAD SPECIAL COMIN' RIGHT UP!
ZOW!!
ZIP!
ZOOM!
ROAR!
WHOOSH!
ZOW!
ZOOM!
ZINZ!
HERE YA' GO, KID... ONE LAUNCHPAD McQUACK SUPER FOAMY CRASH AND BURN SPECIAL!
END

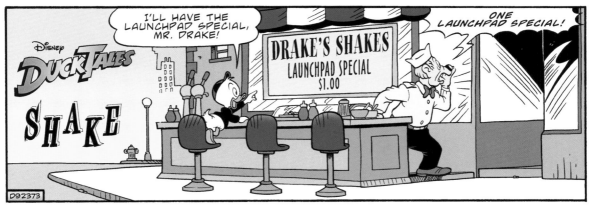

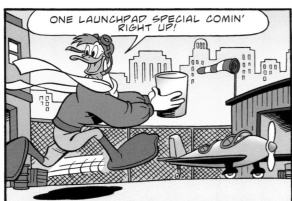

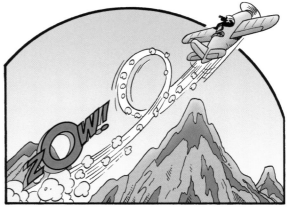

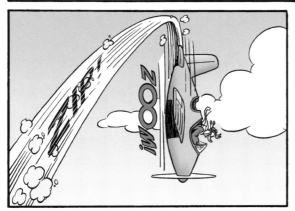

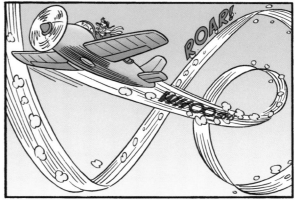

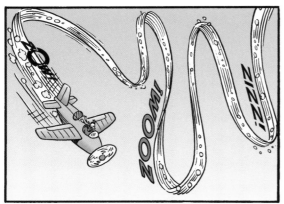

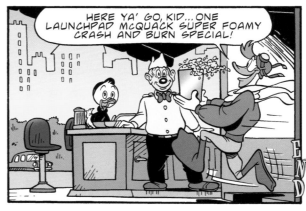

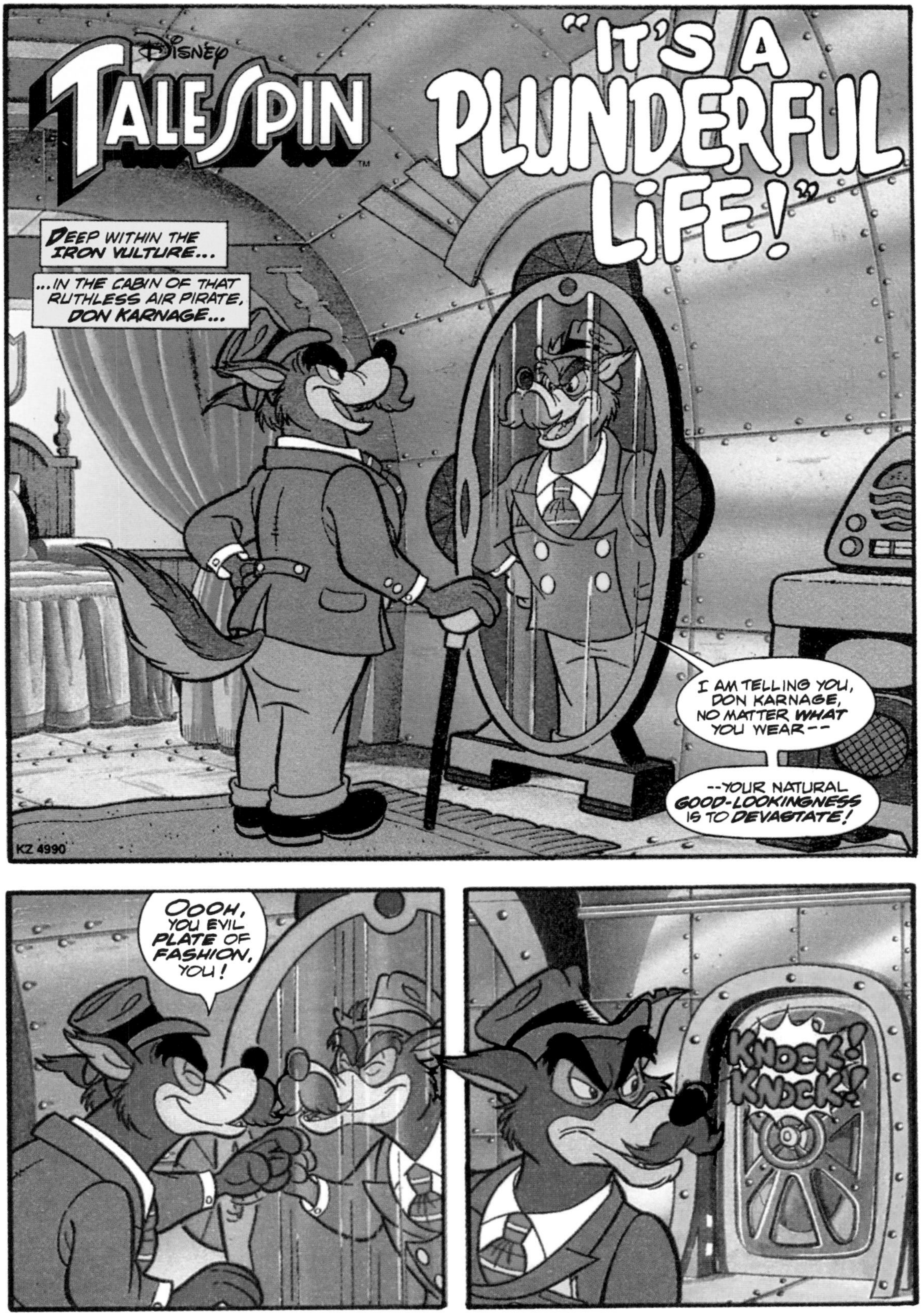
Disney
TaleSpin
"It's a Plunderful Life!"
Deep within the Iron Vulture...
...in the cabin of that ruthless air pirate, Don Karnage...
I am telling you, Don Karnage, no matter what you wear--
--your natural good-lookingness is to devastate!
KZ 4990
Ooooh, you evil plate of fashion, you!
Knock! Knock!

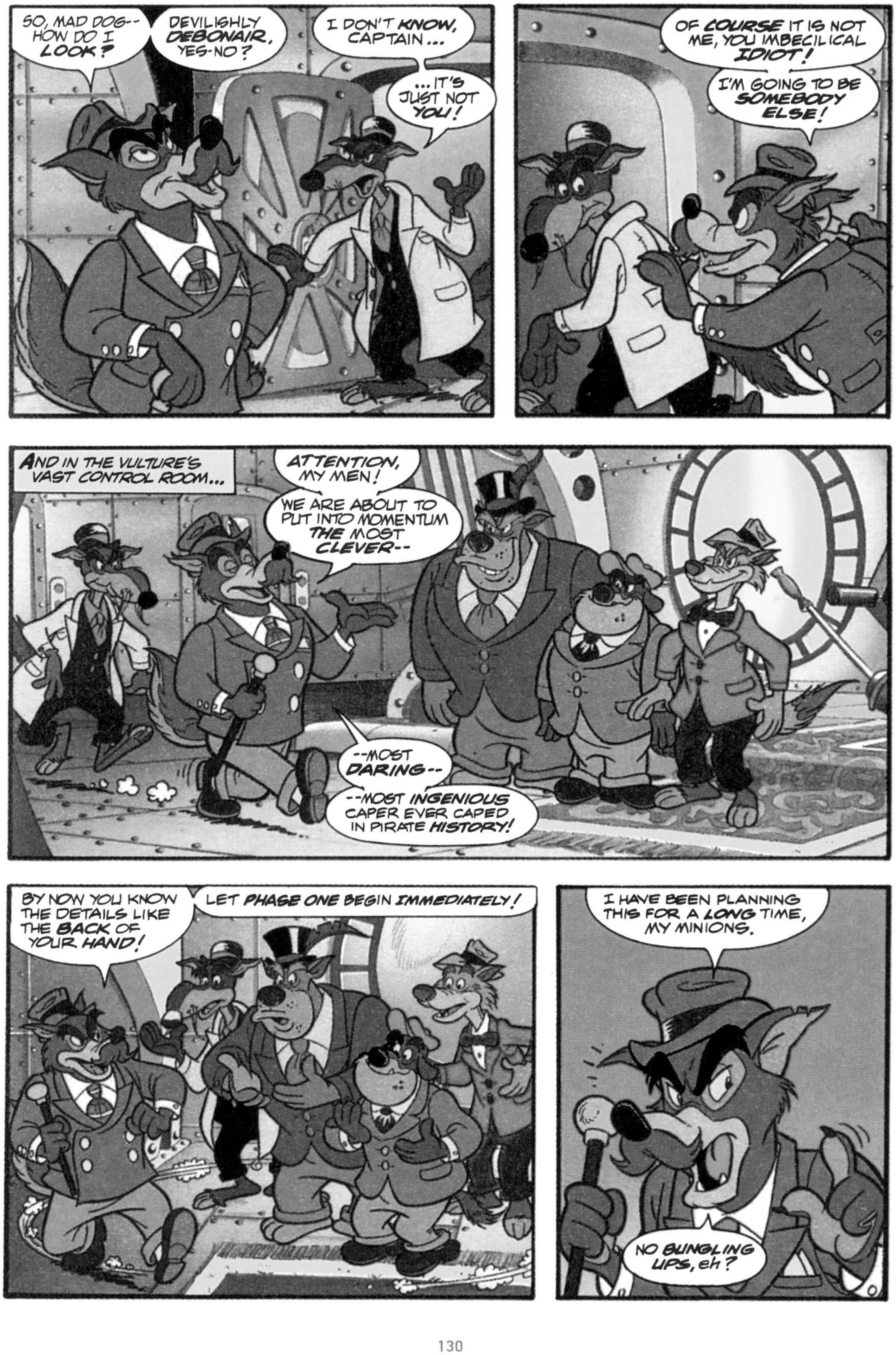
SO, MAD DOG-- HOW DO I LOOK?
DEVILISHLY DEBONAIR, YES-NO?
I DON'T KNOW, CAPTAIN...
...IT'S JUST NOT YOU!
OF COURSE IT IS NOT ME, YOU IMBECILICAL IDIOT!
I'M GOING TO BE SOMEBODY ELSE!
AND IN THE VULTURE'S VAST CONTROL ROOM...
ATTENTION, MY MEN!
WE ARE ABOUT TO PUT INTO MOMENTUM THE MOST CLEVER--
--MOST DARING--
--MOST INGENIOUS CAPER EVER CAPED IN PIRATE HISTORY!
BY NOW YOU KNOW THE DETAILS LIKE THE BACK OF YOUR HAND!
LET PHASE ONE BEGIN IMMEDIATELY!
I HAVE BEEN PLANNING THIS FOR A LONG TIME, MY MINIONS.
NO BUNGLING UPS, eh?

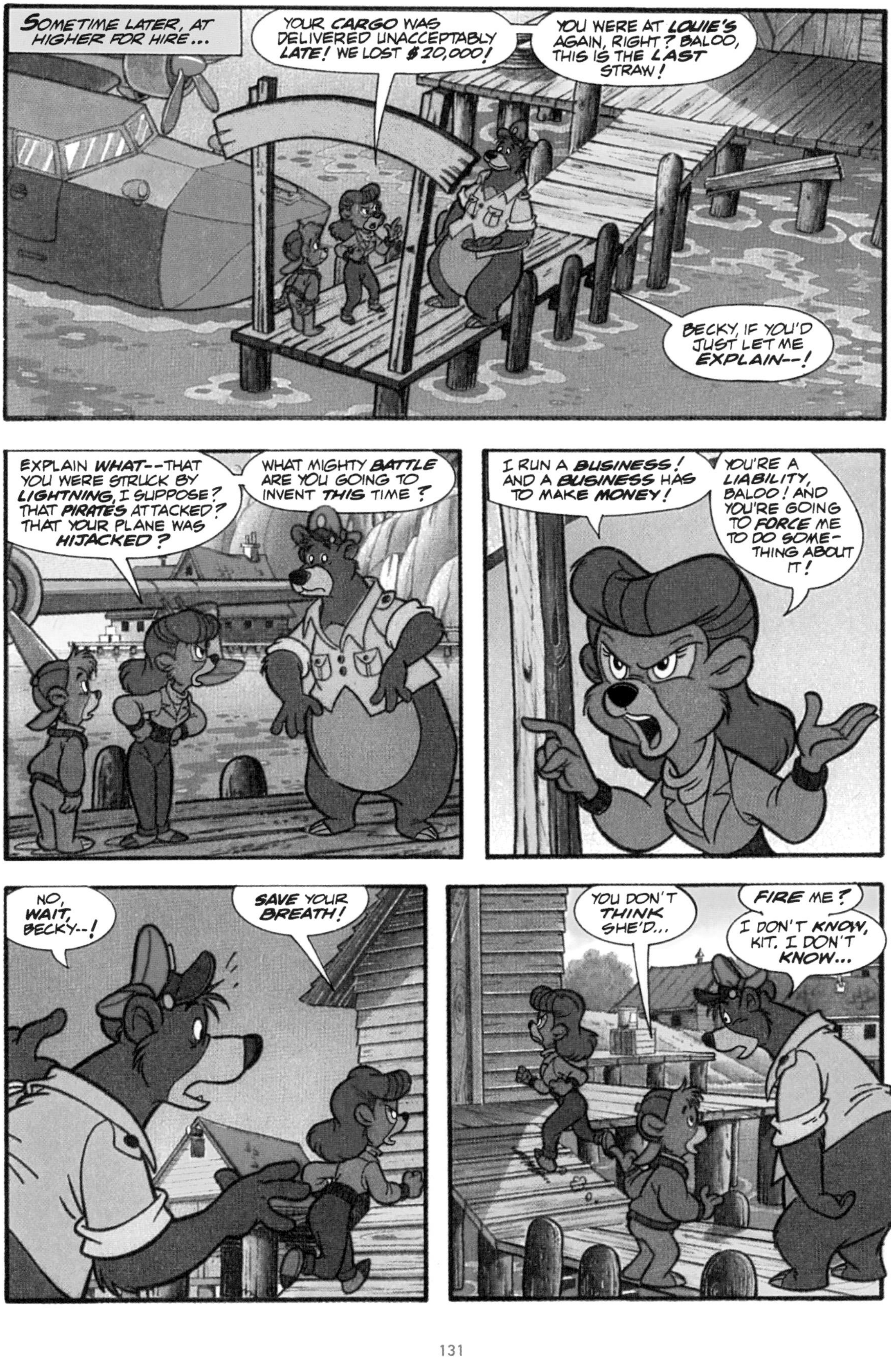
SOMETIME LATER, AT HIGHER FOR HIRE...
YOUR CARGO WAS DELIVERED UNACCEPTABLY LATE! WE LOST $20,000!
YOU WERE AT LOUIE'S AGAIN, RIGHT? BALOO, THIS IS THE LAST STRAW!
BECKY, IF YOU'D JUST LET ME EXPLAIN--!
EXPLAIN WHAT--THAT YOU WERE STRUCK BY LIGHTNING, I SUPPOSE? THAT PIRATES ATTACKED? THAT YOUR PLANE WAS HIJACKED?
WHAT MIGHTY BATTLE ARE YOU GOING TO INVENT THIS TIME?
I RUN A BUSINESS! AND A BUSINESS HAS TO MAKE MONEY!
YOU'RE A LIABILITY, BALOO! AND YOU'RE GOING TO FORCE ME TO DO SOME-THING ABOUT IT!
NO, WAIT, BECKY--!
SAVE YOUR BREATH!
YOU DON'T THINK SHE'D...
FIRE ME?
I DON'T KNOW, KIT. I DON'T KNOW...

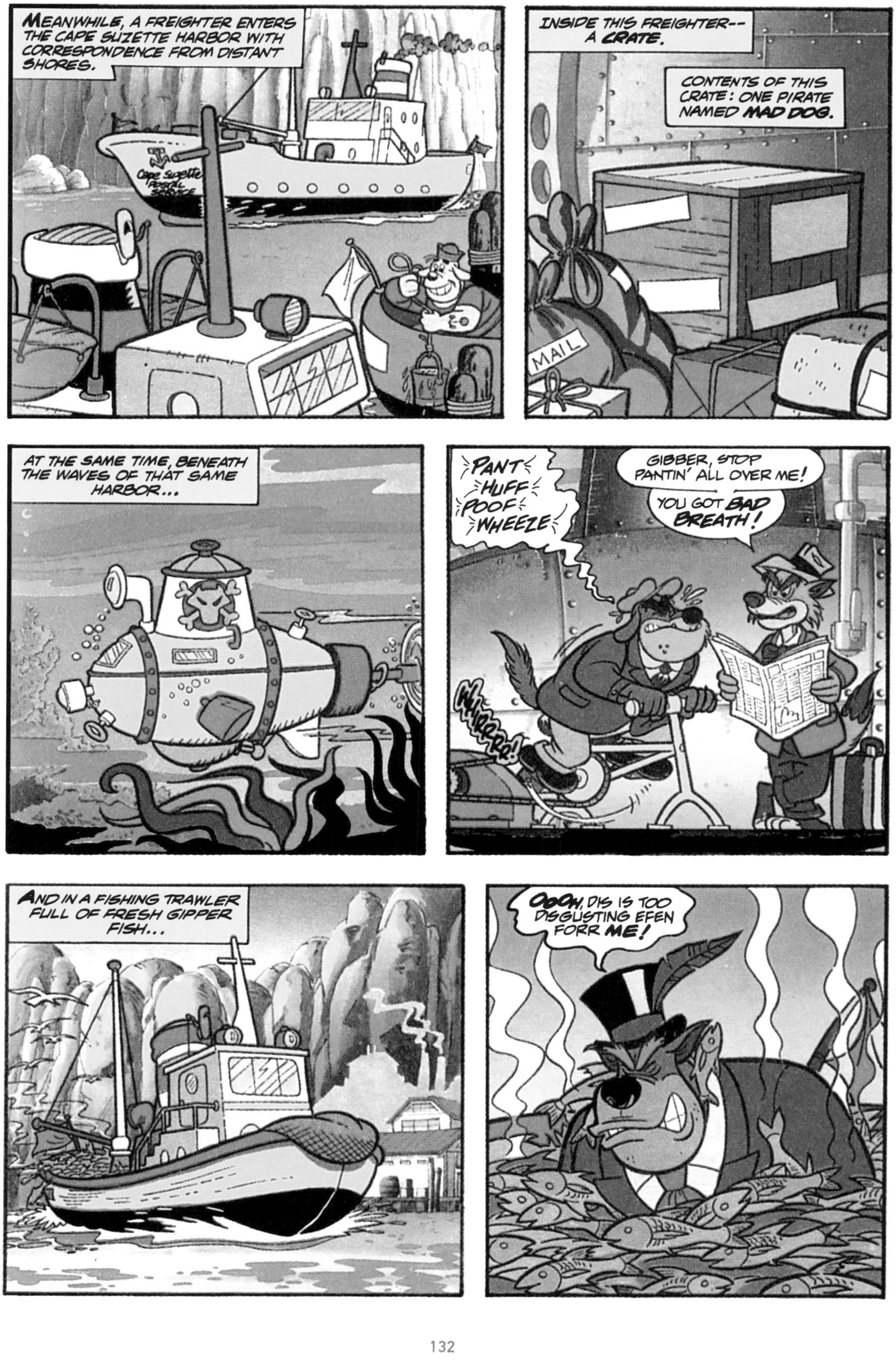
MEANWHILE, A FREIGHTER ENTERS THE CAPE SUZETTE HARBOR WITH CORRESPONDENCE FROM DISTANT SHORES.
Cape Suzette Postal Service
INSIDE THIS FREIGHTER-- A CRATE.
CONTENTS OF THIS CRATE: ONE PIRATE NAMED MAD DOG.
MAIL
AT THE SAME TIME, BENEATH THE WAVES OF THAT SAME HARBOR...
PANT HUFF POOF WHEEZE
GIBBER, STOP PANTIN' ALL OVER ME!
YOU GOT BAD BREATH!
WHIRRRR!
AND IN A FISHING TRAWLER FULL OF FRESH GIPPER FISH...
OOOH, DIS IS TOO DISGUSTING EFFEN FORR ME!

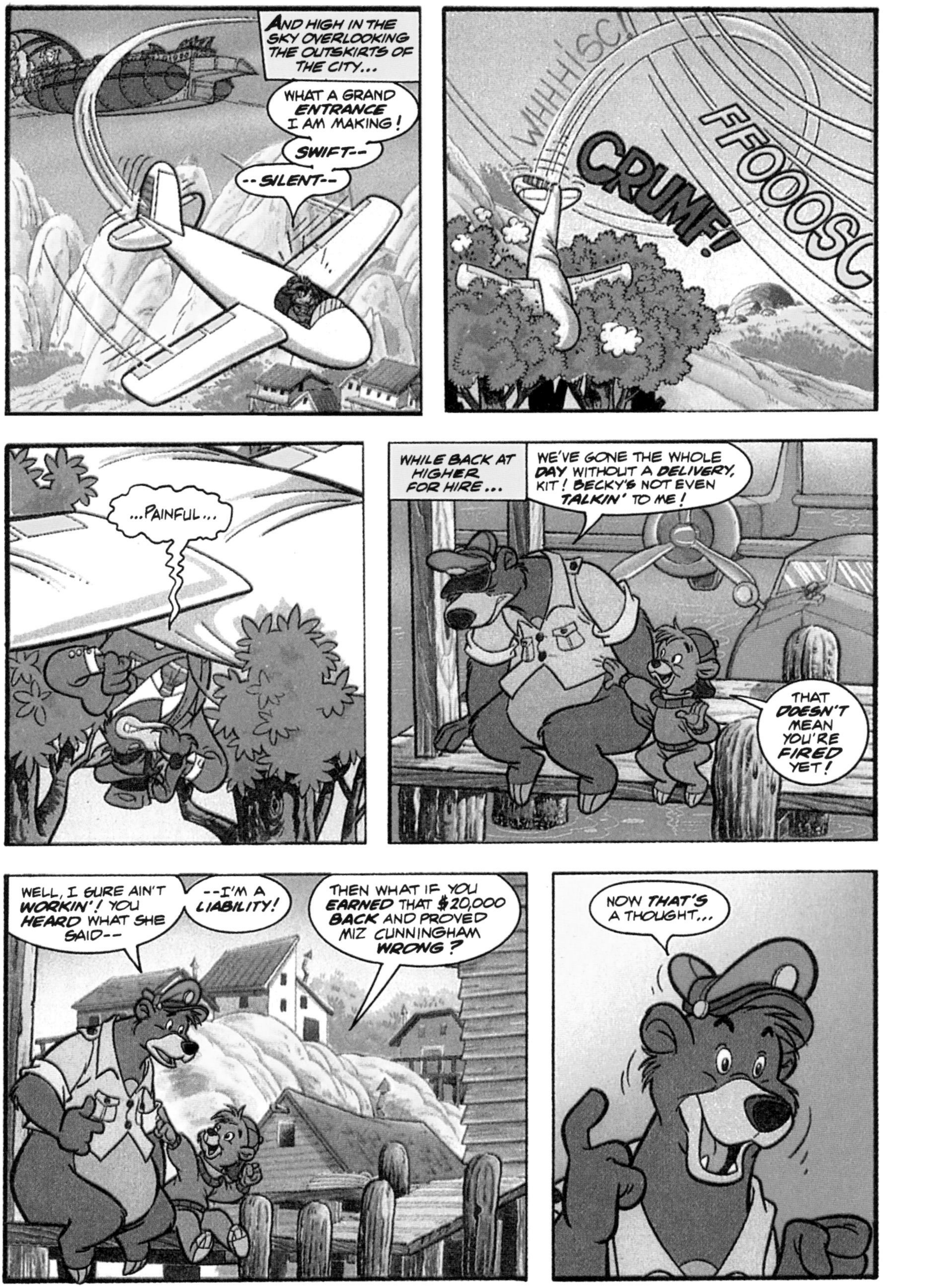

AND HIGH IN THE SKY OVERLOOKING THE OUTSKIRTS OF THE CITY...
WHAT A GRAND ENTRANCE I AM MAKING!
SWIFT--
--SILENT--
WHHHISC!
CRUMF!
FFOOOSC
...PAINFUL...
WHILE BACK AT HIGHER FOR HIRE...
WE'VE GONE THE WHOLE DAY WITHOUT A DELIVERY, KIT! BECKY'S NOT EVEN TALKIN' TO ME!
THAT DOESN'T MEAN YOU'RE FIRED YET!
WELL, I SURE AIN'T WORKIN'! YOU HEARD WHAT SHE SAID--
--I'M A LIABILITY!
THEN WHAT IF YOU EARNED THAT $20,000 BACK AND PROVED MIZ CUNNINGHAM WRONG?
NOW THAT'S A THOUGHT...

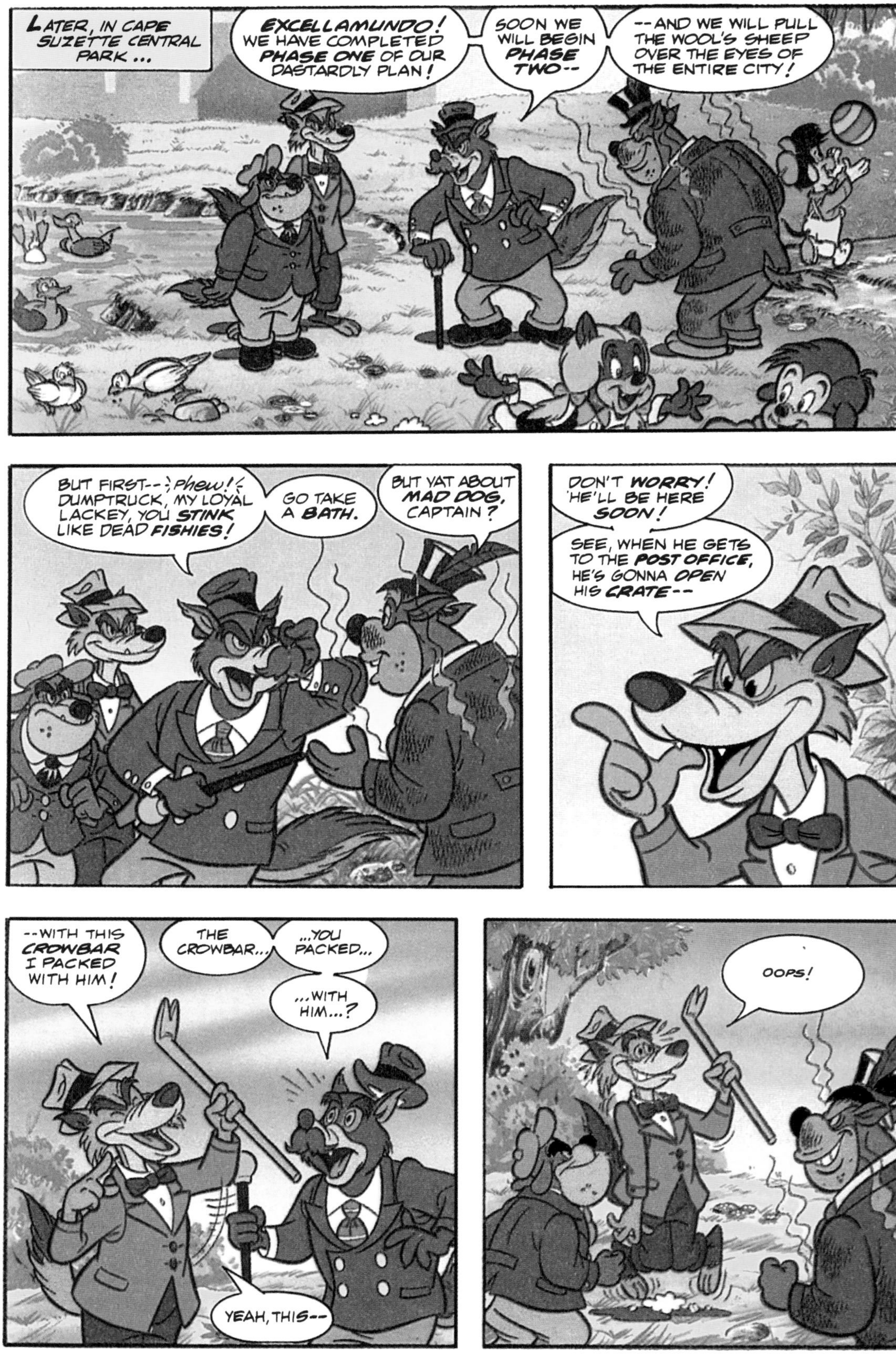
LATER, IN CAPE SUZETTE CENTRAL PARK...
EXCELLAMUNDO! WE HAVE COMPLETED PHASE ONE OF OUR DASTARDLY PLAN!
SOON WE WILL BEGIN PHASE TWO--
--AND WE WILL PULL THE WOOL'S SHEEP OVER THE EYES OF THE ENTIRE CITY!
BUT FIRST-- phew! DUMPTRUCK, MY LOYAL LACKEY, YOU STINK LIKE DEAD FISHIES!
GO TAKE A BATH.
BUT YAT ABOUT MAD DOG, CAPTAIN?
DON'T WORRY! HE'LL BE HERE SOON!
SEE, WHEN HE GETS TO THE POST OFFICE, HE'S GONNA OPEN HIS CRATE--
--WITH THIS CROWBAR I PACKED WITH HIM!
THE CROWBAR...
...YOU PACKED...
...WITH HIM...?
YEAH, THIS--
OOPS!

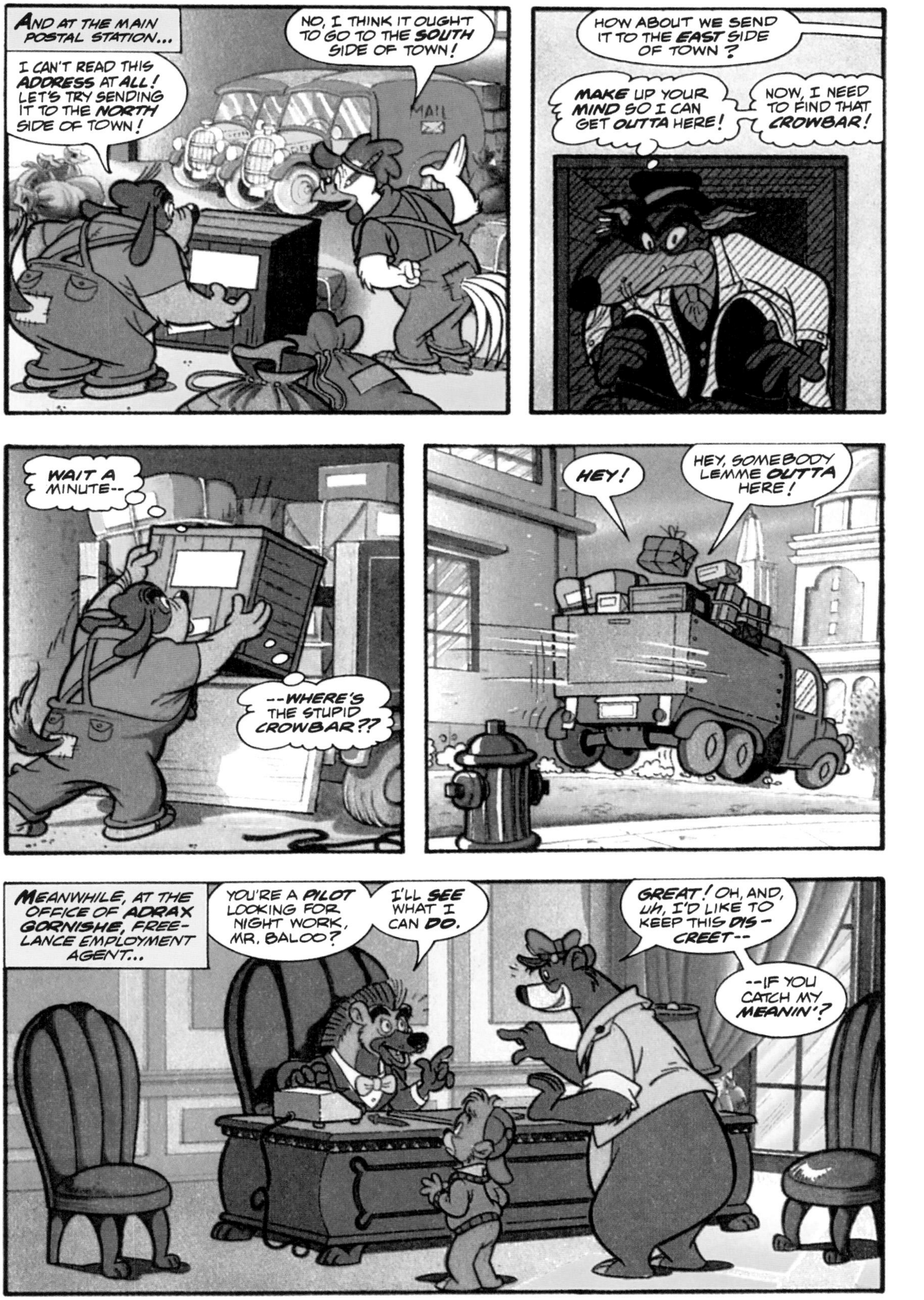
AND AT THE MAIN POSTAL STATION...
I CAN'T READ THIS ADDRESS AT ALL! LET'S TRY SENDING IT TO THE NORTH SIDE OF TOWN!
NO, I THINK IT OUGHT TO GO TO THE SOUTH SIDE OF TOWN!
MAIL
HOW ABOUT WE SEND IT TO THE EAST SIDE OF TOWN?
MAKE UP YOUR MIND SO I CAN GET OUTTA HERE!
NOW, I NEED TO FIND THAT CROWBAR!
WAIT A MINUTE--
--WHERE'S THE STUPID CROWBAR??
HEY!
HEY, SOMEBODY LEMME OUTTA HERE!
MEANWHILE, AT THE OFFICE OF ADRAX GORNISHE, FREE-LANCE EMPLOYMENT AGENT...
YOU'RE A PILOT LOOKING FOR NIGHT WORK, MR. BALOO?
I'LL SEE WHAT I CAN DO.
GREAT! OH, AND, uh, I'D LIKE TO KEEP THIS DIS-CREET--
--IF YOU CATCH MY MEANIN'?

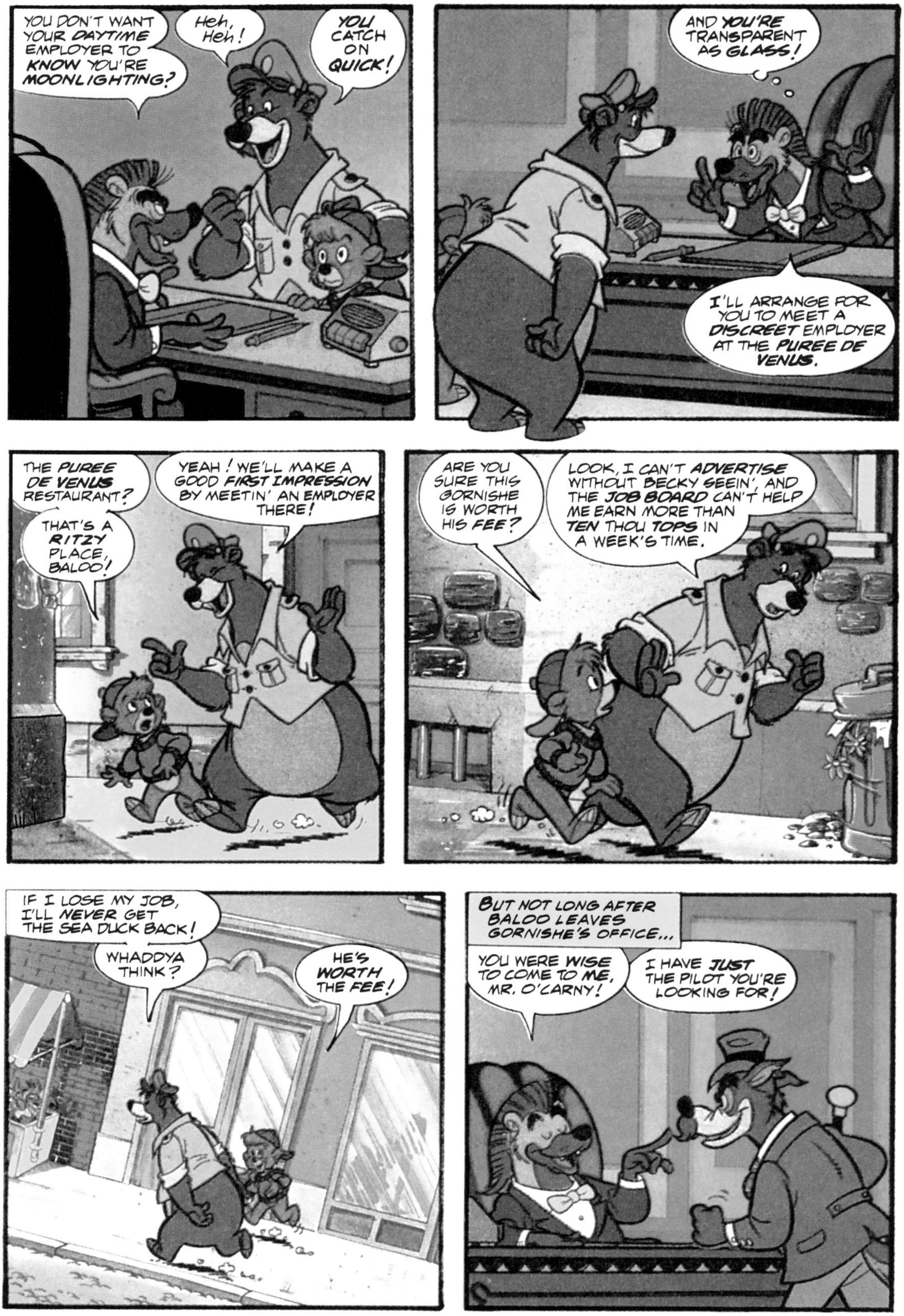

YOU DON'T WANT YOUR DAYTIME EMPLOYER TO KNOW YOU'RE MOONLIGHTING?
Heh, Heh!
YOU CATCH ON QUICK!
AND YOU'RE TRANSPARENT AS GLASS!
I'LL ARRANGE FOR YOU TO MEET A DISCREET EMPLOYER AT THE PUREE DE VENUS.
THE PUREE DE VENUS RESTAURANT?
THAT'S A RITZY PLACE, BALOO!
YEAH! WE'LL MAKE A GOOD FIRST IMPRESSION BY MEETIN' AN EMPLOYER THERE!
ARE YOU SURE THIS GORNISHE IS WORTH HIS FEE?
LOOK, I CAN'T ADVERTISE WITHOUT BECKY SEEIN', AND THE JOB BOARD CAN'T HELP ME EARN MORE THAN TEN THOU TOPS IN A WEEK'S TIME.
IF I LOSE MY JOB, I'LL NEVER GET THE SEA DUCK BACK!
WHADDYA THINK?
HE'S WORTH THE FEE!
BUT NOT LONG AFTER BALOO LEAVES GORNISHE'S OFFICE...
YOU WERE WISE TO COME TO ME, MR. O'CARNY!
I HAVE JUST THE PILOT YOU'RE LOOKING FOR!

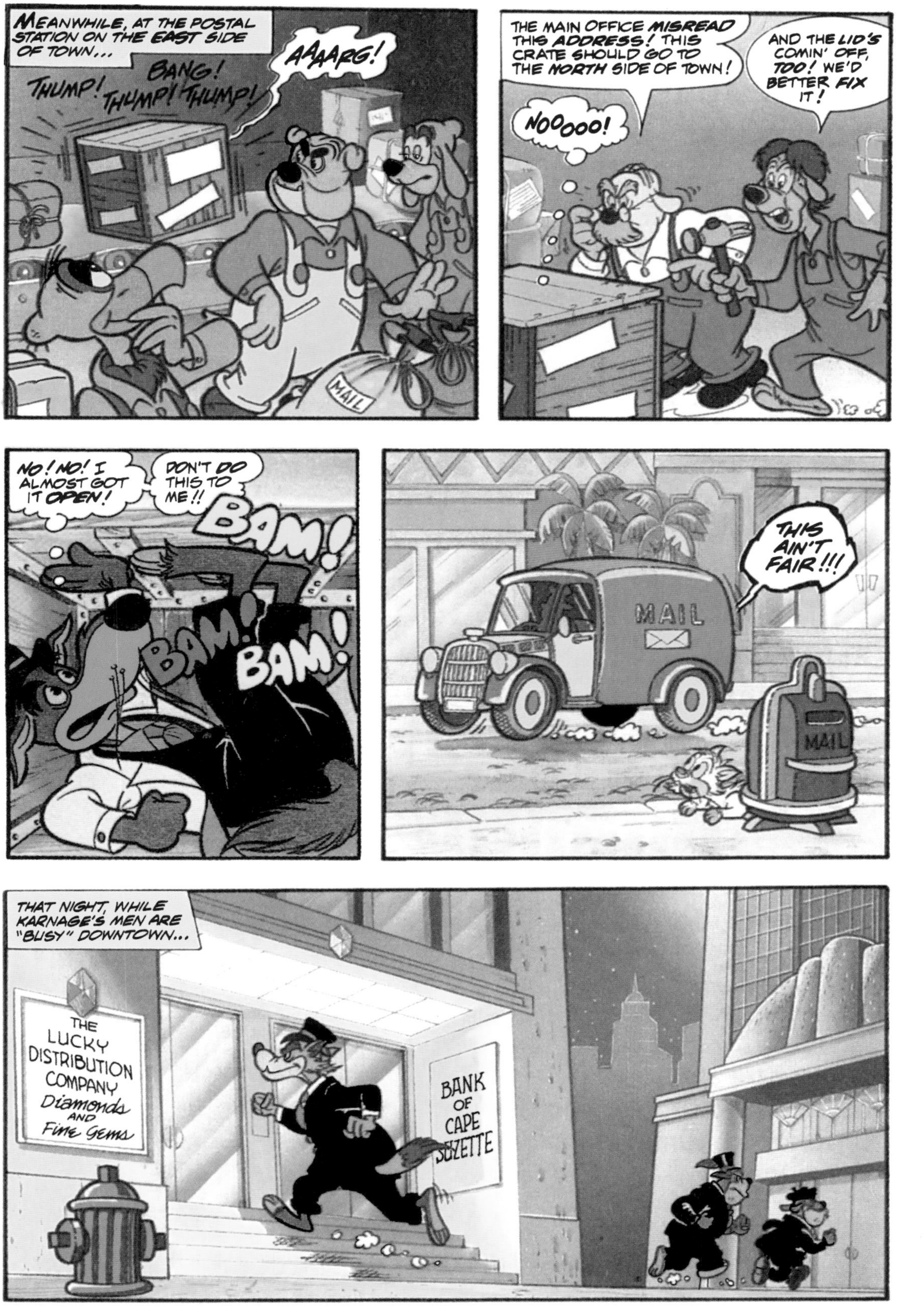

MEANWHILE, AT THE POSTAL STATION ON THE EAST SIDE OF TOWN...
THUMP! BANG! THUMP! THUMP!
AAAARG!
THE MAIN OFFICE MISREAD THIS ADDRESS! THIS CRATE SHOULD GO TO THE NORTH SIDE OF TOWN!
AND THE LID'S COMIN' OFF, TOO! WE'D BETTER FIX IT!
NOOOOO!
MAIL
NO! NO! I ALMOST GOT IT OPEN!
DON'T DO THIS TO ME!!
BAM! BAM! BAM!
THIS AIN'T FAIR!!!
MAIL
MAIL
THAT NIGHT, WHILE KARNAGE'S MEN ARE "BUSY" DOWNTOWN...
THE LUCKY DISTRIBUTION COMPANY Diamonds AND Fine Gems
BANK OF CAPE SUZETTE

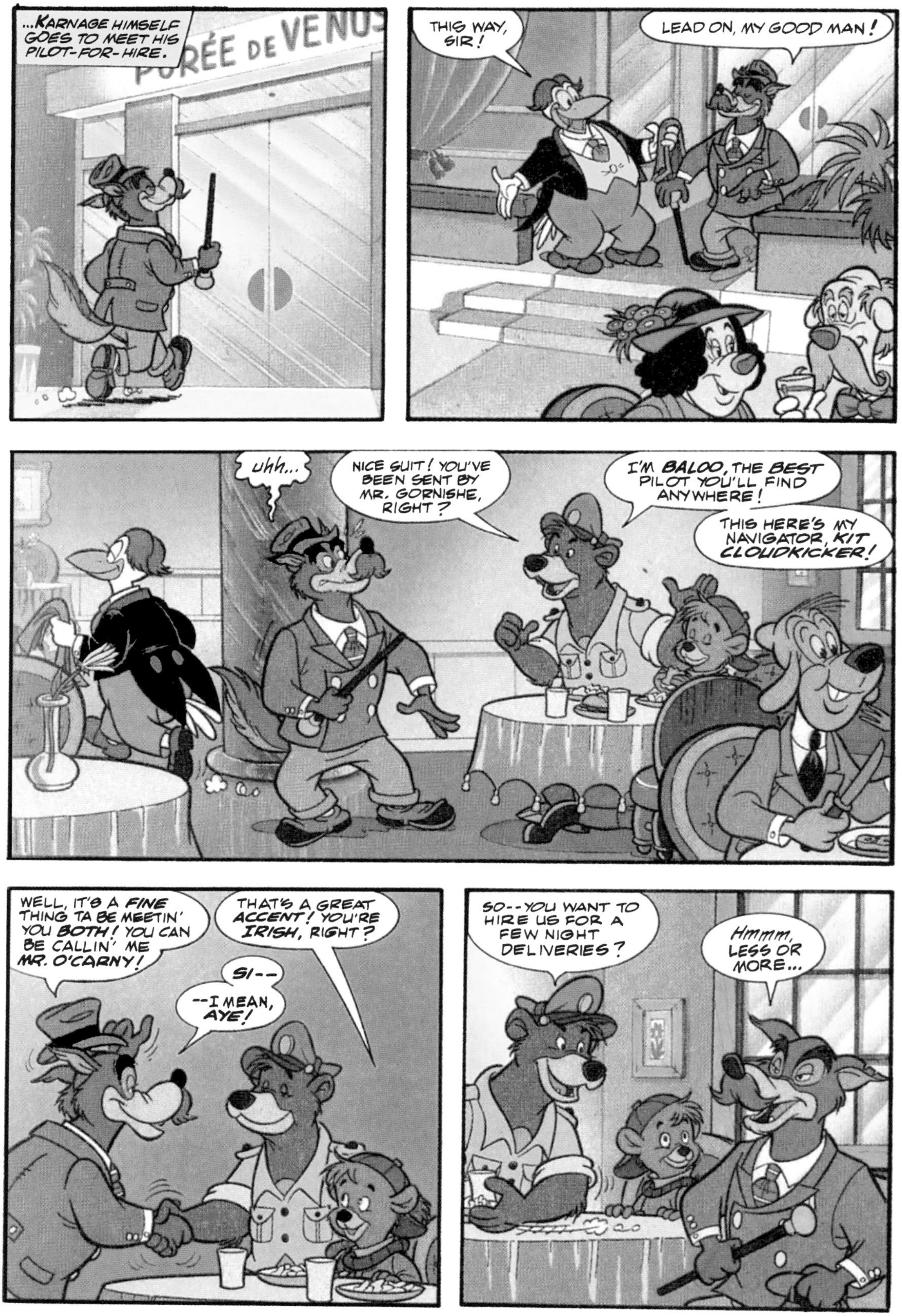
...KARNAGE HIMSELF GOES TO MEET HIS PILOT-FOR-HIRE.
PURÉE DE VENUS
THIS WAY, SIR!
LEAD ON, MY GOOD MAN!
uhh...
NICE SUIT! YOU'VE BEEN SENT BY MR. GORNISHE, RIGHT?
I'M BALOO, THE BEST PILOT YOU'LL FIND ANYWHERE!
THIS HERE'S MY NAVIGATOR, KIT CLOUDKICKER!
WELL, IT'S A FINE THING TA BE MEETIN' YOU BOTH! YOU CAN BE CALLIN' ME MR. O'CARNY!
THAT'S A GREAT ACCENT! YOU'RE IRISH, RIGHT?
SI--
--I MEAN, AYE!
SO--YOU WANT TO HIRE US FOR A FEW NIGHT DELIVERIES?
Hmmm, LESS OR MORE...

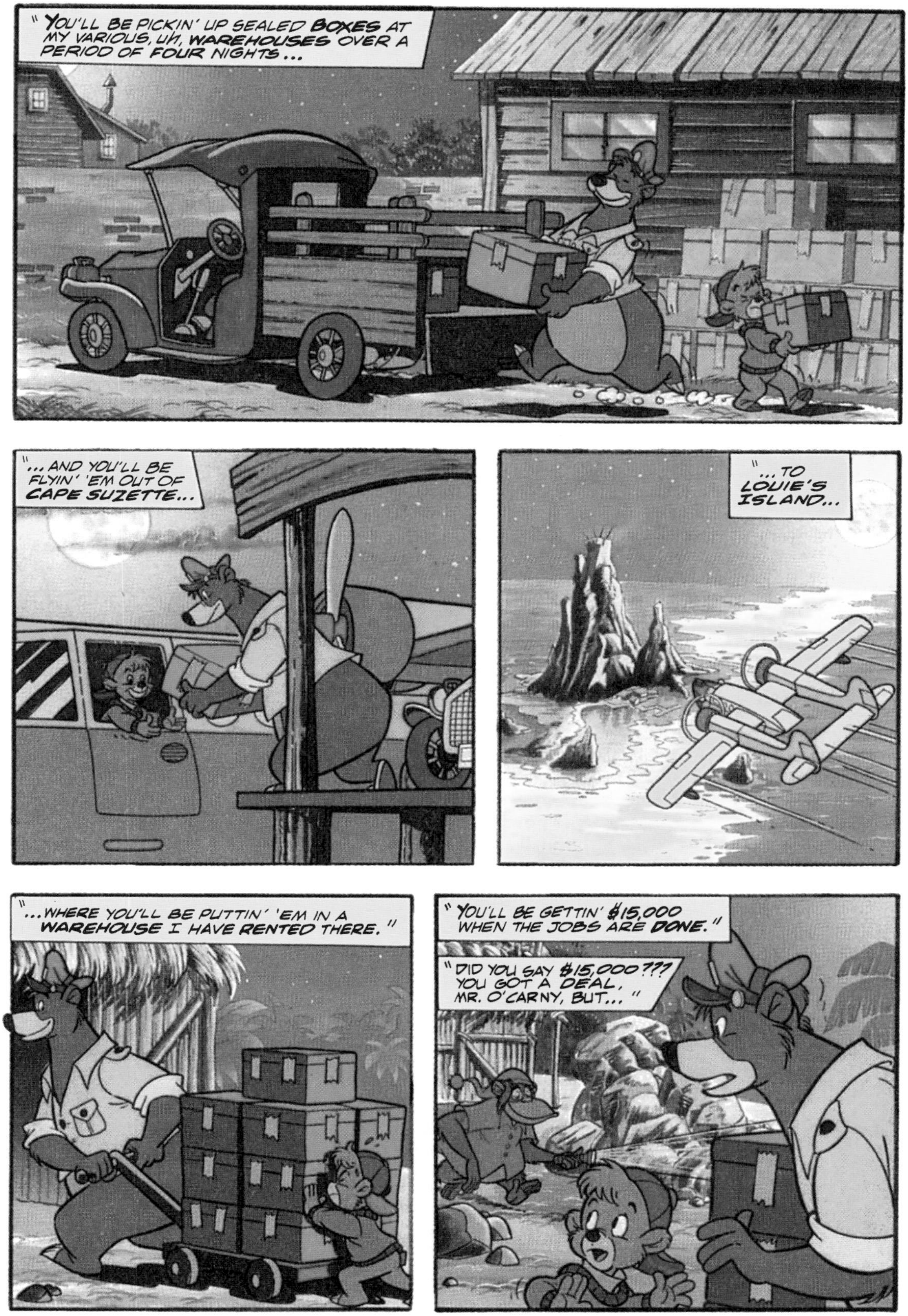
"YOU'LL BE PICKIN' UP SEALED BOXES AT MY VARIOUS, UH, WAREHOUSES OVER A PERIOD OF FOUR NIGHTS...
"...AND YOU'LL BE FLYIN' 'EM OUT OF CAPE SUZETTE...
"...TO LOUIE'S ISLAND...
"...WHERE YOU'LL BE PUTTIN' 'EM IN A WAREHOUSE I HAVE RENTED THERE."
"YOU'LL BE GETTIN' $15,000 WHEN THE JOBS ARE DONE."
"DID YOU SAY $15,000??? YOU GOT A DEAL, MR. O'CARNY, BUT..."

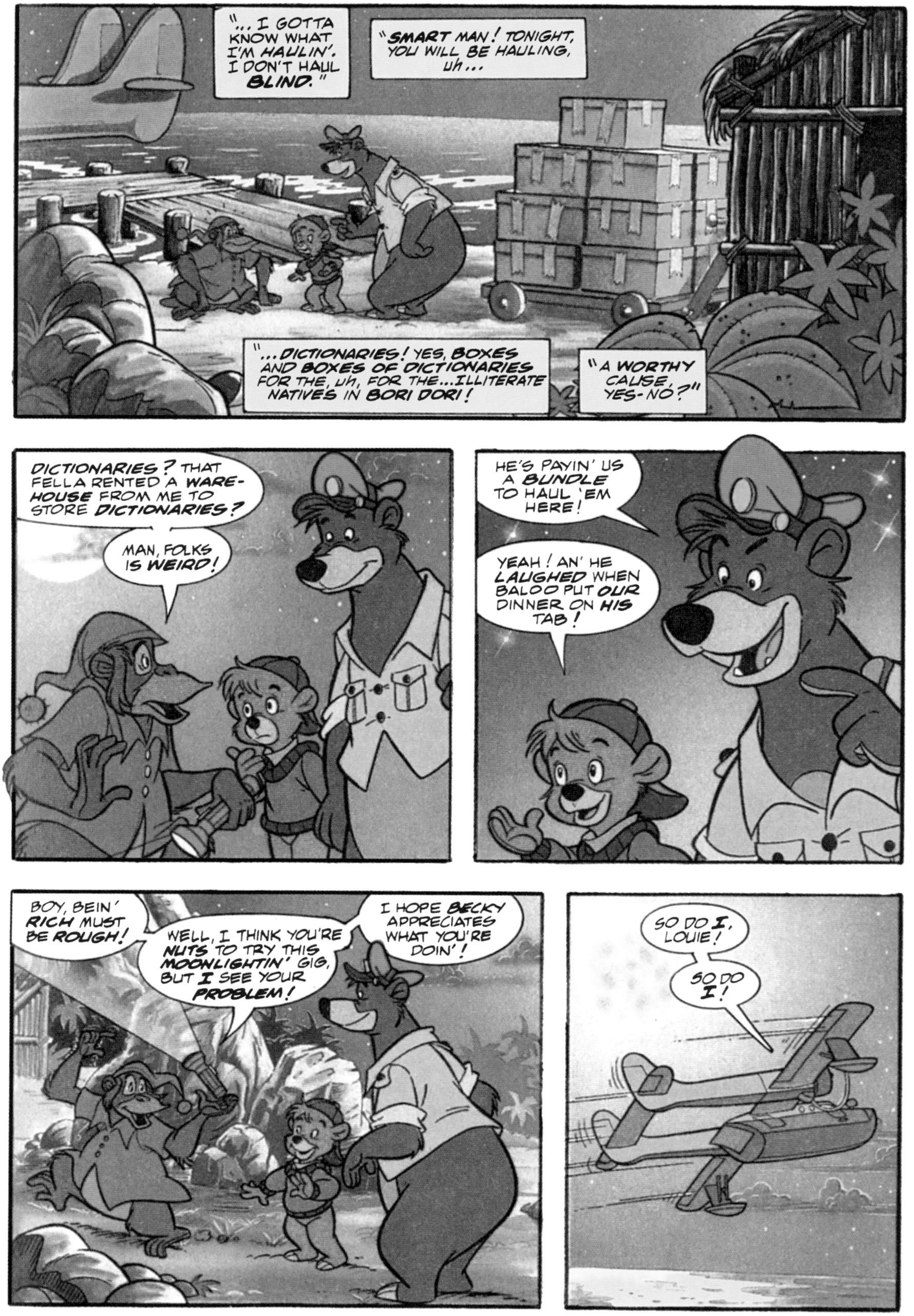
"... I GOTTA KNOW WHAT I'M HAULIN'. I DON'T HAUL BLIND."
"SMART MAN! TONIGHT, YOU WILL BE HAULING, uh ...
"... DICTIONARIES! YES, BOXES AND BOXES OF DICTIONARIES FOR THE, uh, FOR THE... ILLITERATE NATIVES IN BORI DORI!
"A WORTHY CAUSE, YES-NO?"
DICTIONARIES? THAT FELLA RENTED A WARE-HOUSE FROM ME TO STORE DICTIONARIES?
MAN, FOLKS IS WEIRD!
HE'S PAYIN' US A BUNDLE TO HAUL 'EM HERE!
YEAH! AN' HE LAUGHED WHEN BALOO PUT OUR DINNER ON HIS TAB!
BOY, BEIN' RICH MUST BE ROUGH!
WELL, I THINK YOU'RE NUTS TO TRY THIS MOONLIGHTIN' GIG, BUT I SEE YOUR PROBLEM!
I HOPE BECKY APPRECIATES WHAT YOU'RE DOIN'!
SO DO I, LOUIE!
SO DO I!

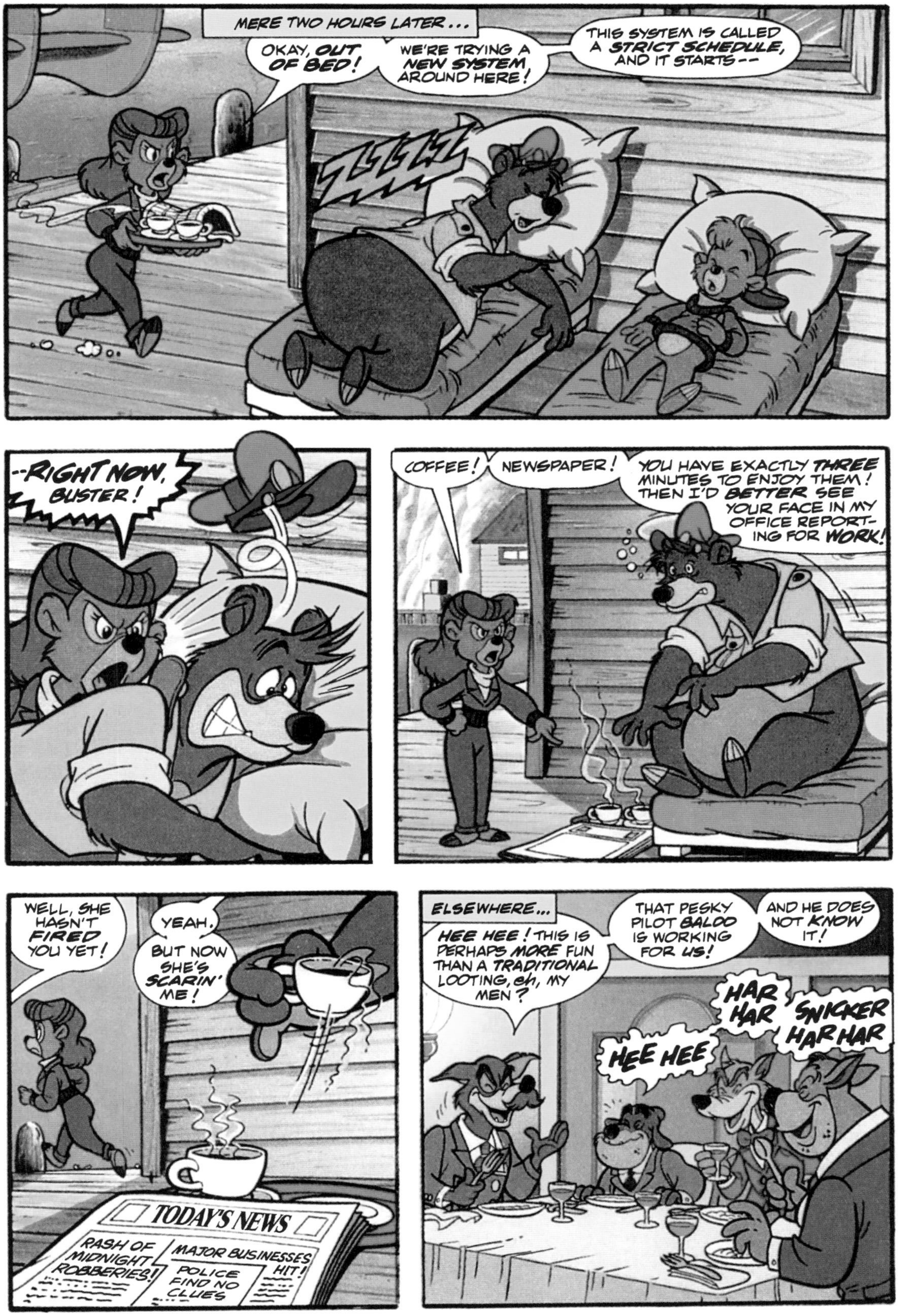
MERE TWO HOURS LATER...
OKAY, OUT OF BED!
WE'RE TRYING A NEW SYSTEM AROUND HERE!
THIS SYSTEM IS CALLED A STRICT SCHEDULE, AND IT STARTS--
ZZZZZ
--RIGHT NOW, BUSTER!
COFFEE!
NEWSPAPER!
YOU HAVE EXACTLY THREE MINUTES TO ENJOY THEM! THEN I'D BETTER SEE YOUR FACE IN MY OFFICE REPORTING FOR WORK!
WELL, SHE HASN'T FIRED YOU YET!
YEAH, BUT NOW SHE'S SCARIN' ME!
TODAY'S NEWS
RASH OF MIDNIGHT ROBBERIES!
MAJOR BUSINESSES HIT!
POLICE FIND NO CLUES
ELSEWHERE...
HEE HEE! THIS IS PERHAPS MORE FUN THAN A TRADITIONAL LOOTING, eh, MY MEN?
THAT PESKY PILOT BALOO IS WORKING FOR US!
AND HE DOES NOT KNOW IT!
HAR HAR
SNICKER HAR HAR
HEE HEE

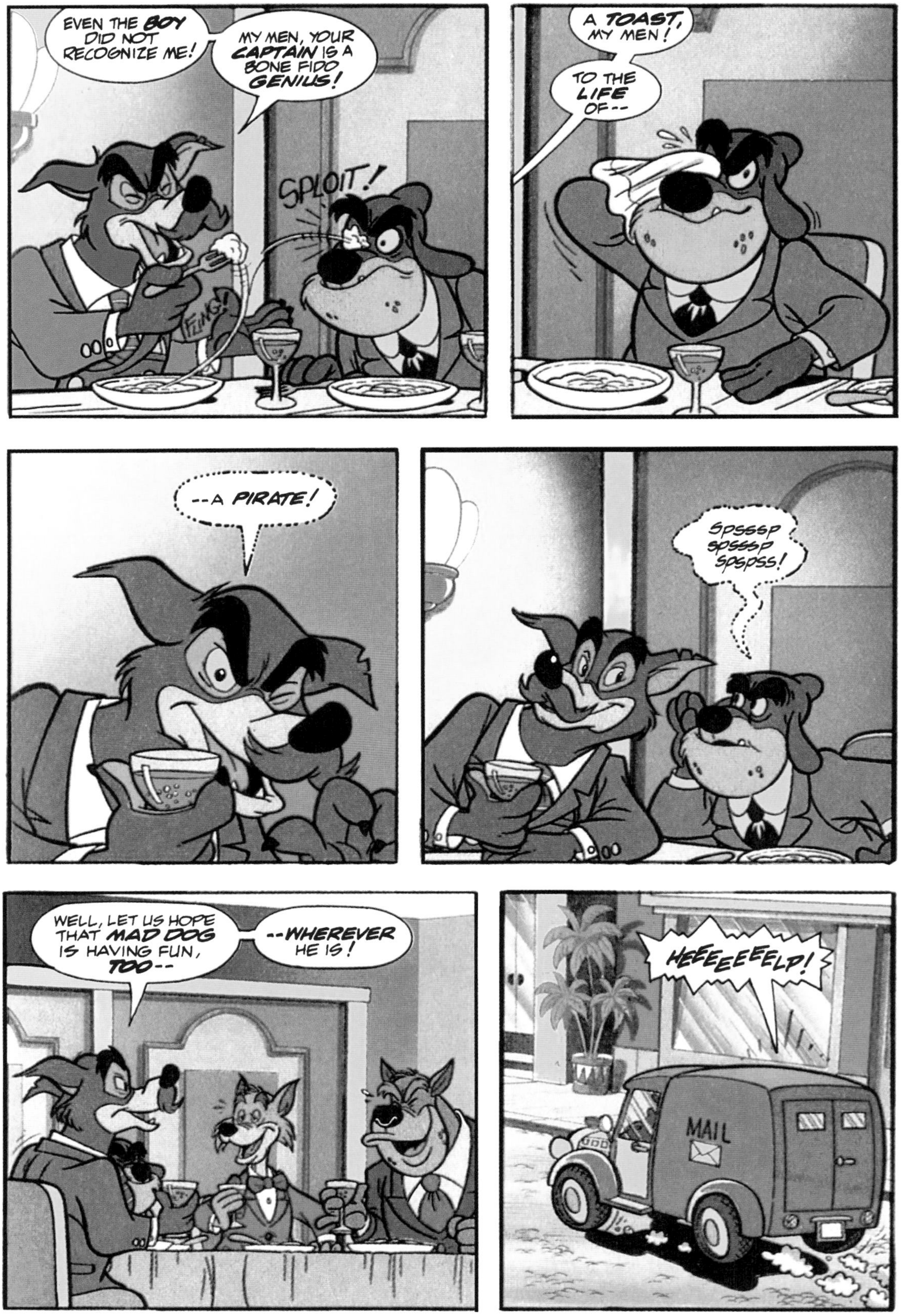

EVEN THE BOY DID NOT RECOGNIZE ME!
MY MEN, YOUR CAPTAIN IS A BONE FIDO GENIUS!
SPLOIT!
FLING!
A TOAST, MY MEN!
TO THE LIFE OF--
--A PIRATE!
Spsssp spsssp spspss!
WELL, LET US HOPE THAT MAD DOG IS HAVING FUN, TOO--
--WHEREVER HE IS!
HEEEEEEEELP!
MAIL

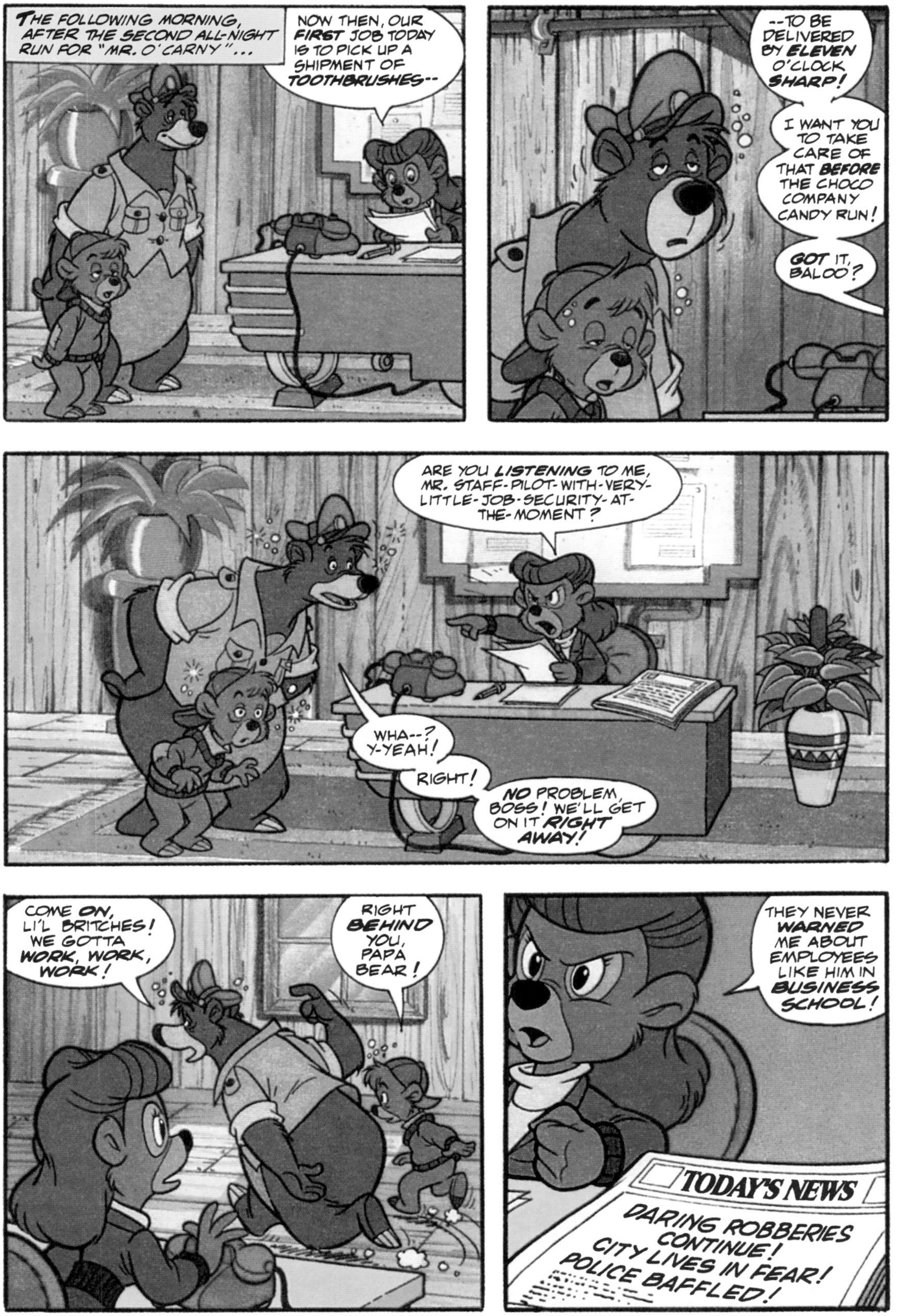
THE FOLLOWING MORNING, AFTER THE SECOND ALL-NIGHT RUN FOR "MR. O'CARNY"...
NOW THEN, OUR FIRST JOB TODAY IS TO PICK UP A SHIPMENT OF TOOTHBRUSHES--
--TO BE DELIVERED BY ELEVEN O'CLOCK SHARP!
I WANT YOU TO TAKE CARE OF THAT BEFORE THE CHOCO COMPANY CANDY RUN!
GOT IT, BALOO?
ARE YOU LISTENING TO ME, MR. STAFF-PILOT-WITH-VERY-LITTLE-JOB-SECURITY-AT-THE-MOMENT?
WHA--? Y-YEAH!
RIGHT!
NO PROBLEM, BOSS! WE'LL GET ON IT RIGHT AWAY!
COME ON, LI'L BRITCHES! WE GOTTA WORK, WORK, WORK!
RIGHT BEHIND YOU, PAPA BEAR!
THEY NEVER WARNED ME ABOUT EMPLOYEES LIKE HIM IN BUSINESS SCHOOL!
TODAY'S NEWS
DARING ROBBERIES CONTINUE! CITY LIVES IN FEAR! POLICE BAFFLED!

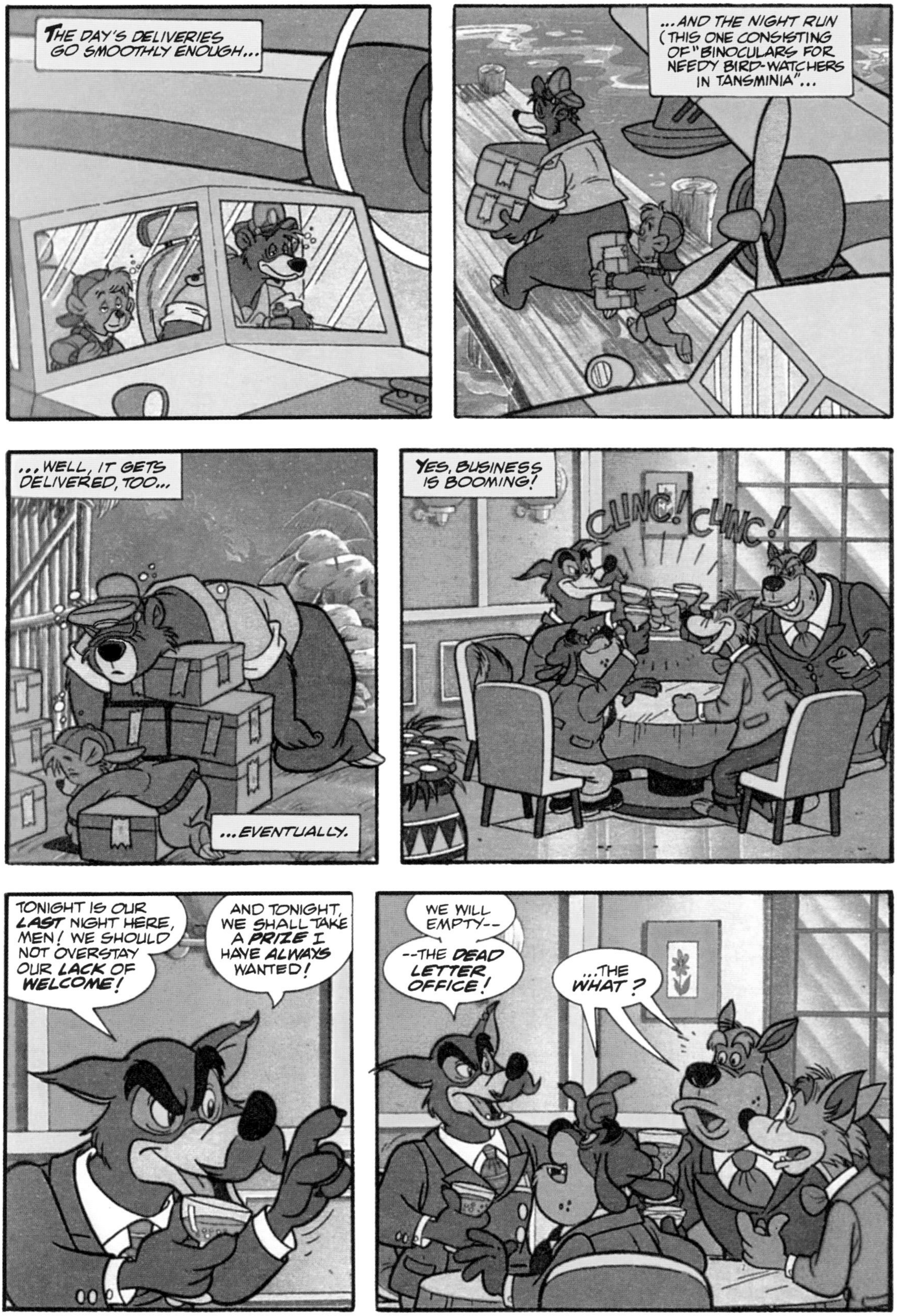

THE DAY'S DELIVERIES GO SMOOTHLY ENOUGH...
...AND THE NIGHT RUN (THIS ONE CONSISTING OF "BINOCULARS FOR NEEDY BIRD-WATCHERS IN TANSMINIA"...
...WELL, IT GETS DELIVERED, TOO...
...EVENTUALLY.
YES, BUSINESS IS BOOMING!
CLINC! CLINC!
TONIGHT IS OUR LAST NIGHT HERE, MEN! WE SHOULD NOT OVERSTAY OUR LACK OF WELCOME!
AND TONIGHT, WE SHALL TAKE A PRIZE I HAVE ALWAYS WANTED!
WE WILL EMPTY--
--THE DEAD LETTER OFFICE!
...THE WHAT?

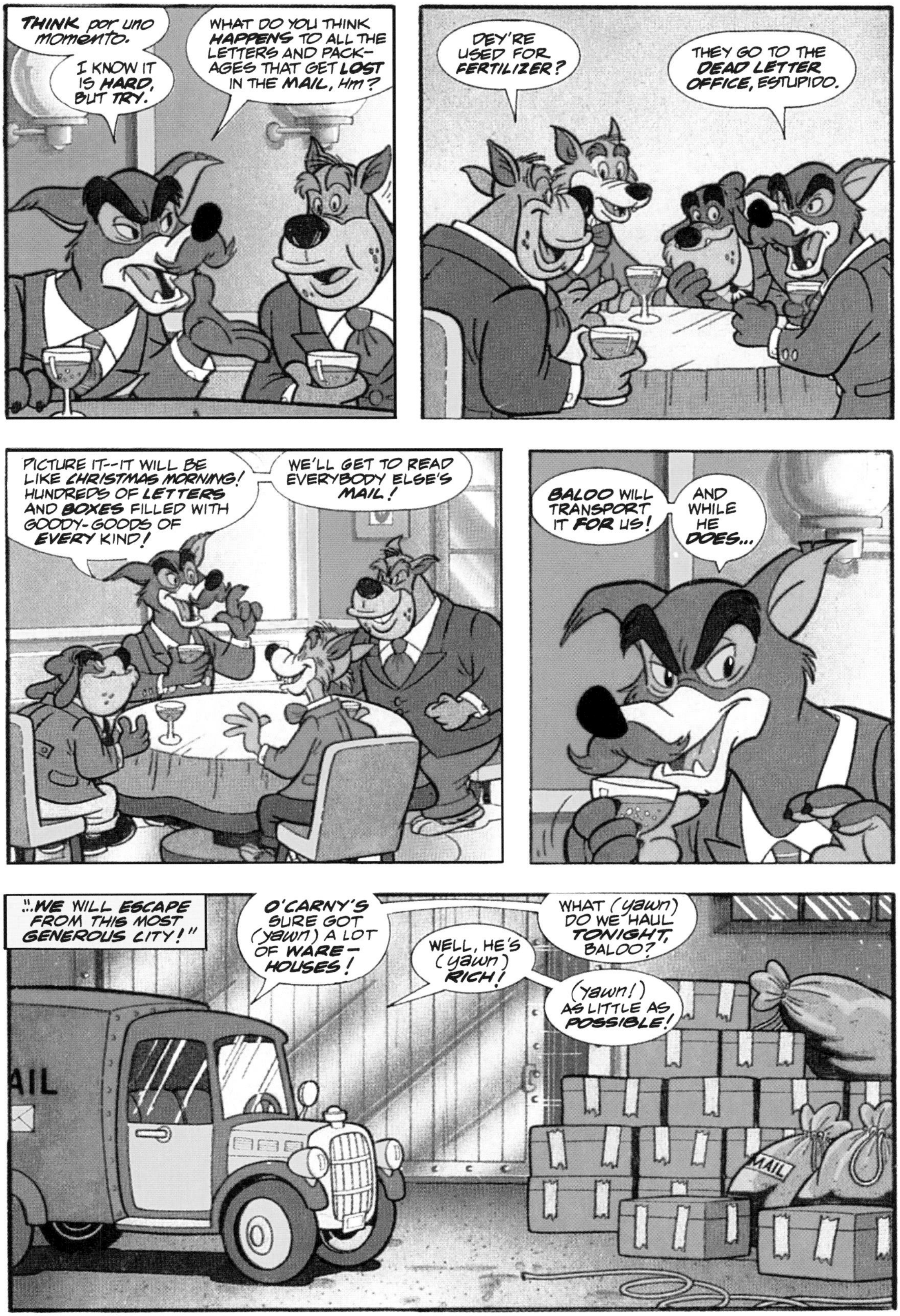
THINK por uno momento.
I KNOW IT IS HARD, BUT TRY.
WHAT DO YOU THINK HAPPENS TO ALL THE LETTERS AND PACKAGES THAT GET LOST IN THE MAIL, Hm?
DEY'RE USED FOR FERTILIZER?
THEY GO TO THE DEAD LETTER OFFICE, ESTUPIDO.
PICTURE IT--IT WILL BE LIKE CHRISTMAS MORNING! HUNDREDS OF LETTERS AND BOXES FILLED WITH GOODY-GOODS OF EVERY KIND!
WE'LL GET TO READ EVERYBODY ELSE'S MAIL!
BALOO WILL TRANSPORT IT FOR US!
AND WHILE HE DOES...
"...WE WILL ESCAPE FROM THIS MOST GENEROUS CITY!"
O'CARNY'S SURE GOT (yawn) A LOT OF WARE-HOUSES!
WELL, HE'S (yawn) RICH!
WHAT (yawn) DO WE HAUL TONIGHT, BALOO?
(yawn!) AS LITTLE AS POSSIBLE!
MAIL
MAIL

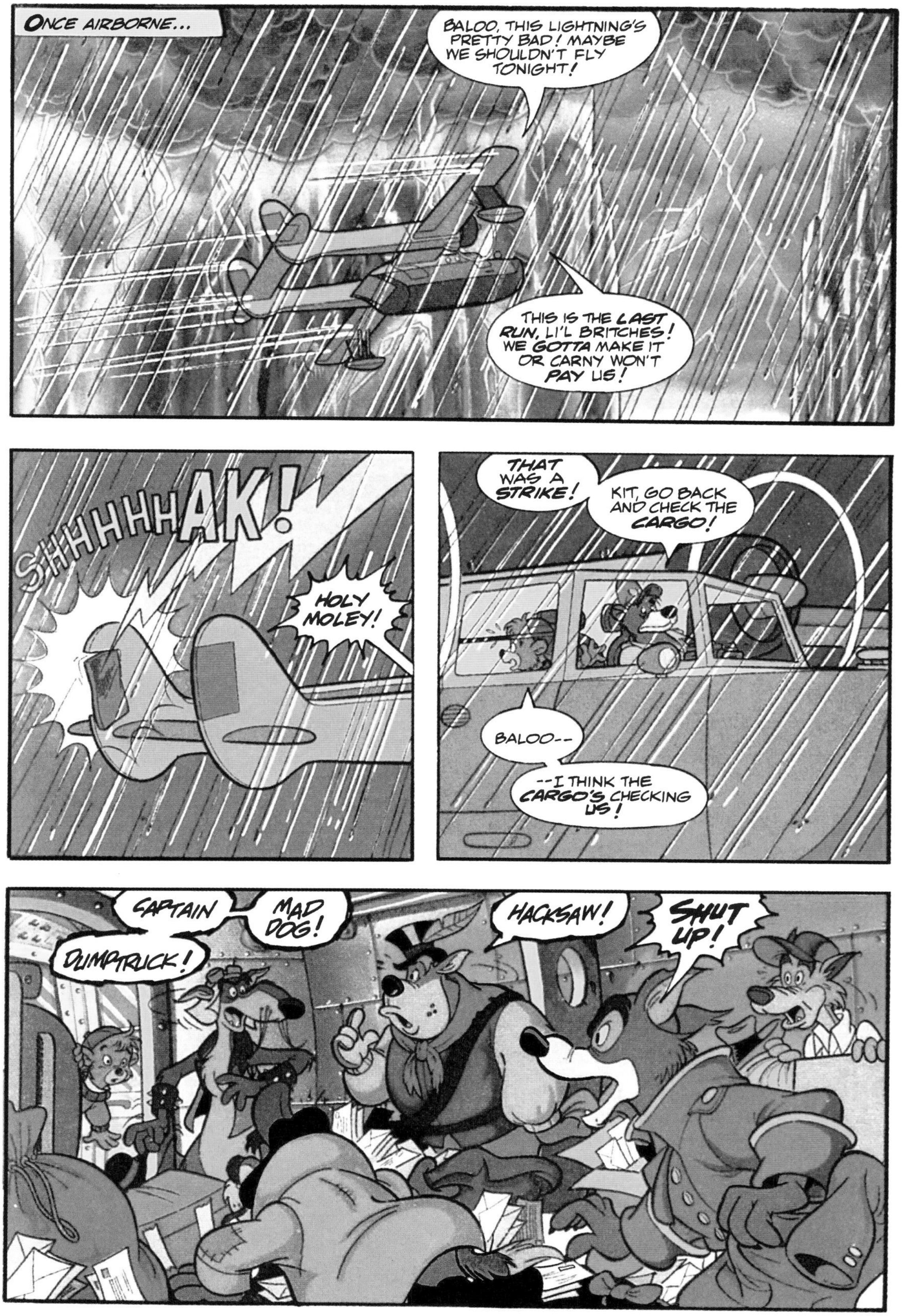
ONCE AIRBORNE...
BALOO, THIS LIGHTNING'S PRETTY BAD! MAYBE WE SHOULDN'T FLY TONIGHT!
THIS IS THE LAST RUN, LI'L BRITCHES! WE GOTTA MAKE IT OR CARNY WON'T PAY US!
SHHHHHAK!
HOLY MOLEY!
THAT WAS A STRIKE!
KIT, GO BACK AND CHECK THE CARGO!
BALOO--
--I THINK THE CARGO'S CHECKING US!
CAPTAIN
MAD DOG!
DUMPTRUCK!
HACKSAW!
SHUT UP!

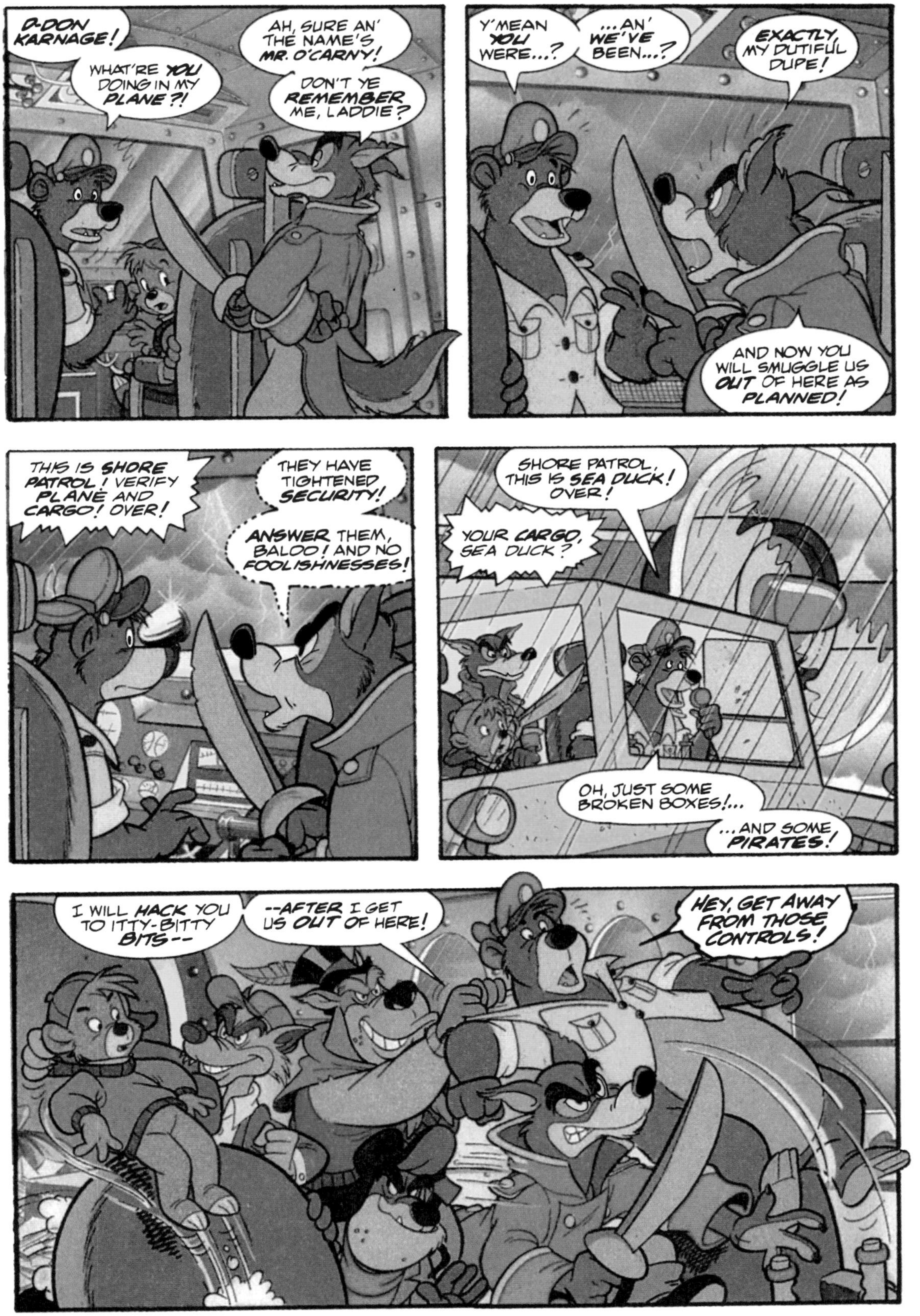
D-DON KARNAGE!
WHAT'RE YOU DOING IN MY PLANE?!
AH, SURE AN' THE NAME'S MR. O'CARNY!
DON'T YE REMEMBER ME, LADDIE?
Y'MEAN YOU WERE...?
...AN' WE'VE BEEN...?
EXACTLY, MY DUTIFUL DUPE!
AND NOW YOU WILL SMUGGLE US OUT OF HERE AS PLANNED!
THIS IS SHORE PATROL! VERIFY PLANE AND CARGO! OVER!
THEY HAVE TIGHTENED SECURITY!
ANSWER THEM, BALOO! AND NO FOOLISHNESSES!
SHORE PATROL, THIS IS SEA DUCK! OVER!
YOUR CARGO, SEA DUCK?
OH, JUST SOME BROKEN BOXES!...
...AND SOME PIRATES!
I WILL HACK YOU TO ITTY-BITTY BITS--
--AFTER I GET US OUT OF HERE!
HEY, GET AWAY FROM THOSE CONTROLS!

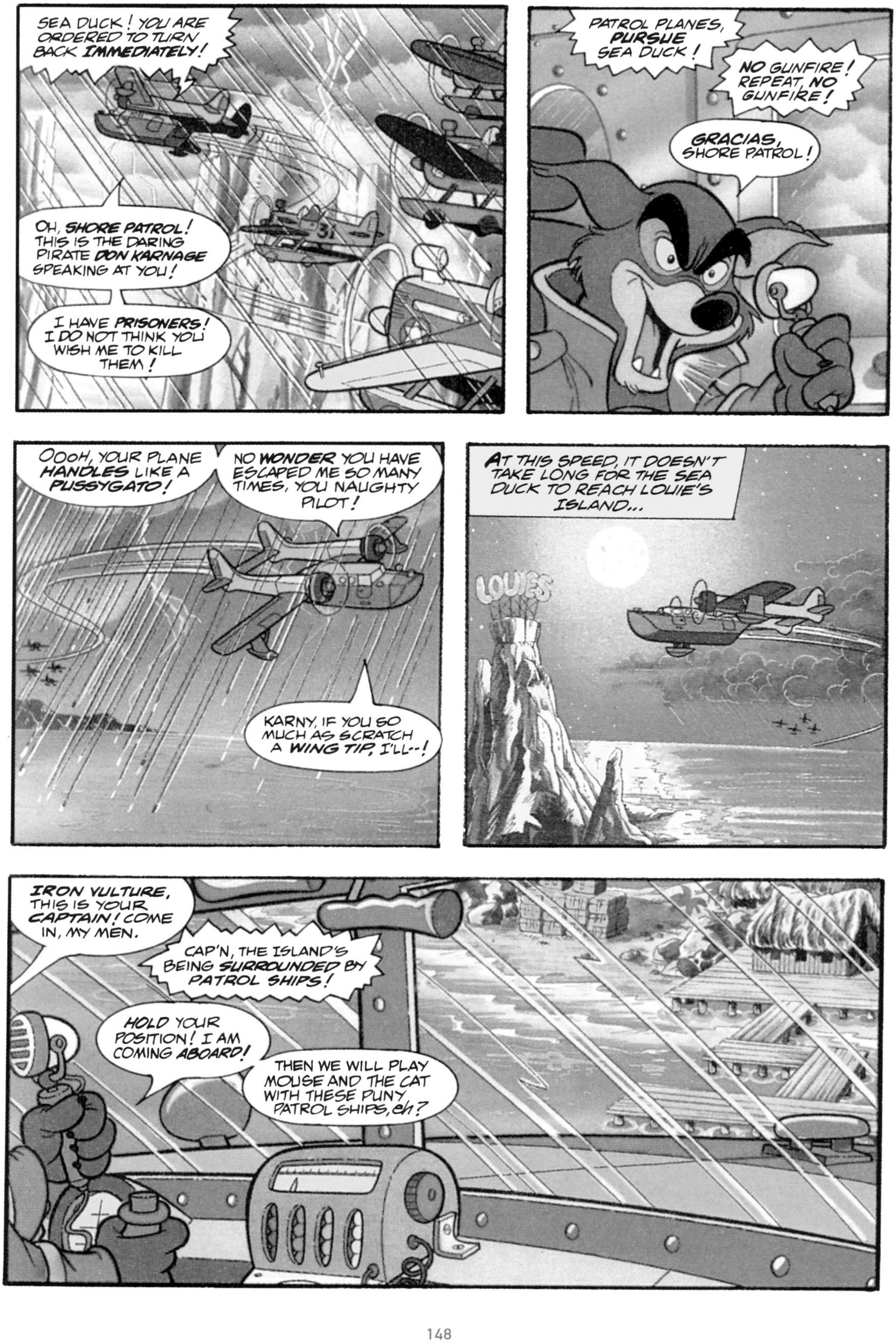
SEA DUCK! YOU ARE ORDERED TO TURN BACK IMMEDIATELY!
OH, SHORE PATROL! THIS IS THE DARING PIRATE DON KARNAGE SPEAKING AT YOU!
I HAVE PRISONERS! I DO NOT THINK YOU WISH ME TO KILL THEM!
PATROL PLANES, PURSUE SEA DUCK!
NO GUNFIRE! REPEAT, NO GUNFIRE!
GRACIAS, SHORE PATROL!
OOOH, YOUR PLANE HANDLES LIKE A PUSSYGATO!
NO WONDER YOU HAVE ESCAPED ME SO MANY TIMES, YOU NAUGHTY PILOT!
KARNY, IF YOU SO MUCH AS SCRATCH A WING TIP, I'LL--!
AT THIS SPEED, IT DOESN'T TAKE LONG FOR THE SEA DUCK TO REACH LOUIE'S ISLAND...
LOUIES
IRON VULTURE, THIS IS YOUR CAPTAIN! COME IN, MY MEN.
CAP'N, THE ISLAND'S BEING SURROUNDED BY PATROL SHIPS!
HOLD YOUR POSITION! I AM COMING ABOARD!
THEN WE WILL PLAY MOUSE AND THE CAT WITH THESE PUNY PATROL SHIPS, eh?

NOT IF *I* CAN HELP IT!

HEY, *WHAT'RE* YOU--!

FLICK!

WHAT DID YOU *DO?!* I CAN'T STOP THE *PLANE!!*

NNEEEEERRRROM!

THAT'S WHAT YOU GET FOR HIJACKING A CUSTOMIZED BABY LIKE *THIS* ONE, KARNY!

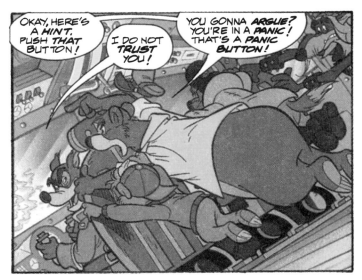

OKAY, HERE'S A *HINT.* PUSH *THAT* BUTTON!

I DO NOT *TRUST* YOU!

YOU GONNA *ARGUE?* YOU'RE IN A *PANIC!* THAT'S A *PANIC* BUTTON!

YOU WILL PAY *DEARLY* FOR THIS, BALOO!

PUNCH

YEAAAAAAH!!

SPRROING!

NOW IF YOU BOYS ARE *SMART,* YOU'LL LET ME TAKE *CONTROL* AGAIN!

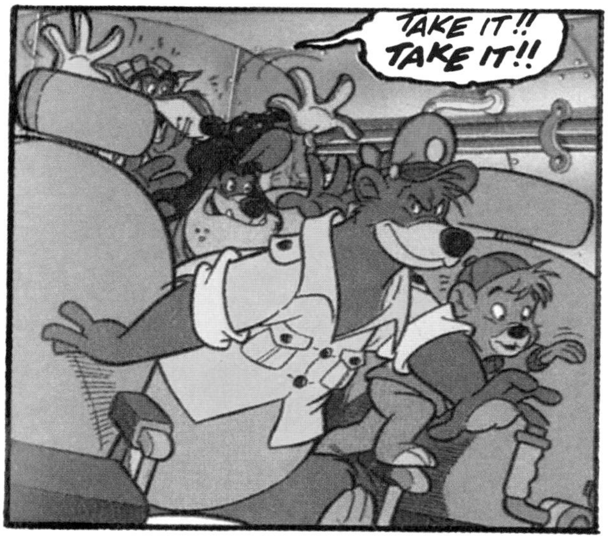
TAKE IT!! TAKE IT!!

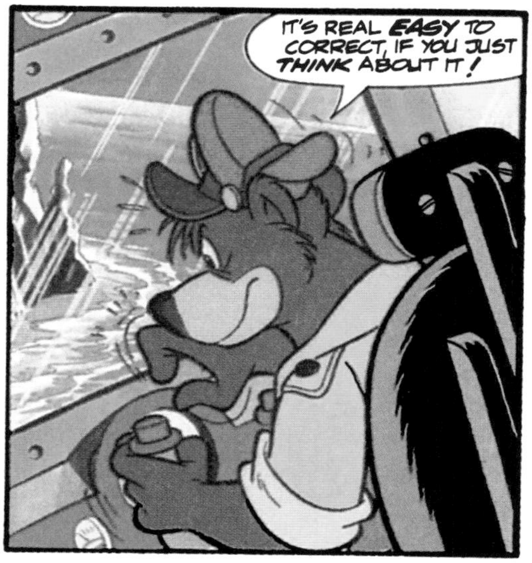
IT'S REAL EASY TO CORRECT, IF YOU JUST THINK ABOUT IT!

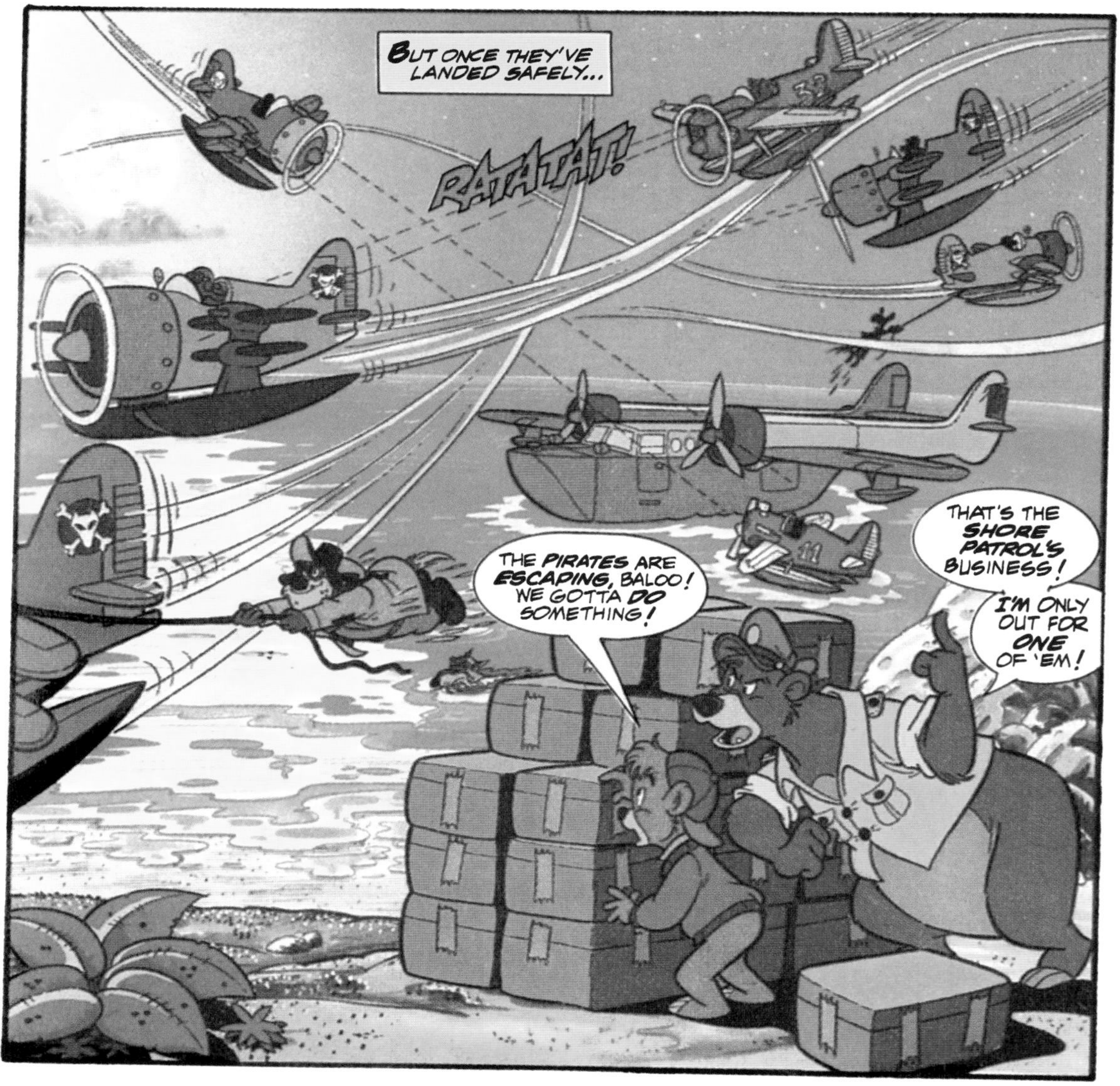
BUT ONCE THEY'VE LANDED SAFELY...
RATATAT!
THE PIRATES ARE ESCAPING, BALOO! WE GOTTA DO SOMETHING!
THAT'S THE SHORE PATROL'S BUSINESS!
I'M ONLY OUT FOR ONE OF 'EM!

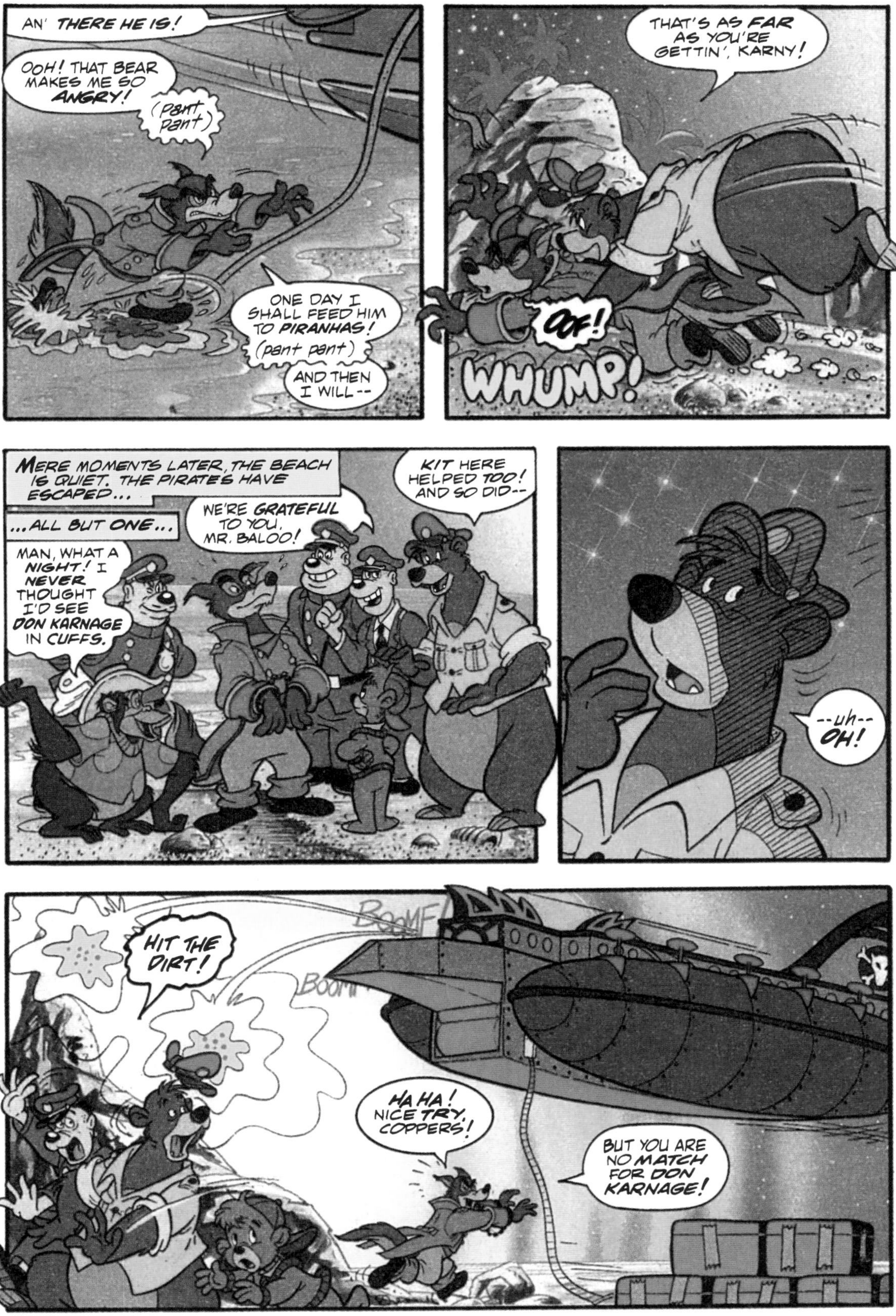
AN' THERE HE IS!
OOH! THAT BEAR MAKES ME SO ANGRY!
(pant pant)
ONE DAY I SHALL FEED HIM TO PIRANHAS!
(pant pant)
AND THEN I WILL --
THAT'S AS FAR AS YOU'RE GETTIN', KARNY!
OOF!
WHUMP!
MERE MOMENTS LATER, THE BEACH IS QUIET. THE PIRATES HAVE ESCAPED...
...ALL BUT ONE...
MAN, WHAT A NIGHT! I NEVER THOUGHT I'D SEE DON KARNAGE IN CUFFS.
WE'RE GRATEFUL TO YOU, MR. BALOO!
KIT HERE HELPED TOO! AND SO DID--
--uh-- OH!
HIT THE DIRT!
HA HA! NICE TRY, COPPERS!
BUT YOU ARE NO MATCH FOR DON KARNAGE!

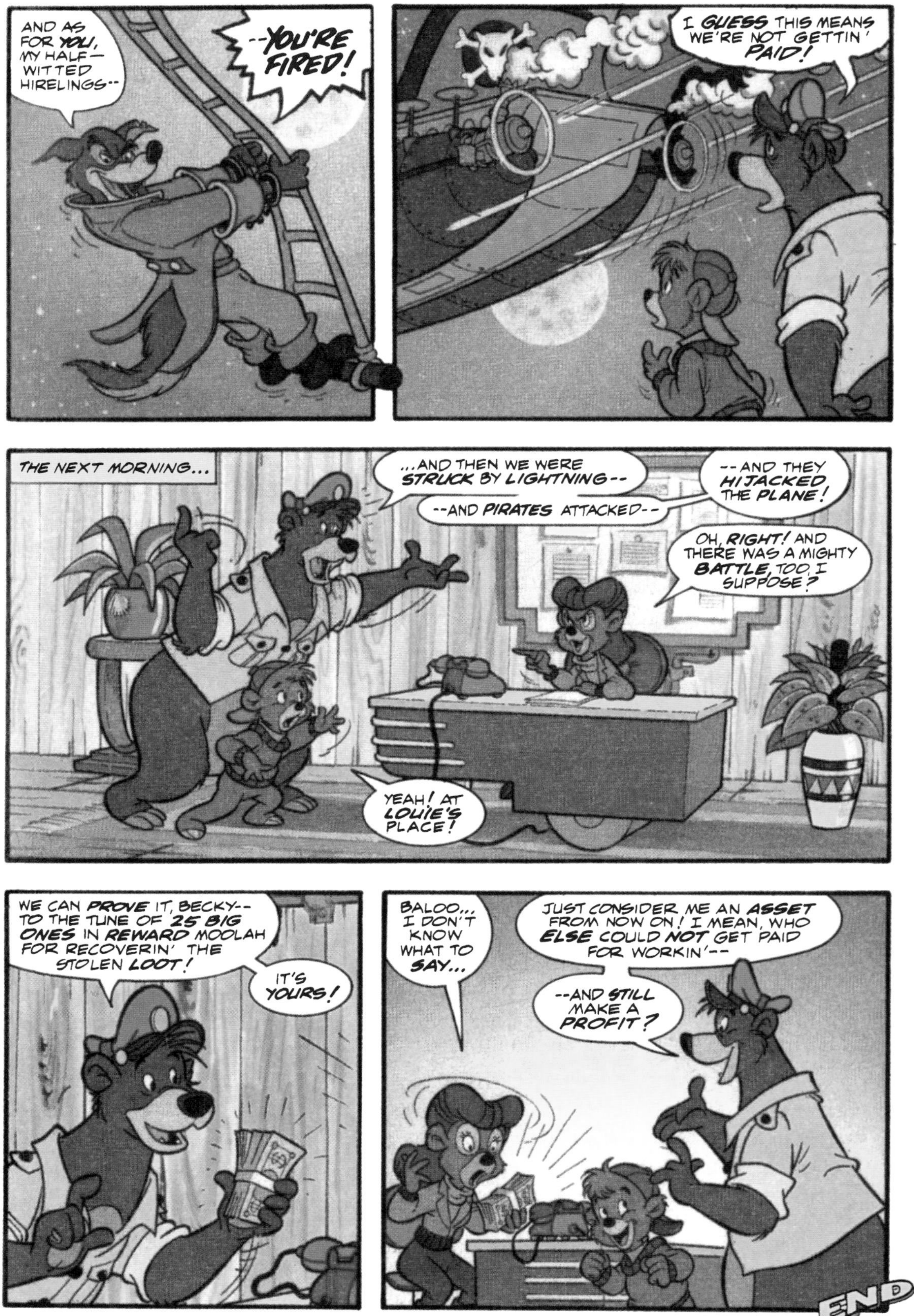
AND AS FOR YOU, MY HALF-WITTED HIRELINGS--
--YOU'RE FIRED!
I GUESS THIS MEANS WE'RE NOT GETTIN' PAID!
THE NEXT MORNING...
...AND THEN WE WERE STRUCK BY LIGHTNING--
--AND PIRATES ATTACKED--
--AND THEY HIJACKED THE PLANE!
OH, RIGHT! AND THERE WAS A MIGHTY BATTLE, TOO, I SUPPOSE?
YEAH! AT LOUIE'S PLACE!
WE CAN PROVE IT, BECKY-- TO THE TUNE OF 25 BIG ONES IN REWARD MOOLAH FOR RECOVERIN' THE STOLEN LOOT!
IT'S YOURS!
BALOO... I DON'T KNOW WHAT TO SAY...
JUST CONSIDER ME AN ASSET FROM NOW ON! I MEAN, WHO ELSE COULD NOT GET PAID FOR WORKIN'--
--AND STILL MAKE A PROFIT?
END

Darkwing Duck in Salad Daze!

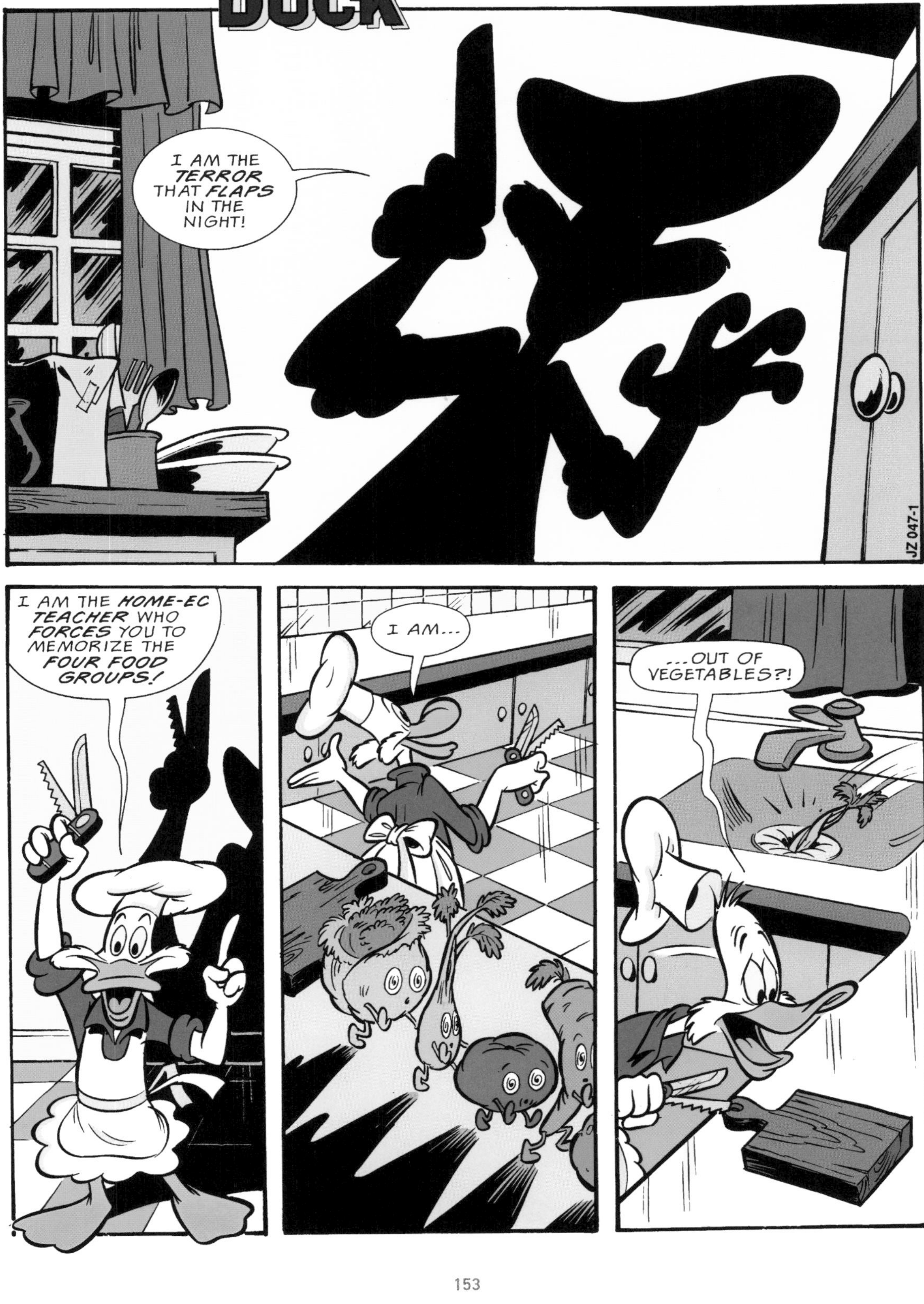
I AM THE TERROR THAT FLAPS IN THE NIGHT!
JZ 047-1
I AM THE HOME-EC TEACHER WHO FORCES YOU TO MEMORIZE THE FOUR FOOD GROUPS!
I AM...
...OUT OF VEGETABLES?!

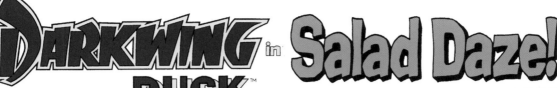

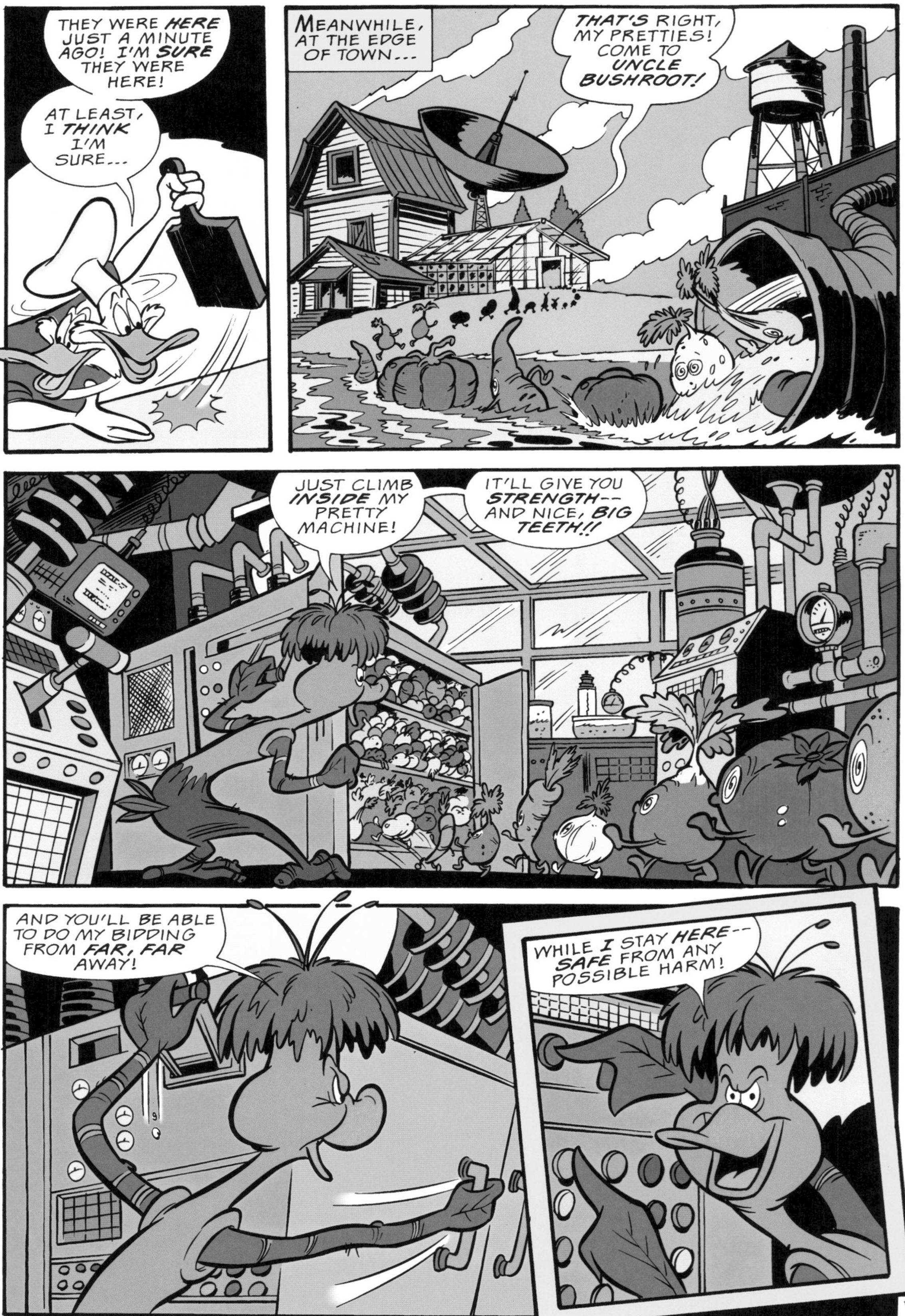
THEY WERE HERE JUST A MINUTE AGO! I'M SURE THEY WERE HERE!
AT LEAST, I THINK I'M SURE...
MEANWHILE, AT THE EDGE OF TOWN...
THAT'S RIGHT, MY PRETTIES! COME TO UNCLE BUSHROOT!
JUST CLIMB INSIDE MY PRETTY MACHINE!
IT'LL GIVE YOU STRENGTH-- AND NICE, BIG TEETH!!
AND YOU'LL BE ABLE TO DO MY BIDDING FROM FAR, FAR AWAY!
WHILE I STAY HERE-- SAFE FROM ANY POSSIBLE HARM!

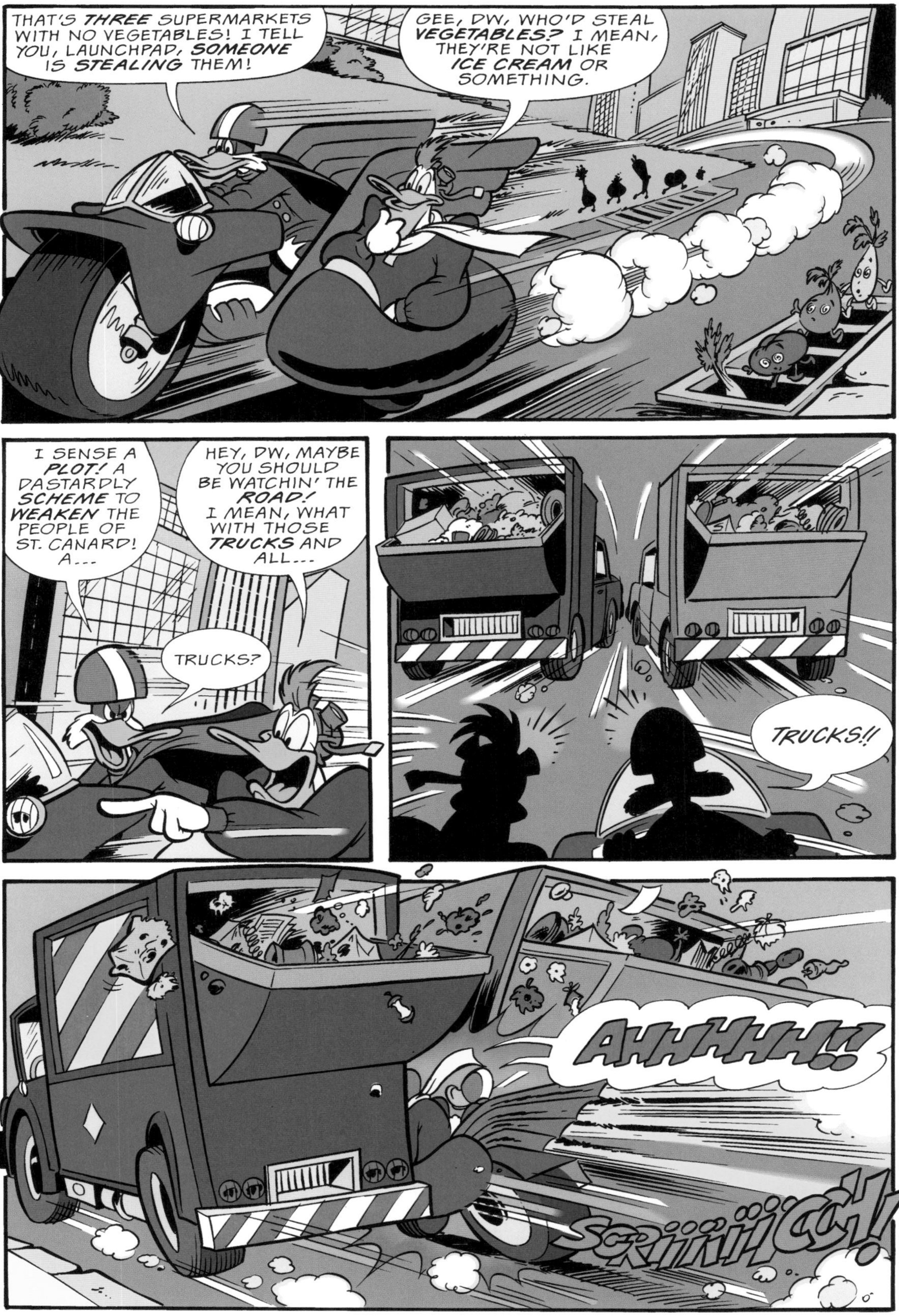
THAT'S THREE SUPERMARKETS WITH NO VEGETABLES! I TELL YOU, LAUNCHPAD, SOMEONE IS STEALING THEM!
GEE, DW, WHO'D STEAL VEGETABLES? I MEAN, THEY'RE NOT LIKE ICE CREAM OR SOMETHING.
I SENSE A PLOT! A DASTARDLY SCHEME TO WEAKEN THE PEOPLE OF ST. CANARD! A...
HEY, DW, MAYBE YOU SHOULD BE WATCHIN' THE ROAD! I MEAN, WHAT WITH THOSE TRUCKS AND ALL...
TRUCKS?
TRUCKS!!
AHHHHH!!
SCRIIIIICCH!

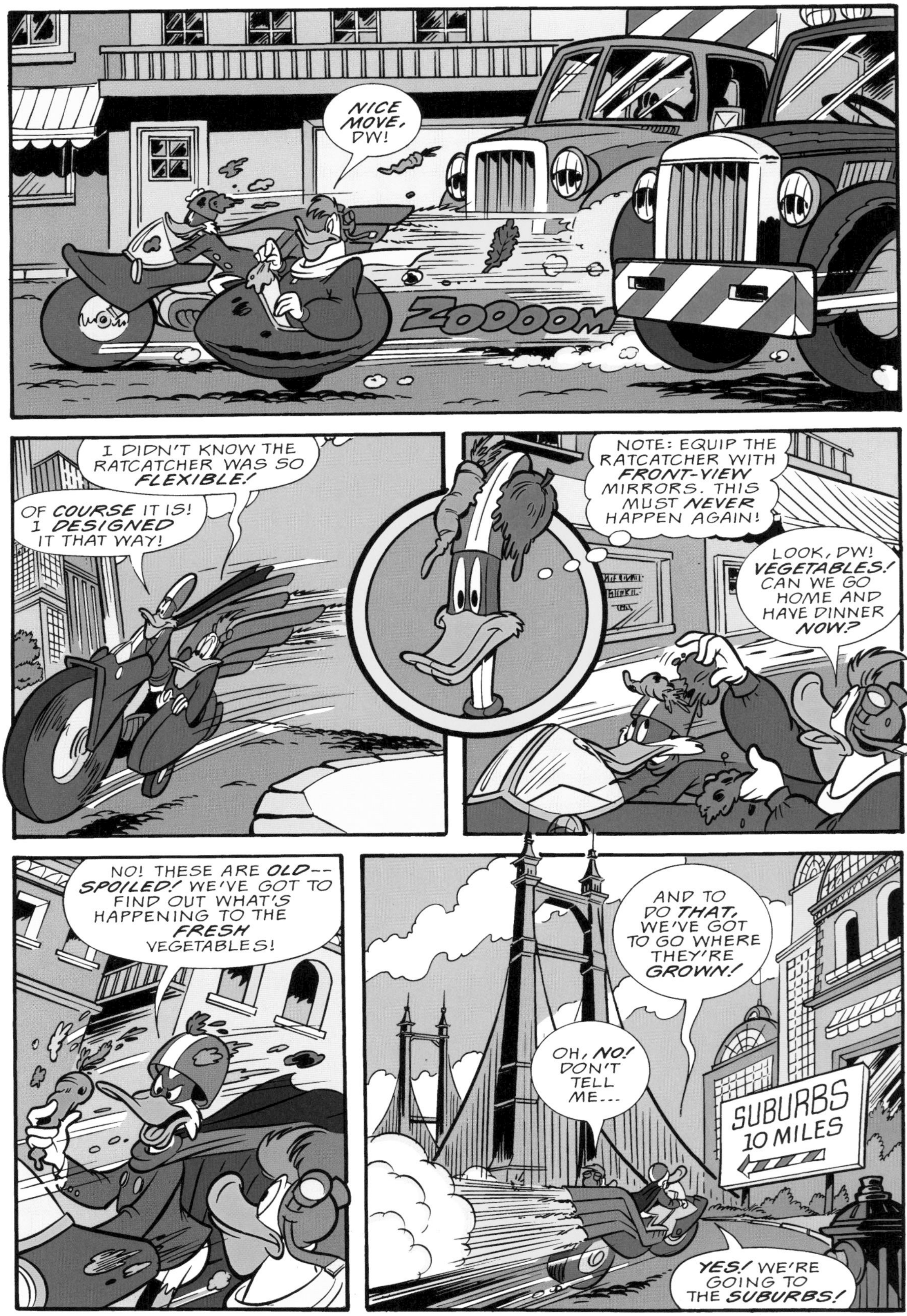
NICE MOVE, DW!
ZOOOOOM
I DIDN'T KNOW THE RATCATCHER WAS SO FLEXIBLE!
OF COURSE IT IS! I DESIGNED IT THAT WAY!
NOTE: EQUIP THE RATCATCHER WITH FRONT-VIEW MIRRORS. THIS MUST NEVER HAPPEN AGAIN!
LOOK, DW! VEGETABLES! CAN WE GO HOME AND HAVE DINNER NOW?
NO! THESE ARE OLD--SPOILED! WE'VE GOT TO FIND OUT WHAT'S HAPPENING TO THE FRESH VEGETABLES!
AND TO DO THAT, WE'VE GOT TO GO WHERE THEY'RE GROWN!
OH, NO! DON'T TELL ME...
SUBURBS 10 MILES
YES! WE'RE GOING TO THE SUBURBS!

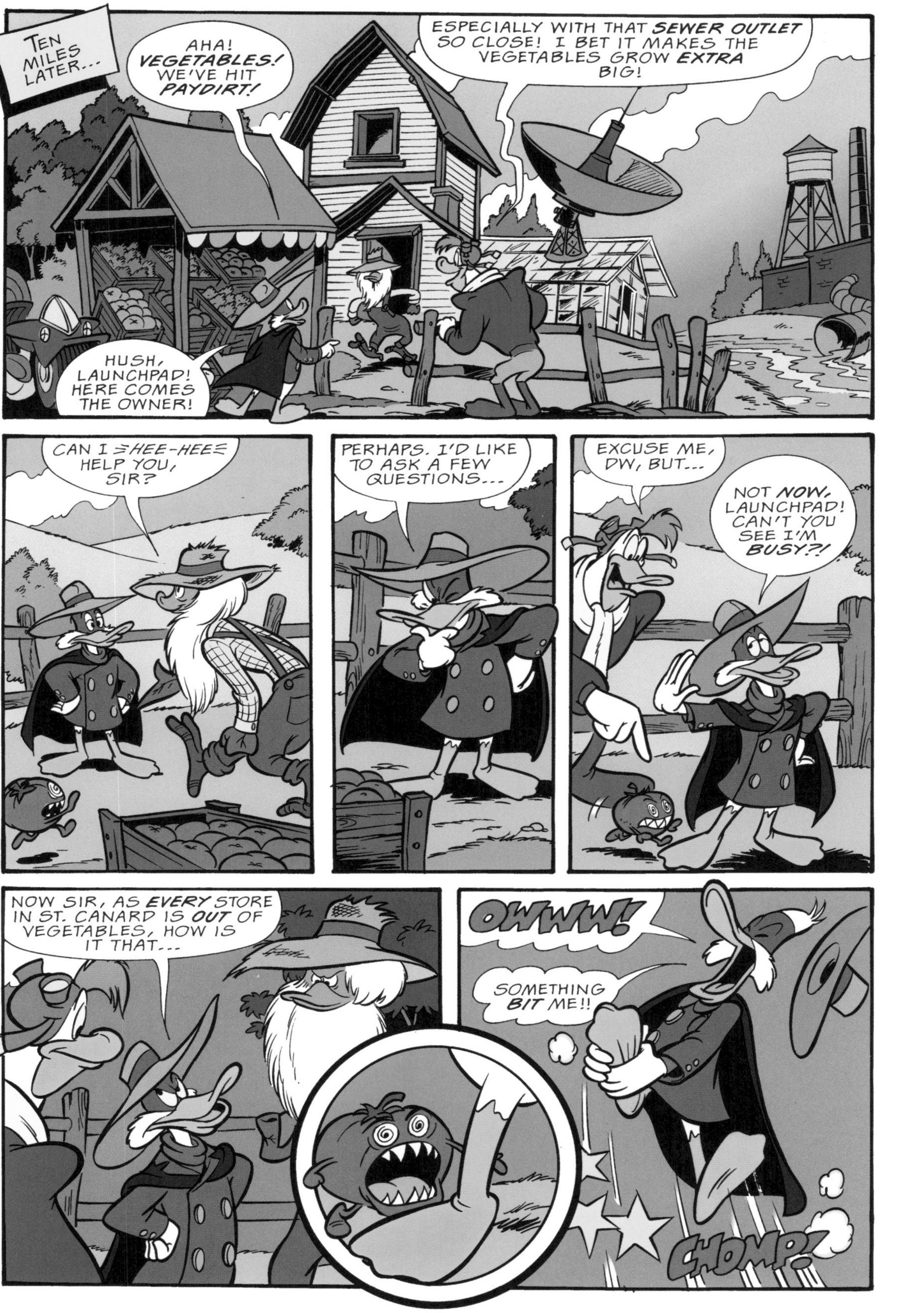
TEN MILES LATER...
AHA! VEGETABLES! WE'VE HIT PAYDIRT!
ESPECIALLY WITH THAT SEWER OUTLET SO CLOSE! I BET IT MAKES THE VEGETABLES GROW EXTRA BIG!
HUSH, LAUNCHPAD! HERE COMES THE OWNER!
CAN I HEE-HEE HELP YOU, SIR?
PERHAPS. I'D LIKE TO ASK A FEW QUESTIONS...
EXCUSE ME, DW, BUT...
NOT NOW, LAUNCHPAD! CAN'T YOU SEE I'M BUSY?!
NOW SIR, AS EVERY STORE IN ST. CANARD IS OUT OF VEGETABLES, HOW IS IT THAT...
OWWW!
SOMETHING BIT ME!!
CHOMP!

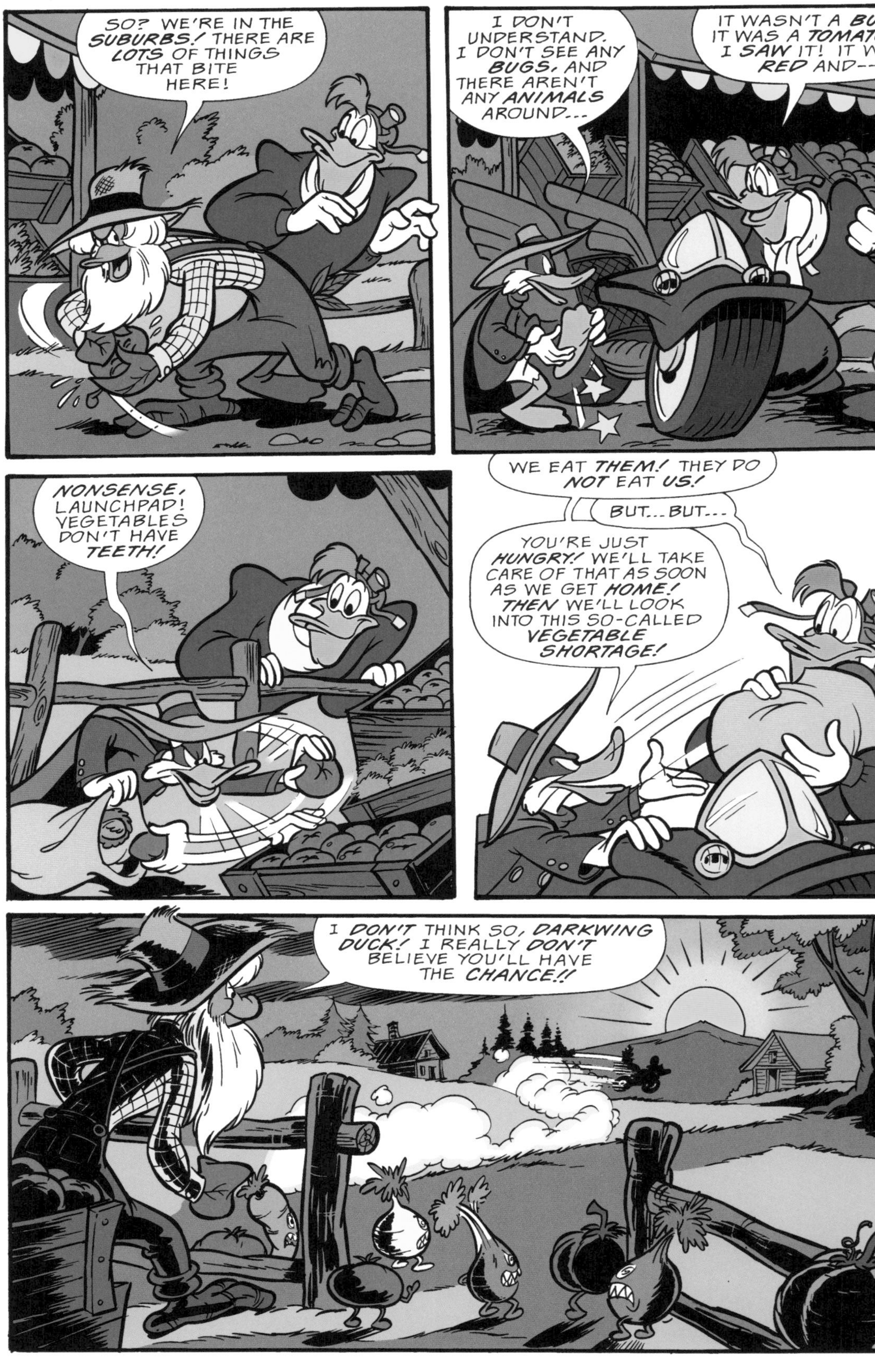
SO? WE'RE IN THE SUBURBS! THERE ARE LOTS OF THINGS THAT BITE HERE!
I DON'T UNDERSTAND. I DON'T SEE ANY BUGS, AND THERE AREN'T ANY ANIMALS AROUND...
IT WASN'T A BUG! IT WAS A TOMATO! I SAW IT! IT WAS RED AND--
NONSENSE, LAUNCHPAD! VEGETABLES DON'T HAVE TEETH!
WE EAT THEM! THEY DO NOT EAT US!
BUT...BUT...
YOU'RE JUST HUNGRY! WE'LL TAKE CARE OF THAT AS SOON AS WE GET HOME! THEN WE'LL LOOK INTO THIS SO-CALLED VEGETABLE SHORTAGE!
I DON'T THINK SO, DARKWING DUCK! I REALLY DON'T BELIEVE YOU'LL HAVE THE CHANCE!!

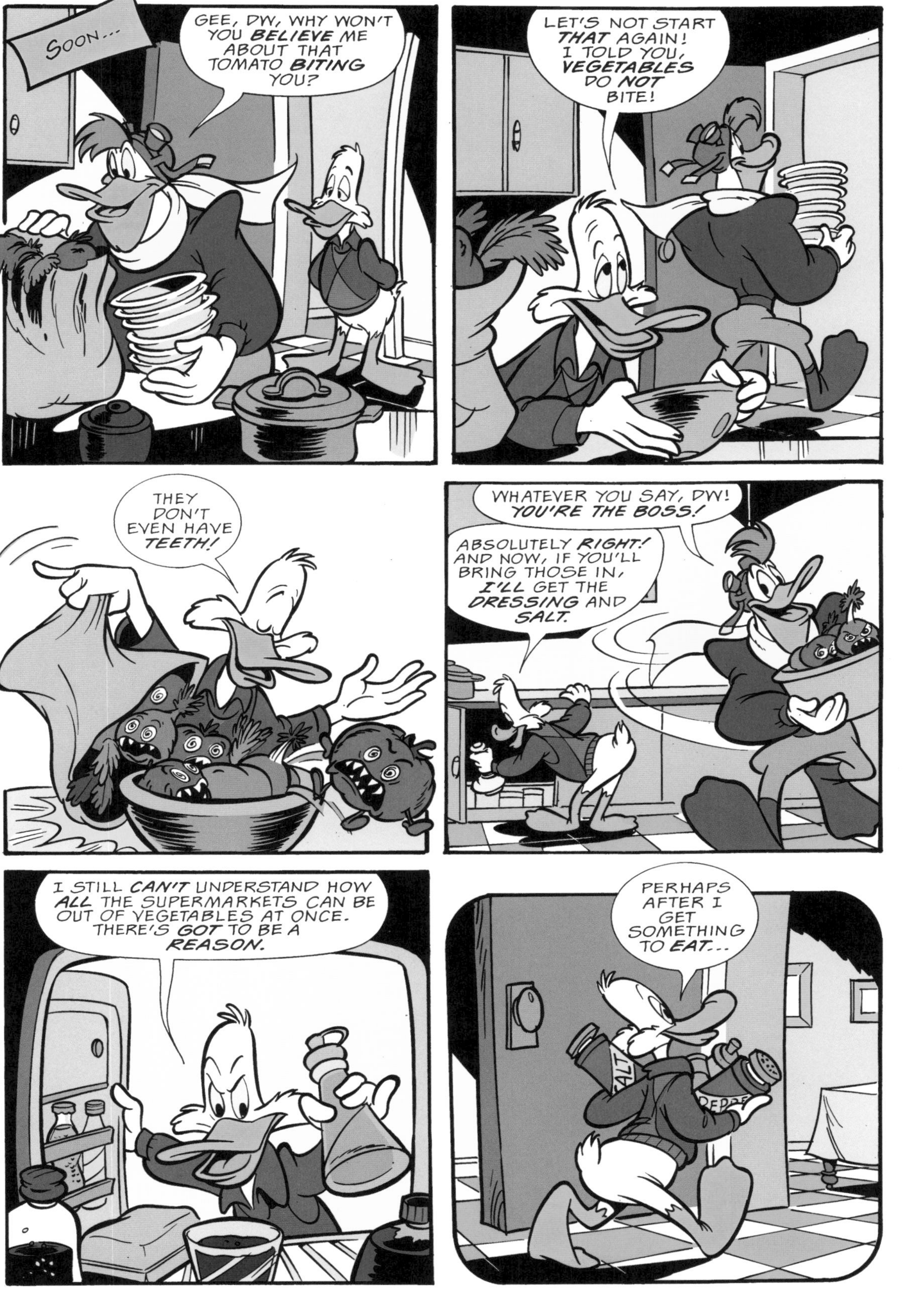
SOON...
GEE, DW, WHY WON'T YOU BELIEVE ME ABOUT THAT TOMATO BITING YOU?
LET'S NOT START THAT AGAIN! I TOLD YOU, VEGETABLES DO NOT BITE!
THEY DON'T EVEN HAVE TEETH!
WHATEVER YOU SAY, DW! YOU'RE THE BOSS!
ABSOLUTELY RIGHT! AND NOW, IF YOU'LL BRING THOSE IN, I'LL GET THE DRESSING AND SALT.
I STILL CAN'T UNDERSTAND HOW ALL THE SUPERMARKETS CAN BE OUT OF VEGETABLES AT ONCE. THERE'S GOT TO BE A REASON.
PERHAPS AFTER I GET SOMETHING TO EAT...

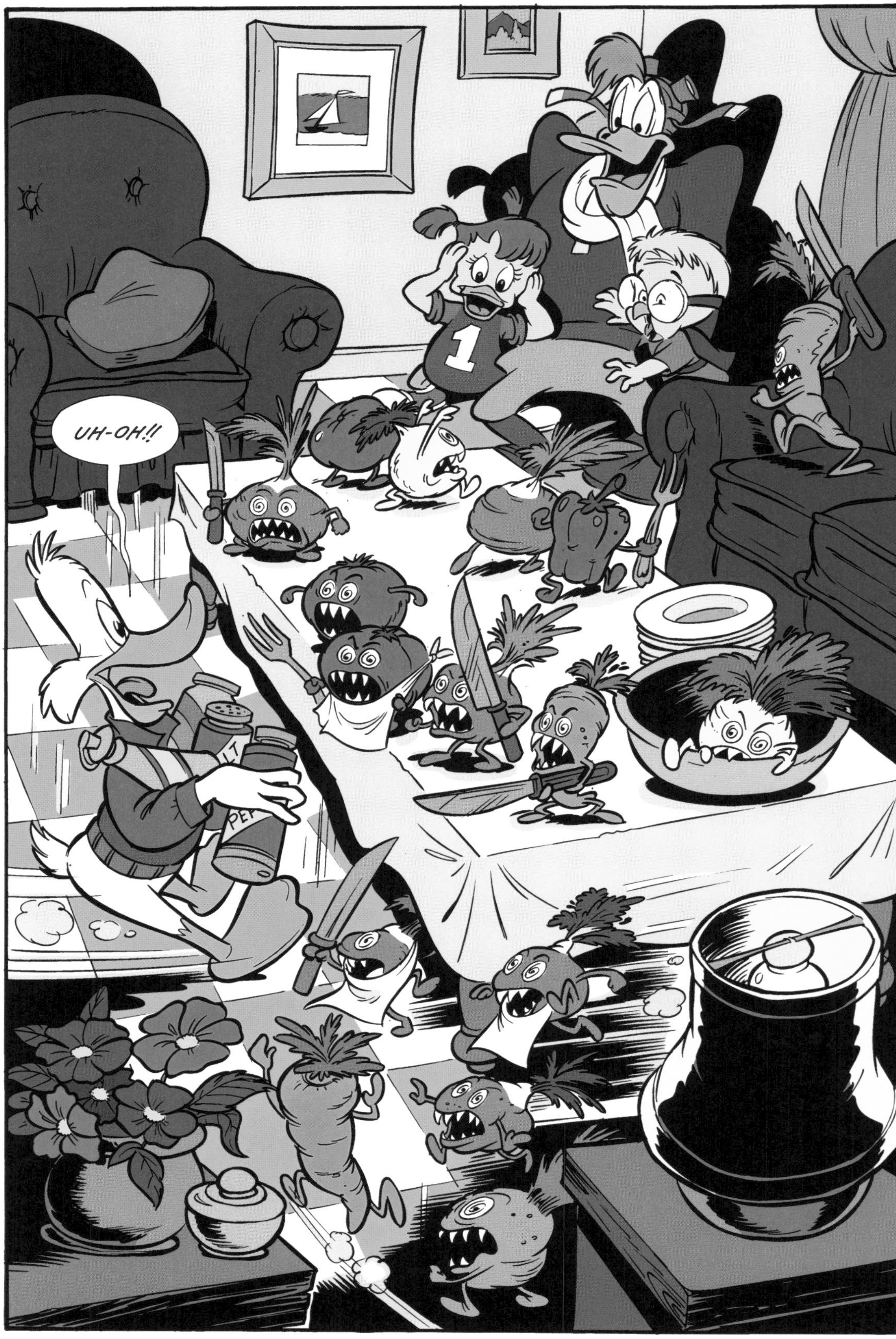
UH-OH!!

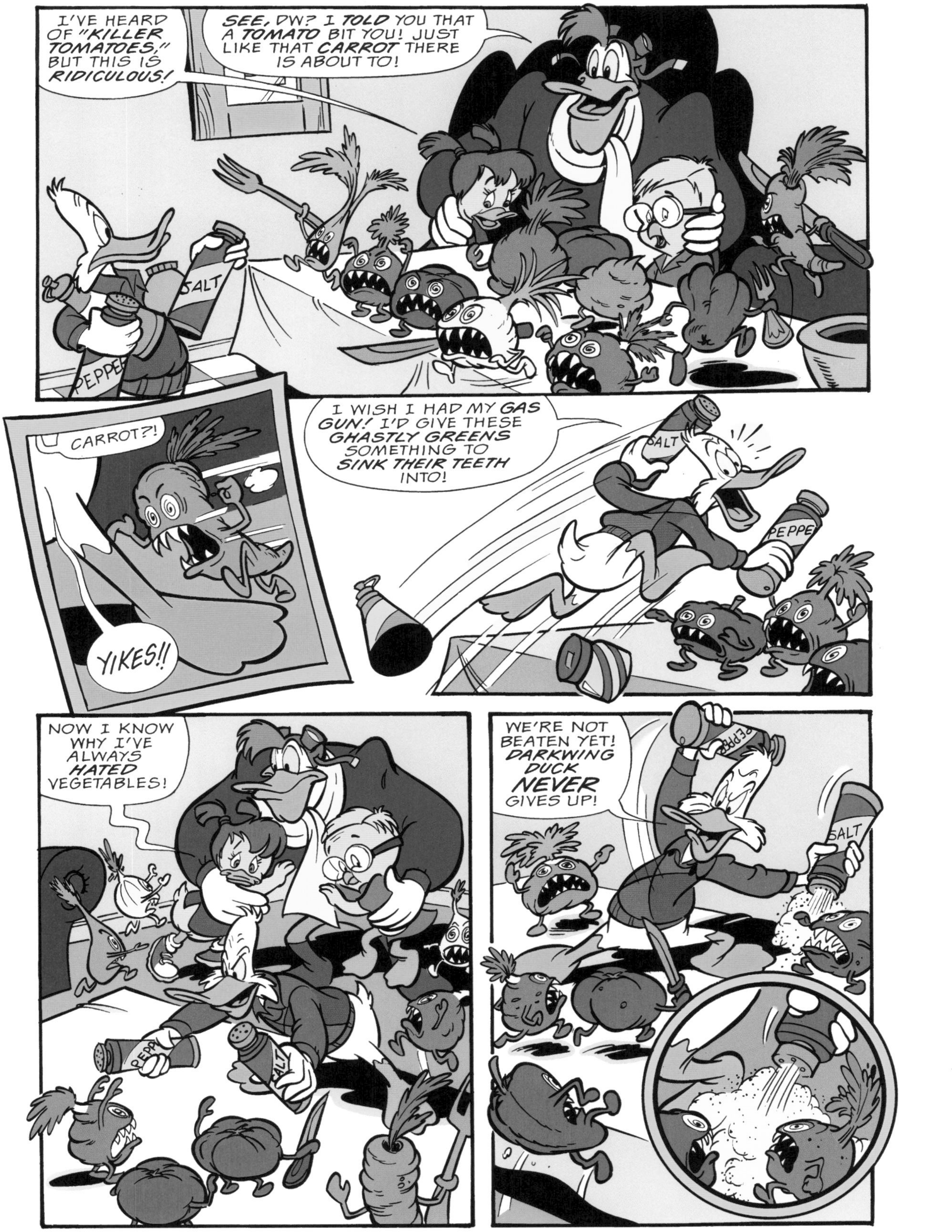
I'VE HEARD OF "KILLER TOMATOES," BUT THIS IS RIDICULOUS!
SEE, DW? I TOLD YOU THAT A TOMATO BIT YOU! JUST LIKE THAT CARROT THERE IS ABOUT TO!
SALT
PEPPER
CARROT?!
YIKES!!
I WISH I HAD MY GAS GUN! I'D GIVE THESE GHASTLY GREENS SOMETHING TO SINK THEIR TEETH INTO!
SALT
PEPPE
NOW I KNOW WHY I'VE ALWAYS HATED VEGETABLES!
PEPPE
SALT
WE'RE NOT BEATEN YET! DARKWING DUCK NEVER GIVES UP!
PEPPER
SALT

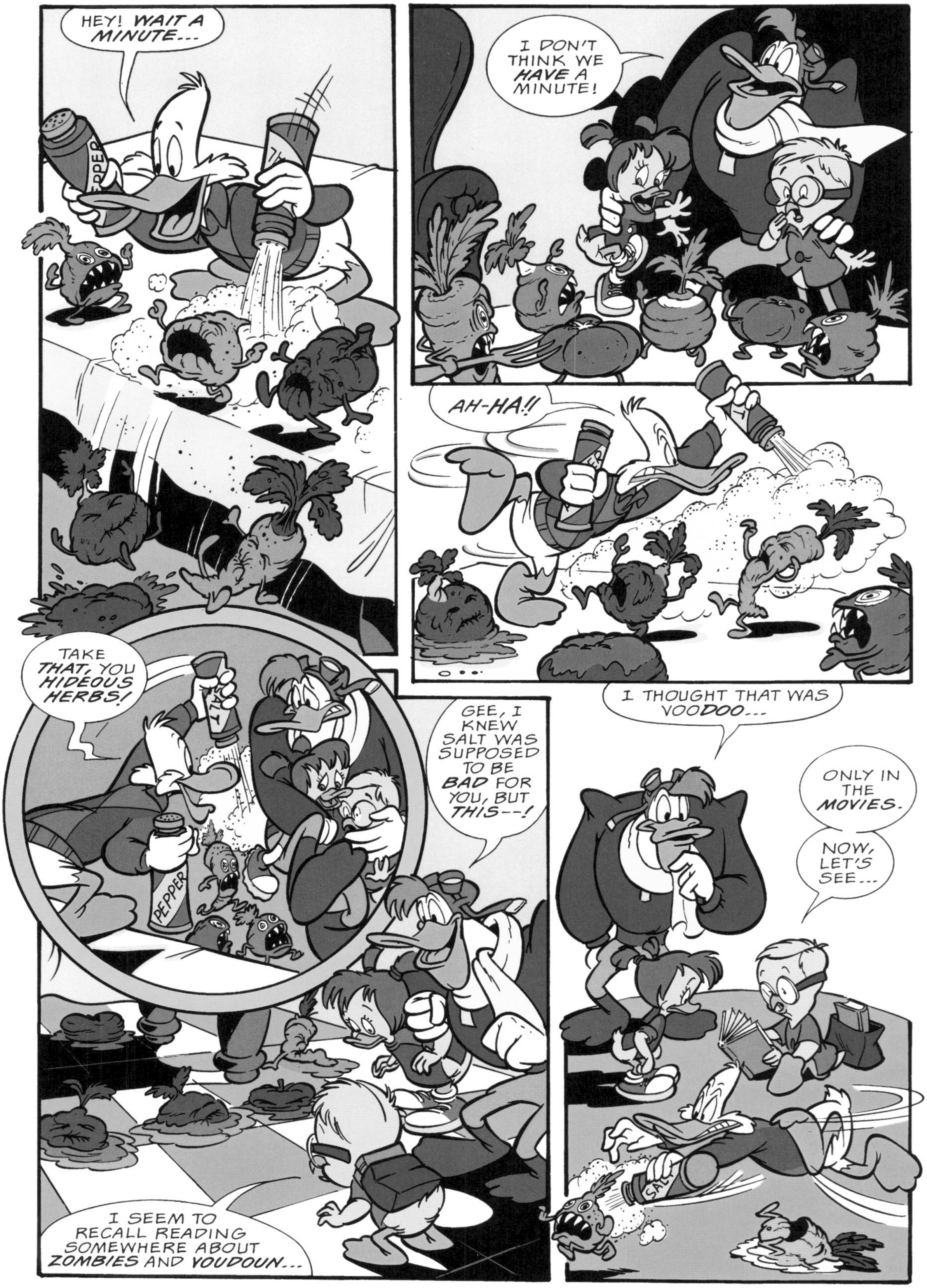
HEY! WAIT A MINUTE...
PEPPER
I DON'T THINK WE HAVE A MINUTE!
AH-HA!!
TAKE THAT, YOU HIDEOUS HERBS!
SALT
PEPPER
GEE, I KNEW SALT WAS SUPPOSED TO BE BAD FOR YOU, BUT THIS--!
I SEEM TO RECALL READING SOMEWHERE ABOUT ZOMBIES AND VOUDOUN...
I THOUGHT THAT WAS VOODOO...
ONLY IN THE MOVIES.
NOW, LET'S SEE...
SALT

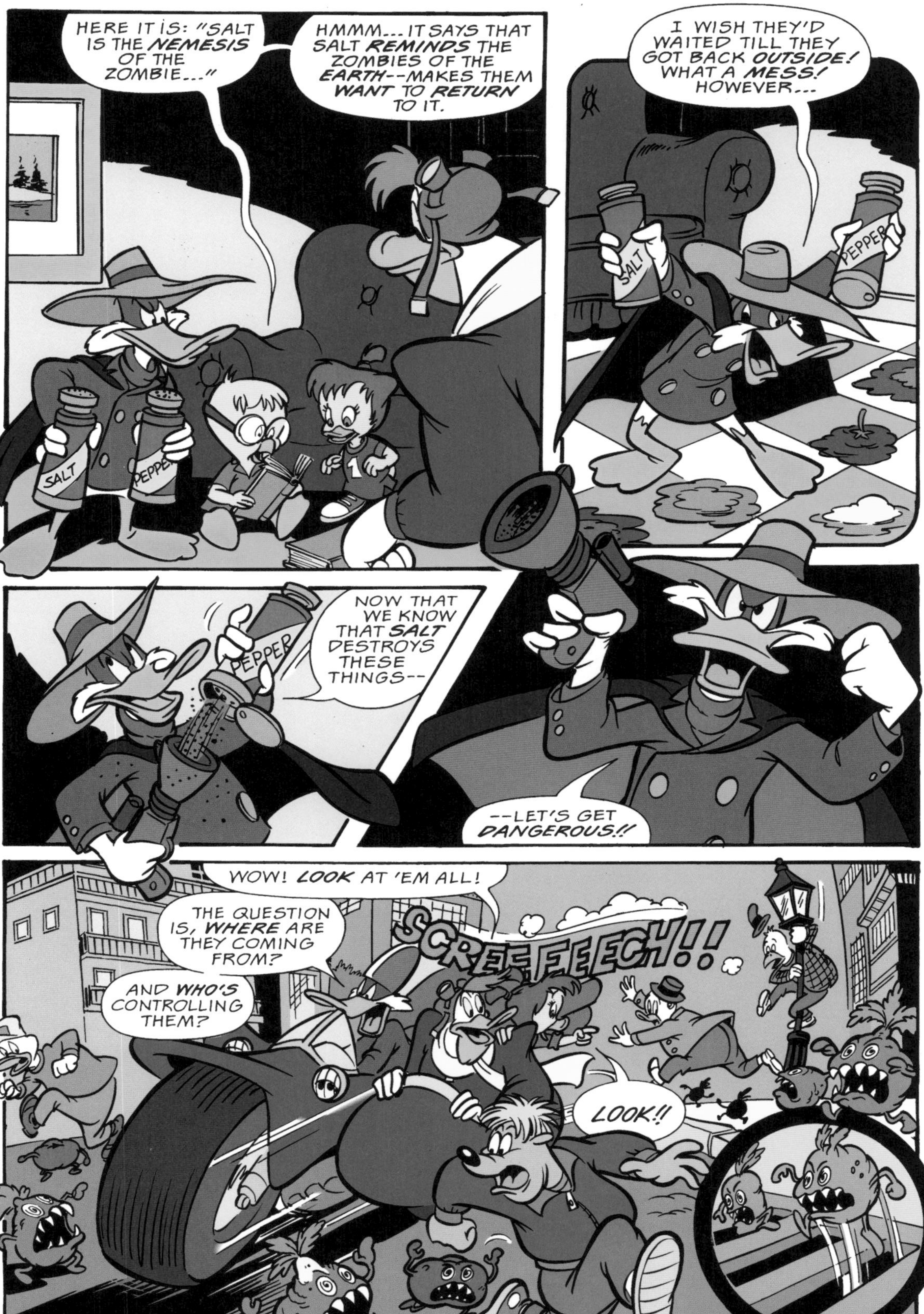
HERE IT IS: "SALT IS THE NEMESIS OF THE ZOMBIE..."
HMMM... IT SAYS THAT SALT REMINDS THE ZOMBIES OF THE EARTH--MAKES THEM WANT TO RETURN TO IT.
SALT
PEPPER
I WISH THEY'D WAITED TILL THEY GOT BACK OUTSIDE! WHAT A MESS! HOWEVER...
SALT
PEPPER
PEPPER
NOW THAT WE KNOW THAT SALT DESTROYS THESE THINGS--
--LET'S GET DANGEROUS!!
WOW! LOOK AT 'EM ALL!
THE QUESTION IS, WHERE ARE THEY COMING FROM?
AND WHO'S CONTROLLING THEM?
SCREEEEEECH!!
LOOK!!

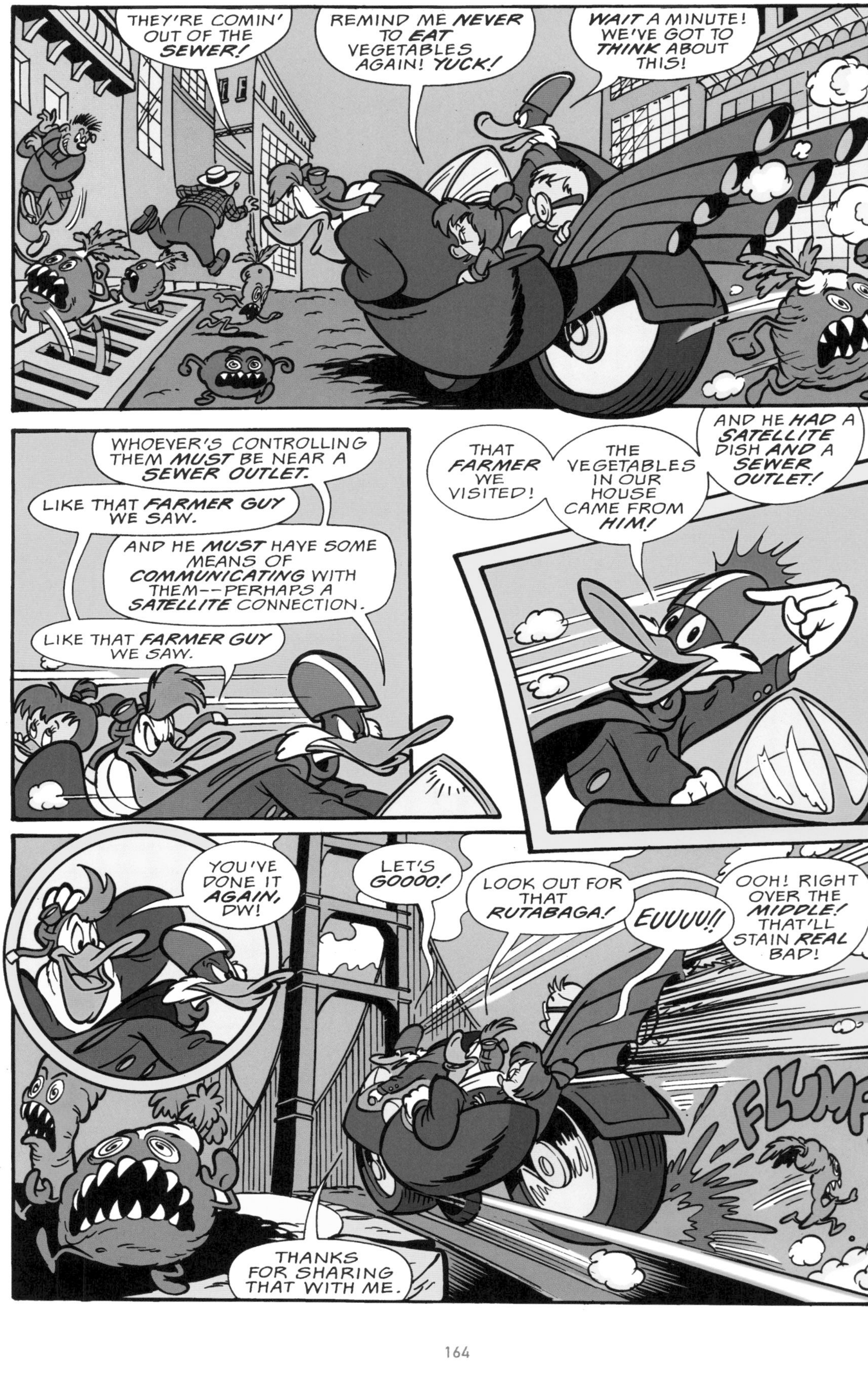
THEY'RE COMIN' OUT OF THE SEWER!
REMIND ME NEVER TO EAT VEGETABLES AGAIN! YUCK!
WAIT A MINUTE! WE'VE GOT TO THINK ABOUT THIS!
WHOEVER'S CONTROLLING THEM MUST BE NEAR A SEWER OUTLET.
LIKE THAT FARMER GUY WE SAW.
AND HE MUST HAVE SOME MEANS OF COMMUNICATING WITH THEM--PERHAPS A SATELLITE CONNECTION.
LIKE THAT FARMER GUY WE SAW.
THAT FARMER WE VISITED!
THE VEGETABLES IN OUR HOUSE CAME FROM HIM!
AND HE HAD A SATELLITE DISH AND A SEWER OUTLET!
YOU'VE DONE IT AGAIN, DW!
LET'S GOOOO!
LOOK OUT FOR THAT RUTABAGA!
EUUUU!!
OOH! RIGHT OVER THE MIDDLE! THAT'LL STAIN REAL BAD!
FLUMP!
THANKS FOR SHARING THAT WITH ME.

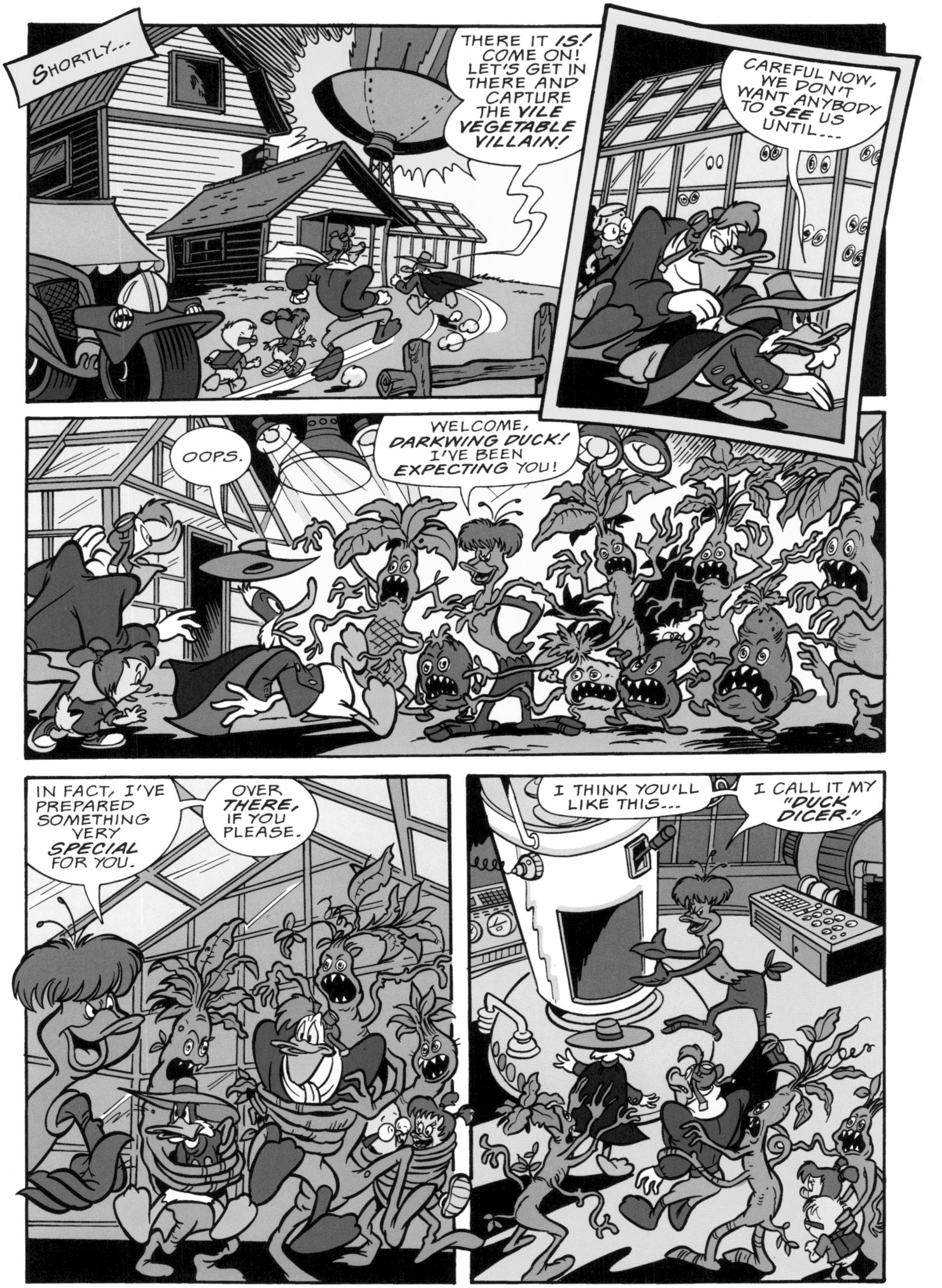
SHORTLY...
THERE IT IS! COME ON! LET'S GET IN THERE AND CAPTURE THE VILE VEGETABLE VILLAIN!
CAREFUL NOW, WE DON'T WANT ANYBODY TO SEE US UNTIL...
OOPS.
WELCOME, DARKWING DUCK! I'VE BEEN EXPECTING YOU!
IN FACT, I'VE PREPARED SOMETHING VERY SPECIAL FOR YOU.
OVER THERE, IF YOU PLEASE.
I THINK YOU'LL LIKE THIS...
I CALL IT MY "DUCK DICER."

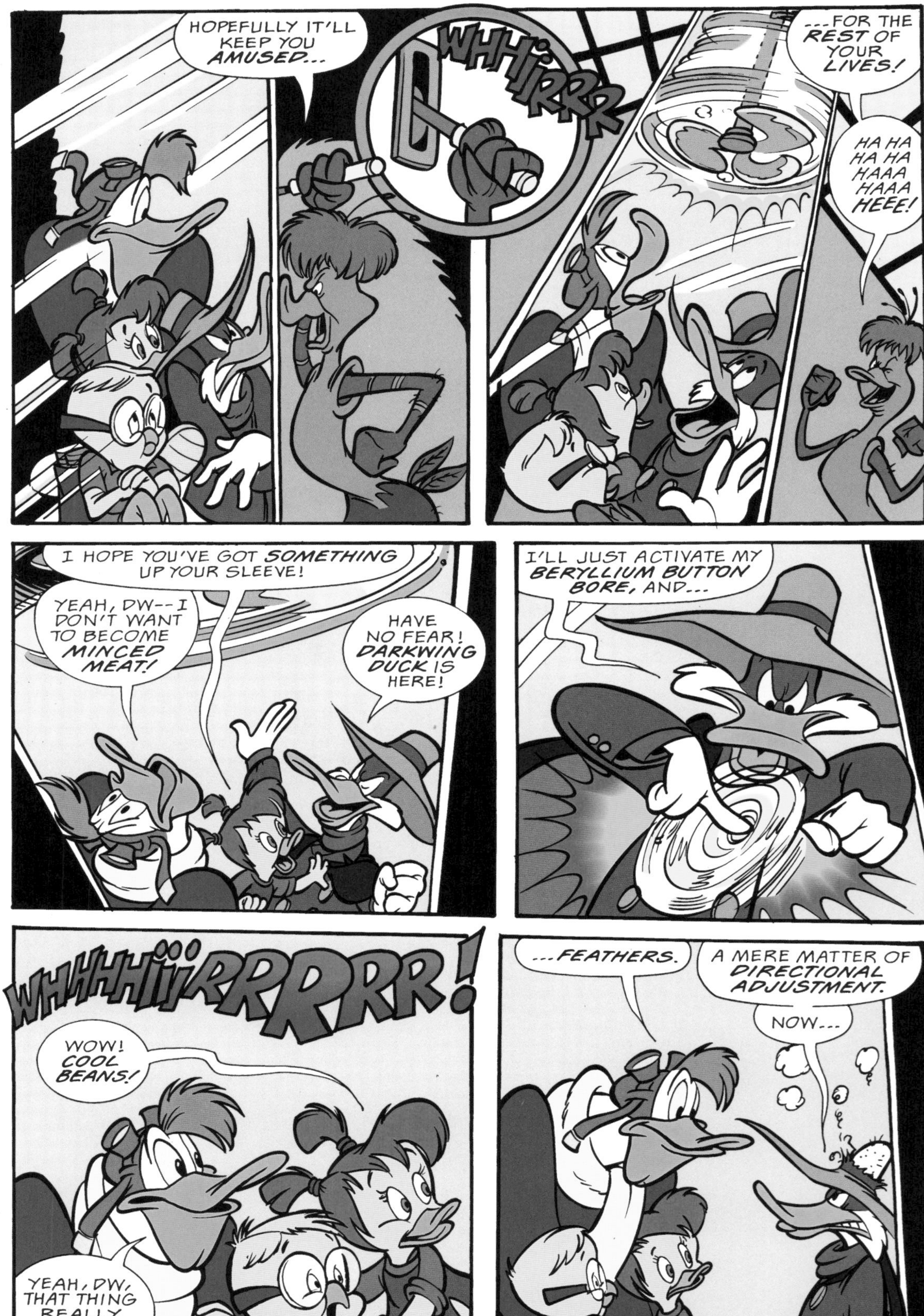
HOPEFULLY IT'LL KEEP YOU AMUSED...
WHHIRRR
...FOR THE REST OF YOUR LIVES!
HA HA HA HA HAAA HAAA HEEE!
I HOPE YOU'VE GOT SOMETHING UP YOUR SLEEVE!
YEAH, DW--I DON'T WANT TO BECOME MINCED MEAT!
HAVE NO FEAR! DARKWING DUCK IS HERE!
I'LL JUST ACTIVATE MY BERYLLIUM BUTTON BORE, AND...
WHHHHIIIRRRRRR!
WOW! COOL BEANS!
YEAH, DW, THAT THING REALLY CAN CUT...
...FEATHERS.
A MERE MATTER OF DIRECTIONAL ADJUSTMENT.
NOW...

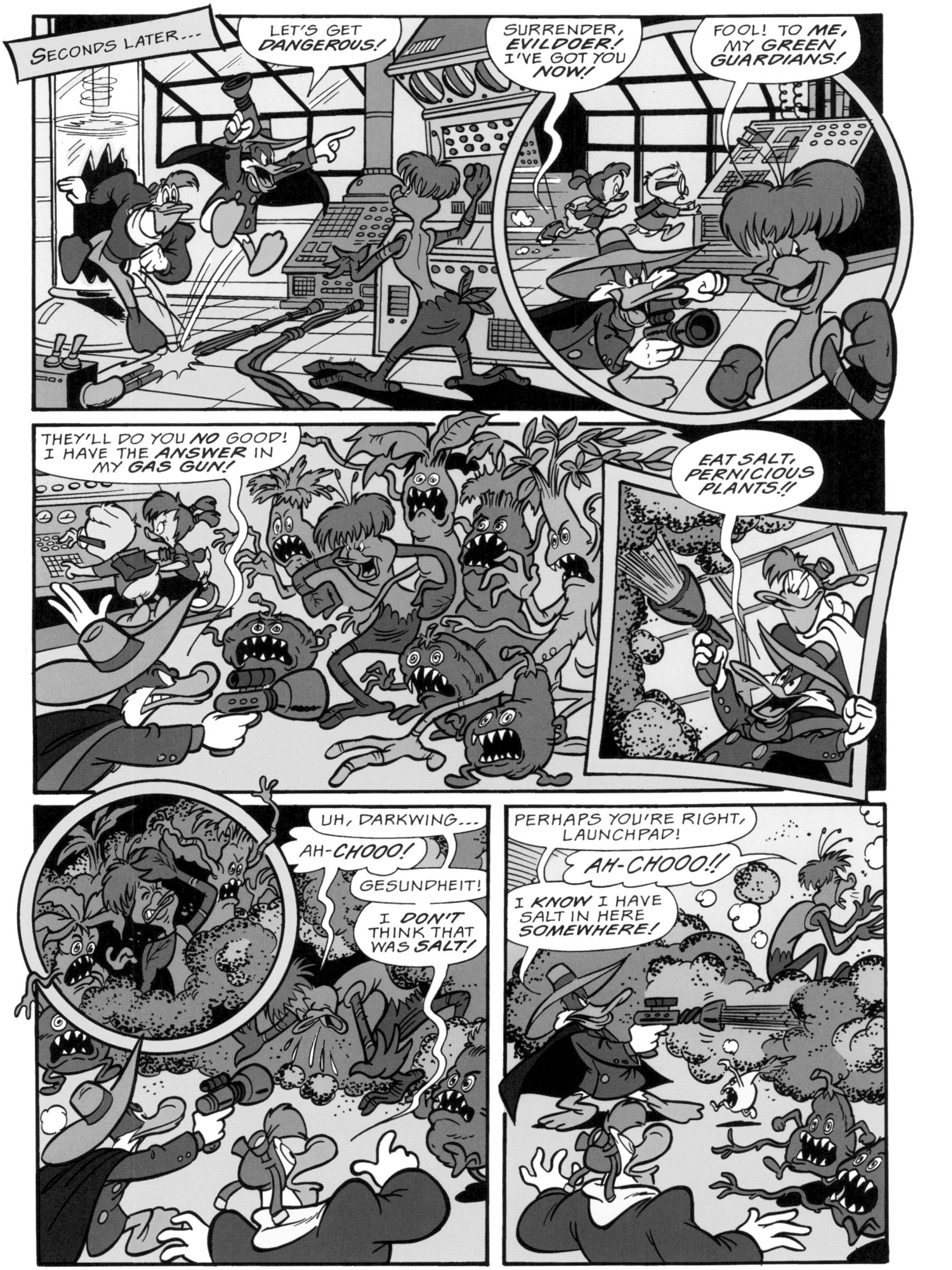

SECONDS LATER...
LET'S GET DANGEROUS!
SURRENDER, EVILDOER! I'VE GOT YOU NOW!
FOOL! TO ME, MY GREEN GUARDIANS!
THEY'LL DO YOU NO GOOD! I HAVE THE ANSWER IN MY GAS GUN!
EAT SALT, PERNICIOUS PLANTS!!
UH, DARKWING...
AH-CHOOO!
GESUNDHEIT!
I DON'T THINK THAT WAS SALT!
PERHAPS YOU'RE RIGHT, LAUNCHPAD!
AH-CHOOO!!
I KNOW I HAVE SALT IN HERE SOMEWHERE!

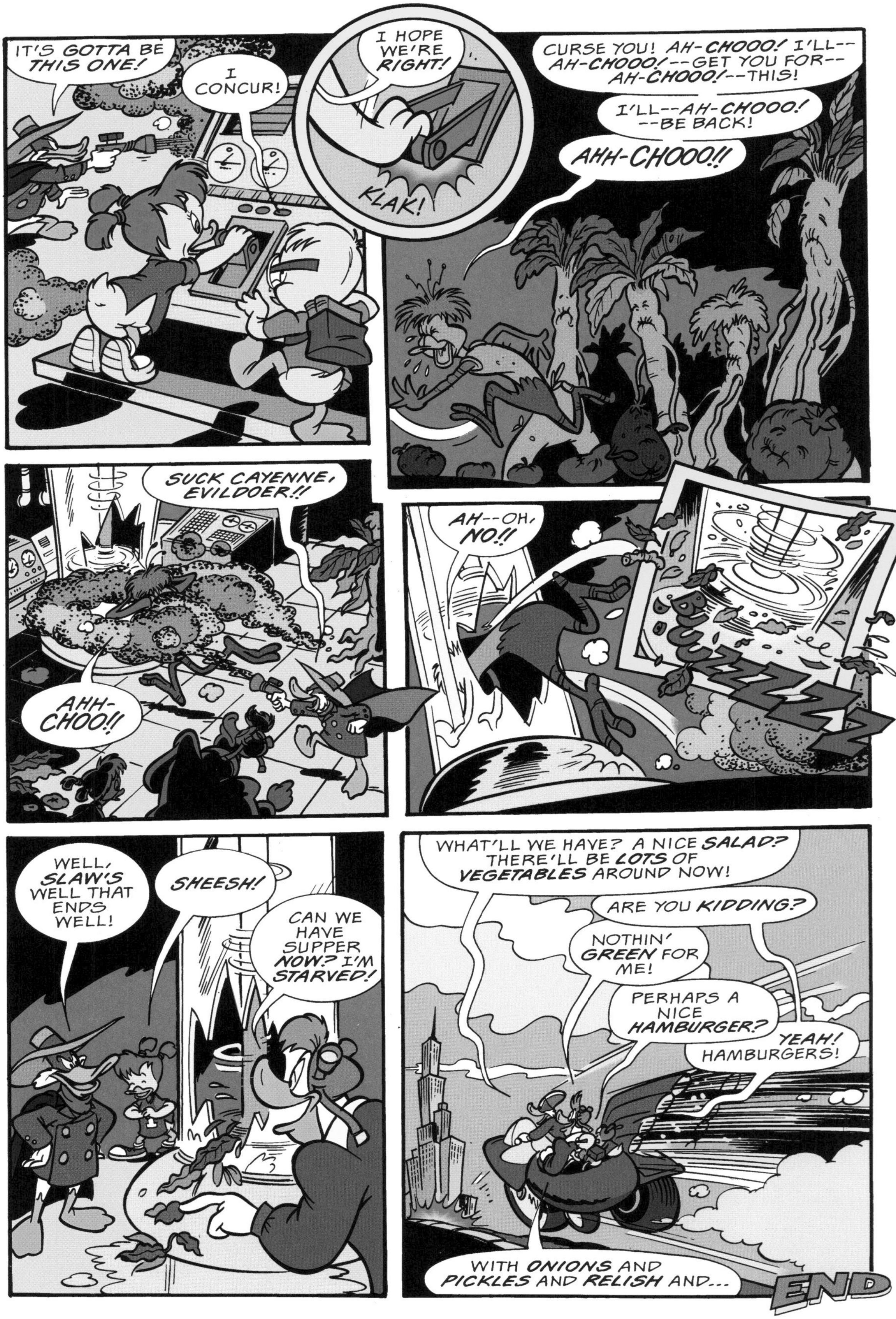
IT'S GOTTA BE THIS ONE!
I CONCUR!
I HOPE WE'RE RIGHT!
KLAK!
CURSE YOU! AH-CHOOO! I'LL-- AH-CHOOO! --GET YOU FOR-- AH-CHOOO! --THIS!
I'LL--AH-CHOOO! --BE BACK!
AHH-CHOOO!!
SUCK CAYENNE, EVILDOER!!
AHH-CHOO!!
AH--OH, NO!!
BUZZZZZ
WELL, SLAW'S WELL THAT ENDS WELL!
SHEESH!
CAN WE HAVE SUPPER NOW? I'M STARVED!
WHAT'LL WE HAVE? A NICE SALAD? THERE'LL BE LOTS OF VEGETABLES AROUND NOW!
ARE YOU KIDDING?
NOTHIN' GREEN FOR ME!
PERHAPS A NICE HAMBURGER?
YEAH! HAMBURGERS!
WITH ONIONS AND PICKLES AND RELISH AND...
END

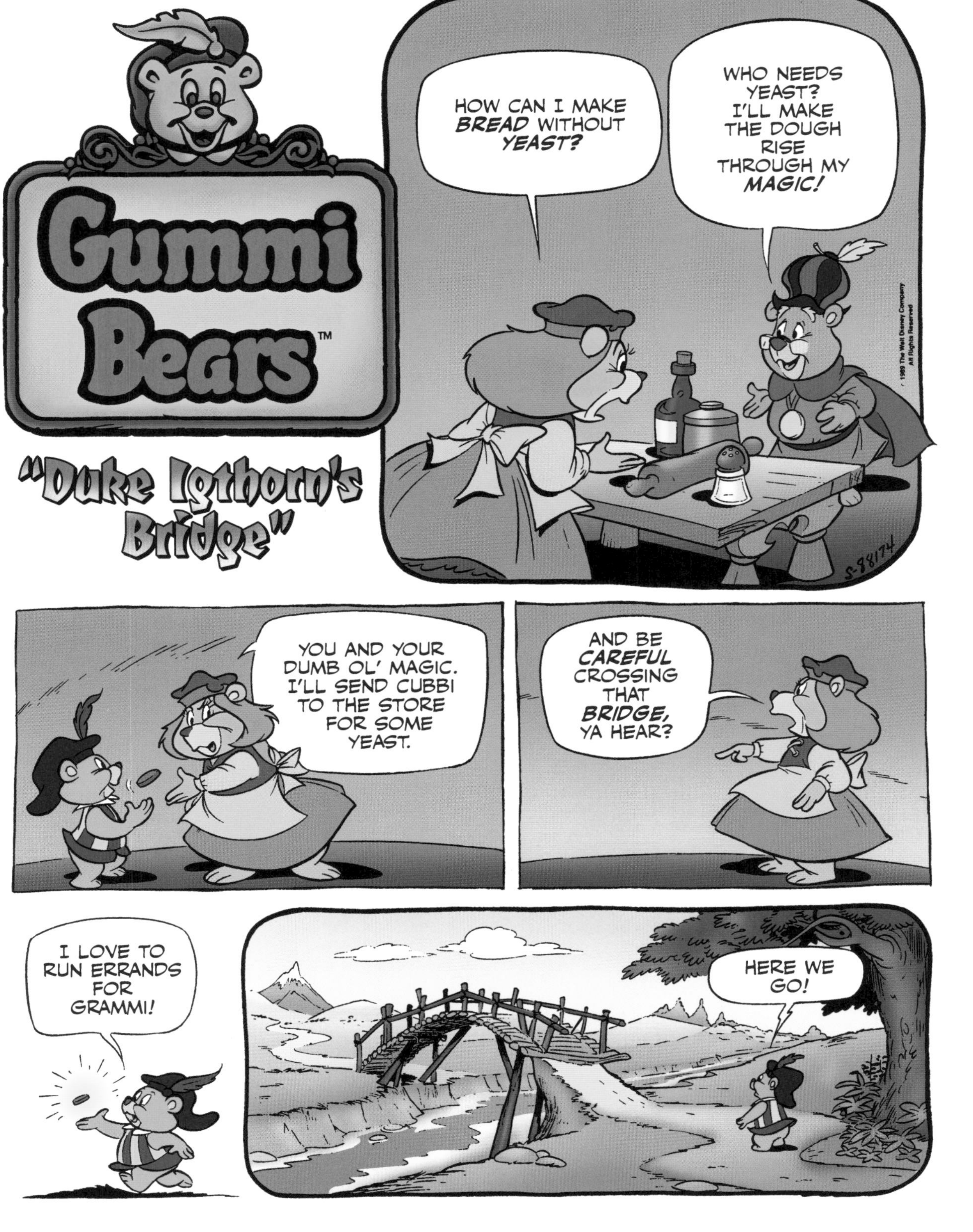
Gummi Bears™
"Duke Igthorn's Bridge"
HOW CAN I MAKE *BREAD* WITHOUT *YEAST?*
WHO NEEDS YEAST? I'LL MAKE THE DOUGH RISE THROUGH MY *MAGIC!*
© 1989 The Walt Disney Company All Rights Reserved
S-88174
YOU AND YOUR DUMB OL' MAGIC. I'LL SEND CUBBI TO THE STORE FOR SOME YEAST.
AND BE *CAREFUL* CROSSING THAT *BRIDGE,* YA HEAR?
I LOVE TO RUN ERRANDS FOR GRAMMI!
HERE WE GO!

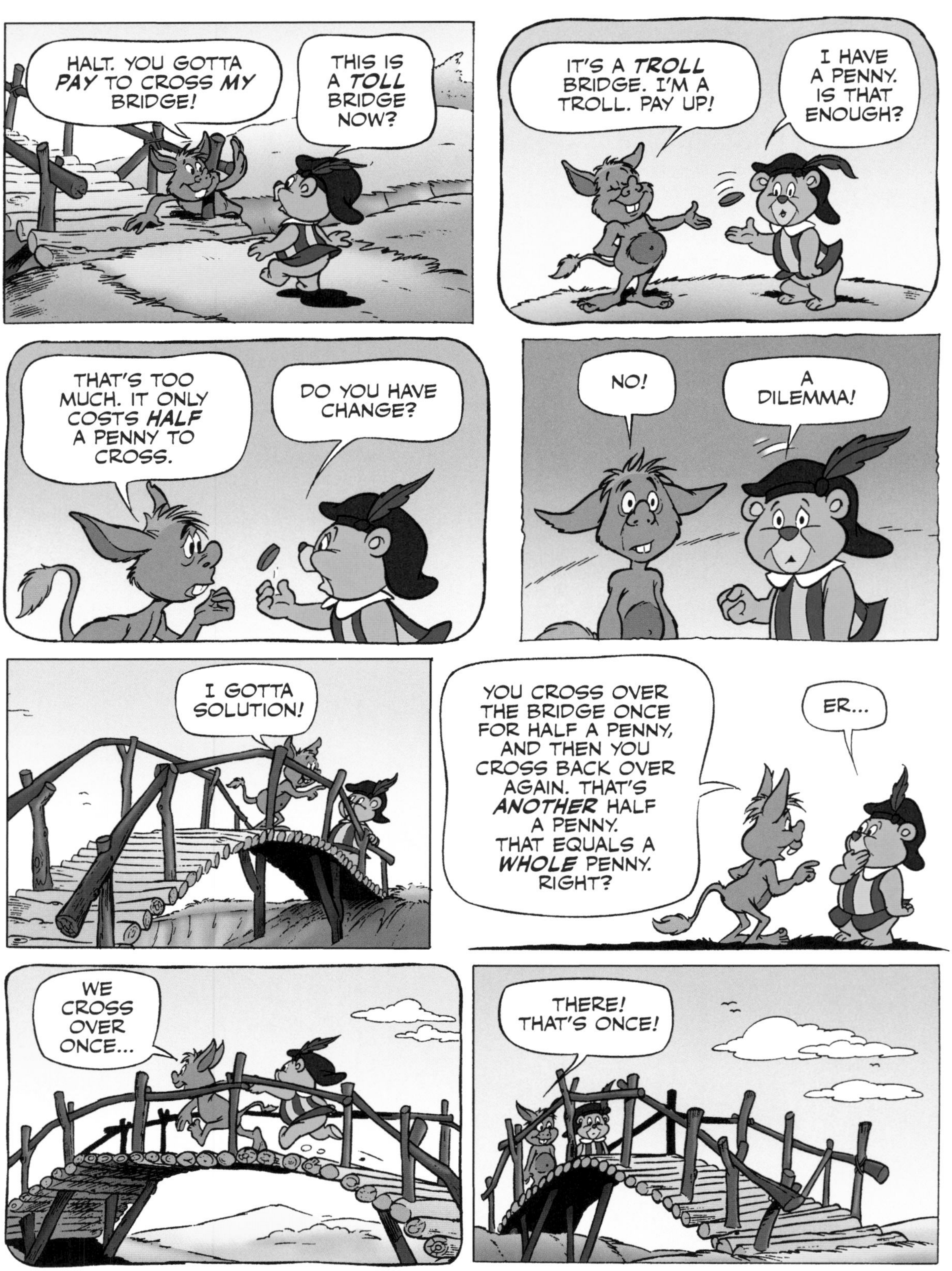

HALT. YOU GOTTA PAY TO CROSS MY BRIDGE!
THIS IS A TOLL BRIDGE NOW?
IT'S A TROLL BRIDGE. I'M A TROLL. PAY UP!
I HAVE A PENNY. IS THAT ENOUGH?
THAT'S TOO MUCH. IT ONLY COSTS HALF A PENNY TO CROSS.
DO YOU HAVE CHANGE?
NO!
A DILEMMA!
I GOTTA SOLUTION!
YOU CROSS OVER THE BRIDGE ONCE FOR HALF A PENNY, AND THEN YOU CROSS BACK OVER AGAIN. THAT'S ANOTHER HALF A PENNY. THAT EQUALS A WHOLE PENNY. RIGHT?
ER...
WE CROSS OVER ONCE...
THERE! THAT'S ONCE!

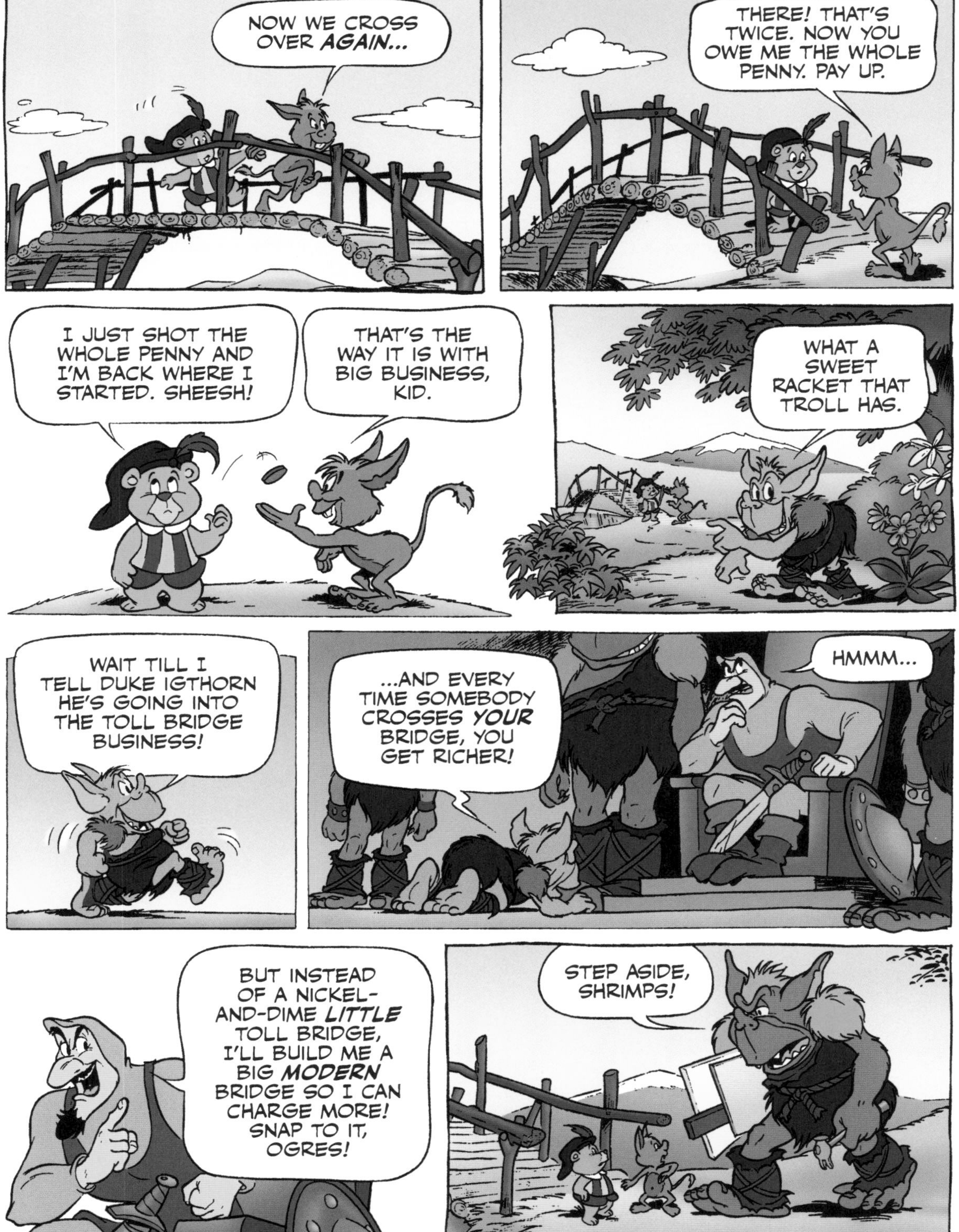
NOW WE CROSS OVER AGAIN...
THERE! THAT'S TWICE. NOW YOU OWE ME THE WHOLE PENNY. PAY UP.
I JUST SHOT THE WHOLE PENNY AND I'M BACK WHERE I STARTED. SHEESH!
THAT'S THE WAY IT IS WITH BIG BUSINESS, KID.
WHAT A SWEET RACKET THAT TROLL HAS.
WAIT TILL I TELL DUKE IGTHORN HE'S GOING INTO THE TOLL BRIDGE BUSINESS!
...AND EVERY TIME SOMEBODY CROSSES YOUR BRIDGE, YOU GET RICHER!
HMMM...
BUT INSTEAD OF A NICKEL-AND-DIME LITTLE TOLL BRIDGE, I'LL BUILD ME A BIG MODERN BRIDGE SO I CAN CHARGE MORE! SNAP TO IT, OGRES!
STEP ASIDE, SHRIMPS!

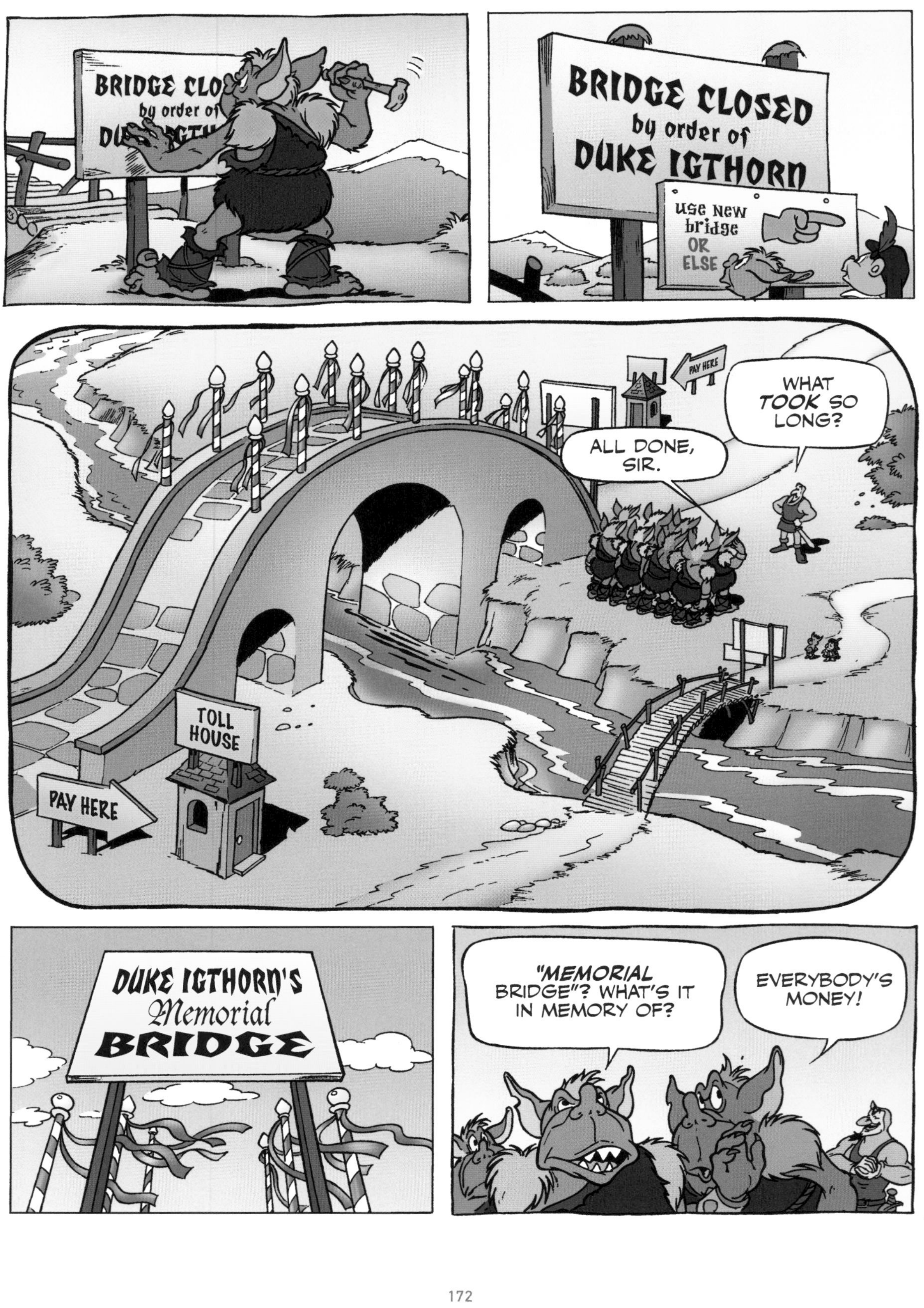
BRIDGE CLO
by order of
BRIDGE CLOSED
by order of
DUKE IGTHORN
use new bridge OR ELSE
PAY HERE
WHAT TOOK SO LONG?
ALL DONE, SIR.
TOLL HOUSE
PAY HERE
DUKE IGTHORN'S Memorial BRIDGE
"MEMORIAL BRIDGE"? WHAT'S IT IN MEMORY OF?
EVERYBODY'S MONEY!

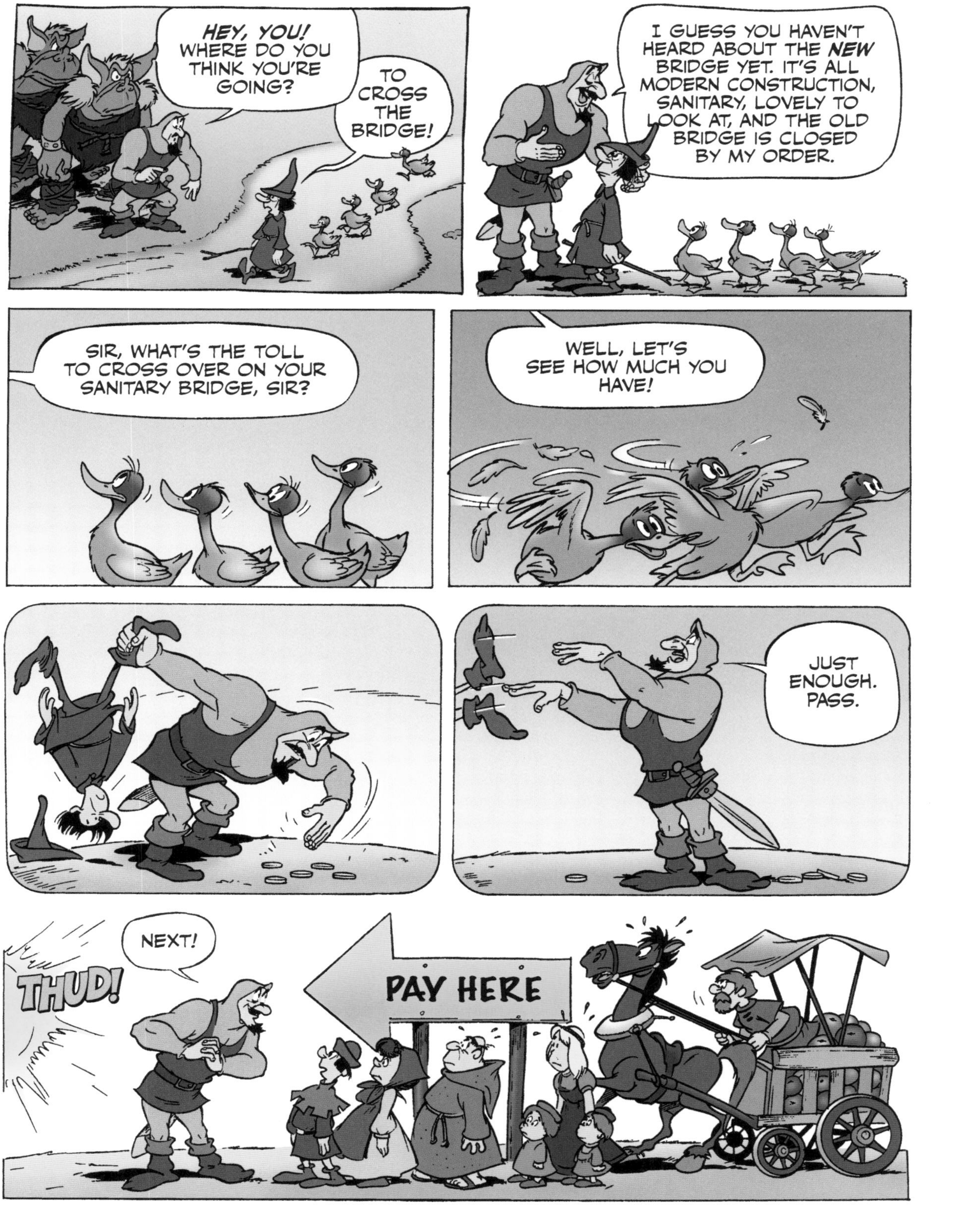
HEY, YOU! WHERE DO YOU THINK YOU'RE GOING?
TO CROSS THE BRIDGE!
I GUESS YOU HAVEN'T HEARD ABOUT THE NEW BRIDGE YET. IT'S ALL MODERN CONSTRUCTION, SANITARY, LOVELY TO LOOK AT, AND THE OLD BRIDGE IS CLOSED BY MY ORDER.
SIR, WHAT'S THE TOLL TO CROSS OVER ON YOUR SANITARY BRIDGE, SIR?
WELL, LET'S SEE HOW MUCH YOU HAVE!
JUST ENOUGH. PASS.
THUD!
NEXT!
PAY HERE

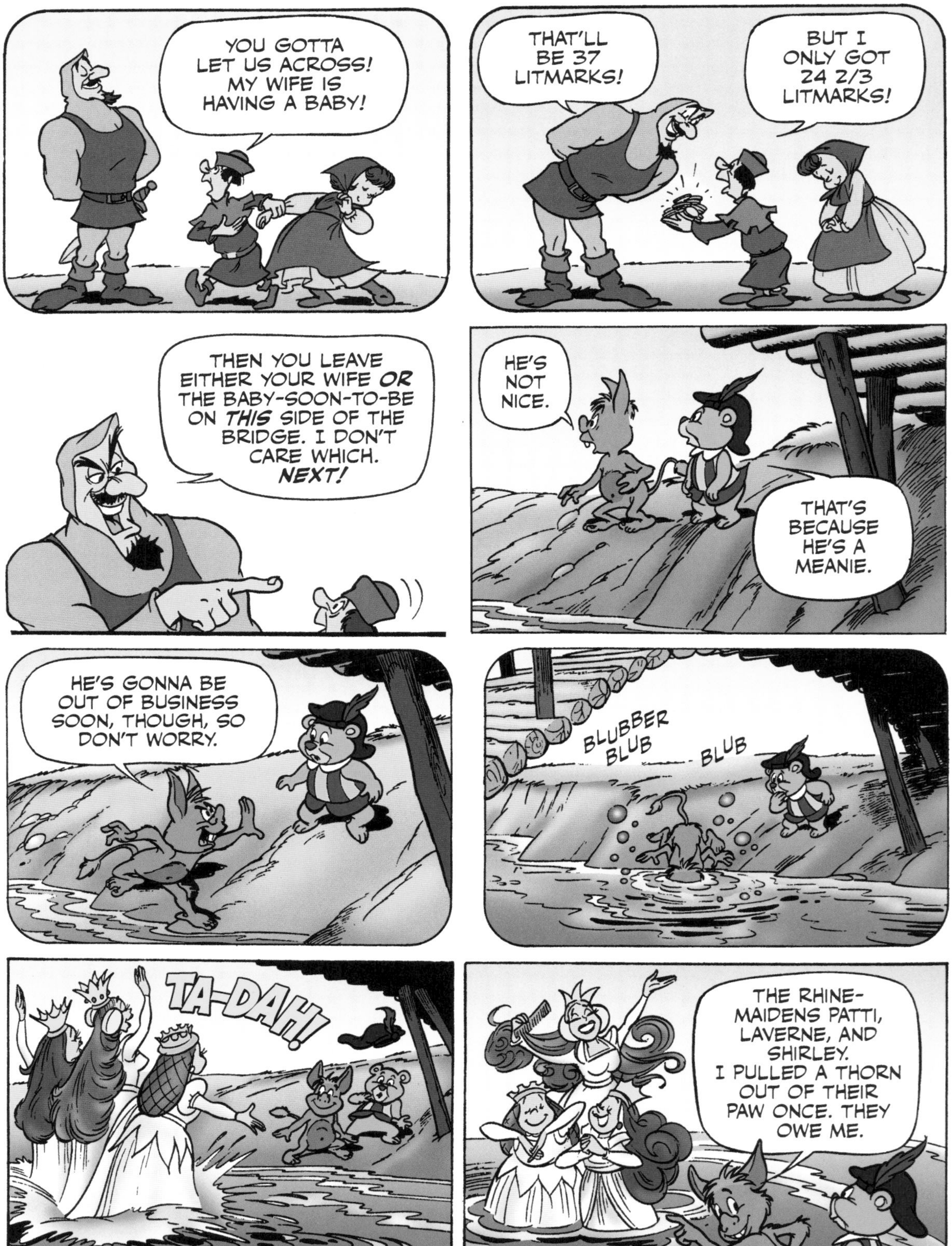
YOU GOTTA LET US ACROSS! MY WIFE IS HAVING A BABY!
THAT'LL BE 37 LITMARKS!
BUT I ONLY GOT 24 2/3 LITMARKS!
THEN YOU LEAVE EITHER YOUR WIFE *OR* THE BABY-SOON-TO-BE ON *THIS* SIDE OF THE BRIDGE. I DON'T CARE WHICH. *NEXT!*
HE'S NOT NICE.
THAT'S BECAUSE HE'S A MEANIE.
HE'S GONNA BE OUT OF BUSINESS SOON, THOUGH, SO DON'T WORRY.
BLUBBER BLUB
BLUB
TA-DAH!
THE RHINE-MAIDENS PATTI, LAVERNE, AND SHIRLEY. I PULLED A THORN OUT OF THEIR PAW ONCE. THEY OWE ME.

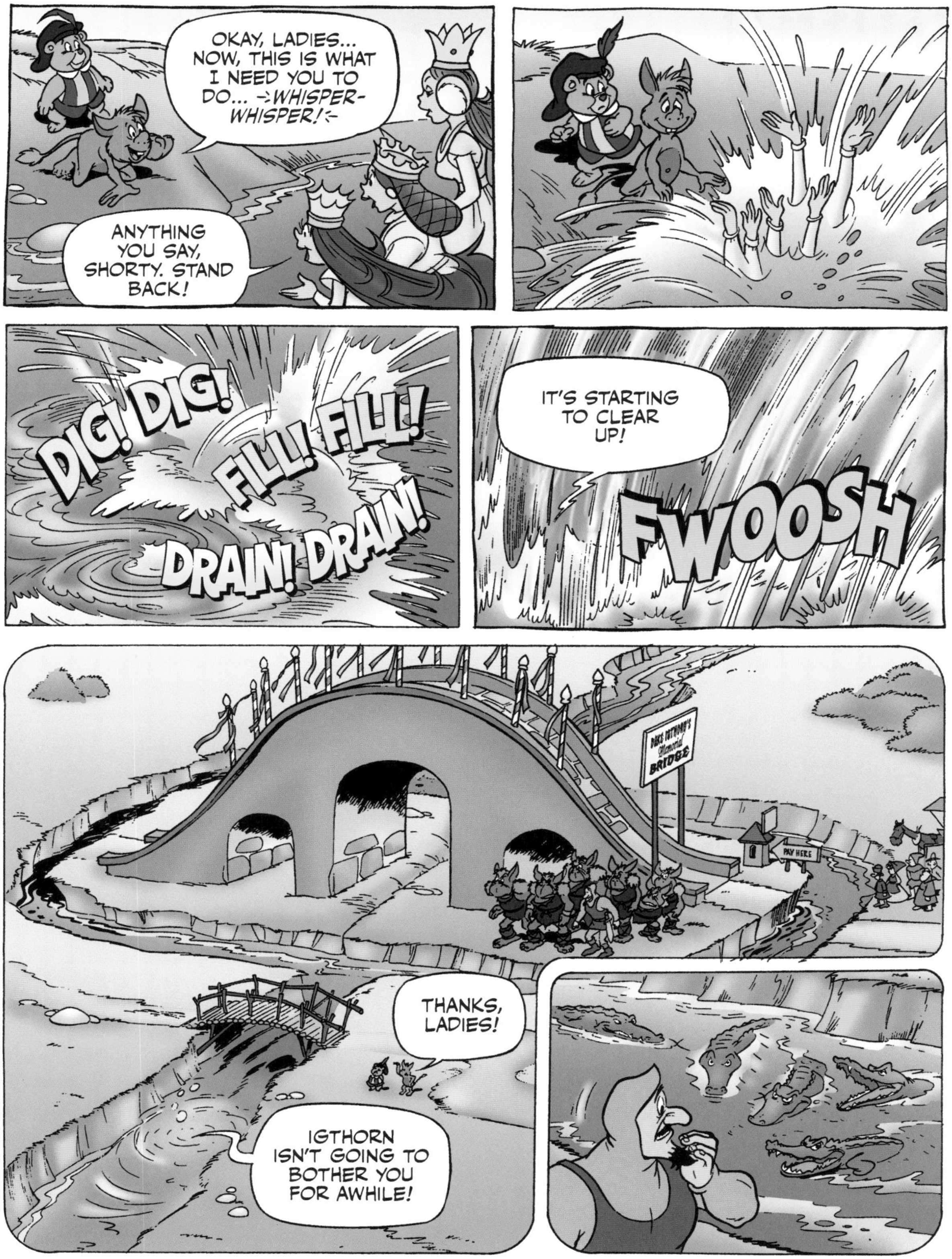
OKAY, LADIES... NOW, THIS IS WHAT I NEED YOU TO DO... ⇢WHISPER-WHISPER!⇠
ANYTHING YOU SAY, SHORTY. STAND BACK!
DIG! DIG!
FILL! FILL!
DRAIN! DRAIN!
IT'S STARTING TO CLEAR UP!
FWOOSH
THANKS, LADIES!
IGTHORN ISN'T GOING TO BOTHER YOU FOR AWHILE!

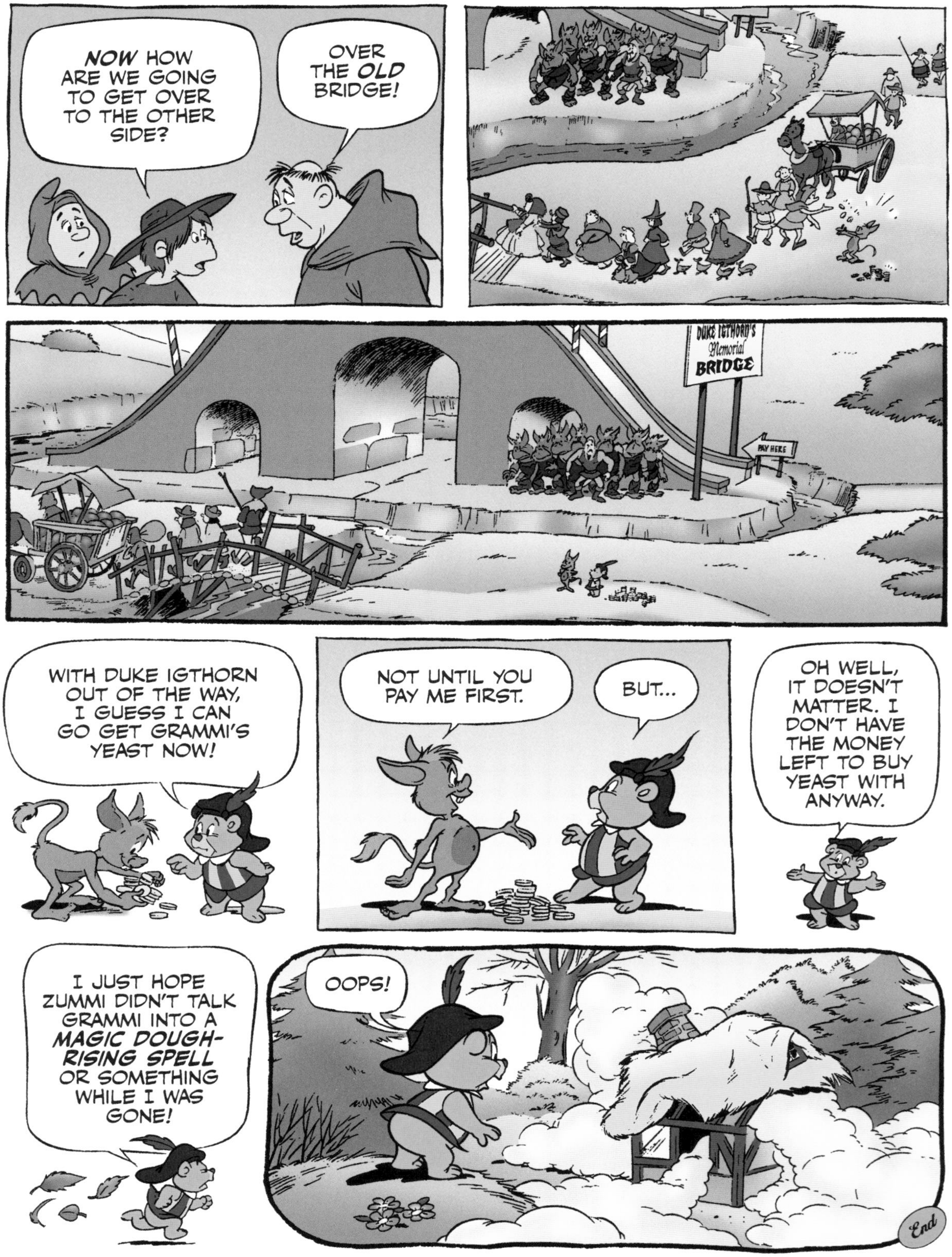
NOW HOW ARE WE GOING TO GET OVER TO THE OTHER SIDE?
OVER THE OLD BRIDGE!
DUKE IGTHORN'S Memorial BRIDGE
PAY HERE
WITH DUKE IGTHORN OUT OF THE WAY, I GUESS I CAN GO GET GRAMMI'S YEAST NOW!
NOT UNTIL YOU PAY ME FIRST.
BUT...
OH WELL, IT DOESN'T MATTER. I DON'T HAVE THE MONEY LEFT TO BUY YEAST WITH ANYWAY.
I JUST HOPE ZUMMI DIDN'T TALK GRAMMI INTO A MAGIC DOUGH-RISING SPELL OR SOMETHING WHILE I WAS GONE!
OOPS!
End

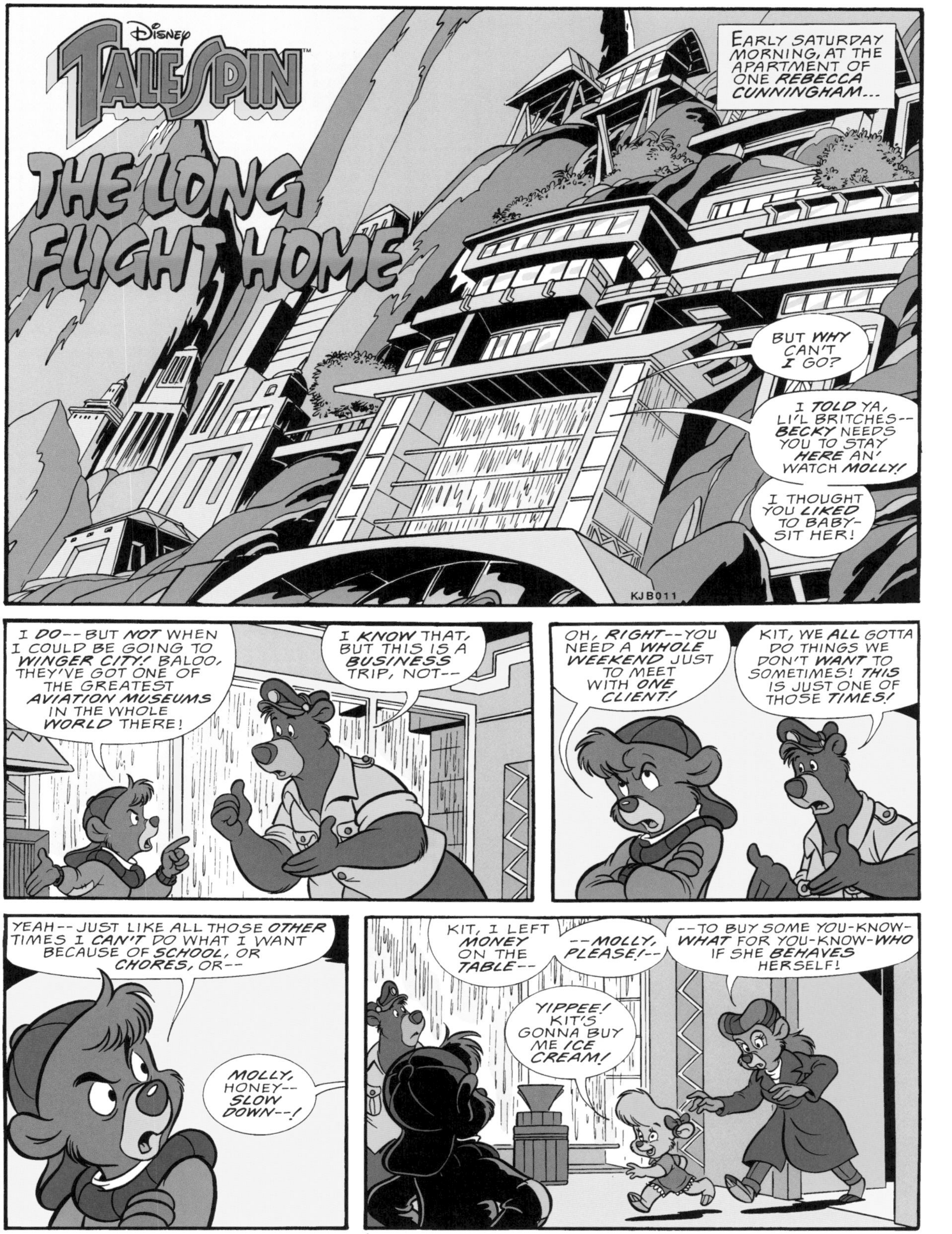
DISNEY
TALESPIN™
THE LONG FLIGHT HOME
EARLY SATURDAY MORNING, AT THE APARTMENT OF ONE REBECCA CUNNINGHAM...
BUT WHY CAN'T I GO?
I TOLD YA, LI'L BRITCHES-- BECKY NEEDS YOU TO STAY HERE AN' WATCH MOLLY!
I THOUGHT YOU LIKED TO BABY-SIT HER!
KJB011
I DO-- BUT NOT WHEN I COULD BE GOING TO WINGER CITY! BALOO, THEY'VE GOT ONE OF THE GREATEST AVIATION MUSEUMS IN THE WHOLE WORLD THERE!
I KNOW THAT, BUT THIS IS A BUSINESS TRIP, NOT--
OH, RIGHT--YOU NEED A WHOLE WEEKEND JUST TO MEET WITH ONE CLIENT!
KIT, WE ALL GOTTA DO THINGS WE DON'T WANT TO SOMETIMES! THIS IS JUST ONE OF THOSE TIMES!
YEAH-- JUST LIKE ALL THOSE OTHER TIMES I CAN'T DO WHAT I WANT BECAUSE OF SCHOOL, OR CHORES, OR--
MOLLY, HONEY-- SLOW DOWN--!
KIT, I LEFT MONEY ON THE TABLE--
--MOLLY, PLEASE!--
--TO BUY SOME YOU-KNOW-WHAT FOR YOU-KNOW-WHO IF SHE BEHAVES HERSELF!
YIPPEE! KIT'S GONNA BUY ME ICE CREAM!

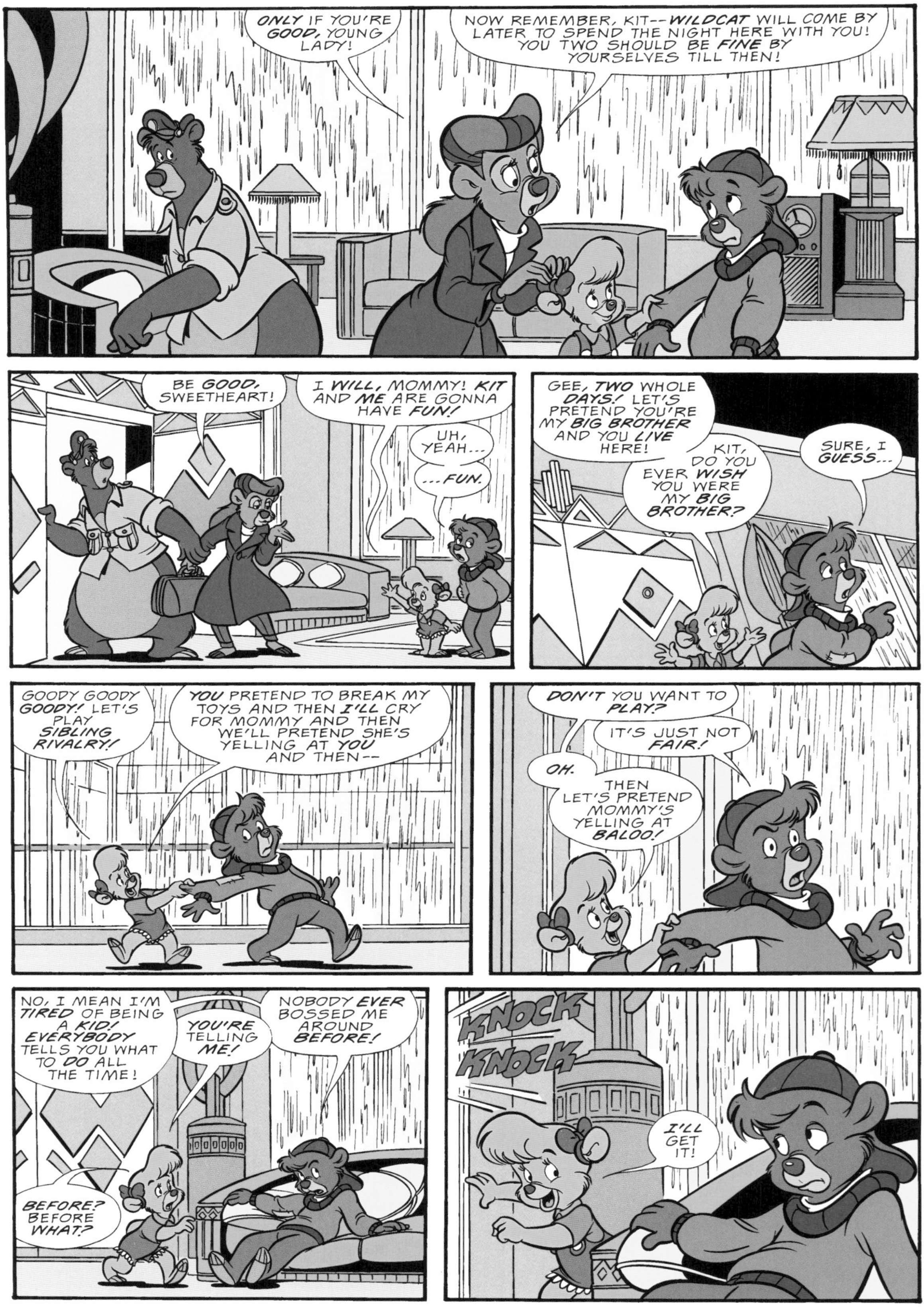
ONLY IF YOU'RE GOOD, YOUNG LADY!
NOW REMEMBER, KIT--WILDCAT WILL COME BY LATER TO SPEND THE NIGHT HERE WITH YOU! YOU TWO SHOULD BE FINE BY YOURSELVES TILL THEN!
BE GOOD, SWEETHEART!
I WILL, MOMMY! KIT AND ME ARE GONNA HAVE FUN!
UH, YEAH...
...FUN.
GEE, TWO WHOLE DAYS! LET'S PRETEND YOU'RE MY BIG BROTHER AND YOU LIVE HERE!
KIT, DO YOU EVER WISH YOU WERE MY BIG BROTHER?
SURE, I GUESS...
GOODY GOODY GOODY! LET'S PLAY SIBLING RIVALRY!
YOU PRETEND TO BREAK MY TOYS AND THEN I'LL CRY FOR MOMMY AND THEN WE'LL PRETEND SHE'S YELLING AT YOU AND THEN--
DON'T YOU WANT TO PLAY?
IT'S JUST NOT FAIR!
OH.
THEN LET'S PRETEND MOMMY'S YELLING AT BALOO!
NO, I MEAN I'M TIRED OF BEING A KID! EVERYBODY TELLS YOU WHAT TO DO ALL THE TIME!
YOU'RE TELLING ME!
NOBODY EVER BOSSED ME AROUND BEFORE!
BEFORE? BEFORE WHAT?
KNOCK KNOCK
I'LL GET IT!

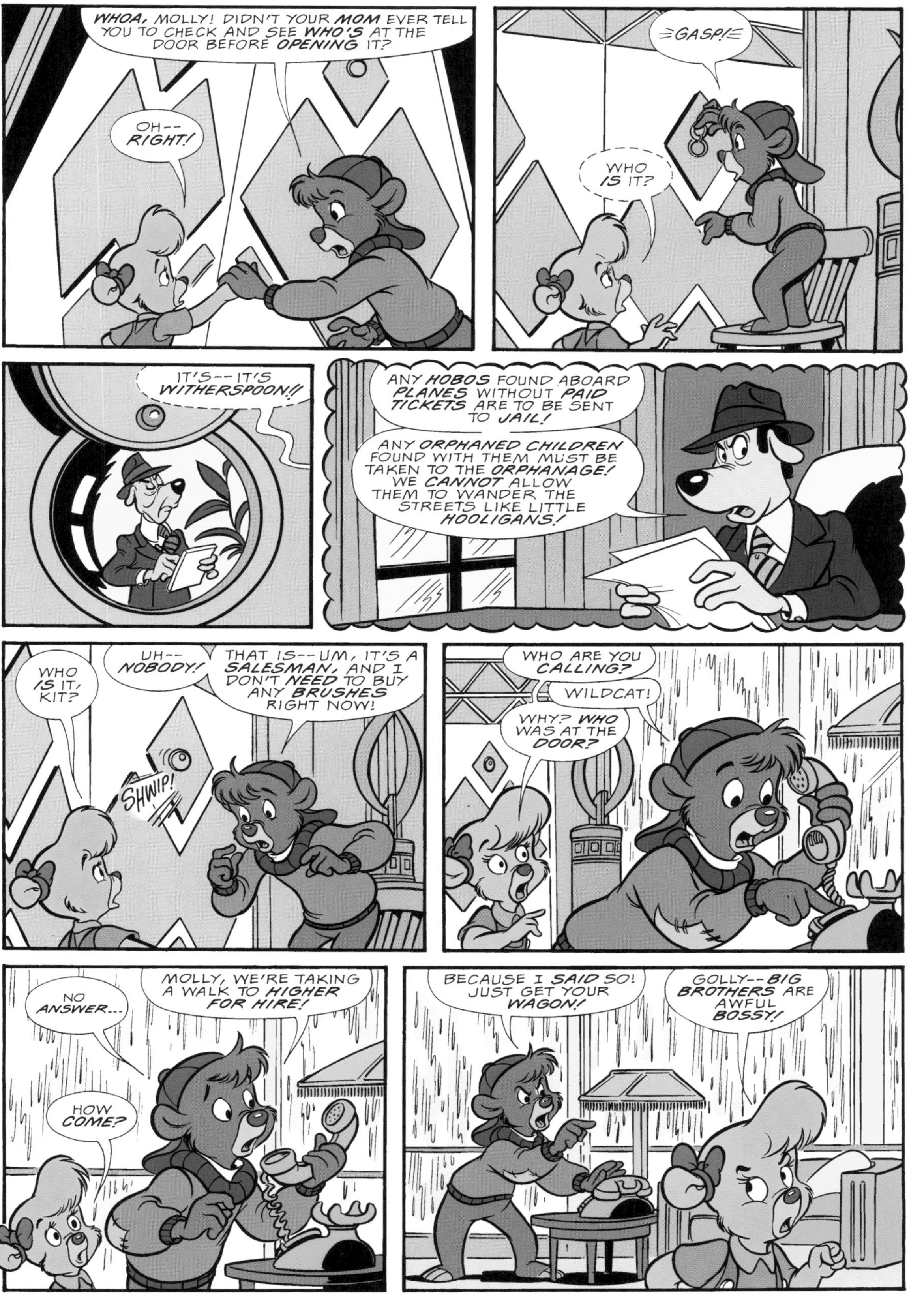
WHOA, MOLLY! DIDN'T YOUR MOM EVER TELL YOU TO CHECK AND SEE WHO'S AT THE DOOR BEFORE OPENING IT?
OH-- RIGHT!
GASP!
WHO IS IT?
IT'S-- IT'S WITHERSPOON!!
ANY HOBOS FOUND ABOARD PLANES WITHOUT PAID TICKETS ARE TO BE SENT TO JAIL!
ANY ORPHANED CHILDREN FOUND WITH THEM MUST BE TAKEN TO THE ORPHANAGE! WE CANNOT ALLOW THEM TO WANDER THE STREETS LIKE LITTLE HOOLIGANS!
WHO IS IT, KIT?
UH-- NOBODY!
THAT IS--UM, IT'S A SALESMAN, AND I DON'T NEED TO BUY ANY BRUSHES RIGHT NOW!
SHWIP!
WHO ARE YOU CALLING?
WILDCAT!
WHY? WHO WAS AT THE DOOR?
NO ANSWER...
MOLLY, WE'RE TAKING A WALK TO HIGHER FOR HIRE!
HOW COME?
BECAUSE I SAID SO! JUST GET YOUR WAGON!
GOLLY--BIG BROTHERS ARE AWFUL BOSSY!

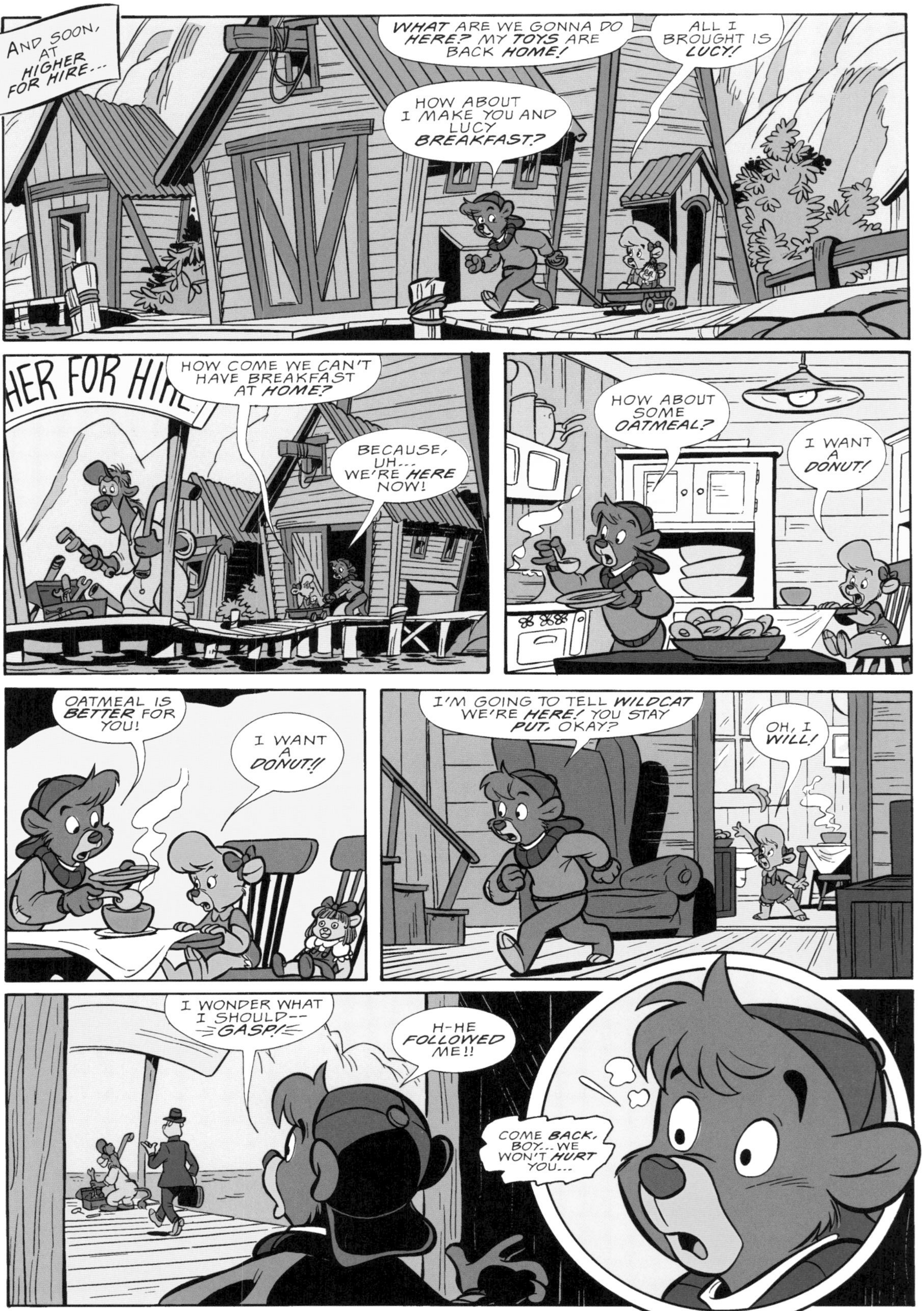

AND SOON, AT HIGHER FOR HIRE...
WHAT ARE WE GONNA DO HERE? MY TOYS ARE BACK HOME!
ALL I BROUGHT IS LUCY!
HOW ABOUT I MAKE YOU AND LUCY BREAKFAST?
HER FOR HIR
HOW COME WE CAN'T HAVE BREAKFAST AT HOME?
BECAUSE, UH... WE'RE HERE NOW!
HOW ABOUT SOME OATMEAL?
I WANT A DONUT!
OATMEAL IS BETTER FOR YOU!
I WANT A DONUT!!
I'M GOING TO TELL WILDCAT WE'RE HERE! YOU STAY PUT, OKAY?
OH, I WILL!
I WONDER WHAT I SHOULD-- GASP!
H-HE FOLLOWED ME!!
COME BACK, BOY... WE WON'T HURT YOU...

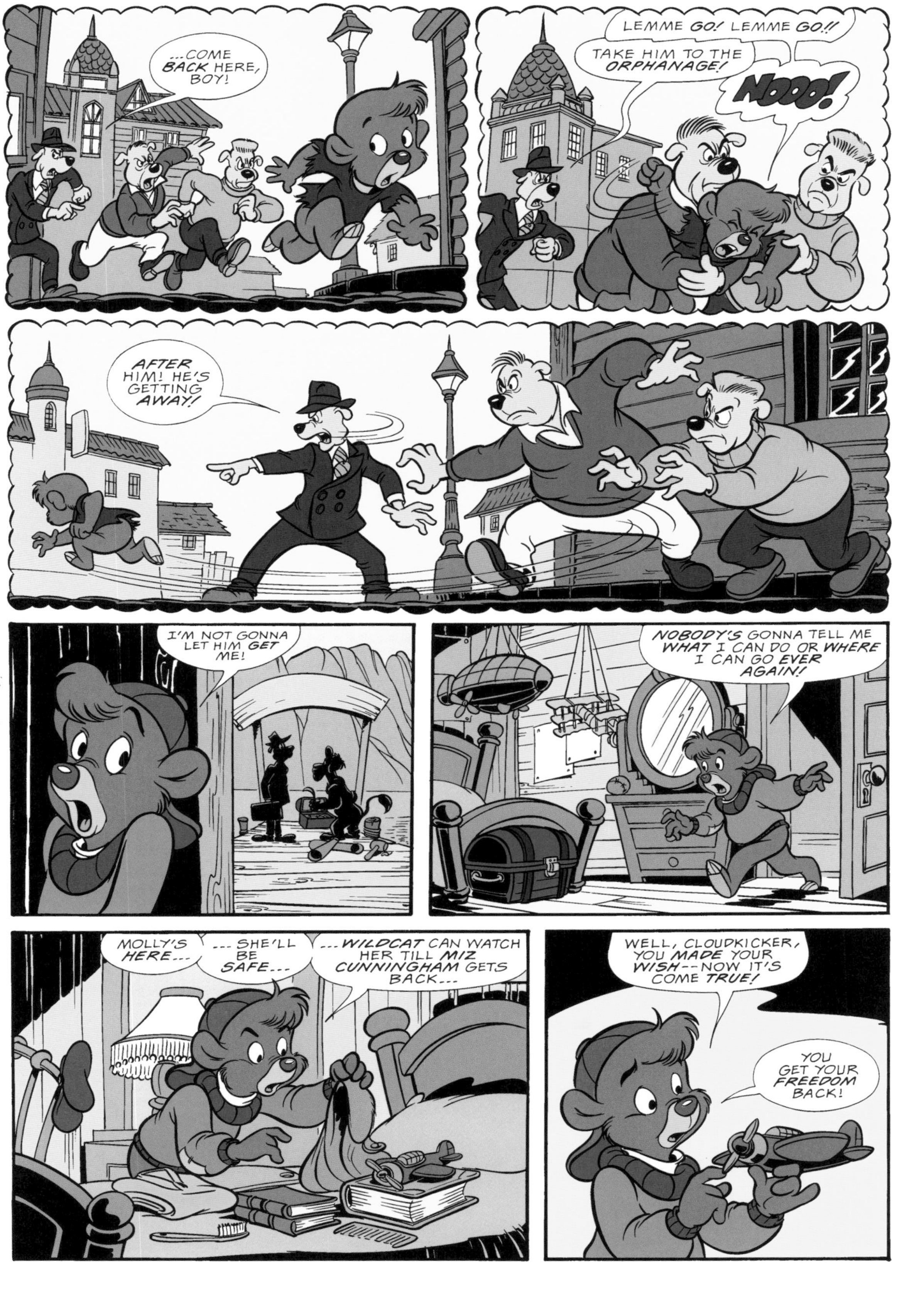

...COME BACK HERE, BOY!
LEMME GO! LEMME GO!!
TAKE HIM TO THE ORPHANAGE!
NOOO!
AFTER HIM! HE'S GETTING AWAY!
I'M NOT GONNA LET HIM GET ME!
NOBODY'S GONNA TELL ME WHAT I CAN DO OR WHERE I CAN GO EVER AGAIN!
MOLLY'S HERE...
...SHE'LL BE SAFE...
...WILDCAT CAN WATCH HER TILL MIZ CUNNINGHAM GETS BACK...
WELL, CLOUDKICKER, YOU MADE YOUR WISH--NOW IT'S COME TRUE!
YOU GET YOUR FREEDOM BACK!

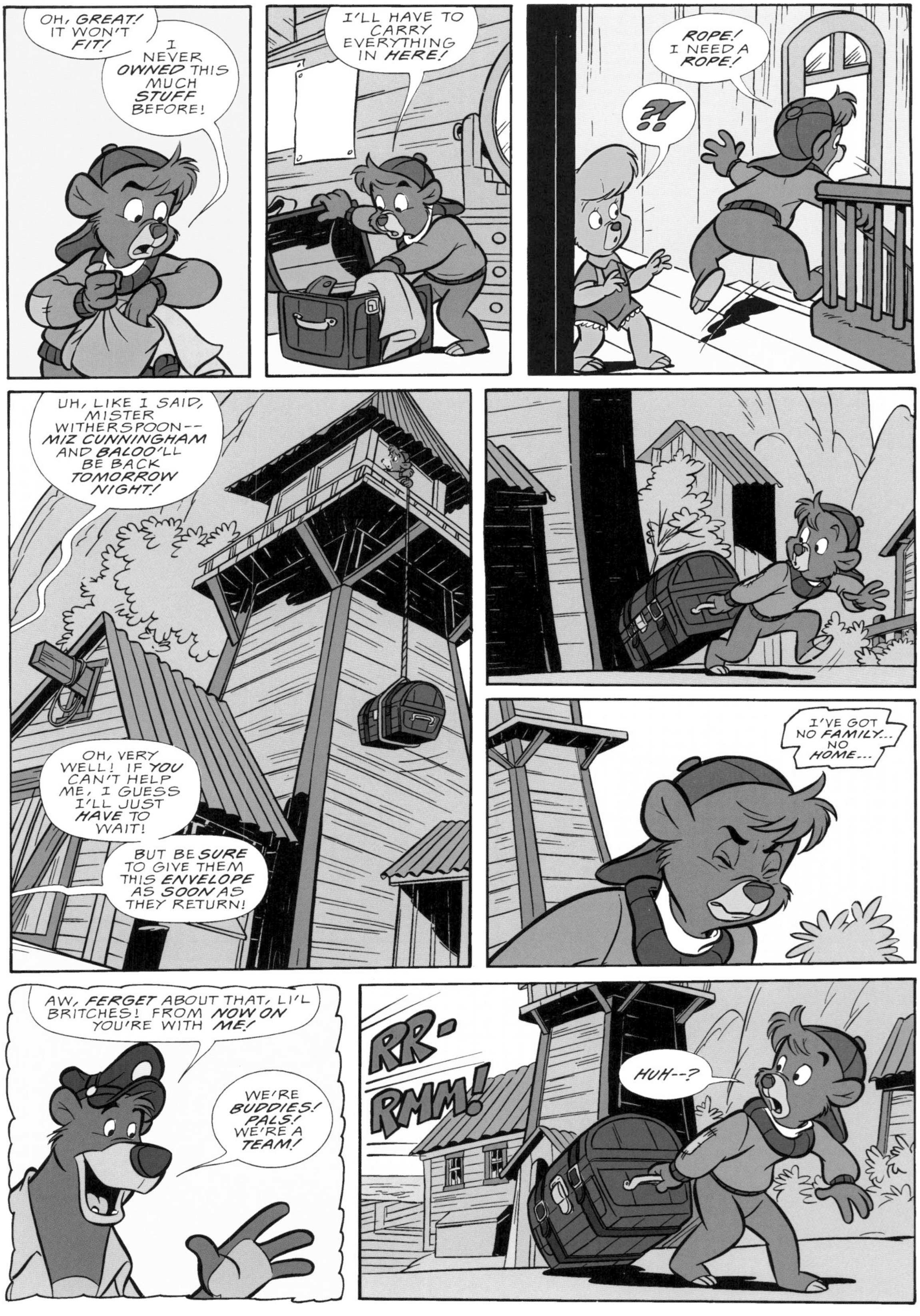

OH, GREAT! IT WON'T FIT!
I NEVER OWNED THIS MUCH STUFF BEFORE!
I'LL HAVE TO CARRY EVERYTHING IN HERE!
ROPE! I NEED A ROPE!
?!
UH, LIKE I SAID, MISTER WITHERSPOON-- MIZ CUNNINGHAM AND BALOO'LL BE BACK TOMORROW NIGHT!
OH, VERY WELL! IF YOU CAN'T HELP ME, I GUESS I'LL JUST HAVE TO WAIT!
BUT BE SURE TO GIVE THEM THIS ENVELOPE AS SOON AS THEY RETURN!
I'VE GOT NO FAMILY... NO HOME...
AW, FERGET ABOUT THAT, LI'L BRITCHES! FROM NOW ON YOU'RE WITH ME!
WE'RE BUDDIES! PALS! WE'RE A TEAM!
RR-RMM!
HUH--?

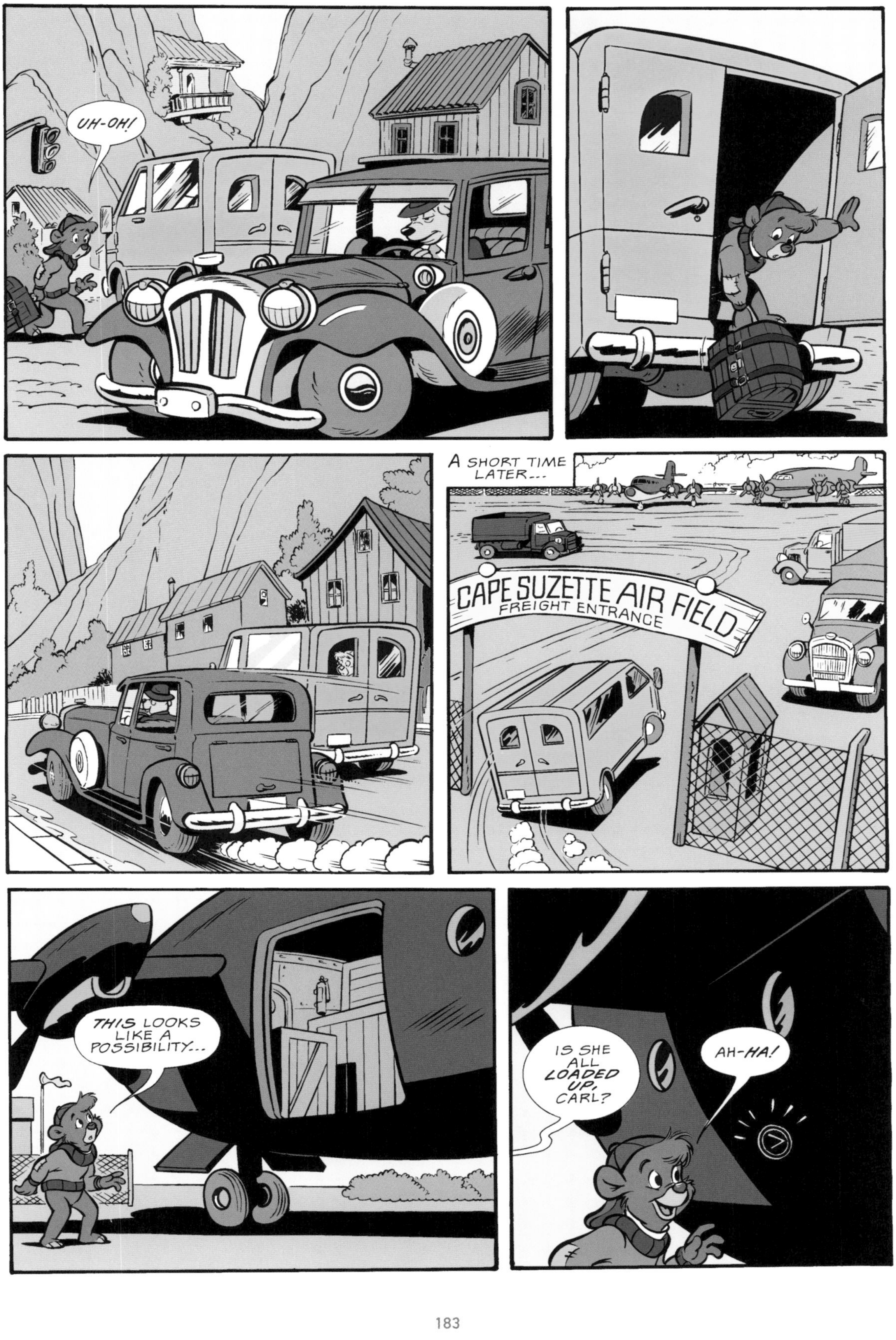
UH-OH!
A SHORT TIME LATER...
CAPE SUZETTE AIR FIELD
FREIGHT ENTRANCE
THIS LOOKS LIKE A POSSIBILITY...
IS SHE ALL LOADED UP, CARL?
AH-HA!

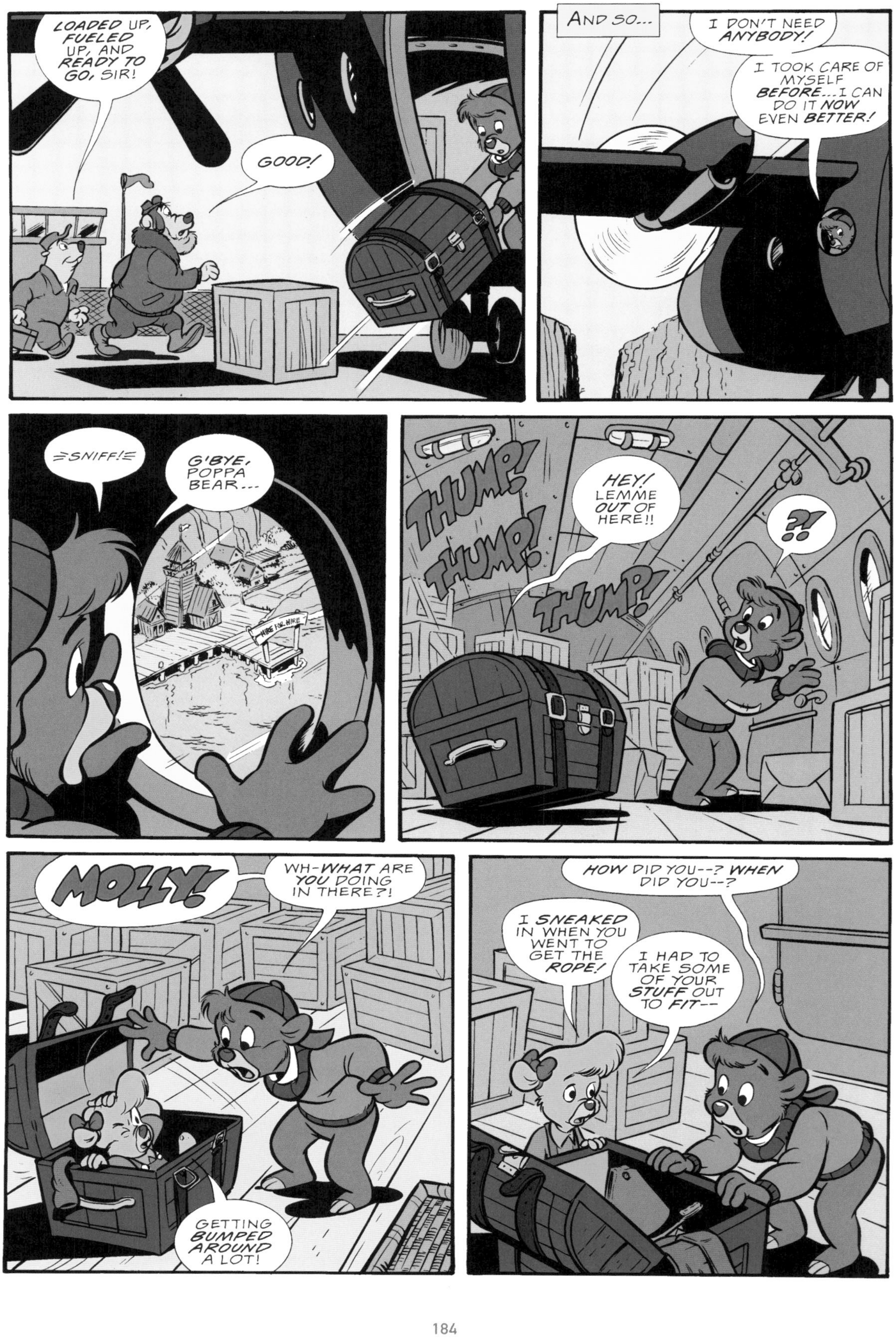
LOADED UP, FUELED UP, AND READY TO GO, SIR!
GOOD!
AND SO...
I DON'T NEED ANYBODY!
I TOOK CARE OF MYSELF BEFORE...I CAN DO IT NOW EVEN BETTER!
=SNIFF!=
G'BYE, POPPA BEAR...
HIRE FOR HIRE
THUMP! THUMP! THUMP!
HEY! LEMME OUT OF HERE!!
?!
MOLLY!
WH-WHAT ARE YOU DOING IN THERE?!
GETTING BUMPED AROUND A LOT!
HOW DID YOU--? WHEN DID YOU--?
I SNEAKED IN WHEN YOU WENT TO GET THE ROPE!
I HAD TO TAKE SOME OF YOUR STUFF OUT TO FIT--

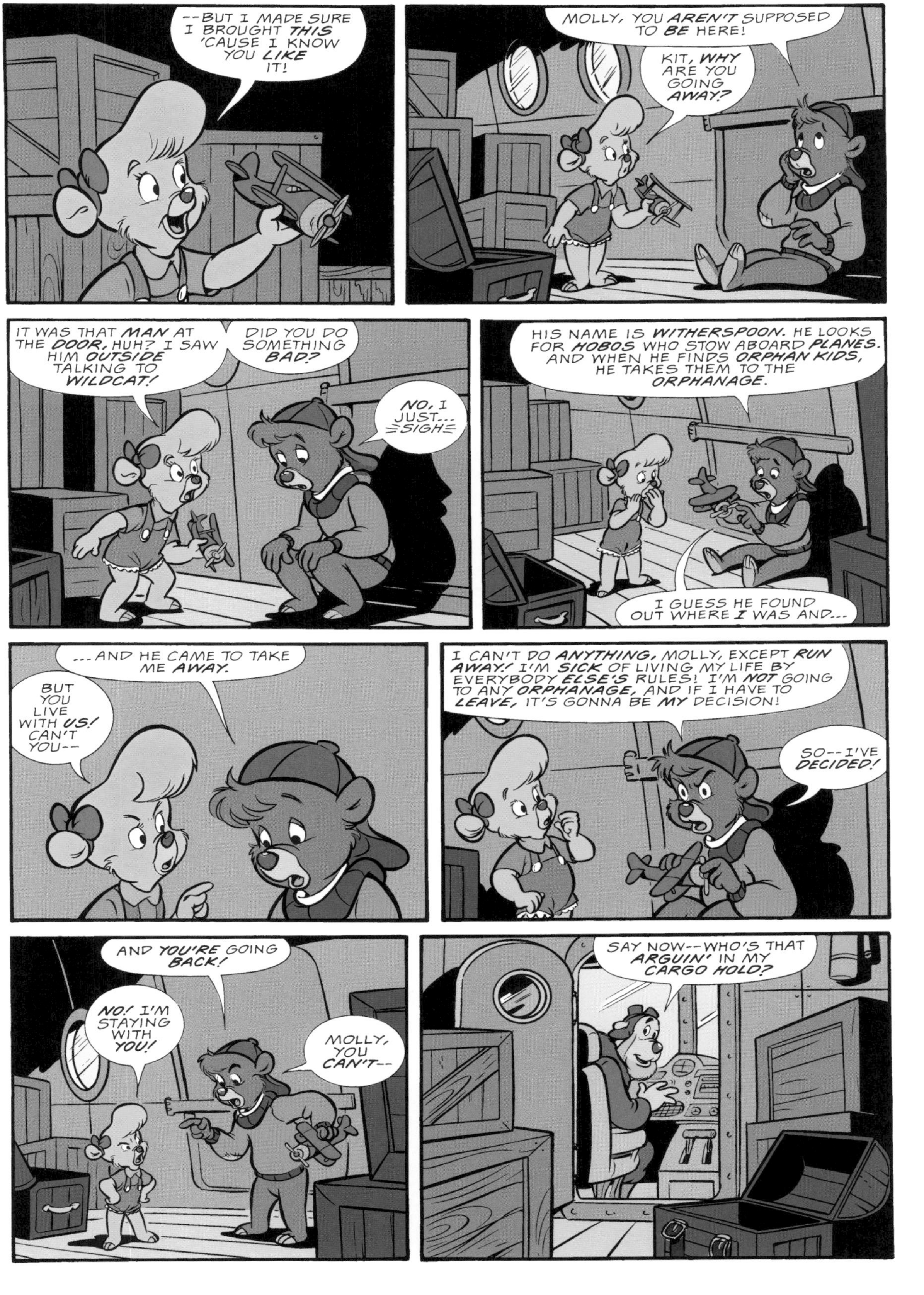
--BUT I MADE SURE I BROUGHT THIS 'CAUSE I KNOW YOU LIKE IT!
MOLLY, YOU AREN'T SUPPOSED TO BE HERE!
KIT, WHY ARE YOU GOING AWAY?
IT WAS THAT MAN AT THE DOOR, HUH? I SAW HIM OUTSIDE TALKING TO WILDCAT!
DID YOU DO SOMETHING BAD?
NO, I JUST... SIGH
HIS NAME IS WITHERSPOON. HE LOOKS FOR HOBOS WHO STOW ABOARD PLANES. AND WHEN HE FINDS ORPHAN KIDS, HE TAKES THEM TO THE ORPHANAGE.
I GUESS HE FOUND OUT WHERE I WAS AND...
...AND HE CAME TO TAKE ME AWAY.
BUT YOU LIVE WITH US! CAN'T YOU--
I CAN'T DO ANYTHING, MOLLY, EXCEPT RUN AWAY! I'M SICK OF LIVING MY LIFE BY EVERYBODY ELSE'S RULES! I'M NOT GOING TO ANY ORPHANAGE, AND IF I HAVE TO LEAVE, IT'S GONNA BE MY DECISION!
SO--I'VE DECIDED!
AND YOU'RE GOING BACK!
NO! I'M STAYING WITH YOU!
MOLLY, YOU CAN'T--
SAY NOW--WHO'S THAT ARGUIN' IN MY CARGO HOLD?

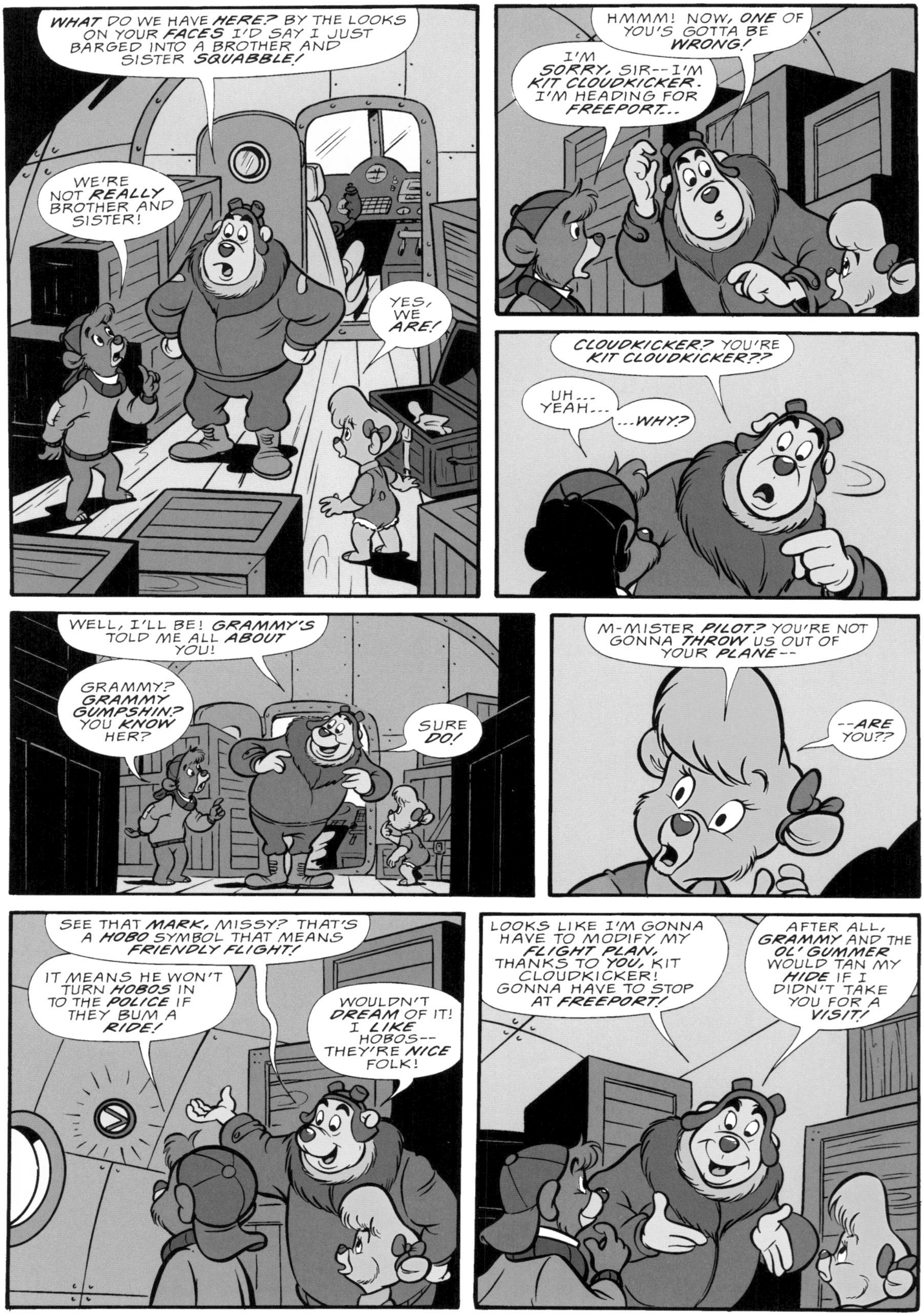
WHAT DO WE HAVE HERE? BY THE LOOKS ON YOUR FACES I'D SAY I JUST BARGED INTO A BROTHER AND SISTER SQUABBLE!
WE'RE NOT REALLY BROTHER AND SISTER!
YES, WE ARE!
HMMM! NOW, ONE OF YOU'S GOTTA BE WRONG!
I'M SORRY, SIR--I'M KIT CLOUDKICKER. I'M HEADING FOR FREEPORT...
CLOUDKICKER? YOU'RE KIT CLOUDKICKER?!?
UH... YEAH...
...WHY?
WELL, I'LL BE! GRAMMY'S TOLD ME ALL ABOUT YOU!
GRAMMY? GRAMMY GUMPSHIN? YOU KNOW HER?
SURE DO!
M-MISTER PILOT? YOU'RE NOT GONNA THROW US OUT OF YOUR PLANE--
--ARE YOU??
SEE THAT MARK, MISSY? THAT'S A HOBO SYMBOL THAT MEANS FRIENDLY FLIGHT!
IT MEANS HE WON'T TURN HOBOS IN TO THE POLICE IF THEY BUM A RIDE!
WOULDN'T DREAM OF IT! I LIKE HOBOS-- THEY'RE NICE FOLK!
LOOKS LIKE I'M GONNA HAVE TO MODIFY MY FLIGHT PLAN, THANKS TO YOU, KIT CLOUDKICKER! GONNA HAVE TO STOP AT FREEPORT!
AFTER ALL, GRAMMY AND THE OL' GUMMER WOULD TAN MY HIDE IF I DIDN'T TAKE YOU FOR A VISIT!

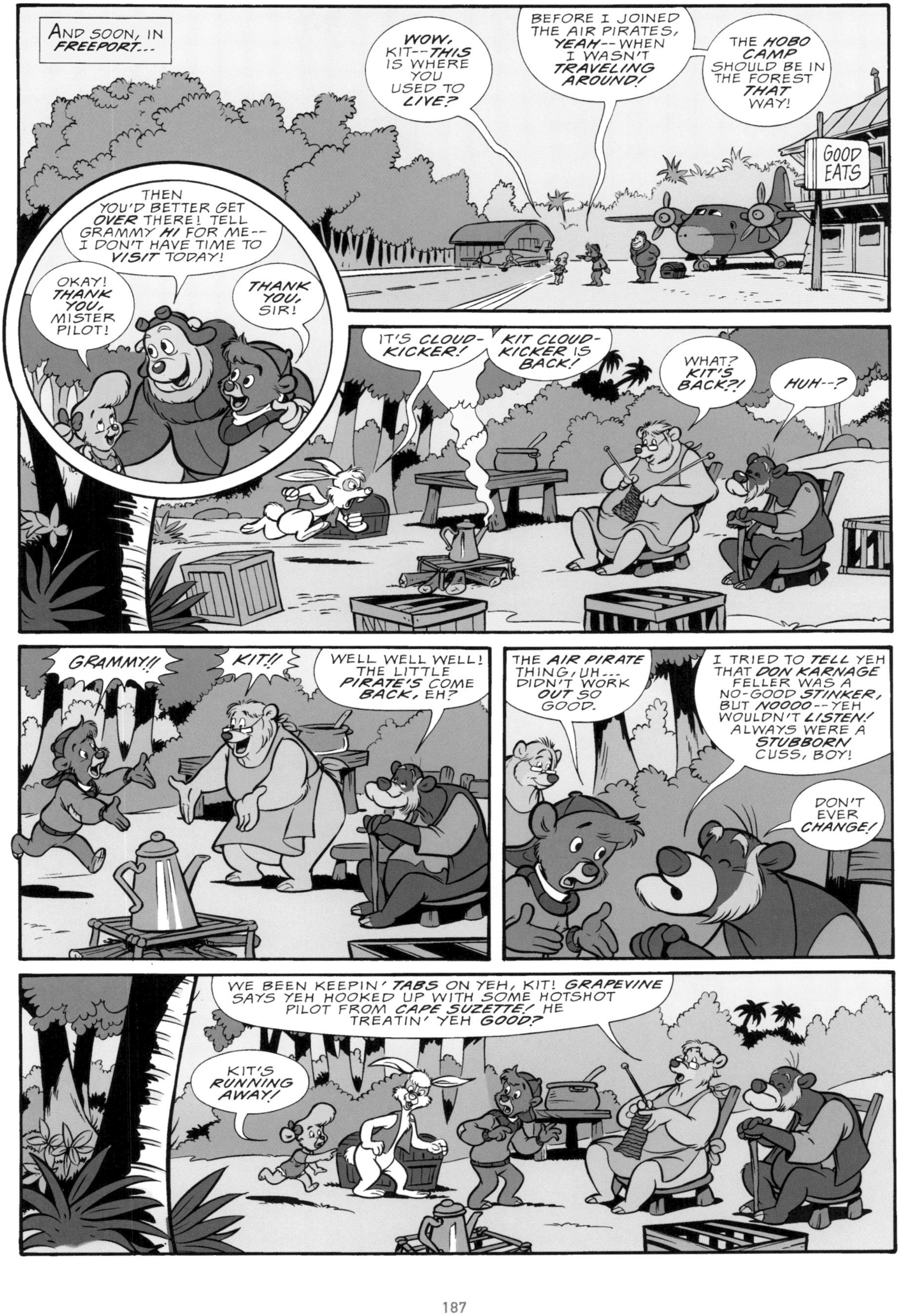
AND SOON, IN FREEPORT...
WOW, KIT--THIS IS WHERE YOU USED TO LIVE?
BEFORE I JOINED THE AIR PIRATES, YEAH--WHEN I WASN'T TRAVELING AROUND!
THE HOBO CAMP SHOULD BE IN THE FOREST THAT WAY!
GOOD EATS
THEN YOU'D BETTER GET OVER THERE! TELL GRAMMY HI FOR ME--I DON'T HAVE TIME TO VISIT TODAY!
OKAY! THANK YOU, MISTER PILOT!
THANK YOU, SIR!
IT'S CLOUD-KICKER!
KIT CLOUD-KICKER IS BACK!
WHAT? KIT'S BACK?!
HUH--?
GRAMMY!!
KIT!!
WELL WELL WELL! THE LITTLE PIRATE'S COME BACK, EH?
THE AIR PIRATE THING, UH... DIDN'T WORK OUT SO GOOD.
I TRIED TO TELL YEH THAT DON KARNAGE FELLER WAS A NO-GOOD STINKER, BUT NOOOO--YEH WOULDN'T LISTEN! ALWAYS WERE A STUBBORN CUSS, BOY!
DON'T EVER CHANGE!
WE BEEN KEEPIN' TABS ON YEH, KIT! GRAPEVINE SAYS YEH HOOKED UP WITH SOME HOTSHOT PILOT FROM CAPE SUZETTE! HE TREATIN' YEH GOOD?
KIT'S RUNNING AWAY!

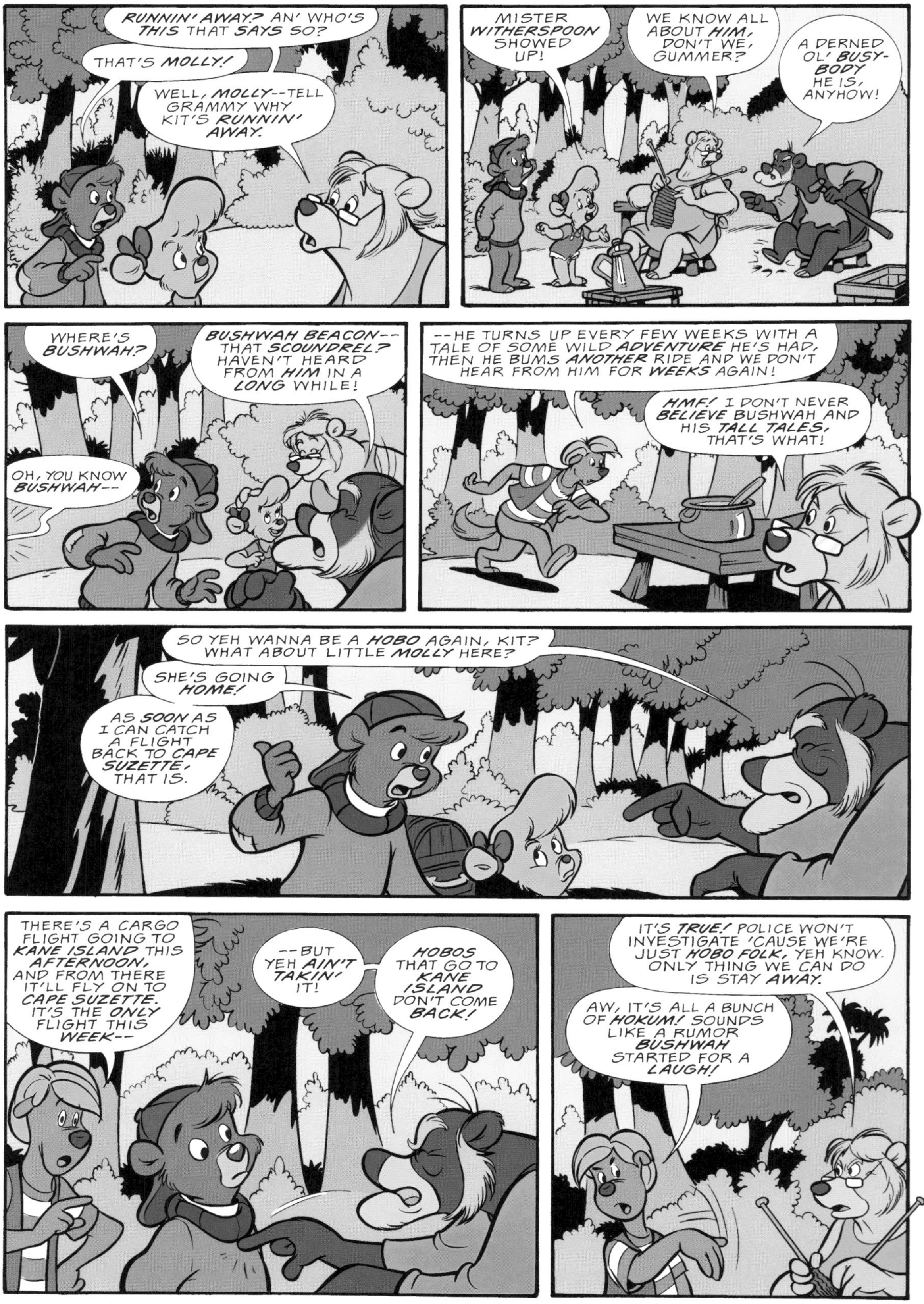
RUNNIN' AWAY? AN' WHO'S THIS THAT SAYS SO?
THAT'S MOLLY!
WELL, MOLLY--TELL GRAMMY WHY KIT'S RUNNIN' AWAY.
MISTER WITHERSPOON SHOWED UP!
WE KNOW ALL ABOUT HIM, DON'T WE, GUMMER?
A DERNED OL' BUSY-BODY HE IS, ANYHOW!
WHERE'S BUSHWAH?
BUSHWAH BEACON--THAT SCOUNDREL? HAVEN'T HEARD FROM HIM IN A LONG WHILE!
OH, YOU KNOW BUSHWAH--
--HE TURNS UP EVERY FEW WEEKS WITH A TALE OF SOME WILD ADVENTURE HE'S HAD, THEN HE BUMS ANOTHER RIDE AND WE DON'T HEAR FROM HIM FOR WEEKS AGAIN!
HMF! I DON'T NEVER BELIEVE BUSHWAH AND HIS TALL TALES, THAT'S WHAT!
SO YEH WANNA BE A HOBO AGAIN, KIT? WHAT ABOUT LITTLE MOLLY HERE?
SHE'S GOING HOME!
AS SOON AS I CAN CATCH A FLIGHT BACK TO CAPE SUZETTE, THAT IS.
THERE'S A CARGO FLIGHT GOING TO KANE ISLAND THIS AFTERNOON, AND FROM THERE IT'LL FLY ON TO CAPE SUZETTE. IT'S THE ONLY FLIGHT THIS WEEK--
--BUT YEH AIN'T TAKIN' IT!
HOBOS THAT GO TO KANE ISLAND DON'T COME BACK!
IT'S TRUE! POLICE WON'T INVESTIGATE 'CAUSE WE'RE JUST HOBO FOLK, YEH KNOW. ONLY THING WE CAN DO IS STAY AWAY.
AW, IT'S ALL A BUNCH OF HOKUM! SOUNDS LIKE A RUMOR BUSHWAH STARTED FOR A LAUGH!

NOW YEH SEE HERE, *ROY-BOY RUDDER*-- GRANNY GUMPSHIN AIN'T LIVED THIS LONG BY *POO-POOIN'* THE *FACTS* IN FRONT OF HER *EYES!*

KANE ISLAND'S A *BAD TICKET!!*

YUP!

BUT I DON'T HAVE A *CHOICE!* MOLLY HAS TO GO BACK BEFORE HER *MOTHER* FINDS OUT SHE'S *GONE!* I CAN'T WAIT A WHOLE *WEEK!*

WELL, YER A *FREE YOUNG 'UN*, KIT! YEH KNOW THE *FACTS* NOW!

THE *CHOICE IS UP TO YOU!*

MEANWHILE, BACK AT *HIGHER FOR HIRE...*

ALMOST DONE! ALL I GOTTA DO IS UNCLOG THAT *LAST* LITTLE *PIPE* AND THE PLUMBING WILL BE *ALMOST SORT OF GOOD AS NEW!*

OOPS! I BETTER NOT GET THAT NICE *ENVELOPE* ALL *MESSY!*

WHATEVER'S *INSIDE* IS PROBABLY *REAL IMPORTANT!*

MISTER WITHERSPOON WAS AWFULLY *ANXIOUS* TO TALK TO MIZ CUNNINGHAM AND *BALOO!*

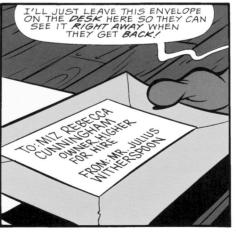

I'LL JUST LEAVE THIS ENVELOPE ON THE *DESK* HERE SO THEY CAN SEE IT *RIGHT AWAY* WHEN THEY GET *BACK!*

TO: MIZ REBECCA CUNNINGHAM OWNER HIGHER FOR HIRE

FROM: MR. JULIUS WITHERSPOON

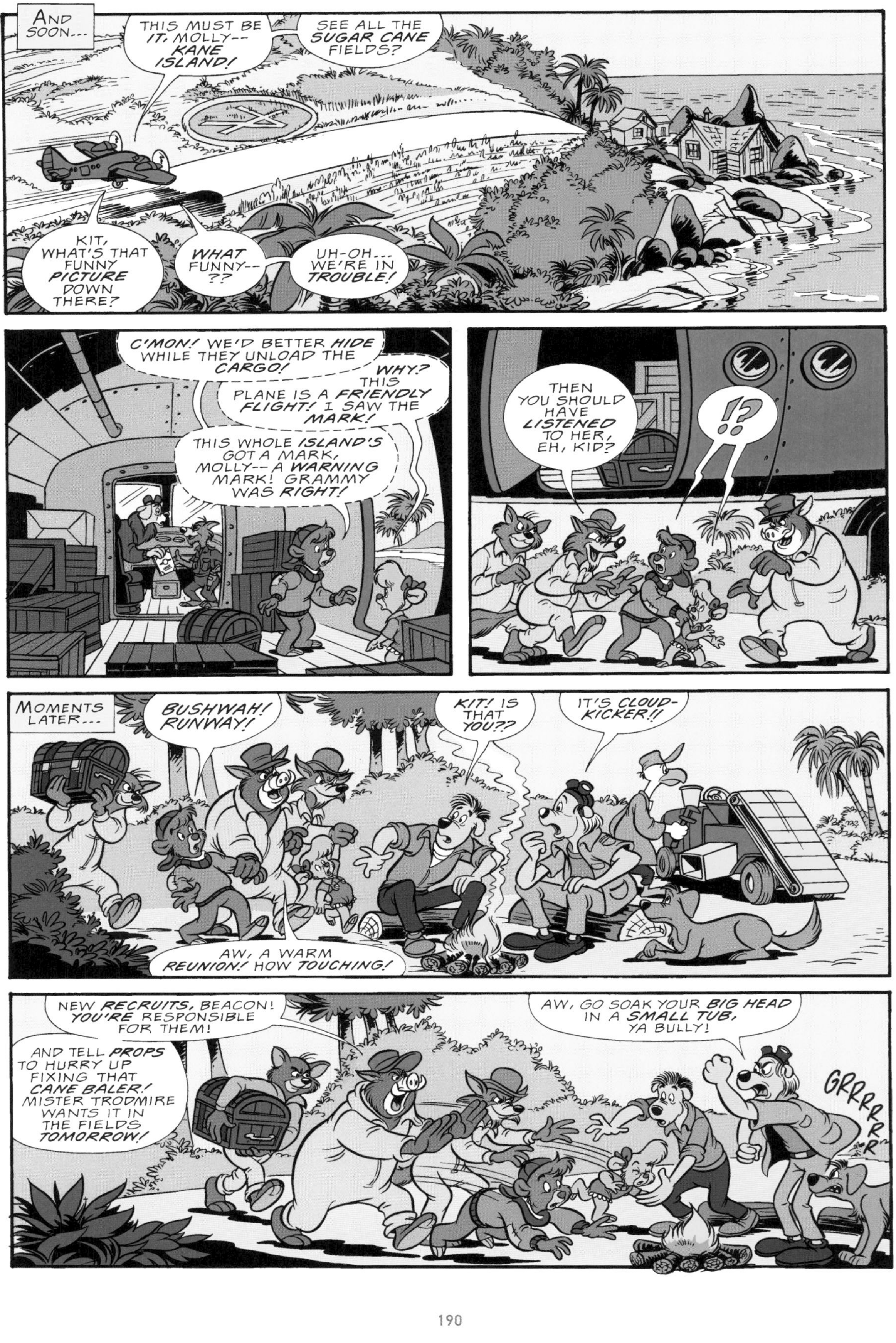

AND SOON...
THIS MUST BE IT, MOLLY-- KANE ISLAND!
SEE ALL THE SUGAR CANE FIELDS?
KIT, WHAT'S THAT FUNNY PICTURE DOWN THERE?
WHAT FUNNY-- ??
UH-OH... WE'RE IN TROUBLE!
C'MON! WE'D BETTER HIDE WHILE THEY UNLOAD THE CARGO!
WHY? THIS PLANE IS A FRIENDLY FLIGHT! I SAW THE MARK!
THIS WHOLE ISLAND'S GOT A MARK, MOLLY-- A WARNING MARK! GRAMMY WAS RIGHT!
THEN YOU SHOULD HAVE LISTENED TO HER, EH, KID?
!?
MOMENTS LATER...
BUSHWAH! RUNWAY!
KIT! IS THAT YOU??
IT'S CLOUD-KICKER!!
AW, A WARM REUNION! HOW TOUCHING!
NEW RECRUITS, BEACON! YOU'RE RESPONSIBLE FOR THEM!
AND TELL PROPS TO HURRY UP FIXING THAT CANE BALER! MISTER TRODMIRE WANTS IT IN THE FIELDS TOMORROW!
AW, GO SOAK YOUR BIG HEAD IN A SMALL TUB, YA BULLY!
GRRRRRR

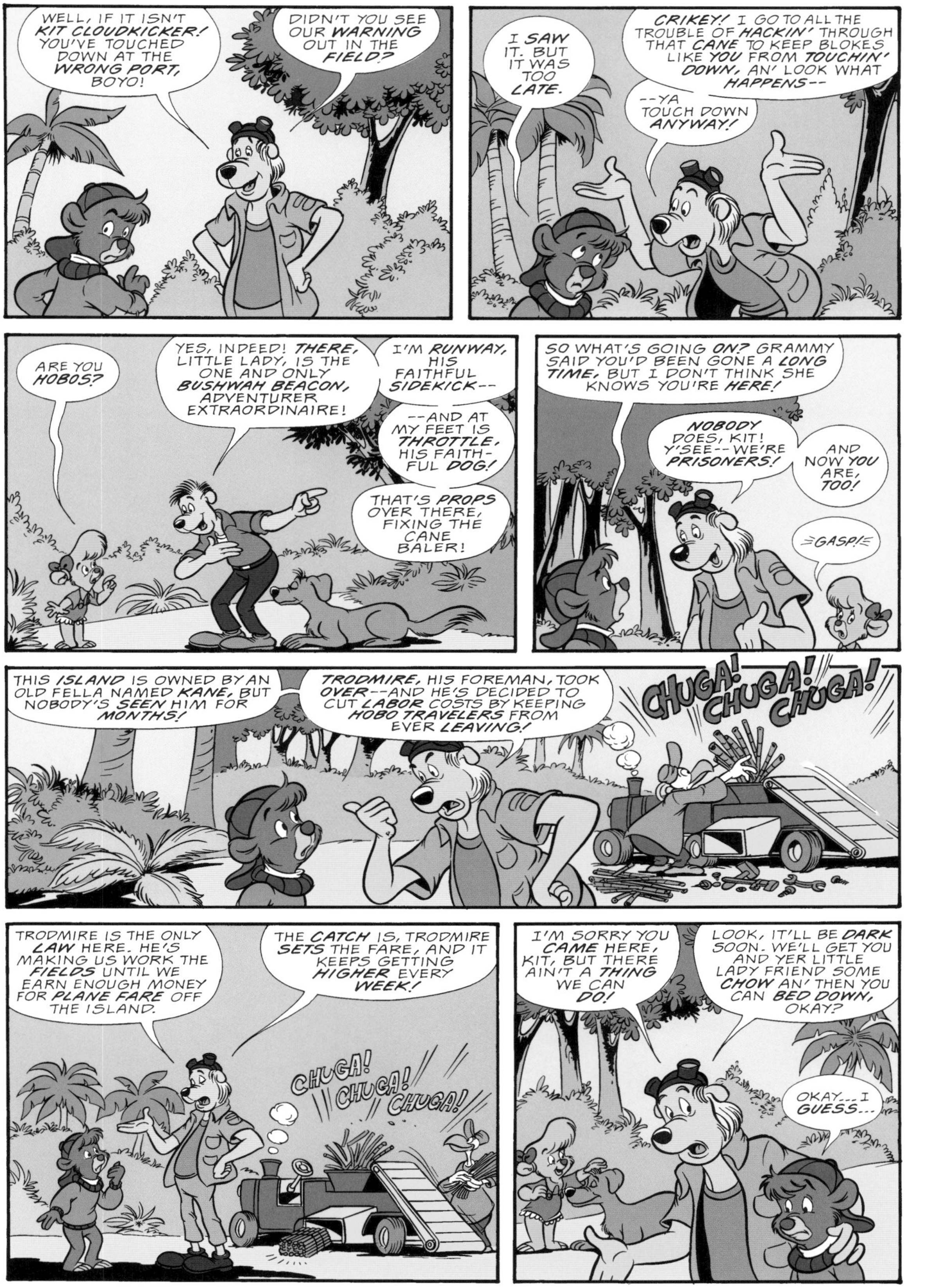
WELL, IF IT ISN'T KIT CLOUDKICKER! YOU'VE TOUCHED DOWN AT THE WRONG PORT, BOYO!
DIDN'T YOU SEE OUR WARNING OUT IN THE FIELD?
I SAW IT. BUT IT WAS TOO LATE.
CRIKEY! I GO TO ALL THE TROUBLE OF HACKIN' THROUGH THAT CANE TO KEEP BLOKES LIKE YOU FROM TOUCHIN' DOWN, AN' LOOK WHAT HAPPENS--
--YA TOUCH DOWN ANYWAY!
ARE YOU HOBOS?
YES, INDEED! THERE, LITTLE LADY, IS THE ONE AND ONLY BUSHWAH BEACON, ADVENTURER EXTRAORDINAIRE!
I'M RUNWAY, HIS FAITHFUL SIDEKICK--
--AND AT MY FEET IS THROTTLE, HIS FAITH-FUL DOG!
THAT'S PROPS OVER THERE, FIXING THE CANE BALER!
SO WHAT'S GOING ON? GRAMMY SAID YOU'D BEEN GONE A LONG TIME, BUT I DON'T THINK SHE KNOWS YOU'RE HERE!
NOBODY DOES, KIT! Y'SEE--WE'RE PRISONERS!
AND NOW YOU ARE, TOO!
GASP!
THIS ISLAND IS OWNED BY AN OLD FELLA NAMED KANE, BUT NOBODY'S SEEN HIM FOR MONTHS!
TRODMIRE, HIS FOREMAN, TOOK OVER--AND HE'S DECIDED TO CUT LABOR COSTS BY KEEPING HOBO TRAVELERS FROM EVER LEAVING!
CHUGA! CHUGA! CHUGA!
TRODMIRE IS THE ONLY LAW HERE. HE'S MAKING US WORK THE FIELDS UNTIL WE EARN ENOUGH MONEY FOR PLANE FARE OFF THE ISLAND.
THE CATCH IS, TRODMIRE SETS THE FARE, AND IT KEEPS GETTING HIGHER EVERY WEEK!
CHUGA! CHUGA! CHUGA!
I'M SORRY YOU CAME HERE, KIT, BUT THERE AIN'T A THING WE CAN DO!
LOOK, IT'LL BE DARK SOON. WE'LL GET YOU AND YER LITTLE LADY FRIEND SOME CHOW AN' THEN YOU CAN BED DOWN, OKAY?
OKAY... I GUESS...

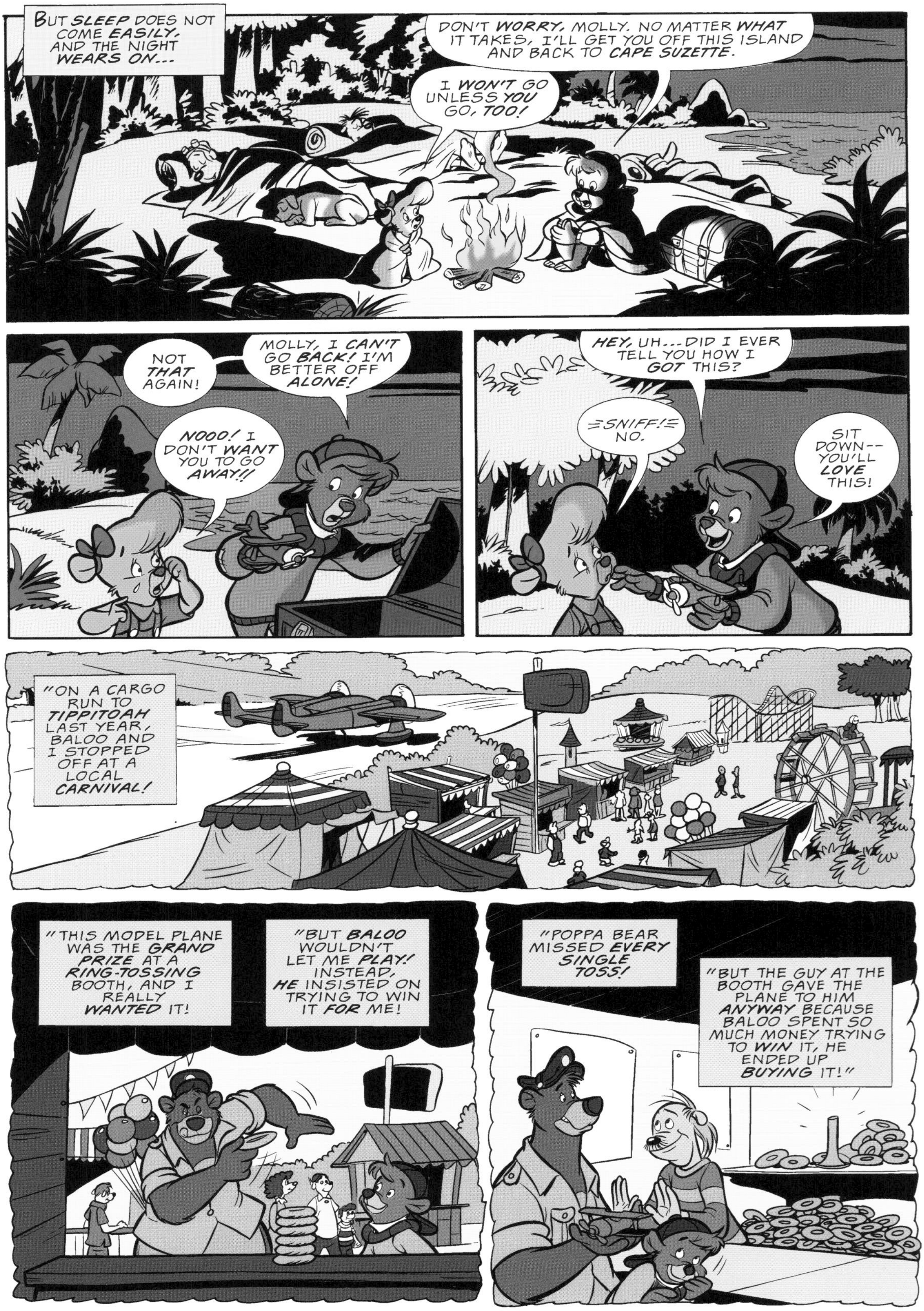
BUT SLEEP DOES NOT COME EASILY, AND THE NIGHT WEARS ON...
DON'T WORRY, MOLLY. NO MATTER WHAT IT TAKES, I'LL GET YOU OFF THIS ISLAND AND BACK TO CAPE SUZETTE.
I WON'T GO UNLESS YOU GO, TOO!
NOT THAT AGAIN!
MOLLY, I CAN'T GO BACK! I'M BETTER OFF ALONE!
NOOO! I DON'T WANT YOU TO GO AWAY!!
HEY, UH... DID I EVER TELL YOU HOW I GOT THIS?
=SNIFF!= NO.
SIT DOWN-- YOU'LL LOVE THIS!
"ON A CARGO RUN TO TIPPITOAH LAST YEAR, BALOO AND I STOPPED OFF AT A LOCAL CARNIVAL!
"THIS MODEL PLANE WAS THE GRAND PRIZE AT A RING-TOSSING BOOTH, AND I REALLY WANTED IT!
"BUT BALOO WOULDN'T LET ME PLAY! INSTEAD, HE INSISTED ON TRYING TO WIN IT FOR ME!
"POPPA BEAR MISSED EVERY SINGLE TOSS!
"BUT THE GUY AT THE BOOTH GAVE THE PLANE TO HIM ANYWAY BECAUSE BALOO SPENT SO MUCH MONEY TRYING TO WIN IT, HE ENDED UP BUYING IT!"

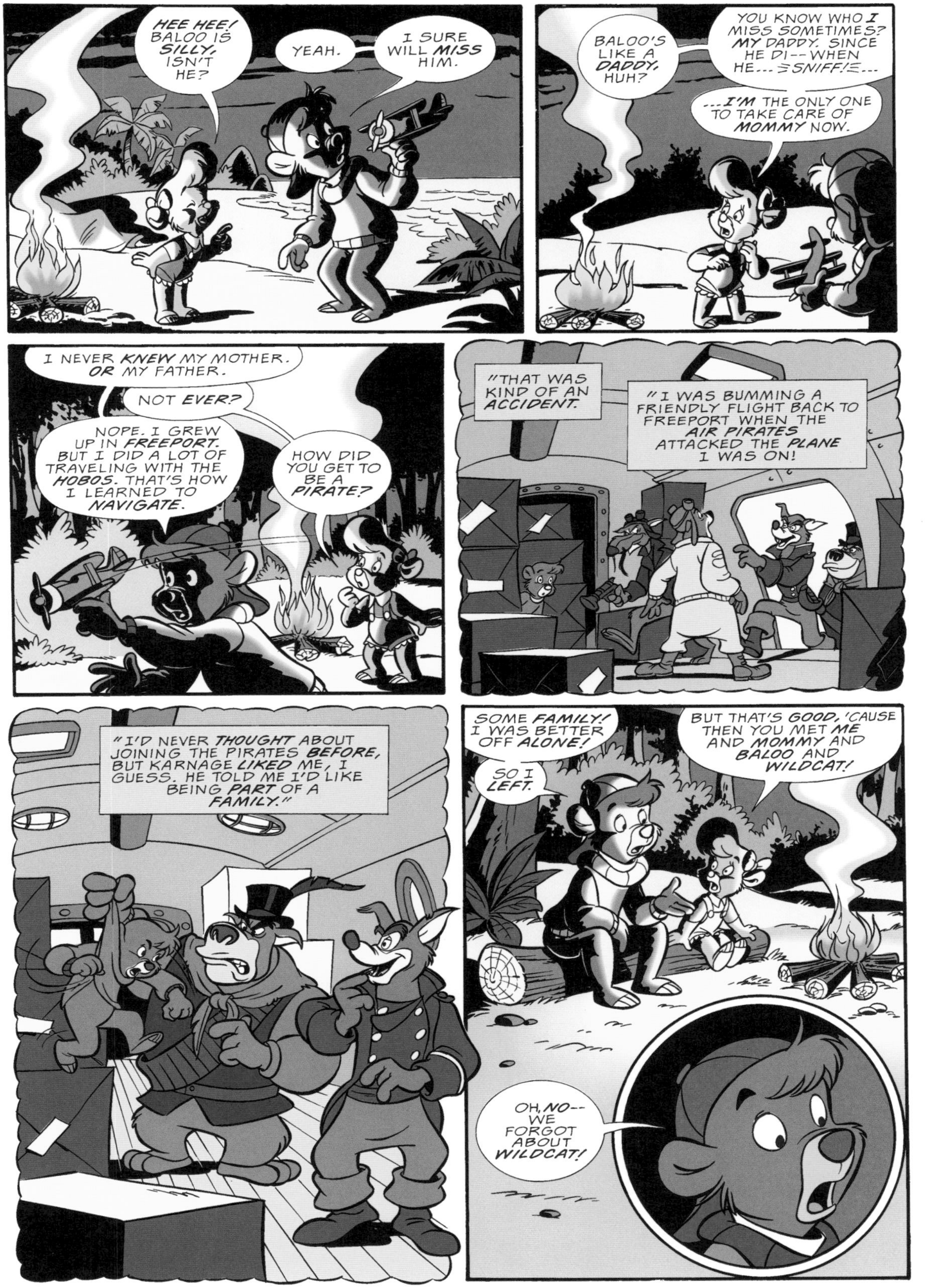
HEE HEE! BALOO IS SILLY, ISN'T HE?
YEAH.
I SURE WILL MISS HIM.
BALOO'S LIKE A DADDY, HUH?
YOU KNOW WHO I MISS SOMETIMES? MY DADDY. SINCE HE DI--WHEN HE... SNIFF!...
...I'M THE ONLY ONE TO TAKE CARE OF MOMMY NOW.
I NEVER KNEW MY MOTHER. OR MY FATHER.
NOT EVER?
NOPE. I GREW UP IN FREEPORT. BUT I DID A LOT OF TRAVELING WITH THE HOBOS. THAT'S HOW I LEARNED TO NAVIGATE.
HOW DID YOU GET TO BE A PIRATE?
"THAT WAS KIND OF AN ACCIDENT.
"I WAS BUMMING A FRIENDLY FLIGHT BACK TO FREEPORT WHEN THE AIR PIRATES ATTACKED THE PLANE I WAS ON!
"I'D NEVER THOUGHT ABOUT JOINING THE PIRATES BEFORE, BUT KARNAGE LIKED ME, I GUESS. HE TOLD ME I'D LIKE BEING PART OF A FAMILY."
SOME FAMILY! I WAS BETTER OFF ALONE!
SO I LEFT.
BUT THAT'S GOOD, 'CAUSE THEN YOU MET ME AND MOMMY AND BALOO AND WILDCAT!
OH, NO-- WE FORGOT ABOUT WILDCAT!

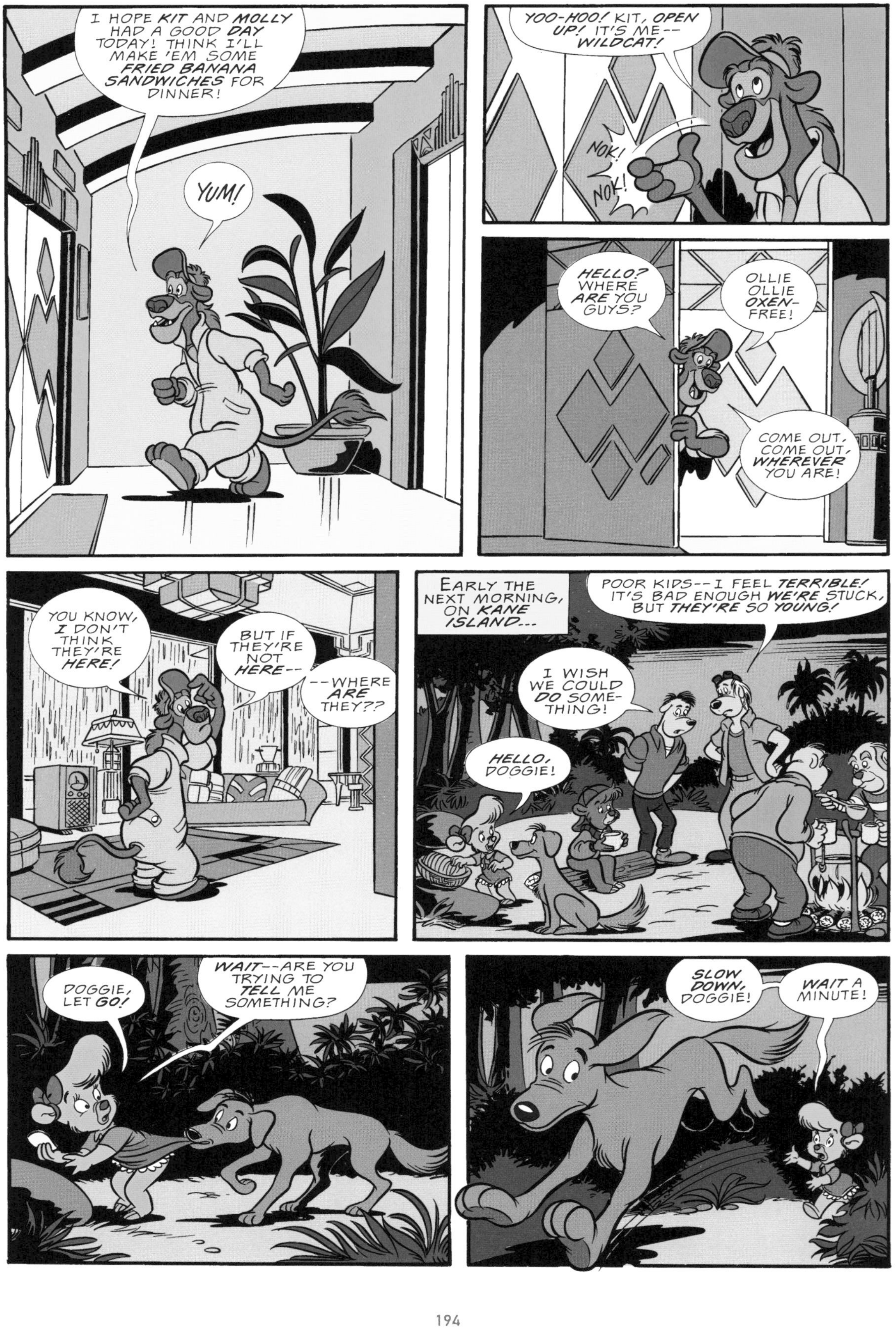
I HOPE KIT AND MOLLY HAD A GOOD DAY TODAY! THINK I'LL MAKE 'EM SOME FRIED BANANA SANDWICHES FOR DINNER!
YUM!
YOO-HOO! KIT, OPEN UP! IT'S ME-- WILDCAT!
NOK! NOK!
HELLO? WHERE ARE YOU GUYS?
OLLIE OLLIE OXEN-FREE!
COME OUT, COME OUT, WHEREVER YOU ARE!
YOU KNOW, I DON'T THINK THEY'RE HERE!
BUT IF THEY'RE NOT HERE--
--WHERE ARE THEY??
EARLY THE NEXT MORNING, ON KANE ISLAND...
POOR KIDS--I FEEL TERRIBLE! IT'S BAD ENOUGH WE'RE STUCK, BUT THEY'RE SO YOUNG!
I WISH WE COULD DO SOMETHING!
HELLO, DOGGIE!
DOGGIE, LET GO!
WAIT--ARE YOU TRYING TO TELL ME SOMETHING?
SLOW DOWN, DOGGIE!
WAIT A MINUTE!

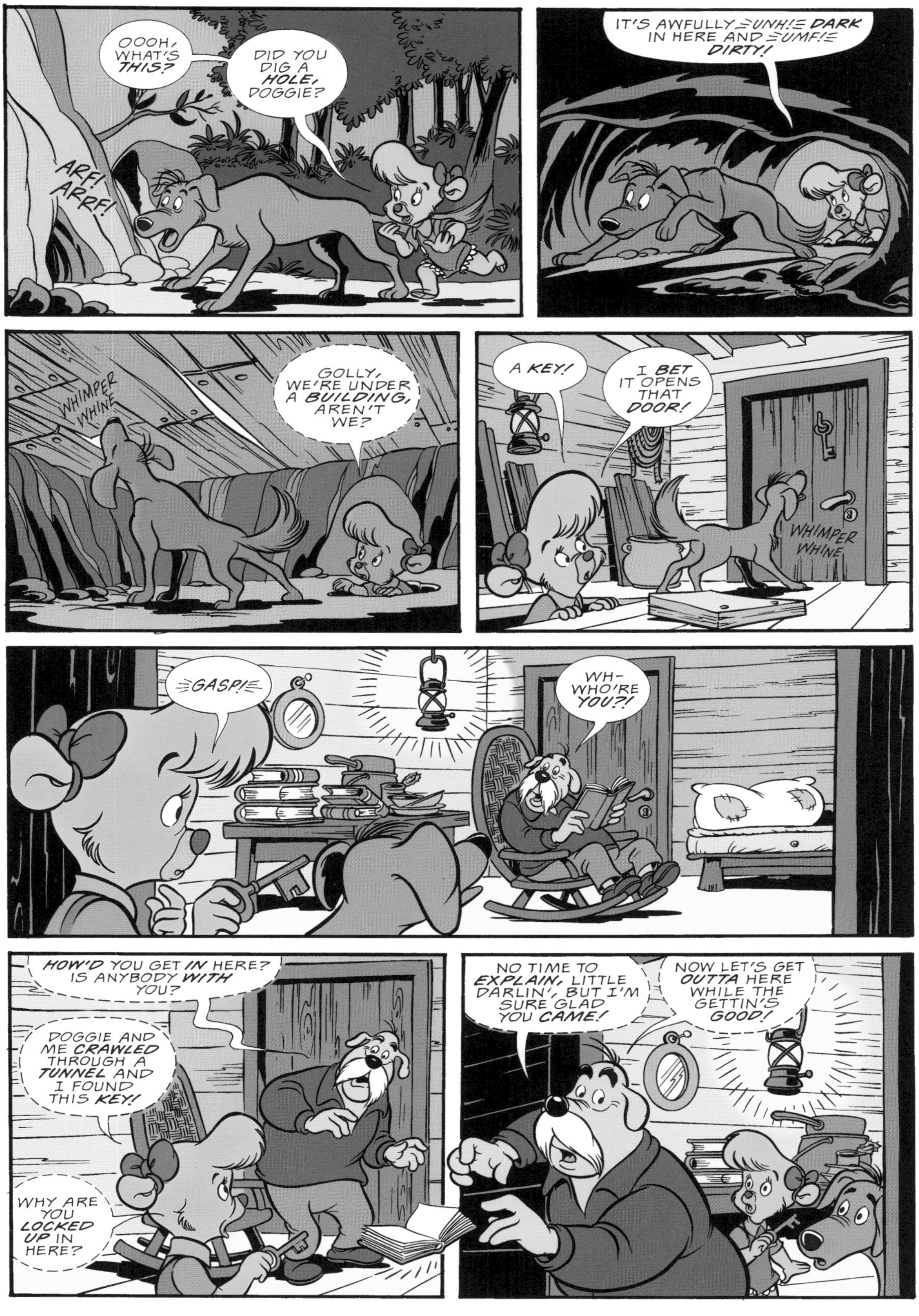
OOOH, WHAT'S THIS?
DID YOU DIG A HOLE, DOGGIE?
ARF! ARRF!
IT'S AWFULLY UNH! DARK IN HERE AND UMF! DIRTY!
WHIMPER WHINE
GOLLY, WE'RE UNDER A BUILDING, AREN'T WE?
A KEY!
I BET IT OPENS THAT DOOR!
WHIMPER WHINE
GASP!
WH- WHO'RE YOU?!
HOW'D YOU GET IN HERE? IS ANYBODY WITH YOU?
DOGGIE AND ME CRAWLED THROUGH A TUNNEL AND I FOUND THIS KEY!
WHY ARE YOU LOCKED UP IN HERE?
NO TIME TO EXPLAIN, LITTLE DARLIN', BUT I'M SURE GLAD YOU CAME!
NOW LET'S GET OUTTA HERE WHILE THE GETTIN'S GOOD!

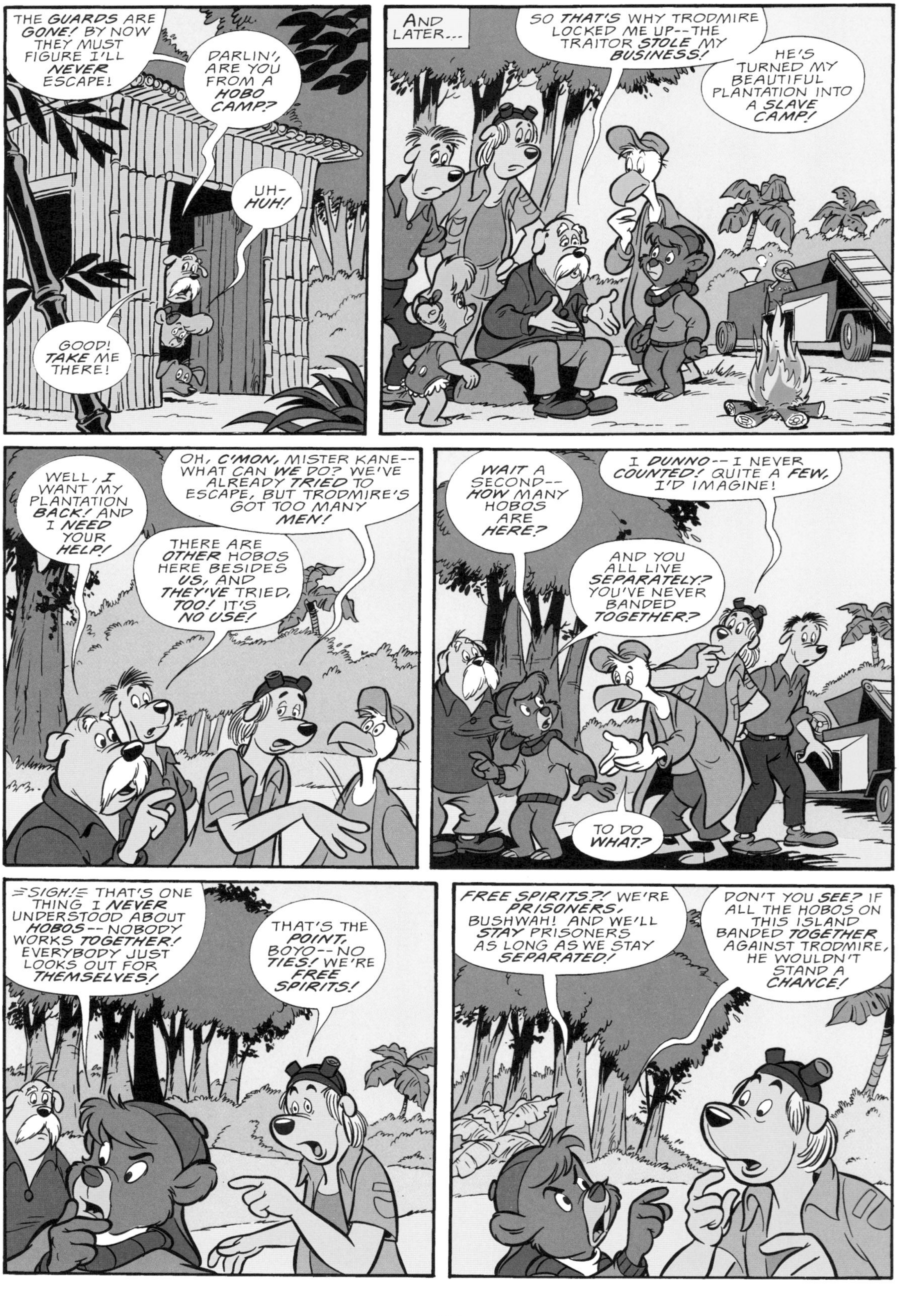
THE GUARDS ARE GONE! BY NOW THEY MUST FIGURE I'LL NEVER ESCAPE!
DARLIN', ARE YOU FROM A HOBO CAMP?
UH-HUH!
GOOD! TAKE ME THERE!
AND LATER...
SO THAT'S WHY TRODMIRE LOCKED ME UP--THE TRAITOR STOLE MY BUSINESS!
HE'S TURNED MY BEAUTIFUL PLANTATION INTO A SLAVE CAMP!
WELL, I WANT MY PLANTATION BACK! AND I NEED YOUR HELP!
OH, C'MON, MISTER KANE--WHAT CAN WE DO? WE'VE ALREADY TRIED TO ESCAPE, BUT TRODMIRE'S GOT TOO MANY MEN!
THERE ARE OTHER HOBOS HERE BESIDES US, AND THEY'VE TRIED, TOO! IT'S NO USE!
WAIT A SECOND--HOW MANY HOBOS ARE HERE?
I DUNNO--I NEVER COUNTED! QUITE A FEW, I'D IMAGINE!
AND YOU ALL LIVE SEPARATELY? YOU'VE NEVER BANDED TOGETHER?
TO DO WHAT?
=SIGH!= THAT'S ONE THING I NEVER UNDERSTOOD ABOUT HOBOS--NOBODY WORKS TOGETHER! EVERYBODY JUST LOOKS OUT FOR THEMSELVES!
THAT'S THE POINT, BOYO--NO TIES! WE'RE FREE SPIRITS!
FREE SPIRITS?! WE'RE PRISONERS, BUSHWAH! AND WE'LL STAY PRISONERS AS LONG AS WE STAY SEPARATED!
DON'T YOU SEE? IF ALL THE HOBOS ON THIS ISLAND BANDED TOGETHER AGAINST TRODMIRE, HE WOULDN'T STAND A CHANCE!

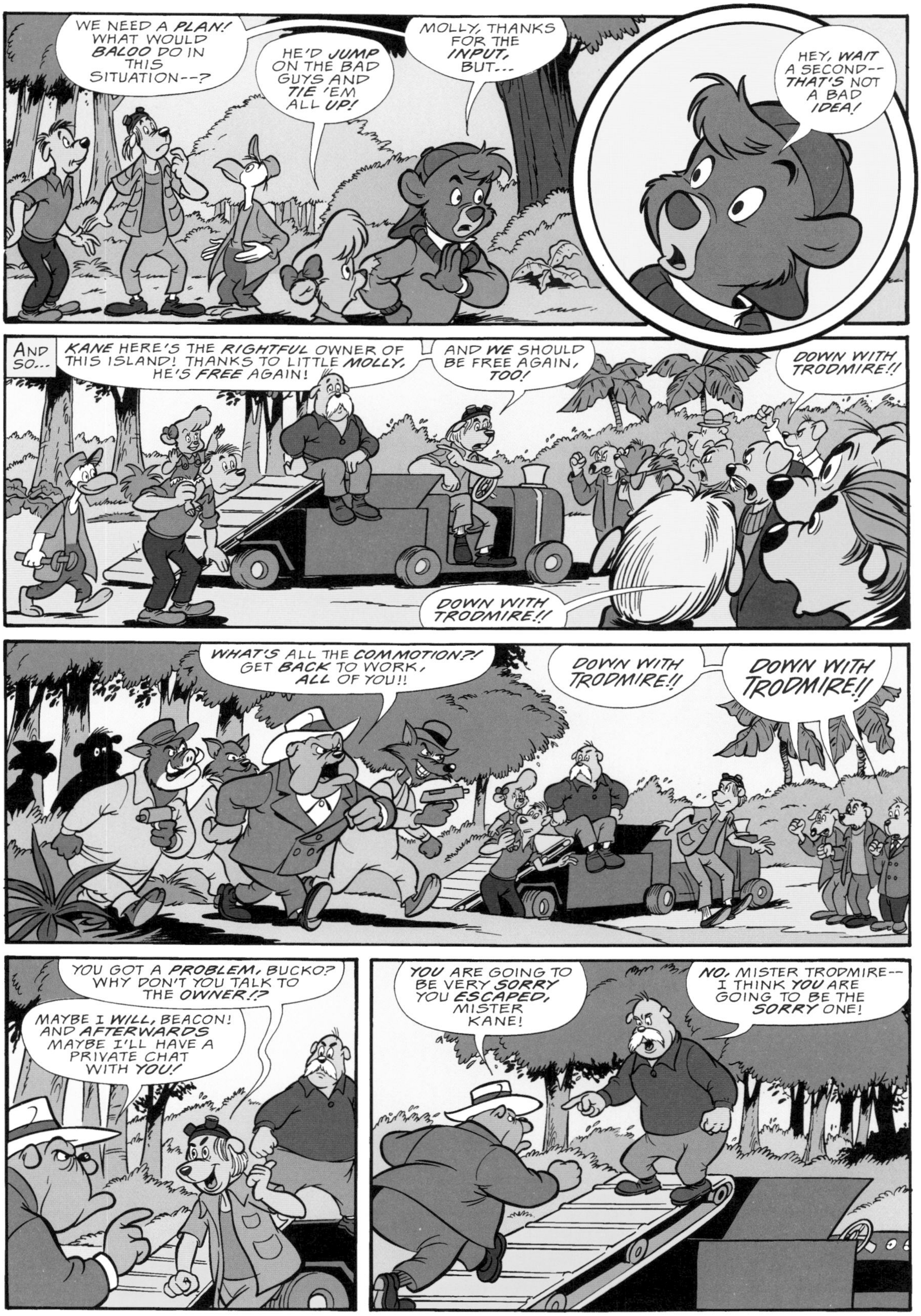

WE NEED A PLAN! WHAT WOULD BALOO DO IN THIS SITUATION--?
HE'D JUMP ON THE BAD GUYS AND TIE 'EM ALL UP!
MOLLY, THANKS FOR THE INPUT, BUT...
HEY, WAIT A SECOND--THAT'S NOT A BAD IDEA!
AND SO...
KANE HERE'S THE RIGHTFUL OWNER OF THIS ISLAND! THANKS TO LITTLE MOLLY, HE'S FREE AGAIN!
AND WE SHOULD BE FREE AGAIN, TOO!
DOWN WITH TRODMIRE!!
DOWN WITH TRODMIRE!!
WHAT'S ALL THE COMMOTION?! GET BACK TO WORK, ALL OF YOU!!
DOWN WITH TRODMIRE!!
DOWN WITH TRODMIRE!!
YOU GOT A PROBLEM, BUCKO? WHY DON'T YOU TALK TO THE OWNER!?
MAYBE I WILL, BEACON! AND AFTERWARDS MAYBE I'LL HAVE A PRIVATE CHAT WITH YOU!
YOU ARE GOING TO BE VERY SORRY YOU ESCAPED, MISTER KANE!
NO, MISTER TRODMIRE--I THINK YOU ARE GOING TO BE THE SORRY ONE!

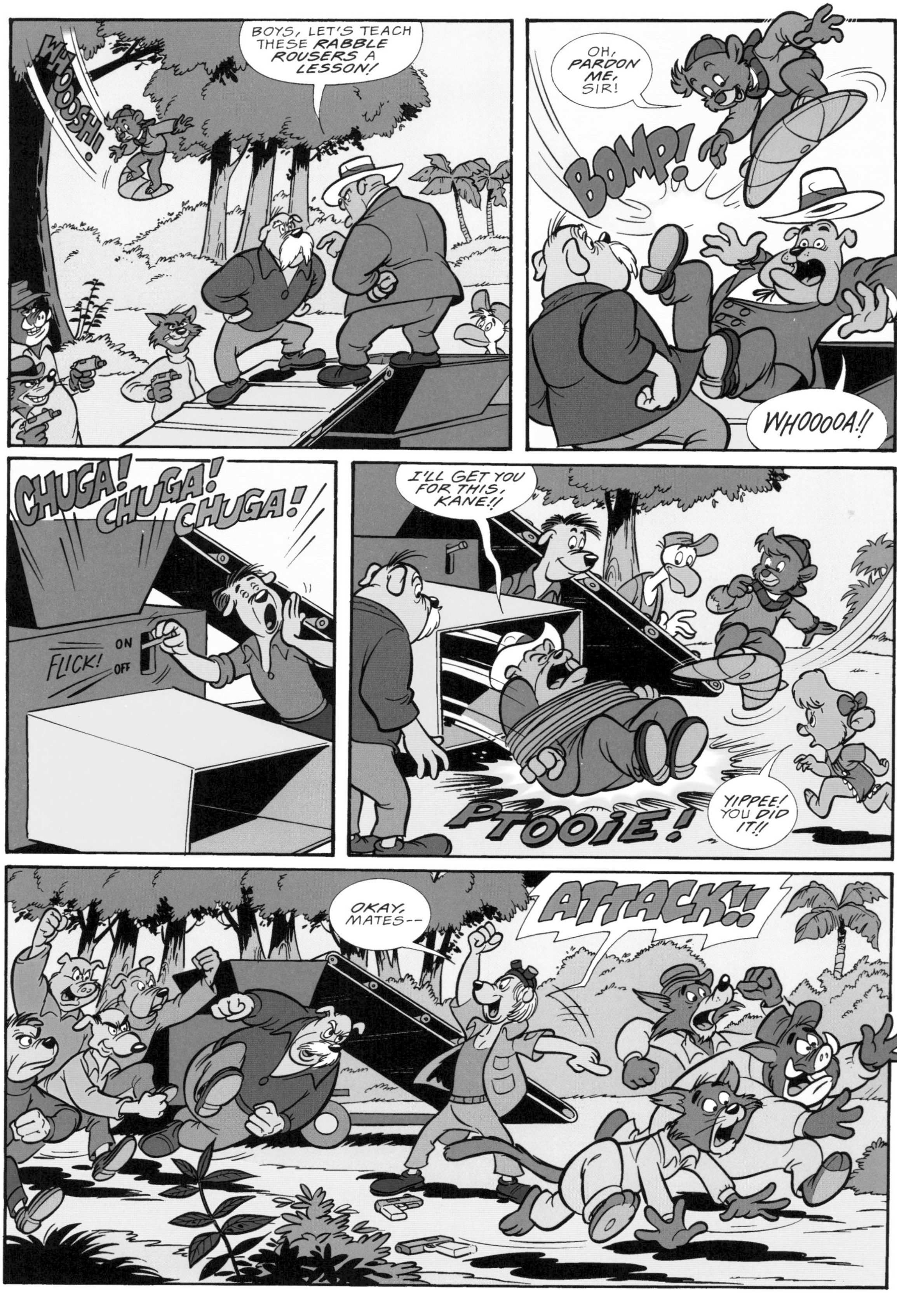
WHOOOSH!
BOYS, LET'S TEACH THESE RABBLE ROUSERS A LESSON!
OH, PARDON ME, SIR!
BOMP!
WHOOOOA!!
CHUGA! CHUGA! CHUGA!
ON
OFF
FLICK!
I'LL GET YOU FOR THIS, KANE!!
PTOOIE!
YIPPEE! YOU DID IT!!
OKAY, MATES--
ATTACK!!

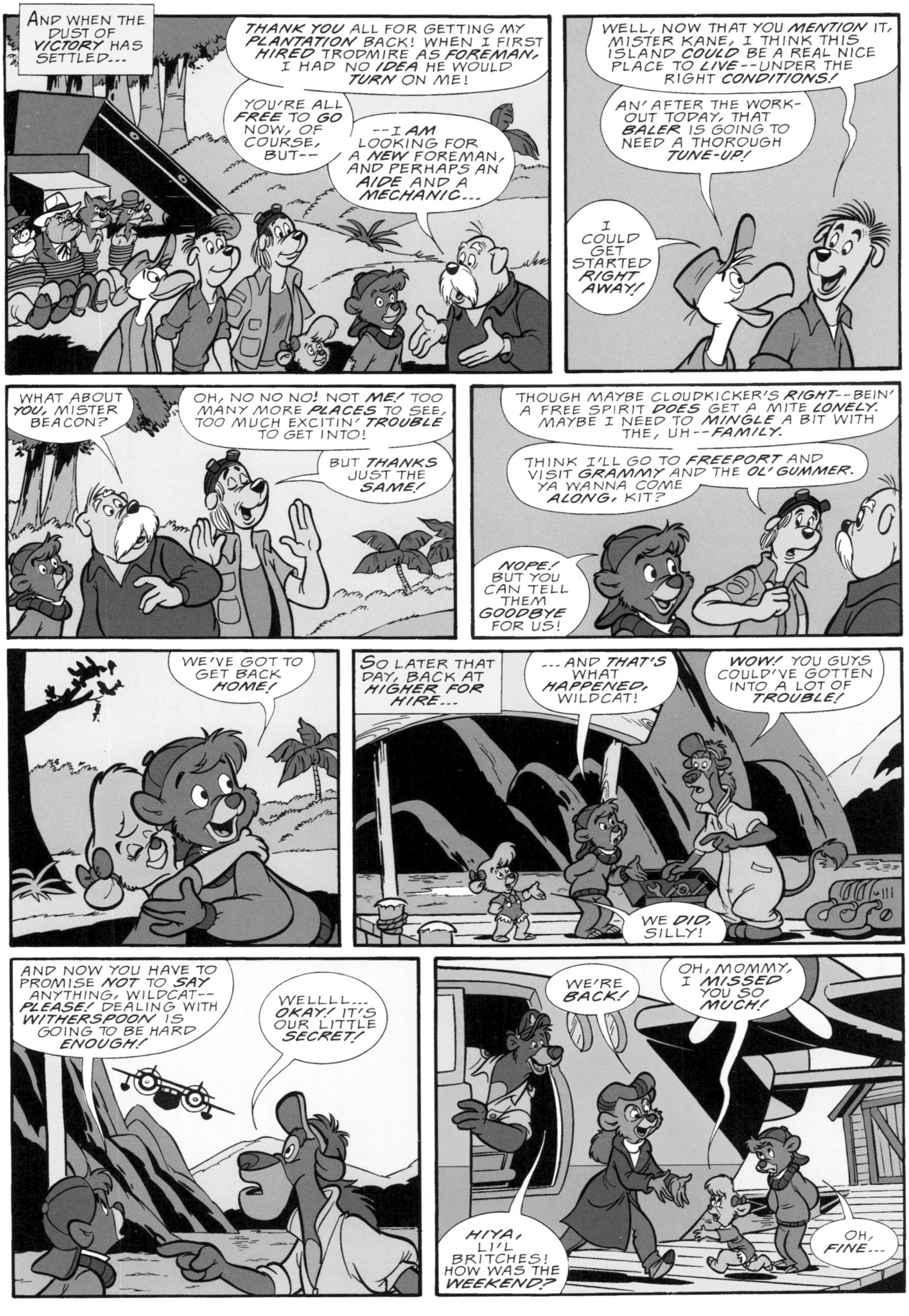
AND WHEN THE DUST OF VICTORY HAS SETTLED...
THANK YOU ALL FOR GETTING MY PLANTATION BACK! WHEN I FIRST HIRED TRODMIRE AS FOREMAN, I HAD NO IDEA HE WOULD TURN ON ME!
YOU'RE ALL FREE TO GO NOW, OF COURSE, BUT--
--I AM LOOKING FOR A NEW FOREMAN, AND PERHAPS AN AIDE AND A MECHANIC...
WELL, NOW THAT YOU MENTION IT, MISTER KANE, I THINK THIS ISLAND COULD BE A REAL NICE PLACE TO LIVE--UNDER THE RIGHT CONDITIONS!
AN' AFTER THE WORK-OUT TODAY, THAT BALER IS GOING TO NEED A THOROUGH TUNE-UP!
I COULD GET STARTED RIGHT AWAY!
WHAT ABOUT YOU, MISTER BEACON?
OH, NO NO NO! NOT ME! TOO MANY MORE PLACES TO SEE, TOO MUCH EXCITIN' TROUBLE TO GET INTO!
BUT THANKS JUST THE SAME!
THOUGH MAYBE CLOUDKICKER'S RIGHT--BEIN' A FREE SPIRIT DOES GET A MITE LONELY. MAYBE I NEED TO MINGLE A BIT WITH THE, UH--FAMILY.
THINK I'LL GO TO FREEPORT AND VISIT GRAMMY AND THE OL' GUMMER. YA WANNA COME ALONG, KIT?
NOPE! BUT YOU CAN TELL THEM GOODBYE FOR US!
WE'VE GOT TO GET BACK HOME!
SO LATER THAT DAY, BACK AT HIGHER FOR HIRE...
...AND THAT'S WHAT HAPPENED, WILDCAT!
WOW! YOU GUYS COULD'VE GOTTEN INTO A LOT OF TROUBLE!
WE DID, SILLY!
AND NOW YOU HAVE TO PROMISE NOT TO SAY ANYTHING, WILDCAT--PLEASE! DEALING WITH WITHERSPOON IS GOING TO BE HARD ENOUGH!
WELLLL... OKAY! IT'S OUR LITTLE SECRET!
WE'RE BACK!
OH, MOMMY, I MISSED YOU SO MUCH!
HIYA, LI'L BRITCHES! HOW WAS THE WEEKEND?
OH, FINE...

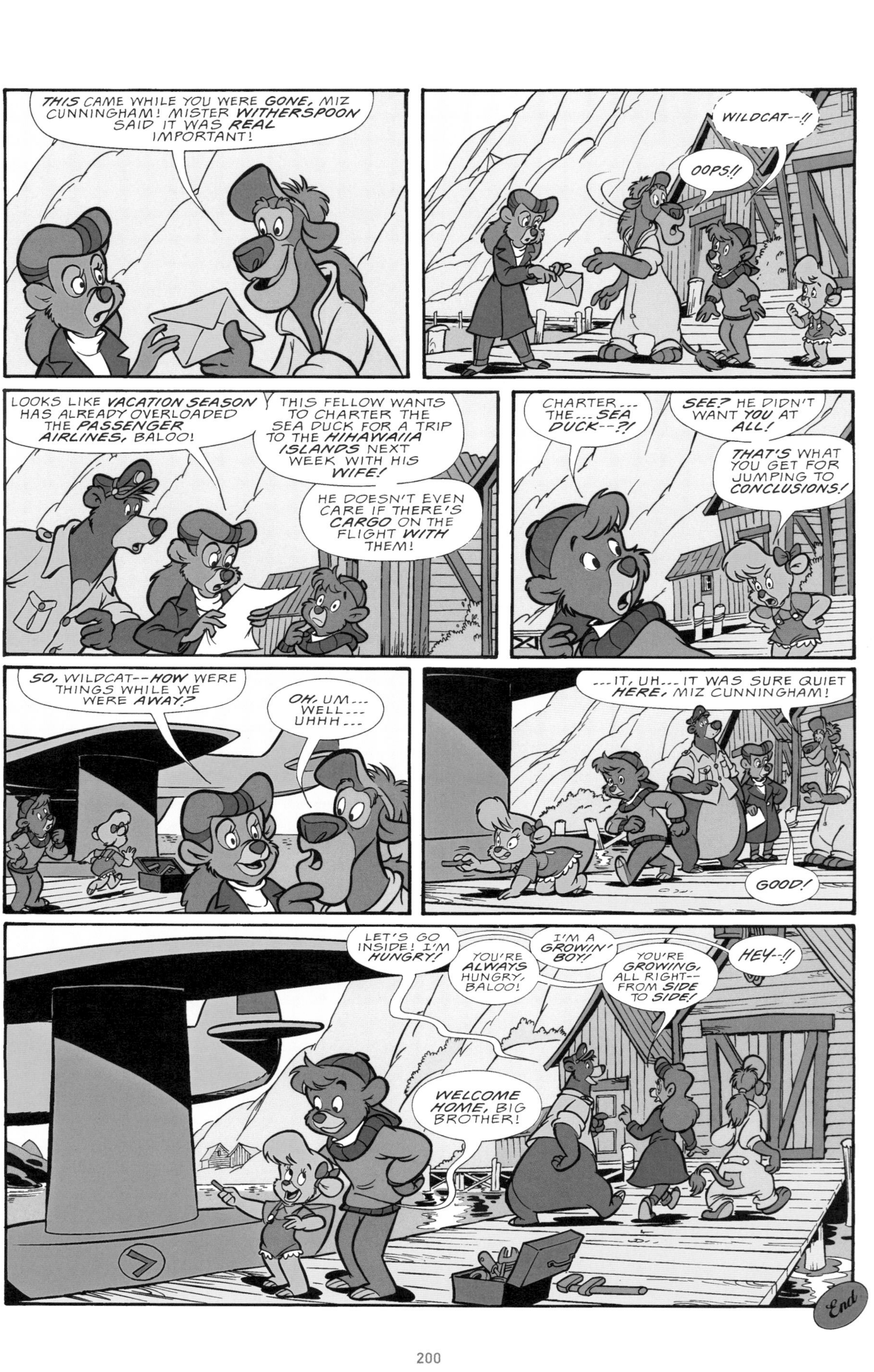
THIS CAME WHILE YOU WERE GONE, MIZ CUNNINGHAM! MISTER WITHERSPOON SAID IT WAS REAL IMPORTANT!
WILDCAT--!!
OOPS!!
LOOKS LIKE VACATION SEASON HAS ALREADY OVERLOADED THE PASSENGER AIRLINES, BALOO!
THIS FELLOW WANTS TO CHARTER THE SEA DUCK FOR A TRIP TO THE HIHAWAIIA ISLANDS NEXT WEEK WITH HIS WIFE!
HE DOESN'T EVEN CARE IF THERE'S CARGO ON THE FLIGHT WITH THEM!
CHARTER... THE... SEA DUCK--?!
SEE? HE DIDN'T WANT YOU AT ALL!
THAT'S WHAT YOU GET FOR JUMPING TO CONCLUSIONS!
SO, WILDCAT--HOW WERE THINGS WHILE WE WERE AWAY?
OH, UM... WELL... UHHH...
...IT, UH... IT WAS SURE QUIET HERE, MIZ CUNNINGHAM!
GOOD!
LET'S GO INSIDE! I'M HUNGRY!
YOU'RE ALWAYS HUNGRY, BALOO!
I'M A GROWIN' BOY!
YOU'RE GROWING, ALL RIGHT-- FROM SIDE TO SIDE!
HEY--!!
WELCOME HOME, BIG BROTHER!
End

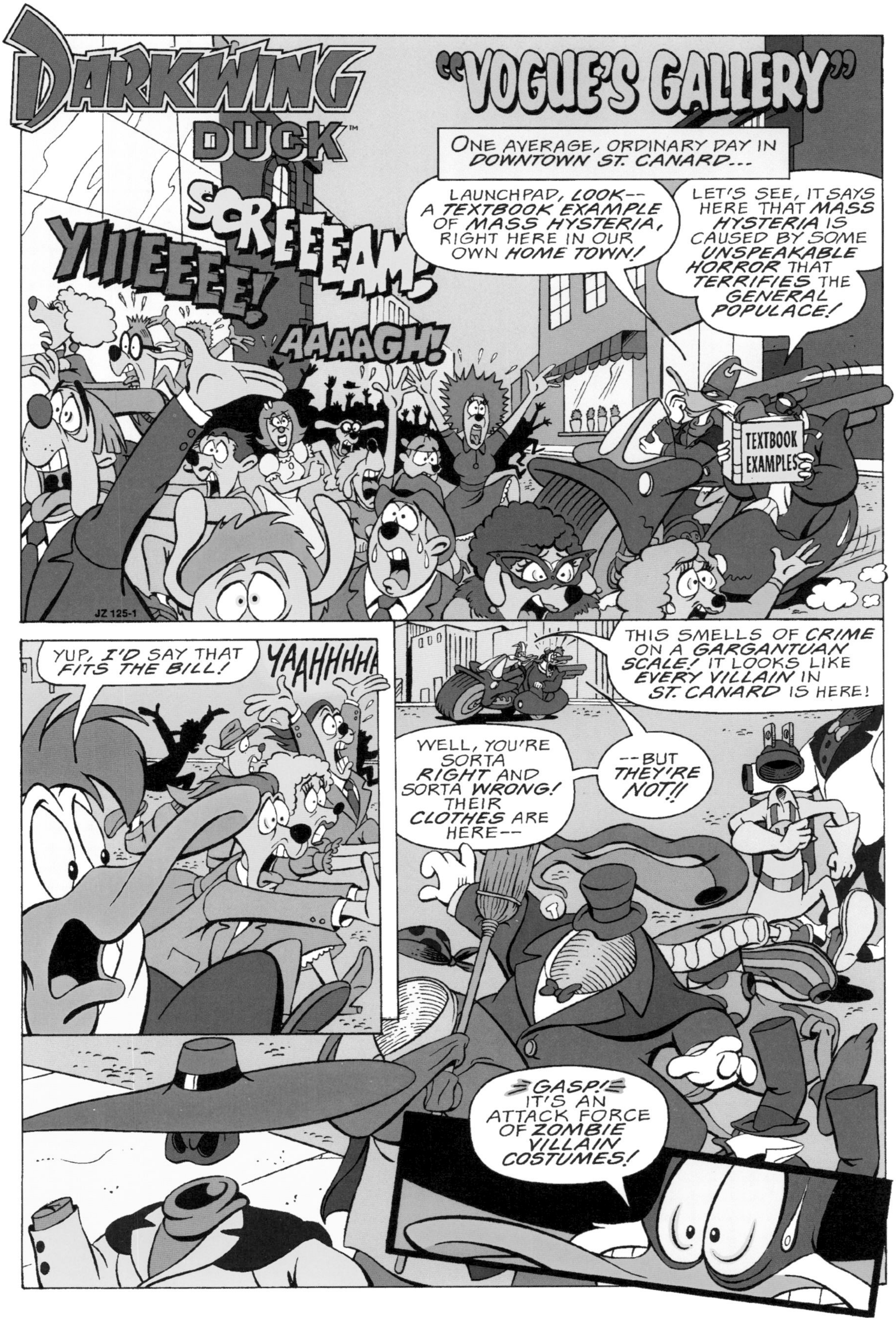
DARKWING DUCK™
"VOGUE'S GALLERY"
ONE AVERAGE, ORDINARY DAY IN DOWNTOWN ST. CANARD...
SCREEEEAM!
YIIIEEEEE!
AAAAGH!
LAUNCHPAD, LOOK-- A TEXTBOOK EXAMPLE OF MASS HYSTERIA, RIGHT HERE IN OUR OWN HOME TOWN!
LET'S SEE, IT SAYS HERE THAT MASS HYSTERIA IS CAUSED BY SOME UNSPEAKABLE HORROR THAT TERRIFIES THE GENERAL POPULACE!
TEXTBOOK EXAMPLES
JZ 125-1
YUP, I'D SAY THAT FITS THE BILL!
YAAHHHHA
THIS SMELLS OF CRIME ON A GARGANTUAN SCALE! IT LOOKS LIKE EVERY VILLAIN IN ST. CANARD IS HERE!
WELL, YOU'RE SORTA RIGHT AND SORTA WRONG! THEIR CLOTHES ARE HERE--
--BUT THEY'RE NOT!!
GASP! IT'S AN ATTACK FORCE OF ZOMBIE VILLAIN COSTUMES!

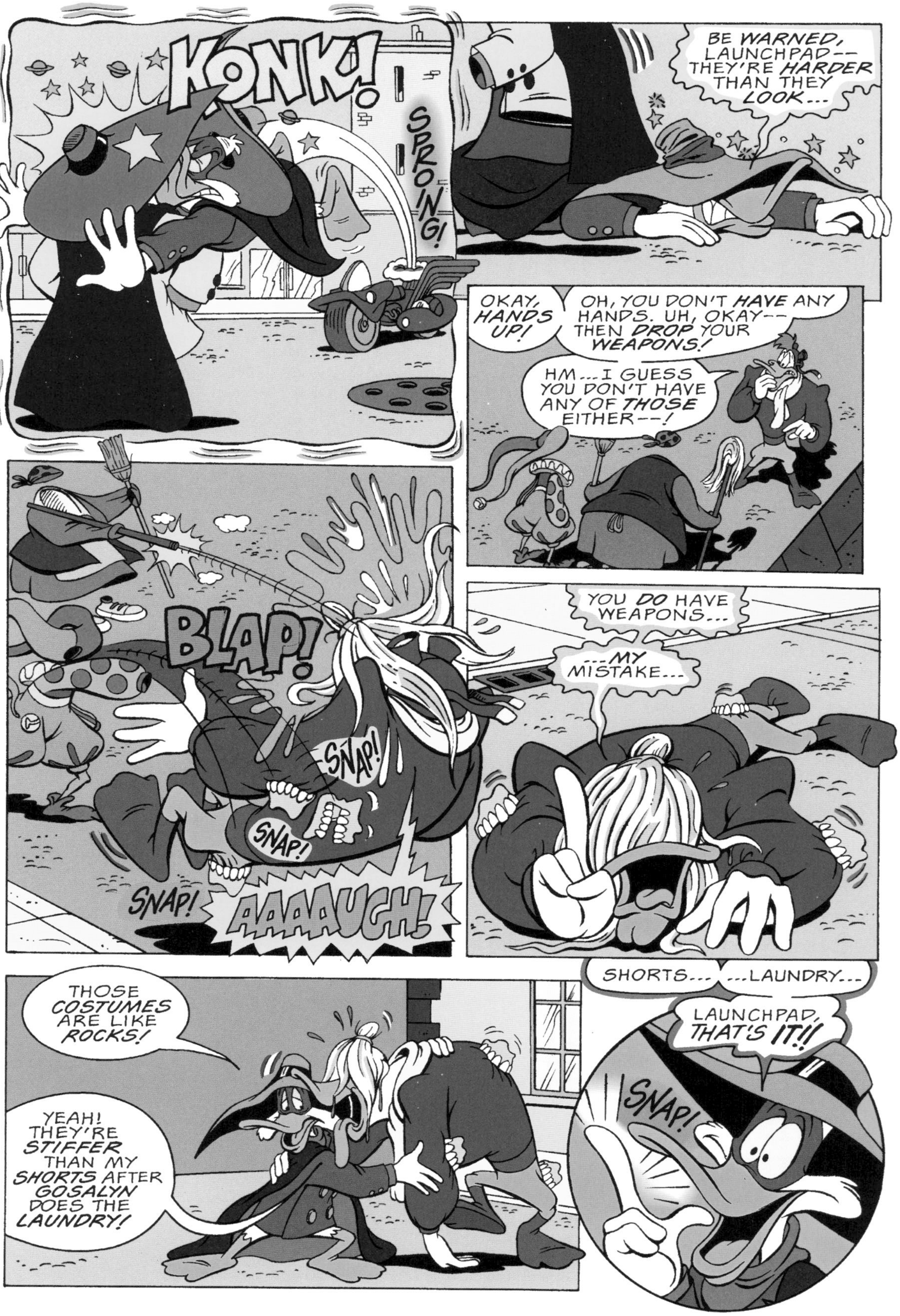
KONK!
SPROING!
BE WARNED, LAUNCHPAD-- THEY'RE HARDER THAN THEY LOOK...
OKAY, HANDS UP!
OH, YOU DON'T HAVE ANY HANDS. UH, OKAY-- THEN DROP YOUR WEAPONS!
HM...I GUESS YOU DON'T HAVE ANY OF THOSE EITHER--!
BLAP!
SNAP!
SNAP!
SNAP!
AAAAUGH!
YOU DO HAVE WEAPONS...
...MY MISTAKE...
THOSE COSTUMES ARE LIKE ROCKS!
YEAH! THEY'RE STIFFER THAN MY SHORTS AFTER GOSALYN DOES THE LAUNDRY!
SHORTS...
...LAUNDRY...
LAUNCHPAD, THAT'S IT!!
SNAP!

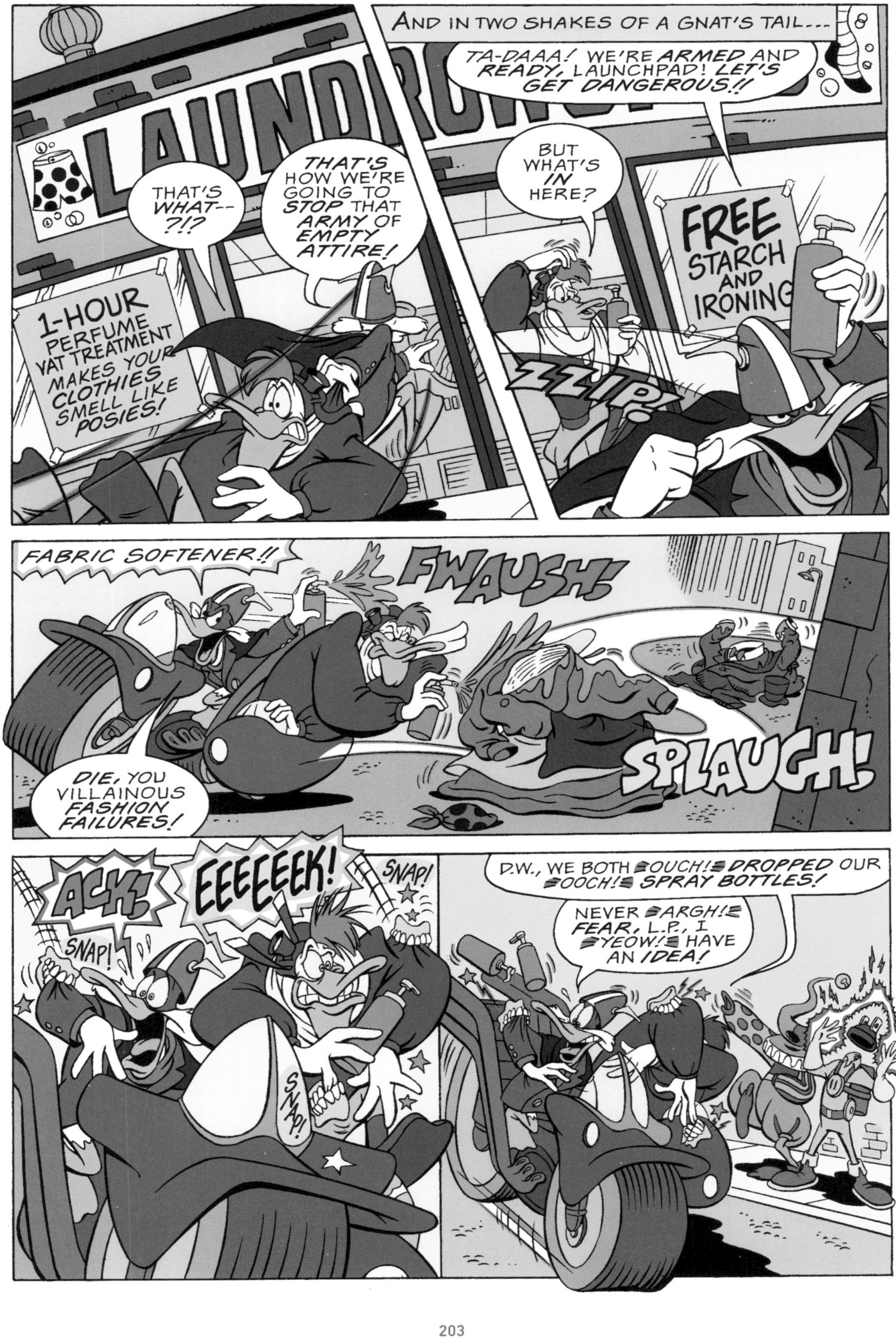
LAUNDROMAT
1-HOUR PERFUME YAT TREATMENT MAKES YOUR CLOTHIES SMELL LIKE POSIES!
THAT'S WHAT-- ?!?
THAT'S HOW WE'RE GOING TO STOP THAT ARMY OF EMPTY ATTIRE!
AND IN TWO SHAKES OF A GNAT'S TAIL...
TA-DAAA! WE'RE ARMED AND READY, LAUNCHPAD! LET'S GET DANGEROUS!!
BUT WHAT'S IN HERE?
FREE STARCH AND IRONING
ZZIP!
FABRIC SOFTENER!!
FWAUSH!
DIE, YOU VILLAINOUS FASHION FAILURES!
SPLAUGH!
ACK!
EEEEEEK!
SNAP!
SNAP!
SNAP!
D.W., WE BOTH OUCH! DROPPED OUR OOCH! SPRAY BOTTLES!
NEVER ARGH! FEAR, L.P., I YEOW! HAVE AN IDEA!

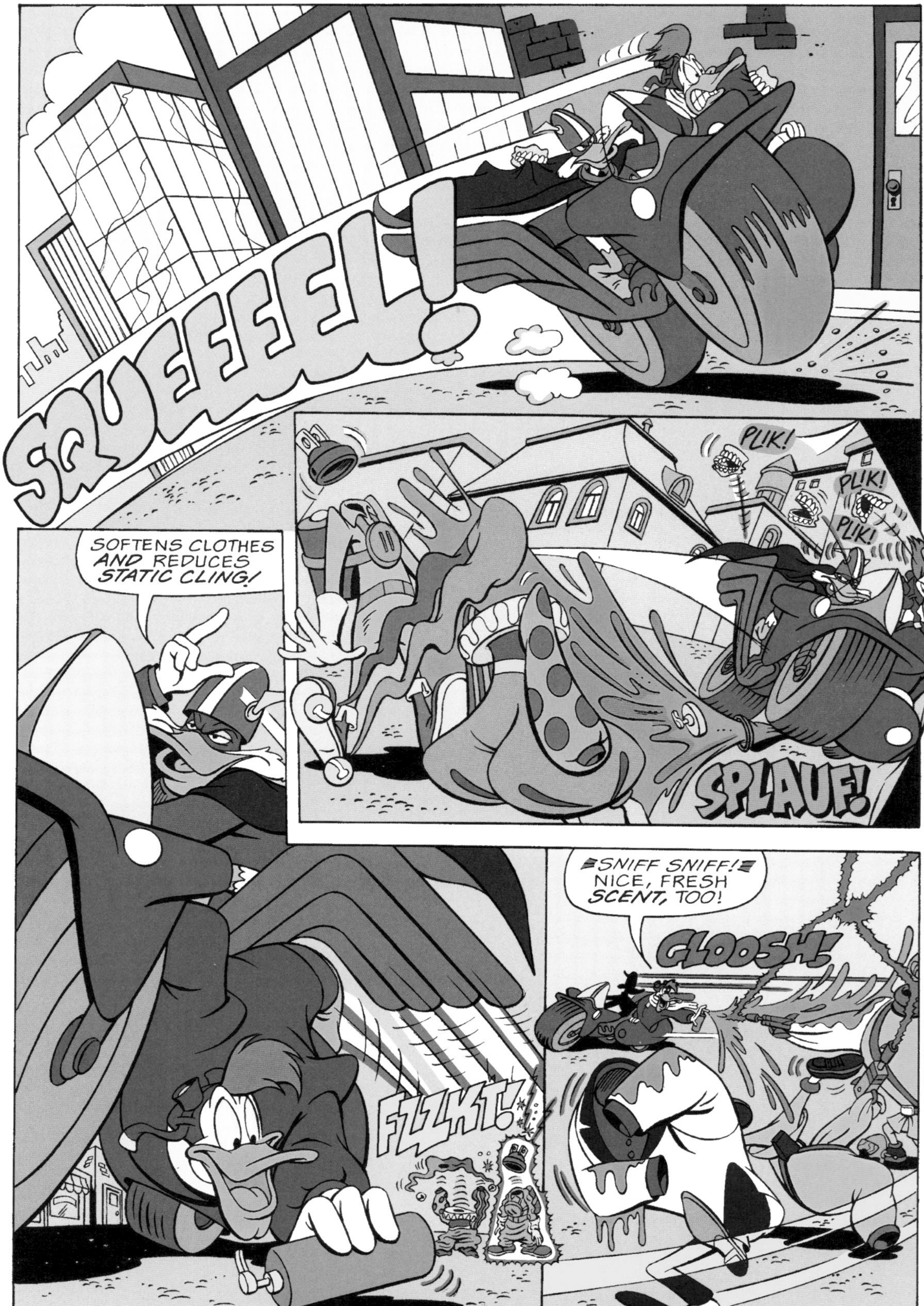
SQUEEEEL!
SOFTENS CLOTHES AND REDUCES STATIC CLING!
PLIK!
PLIK!
PLIK!
SPLAUF!
SNIFF SNIFF! NICE, FRESH SCENT, TOO!
GLOOSH!
FZZKT!

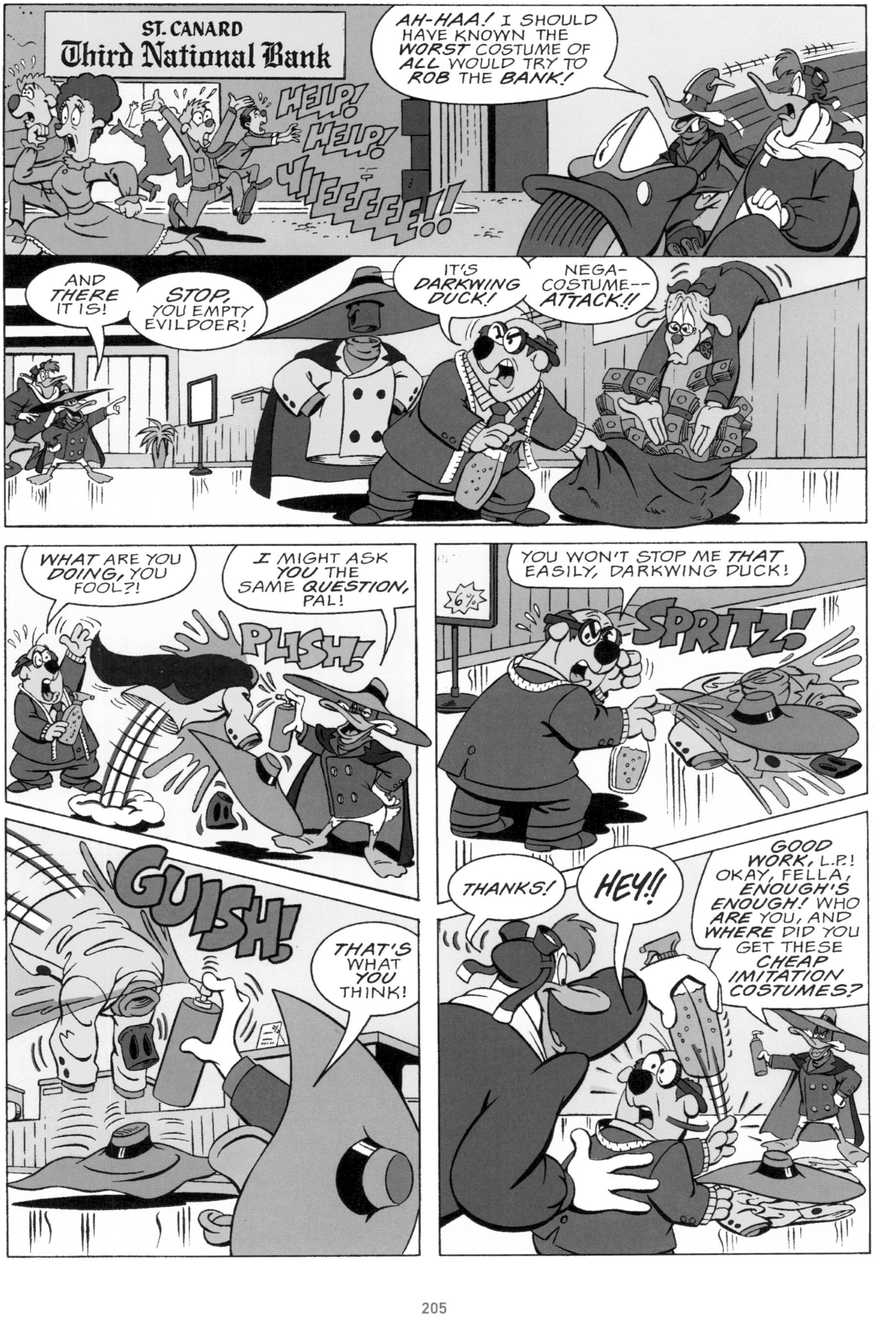

ST. CANARD
Third National Bank
HELP! HELP! YIIEEEEE!!
AH-HAA! I SHOULD HAVE KNOWN THE WORST COSTUME OF ALL WOULD TRY TO ROB THE BANK!
AND THERE IT IS!
STOP, YOU EMPTY EVILDOER!
IT'S DARKWING DUCK!
NEGA-COSTUME-- ATTACK!!
WHAT ARE YOU DOING, YOU FOOL?!
I MIGHT ASK YOU THE SAME QUESTION, PAL!
PLISH!
YOU WON'T STOP ME THAT EASILY, DARKWING DUCK!
6%
SPRITZ!
GUISH!
THAT'S WHAT YOU THINK!
THANKS!
HEY!!
GOOD WORK, L.P.! OKAY, FELLA, ENOUGH'S ENOUGH! WHO ARE YOU, AND WHERE DID YOU GET THESE CHEAP IMITATION COSTUMES?

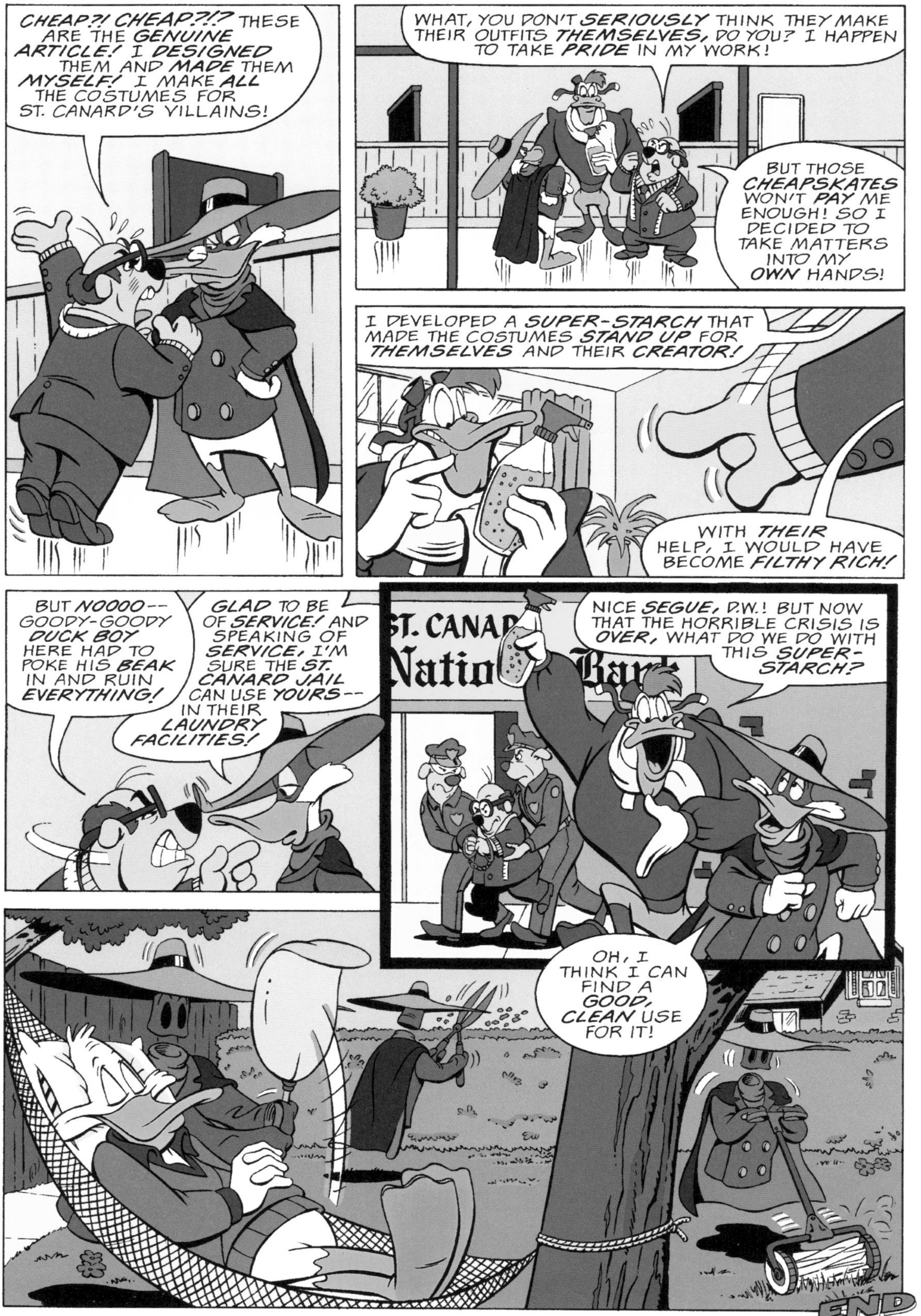
CHEAP?! CHEAP?!? THESE ARE THE GENUINE ARTICLE! I DESIGNED THEM AND MADE THEM MYSELF! I MAKE ALL THE COSTUMES FOR ST. CANARD'S VILLAINS!
WHAT, YOU DON'T SERIOUSLY THINK THEY MAKE THEIR OUTFITS THEMSELVES, DO YOU? I HAPPEN TO TAKE PRIDE IN MY WORK!
BUT THOSE CHEAPSKATES WON'T PAY ME ENOUGH! SO I DECIDED TO TAKE MATTERS INTO MY OWN HANDS!
I DEVELOPED A SUPER-STARCH THAT MADE THE COSTUMES STAND UP FOR THEMSELVES AND THEIR CREATOR!
WITH THEIR HELP, I WOULD HAVE BECOME FILTHY RICH!
BUT NOOOO-- GOODY-GOODY DUCK BOY HERE HAD TO POKE HIS BEAK IN AND RUIN EVERYTHING!
GLAD TO BE OF SERVICE! AND SPEAKING OF SERVICE, I'M SURE THE ST. CANARD JAIL CAN USE YOURS-- IN THEIR LAUNDRY FACILITIES!
ST. CANAR
Natio
Bank
NICE SEGUE, D.W.! BUT NOW THAT THE HORRIBLE CRISIS IS OVER, WHAT DO WE DO WITH THIS SUPER-STARCH?
OH, I THINK I CAN FIND A GOOD, CLEAN USE FOR IT!
END

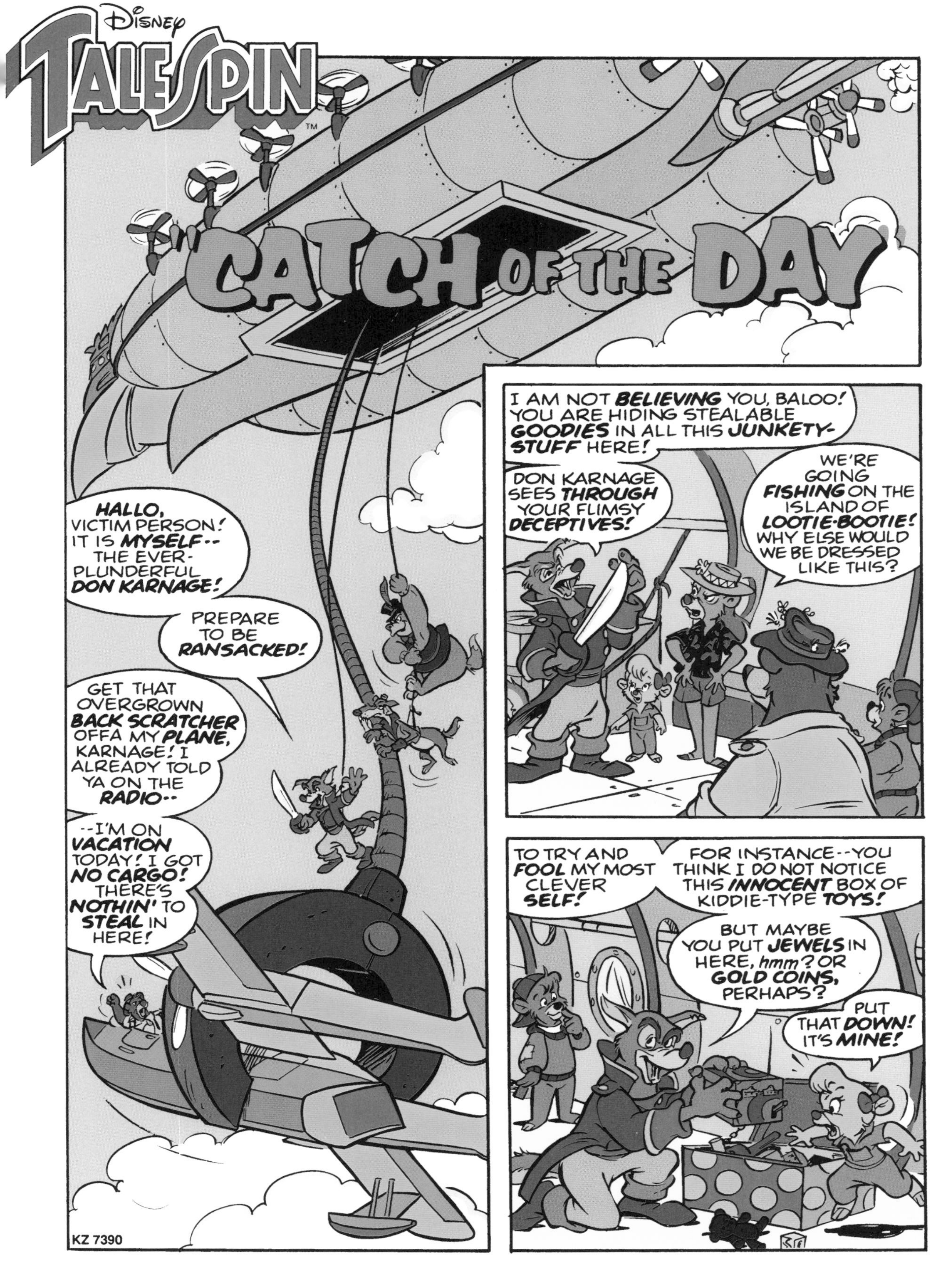
Disney
TaleSpin
"CATCH OF THE DAY"
HALLO, VICTIM PERSON! IT IS MYSELF-- THE EVER-PLUNDERFUL DON KARNAGE!
PREPARE TO BE RANSACKED!
GET THAT OVERGROWN BACK SCRATCHER OFFA MY PLANE, KARNAGE! I ALREADY TOLD YA ON THE RADIO--
--I'M ON VACATION TODAY! I GOT NO CARGO! THERE'S NOTHIN' TO STEAL IN HERE!
KZ 7390
I AM NOT BELIEVING YOU, BALOO! YOU ARE HIDING STEALABLE GOODIES IN ALL THIS JUNKETY-STUFF HERE!
DON KARNAGE SEES THROUGH YOUR FLIMSY DECEPTIVES!
WE'RE GOING FISHING ON THE ISLAND OF LOOTIE-BOOTIE! WHY ELSE WOULD WE BE DRESSED LIKE THIS?
TO TRY AND FOOL MY MOST CLEVER SELF!
FOR INSTANCE--YOU THINK I DO NOT NOTICE THIS INNOCENT BOX OF KIDDIE-TYPE TOYS!
BUT MAYBE YOU PUT JEWELS IN HERE, hmm? OR GOLD COINS, PERHAPS?
PUT THAT DOWN! IT'S MINE!

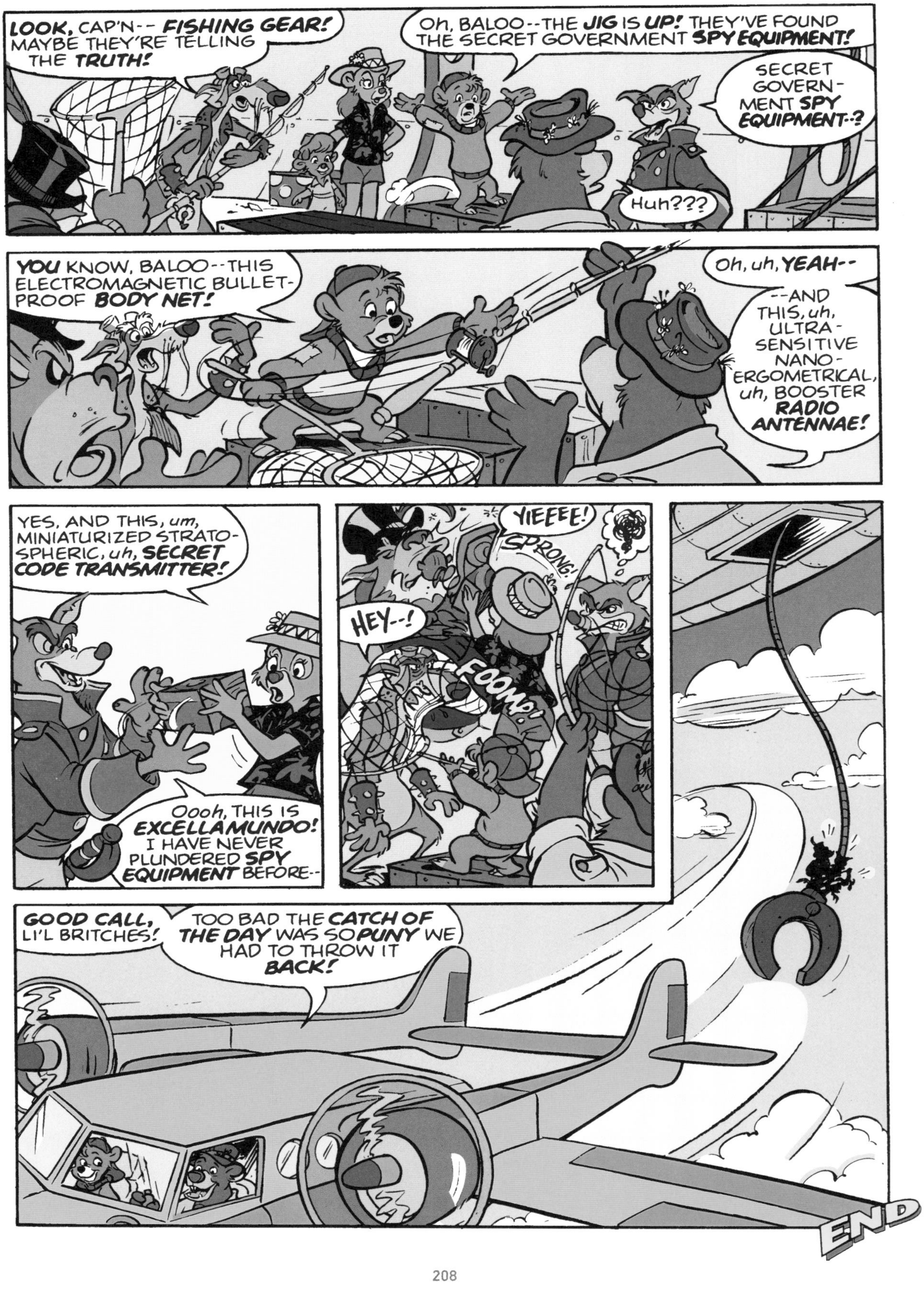
LOOK, CAP'N-- FISHING GEAR! MAYBE THEY'RE TELLING THE TRUTH!
Oh, BALOO--THE JIG IS UP! THEY'VE FOUND THE SECRET GOVERNMENT SPY EQUIPMENT!
SECRET GOVERN-MENT SPY EQUIPMENT-?
Huh???
YOU KNOW, BALOO--THIS ELECTROMAGNETIC BULLET-PROOF BODY NET!
Oh, uh, YEAH--
--AND THIS, uh, ULTRA-SENSITIVE NANO-ERGOMETRICAL, uh, BOOSTER RADIO ANTENNAE!
YES, AND THIS, um, MINIATURIZED STRATO-SPHERIC, uh, SECRET CODE TRANSMITTER!
Oooh, THIS IS EXCELLAMUNDO! I HAVE NEVER PLUNDERED SPY EQUIPMENT BEFORE--
YIEEEE!
SPRONG!
HEY--!
FOOMP!
GOOD CALL, LI'L BRITCHES!
TOO BAD THE CATCH OF THE DAY WAS SO PUNY WE HAD TO THROW IT BACK!
END